THE SUPERVILLAIN READER

THE SUPERVILLAIN READER

Edited by Robert Moses Peaslee and Robert G. Weiner

Foreword by Stephen Graham Jones

Afterword by Randy Duncan

UNIVERSITY PRESS OF MISSISSIPPI • JACKSON

The University Press of Mississippi is the scholarly publishing agency of
the Mississippi Institutions of Higher Learning: Alcorn State University,
Delta State University, Jackson State University, Mississippi State University,
Mississippi University for Women, Mississippi Valley State University,
University of Mississippi, and University of Southern Mississippi.

www.upress.state.ms.us

The University Press of Mississippi is a member of the Association of University Presses.

First printing 2020
∞

Library of Congress Cataloging-in-Publication Data available
LCCN 2019032127

Hardback	ISBN 978-1-4968-2646-6
Trade paperback	ISBN 978-1-4968-2647-3
Epub single	ISBN 978-1-4968-2648-0
Epub institutional	ISBN 978-1-4968-2649-7
PDF single	ISBN 978-1-4968-2650-3
PDF institutional	ISBN 978-1-4968-2651-0

British Library Cataloging-in-Publication Data available

CONTENTS

SECTION 2. SUPERVILLAINY IN MYTH AND LITERATURE

SECTION 3: SUPERVILLAINY IN CINEMA AND TELEVISION

SECTION 4: SUPERVILLAINY IN COMICS AND SEQUENTIAL ART

ACKNOWLEDGMENTS

VOLUMES LIKE THIS ONE ARE BROUGHT INTO EXISTENCE THROUGH THE INTEN-sive efforts of a true rogues' gallery of collaborators. We must first thank the University Press of Mississippi for seeing the value of this contribution, and especially Vijay Shah, UPM's incredibly patient acquisitions editor, who over-saw the nurturing and development of what you will read below. This volume also required significant additional effort in securing permissions for reprints, something we encountered here for the first time, and we must thank Lisa McMurtray for shepherding us through that process.

Of course, the collection would still be merely an idea without the efforts of our authors and the generosity of those from whom we've sought permission to reprint previously published work. Each of them has placed enormous trust in us, and we hope that all of them feel that their work is positioned productively and provocatively among the other pieces in the book. Because of the com-plexity of this project, our authors have also had to be a bit more patient than they might have expected in waiting for the book to come out, and for that, too, we are very grateful. We hope it was worth the wait. In addition, thanks to our peer reviewers, whose insights and provocations were cogent and vital, and helped us produce a better piece of scholarship.

Several people helped us at different stages of this book's completion. Thanks to Oluseyi Adegbola, Harper Anderson, Tess Greenlees, Derrick Holland, Duncan Prettyman, and Jonathan Villareal, all of whom performed great feats of strength under significant time pressures in order to keep the project moving more or less on schedule.

In addition, each of the editors would like to offer some individual words of appreciation.

LOVED ONES ALWAYS SUFFER FOR OUR OBSESSIONS, AND IN THE CASE OF THIS particular obsession I must thank Kate, Coen, Hazel, and Nora Peaslee for suffering absences both physical and mental at key moments in this volume's evolution. Your love and support is the single greatest treasure I could ask for. My adoration, respect, and gratitude are boundless.

Also, I must thank my colleagues in the College of Media and Communication at Texas Tech University; in particular, thanks to Dean David Perlmutter and Associate Dean Amy Koerber for the space and resources to pursue projects like this while also serving in an administrative role. Thanks to the faculty in the Department of Journalism and Creative Media Industries, whose e-mails may at times have been answered a bit later than they might have expected as a result of my focus on this project. Your work inspires mine.

Several Texas Tech colleagues have been particularly influential coconspirators over the past ten years, and I'd like to single them out for special thanks: Drs. Jerod Foster, Todd Chambers, Kent Wilkinson, Glenn Cummins, Aliza Wong, Wyatt Phillips, Allison Whitney, Jimmie Reeves, Dennis Harp, and Dean Jerry Hudson. To the Tribe: thanks for helping me keep it all in perspective. And of course, my coeditor, Robert G. Weiner, an excellent, generous human—not a trace of supervillain—who has taught me so much about the right way to be in the world.

Finally, to my students, the readers of this volume, and the pop culture fans who come out to meet us at conventions and conferences—thank you for your enthusiasm, passion, critique, and commitment. It is truly humbling to stand with you and share in whatever geeks you out. I look forward to reading your book someday.

—ROBERT MOSES PEASLEE

THANKS TO MY COLLEAGUES AT THE TEXAS TECH LIBRARY AND AT RESEARCH, Instruction, and Outreach (RIO). Thanks to RIO head Donell Callender for being supportive of what I do in my scholarship and work, Miss Denise Caspell for keeping me in line, and Laura Heinz for always having an open ear. Thanks also to President Lawrence Schovanec for being concerned. Thanks to Ryan Cassidy, Marina Oliver (thank you for listening and for your support), Joshua Salmans, Dr. Edgar Cizko, Kim Vardmann, Brett Brock, Dr. Joar Mahkent, Roman Sionis, Dr. Miles Warren, Drs. Chris and Angie Smith, Hank Henshaw, Melissa Gold, Sebastian Shaw, S. Aitan, Police Lieutenant Danny Quon, Tom Lopaka, Dr. Roger Landes, Steve Stallings, Dr. Gary Elbow, and Cheyenne Belew. Special thanks to Dr. Floyd Pirtle, Dr. Fatima Salas, Dr. Joaquin Lado, Dr. Tam Nguyen, and Dr. Benedicto Baronia. Thanks also to the Honors College faculty and staff (especially Dean Michael San Francisco, Cheyanne, Stacy, Sharon, Dr. Wong, and the whole staff) and to the libraries' faculty and staff, especially those in Information Technology (Mark, Blake, Stokes, Dalton, Max, Mario, and the whole staff), Acquisitions (John Brown and the whole staff), and Document Delivery (Katie and the whole staff). Thanks to Ghi and Lando, and thanks to

Dr. Aliza Wong for her continued support. Thanks to Lynda Watson and Gena Seaburg, who are always there with caring and helpful advice for my furry pals. Love and thanks to my furry friends, Lexi, Paws, Lovemore, Gardena, Lee, and Kirby. This book is in memory of Persia, Mr. Eddie, Grant, Blossom, and especially Miss Tess, my best pal who always had a "Yahoo" for me, and Rocket, who always surprised me.

Special thanks to Kate Peaslee, Darren Hick, Mark Charney and the School of Theater and Dance, Rachel McEniry, Ryan Litsey, Damon Greer, John Oyerbides, Mike Blevins, Donna McDonald, Joe Gulick, Bill McDonald, Matt McEniry, Amy Kim, Lisa Day, Lauren McDonald, Tim Day, Paul Reinsch, Hanna Marie Sawka, Nora Hyman, Tom Blackburn, Todd Chambers, MM (thanks for the apple pie), Rev. Jeffery Vayda, Wyatt Phillips, and Larry Weiner (love to you all and thanks for being there and caring).

An extra special thanks to Marissa Blanco, Alicia Goodman, Darren Hick, Vicky Weiner, Marilyn Weiner, Sara Dulin, Morgan Hyman, Joe Ferrer, Geraldine Ferrer, and Tom Gonzales for everything you did for me during my difficult time. You are all appreciated.

Thanks to my honors students past and present for teaching me new ways to critically think about popular culture. Go forth and make the world a better place.

Finally, thanks to Dr. Robert Moses Peaslee. Thanks for your hard work, determination, and friendship. Working with you on these various projects has been such a joy and one of the high points of my entire life. Rob, you never cease amazing me. You are truly a class act.

—ROBERT G. WEINER

BUILDING A BETTER BAD GUY

STEPHEN GRAHAM JONES

WITHOUT SUPERVILLAINS, THERE CAN BE NO SUPERHEROES. THIS IS AN AXIOM in the world of capes and tights—it's going to be a boring comic book if there's no one to fight—but it goes for the world at large, too, since forever, which you can trace out baddie by baddie throughout the course of this book. The differences from culture to culture and era to era are fascinating and telling, but so are the similarities—so is this impulse we have to seed our world with antagonists. It would seem we do this less to "prove" our own heroics and more because these evil forces are the dynamo at the center of creation, always stirring things up, and in the most generative and necessary fashion. Without Loki, all of Asgard tends to just drink itself to sleep each night, doesn't it? With nothing to strive against, forward motion dissipates and life feels stagnant, and soon enough, just because we want some excitement, we step out into those dark hinterlands, and we find a bear to poke.

Thing is, that bear, it's been waiting; it's been scheming, and it's got a plan to pull everything down around us. And it goes by many names, most of which you can find in the table of contents Robert Moses Peaslee and Robert G. Weiner have assembled here. You expect Iago, you're ready for Milton's version of Satan, you imagine that a book about supervillains can't be complete without some Darth Vader—but are you familiar with Aṅgulimāla? Do you know Voldemort as well as you think you do? Did you expect GI Joe and Cobra to make an appearance here? Prepare to dial back to the *Iliad* and then all the way up to Harley Quinn and Catwoman, and get, from that mad rush, a sense of what we talk about when we talk about bad guys.

Though, let me tell you how I use this text, and how I plan to keep on using it. It's meant to be descriptive—a comprehensive taxonomy, with exegesis—but you can take it as prescriptive, too. You can read *A Supervillain Reader* as a template, as a model, as a mold. You can use it to create better bad buys.

Do you want your story, your comic, your movie, your play—your whatever—to be infectious and addictive and engaging, to pull the reader or audience in by the face, leave them unable to stop turning the pages? Then build your antagonist like Satan, with grandiose schemes and a need to articulate them. Be sure to make that antagonist as devious as Moriarty, as driven as Thanos, as charismatic as Lex Luthor, and as slippery as Iago.

After you've done that? *Then* sketch out your protagonist, your hero, and never forget that your protagonist isn't the real main character here. Yes, heroes are the ones who will experience "change" through the struggle of the story; yes, they're the ones whose shoulder we're most often looking over; and yes, they're the ones we want to pull through, to overcome. But, what they're overcoming? It's all the obstacles thrown up by the antagonist, by the supervillain, who is the one actually charting the shape of the story. Joseph Campbell's "Call to Adventure" in his *The Hero's Journey* is never something of the hero's making, but the hero's opposite: the supervillain. The antagonist provides the catalyst. The bad guy pushes that first rock downhill that becomes the avalanche.

It is important to remember, too, that the hero is always weaker than the supervillain, be it in muscles, or intelligence, or finances. This is key, so I'll say it again: the protagonist is always weaker than the antagonist. If the protagonist weren't? Then there's no tension, as we know exactly how this story will turn out. When the hero is at a disadvantage, though, then it's an uphill battle the whole way, and we invest in the outcome—we hope, we root for the ending we want.

And, even in those rare cases where it would seem the hero is more capable than the supervillain in every regard—Superman and Luthor, say—then, still, the supervillain has the upper hand, simply because that supervillain isn't constrained by morals or society. He can do things the hero never can.

Think Joker and Batman, right? Two sides of the same coin, but the Joker always, somehow, lands faceup and smiling, not because his grin has been etched on but because the Batman doesn't kill. The Joker can use guns, Batman can't. The Joker can take hostages, Batman can't. Each of Batman's victories means so much more, since he's forever outmatched.

This is what *A Supervillain Reader* can teach us: always tilt your process toward building a better bad guy. And take all the supervillains you find in this book as models. Fall into the Bible, come out in the pages of *The Maxx*, and, while nobody's exactly watching, maybe pretend you're Loki at your desk, forever messing things up for the boring, normal world, but messing them up in the most wonderful, productive ways.

Long live supervillains.

Without them, there's no story.

IT'S ALL ABOUT THE VILLAIN!

ROBERT G. WEINER, ROBERT MOSES PEASLEE, AND DUNCAN PRETTYMAN

I don't need a teacher. I need an enemy. The greatest villains have always been defined by the [people] who try and stop them.

THE RIDDLER, GOTHAM TELEVISION SERIES

LITERARY AND FILMIC SUPERVILLAINS HAVE BECOME AN INTEGRAL PART OF popular consciousness. Grendel, Darth Vader, Snidely Whiplash, Sauron, Blofeld, Dracula, Lady Macbeth, Long John Silver, Bluto, Sweeney Todd, Uriah Heep, Edward Hyde, Fu Manchu, Fantomas, Moriarty—all of these characters and many more have become to varying degrees as important to our understanding of what makes up human nature and evil as any religious text. Today, the villain is newly ubiquitous in popular culture; this villainous turn is chief among the reasons this collection has been produced. While we should be careful about assigning to this trend any undue novelty (toys featuring supervillains go back several decades, after all, including plastic models of figures like the Joker, the Riddler, the Green Goblin, the Lizard, and Doctor Doom), it seems apparent to anyone paying attention that, as Heath Ledger's Joker suggests, "things have changed."

In some cases, villain toys, puzzles, games, and video games provide a way for children (and adults) to live vicariously as the bad guy while, hopefully, keeping their moral compasses intact. Villains can be used to teach children traditional human values, like sharing and helping others, as they are in books like *DC Superheroes: My First Book of Super-Villains*—Lex Luthor is selfish, while Superman is caring; the Joker plays tricks on everyone, while Batman wants to keep them safe.[1] Superheroes are to be held up as exemplars of good decision making while villains are not (fig. 1).

But supervillains are by no means featured today only as straw men or negative examples; readers and viewers have for some time been invited to revel in the bad guys' beguiling sociopathy and sympathize with their plight. As

Figure 1. A tool for teaching young children that superheroes do what is right (from Katz and Katz, *DC Super Heroes: My First Book of Super-Villains*, 2014).

early as 1976, Simon and Schuster published a collection of stories recounting the origins of Marvel villains called *Bring On the Bad Guys*, featuring Loki, Mephisto, Dormammu, the Red Skull, the Green Goblin, Doctor Doom, and the Abomination. Stan Lee's introduction to the 1998 revised edition of that volume is characteristic of his inimitable voice and one of the early indicators of contemporary trends in popular culture storytelling:

> The viler the villain, the more heroic the hero!
>
> Think about it. Would David have seemed so heroic battling Goliath if Goliath had been a five-foot-tall accountant? Would legend have paid homage to the battle between Ulysses and Cyclops if Cyclops had merely been a mild-mannered optician? Would you have thrilled to the exploits of Robin Hood quite as much if the Sheriff of Nottingham had been a charitable official famed for his kindness and charity?
>
> Now let's take some examples that are closer to home . . .
>
> Would loyal readers have followed the exploits of the Fantastic Four all these years if their arch-enemy, Dr. Victor von Doom, was a beloved Bavarian pediatrician? And what about SpiderMan? How exciting would his adventures have been if Carnage was a gentle, fun-loving philanthropist whose greatest pleasure was helping those who were less fortunate than he? Take the mighty Thor. Imagine how excited you'd be about his battles with Loki if Loki was a sensitive and caring brother who spent his time writing poetry and wrapping bandages for the Asgardian branch of the Red Cross![2]

That Lee had the foresight to publish this collection long before the deluge of villain-centric media being produced today speaks to just how powerful these characters are and to the rich conceptual value of villainy. Two decades later, Marvel published a sequel titled *Bring Back the Bad Guys*,[3] and Stan Lee edited a volume of prose stories featuring Marvel villains called *The Ultimate Super-Villains*.[4] DC has also recently published a number of volumes bringing their villains front and center, including *Forever Evil*, *Villains United*, *DC Comics Super-Villains: The Complete Visual History*, and several volumes featuring the Secret Society of Super Villains.[5] There are many more volumes featuring specific villains like the Joker, Doctor Doom, the Green Goblin, the Kingpin, Galactus, Thanos, the Riddler, Two-Face, Lex Luthor, and Magneto. *Supervillains and Philosophy* and *The Science of Supervillains* are popular academic works.[6] There are also tongue-in-cheek "handbooks" on villainy,[7] and one should not miss Jon Morris's *The Legion of Regrettable Supervillains: Oddball Criminals from Comic Book History*. Morris catalogues the most bizarre supervillains from sequential art, including Brickbat (who throws poison bricks) and the Jingler, who uses poetry to kill and the blood of his victim as ink. Other oddball villains have names like Balloon Maker, the Roach Wrangler, the Human Flying Fish, and the Seaweed Queen.[8]

One reason that villains are so compelling to contemporary audiences may be that, as Peter Coogan suggests, villains are proactive while heroes are reactive.[9] The villain presents freedom of choice and free will, while the hero represents repression and the stable order of things. Ryan Litsey, writing in this volume on the Kingpin and earlier on the Joker,[10] suggests that not only are villains attractive as cathartic proxies for the reader; they may present a reader's most authentic possible point of reference. Such ruminations on the attraction of mavericks, rule breakers, and narcissists take on new urgency and relevance in the current era of populism heralded by the 2016 election of US president Donald Trump, a candidate who subscribed to "winning" as an ethos rather than that nonsense about great power and great responsibility—a candidate marked not by traditionally heroic ideals of sacrifice, piety, and commitment to social order but by traditionally deviant ideals of compulsive acquisition, irreverence, and disruption of the status quo. While the latter qualities have been enjoyable in fictional characters for generations, their presence in a viable candidate for—and, of course, winner of—the highest office in the land is a new and urgent development. We feel that this volume, then, may contribute to our understanding of such social phenomena, if only obliquely.

THE CHARACTERIZATION OF EVIL

Villains have a long history in the narrative and folklore of humanity: Ishtar from the *Epic of Gilgamesh*, Kali the Hindu goddess of death, the demonic Rolangs in Tibetan culture, Hera and Cronos in Greek mythology, Pluto from the Roman tradition, the trickster in some Norse and Native American stories, Set in the Egyptian tradition, and Gaunab and Ardo from African traditions. Perhaps the most recognizable example in the Western tradition is Satan, featured in the biblical story of Adam and Eve from the book of Genesis, taking the form of a serpent who temps Eve with the apple as a means to gain divine knowledge. According to some interpretations of Isaiah 14:9–22, Satan's greatest crime was being prideful and thinking himself equal to God; this of course leads to his expulsion from heaven to Sheol (Hades/Hell/the Underworld/the Place of the Dead), to endure eternal damnation and harvest the souls of the ungodly. The Koran, in "The Heights," 7:11–18, makes a similar mention of Satan's pride. Satan refuses to prostrate before Adam when commanded to do so by God:

"Why did you not prostrate yourself when I commanded you?" He asked. "I am nobler than he," he replied. "You created me out of fire, but You created him of Clay." He said: "Off with you hence! There is no place for your contemptuous pride. Away with you! Henceforth you shall be humble."[11]

Certainly, with the advent of Christianity and stories of Satan tempting Jesus in the book of Matthew and the Great Beast in the book of Revelation (not to mention Satan's attempt to destroy Job in the Old Testament), Satan is presented as the author of all evil in the world, acting with assistance from demons to tempt the faithful into sin and wickedness. The apocryphal literature did much to ensure that this idea was propagated. For example, in the book of Infancy, which tells the story of Jesus's early years, Satan is consistently a thorn in Jesus's side, always trying to hurt him in some way—he even possesses a young Judas Iscariot.[12]

Satan, however, has experienced a popular culture rehabilitation. The television show *Lucifer* (2016–) has turned the Devil into nothing less than a hero. Based on Neil Gaiman, Sam Kieth, and Mike Dringenberg's version of Satan in the DC Comics series *The Sandman* (first appearing in *The Sandman*, no. 4 [1989]), the Fox adaptation portrays the character as prideful and sexually promiscuous, but also as a punisher of evil. This likely strikes the mainstream television viewer as novel, but the Devil has enjoyed a robust representation in comics for some time. While not always positioned theologically as Jewish, Christian, or Islamic in nature, Satan's various iterations consistently feature him harvesting souls and employing minions to do his bidding. For example, Marvel's (or Timely Comics') original Golden Age Black Widow is employed by Satan to kill evildoers so that their souls can enter Hell and nourish Satan's never-ending hunger for them.[13] In 2015, as part of his "Chilling Archives of Horror" series, comics historian Craig Yoe published *Devil Tales*, featuring stories of old Scratch from the pre–Comics Code days (and featuring the work of artists like Don Heck, Gene Colon, and Dick Ayers).[14] There are Satan-like characters scattered through the respective universes of Marvel and DC, and others who live in the underworld: Marvel has Mephisto, Blackheart, Zarathos, and occasionally even Satan himself (one of Marvel's most famous supernatural characters is the Son of Satan, Daimon Hellstrom); DC has its own versions of Satan (and characters like Neron and the Blue Devil); and Image Comics in their Spawn universe also deploys a version of Satan and the character Malebolgia.[15]

Satan's influence on popular culture storytelling forms is well articulated in one particular sequential art example: 2011's *Fear Itself: Ghost Rider*. Here, former Ghost Rider Johnny Blaze and Mephisto dialogue about the nature of evil and sin. In this iteration, Blaze has given up being the Ghost Rider, and the mantle has been taken up by a young female. The story revolves around the first human, Adam, who brought sin into the world. Adam and his followers are using the Ghost Rider to wipe away all sin and make the world a godlier place. All is not what it seems, however; once the Ghost Rider wipes the sin out of someone, that person is reduced to a mindless zombie. Responding to Blaze, Mephisto suggests: "Sin may be a bad. But it's also part of what makes humanity. It's inherent in your flaws and foibles, your desires, your drives. Without these things, you have no creativity. No goals or 'Demons' to overcome. No urge to improve as individuals. This cold emotionless existence is what happens if Adam takes the sin away from humanity."[16] Blaze is not convinced, however, and believes that Mephisto has a more sinister idea in mind (fig. 2). Stan Lee had Satan in mind when he introduced Mephisto in *Silver Surfer*, no. 3 (1968), but he "didn't want to hit the reader over the head with religious implications."[17] He had wanted to create a villain who was the "most universally recognized symbol of evil on the face of the earth—the specter of Satan."[18] Mephisto attempts to pervert and destroy the Silver Surfer, whom Lee saw as an "allegorical representation of all that is good, all that is pure and unsullied in the human condition. . . . His total selflessness, and loathing of violence, greed, and deceit seem to place him on par with the greatest heroes in the annuals of religious legend."[19]

This characterization of Satan is some distance from classic representations of evil. Nathan Alan Breen's analysis of demonic characters in Old English poetry shows how the protagonists' demonic opponents were shown to be inferior to the subjects in various ways (such as knowledge and agency).[20] Breen points out that showing demonic characters as inferior was a form of "othering" that distanced them from readers and subjects, which in turn reduced feelings of empathy and/or pity. Part of the reason that this distance was created was so that when subjects (heroes) use their opponents' (villains') methods against them, readers do not consider the subjects' use of such methods "evil." For example, when superheroes use violence to stop supervillains in comic books, readers do not consider the superheroes' acts "evil." The reason for this is twofold. First, by othering the villain, the author ensures that audiences don't feel

Figure 2. The Satan-like Mephisto tells Johnny Blaze that sin is a necessary part of humanity; without sin, we lose an important part of who we are as humans (from Williams, Clark, Ching, et al., *Fear Itself: Ghost Rider*, 2011).

bad or pity them when bad things happen to them; and, second, because the violence is being used against an other, audiences do not generally consider it a negative "mark" against the superhero. What normally would be considered an evil act (using violence against another human/sentient being) is in this case not considered evil; in fact, it may be lauded as good, righteous, or just. In an analysis of justice paradigms in comic books, Nickie Phillips and Staci Strobl argue that the dominant paradigm is vigilantism, "in which moral justice trumps legitimate criminal procedure."[21] The reason that this paradigm dominates comic books (or at least superhero comics) is its appeal to a "retributive" view of justice popular in the United States. Thus, "the irony of comic books as a revenge fantasy is that evil is employed against evil in hopes of giving birth to good, a uniquely Judeo-Christian notion of apocalyptic redemption."[22] Unfortunately, the "irony of comic books" is not limited to comic books, or even US culture. Examples of the "irony of comic books" can be seen in other media from other cultures around the world.

For example, in the story of Shuten Dōji from medieval Japan, the titular evil demon welcomes the heroes, disguised as priests, who have come to kill him, into his fortress.[23] Shuten Dōji is shown to be a generous and trusting host; however, these qualities are ultimately his downfall, as the heroes use their subterfuge to slay him while he sleeps. Here, we are expected to praise the heroes for their cleverness and use of deception and lies to kill the demon, who had acted generously. This example illustrates how, by othering the villain, we can justify the acts of the heroes, even if we would normally condemn such actions. This process of othering the villain or villainizing the other is central to the concept of the villain and is rooted deep within the human experience.

According to Jens Kjeldgaard-Christiansen, evil, and consequently the villain, serve evolutionary purposes for the human psyche: evil is "an agentic designation reserved for a marked, sustained mismatch between the expected welfare tradeoffs of others toward us and our groups—be it real or imagined."[24] In other words, evil does not exist and is only a convenient label for competing interests or world views. In fact, many characteristics of villains, such as "foreign" accents or disgusting appearances, help to make othering them even easier. Thus, when we can simply justify a person's action as "evil," we do not consider what may have caused that person to act the way he or she did, often justifying "draconian punishment" against the other.[25] The contemporary reengagement with Satan is perhaps symptomatic of a new generation coming to terms with this perspectival nature of evil.

NARRATOLOGY AND THE SUPERVILLAIN

Discussing the Joker, Janet Pate argues that "every superhero must have a supervillain to exercise his brain and muscle power and keep him on his toes."[26] It is often a matter of being two sides of the same coin, or matched opposites: Batman/Joker, Reed Richards/Doctor Doom, the Flash/Reverse Flash, Wonder Woman/Cheetah, Iron Man/Mandarin, and so on. As the Mandarin tells Tony Stark (Iron Man): "We are linked you and I. By the strands of FATE. We are Yin and Yang, East and West, Black Science and Mystic Purity. The Living and the Dying" (fig. 3).[27]

This duality of actant and reactant is an important dimension of the superhero/supervillain narrative, one explored in detail by the discipline of narratology. In *Narratology: Introduction to the Theory of Narrative*, Mieke Bal defines narratology as "the theory of narratives," the goal of which is to deconstruct its subjects for deep analysis. Narratology as a project seeks to provide a

Figure 3. The supervillain is often the matched opposite of the superhero, as the Mandarin tells Tony Stark's Iron Man (from Benson, Kaminski, Abnett, et al., *Iron Man/War Machine: Hands of the Mandarin*, 2013).

vocabulary for describing any given narrative text, which Bal defines as "a text in which an agent relates ('tells') a story in a particular medium,"[28] including anything from books to movies. A story is a presented within a fabula, which Bal defines as "a series of logically and chronologically related events that are caused or experienced by actors."[29] Actors are simply "agents that perform actions," and events are "transitions from one state to another."[30] Thus, Bal suggests, agents tell stories, which are presented as fabula within which actors perform actions in order to cause or experience events, which are transitions from one state to another. Narratologists distinguish between three different layers of analysis—(narrative) text, story, and (fabula) elements—each of which is made up of several particular topics that distinguish one layer from the others.

The first topic of importance in the present discussion is the *narrator*. The narrator is part of the text layer and is defined as a "fictitious spokesman" who "'utters' the signs" that make up a story.[31] The narrator may or may not be a character in the story but is always separate from the text's creator. Narrators can cede control at times to allow characters to speak directly, and they can play important roles in narratological analysis, as will be shown later. Now we turn attention to two important topics in the second layer of analysis, *story*. The first of these two topics is *sequential ordering*, simply the relations between "events in the story and their chronological sequence in the fabula."[32] Narrative texts can obviously have a wide range of different orderings. The second topic is *focalization*, "the relation between the vision and that which is 'seen,' perceived."[33] Put another way, focalization is about identifying the lens through which we see a story (its characteristics, etc.) and how it relates to what is seen.

The final layer, *elements*, contains the topic of *classes of actors*. These are particularly important to this volume, which is concerned with a particular class of actor, the villain, or, as shall be described below, the "opponent." According to Bal, there are six classes of actors, each of which is based on certain shared characteristics of its members. The first two classes of actors are related *subjects* and *objects*. A subject is an actor who aspires toward some object, while an object is what the subject aspires toward. For example, Superman wants to defeat Lex Luthor: Lex Luthor would be the object and Superman the subject. The object does not have to be a person, nor does it even have to be material. For example, Indiana Jones wants to find the Holy Grail (material), and Miss America wants world peace (immaterial). The next two classes of actors are also related: *power* and *receiver*. Power is that which gives the object. Bal notes that "in many cases [power is] not a person but an abstraction: e.g. society, fate, time, human self-centredness, cleverness."[34] Thus, power could be something within the subject, like a personal trait, or it may be external to the subject, like a king. A receiver is "the person to whom the object is given"[35]—generally the subject is also the receiver but does not have to be. Finally, the last two classes of actors are *helpers* and *opponents*. Helpers help the subject get the object; for example, Robin helps Batman defeat the Joker. However, the magic sword that can cut the giant's chain, or the moonless night that allows the detective to slip into the gangster's hideout, are also helpers. Opponents, then, hinder the subject from getting the object. Again, the opponent does not have to be an actor. It could be the detective's alcoholism, or the knight's fear of snails. Collectively, these six classes can be used to describe all actors in a narrative text.

Throughout history and across genres, authors have used narratological techniques to set apart villains, antagonists, and opponents from other characters in a narrative text. One way that authors and/or narrators do this is to exert a certain amount of control over villains. Villains, while necessary for an interesting story, must be carefully controlled by creators lest they confuse or mislead other characters and/or readers. Creators therefore use a variety of narratological techniques to clearly show that villains are inferior to the hero(es) and should not be listened to. Additionally, showing villains as inferior is another way for creators to "other" them so that readers do not identify with or pity them, which could lead readers to turn on the hero (who is now seen as a bully).

Breen's analysis of the representation of demonic characters in Old English poems provides an apt illustration. Breen focuses on how the narrative elements and narrator are used to control demonic characters so that they are ultimately shown as inferior and/or disadvantaged compared to the forces of good, arguing that "precise arrangement of the narrative and characters' speech" is needed to control the demonic character.[36] In other words, authors carefully choose their words to ensure that demonic character(s) are seen as wrong and bad. Breen suggests that many Old English authors made use of their narrators in this way; through the narrator, the author maintains control of all the characters in the story by selectively deciding when they are allowed to speak directly. This allows the author to remain in control even when allowing demonic characters to offer contradictory utterances. Breen discusses another method for controlling demonic characters, namely limiting or restricting their knowledge and/or agency: they are thus seen as inferior to other characters who possess more knowledge and freedom. Finally, Breen demonstrates how time can be used to create a hierarchy of power among characters: the more clearly and chronologically a character can present a narrative, the more power they have. Thus, demonic characters fail to present coherent narratives and are cast as lacking power. Breen's analysis shows that villains, at least in Old English poetry, are characterized by a lack of control. They are too dangerous to be given freedom for fear that they will affect the other characters and/or the reader. The idea of control as it relates to villains runs through many narratological accounts of villains, albeit in different forms.

Another way authors set villains apart from other characters is by denying them full control over their desires. Often, villains have the ability to sate all of their desires, and yet they remain unsatisfied. Samuel Toman Rowe argues that in the eighteenth-century novel it is the villain's desire, *not* the hero's, that pushes the narrative forward.[37] Rowe labels this idea—that villains are the instigators of the plot but are nevertheless swept up by it involuntarily—the "persecutory plot." In his analysis, Rowe demonstrates how the persecutory plot plays out in the stories of four archetypal eighteenth-century villains: (1) the criminal, (2) the rake, (3) the "oriental" despot, and (4) the gothic villain. The criminal is characterized by tragicomedy, a preoccupation with the proletarian lifestyle, and the demeanor of a picaro, "cunning in response to a contingent circumstance."[38] The rake is essentially a rapacious playboy, while the "oriental" despot is "an insatiable, capricious, and violent being weltering in sexual and gustatory enjoyments."[39] Lastly, the gothic villain is characterized by "gothic faciality,"[40] conjuring the idea of readable versus unreadable faces: the "insatiable desire of others is focused in the face, thus gothic fiction makes the negativity of [the villain's] desire visible on his face."[41] What Rowe's analysis shows is that another characteristic of villains, at least in the eighteenth-century English novel, is insatiability, which puts the plot of the story into motion.

The idea of the villain as the driver of the plot is also seen in another context, that of video games. Here, the villain/antagonist often serves the purpose of not only setting the plot in motion but also establishing the terms of gameplay. Thus, another way that villains can be identified is by looking at which characters instigate the plot of a narrative. In his analysis of video game antagonists, James Neel shows how they have evolved from purely gameplay elements to story elements, ultimately serving both functions.[42] Neel suggests that antagonists in video games have "four primary functions": (1) "the antagonist is the primary source of the game's conflict," (2) "the actions of the antagonist define the player's goals," (3) "the antagonist presents players with obstacles to overcome," and (4) "the antagonist is the final obstacle, and their defeat resolves the conflict."[43] Additionally, Neel notes that video game antagonists are mainly denoted through their characterization. In other words, in video games you can pick out a character as a villain by his or her dialogue and actions. Therefore, another method of identifying villains is to look for who acts as the genesis of a narrative's action.

No stranger to narrative action, Christian intellectual C. S. Lewis has argued that evil is simply good spoiled, contending that "there can be good without evil, but no evil without good. You know what the biologists mean by a parasite—an animal that lives on another animal. Evil is a parasite. It is there only because good is there for it to spoil and confuse."[44] Lewis saw the human condition and its propensity for heroic acts, but he also understood that humanity has within it those parasitic tendencies for villainy. The villain, for Lewis, is thus one who is unhampered by societal morality, with the free will to do as one pleases without thought to consequences. Mike Alsford suggests that "true villainy has to do with the desire to dominate, to subsume the other within the individual self. . . . The villain would appear to lack empathy, the ability to feel for others, to see themselves as part of a larger whole. The villain uses the world and the people in it from a distance, as pure resource."[45] This definition covers many aspects of villainy, but it is too boilerplate. As this volume shows, the line between villainy and heroism is often a thin one. For some villains, there can be redemption; a single evil act does not necessarily make one pure evil. For example, in Sam Raimi's film *Spider-Man 3*, Uncle Ben dies because he got in the way of Sandman, who was stealing to get money for his daughter's operation. Uncle Ben was a victim of circumstance. This does not excuse Sandman's killing of Ben, but it does explain how one can commit an evil act without evil motivations. As Jeff Rovin argues in *The Encyclopedia of Super Villains*: "The truth is, super villains also teach us about ourselves. We may admire the hubris of super villains, identify with their frustrations, and even . . . find their freedom alluring. But the bottom line is that in life, as in art, herodom is a chronicle of successes while villaindom is a catalogue of failures."[46]

DEFINING SUPERVILLAINS: A SPECTRUM OF IDENTIFICATION

Like their foes, supervillains have origin stories, and this is one of the attributes that sets them apart from average criminals. There are those who arise as a result of a freakish accident (the Joker falling into a vat of chemicals); others who are spurned by a romantic interest, often because of their appearance (the Mole Man or Venom, the latter spurned not by a love interest but by Peter Parker/Spider-Man); and those who are created for a purpose (the Scorpion, created to take down Spider-Man). Others, like Darkseid, are simply forces of nature. But the origin story, while possibly a viable mode of categorization, is not the most useful. In addition to sorting varieties of supervillain, we must also determine what separates the supervillain from the superhero.

They have much in common, after all. In terms of comic studies, however, the defining characteristic is that, historically, the hero does not kill. The boundary for superheroes is often killing, which is "generally regarded as a line that superheroes will not cross because it makes them too much like the criminals they fight. Killing also takes the hero from being reactive . . . to proactive, taking the powers of the jury and judge into their own hands."[47] Today, even seemingly incorruptible characters like Jim Gordon can cross that line. In the series *Gotham*, Gordon kills for the Penguin, and he also has no problem taking out evildoers, like mayor Theo Galavan. The Sub-Mariner, the Punisher, Deadpool, and similar characters, while fascinating to watch, are not superheroes in the traditional sense (since they have no compunction about killing), even though their actions may do some good and take out criminals. Spawn kills child-killer Billy Kincaid, who would, no doubt, continue to kidnap and murder children if he were not taken out. But Batman will never kill the Joker (even though the Joker often wants him to), because it would go against his moral code, no matter how many people the Joker murders. Likewise, the Fantastic Four will not kill Doctor Doom, nor will Spider-Man kill any of his rogues' gallery, no matter how many times these villains try to kill the heroes. This begs the question: are heroes like Batman and Spider-Man at fault for all the serial murders the Joker or Carnage commit? Have they sacrificed lives that could have been saved if they had just crossed that line and eliminated the villains in question? Does that make Batman or Spider-Man less of a hero and more a villain?

As we discussed above, narratology tells us that opposing forces in any story are subjects and opponents, but it is clear that the binary of hero/villain does not map comfortably onto that of subject/opponent. The subject is the actor within the narrative with whom the audience is invited to empathize and experience the action, but that actor need not be heroic. When they are, the opponent is sometimes a true villain, but the heroic actor may also face off against an antivillain (a villain with sympathetic qualities who invites the audience into some degree of identification based on shared characteristics or desires). Alternatively, the subject may be an antihero, a protagonist who invites identification through their centrality in the story but whose actions may at times be repulsive or objectionable. In the middle of the spectrum—hero, antihero, antivillain, villain—sits the chaotic-neutral presence of the trickster, a subject position very seldom offered to the audience.

"Evil" Villains: Low Identification

Western popular culture villainy might be said to have begun self-consciously at the beginning of the twentieth century with a low degree of ambiguity. The cartoonish, villainous foil to the hero, unavailable to the audience as a point of identification and replete with designs on evil for its own sake, emerges with Dr. Quartz and Dr. Mabuse. Dr. Quartz, the nemesis of America's version of Sherlock Holmes, Nick Carter, first appeared in *Nick Carter Library*, no. 13 (1891), two years before Moriarty would appear as Holmes's chief foe. Quartz faced off against Carter in twenty-seven encounters, including a comic book appearance the third issue of *Shadow Comics* (1940).[48] Like later characters such as the Red Skull and the Joker, Dr. Quartz seemingly dies many times, but he always reappears to match wits with Carter another day (lest anyone think that comic storytelling is only type of narrative in which characters die and reappear consistently). Coogan describes Quartz as "an amoral hypnotist and vivisectionist who most enjoys slicing up living women [like the real-life Jack the Ripper] and playing against Carter with lives as pawns in his twisted game of chess. In many ways he presages the fictional villains and real serial killers of the twentieth century."[49] Quartz is not without his weaknesses, one of which is characteristic of many villains: hubris. "His egotism, his conceit, his unlimited belief in himself is also his greatest weakness, but even knowing this Nick cannot let his guard down against Doctor Quartz for a moment."[50] Coogan quotes Carter from *New Nick Carter Weekly*, no. 692, concerning Quartz: "His intelligence is quite the most profound of any person I have ever known. ... He is totally without two qualities possessed by other humans ... [namely] [m]orality and conscience. The man recognizes no moral responsibility. ... Compassion in any form, is a meaningless term."[51]

Like Quartz, Dr. Mabuse is a fascinating study in villainy. Created by Norbert Jacques, who published the novel *Dr. Mabuse, der Spieler* (*Dr. Mabuse, the Gambler*) in 1921, the character has been the subject of at least five novels and twelve films. These include three films directed by German auteur Fritz Lang: *Dr. Mabuse the Gambler* (1922; released in two parts, this four-hour opus is one the greatest silent films ever made); *The Testament of Dr. Mabuse* (1933) (banned by the Nazi Party in Germany and not shown there until 1961); and *The Thousand Eyes of Dr. Mabuse* (1960). It was Lang's films that made Mabuse a villain of notoriety worldwide. Like Lex Luthor or the Kingpin, Dr. Mabuse's criminal empire is methodically well thought out, leaving little to chance. His is a well-oiled machine, and he has a hand in everything—from stock market manipulation, to political agitation, to gambling, to staging psychoanalysis lectures and hypnotism shows. Like the Joker, Mabuse never seems to run out of henchmen, and he is a master of disguise (always seemingly one step ahead of the law, like Prometheus in the fifth season of *Arrow*). Mabuse is an intellectual, trained in psychiatry—like the female villains Dr. Harleen Frances Quinzel (Harley Quinn) and Dr. Karla Sofen (Moonstone)—and uses his training to gain advantage over others. For Mabuse, "[e]verything in the world gets boring in the long run—except one—the game with people—and their faith—no such thing as luck, only the will to gain power."[52] He is interested in the force of will and is the Nietzschean superman (*Übermensch*) in its purest form. "When humanity, subjugated by the terror of crime, has been driven insane by fear and horror, and when chaos has become supreme law, then the time will have come for the empire of crime."[53] Presaging the Joker and Harley Quinn's codependent, abusive relationship, Mabuse has a female henchwoman, Carozza, who views him as "the greatest man alive" and deludes herself into thinking that Mabuse actually has feelings for her.[54] Viewed with contemporary eyes, Lang's two earlier films and Jacques's original novel are chilling prophecies of the rise of fascism and the Nazis. The story of Dr. Mabuse is a story of surveillance that resonates across two world wars, the Cold War, and the War on Terror. As film scholar Tom Gunning argues: "Today [Mabuse] does not simply seem a figure from past history, but a compelling contemporary image of terrorism in an age of universal conspiracy and advanced technology."[55] Mabuse would no doubt feel right at home in our time.

Antivillains and Antiheroes: Identification at a Cost

Comic villains in the Golden Age would largely be characterized according to this unambiguously evil profile, informed to a great degree by these doctors of pulp fiction, who in turn were informed by many of the "othered" villains of myth, religion, and literature we will discuss in section 2 below. But with the advent of the Silver Age, villain characters would begin to invite meaningful identification opportunities for the audience. Magneto presents an interesting case study of the antivillain. Due to his experiences as a Jewish prisoner in Auschwitz, he fights for mutant rights (and superiority) with a much more militant stance than Professor X, who dreams of peaceful coexistence with the human community. Magneto can be seen as a Malcolm X type, while Xavier can be compared to Martin Luther King Jr. As former *X-Men* editor Bob Harris argues:

> I remember an old saying that every hero is defined by the villain he or she fights—and I think that's really true when it comes to the X-Men and Magneto. Both want a better place—a better world—for their kind, they just go about it in very different ways. The X-Men hope for the best—where humans and mutants live together in peace. Magneto fears the world and believes that only force can bring change. He doesn't view himself as evil—and to some minds he isn't—and that's what makes him so fascinating and the X-Men's job so difficult.[56]

Similarly, in the short story "Connect the Dots," Adam Troy Castro presents Magneto as

> not a demon and . . . not a villain. . . . [I]t was his most cherished dream to conquer the world, not out of any personal lust for power, but to make it a safe place for the race of superpowered people . . . mutants, people born with extraordinary powers. . . . He'd committed any number of atrocities in pursuit of that goal—he killed, and waged war, ravished countries. It gave him no pleasure, but it was necessary. Homo sapiens had proven it could not be trusted. Homo superior had to fight for survival.[57]

Magneto doesn't want to kill Professor X or the X-Men, but they stand in his way, so he will fight them. In fact, one of the most common tropes in the villain/hero narrative is that they start out as friends working together in some way. Professor X and Magneto were close friends, but their views on how to achieve social change diverged. Other examples include Doctor Doom/Reed Richards, Batman/Two-Face (or, rather, Bruce Wayne/Harvey Dent), and Mr. Glass (Elijah Price) and David Dunn from M. Night Shyamalan's film *Unbreakable* (2000).

A recent documentary, *Necessary Evil Super-Villains of DC Comics* (2013), suggests that "the function and role of the hero and the villain is all simply a matter of perspective. If we reversed focus and considered the story from the point of view of the villain, wouldn't the hero be the villain and the villain the hero?"[58] The doppelgängers of the *Justice League on Earth 3*, the Crime Syndicate, are a telling example of this. On their world, doing good is evil and doing bad is good. In the very first superhero feature film released to theaters (that was not a serial), *Superman and the Mole Men* (1951), the villains of the movie, the mole men, are really victims. The film is an interesting study in mass hysteria, the lynching mentality, and how, due to unfortunate circumstances, "the other" is often vilified.

The obverse of the (sometimes) sympathetic villain is the antihero, a character type that has emerged, it seems, as our contemporary popular culture's most compelling. This is, perhaps, because the antihero has blurred the line between heroism and villainy, reflecting the ethical or moral ambiguity that most individuals have found in their own lives. But the antihero is certainly not new. If we consider only comics, Marvel's first antihero was the Sub-Mariner Prince Namor, created by Bill Everett, who first appeared in *Marvel Comics*, no. 1 (1939) and proved to be enormously popular. The Sub-Mariner felt wronged by what the surface world had done to his race of underwater Atlanteans (such as killing and poisoning them). Namor would fight against the Human Torch and try to destroy the surface world, and then he would be on the side of humanity fighting the Nazis and the Axis powers. He has a volatile temper and has little respect or regard for surface dwellers. It is precisely this back-and-forth that helped make the Sub-Mariner one of the most popular and fascinating characters during the Golden Age of comics and beyond.[59]

Morally ambiguous antiheroes, such as *Breaking Bad*'s Walter White and *Mad Men*'s Don Draper, have enjoyed enormous popularity despite that fact there is little to admire in them—except, perhaps, their ruthless arrogance. Other shows like *House of Cards, Prison Break, Orange Is the New Black, The Sopranos, Sons of Anarchy*, and *Shameless*, to name a few, all feature protagonists behaving in ways that fall outside the traditional boundaries of heroism. We have even watched and empathized with Dexter Morgan, a serial killer who kills other serial killers while working as a forensics technician for the

Miami-Metro Police Department. *Deadpool* (2016), an R-rated "superhero" movie, was a worldwide sensation, making it at the time the second-highest-grossing R-rated film in America (just behind *The Passion of the Christ* [2004]).[60] Deadpool's predecessor, the Punisher, who first appeared in 1974's *The Amazing Spider-Man*, no. 129, was at the time a new kind of comics protagonist: a vigilante who killed bad guys (crime lords, gangsters, drug traffickers, and rapists). The Punisher was created at a time when revenge films like *Death Wish* (August 1974, appearing five months after the Punisher's February 1974 debut) and *Dirty Harry* (1971) were enormously popular[61]—judge, jury, and slayer all rolled into one. The Punisher has proven to be a popular staple in the Marvel universe. The character appeared in three feature films (1989, 2004, 2008) and proved popular in season two of Netflix's *Daredevil*; fans clamored for the character to get his own series (which, in turn, debuted in 2017). Jessica Jones, who, unlike every other character described in the preceding paragraph, is not a white male, is among a new class of female characters increasingly allowed to be deeply flawed as well.

We should perhaps not be surprised. Although there are those supervillains who are pure evil (e.g., the Red Skull), villains are most often rather more complicated. They may do immoral, narcissistic things, but they can also act with dignity and show selflessness. For example, Doctor Doom may be a dictator of his kingdom of Latveria, but he genuinely loves the kingdom's citizens. They may not have the freedom to do as they please, but they both love and fear Doom. Doom sees himself as a benevolent dictator even though his ultimate goal is world conquest. In *The Amazing Spider-Man*, no. 36 (2001), Doom sheds a tear over the fall of the Twin Towers on 9/11 (as the Kingpin and Magneto look on): "Because even the worst of us . . . however scarred . . . are still human. Still feel! Still mourn the random deaths of innocents."[62]

Today, as the moral authority of Western democracies is questioned on several fronts, even the most sacred of heroes can descend into villainy. Recently, in its *Secret Empire* storyline, Marvel made no less an icon than Captain America a Nazi/Hydra agent.[63] The character who embodied "life, liberty, and the pursuit of happiness" becomes a villain fighting for totalitarian ideals and kills fellow Avenger Black Widow. This could easily be read as a slap in the face to Cap's Jewish creators Jack Kirby and Joe Simon, the soldiers who fought in World War II, and the victims who died in the Holocaust concentration camps. Although it's now been revealed that this evil version of Cap was not the real Steve Rogers (who has returned), one could argue that the damage to the character is already done. While Marvel's *Civil War* storyline (2006) proved to be immensely popular, *Secret Empire* is the most unpopular crossover in the company's seventy-five-plus-year history.[64] Although, in *Civil War*, Captain America and Iron Man are at odds, the character keeps his dignity by holding to the rights of the individual. While Marvel has a history of turning its heroes into villains (Daredevil, the Angel, and the Scarlet Witch, among others),[65] it is possible that Marvel has, at least in the case of Captain America, lost touch with its fan base. Could this episode mark a reactive swing of the pendulum back to traditional hero/villain binaries?

The Trickster: Seduction as Identification

One character trope that will always trouble that binary is the trickster, who occupies a middle ground between the poles of good and evil (or perhaps, more accurately, who is simply groundless and rejects the notion of polarity). While the trickster is often unique and separate from the villain, trickster characters often take antagonistic roles within narrative texts. For example, within Norse mythology, Loki is an archetypal trickster, but he also acts as an antagonist in many Norse myths, comic book storylines, and film adaptations. According to Lewis Hyde, trickster characters and stories have several key characteristics.[66] First, appetite is the core of the trickster story; a trickster's appetite can, and often does, take any form (e.g., hunger or lust), and that desire drives the action of the story. A second characteristic of tricksters, according to Hyde, is that they live on the road. A trickster is transient and constantly on the move, in search of ways to satisfy desires. Third, the "trickster embodies consciousness coming into being."[67] Trickster stories show how, without consciousness, we suffer, but with it we can control events; these stories bear witness to the trickster's awakening to self-awareness and the benefits it brings. In addition to these three major characteristics, Hyde also notes three key themes of trickster stories: (1) chance and accident, (2) divination, and (3) the lucky find. These themes are consistently found within trickster stories and are another way we can identify them. Hyde provides several other notes about tricksters and their stories: tricksters are shameless and can't keep their mouths shut; trickster stories describe the pure and the impure as well as the opposition between gift and theft; and tricksters reveal, and therefore disrupt, the blind spots of conventional cultural norms. Overall, Hyde argues, tricksters help us see to the heart of things.

Of course, the most prominent trickster in popular culture is the Joker. A changeable being, the Joker invites wildly varying degrees of identification, depending on his mode of deployment. In Alan Moore's hands, the Joker is abhorrent (even if we can sympathize with his circumstances as a failed comedian stricken with grief); embodied in Heath Ledger's incredible performance, the Joker becomes, at times, someone we'd rather like to be (at least in a few key moments). In 2015, we published an edited collection entitled *The Joker: A Serious Study of the Clown Prince of Crime*.[68] In that volume, the Joker's impact, provenance, nature, and evolution were discussed at length, so in preparing the current manuscript, which was largely inspired by our experience working on *The Joker*, we have made the perhaps controversial decision *not* to spend valuable column inches discussing this most compelling of pop culture bad guys at any length. This is but one of many difficult choices a project like this one presents.

ABOUT THIS VOLUME

While we have herein tried to produce a vital and lasting impression of the supervillain as a rich and significant concept, with many various forms and manifestations, we cannot possibly be comprehensive. There are simply too many examples, and most readers will likely find one of their favorites overlooked in the pages that follow. Among them are characters who have become (or will very soon become) mainstreamed in popular culture: Loki, Thanos, Dormammu, and Darkseid, robust and rich characters all, find only passing mention below. Also passed over is any sustained discussion of Klingons or Khan, Daleks or Disney queens, Sauron or Saruman. Jason Voorhees, Michael Myers, and Freddy Krueger all linger restlessly on the sidelines; the Xenomorph and the Predator do battle elsewhere. There will no doubt be criticisms of the choices we've made. What we have endeavored to craft might best be called a mosaic rather than a list—fragmented, overlapping, more comprehensible and profound in aggregate, perhaps, than in any one part.

Our volume is influenced by two previous publications: *The Superhero Reader* and *The Comics Studies Reader*.[69] However, unlike those volumes, which almost exclusively feature previously published material, we present a combination of reprinted and original work. Our intent is to put the past and present in conversation, to better understand the future of this literature, of our popular culture, and, if it is not too indulgent to suggest it, of our society. Our volume also differs from the above in that, while the bulk of our tome is dedicated to the study of villainy in comics and sequential art, we have chosen to include discussion of other popular culture forms. In juxtaposing comics villains with witches and henchmen, Voldemort, Shakespeare's Coriolanus, Godzilla, and Darth Vader, we hope to point out the rich intermedia presence of the supervillain construct as well as some of its chronological development. As Peter Coogan suggests, the supervillain is "not unique" to the superhero genre, and thus our volume provides a glimpse into supervillainy of all kinds.[70] We hope that what follows, organized in such a way as to move chronologically—after a sustained consideration of typology and philosophy—with the development of media technologies (myth/literature, motion pictures, and, finally, the comic book and sequential art forms that emerge from it), can be useful for both undergraduate and graduate students, and that scholars can find here a place of departure. Each of the four sections that follow are designed to take the reader on a journey toward greater understanding of the supervillain character type—its long history, its morphology, and its intimate relationship to cultural discourses of right and wrong.[71]

It is ultimately the eternal struggle between villain and hero that keeps us coming back to these stories over and over again—whether in comics, films, novels, religious literature, or video games. No matter how many times we see the Joker face off against Batman or Daredevil confront the Kingpin, it never grows stale for us. As Iron Man tells Spider-Man: "The Bad Guys knock us over and we get back up on our feet, better than ever and twice as tough. It's what we do."[72] At the heart of this collection is a nagging apprehension that it's the knocking over—rather than the getting back up—that is increasingly attractive to us as readers of popular culture texts.

We begin our journey in Section 1 with a series of pieces that attempt, in their various ways, to build a moral philosophy within which we might account for villainy and, for analytical purposes, parse out its many forms into workable taxonomies. A. G. Holdier, in chapter 1, deepens the discussion only hinted at above about the relationship between heroes, antiheroes, antivillains, and villains and their respective moral identities. In this new piece, Holdier suggests that "moral identity is the field on which any talk of 'hero,' 'villain,' or some mixture of the two is played." Following Holdier's discussion, we include a previously published essay by Robert Moses Peaslee, who utilizes the work of British cultural historian E. P. Thompson and German sociologist Max Weber to unpack the "moral economy" of superheroism and, by association, supervillainy. Although not primarily concerned with villain characters, Peaslee's chapter is included for the contribution it makes to our discussion about moral choices in superhero/villain texts, choices that often lead the subjects of such texts to reject what is "legal" for what is "right." Jared Poon takes a lighthearted but challenging philosophical approach to the character of Magneto in the next chapter, showing that the Master of Metal, perhaps the most compelling villain in comics, asks a great deal of us as readers: how do we proceed when the means justify the end?

In the second half of Section 1, we move to definition and categorization, beginning with excerpts from Vladimir Propp's 1968 masterwork, *Morphology of the Folktale*. In the excerpted chapter, "The Functions of Dramatis Personae," Propp outlines the responsibilities of the villain as a story engine, underpinning much of what Mieke Bal proposes in the above discussion of narratology. Following Propp, we include an extended excerpt from Peter Coogan's much-cited work *Superhero: The Secret Origin of a Genre*. Here, we reproduce the majority of his chapter "The Supervillain," not only because it is cited extensively throughout the rest of the book but also because it (along with the other chapters in *Superhero*) has served as a framework upon which the field of comics studies has hung its hat for the better part of a decade. Lennart Soberon takes the baton from Coogan to explore, in a new piece, how "throughout the history of narrative film, filmmakers have been occupied with creative decisions regarding enemy-making." Soberon proposes a useful framework illustrating how "the spectator is guided through gradually intensified layers of opposition" through the creative decisions of filmmakers. Robin S. Rosenberg, in a piece reprinted from her 2013 collaboration with Coogan, takes the latter's 2006 categories into new territory, expanding and troubling some of the boundaries proposed seven years earlier (a lifetime, it turns out, in terms of how these characters and the media that deploy them have evolved). Finally, Cait Mongrain and David D. Perlmutter round out the section with an investigation of villainy's unsung heroes, the henchmen. Taking us from the very earliest manifestations of this tropic story device all the way up to contemporary video game narrative, Mongrain and Perlmutter show that it is his "intrinsically ancillary role that, almost paradoxically, makes the henchman essential."

Section 2 moves from definitions to what we might call the "source code" of the modern supervillain. Here we explore proto-supervillainy in a number of examples of myth (understood broadly to include both explicitly religious stories and those told in more secular circles that are nonetheless constitutive of "the way things are") and literature. Expanding the above discussion regarding Satan's (and Christianity's) role in establishing an ultimate cipher of evil, we begin with John Thompson's discussion of Aṅgulimāla, ancient India's supervillain and "a vicious murderer/brigand who, subdued by the Buddha, renounces his outlaw ways for monastic life and attains nirvana." Then, fast-forwarding to the Elizabethan era, we engage with one William Shakespeare and his approach to villainy—in some ways, the first popular culture examples of the character trope. Maurice Charney's is the first of two articles concerned with the Bard, and in his reprinted introduction from his book *Shakespeare's Villains* (2011), Charney takes us on a tour of the most ignominious and devious of Shakespeare's antagonists. One character he doesn't linger over, however, is Coriolanus, an oversight addressed in a new piece by Jerold J. Abrams, who suggests that "Shakespeare's supervillain" is actually a precursor of the first modern superhero, Superman himself. In chapter 12, we return to Christianity and take a deep dive into Restoration poet John Milton's *Paradise Lost*. Here, in a reprinted piece from 1999, John Carey investigates Milton's attempts to encapsulate evil within the character of Satan, an effort he deems unsuccessful in a way that perhaps resonates in consideration of today's depictions of the character: "[T]hose readers [of Milton] who have left their reactions on record have seldom been able to regard Satan as a depiction of pure evil, and some of the most distinguished have claimed that he is superior in character to Milton's God."

Moving to the modern period, the second half of Section 2 begins with Tony Magistrale's reprinted analysis of Herman Melville's *Moby-Dick*, and in particular of Captain Ahab as a gothic villain. Magistrale shows that, in Melville's characterization of Ahab, "the standard, eighteenth-century gothic apparatus—blood bonds with evil, haunted castles, a reliance on supernatural terror—evolved to tell a more complicated story, focusing on the profoundly tragic imperfections inherent in man and his institutions." In chapter 14, Richard Heldenfels explores the Sherlock Holmes literary canon, in particular Holmes's female foil, Irene Adler, for early traces of the Catwoman character, arguing: "The more closely you look at Holmes and Adler, the more you see the roots of Batman and Catwoman: two closely matched opponents; villains whose criminality has in both cases a sense of ambiguity; wronged women and damaged men; an attraction that is as confusing as it is powerful for the men in the equation; and an upheaval in gender roles." Speaking of gender roles, we next move into a consideration of witches, wicked and otherwise, as they have been constructed in the popular consciousness by religious and secular texts. Hannah Ryan, taking us from the fifteenth to the twenty-first century, shows how midwives, "these educated and trusted, yet nonconforming women were *uniquely imperiled by their learnedness and vocation*, which were critical to the survival, health, and well-being of their communities," and how this conflation of knowledge, gender, and persecution continues (and is sometimes contested) in contemporary pop culture representations. Finally, Section 2 concludes with a pivot from witches to wizards, as Adam Davidson-Harden considers J. K. Rowling's supervillain, the dark sorcerer Voldemort. Davidson-Harden suggests that "Voldemort represents an essentially humanistic hermeneutics of evil, and this approach contrasts with that of an author to whom Rowling owes inspiration, namely J. R. R. Tolkien, whose 'evil' characters are firmly rooted in his own fully articulated religious/divine framework."

Chapter 17 begins our third section, which engages with how cinema and, later, television have adapted the archetype of the supervillain for the screen. In "Caligari," reprinted from his hugely influential monograph *From Caligari to Hitler: A Psychological History of the German Film*, Siegfried Kracauer details the history of *The Cabinet of Dr. Caligari*, the German expressionist masterpiece that established the cinematic template for the "mad scientist" character trope. In particular, Kracauer outlines the process by which "a revolutionary film was thus turned into a conformist one," both presaging and helping to pave the way, in his estimation, for rise of the Third Reich. Following this, Stefan Danter explores the evolution of Godzilla, at once, paradoxically, the embodied demonization of atomic power in the twentieth century's second half and the benevolent protector of postwar Japan. Joe Cruz and Lars Stoltzfus-Brown follow Danter by cataloging the adventures of Harley Quinn, perhaps the most compelling and confounding female supervillain in the history of comics—but who has the rarified distinction of entering the canon through the door of an animated television series. Tara Lomax then asks us to consider Darth Vader in light of the practices of storytelling, suggesting that "the *Star Wars* franchise's episodic plot structure is fundamental to understanding the dynamics of Vader as a complex villain." Part of her analysis deals with the *Star Wars* prequels' capacity (however imperfectly) to show us Vader's point of view, a dynamic taken up in the following chapter by Víctor Hernández-Santaolalla and Alberto Hermida, who, in the contemporary television serial killer narrative, detect "a dramatic change in the focalization of the discourse, redirecting interest into getting to know [villainous or ambiguous characters] better." Relatedly, Ryan Litsey closes out the third section, remaining in the universe of television with a Machiavellian discussion of Netflix's treatment of a "heroic villain"—the Kingpin—in its *Daredevil* series.

In Section 4—our most substantial by design—we turn things over to the sequential art scholars to discuss, among many other things, how all of the intermedia influences explored in the previous sections find their way into comic books, manga, and graphic novels. We set the table initially, however, by reprinting the Code of the Comics Magazine Association of America (1954), otherwise known as the Comics Code, because it has directly impacted the characterization of villains in comics for generations. A creator who had a hand in leading comics out from under the code, Grant Morrison, is excerpted in the following chapter, providing his thoughts on the villain's villain, the Joker. In chapter 25, José Alaniz, in an excerpt from his 2014 book *Death, Disability, and the Superhero: The Silver Age and Beyond*, helps us understand representations of (dis)ability during this era, comics' so-called Silver Age, an era in which Captain America would reemerge from his Allied war hero persona to combat none other than President Richard Nixon (as Richard Hall tells us in the following chapter). Phillip Cunningham follows with his 2010 discussion of his experience growing up an African American fan of comics who found not only a dearth of superheroes who looked like him, but also a corresponding absence of black supervillains. The distinction here between villain and supervillain, and how that distinction maps over racial representation, is particularly important. J. Richard Stevens, in chapter 28, then prosecutes a cogent and detailed analysis of 1980s *GI Joe* villain Cobra Commander, whose organization, upon closer examination, bears "more resemblance to the neoliberal ethos of the Ronald Reagan administration itself than to its clandestine nonstate opponents."

Returning to DC Comics, we continue with Dan Vena's discussion of the supervillain Bizarro as a "trans-monster," then back to Marvel once again with

Naja Later's examination of the *Captain America* character Bucky Barnes, who, she argues, "creates a highly self-reflexive engagement with the generic lore of the superhero, prompting a corresponding engagement with the lore of American nationhood." Flying across the Pacific to connect the volume with Japanese manga and anime, we then reprint Noriko Reider's 2010 discussion of changing representations of *oni*, demonic characters from different dimensions who provide a complex array of challenges and opportunities for the protagonists with whom they interact.

Integrating East and West, we present Wyatt D. Phillips's essay on *Superman: Red Son*, in which Superman's story is reimagined in such a way that he becomes a Soviet rather than an American hero. Here, Phillips suggests that, "[i]n separating Superman's idealized morality from his ideological association with America, this comic book raises questions of morality's source (innate or learned) and, more significantly, the influence that political ideologies have on our conceptions of 'good' and 'evil' and ends versus means." In chapter 33, Matthew McEniry examines the books *Irredeemable* and *Injustice: Gods Among Us*, asking what happens when the trust placed in power—perhaps more fragile than we care to consider—breaks down. Finally, Tiffany Hong closes out our substantive chapters with a tour of the Image Comics work of Sam Kieth, whose storytelling in *The Maxx*, in which "the titular superhero is in reality a mere inhabitant of a rape survivor's unconscious writ large . . . destabilizes the [superhero] genre's assumptions of narrative hierarchy and linearity." Hong here examines "the prioritization of voice and narrative authority from hero, to villain, to the oft-silenced or absent victim, and heroic action as a response to or a preempting of villainous action."

Notes

1. David Bar Katz and Morris Katz, DC Super Heroes: My First Book of Super-Villains; Learn the Difference between Right and Wrong (New York: Downtown Bookworks, 2014).

2. Stan Lee, introduction to Bring On the Bad Guys: Origins of the Marvel Comics Villains (New York: Marvel Enterprises, 1998), 1–4. The book was first published in 1976 and has been updated, with characters created much later than 1976.

3. Stan Lee, Jack Kirby, John Romita et al., Bring Back the Bad Guys (New York: Marvel Enterprises, 1998).

4. Stan Lee, ed., The Ultimate Super-Villains: New Stories Featuring Marvel's Deadliest Villains (New York: Berkley Trade, 1996).

5. Geoff Johns, David Finch, and Richard Friend, Forever Evil (New York: DC Comics, 2015); Gail Simone, Dale Eaglesham et al., Villains United (New York: DC Comics, 2006); Daniel Wallace, DC Comics Super-Villains: The Complete Visual History (New York: Insight Comics, 2017) (originally published as a hardback in 2014); Gerry Conway, Bob Rozakis, David Anthony Kraft et al., The Secret Society of Super-Villains, vol. 1 (New York: DC Comics, 2011); and Paul Levitz, Gerry Conway et al., The Secret Society of Super-Villains, vol. 2 (New York: DC Comics, 2012).

6. Ben Dyer, ed., *Supervillains and Philosophy: Sometimes, Evil Is Its Own Reward* (Chicago: Open Court, 2009); and Lois H. Gresh and Robert Weinberg, *The Science of Supervillains* (New York: Wiley, 2004).

7. See King Oblivion, Adam Wallenta, and Matt Wilson, *The Supervillain Field Manual: How to Conquer (Super)Friends and Incinerate People* (New York: Skyhorse Publishing, 2013); and Neil Zawacki and James Dignan, *How to Be a Villain: Evil Laughs, Secret Lairs, Master Plans, and More!!!* (San Francisco: Chronicle Books, 2003).

8. Jon Morris, *The Legion of Regrettable Super Villains: Oddball Criminals from Comic Book History* (Philadelphia: Quirk Books, 2017).

9. Coogan argues: "The villains' machinations drive the plot. The hero reacts to the villain's threat, which justifies the hero's violence. But on generic level, the villain is reactive; that is supervillains are created in reaction to the hero's ability to defeat ordinary criminals in order to create narrative tension." Peter Coogan, *Superhero: The Secret Origin of a Genre* (Austin, TX: MonkeyBrain Books, 2005), 110.

10. Ryan Litsey, "The Joker, Clown Prince of Nobility: The 'Master' Criminal, Nietzsche, and the Rise of the Superman," in *The Joker: A Serious Study of the Clown Prince of Crime*, ed. Robert Moses Peaslee and Robert G. Weiner (Jackson: University Press of Mississippi, 2015), 179–93.

11. The Koran, "The Heights," 7:12–15, trans. Nessim Joseph Dawood (New York: Penguin, 1990), 109.

12. Rutherford Hayes Platt, ed., *The Lost Books of the Bible and the Forgotten Books of Eden* (New York: Alpha House, 1926).

13. The Black Widow first appeared in *Mystic Comics*, no. 4 (1940). See Jack Binder, Fred Schwab et al., *Marvel Masterworks: Golden Age Mystic Comics*, vol. 1 (New York: Marvel Enterprises, 2011).

14. Steve Banes, ed., *Devil Tales* (San Diego: IDW Publishing, 2015).

15. For more information on the Devil in comics, see Benito Cereno, "The Devil in Disguise: The History of the Devil as a Comic Book Supervillain," Comics Alliance, October 8, 2015, available at http://comicsalliance.com/history-devil-comic-book-supervillain/; and Remy Carreiro, "Five Interesting Interpretations of the Devil in Comics," *Unreality Magazine*, August 16, 2012, available at http://unrealitymag.com/lists/five-interesting-interpertations-of-the-devil-in-comics/.

16. Rob Williams, Matthew Clark, Brian Ching et al., *Fear Itself: Ghost Rider* (New York: Marvel Enterprises, 2011), n.p.

17. Stan Lee, "Blaze of Fire! Scent of Brimstone," in Stan Lee, Jack Kirby et al., *Bring On the Bad Guys: Origins of the Marvel Comics Villains* (New York: Marvel Enterprises, 1998), n.p.

18. Lee, "Blaze of Fire!"

19. Lee, "Blaze of Fire!"

20. Nathan Alan Breen, "The Voice of Evil: A Narratological Study of Demonic Characters in Old English Literature," PhD diss., University of Illinois, 2003.

21. Nickie D. Phillips and Staci Strobl, "Cultural Criminology and Kryptonite: Apocalyptic and Retributive Constructions of Crime and Justice in Comic Books," *Crime, Media, Culture* 2, no. 3 (2006): 304.

22. Phillips and Strobl, "Cultural Criminology and Kryptonite," 325.

23. Noriko Reider, "Carnivalesque in Medieval Japanese Literature: A Bakhtinian Reading of *Ōeyama Shuten Dōji*," *Japanese Studies* 28, no. 3 (2008): 383–94.

24. Jens Kjeldgaard-Christiansen, "Evil Origins: A Darwinian Genealogy of the Popcultural Villain," *Evolutionary Behavioral Sciences* 10, no. 2 (2016): 115.

25. Kjeldgaard-Christiansen, "Evil Origins," 119.

26. Janet Pate, *The Great Villains* (Indianapolis: Bobbs-Merrill, 1975), 68.

27. Scott Benson, Len Kaminski, Dan Abnett et al. *Iron Man/War Machine: Hands of the Mandarin* (New York: Marvel Enterprises, 2013), 154.

28. Mieke Bal, *Narratology: Introduction to the Theory of Narrative*, 3rd ed. (Toronto: University of Toronto Press, 2009), 5.

29. Bal, *Narratology*, 5.

30. Bal, *Narratology*, 5.

31. Bal, *Narratology*, 8.

32. Bal, *Narratology*, 80.

33. Bal, *Narratology*, 142.

34. Bal, *Narratology*, 198.

35. Bal, *Narratology*, 199.

36. Breen, "The Voice of Evil," 23.

37. Samuel Toman Rowe, "Imaginary Wants: Desire, Villainy, and Capital in Eighteenth-Century Fiction," PhD diss., University of Chicago, 2017.

38. Rowe, "Imaginary Wants," 50.

39. Rowe, "Imaginary Wants," 130.

40. Rowe, "Imaginary Wants," 176.

41. Rowe, "Imaginary Wants," 178.

42. James Neel, "Anatomy of a Villain: Play, Story, and Conflict in Single-Player Video Games," PhD diss., Arizona State University, 2012.

43. Neel, "Anatomy of a Villain," 22.

44. C. S. Lewis, *Words to Live By: A Guide for the Merely Christian* (New York: HarperCollins, 2007), 98.

45. Mike Alsford, *Heroes and Villains* (Waco, TX: Baylor University Press, 2006), 120.

46. Jeff Rovin, *The Encyclopedia of Super Villains* (New York: Facts on File, 1987), ix.

47. Coogan, *Superhero*, 112. Coogan points out that, for brief moment in the Golden Age, both Superman and Batman killed, and characters like the Spectre have as well. It should be noted, too, that Golden Age characters Captain America and Bucky had no problems killing Nazis, and in the case of the first Red Skull, Cap did not try to stop George Maxon from dying.

48. This story, "Nick Carter, Super Sleuth: Mystery of the Opera Star's Death," was reprinted in Anthony Tollin, ed., *Nick Carter*, vol. 3 (San Antonio: Sanctum Books, 2014), 139–44.

49. Coogan, *Superhero*, 68.

50. J. Randolph Cox, "The Magician of Crime," in *Nick Carter*, vol. 3, ed. Anthony Tollin (San Antonio: Sanctum Books, 2014), 4.

51. Coogan, *Superhero*, 68–69, quoting *New Nick Carter Weekly*, no. 692.

52. Fritz Lang, dir., *Dr. Mabuse, the Gambler* (New York: Kino Video, 2006). See also Norbert Jacques, *Dr. Mabuse*, trans. Lillian A. Clare (1923; repr., Eugene, OR: Bruin Books, 2015).

53. Fritz Lang, dir., *The Testament of Dr. Mabuse* (New York: Criterion Collection, 2004).

54. Lang, *Dr. Mabuse, the Gambler*.

55. Tom Gunning, liner notes to Fritz Lang, dir., *The Testament of Dr. Mabuse* (New York: Criterion Collection, 2004).

56. Bob Harris, quoted in *X-Men: Creator's Choice*, no. 2 (December 1993), 1.

57. Adam Troy Castro, "Connect the Dots," in *The Ultimate Super-Villains: New Stories Featuring Marvel's Deadliest Villains*, ed. Stan Lee (New York: Berkley Trade, 1996), 33.

58. Scott Devine and J. M. Kenny, dirs., *Necessary Evil: Super-Villains of DC Comics* (New York: Warner Brothers/DC Comics, 2013).

59. Carl Burgos, Bill Everett, Paul Gustavson et al., *Golden Age Marvel Comics Masterworks*, vol. 3 (New York: Marvel Enterprises, 2008); and Carl Burgos and Bill Everett, *Golden Age Human Torch Masterworks*, vol. 2 (New York: Marvel Enterprises, 2007).

60. "Domestic Grosses by MPAA Rating," Box Office Mojo, available at http://www.boxofficemojo.com/alltime/domestic/mpaa.htm, last modified August 15, 2017.

61. See John Cline, "Bernie's 'Deathwish': History and Transgression in New York City," in *Cinema Inferno: Celluloid Explosions from the Cultural Margins*, ed. Robert G. Weiner and John Cline (Lanham, MD: Scarecrow Press, 2010), 145–56. Cline argues that the "Punisher is derived arguably from Don Pendleton's *The Executioner* series with 'Mack Bolon' serving as a model for

Frank Castle" (156). See also Gerry Conway et al., *The Essential Punisher*, vol. 1 (New York: Marvel Enterprises, 2006).

62. J. Michael Straczynski, John Romita Jr., Scott Hanna et al., *The Amazing Spider-Man*, no. 36 (December 2001), n.p.

63. Nick Spencer, Steve McNiven et al., *Secret Empire* (New York: Marvel Enterprises, 2017).

64. Carlos Rosario Gonzalez, "Grab Your Pitchforks: Captain America Just Killed a Fellow Avenger in Marvel Comics' Most Unpopular Storyline Ever," MoviePilot.com, available at https://moviepilot.com/p/captain-america-kills-black-widow-secret-empire-marvel-comics/4333897.

65. Conversely, villains have become heroes, as the Sandman was once in the Avengers, Magneto was headmaster of Xavier's School for Gifted Youngsters, Juggernaut joined the X-Men, and Catwoman was in the Justice League of America. Hawkeye, Black Widow, Quicksilver, and the Swordsman were all villains before they were heroes. See also Christopher Gates, "How Marvel Turned These Heroes into the Greatest Villains," *Looper*, August 17, 2017, available at http://www.looper.com/48755/marvel-turned-heroes-greatest-villians/s/image-8085/.

66. Lewis Hyde, *Trickster Makes This World: Mischief, Myth, and Art* (New York: Farrar, Straus and Giroux, 1998).

67. Hyde, *Trickster Makes This World*, 56.

68. Robert Moses Peaslee and Robert G. Weiner, eds., *The Joker: A Serious Study of the Clown Prince of Crime* (Jackson: University Press of Mississippi, 2015).

69. Charles Hatfield, Jeet Heer, and Kent Worcester, eds., *The Superhero Reader* (Jackson: University Press of Mississippi, 2013); and Jeet Heer and Kent Worcester, eds., *A Comic Studies Reader* (Jackson: University Press of Mississippi, 2008).

70. Coogan, *Superhero*, 61.

71. While there is a tendency to think of cinema as coming before the rise of comics, both formats became cultural phenomena at nearly the same period of the 1890s (although comics and proto-comics have a much longer history). Cinema, however, developed into a mass culture form around the world shortly after its inception. In fact, almost immediately, cinema started poaching from comics for its story material. As film historian Emmanuelle Toulet points out:

> The comics supplied the cinema with ideas for scripts, and characters. . . . The structure of the comic strip also had an influence on the emergence of cinematic language: Full-page features were divided into panels equivalent to film shots which furthered the story while varying the viewing angle, scale, and location. Several comic strips like *Buster Brown* [1904] or *Little Nemo* [1911, created by Winsor McCay] began with full page drawings that introduced the story but were not a real part of it. This initial image can be compared with the close-up with which many films opened. But all parallels aside, in the first years of the century, film directors were far from attaining the cartoonists' narrative virtuosity. (Emmanuelle Toulet, *Cinema Is 100 Years Old* [London: Thames and Hudson, 1995], 113–14)

Other comics adapted in the early years of cinema include McCay's *Dream of the Rarebit Fiend* (1906), *Happy Hooligan* (1903), *Krazy Kat* (1916), *Trouble in Hogan's Alley* (1900), and *The Katzenjammer Kids* (1898). See also Blair Davis, *Movie Comics: Page to Screen/Screen to Page* (New Brunswick, NJ: Rutgers University Press, 2017). Davis traces the history of how film adapted comics as well as the impact films have had on comics. Another useful volume is Wheeler Winston Dixon and Richard Graham, *A Brief History of Comic Book Movies* (Cham, Switzerland: Palgrave Macmillan, 2017).

72. Matt Fraction, Salvador Larroca, Frank D'Armata et al., *The Invincible Iron Man*, vol. 1, *The Five Nightmares* (New York: Marvel Enterprises, 2009), n.p.

Section 1

MORAL PHILOSOPHIES AND TAXONOMIES OF VILLAINY

CHAPTER 1

Dividing Lines

A Brief Taxonomy of Moral Identity

A. G. HOLDIER

IN 1972, UMBERTO ECO AND NATALIE CHILTON PUBLISHED THE SEMINAL ESSAY "The Myth of Superman," a groundbreaking work that looks at the iconic hero as an archetypical protagonist paradoxically constrained in a genre that precludes genuine narratival development. Eco argues that the god-like Superman must be shown to change and grow if the reader is to relate to him as a hero, but the nature of the comic book medium requires that the character of Superman never change significantly enough, lest he become unrecognizable and thereby threaten the continued profitability of his serial publications. Eco contends that this "inconsumable-consumable" tension, combined with the invincible prowess of the superhero, results in a temporally locked narrative that can never advance; as he says, "Superman, by definition the character whom nothing can impede, finds himself in the worrisome narrative situation of being a hero without an adversary and therefore without the possibility of any development."[1] Strangely, across more than eight thousand words, Eco's essay never considers the role of the supervillain.

Although it might be true that Superman's abilities make it more difficult to challenge him in a believable fashion, the array of similarly overpowered enemies in his rogues' gallery have been doing precisely that for decades. And while Superman has been known to battle realistic enemies ranging from bank robbers to Hitler, it is the exaggerated moral duality of the superhero-supervillain relationship that may be at the core of the perennial popularity of superhero stories. According to David Pizarro and Roy Baumeister, the human brain enjoys analyzing and categorizing the moral character of others in precisely the pleasure-eliciting fashion that pro-survival evolutionary developments would predict, but such calculations are difficult and often inaccurate. A fictional world wherein little moral ambiguity exists between the easily identifiable main characters functions as a moral equivalent of pornography: "Just as sexual pornography depicts a world where the desired outcomes occur reliably and the difficulties and ambiguities of actual life are pleasantly and effortlessly absent, comic books depict a world where desired outcomes occur reliably (good triumphs over evil) and the difficulties and ambiguities of moral prediction are absent."[2] Following this line of thinking, because Superman and Lex Luthor are easily identifiable as hero and villain, the reader can enjoy the pleasurable chemical feedback of that moral analysis with little effort needed.

However, not only does this thesis leave open many questions about the current popularity of supervillains in themselves, but it also torpedoes the possibility of analyzing any character who spans the gap between the two moral poles. With the recent rise of interest in protagonists whose moral identity is shrouded in ambiguity, the pornographic hypothesis must be adapted to consider both the antihero and the antivillain, in addition to the classical hero and villain roles. What follows is a brief taxonomy of these four categories, analyzing their unique characteristics but especially their differences (what distinguishes a villain from an antihero, for example) and, crucially, their interdependencies.

MORAL IDENTITY

When one reads a text, the characters are identifiable by their physical descriptions, historical backgrounds, relationships with other characters, and more, but to label an individual as "hero," "villain," or something else forces the reader to rely on a particular factor of character classification based on normative grounds: moral identity. Sitting at the confluence of psychology and ethical philosophy, moral identity isolates and considers the moral traits within the multilayered matrix of a character's personality, rated both internally via the character's reflective self-conception (as such might be available in the text) and externally via his or her actions and interactions with others, to categorize the moral nature of the character in general.[3] To be able to identify a character as generous, patient, honest, or kind (each an example of a moral trait) requires the reader to consider not simply a single conscious choice that the character makes but rather what the sum total of a series of choices appears to reveal about the character's personality; as Karl Aquino and Americus Reed explain, "moral identity is . . . linked to specific moral traits, but it may also be amenable to a distinct mental image of what a moral person is likely to think, feel, and do."[4] Taken as a whole, moral identity is the field on which any talk of "hero," "villain," or some mixture of the two is played.

However, as a heuristic for literary analysis, moral identity can be limited in its scope; in the absence of an intentionally self-revelatory monologue, internal information about a character's psyche is often hard to come by. Instead, the reader is primarily left to draw on data external to the character's subjective thought process, typically in the form of the individual's dialogue or physical actions, in order to categorize that person. But if this is the case, then Eco's tension remains problematic: without narratival development, the available data for analysis will inevitably become repetitive, thereby allowing for, at best, a flat interpretation or, at worst, a conclusion anemic in its insipidity. A robust analysis of moral identity requires a variety of data taken in a multiplicity of scenarios; if Superman truly cannot grow, then discussions of him as a character will quickly become listlessly overwrought.

And yet, Superman and many other superpowered characters continue to fascinate and capture the hearts and minds (and wallets) of large audiences. In part, as already mentioned, Eco's suggestion that overpowered individuals are "heroes without adversaries" has been patently debunked by decades of narratives spun around the machinations of similarly overpowered supervillains; though he always prevails in the end, Superman has indeed found balanced matches against plenty of evil characters, even dying at the hands of one (albeit only temporarily). And, although comics may have once functioned with a continuous reset parameter at the end of each issue, the mid-1980s (particularly in the wake of 1985's *Crisis on Infinite Earths* series) saw a shift in comic storytelling technique that began to emphasize a continuous setting for the characters that could feasibly carry the consequences of one story over into the next, thereby setting the stage for genuine plot development and the possibility of acquiring a full-bodied picture of a character's moral identity.

HERO/VILLAIN

With continuity comes a library of data for synthesizing an assessment of an individual's moral identity, primarily in the form of that individual's outward activity (though tempered also with moments of internal insight). In the classic dichotomy, the only ultimate question is whether or not a character is a "good person"—is the figure a hero or a villain, based on the general pattern of their actions?

An easily adaptable technique for approaching such an inquiry comes from Aristotle's description of the ethical life: a good person is one who succeeds at living a "life shaped by exercise of the virtues of intellect and character."[5] Although debates about his conclusions (and even some of his terms) continue today, Aristotle's definition of εὐδαιμονία (*eudaimonia*) captures this sense of successfulness: if a person flourishes and cultivates well-being over the course of their life, then that life could be described as eudaimonistic. And while "flourishing" and "well-being" are two common translations of *eudaimonia*, given that Aristotle also connects the concept with the ultimate purpose of human existence, the arguably most popular rendering of the term is "happiness."

On this view, virtues are the technical, skillful aspects of an agent's behavior that ensure a given action to be performed excellently. Virtues to Aristotle are not merely personality traits to admire but components of actions that must be demonstrated; as D. S. Hutchinson puts it, "only those who make active use of their virtues can be said to be living successfully—just as only those who actually compete in the Olympics can win."[6] Aristotle's skillfully orientated virtues, particularly in a literary framework, are also what were described above as moral traits, but the key from Aristotle is that these moral traits must be exercised in order to accomplish *eudaimonia* and be considered a good person.

With this in mind, the twin elements of (a) moral traits and (b) the application of those traits within an individual's actions offer two key factors for differentiating between heroic and villainous characters. Heroes are not simply good people who happen to possess ideal moral viewpoints or beliefs (as demonstrated through dialogue or omniscient narration), but they demonstrate their heroic character by working out those moral traits in their plot-driving behavior; conversely, villainous characters both possess and demonstrate the opposite. These bilateral touchstones function in tandem and might be diagrammed as in table 1. Therefore, characters like Superman, Sam Gamgee, and Luke Skywalker are heroic in virtue of their approach toward Aristotelian *eudaimonia* insofar as they develop ideal moral traits as revealed through their actions; villains like Voldemort, Saruman the White, and Joffrey Baratheon, drenched in vicious moral traits applied to nefarious ends, are necessarily precluded from Aristotle's conception of the "good life."

TABLE 1	Acts Morally	Acts Immorally
Possesses Moral Traits	Hero	
Lacks Moral Traits		Villain

A final point from Aristotle's work is instructive: it is only once a character's story is complete that their moral identity can be best assessed.[7] This helps to explain how villainous characters might redeem themselves prior to their death, demonstrating with finality (particularly in the case of redemption-through-sacrifice) that their moral identity is defined ultimately by virtuous and not vicious traits. Whether thanks to a diegetic moral epiphany (such as in the case of Darth Vader) or the device of an unreliable narrator (as with a character like Severus Snape), villains can become heroes when they reveal an underlying commitment to virtuous activity, even after a pattern of immoral behavior, through a particularly noteworthy moral act.

ANTIHERO/ANTIVILLAIN

In his magnum opus, *The Gulag Archipelago*, Aleksandr Solzhenitsyn laments the complexity of moral identity in the real world: "If only it were all so simple! If only there were evil people somewhere insidiously committing evil deeds, and it were necessary only to separate them from the rest of us and destroy them. But the line dividing good and evil cuts through the heart of every human being. And who is willing to destroy a piece of his own heart?"[8] Much like Pizarro and Baumeister's pornographic thesis, Solzhenitsyn's observation strikes at the heart of a perennial issue with heroic—particularly superheroic—characters: they are jarringly unrealistic, not simply thanks to their gravity-defying powers of flight or their unfashionable proclivity for skin-tight spandex, but as recognizable people to whom an audience can relate. Perhaps this explains the rise of characters whose moral identity is cloudy with paradox: the antihero and the antivillain.

Superman's invincibility elevates him not only above the average villain but above every actual reader to a degree that undermines what J. R. R. Tolkien called the "Secondary Belief" necessary for any fantasy story to function properly: "Anyone inheriting the fantastic device of human language can say *the green sun*. Many can then imagine or picture it. But that is not enough. . . . To make a Secondary World inside which the green sun will be credible, commanding Secondary Belief, will probably require labour and thought, and will certainly demand a special skill, a kind of elvish craft."[9] As Eco points out, omnipotent characters can transfix audiences only temporarily: "An immortal Superman would no longer be a man, but a god, and the public's identification with his double identity would fall by the wayside."[10] However, an ardent antihero who lacks moral traits or a chivalrous antivillain who fails to act morally cannot help but pique a reader's interest precisely because of the character's seemingly contradictory nature.

Antiheroes are characters who act morally, but typically for reasons disconnected from an inner sense of virtue; antivillains are their complementary counterparts, characters who retain moral traits while failing to put them into practice. Examples range from Han Solo to Anne Rice's Lestat to the Punisher for the former, with the latter's ranks filled with characters like Magneto, Captain Nemo, and Milton's Lucifer; in each case, the character appears to possess a given set of virtuous or vicious traits, but then performs actions that run contrary to what might be reasonably expected. The Punisher rightly seeks to rid the world of evil, but has no qualms about committing murderous actions to do so; Nemo unhesitatingly destroys another ship, but not before demonstrating congenial hospitality to Aronnax and his friends. This complexity of moral identity is difficult to explain based on a simple bivalent framework—even scalar models that would rank "antihero" simply as a "less heroic" form of hero fail to capture the nuances of the bilateral concerns drawn above from Aristotle.[11] However, these two contradictory forms of moral identity can easily be mapped into the quadrants left empty in table 1, as shown in table 2. In this view, an antihero fails to cultivate moral traits, but still (for a variety of possible reasons) seeks to accomplish otherwise good ends; similarly, an antivillain maintains a personal sense of morality, but either applies that code toward immoral ends or fails to apply it whatsoever.

TABLE 2	Acts Morally	Acts Immorally
Possesses Moral Traits	Hero	Anti-Villain
Lacks Moral Traits	Anti-Hero	Villain

To further explore this complexity, the French philosopher Paul Ricoeur's two-part philosophy of identity is instructive. Ricoeur distinguishes two forms of identity akin to the two senses of the passage of time for a person: the external, objective sense that passes identically for a group of people versus the internal, subjective sense that can make time feel shorter or longer than it really is for an individual. To Ricoeur, these two senses of time lead to two ways of talking about a character's identity through time. The external data Ricoeur dubs the *idem*-identity of a subject, which comprises everything seen from a third-person viewpoint—what has been discussed above as the visible external actions of an individual. The internal perspective Ricoeur calls the *ipse*-identity, and this first-person sense of selfhood captures the subjective perception of an individual's character—what has previously here been mentioned as the inner moral traits of the person.

For Ricoeur, one's *ipse*-identity changes and grows, fluctuating over time as a person learns and reacts to events in the world around, but always remaining essentially constant in a conscious sense: the individual having the differing experiences maintains a certain cohesive sameness throughout that perspectival change. *Ipse* substantiates what is often taken to be the natural sense of self-identity: a subject's personal view of the world. Conversely, the *idem*-identity never fundamentally changes, for it is always the totality of the external observations about the activity of a character as would be told by an impartial witness. In short, Ricoeur sees *ipse*-identity as the answer to the question "Who am I?," whereas *idem*-identity answers, "What am I?" (where that "what" is most easily marked as an object acting in the world). Crucially, these two components are necessarily overlapping and ultimately inextricable. Ricoeur explains: "This overlapping, however, does not abolish the difference separating the two problematics: precisely as second nature, my character is me, myself, *ipse*; but this *ipse* announces itself as *idem*."[12]

Therefore, the Ricoeurian element of *ipse*-identity can function to explain the first-person beliefs, emotions, and properties that make up the list of an individual's moral traits previously discussed; similarly, the notion of *idem*-identity is comparable to the external view of the person's chosen actions (see table 3). The benefit of this exercise comes in Ricoeur's ultimate conclusion about the union of the *ipse/idem* contradistinction, insisting that the "suturing" of these two elements together creates a robust sense of one's "narrative" identity that can encapsulate both who a figure is and what he or she is like; as Kim Atkins describes, "Ricoeur argues that the narrative model provides the means for creating such a temporally continuous, conceptual whole by bringing the elements of life into relations of 'emplotment,' just as a story's plot configures its constitutive elements to create a unified entity."[13] In general, Ricoeur wanted to adapt hermeneutical concepts to describe real-world experiences of identity as if they were stories; what is proposed here is essentially a recursive application of Ricoeur's own concepts back into a hermeneutical context.

TABLE 3	Moral Idem	Immoral Idem
Moral Ipse	Hero	Anti-Villain
Immoral Ipse	Anti-Hero	Villain

This injection of Ricoeur's narratival identity into the conversation about antiheroes and antivillains allows the reader to juxtapose the charted bivalent conditionals in a manner that was precluded by the simple dichotomy from earlier. A character might well possess an *ipse*-identity marked by villainous moral traits, but if their external *idem*-identity appears heroic, then this tension need not be described as vaguely belonging to a somehow lesser form of hero, but simply to someone categorized separately as an antihero. Similarly, if a villain appears to possess an honorable moral code within their *ipse*-identity, that does not excuse their ultimately villainous actions carried out as a part of their *idem*-identity. Such an approach avoids collapsing these complex tensions into an oversimplified rating and instead maintains the distinct concerns of internal traits and external actions.

THE DIVIDING LINE

Finally, a Ricoeurian look at the moral identity of characters allows a final suggestion to explain the appeal of the antitypes: they are, potentially, the most realistic characters possible. To Ricoeur, the term "character" "designates the set of lasting dispositions by which a person is recognized. In this way character is able to constitute the limit point where ... *ipse* becomes indiscernible from ...

idem, and where one is inclined not to distinguish them from one another."[14] The ideal situation—Ricoeur's variation of Aristotle's *eudaimonia*—is when one's inward life and outward life come to be marked in an identical moral fashion, just as in the case of the hero. Both the antihero and the antivillain are progressing toward this goal, albeit along different tracks, but each still carries profound moral flaws—in precisely the same way that the audience of the work inevitably will and will recognize.

Not only do these flaws maintain a reader's interest with their familiarity, but the excitement of the story likewise captures what Tolkien calls the hopeful "recovery" that fantasy stories engender: "Recovery (which includes return and renewal of health) is a re-gaining—regaining of a clear view. I do not say 'seeing things as they are' and involve myself with the philosophers, though I might venture to say 'seeing things as we are (or were) meant to see them'—as things apart from ourselves."[15] Such characters allow a reader to easily reflect on his or her own moral identity precisely because antitypes are far from morally pornographic; they apprehend and present a realistic picture of a conflicted moral agent who is often uncertain and inconsistent in their choices.

Notably, several of the critiques Eco makes in his original essay have been answered naturally as superhero comics, in particular, have matured over the intervening decades since its publication. Not only have the supervillains that Eco ignored become a mainstay in the medium, but various methods of introducing flaws into the heroes' stories have been tried, just as Eco recommended (it is particularly noteworthy that roughly twenty years after Eco joked about an immortal Superman, DC Comics saw fit to have the character killed—even if only for a limited time). But the resurgence of interest in antitypes stems, perhaps, from Eco's original point: if a character requires an adversary in order for the narrative to advance, then the internally conflicted antihero or antivillain will never fail to motivate the story. These realistic characters can be their own adversaries and, precisely because of the ubiquity of Solzhenitsyn's dividing line, they can be our entertaining mirrors as well.

Notes

1. Umberto Eco, "The Myth of Superman," trans. Natalie Chilton, *Diacritics* 2, no. 1 (1972): 16. This essay is also available in Jeet Heer and Kent Worcester, eds., *Arguing Comics: Literary Masters on a Popular Medium* (Jackson: University Press of Mississippi, 2004).

2. David A. Pizarro and Roy Baumeister, "Superhero Comics as Moral Pornography," in *Our Superheroes, Ourselves*, ed. Robin S. Rosenberg (New York: Oxford University Press, 2013), 33.

3. This definition relies heavily on Karl Aquino and Americus Reed II, "The Self-Importance of Moral Identity," *Journal of Personality and Social Psychology* 83, no. 6 (2002): 1424, although it is here adapted to relate more specifically to fictional characters (who, for example, must only be observed and cannot be directly interrogated).

4. Aquino and Reed, "The Self-Importance of Moral Identity," 1424.

5. C. C. W. Taylor, "Politics," in *The Cambridge Companion to Aristotle*, ed. Jonathan Barnes (New York: Cambridge University Press, 1995), 237.

6. D. S. Hutchinson, "Ethics," in *The Cambridge Companion to Aristotle*, ed. Jonathan Barnes (New York: Cambridge University Press, 1995), 199.

7. See Aristotle's treatment of Solon's thesis along these lines in *Nicomachean Ethics* 1100a–1103a.

8. Aleksandr I. Solzhenitsyn, *The Gulag Archipelago, 1918–1956: An Experiment in Literary Investigation*, vol. 1, trans. Thomas P. Whitney (New York: Harper and Row, 1973), 168.

9. J. R. R. Tolkien, "On Fairy-Stories," in *Tolkien on Fairy-Stories*, ed. Verlyn Flieger and Douglas A. Anderson (London: HarperCollins, 2014), 61. To Tolkien, Secondary Belief in a reader surpasses a mere suspension of disbelief to achieve a consistent atmosphere of imagined realism within the constraints of the fictional world. Just as in the real world, the internal logic of a fantasy setting must be valid given whatever parameters are defined as "normal," even if those parameters are vastly different from those of the real world.

10. Eco, "The Myth of Superman," 16.

11. For one such example of a scalar model, see Travis Langley, "Our Superheroes, Our Supervillains: Are They All That Different?," in *Our Superheroes, Ourselves*, ed. Robin S. Rosenberg (New York: Oxford University Press, 2013), 99.

12. Paul Ricoeur, *Oneself as Another*, trans. Kathleen Blamey (Chicago: University of Chicago Press, 1992), 121.

13. Kim Atkins, "Narrative Identity, Practical Identity, and Ethical Subjectivity," *Continental Philosophy Review* 37, no. 3 (2004): 348.

14. Ricoeur, *Oneself as Author*, 121.

15. Tolkien, "On Fairy-Stories," 67.

CHAPTER 2

Superheroes, "Moral Economy," and the "Iron Cage"

Morality, Alienation, and the Super-Individual[1]

ROBERT MOSES PEASLEE

IN "THE MYTH OF SUPERMAN," UMBERTO ECO COMMENTED THAT THE PREVAIL-ing view of Superman (and superheroes generally) as mythical saviors was, by way of myopia, in error; instead, Eco pointed out, analysts should be attuned to the particularly American qualities of Superman, who eschews fighting injustice on the macro or structural level and prefers instead to wage smaller battles of immediate and palpable significance.[2] The effect of this decision, according to Eco, is an implicit acceptance and defense on the hero's part of the tenets of capitalism and bureaucracy, such as property ownership, legality, and due process. In sum, Superman is ideology.

Since the early 1970s, the presence of superheroes (and comic book characters in general) in popular culture has become increasingly pronounced. In particular, cinematic adaptations abound, largely beginning with *Superman* (1978) and continuing through the 1990s and 2000s with ever-increasing sophistication. If Eco is correct, then, it becomes important to consider the relationship of these characters to the societies in which they operate (both in narrative and in "real" life); these characters occupy unique positions in relation to power, and how they negotiate these positions has much to tell the viewer about the value and legitimacy of the institutions in which such power is situated.

It is the goal of this chapter to offer one way of imagining the role of the superhero in contemporary society, a way that recognizes the superhero as an extreme example of the individual in an alienating and diffuse society. The tradition holds, after all, that superhero characters are both Superman and Everyman, alter ego and superego. The character of Aunt May, in an enormously interesting scene in *Spider-Man 2* (2004), reminds her reticent super-nephew that "there's a hero in all of us." We are meant to both identify with and distance ourselves from such otherworldly characters, and, clearly, these films are manifestations of contemporary negotiations between the self and the whole, between desire and responsibility, between chaos and order.

Two theorists offer compelling ways of understanding Hollywood's superhero tradition. E. P. Thompson's work on the concept of the "moral economy," which analyzes the behavior of the eighteenth-century British rural peasantry during that era's occasional bread riots, is of central value to the following analysis.[3] Thompson maintains that the traditional view of riot activity as sporadic, primal responses to physical deprivation (which evokes a rather animalistic view of rioters) is incomplete. What such a summation lacks is an awareness of the reasoned moral argument underpinning such activities, an argument that values implicit social "goodness" over the doctrine of codified law and an emerging sense of the infallible market economy.

As characters who act variously toward (in tandem with, outside of, in opposition to) explicit expressions of social cohesion (police and government are prevalent examples), superheroes evoke a correspondent implicit goodness, a commonsense approach to doing right that often operates outside the acceptable parameters of bureaucratic authority. It is in consideration of bureaucracy, in fact, that the work of Max Weber becomes vital. According to Weber, the human construction of society, the "technical and economic conditions of machine production which . . . determine the lives of all the individuals who are born into this mechanism," becomes an "iron cage" of constraint; in fact, bureaucracy in full flower comes to act in opposition to the very democracy responsible for its creation.[4] Since superheroes do not reject bureaucracy outright (though they certainly could) but exist to varying degrees within it, the dialectical nature of the human relationship with law and propriety are vividly expressed in their activities.[5] What is of interest is the degree to which Eco's thesis, related above, concerning the ideological nature of superhero characters holds; that is, are viewers discouraged by such characters to think and act outside the established parameters of control and normalcy? This chapter aims to add to the discussion of whether or not this is an accurate assessment and raises the possibility that, rather than being ideological, superheroes represent a gap in ideology, what Janice Radway has called an "ideological seam."[6]

The study will commence with analyses of three films, each of which was released during the US summer blockbuster season of 2004: *Spider-Man 2*, *Hellboy*, and *Catwoman*. The selection of these particular films is not meant to imply any scientific sampling method. Rather, they were chosen qualitatively based on their roots to comic book culture, their similarities and differences, and the various discourses and institutions they address. Other films could have been used. In fact, the term "superhero" could easily be extended to encompass characters such as Harry Potter and Jesus Christ himself (as portrayed in Mel

Gibson's *The Passion of the Christ* [2004]). But that is another paper, and I encourage someone to write it if I do not find the time.

SPIDER-MAN, HELLBOY, AND CATWOMAN: ARTICULATIONS OF HUMANITY

In this section, I would like to make some comments about the role of these three characters (and the texts in which they appear) in articulating the sentiments expressed in the work of Thompson and Weber. In order to make clear the degree to which the trope of the superhero addresses issues of sociality, governance, and alienation, I will make several particular comments about key sequences in each of the films under study.[7] First, however, I would like to make some holistic observations that help couch the finitude of each text in a larger cultural and cinematic discourse.

For example, the setting for each of these narratives is one of extreme urbanity. *Spider-Man 2* takes place expressly in New York, while *Hellboy* and *Catwoman* are both implied to unfold in the Big Apple. In all three films, the geography of skyscrapers, subways, sewers, and compartmentalizing spaces such as apartments and cubicles plays a constitutive role in not only the mood but also the action of the story. Peter Parker lives in a tiny apartment and is constantly bumped, jostled, and impeded as he moves throughout the city. Only when he is Spider-Man is he capable of transcending the maze of urban structure, as he leaps from building to building with the aid of his webs. Patience Phillips, similarly inept as an average citizen, finds liberation from her inhuman pod of a workspace at the moment she quits her design job and embraces her Catwoman chutzpah. Hellboy is perhaps the most confined of the three, as he is essentially jailed under maximum security between episodes with supernatural bad guys. His constant propensity to escape, aided (like his previous two counterparts) by his ability to navigate the rooftops and underground mazes of the city, is a clear expression of a desire for sociality. And yet the city, the apex of sociality, is impossible without the mechanical and bureaucratic structures that act to dehumanize it. Superheroes thus toe the line between integration with and transcendence of the social whole. The urban setting has a fraternal association with the superhero tradition, one that holds its main characters responsible for elevating the plight of humanity, both by their actions and by their very existence, above the calculable and administrative matrix of urban structure and organization.[8]

Origin stories, also, are of great interest to our current discussion. Each of the three main characters under study, once they assume the role of superhero in earnest, do so in reaction to a perceived need, a need that cannot be met by the sanctioned bodies of force and authority currently in existence. Spider-Man, created by the accidental bite of a genetically engineered "super-spider," is motivated to fight crime largely by the death of his uncle (for which Parker feels continuously responsible). Parker's decision to become a crime fighter stems largely from the realization that the police, who are always a step behind the criminals, cannot stop crime before it happens. To a large extent, they can only prosecute it. With his powers, Spider-Man comes to realize that he can act preemptively against crime, and he does just that. Catwoman, meanwhile, imagines her mission initially as one of revenge. This desire for revenge as a motivating force highlights another shortcoming of the urban peacekeeping apparatus—the police and courts cannot mete out revenge, only justice. Justice is both imperfect and impersonal, and therefore largely unsatisfying. Revenge, on the other hand, is a visceral act, an eminently human (though perhaps not social) act. Catwoman's appeal, like her Gotham counterpart Batman's, is that she is driven by this personal desire to confront her trespassers. That this desire gives way to a more ecumenical concern with wrongdoing is indicative of the degree to which the superhero simultaneously moves within, and not simply outside, the bureaucracy.

Hellboy, finally, is perhaps the clearest example of a character who is needed to do the things that police, military, and government authorities cannot. Employed by a government simultaneously fighting and covering up supernatural threats, Hellboy stands as an example of bureaucratic insufficiency par excellence. But he also stands apart from his two super counterparts in that he was never human. His omnipotence comes from the fact that he, too, is a supernatural being—one, in fact, who must grind down his horns to appear even remotely docile. The fact that Hellboy submits to this kind of regimen, as well as his virtual incarceration, is due to his relationship with and commitment to his father, a device that suggests the preeminent position of personal relationships over the maintenance of the social whole. Hellboy's resolve, like Spider-Man's, is based on a promise to a loved one, not to a municipality.

The utopian wish to halt violence before it occurs, the legitimate desire for revenge, and the commitment to familial and other personal relationships are all ends to which a variety of means may be tolerated by a society in which codified law largely cannot offer them. This is the essence of Thompson's "moral economy": "[I]n one respect the moral economy of the crowd broke decisively with that of the paternalists [contemporary government]: for *the popular ethic sanctioned direct action by the crowd, whereas the values of order underpinning the paternalist model emphatically did not.*[9] That citizens do not generally form mobs in contemporary society should not lead one to presume that this tendency does not still exist, even if only in latent form. In addition, to see this tendency as directed only against those who would disrupt "normalcy" through criminal activity would be myopic. Indeed, the nature of these superheroes is at once to support and critique the social systems in which they operate. Weber points out that "the most decisive thing here—indeed it is rather exclusively so—is the *leveling of the governed* in opposition to the ruling and bureaucratically articulated group, which in its turn may occupy a quite autocratic position, both in fact and in form."[10] That agents of this "leveling" are continually portrayed in superhero texts as inadequate, unreasonable, and often simply annoying speaks to a disfavor with modern social and technological systems, necessary as they may be.

Spider-Man 2 and System Fallibility

In addition to battling villains and personal ambivalence, Spider-Man comes into frequent and often conflictual contact with two major systems or mechanisms. The first of these, what can broadly be termed "science" or "technology," is a long-standing cliché of the superhero genre. One need look no further than the origin stories of many heroes and most villains to establish this generalization. Similarly, the second system, that of the judicial apparatus, appears with equal frequency as a common set of characters (e.g., *Batman*'s Commissioner Gordon) often working alongside but, in the end, far behind the hero. *Spider-Man 2*, in many ways, does not deviate greatly from these general formulas, yet the degree to which both of these mechanisms, ostensibly created to ensure human safety, fail utterly to do so in the film is remarkable. Some examples will make this clear.

The genre of science fiction, at its root, is about the ongoing interface between human and machine, between the mind and its products. The central question in much of the congruent fiction and cinema deals with the nature of control and in whose (or what's) hands it rests. Often, it is the inequity, or "madness," of the scientist that looses the deleterious and catastrophic effects of his creations upon the world. But in the case of *Spider-Man 2* villain Dr. Otto Octavius, such a summation seems inappropriate. Octavius is portrayed as an eminently reasonable man, a researcher and scholar passionate about the social responsibility of those individuals whose intellectual gifts allow them to achieve greatness. He is an attractive (that is, sympathetic) character with an equally attractive dream: to supply cheap, renewable energy to the world through the harnessing of fusion technology.

In discussing Octavius's work over dinner, Parker voices the concern of society at large when he probes the doctor's certainty of containing the reaction (since failing to do so would mean disaster). Octavius laughs off the concern, his confidence in mathematical calculation unshakeable. When the reaction fails, Spider-Man is on the scene to shut down the doctor's machine before it can consume the entire building in flames and destruction. Strangely, given the undoubtedly complex nature of the computation that brought such a monstrous technology into existence, all Spider-Man must do to stop the reaction is pull the plug (or, rather, several large plugs), and the city is once again safe. Octavius, now fused together with his artificially intelligent arms (minus the "inhibitor chip" that directs his thoughts and intentions to them), falls under the influence of technology itself. His desire to rebuild and his returned confidence in his calculations are a clear representation of human pride, but also of the lusty progress of science for science's sake. When his second, more powerful fusion device also spins predictably out of control, it is only a reawakened Octavius, released from the influence of the arms, who can save the city. He sacrifices himself to the depths, acknowledging his inability to control such a technology in any other way but by simply destroying it.

Octavius's crime, in the end, is the removal of scientific knowledge from the context of society. Parker is a continuous cautionary presence for the doctor, whose own intentions are very much in line with the improvement of life quality for a great majority of the population. But when the science becomes removed from these intentions, as it so often does in these films (the initial film in the franchise offered a similar plot device), it invariably morphs into something terrible to behold. Spider-Man, then, becomes the restraint, literally pulling back on the reins (in the form of electrical cables) to stop the impending technological doom. The omnipotence of the superhero offers a foil to human pretension, through scientific discovery, to the same.

Technology spinning out of control is thus a constant presence in *Spider-Man 2*. The centerpiece action sequence of the film, in which Spider-Man and Doc Ock duke it out all over New York, climaxes on an elevated train careening through the midtown skyscrapers. In an attempt to divert Spider-Man's attention, Ock disables the brakes on the train, requiring the hero to find a way to arrest its progress and save the innocent citizens inside. This scenario, again, will not be unfamiliar to readers and viewers of superhero lore. All at once, the technological safety and security of a commuter subway train (in terms of reliability, failsafe systems of stoppage and control, etc.) is utterly forgotten, and those on board, hastening toward the end of the line and their certain demise, are without options. Science has failed them—turned against them, even. It is only Spider-Man, with a generous application of webs to the passing buildings, who is able to stop the train in time, splayed Christ-like across the front of the train, arms wide, and in physical agony. And should one miss the savior metaphor, his unconscious body is passed back through the train, still in crucifixion pose, where his calm, boyish face is gazed upon by adoring and grateful citizens.

In addition to minimizing the impact of clearly fallible technological systems, Spider-Man spends much of the remainder of his days in places where an equally inept judicial system cannot be (or simply isn't). In the opening sequence of the film, in which Parker is forced to assume his super-identity to keep his pizza delivery job, Spider-Man swoops in to rescue two wayward, ball-chasing children from an oncoming truck. Later, when the hero joins a police chase in progress, only a well-placed web saves a group of innocent bystanders from being crushed by an out-of-control police car (which, as another example of unchecked technology, is seen as a highly imperfect means of pursuit compared to a nimble webslinger). When Doc Ock robs a bank from which Aunt May is seeking a loan, no vault or security guard is of any use, nor can "the authorities," as they are so often referred to, do anything about the aforementioned calamities with the train and the fusion reactor. Time and again, the tools of security and law enforcement are unable to counter the immediacy or the enormity of the dangers to which their citizens are exposed. In fact, during a key sequence in the film when Parker renounces his heroic identity and ceases his activity as Spider-Man, we see both an alley street fight and a house fire in which members of society are victimized. This is what the normal world looks like. A world without superheroes is one largely without safety, and this fact is presented so clearly to Parker as to compel him to ascetically renounce his personal desires (primarily for a relationship with his love interest) and return to crime fighting. There is little ambivalence here on the effectiveness of law and the agencies entrusted with its enforcement in preventing crime.

Hellboy, Bureaucratic Inadequacy, and Individuality

Despite working as part of a team (the Bureau of Paranormal Research), Hellboy insists upon undertaking his missions alone. While this tendency is partially and playfully explained by his colleague Abe Sapien as the "whole lonely hero thing," the wisdom of Hellboy's preference becomes clear as the film unfolds. In every altercation that ensues between the Bureau and various forces of evil, human action and technology are of virtually no use. Sammael, the demon whose initial breakout in the museum is the impetus for the first action sequence of the film, disposes of (or, rather, digests) six armed security guards with no effort. Later in the chase, when young Agent Myers tries to assist Hellboy, he finds himself caught in the middle of a busy highway and is saved at the last minute only by the gigantic fist of the hero. Hellboy punches straight down onto the hood of an oncoming vehicle, causing it to flip (in one of the few nifty shots in the film) harmlessly over them. He loses ground, however, on Sammael, and the agent is seen as no more than a bald inconvenience.

It becomes difficult, in fact, to see the Bureau and the agents who work for it as anything more than a restriction on the hero. Hellboy is locked into his living space, let out only to foil supernatural wrongdoing. After initially defeating Sammael, Hellboy disappears into the darkness, and then is found a few hours later. Interestingly, when found, Hellboy returns quietly. Much of this quiescence may be attributed to the respect he feels for his father, Broom (who heads the Bureau), but the indication that seems most apt is that Hellboy resents his mission far less than the system in which he must accomplish it.

Later in the film, once the Bureau has learned of Sammael's ability to clone himself, Hellboy and his team search the underground catacombs of the city for the villain's lair. After Abe is able to pinpoint the location of the den on the other side of a wall, the agent's first response is to suggest obtaining a permit to inspect the location. Exasperated, Hellboy uses his concrete fist to obliterate the need for such paperwork. Once the villains are found, Hellboy separates from the team in the ensuing chase. Predictably, all agents concerned (Myers excepted) are killed. Manning, a Justice Department appointee furious at what he sees as an ongoing pattern of damaging, individualistic behavior, lectures Hellboy on the importance of working as a team, to which the hero responds by destroying the room in which they are arguing.

The foregoing sequence is vital at a number of points. First, once again the human forces charged with securing the safety and well-being of their citizens are seen as woefully inadequate. Only the superhero can approach evil and succeed. What is more, the agents are lampooned in the sequence as largely impotent bureaucrats in their adherence to law and policy (e.g., the permit). The audience is clearly meant to laugh at the suggestion, all the more so after Hellboy finds a much more direct, though unsanctioned, means to the end. But what is most interesting is Hellboy's reaction to the admonition by Manning. The righteousness with which Manning approaches the hero is intolerable to him exactly because he has always told everyone concerned that he works alone. Hellboy knows that his human counterparts are no help to him, and yet he is chastised for not working with them properly. There is blame to be handed out in the aftermath of so much death, and the question posed by the dialogue between Hellboy and Manning is, do we blame the individual who left the agents behind or the system that insisted on putting them there?

Shortly after this sequence, Broom, Hellboy's adoptive father, is murdered in his study at the Bureau. The irony here is that the maximum-security installation that has contained the demon hero for sixty years could not protect his father, a fact not lost on the grieving son. His mission to find the reincarnate villain Rasputin is now personal, and his tolerance for Manning—the clearest symbol of bureaucracy in the film—is absolutely zero. Paired together in the final hunt for Rasputin and his minions, Manning and Hellboy disagree at several points along the way. Hellboy simply dismisses Manning outright, exhibiting rank insubordination at every turn. When Manning later finds himself in mortal danger, it is the action of the hero that saves his life, a fact that leads to a reconciliation of sorts between the two characters. What this reconciliation means, however, is unclear. Has Hellboy returned to the fold, as it were, recognizing that he is needed by his human coworkers? Has Manning come to accept the hero's maverick nature? We are left to speculate. But Hellboy's greatest test is yet to come.

When, in the climactic sequence of the film, Hellboy is given the choice of opening a cosmic lock and unleashing the incarcerated Seven Gods of Chaos upon the world, or refusing and ensuring his love interest's demise, his ultimate refusal to open the lock is played as a reaffirmation of his commitment to his father and, by extension, humanity generally. Once the injured Myers is able to toss Broom's rosary to the hero (who had carried the beads with him since his father's death), Hellboy is then able to resist the temptation to choose poorly. Another interpretation, however, is of interest, and it concerns the degree to which Hellboy does or does not simply fulfill a function. On more than one occasion, Rasputin encourages Hellboy to become that which he was meant to be. What this means is that the hero was conceived as no more than a key brought into the world, along with his giant concrete fist (evil assistant Ilsa asks mockingly, "What did you think it was for?"), simply to open the lock and end the imprisonment of the Seven Gods. In a sense, then, his final decision is very much about the place of an individual in a proscribed system. On the one hand (literally), Hellboy can fulfill his "destiny" and perform the role he was created to perform. On the other, he can choose not to act in the way in which the system assumed he would. He can transcend the role given him and make a choice as a feeling, thinking individual. This is, of course, the path he chooses, presumably to the impassioned delight of most audiences. The interesting question, I would offer, is whether this delight stems from the textual fact of deliverance or the more extratextual demonstration of individual empowerment.

In the end, the refusal on the hero's part to be no more than a "key" is closely akin to his discomfited role within the Bureau. Hellboy, like many of his super-contemporaries, desperately wants the many components of a "normal" human life: love, friendship, and freedom, to name a few. His workaday sensibility, constantly reinforced by his insistence that his heroic exploits are simply "his job," helps to further place his sensational circumstances on very common ground. His rejection of the bureaucratic apparatus of his employer is thus never a rejection of the mission. It is rather the same rejection given to Rasputin as Hellboy stands before the lock. As the opening lines of the film, and their reprise at the conclusion, attest, what makes a man is not his origins, but the choices he makes. This is a very populist sentiment indeed.

Catwoman, Patriarchy, and Corporate Greed

Catwoman, as a film, seems so obviously engineered as a feminist allegory that pointing it out seems almost redundant.[11] First, there is the bifurcation of our main character: Patience Phillips, whose first name indicates without subtlety her approach to life, and Catwoman, who is powerful, sexy, and independent. Second, there is the ongoing integration of Catwoman's origin story, relayed by Ophelia Powers as a quick lesson on feminist spirituality in which the chosen woman is given "both a blessing and a curse": freedom without hope for personal attachment. Later, there are sporadic but considerable moments of feminine power, such as the sequence in which Catwoman foils a group of male jewelry thieves, keeps the loot for herself, then returns the haul to the police minus a few baubles (including a huge diamond ring that she puts, after some consideration, on her right—rather than the engagement-laden left—hand). Finally and most significantly, there is the villainous power against which Catwoman must fight.

Hedare Beauty is positioned for much of the film as a company run by a man but making products for women. Its most important commodity is Beauline, a skin cream that reverses the signs of aging in female skin (significantly, no man is ever seen applying the cream), and Laurel Hedare is portrayed for much of the film as a prisoner of this man, his company, and its addictive produce. When she is cast aside after many years for a new, younger public face (one with whom George Hedare has become romantically involved), Laurel and Catwoman, both in terms of the narrative and in terms of character development, share a certain sympathy. Catwoman, as the reincarnation of a young woman who is killed by the company after discovering the truth about its product (killed, it seems worth noting, by being literally ejaculated out of a waste-drainage pipe), seems to hold a comparable position to the summarily discarded Laurel. Either woman is a threat to the success of the company.

In the end, however, *Catwoman* seems to offer mixed messages regarding feminine empowerment. Most obviously, the true villain in all of this turns out to be Laurel herself, who has been empowered indeed in killing several people in her desire to make the success of Beauline ironclad. The climactic battle of the film is not between Catwoman and some patriarchal oppressor, but between the two strongest female characters in the film. Also of interest is the fact that, if the logic of Beauline as presented in the film is to be trusted, all women who continued to apply Beauline would become, like Laurel, largely indestructible. Such a possibility seems almost Edenic in its feminist implications, yet it is rejected by both Catwoman and the general mood of the film. Finally, and perhaps most banally, there is the matter of Catwoman's costume, a getup engineered as much for a young, male audience as much or more than it is for strong women. It is a fair question to ask why Patience's newfound pride and power must be displayed sexually, as though it were only once she can get into that strategically torn leather catsuit, grab her whip, and strut seductively around the city that she can make her mark in the world. It is nearly, if not completely, a caricature.

What is most interesting about this conflicting stance toward female empowerment is that it ultimately plays second fiddle to a more pervasive cautionary tale. This tale recalls the Thompsonian "moral economy" in its critique of unfettered corporate conduct. Initially, Patience's plight stands in contravention to the idea that one's hard work is paid in kind, that the pressures of market profitability will require entrepreneurs to act in accordance with the well-being of the community. Later, Catwoman herself stands as the only safeguard in a system that would have stocked every shelf in the country, if not the world, with a grossly unsafe product overnight. Science, portrayed in the film as only superficially uncorrupted by financial desire, is of no assistance whatsoever in stopping the distribution of Beauline. Judicial systems, barely aware of much of anything in the film, are similarly inadequate. Only the superhero, once again, is capable of meeting this systemic failure to keep the community safe.

Catwoman thus evokes the ethic of Thompson's "moral economy" in a number of senses. Clearly, her very presence in a narrative of this fashioning is indicative of a cultural sensibility that the market, which we tend to speak of in roughly anthropomorphic terms, most assuredly does not, by its very nature, have everyone's best interests at heart. The market is a mechanism, like all bureaucracies, that may be manipulated to specific ends. As Weber relates, "bureaucracy has been and is a power instrument of the first order—for the one who controls the bureaucratic apparatus. . . . And where the bureaucratization of administration has been completely carried through, a form of power relation is established that is practically unshatterable."[12] Catwoman, and I, would argue that superheroes in general act as an anomaly in the system, or, as the hero Neo was referred to in *The Matrix* trilogy, a remainder.

But Catwoman and Patience also evoke Thompsonian approaches to economic life in their individual character roles. Patience, on the one hand, is morally outraged when she discovers the truth about Beauline. After she dies, however, and Catwoman becomes her primary identity and attitude base, our hero fosters a new sense of entitlement. She destroys the property of her noisy neighbors because she has asked them to be quiet on numerous occasions and needs to sleep. She steals motorcycles when she needs transportation. She keeps jewelry when she likes the way it looks. Much of the character's adjustment to her new identity is expressed in very selfish terms, not unconscionable for a character who has, by all indications, spent much of her life as a doormat. We can read this as a character simply advocating for herself in an impersonal and unforgiving system. But when Catwoman comes to realize the enormity of the Beauline scheme, she makes the significant observation that "it's not about me anymore." It is at this moment that she becomes a community advocate and most elegantly embodies the Thompsonian model of direct action sanctioned by a popular ethic. It is most definitely "against the law" to escape from jail, steal a car, and destroy a dozen or so freight vehicles, and yet these are steps Catwoman must take to ensure the failure of Hedare's plot and the safety of what she understands to be her community. The bread riots in eighteenth-century England are not so dissimilar in kind or scope.

CONCLUSION

The preceding discussion has offered one way of interpreting the superhero, a trope important in contemporary society if only for its stubborn ubiquity and longevity. I propose an added importance that posits the character, in its many manifestations, as a product of a collective imagination expressing a strained liberalist normativity, the rattling of the tin cup, if you will, against the "iron cage." The relationship of the superhero to the social whole has always been one of alienation of one kind or another. What I find interesting about using Thompson and Weber to read the cinematic superhero text, however, is the degree to which it may explicate the changing nature of that text's protagonist. The movement from an unequivocally moral superhero to one who exhibits the eminently human capacity for ambiguity is indicative of more than just the changing tastes of viewers and readers.

Embedded in this movement is the articulation of a nebulous but nonetheless palpable unease with social organization, an unease that pervades American cinema well beyond the superhero genre. During a recent lecture I gave on superheroes in American cinematic culture, a student asked what I thought of characters like *Fight Club*'s Tyler Durden and *One Flew Over the Cuckoo's Nest*'s R. P. McMurphy—were they superheroes too? I asked him to flesh out his question, to which he responded that, given their extraordinary abilities to act outside the realm of normal human activity and their respective emancipatory ideals, Durden and McMurphy fit the paradigm. This statement caught me off balance, mostly because I sensed that he was right in ways I had not considered. The chaotic, even anarchic nature of these latter two characters is certainly indicative of the mood this chapter seeks to point out: both cry out on behalf of individuals immersed in technocratic and institutional mechanisms of control. But Durden and McMurphy are not superheroes as we have come to understand them generically. They lack certain accoutrements such as masks, capes, and truly supernatural powers. More interesting, especially given the recent release of the ambiguously moral *V for Vendetta*, is the discussion concerning the degree to which characters like Spider-Man, Hellboy, and Cat-woman are actually Durden or McMurphy in disguise.

If they are, then Eco's thesis on the ideological nature of superheroes is in question. If superheroes, in their constant negotiation with the established mechanisms of society, consistently show those mechanisms to be faulty and inadequate, it becomes difficult to posit their implicit support for them. In fact, it may be possible to see in superheroes examples of what Radway has called "ideological seams,"[13] places where the tightly woven fibers of social cohesion and control become more or less transparent. Whether or not we can see these characters in this way deserves further study, but for now it is enough to show, as I hope this chapter has done, that such study will be fruitful. If we are indeed moving into a time when we no longer look to the skies but to the masses for our mythical saviors—if our idea of a superhero is moving away from the "caped crusader" to the Durdenesque nihilistic sociopath—then we as a society are tempted to ask what it is about our realities that make our fantasies evolve in such a way.

Notes

1. Reprinted from Robert Moses Peaslee, "Superheroes, 'Moral Economy', and the 'Iron Cage': Morality, Alienation, and the Super-Individual," in *Super/Heroes: From Hercules to Superman*, ed. Wendy Haslem, Angela Ndalianis, and Chris Mackie (Washington, DC: New Academia, 2007), 37–50. The chapter has been lightly edited for style for the purposes of the present publication.

2. Umberto Eco, "The Myth of Superman," trans. Natalie Chilton, *Diacritics* 2, no. 1 (Spring 1972): 14–22.

3. E. P. Thompson, "The Moral Economy of the English Crowd in the Eighteenth Century," *Past and Present*, no. 50 (February 1971): 76–136.

4. Max Weber, *The Protestant Ethic and the Spirit of Capitalism*, trans. Talcott Parsons (New York: Charles Scribner's Sons, 1958), 181.

5. Since the bulk of this chapter was completed, another interesting entry into the genre has addressed Weber's thesis directly. Brad Bird's computer-animated film *The Incredibles* (2004), about which an entire essay could be written in this regard, is an explicit commentary on individuality in society, with particular emphasis on the atrophy of special abilities circumscribed within bureaucratic expressions of normativity (industry, public schools, etc.). (*Incredibles 2*, also by Bird, was released to theaters worldwide in 2018.)

6. Janice Radway, "Identifying Ideological Seams: Mass Culture, Analytical Method, and Political Practice," *Communication* 9, no. 1 (1986): 93–124.

7. The analyses of these three films assume some level of familiarity with their narrative structure, although I have tried to fill in the gaps where appropriate. Space does not allow for full synopses of the films.

8. New York as a setting since September 11, 2001, also carries a great deal of semiotic weight. The first *Spider-Man* (2002), which was famously altered prior to release due to its inclusion of the World Trade Center buildings in its action sequences, is especially imbued with this coloration. An argument I have chosen not to engage here would position law enforcement and science as

systems that have particular difficulty addressing the urgencies of terrorist activity. Alternatively, my comparison at the end of the chapter of traditional superheroes with characters like *Fight Club*'s Tyler Durden also positions terrorist activity itself as a more provocative expression of the superhero ethos (see *V for Vendetta*, released in 2006). My thanks to my reviewers for suggesting this brief discussion.

9. Thompson, "The Moral Economy of the English Crowd," 98, my italics.

10. Max Weber, "Bureaucracy," in *From Max Weber: Essays in Sociology*, ed. Hans Heinrich Gerth and C. Wright Mills (London: Kegan Paul, 1947), 215.

11. My thanks to Angela Ndalianis, who pointed out the cinematic decision to not only change Catwoman's alter ego from Selina Kyle to Patience Phillips in translation from the comic, but also to elide her past as a prostitute. Clearly this is another consideration in framing *Catwoman*'s feminist message.

12. Weber, "Bureaucracy," 228.

13. Radway, "Identifying Ideological Seams."

CHAPTER 3

What Magneto Cannot Choose[1]

JARED POON

MAGNETO, OUR FAVORITE MASTER OF MAGNETISM, IS WALKING DOWN ONE OF the hallways of his stronghold in the Savage Land, on his way to a poetry recital by his daughter, the Scarlet Witch. He passes his benevolent gaze over the mutant children that throng the place, precocious and carefree.

Suddenly, alarms wail—the Sentinels have found his mutant utopia and are attacking en masse! Beams of energy crash through glittering domes and tall spires as the Sentinels hunt down the mutant residents. Magneto is furious! Rising high into the air on eddies of magnetic force, he bends his will toward the attacking robots and reels them in, exerting his mutant mastery over magnetism to rewire their neural circuits. The Sentinels, now reprogrammed to terminate regular humans rather than mutants, fly off toward New York City, Magneto himself leading from the front. "You have my word, my brothers," he promises his subjects, "a thousand—no, a hundred thousand—human beings will die tonight for every mutant lying bleeding at your feet."[2]

Magneto means to kill every human man, woman, and child in the United States of America, and that is a monstrous act, right? At first glance, the moral metaphysics of the world of comics is about as sophisticated as the primary-colored spandex (or unstable molecular) costumes of the superheroes and supervillains that inhabit it. There are good guys and bad guys. The good guys are dashing and beautiful and fight for what most of regard as noble and good. They are people like Charles Xavier, who preaches harmony between humans and mutants; Spider-Man, who fights crime because such great responsibility comes with great power; and Superman, the moral paragon who stands for truth, justice, and the American way.

The bad guys are people like Magneto, cruel and evil, often bent on either destruction or world domination. Not only are they usually not as pretty as their heroic counterparts (consider how many supervillains are outwardly scarred— the Joker, Victor von Doom, and Weapon-X's Colonel Wraith, just to name a few), their maniacal laughs, tendency to monologue at crucial moments, and callous disregard for life makes it hard to think of them as credible evildoers, that is, as *anything but* two-dimensional supervillains.

Take a moment, however, to step behind the eyes (and mask) of a supervillain—say, Mister Mxyzptlk, or Moses Magnum, or Magneto himself. Does a supervillain see himself as a supervillain? Does he see his own actions as evil? I believe the answer to both of these questions is *no*. Supervillains, from the vile Annihilus to the time-traveling Professor Zoom, see themselves as acting not for the sake of evil but for the sake of the good. That is, supervillains always direct their actions at what is good: the monster never sees a monster in the mirror.

I can hear the grunts of outrage even from here. But don't commit me to Arkham Asylum just yet—even a poor philosopher deserves a fair hearing.

THE CHOICES OF THE MASTER OF MAGNETISM

Just as every superhero or supervillain worth his salt requires an origin story, our discussion about how supervillains see themselves will be well served by a brief examination of the historical background. For that, let us return to the thirteenth century, where our key figures reside. On the one side, we have the *intellectualists* (we'll see what they're all about shortly), fronted by Saint Thomas Aquinas. Thomas famously dictated several different texts to several different secretaries at the same time—not that flashy as a power, but still useful. Arrayed against the intellectualists, we have the *voluntarists* with their poster boy, William of Ockham. William is, of course, the very razor-wielding individual who reminds us not to multiply entities beyond necessity, something Jamie Madrox would do well to remember.

The disagreement between the intellectualists and voluntarists was about the nature of *choice*. Both sides agreed on the general picture of how choices are made—there are three steps. The *senses* first gather information from the surroundings. This information is sent to the *intellect*, which looks at the various options and judges which one is better. The judgment of the intellect is then presented to the *will*, which chooses. Here's how this might work in Magneto's case.

Recall Magneto, hovering over his island sanctuary in the Savage Land, ready to depart and wreak havoc on the human race. How does he come to make that choice? The senses are first engaged—Magneto *sees* the giant robots of purple and chrome, he *hears* the cry of injured mutants, he *smells* the acrid mixture of blood and fire. This sensory information is presented to the intellect, which sorts through them, lays out several courses of action, and judges which are better and which are worse. For the sake of simplicity, let us say that there are three options, as determined by the intellect:

1. Help the Sentinels burn everything to the ground.
2. Destroy the Sentinels in the skies over the Savage Land.
3. Reprogram the Sentinels to hunt humans instead of mutants, and send them back at New York.

The work of the intellect is not done. Not only is it in charge of figuring out what the options are, it is in charge of figuring out which one is best. Magneto's intellect would find options 1 and 2 less than satisfactory, so option 3 it is! The options are all presented to the will, along with which one has been judged to be the best. The will then chooses, or moves the person to act, which in this case means that Magneto sets off to New York to kill several million people. It's worth taking a moment to make sure the terms and concepts remain clear. Ordinarily, when people talk about choosing something, they mean they're just making up their mind. However, in the three-step model above, making up one's mind is not choosing but making an intellectual judgment. For both Thomas Aquinas and William of Ockham, choosing means the will engages you to *act*.

But just what the will can choose is where the intellectualists and voluntarists part ways. For Thomas and his intellectualist friends, the will *must* choose what the intellect presents as being better. If Magneto's intellect judges that protecting his people and taking revenge on his enemies is the best option, his will cannot choose otherwise, and on that basis he *will* then act. On the other hand, for Ockham and his voluntarist buddies, the will is free to choose even the option that is presented as worse. If the voluntarists are right, then Magneto could choose to destroy the Sentinels in the skies over the Savage Land, or help the Sentinels burn everything to the ground, even if these were judged to be in every way worse than another option.

Common sense might side with the voluntarists at first glance. After all, it's surely possible for Magneto to have stopped at merely destroying the Sentinels, no matter what judgments his intellect might have produced. But this intuition deserves careful examination—just what is going on when we do the things we do?

HIS JUDGMENTS REVEALED

The things we do come in at least two flavors. There are things we do intentionally, and things we do unintentionally. In the first category are actions we *choose* to do: discussing the latest Batman movie or cutting the green wire to defuse the gamma bomb. In the second category are things like sneezing, or ab-sent-mindedly scratching an itch, or falling over when shoved. Only the actions that belong in the first category seem morally interesting. After all, if Superman sneezes and incidentally puts out a fire, we don't consider him a virtuous person just for that, nor do we consider the sneezing a morally praiseworthy action. Since we are concerned with good and evil here, let us focus on the kinds of actions that are intentional.

These kinds of actions have a peculiar structure—one might think of them as *acts for ends*. That is, there are at least two components to the action—the thing we do, and why we do it. What it is that we do is often the outwardly ob-servable part of the action. When Magneto exerts his formidable control over magnetic fields to stop a jet from crashing to the ground, that is certainly an awe-inspiring act, but we don't understand the action fully until we know why he did it. In other words, we look for *reasons* for his doing what he did. Was it compassion that moved him, or was it a mere arrogant display of power? The *reasons* behind the act are called *ends*, and they matter to our understanding and evaluation of people's choices.

If this is right, then we need more information to have a complete story about Magneto's choice to give the Sentinels a new directive to seek and kill humans. We need to know not just Magneto's options (and their corresponding acts), but the ends those acts would serve. Only then can we really understand how Magneto's intellect weighs the options against one another and comes to a judgment.

Consider option 1, that Magneto helps the Sentinels burn everything to the ground. It's certainly possible that this is an option that serves one of Magne-to's ends. He might want to spite his son Quicksilver, or he might think that burning it all to the ground would help get rid of the Savage Land's mosquito problem. Compare this with option 3, that Magneto neutralizes the Sentinels' attack and reprograms them for revenge. This might serve another of Magneto's desired ends, namely, to protect his people and build a world where they can live without fear or ostracism. Coming to a judgment about which of those two options is best involves some sort of weighing. Is protecting his fellow mutants a more desirable end than getting rid of the mosquitoes? Magneto has to give up one to pick the other, and so it is necessary to figure out which end is more important. Not surprisingly, he chooses to help his subjects.

Our question was, can Magneto choose to help the Sentinels burn down his stronghold, even if doing so appears in no way the better option? Now we can be more precise about what we're asking. Can Magneto act contrary to his own best judgment that there are no better ends, or combinations of ends, than are served by reprogramming the Sentinels as vengeance weapons against humanity?

It would not just be strange for Magneto to make a choice like this in the scenario we have described, but impossible if it's also true that making choices requires voluntary action. We observed earlier that voluntary choices (the kind open to moral assessment) require intentions. If Magneto has no prior intention behind his action, then reprogramming the Sentinels can be no more than a spastic flailing of limbs and a haphazard release of magnetic power. But if intentions pick out the reasons why we act in any case when we do, then because reasons are the province of the intellect, intentions actually *reveal* the intellect's judgments.

Maybe you don't find this compelling so far. Perhaps you have the intuition that Magneto *could* of course choose to help the Sentinels burn everything to the ground. The above account does not deny this possibility. What is denied is that this can be *chosen*—acted upon—if Magneto's intellect judges that this is not the best option. For Magneto to choose otherwise means that his intellect sees reasons to choose this option that outweigh whatever reasons there are to choose the alternative. These might be the aforementioned pique at Quicksilver, or annoyance at mosquitoes, or perhaps part of a grand plan to lull Professor Xavier into complacence. Without reasons of this sort that make this option better than the others, all things considered, Magneto cannot choose it. Ockham and the voluntarists are wrong, and Aquinas and the intellectualists are right—the will cannot choose against the judgment of the intellect.

Notes

1. Excerpted from Jared Poon, "What Magneto Cannot Choose," in *Supervillains and Philosophy: Sometimes, Evil Is Its Own Reward*, ed. Ben Dyer (Chicago: Open Court, 2009), 53–58. The chapter has been lightly edited for style for the purposes of the present publication.

2. Mark Millar, Chris Bachalo, Tim Townsend, et al., *Ultimate X-Men*, vol. 5 (New York: Marvel Enterprises, 2006).

CHAPTER 4

Excerpts from "The Functions of Dramatis Personae"[1]

VLADIMIR PROPP

AT THIS POINT A NEW PERSONAGE, WHO CAN BE TERMED THE *VILLAIN,* ENTERS the tale.[2] His role is to disturb the peace of a happy family, to cause some form of misfortune, damage, or harm. The villain(s) may be a dragon, a devil, bandits, a witch, or a stepmother.... Thus, a villain has entered the scene. He has come on foot, sneaked up, or flown down, ... and begins to act.

IV. THE VILLAIN MAKES AN ATTEMPT AT RECONNAISSANCE

1. *The reconnaissance has the aim of finding out the location of children, or sometimes of precious objects, etc.* A bear says: "Who will tell me what has become of the tsar's children? Where did they disappear to?" ...
2. *An inverted form of reconnaissance is evidenced when the intended victim questions the villain.* ...
3. *In separate instances, one encounters forms of reconnaissance by means of other personages.*

V. THE VILLAIN RECEIVES INFORMATION ABOUT HIS VICTIM

1. *The villain directly receives an answer to his question.* The chisel answers the bear: "Take me out into the courtyard and throw me to the ground; where I stick, there's the hive." ... Once again we are confronted with paired functions. They often occur in the form of dialogue.... As in other instances, the second half of the paired function can exist without the first. In these cases,

the delivery takes the form of a careless act: A mother calls her son home in a loud voice and thereby betrays his presence to a witch....

2–3. *An inverted or other form of information gathering evokes a corresponding answer.* ...

VI. THE VILLAIN ATTEMPTS TO DECEIVE HIS VICTIM IN ORDER TO TAKE POSSESSION OF HIM OR OF HIS BELONGINGS

The villain, first of all, assumes a disguise. A dragon turns into a golden goat, or a handsome youth; a witch pretends to be a sweet old lady.... Then follows the function itself.

1. *The villain uses persuasion.* A witch tries to have a ring accepted; a godmother suggests the taking of a steam bath; a witch suggests the removal of clothes and bathing in a pond; a beggar seeks alms.
2. *The villain proceeds to act by the direct application of magical means.* The stepmother gives a sleeping potion to her stepson. She sticks a magic pin into his clothing.
3. *The villain employs other means of deception or coercion.* ... A dragon re-arranges the wood shavings that are to show a young girl the way to her brothers.

VII. THE VICTIM SUBMITS TO DECEPTION AND THEREBY UNWITTINGLY HELPS HIS ENEMY

1. *The hero agrees to all of the villain's persuasions* (e.g., takes the ring, goes to steam bathe or to swim). One notes that *interdictions* are always *broken* and, conversely, *deceitful proposals* are always *accepted* and fulfilled.
2–3. The hero mechanically reacts to the employment of magical or other means (e.g., falls asleep or wounds himself). It can be observed that this function can also exist separately. No one lulls the hero to sleep: he suddenly falls asleep by himself in order, of course, to facilitate the villain's task....

VIII. THE VILLAIN CAUSES HARM OR INJURY TO A MEMBER OF A FAMILY

This function is exceptionally important, since by means of it the actual movement of the tale is created. Absentation, the violation of an interdiction, delivery, the success of deceit, all prepare the way for this function, create its possibility of occurrence, or simply facilitate its happening. Therefore, the first seven functions may be regarded as the preparatory part of the tale, whereas the complication is begun by an act of villainy. The forms of villainy are exceedingly varied.

1. *The villain abducts a person.* A dragon kidnaps the tsar's daughter, or a peasant's daughter; a witch kidnaps a boy....

2. *The villain seizes or takes away a magical agent.* The "uncomely chap" seizes a magic coffer; a princess seizes a magic shirt....

3. *The villain pillages or spoils the crops....*

4. *The villain seizes the daylight....*

5. *The villain plunders in other forms.* The object of seizure fluctuates to an enormous degree, and there is no need to register all of its forms. The object of plunder, as will be apparent later on, does not influence the course of action....

6. *The villain causes bodily injury.* A servant girl cuts out the eyes of her mistress. A princess chops off Katoma's legs. It is interesting that these forms (from a morphological point of view) are also forms of seizure....

7. *The villain causes a sudden disappearance.* Usually this disappearance is the result of the application of bewitching or deceitful means; a stepmother puts her stepson into a sleep—his bride disappears forever....

8. *The villain demands or entices his victim.* Usually this form is the result of a deceitful agreement. The king of the sea demands the tsar's son, and he leaves home.

9. *The villain expels someone.* A stepmother drives her stepdaughter out; a priest expels his grandson.

10. *The villain orders someone to be thrown into the sea.* A tsar places his daughter and son-in-law in a barrel and orders the barrel to be thrown into the sea. Parents launch a small boat, carrying their sleeping son, into the sea.

11. *The villain casts a spell upon someone or something.* At this point, one should note that the villain often causes two or three harmful acts at once....

12. *The villain effects a substitution.* This form also is mostly concomitant. A nursemaid changes a bride into a duckling and substitutes her own daughter in the bride's place....

13. *The villain orders a murder to be committed.* The form is in essence a modified (intensified) expulsion: the stepmother orders a servant to kill her stepdaughter while they are out walking....

14. *The villain commits murder.* This is also usually only an accompanying form for other acts of villainy, serving to intensify them. A princess seizes her husband's magic shirt and then kills him....

15. *The villain imprisons or detains someone....*

16. *The villain threatens forced matrimony.* A dragon demands the tsar's daughter as his wife. . . .
17. *The villain makes a threat of cannibalism.* A dragon demands the tsar's daughter for his dinner. . . .
17a. The same form among relatives. A sister intends to devour her brother.
18. *The villain torments at night.* A dragon or a devil torments a princess at night; a witch flies to a maiden and sucks at her breast.
19. *The villain declares war.* . . .

XVI. THE HERO AND THE VILLAIN JOIN IN DIRECT COMBAT

1. *They fight in an open field.* Here, first of all, belong fights with dragons. . . . and also battles with an enemy army or a knight. . . .
2. *They engage in a competition.* . . . The hero wins with the help of cleverness: a gypsy puts a dragon to flight by squeezing a piece of cheese as if it were a stone. . . .
3. *They play cards.* . . .

XVIII. THE VILLAIN IS DEFEATED

1. *The villain is beaten in open combat.*
2. *He is defeated in a contest.*
3. *He loses at cards.*
4. *He loses on being weighed.*
5. *He is killed without a preliminary fight.* A dragon is killed while asleep. . . .
6. *He is banished directly.* A princess, possessed by a devil, places a sacred image around her neck: "The evil power flew away in a puff of smoke." . . .

XXVIII. THE FALSE HERO OR (SECOND) VILLAIN IS EXPOSED

. . . Sometimes it is the result of an uncompleted task (the false hero cannot lift the dragon's heads). Most often it is presented in the form of a story ("Here the princess told everything as it was"). Sometimes all the events are recounted from the very beginning in the form of a tale. The villain is among the listeners, and he gives himself away by an expression of disapproval. Sometimes a song is sung telling of what has occurred and exposing the villain. Other unique forms of exposure also occur. . . .

XXX. THE VILLAIN IS PUNISHED

The villain is shot, banished, tied to the tail of a horse, commits suicide, and so forth. In parallel with this we sometimes have a magnanimous pardon. Usually only the villain of the second move and the false hero are punished, while the first villain is punished only in those cases in which a battle and pursuit are absent from the story. Otherwise he is killed in battle or perishes during the pursuit (a witch bursts in and attempts to drink up the sea, etc.). . . .

Now we shall give several individual, though highly important, deductions. We observe that a large number of functions are arranged in pairs (prohibition-violation, reconnaissance-delivery, struggle-victory, pursuit-deliverance, etc.). Other functions may be arranged according to groups. Thus villainy, dispatch, decision for counteraction, and departure from home constitute the complication. . . . Alongside these combinations there are individual functions (absentations, punishment, marriage, etc.).

Notes

1. Excerpted from Vladimir Propp, *Morphology of the Folktale*, trans. Laurence Scott (Austin: University of Texas Press, 1968), 25–65. The chapter has been lightly edited for style for the purposes of the present publication.

2. Throughout this excerpted chapter, Propp makes reference to countless examples through the use of notations, which are excluded here for purposes of clarity; elided passages are indicated by ellipsis points.

CHAPTER 5

The Supervillain[1]

PETER COOGAN

THE SUPERVILLAIN IS ONE OF THE SIGNIFICANT MARKERS OF THE SUPERHERO genre, but as with the secret identity, it is not unique to the genre. When used as a defining element of the superhero, the supervillain artificially expands the genre to include character types who fight supervillains but are super heroes (heroes who are super) instead of superheroes (protagonists of the superhero genre). The discussion that follows explores the broad spectrum of genres that employ the supervillain trope, particularly in the discussion of supervillains from the James Bond novels of Ian Fleming. Fleming might be called the poet laureate of supervillainy because many of his novels feature villains discoursing on their criminal careers, so his works are very useful in developing theories about and explanations of supervillains.

THE FIVE TYPES

Supervillains come in five types: the monster, the enemy commander, the mad scientist, the criminal mastermind, and the inverted-superhero supervillain. These types are nonexclusive; that is, a supervillain like Spider-Man's foe the Lizard is both a monster and a mad scientist. Doctor Doom, ruler of Latveria and a scientific genius, is an enemy commander and a mad scientist. But most supervillains fit pretty firmly into one of these categories. All these types except the inverted-superhero supervillain predate the superhero. Just as a hero represents the virtues and values of a society or culture, a villain represents an inversion of those values. But more than that, a supervillain has the ability to enact that inversion, to bring the normal activities of a society to a halt and force a hero to arise to defend those virtues.

The Monster

The oldest type of supervillain is the monster. The monster is monstrous because it figures as the inverse of humanity and typically appears in some sort of beast form—thus a werewolf or giant reptile is a monster. When a monster has a human form, it is monstrous morally—it has no moral sense of right or wrong, or a perverted one, which is symbolically expressed by the monster's lack of a soul. Thus vampires and Frankenstein's creature are monsters as they lack the divine spark—the soul—that separates man from beast. This is also why a serial killer, who is a human being, is referred to as a monster—he lacks human compassion; he seems to lack a soul.

The oldest mythological supervillains to oppose heroes were monsters, whether Khumbaba, guardian of the Cedar Forest, or the gigantic Bull of Heaven, both of whom Gilgamesh kills and both of whom were set in place by the gods to limit humankind's reach; or the Nemean Lion or the Hydra, both of which terrorize the Greek countryside and prevent the people from using the land.

Grendel is the classic image of the monster as supervillain. Like Milton's Satan, Grendel is a very different adversary from most epic or mythological monsters. The Celestial Bull that Gilgamesh fought or the Harpies that the Argonauts defeat are monsters set upon mortals by the gods for displeasing them. Grendel has a personal motivation and is not merely the instrument of divine vengeance. He is not a mindlessly destructive beast like the Calydonian Boar, or a creature of another order living a separate existence from humankind without interaction like Medusa and the Gorgons. Grendel has real motivation, like a supervillain. Stan Lee, in introducing a collection of supervillain stories *Bring On the Bad Guys*, writes that supervillains have "also got to be unusual, exciting, provocative, and surprising.... [W]e always try to motivate our miscreant as much as we do our hero. We have to have a varlet doing evil just for the sake of being naughty. We try to indicate why he does the things he does, what made him the way he is."[2] Grendel fits this characterization. One indication of his motivation and interests as a character might be the fact that John Gardner, in 1971, was able to write the novel *Grendel* about him—a rarity among monsters from heroic epics.

In the Viking epic *Beowulf*, the hero is called by King Hrothgar to defeat the monstrous Grendel, who besieges the Danish king's mead hall, Heorot. As the supervillain is the inverted image of the superhero, so too is the outlaw Grendel the inverted image of the heroes of Heorot. Grendel lives a bitter and lonely exiled existence, jealous of the crowded warmth of the Danish feasting hall with its singing bards. He descends from Cain, the first murderer, who inverted family relations and turned brotherly love into fratricide. Grendel's invulnerability and preternatural strength make him invincible against the attacks of Hrothgar's warriors, just as the supervillain's power defies the limited abilities of the authorities. He refuses to pay *wer-gild*, the man-price, for his murders, "offering / No truce, accepting no settlement, no price / In gold or land, and paying the living / For one crime only with another," thus flouting and denying the norms of Viking society.[3] When he makes feasting and fellowship impossible, Grendel conquers the world of the Danes and rules their mead hall.

A contemporary monster, with a dash of mad scientist thrown in, is the Lizard. He is Dr. Curtis Connors, a surgeon who lost an arm in World War II. He synthesizes a serum from lizards that duplicates their rejuvenative abilities in an attempt to regenerate his arm. He is successful—his arm regrows—but perhaps too successful, as the lizard nature of the serum takes over. He acquires the physical characteristics of a lizard—tough green skin, long strong tail—and a measure of its antipathy to humankind. He plans to use his serum on other lizards, crocodiles, and alligators and create a lizard army—the fact that Connors says "other lizards" indicates that he no longer affiliates with humanity.[4]

The Enemy Commander

The second-oldest type of supervillain is the enemy commander. An enemy commander has the resources of a state behind him and is in a position of legal authority within that society. He might be a king, tyrant, dictator, or other absolute ruler, or the true power behind the throne, or a military commander. Satan—John Milton's Satan from *Paradise Lost*—might be said to be the very model of the enemy commander supervillain. He rules the kingdom of Hell, commands numberless demons, and stands in absolute opposition to the will of Heaven and God.

The tyrant as enemy commander appears in epics such as *The Song of Roland* in the person of Marsile, king of Sarraguce and the last Muslim ruler in Spain; and in stories of the Spartans facing down Xerxes and the Persians at Thermopylae. A variation on the enemy commander is the tyrannical ruler, like the Norman Prince John in the tales of Robin Hood. Often these rulers are members of a conquering culture; but because they represent the government of the hero's land, the hero is posited as a rebel and therefore represents the virtues of the conquered peoples—Saxons in the case of Robin Hood.

Enemy commanders represent alien societies whose values are at odds with those of the culture producing the stories. But they are not viewed as villains in their own lands. In America, Adolf Hitler was considered a supervillain, which is why he is so often featured on the cover of World War II–era comics.[5] But in Nazi Germany, Hitler was the heroic ruler, the savior of the German *Volk* and founder of the Thousand-Year Reich. In contemporary times, Osama bin

Laden plays a similar role—US president George W. Bush figures bin Laden as absolutely evil, yet a significant body of Muslims view him as a courageous jihadist, fighting to drive the infidel crusader from the Holy Land.

In US literature, the Native American enemy commander figures as the first supervillain. Native Americans represent an alien culture, constantly threatening apocalyptic violence. Richard Slotkin develops the notion of "savage war" to describe and define the attitude of white settlers toward conflict with Natives. Savage war allows the projection of guilt onto the victims of development, displacement, and genocide. It depends on a belief in the inherent violence of the enemy "other." The savage-war doctrine requires picturing the enemy as capable of extreme violence, which is seen as fundamentally different from the "civilized" warfare engaged in by European armies. Instead, the Native is seen as the absolute opposite of the white settler, an enemy who cannot be appeased or converted, only exterminated. The contest between the two forces is proposed as a zero-sum game in which the outcome can only be complete devastation or complete victory because of the implacable nature of the enemy. The Native is seen as possessing overwhelming force and numbers, and is responsible for initiating and escalating the violence of the conflict. Finally, the enemy Native is portrayed as invading land held rightfully by the white settler; the Native is the interloper and invader. Thus, responsibility for all acts is projected upon the victim of genocide.[6]

Native enemy commanders are thus positioned as commanding an endless and potentially overwhelming supply of savage warriors who threaten the extermination of American—or white—culture. The classic literary Native enemy commander is Magua from James Fenimore Cooper's *The Last of the Mohicans*. Cooper's plot is driven by Magua's thirst for vengeance against the British Colonel Munro, who once had Magua whipped for drunkenness while Magua was serving the British army as a scout. In Cooper's construction of Indian culture, Magua embodies the best and worst of Indian virtues and vices, what Cooper referred to as "gifts." Natives in Cooper's fiction value honor above all. "The American Indian always deemed his moral victories the noblest."[7] Thus honor, not money or territory, is at the center of Native warfare. A consequence of valuing honor is that Cooper's Native Americans prize vengeance. As Magua puts it, "The memory of an Indian is longer than the arm of the palefaces; his mercy shorter than their justice."[8] In the view of Natty Bumppo, hero of Cooper's *Leatherstocking Tales*, revenge is lawful to Native Americans and is one of their "gifts." Similarly, scalping, which is committed for purposes of both honor and revenge, is "the gift and nature of an Indian" but would be "a cruel and unhuman act for a whiteskin."[9] Magua seeks revenge on Colonel Munro through his daughters, and achieves it when Tamenund, the ancient Delaware chief, rules that Magua may rightfully keep the kidnapped Cora Munro as his wife. Cora rejects this verdict, and it seems monstrous to the white characters, but within the Native American society Cooper has established, it is right and proper.

Darth Vader is an excellent example of the enemy commander as supervillain. He is not an emperor but commands the emperor's forces and has the weight and resources of the Empire behind him, besides his own Jedi power. Vader is a hero of the Empire. Luke Skywalker and the rebels violate the primary virtue of the Empire, obedience to the emperor, but embody the values of self-reliance, individualism, and democracy that are at the mythological core of American culture, the milieu in which *Star Wars* was produced.

In superhero comics, the two foremost enemy commanders are Doctor Doom and the Red Skull. Doctor Doom commands the resources of Latveria and as its ruler maintains diplomatic immunity, allowing him to flout the rule of law that is central to democratic culture. But Doom leans significantly toward the inverted-superhero supervillain because Latveria itself is not at war with the United States and Doom is a totalitarian tyrant who suppresses his people's yearning to be free. The Red Skull is a purer example of the enemy commander in superhero comics. As developed in the Silver Age by Stan Lee and Jack Kirby, the Red Skull is second only to Hitler in power in Nazi Germany, and even Hitler fears him. He commands the scientific and military resources of the Third Reich and is actively involved in the attempt to defeat and subjugate America and its allies.[10] Racist, genocidal, and totalitarian, the Nazi ideology stands in stark contrast to the American creed of life, liberty, and the pursuit of happiness. Captain America embodies that creed, so battles between him and the Red Skull are symbolic of the literal battles between American and German forces.

The Mad Scientist

The mad scientist's provenance is grounded in science fiction in the character of Dr. Victor Frankenstein. Mary Shelley subtitles her work *The Modern Prometheus*, and it is in Prometheus that the Western idea of the excessive pursuit of knowledge finds mythic embodiment. Peter Goodrich finds a parallel between Prometheus's gift of fire to man and the mad scientist's pursuit of knowledge: "In his quest for insight into the laws of nature, however altruistic, the mad scientist, too, often misinterprets or altogether fails to perceive the full moral dimensions of his experimentation; and this failure in foresight radically flaws his forethought."[11] The lineage of the mad scientist extends back beyond Frankenstein to medieval alchemists like Doctor Faust, Doctor Pretorius, John Dee, and Roger Bacon; "the mad scientist's insight suggests a supernatural power, which links him to the world of magical practitioners . . . and especially to black magic or sorcery because the application of his principle threatens human society."[12] Alchemists thus bridge the mad sorcerer and mad scientist figures—both are types of wizards "who possess either empirical or magical knowledge," and the "archetypal figure who has been the touchstone for the lineage of wizards since the Middle Ages is Merlin."[13] Merlin is thus a "significant forerunner of all mad scientists . . . a marriage of creative idealism" in his dream of Camelot "and corrupting lust" in his pursuit of Nimue, which takes him away from his oracular role as Arthur's adviser.[14]

"Mad scientists are typically characterized by obsessive behavior and the employment of extremely dangerous or unorthodox methods. They often are motivated by revenge, seeking to settle real or imagined slights, typically related to their unorthodox studies."[15] The pre-Crisis Lex Luthor is the foremost comic book mad-scientist supervillain, but the Ultra-Humanite is particularly important to comic book superheroes, as he was Superman's first supervillain, and Luthor's baldness recalls the Ultra-Humanite's baldness and links them.

The criminal mastermind has also been around much longer than the superhero. John Cawelti traces the criminal mastermind to Edgar Allan Poe's Minister D. in "The Purloined Letter."[16] In Cawelti's view, the criminal mastermind offers a trap for the writer of mystery stories as well as for the hero; he is "too fascinating, too surrounded with ambiguous fantasies, and therefore extremely difficult to keep subordinated to the detective."[17] Minister D. is Monsieur C. Auguste Dupin's mirror image—they are "brilliant, aristocratic, eccentric, both poets and men of the sharpest reasoning powers."[18] He is a worthy adversary for the great detective, and because such villains offer a challenge for their heroes, they recur both as types throughout the metagenre of crime fiction as well as individuals, rising again and again to threaten the stability and safety of the hero and his world.

Dr. Jack Quartz returned time after time—after apparently being shot, hanged, burned, and blown up—at least twenty-five times to face dime-novel detective Nick Carter. More a master criminal than a crime lord, Quartz debuted two years before Dr. Moriarty, in *The Nick Carter Library*, no. 13 (October 31, 1891). Quartz is an amoral, skilled hypnotist and vivisectionist who most enjoys slicing up living women and playing against Carter with lives as pawns in his twisted game of chess. In many ways he presages the fictional villains and real serial killers of the twentieth century. Like the Joker or the Riddler, Quartz sends Carter boastful clues about his crimes. Like many later villains, he keeps his word and has a sense of honor about the rules of the game—rules he himself sets, but which he nonetheless follows scrupulously. Like nearly every archenemy, he values his adversary's life highly, because playing against an equally skilled opponent brings him one of the greatest pleasures of his life. Carter's description of Quartz has many echoes—particularly in Sherlock

Holmes's description of Moriarty and Nayland Smith's of Dr. Fu Manchu—and serves as a useful index of the supervillain personality:

> Intellectually, he is the most remarkable man I have ever known. His intelligence is quite the most profound of any person I have ever known. In education, he is thoroughly versed in every branch of science. I believe that he speaks, fluently, every language that is worth speaking at all—many more of them than I do, myself, and I have mastered twelve. Physically, he is a stronger man than [turn-of-the-century strongman Eugen] Sandow, or I. His manners are perfect. He is at home amid any surroundings, in any costume, under all circumstances. He has always seemed to know everything, and to be ready to make use of anything whenever the occasion should arrive. He is handsome of feature, and has the most wonderful eyes that ever looked out of a human head. . . .
>
> He is totally without two qualities possessed by other humans . . . [m]orality and conscience. The man recognizes no moral responsibility, and he has no conscience at all. Compassion, in any form, is a meaningless term to him. Consideration for another, or for the sufferings of others, he does not know. The only law he recognizes at all is the law of power, of might, of attainment, of succeeding in whatever he undertakes to do. He worships beauty, as beauty alone, but destroys it with the same lack of compunction that he would manifest in plucking a blade of grass from the ground. He loves women, but only just so far as they can serve him, and that done, he destroys them just as he would do with that same blade of grass I have mentioned.[19]

These characteristics are used repeatedly in describing supervillains, and much of Ian Fleming's description of Bond's villains' motives, intellectual prowess, and physical capabilities seems cribbed from Carter's exposition; that is not to say that Fleming did so, but that Frederick van Rensselaer Dey, Carter's creator, so neatly anticipated (or perhaps established) the tropes of the criminal mastermind in his dime novels.

While Jack Quartz stood at the summit of fictional criminals in dime novels, a real man stood at the apex of actual crime in London, the real-life Napoleon of Crime, Adam Worth. Worth was the greatest criminal of the late nineteenth century and controlled or influenced much of London's underworld in his heyday. Interestingly, Worth's life bears many of the marks of the fictional supervillain's existence as laid out in the definition discussion below. Many supervillains suffer a wound—typically psychological and emotional but often with a physical component—that shapes their lives and that they are unable to recover from. Worth's wound was a literal one. His parents were German Jews who emigrated to the United States when the boy was just five years old to set up a tailor shop in Cambridge, Massachusetts. When Worth was six, a school-mate traded him one bright new penny for two of Worth's old ones. Showing his father the fruits of his trade earned him a vicious whipping. And, in the words of the great detective William Pinkerton: "From that day until his death, no one, be he friend or foe, honest or dishonest, Negro or Indian, relative or stranger, ever got the better of Adam Worth in any business transaction, regular or irregular."[20] Worth developed a kind of mania to never again be poor, and a contempt for legal authority. He stole *Portrait of Georgiana, Duchess of Devonshire*—a painting by Thomas Gainsborough of Georgiana Cavendish, wife of the Duke of Devonshire and one of the most celebrated and wicked beauties of eighteenth-century London—and held onto it for twenty-five years, all the while living a double life as both a master thief and a respectable man about town under the alias Henry J. Raymond, a name stolen from Henry Jarvis Raymond, founder of the *New York Times*. As much as he desired money, Worth desired to stick his thumb in the eye of the upper crust of society. His biographer, Ben Macintyre, sums him up thus: "In some ways Worth was an archetypal product of his time: determined to better himself, caring little what moral compromises were made along the way, at once utterly upright and utterly corrupt. But while he was clearly in thrall to society and its rules, he was at the same time bitterly, implacably at war with them. He aped his bourgeois contemporaries, and stole from them, and all the time he despised them."[21] Worth was a real-life criminal mastermind, but he was also the basis for the character most often touted as the archetype of the crime lord, Sherlock Holmes's nemesis, Dr. Moriarty.

That Worth was Sir Arthur Conan Doyle's primary model for Moriarty is not in doubt—the phrase "Napoleon of Crime" made famous in Holmes's introductory description of Moriarty was first used by Scotland Yard detective Robert Anderson in reference to Worth.[22] But what is odd about Moriarty is how little Doyle actually wrote about him. He appears in only one story, "The Final Problem," and is mentioned again only in the novel *The Valley of Fear*. All claims about him seem to be based upon two paragraphs from "The Final Problem":

> For years past I have continually been conscious of some power behind the malefactor, some deep organizing power which forever stands in the way of the law, and throws its shield over the wrongdoer. Again and again in cases of the most varying sorts—forgery cases, robberies, murders—I have felt the presence of this force, and I have deduced its action in many of those undiscovered crimes in which I have not been personally consulted. For years I have endeavored to break through the veil which shrouded it, and at last the time came when I seized my thread and followed it, until it led me, after

a thousand cunning windings, to ex-Professor Moriarty, of mathematical celebrity.

He is the Napoleon of crime, Watson. He is the organizer of half that is evil and of nearly all that is undetected in this great city. He is a genius, a philosopher, an abstract thinker. He has a brain of the first order. He sits motionless, like a spider in the centre of its web, but that web has a thousand radiations, and he knows well every quiver of each of them. He does little himself. He only plans. But his agents are numerous and splendidly organized. Is there a crime to be done, a paper to be abstracted, we will say, a house to be rifled, a man to be removed—the word is passed to the professor, the matter is organized and carried out. The agent may be caught. In that case money is found for his bail or his defense. But the central power which uses the agent is never caught—never so much as suspected. This was the organization which I deduced, Watson, and which I devoted my whole energy to exposing and breaking up.[23]

From these paragraphs come the impression that Moriarty's rich life off the page is worth pursuing on the page, and so he has become the standard for the criminal mastermind and the often unseen presence lurking behind the scenes in Holmes pastiches.

The criminal mastermind is the most common supervillain in the pulps, where they tend to wear Ku Klux Klan–inspired robes and hoods. Doc Savage and the Shadow faced numerous such villains—the Roar Devil, the Midas Man, the Black Master, and Q. Sometimes, the criminal mastermind is blended with the enemy commander type, as in the Red Menace, a corrupt Soviet agent who faced off against the Shadow and lost in 1931. In comics, the Kingpin and post-Crisis Lex Luthor stand as the best-known examples.

The Inverted-Superhero Supervillain

The inverted-superhero supervillain is limited to the superhero genre, primarily because he has superpowers, codenames, and costumes. Although there are earlier costumed supervillains in comics—such as the vampiric Monk, whose schemes Batman ruins in *Detective Comics*, no. 31 (September 1939)—the Joker and Catwoman are probably the best early examples of inverted-superhero supervillains. Prior villains like the Monk draw on masked and robed pulp predecessors, and mad scientists like Lex Luthor or Hugo Strange have a long lineage outside of comics. But the Joker and Catwoman mark an innovation in villainy because they are such direct responses to the superhero by creators looking to expand the superhero genre.

What makes the inverted-superhero supervillain different from other types of supervillain is that they can become superheroes. Marvel Comics features many supervillains who join the good guys—Hawkeye, the Black Widow, Quicksilver, the Scarlet Witch, and even Sandman. This ability to switch from villain to hero can be traced back to the Sub-Mariner, who debuted as an outsider figure, a bitter enemy of the surface world. He could then be positioned as a superhero investigating crimes, an ally of the United States fighting Nazis alongside the Human Torch, or an enemy of humankind taking on the Torch in an epic battle that threatened New York City's existence. The Sub-Mariner's mixed heritage and the tensions in identity it produced allowed him to be treated as an antihero, neither hero nor villain but one whose allegiance and loyalty to American society could fluctuate with the times.

Marvel's other reformed villains are typically reluctant villains, tricked or forced into evil, so their reformations are plausible. Hawkeye is forced into crime by his circus mentor, the Swordsman, and later fights Iron Man as a way of serving his lover, the Soviet agent Mada.[24] Hawkeye joins the Avengers after the Black Widow's supposed death. His former villain status is a useful plot device, as it contrasts him with the Avenger's noble, straight-arrow leader, Captain America. The Black Widow was herself forced into the life of a spy by Soviet commissars who threatened the destruction of her village and held her husband hostage. She comes to serve SHIELD as a double agent but truly turns her back on supervillainy when the death of Soviet super-agent the Red Star, who turns out to be her husband, reveals that in fact he had been an active part of duping her into working as a spy. Quicksilver and the Scarlet Witch debut as members of the Brotherhood of Evil Mutants, but time reveals them to be just confused and misled teenagers who reform once they are freed of Magneto's evil influence.

In all these instances, the supervillain's reformation is built on an ambivalence that is part of the villain's character. Not so in the case of Sandman, a hardened criminal who gains superpowers while escaping from prison. His reversal into a hero is sudden and without any historical basis, which may be why John Byrne found it so easy to retcon away, something that would be much more difficult to do convincingly with Marvel's other reformed miscreants.

Four Subtypes

There are four additional subtypes of supervillain: the alien, the evil god, the femme fatale, and the super-henchman. These subtypes are character tropes that appear in any number of genres. In superhero stories, they serve as supervillains, typically leaning toward one of the main types in their characterization.

Aliens can be monsters, mad scientists, criminal masterminds, enemy commanders, or inverted-superhero supervillains. The Super-Skrull is a monster but also an inverted-superhero supervillain—with all the powers of the Fantastic Four, he could plausibly defect from the Skrull Empire and defend the earth, as the Kree captain Mar-Yell did.[25] Evil gods are those characters who due to their unlimited supernatural power are essentially gods, but who act in evil ways. Loki is an evil god, but he is also an inverted-superhero supervillain—he could start fighting crime on earth as Thor does. Thanos, Darkseid, and Dormammu are all evil gods and enemy commanders—all rule their own worlds, command massive forces, and threaten the earth with invasion.[26] Because the femme fatale role requires a certain element of sexual allure, she cannot be a physically repulsive monster, and she rarely is a mad scientist, as her mania would similarly render her unattractive. The Dragon Lady from *Terry and the Pirates* is a femme fatale but also a criminal mastermind. The Black Widow was a femme fatale and an inverted-superhero supervillain until she defected from the Soviet Union to become an American superhero.

Super-henchmen are underlings who are have enhancements, superpowers, or superior abilities and so would seem to qualify as supervillains themselves. But as underlings, they lack the mania and drive of the supervillain. If the assassin Fat Bastard in the film *Austin Powers in Goldmember* were operating on his own to kill Austin Powers, as Francisco Scaramanga in the James Bond film *The Man with the Golden Gun* does with 007, he would be a criminal mastermind, but because he serves Dr. Evil, he is just a super-henchmen. The same is true of the Bond villains Jaws in *The Spy Who Loved Me* and Oddjob in *Goldfinger*. In superhero comics, super-henchmen count as full supervillains because when they are enhanced and given superpowers, they become inverted-superhero supervillains and do not need the mania to qualify. The Absorbing Man is an excellent example of the super-henchmen. To get at Thor, Loki empowers convicted criminal Carl "Crusher" Creel with the ability to absorb the qualities of whatever objects he touches. Touching steel makes him nearly invulnerable; touching silk allows him to slip from a pursuer's grasp. Touching Mjolnir, Thor's enchanted hammer, gives him the power to go toe to toe with the thunder god.[27] The Absorbing Man has no great mission or plan but just seeks wealth through robbery, so he would not seem to have the mania to be a supervillain. But since he has superpowers and a codename, he could become a superhero. He chooses not to, and so counts as an inverted-superhero supervillain.

DEFINITION

What is a supervillain? The easiest definition is simple: a villain who is super, that is, someone who commits villainous or evil acts and does so in a way superior to ordinary criminals or at a magnified level. But that definition is not satisfying. Another way to look at the supervillain is as the reverse of his foe, the superhero, and thus to reverse the definition of the superhero. . . . But it is important to note that supervillains precede the creation of the superhero genre and in fact oppose superheroes, super heroes, and ordinary authorities; consequently, generic distinction does not play a role in defining the supervillain because the supervillain trope belongs to many genres, certainly those of the adventure metagenre including the Western, spy/secret agent, superhero, war, and science fiction genres as well as many varieties of the detective genre. But the superhero's primary triad of mission, powers, and identity is useful in looking at the supervillain, although this triad operates differently with the supervillain.

Mission

The supervillain has a selfish, antisocial mission. He seeks something—typically wealth or power, but often fame or infamy in addition—that will serve his interests and not those of others or the larger culture. He works at cross-purposes to contemporary society.

It is possible, and even typical, for a monster to act without malice. Destructiveness comes out of its nature—a werewolf is driven by its beast nature to kill; a vampire needs blood to stay alive; the *Astro City* supervillain the Living Nightmare, an externalized distillation of fear, fights superpowered heroes to leech their power to draw on their fears. Most monsters express a force of nature in their destructiveness. They become supervillains when they are set on humankind as a punishment, as many mythical monsters were set on humanity by the gods to punish a transgression or to teach people a lesson.

Enemy commanders are ideologically motivated to conquer or subvert the nations and societies they are at war with. The mad scientist's mission arises from his desire to pursue knowledge past the point of safety—the Frankenstein myth—which always brings harm, because the mad scientist is willing to sacrifice anything for that knowledge. Criminal masterminds are driven by greed and a lust for power.

The mission for inverted-superhero supervillains comes from whatever personal defect a character has before gaining his powers. This defect is what prevents the transformative experience of the origin from turning him into a hero—his character is already flawed, and his new power simply magnifies the flaw and gives him the ability to inflict harm upon others, to seek revenge for the wrongs, or imagined wrongs, done to him. The Red Skull is an abandoned orphan who was treated badly by others as a child, but he is taken up by Hitler and turned into a super-Nazi. He uses his authority to strike back at the world for his suffering. Industrialist Norman Osborn desires wealth and power. He steals the inventions of his business partner, Professor Mendel Stromm, and sets him up on a charge of embezzlement. He suffers brain damage while experimenting with Stromm's formulas, which he hopes to cash in on. He becomes more self-centered and ambitious and creates the Green Goblin identity to pursue even more wealth and power.

Criminal Artistry

The supervillain's dream reaches far beyond the acquisitive schemes of the ordinary crook. The supervillain is an artist whose medium is crime. In Tim Burton's film version of *Batman* (1989), the Joker, played by Jack Nicholson, tells photojournalist Vicki Vale about his vision of himself: "Let me tell you what I'm thinking about, sweetie, I was in the bath one day when I realized why I was destined for greatness. You know how concerned people are about appearances. This is attractive, that is not. Well, that's all behind me. I now do what other people only dream, I make art until someone dies. See? Hee, bee, bee. I am the world's first fully functioning homicidal artist." The Joker sees his crimes as art. When his gang invades the Gotham art museum and defaces masterpieces, the Joker adds his signature to the destroyed paintings—his destruction, in his view, is a creative, artistic act, as are the murders he commits, in which he transforms the unhappy living into the eternally smiling and perfect dead.[28] James Bond's villain Auric Goldfinger shares the view of crime as art. He considers himself a "poet in deeds."[29] To Goldfinger, crime is the unplanted field of human endeavor that he can distinguish himself in:

> Man has climbed Everest and he has scraped the depths of the ocean. He has fired rockets into outer space and split the atom. He has invented, devised, created in every realm of human endeavor, and everywhere he has triumphed, broken records, achieved miracles. I said in every realm, but there is one that he has neglected, Mr. Bond. That one is the human activity loosely known as crime. The so-called criminal exploits committed by individual humans—I do not of course refer to their idiotic wars, their clumsy destruction of each other—are of miserable dimensions: little bank robberies, tiny swindles, picayune forgeries. And yet, ready to hand, a few hundred miles from here, opportunity for the greatest crime is offered. Only the actors are missing. But the producer is at last here, Mr. Bond, and he has chosen his

cast. This very afternoon the script will be read to the leading actors. Then rehearsals will begin and, in one week the curtain will go up for this single, the unique performance. And then will come the applause, the applause for the greatest single extra-legal coup of all time. And, Mr. Bond, the world will rock with that applause for centuries.[30]

Crime here is as legitimate a field of creative expression as exploration, rocket science, or atomic physics. Further, crime is a theatrical art, with actors, audience, and performance, and it can be appreciated aesthetically. The great criminal, the supervillain, is the impresario who puts on a show for the world that is far superior to the pecuniary plunderings of ordinary bad guys.

In the film version of *The Man with the Golden Gun*, Francisco Scaramanga is a high-priced assassin who seeks "a duel between titans" with Bond to test and prove himself the best killer in the world. He lures James Bond to his island base and during dinner says that it would have been ridiculously easy to have shot Bond down when 007 first landed on the island, but explains: "You see Mr. Bond, like any great artist I want to create an indisputable masterpiece once in my lifetime. The death of 007, mano-a-mano, face-to-face, will be me." He sees killing Bond as an artistic act, but added to the typical supervillain view of crime as art is the importance of the hero's greatness. It is Bond's status as a superior killer that makes his death into art. . . .

The Wound

This grandiose self-aggrandizement arises from a sense of victimhood, originating in a wound that the supervillain never recovers from. He develops a superiority complex that most often emerges as a defense mechanism to make up for feelings of inferiority and inadequacy that arose from maltreatment received when he was younger, often in childhood. But often supervillains are indeed inferior—they are defective physically or socially (or both) and are only superior mentally. They are, as therapists say, in love with the story of their wound, unable to get beyond whatever happened in their past and turn their energies toward healing or redemptive therapy.

Ian Fleming's Dr. No blames everything on his parents—a German Methodist missionary and a Chinese girl of good family who paid an aunt to raise their child: "No love, you see . . . lack of parental care."[31] For No, crime represents "revolt against the father figure who had betrayed" him.[32] Instead of learning from his injury and following the golden rule, he inverts it. Dr. No tells 007 that he seeks power, "the power, Mr. Bond, to do unto others what had been done unto me, the power of life and death, the power to decide, to judge, the power of absolute independence from outside authority."[33] Dr. No cannot, will not forgive his parents. Too much of his identity and sense of self is bound up in his rejection of his father, in inverting the Christian mission that led to his own birth.

Almost all villains share this early injury and subsequent inability to move past their injury. Hugo Drax, villain of Fleming's *Moonraker*, was once a Nazi and cannot forgive Britain for defeating the Third Reich. He plans to drop a nuclear missile on London, and when England learns that it has been threatened by a single German, he fumes, "Perhaps they'll stop calling us Krauts—BY ORDER!"[34] William Carpenter, the villain of Philip Wylie's novel *The Murderer Invisible*, believes that the world has hated him since his birth, and he wishes vengeance: "From the day I was born—fourteen pounds of gangling joints—every one I have encountered has laughed at me behind his face. The world has hated me. Women have turned from me. Men have sought to bring my ruin. I have endured every persecution that society, smug in a flabbier and impotent flesh, can contrive."[35] He sees himself as a special and unique victim, and this victimhood justifies his actions. . . .

This sense of injury and need for vengeance reaches parodic heights with the Silver Age origin of Lex Luthor.[36] As a teenager living in Smallville, Luthor created life in a test tube, but a fire broke out. Superboy extinguished the fire with his superbreath, and chemicals ignited, blowing over Luthor and causing his hair to fall out, so he set himself against Superboy and later Superman, becoming the greatest supervillain of the DC universe—all for the loss of his hair.[37]

The Joker offers another theory on the supervillain in *Batman: The Killing Joke*. As a young man, an unsuccessful comedian named Jack suffers a horrendous tragedy when his wife and baby die in a fire caused by a malfunctioning baby-bottle heater. His subsequent short criminal career as the Red Hood ends after the robbery of the Monarch Playing Card Company, when he seeks to escape through the Ace Chemical Works plant, where he once worked. He eludes Batman by plunging into a soup of chemical waste and swimming through drainage pipes, from which he emerges with white skin and green hair and takes on the identity of the Joker. As the Joker, he shoots and cripples Barbara Gordon in front of her father, Commissioner James Gordon (and presumably rapes her, though this is not explicitly stated). He then takes Gordon captive and attempts to drive him mad in a horrible parody of a carnival by showing Gordon images of his daughter's violation. He argues that in a psychotic world in which innocents die, when "faced with the inescapable fact that human existence is mad, random and pointless," the only reasonable response is madness.[38] He wants to demonstrate that one bad day would drive anyone mad, that there is no difference between himself and anyone else, and so he is not inferior or weak for his madness and ultimately not at fault for his actions. He accuses Batman of having a similar bad day and going mad, but refusing to admit the meaninglessness of existence and insisting on "pretending that life makes some sense, that there's some point to all this struggling."[39] So for the Joker, the mania that drives the supervillain is a reasonable and understandable reaction to the universe—it is an attempt to impose meaning on the void, a god-like act emerging out of an ego folded in on itself in an attempt to defend its sovereignty against injury.

A few supervillains have a nonpersonal wound—they feel for a class of beings whom they represent and who have been wounded in some way, or who are mistreated or oppressed (or are presented as being mistreated or oppressed). Dracula, Dr. Fu Manchu, and Ra's al Ghul share a desire to overturn the status quo and reverse the ruling order, because that status quo negatively affects their kind. Their missions are socially transformative....

Monologue and Soliloquy

The supervillain's wound prompts him to monologue, to sit the hero down—whether to dinner or bound in a death trap—and tell his story. The villain seeks, as the Joker does, confirmation of the virtuousness and reasonableness of his decisions, of his mania. He wants the approval of the hero, who is by definition superior and not afflicted with the inferiority complex of the villain. The hero is not damaged, not physically, socially, or morally deformed. If the villain can gain the hero's respect and approval—the respect and approval he so missed in his early life—then his life and villainy are justified, and he is recuperated back into the community that ostracized and rejected him. Approval by the hero will heal the supervillain's wound. But the hero never gives this approval, and that is what keeps the villain coming back to the same hero over and over again, especially if the hero—as in the case of Superman with Lex Luthor and Batman with the Joker—is in some sense responsible for the villain's wound. The hero's refusal often drives the supervillain into a frenzy, leading to a critical error that allows the hero to vanquish his stronger foe, thereby reinforcing the hero's superiority and villain's inferiority and pouring salt into his wound.

In the middle of listening to Dr. Octopus brag about his power, Spider-Man once asked, "Tell me something, Ock, . . . are you trying to defeat me by talking me to death?!"[40] The answer—based upon the propensity of villains to talk, talk, talk—appears to be "yes." Supervillains are given to two forms of speechifying: the soliloquy and the monologue. The theatrical origin of these terms points to an aspect of supervillainy—the artistic and exhibitionist nature of villains' crimes. They are not merely involved in crime for its pecuniary reward; they are impresarios, putting on a show of sorts, and the heroes who oppose them are their audience.

The term "monologuing," coined in Brad Bird's computer-animated film *The Incredibles* (2004), refers to supervillains' tendency toward self-absorbed, self-destructive talking; instead of killing the hero, they spout off on their greatness, the hero's feebleness, and the inevitability of their victory. Ozymandias noted the foolishness of monologuing: "I'm not a Republic serial villain. Do you seriously think I'd explain my master stroke if there remained the slightest chance of you affecting its outcome?"[41] . . .

But if monologuing were only a tool for the creators, it would not have lasted. Monologuing embodies central aspects of supervillainy; it is a form of hubris that comes out of the villain's belief in his absolute supremacy and the assurance that his plans are unstoppable. Hugo Drax, villain of *Moonraker*, conducts a classic death-trap monologue with James Bond bound to a chair in the exhaust pit of a rocket launching pad. Drax says, "You don't know how I have longed for an English audience . . . to tell my story."[42] He then tells Bond the story of his life, finishing with the details of his plan to launch a nuclear missile at London, and closes by asking, "What do you think of my story?" Bond dismisses Drax's life as "sad business," which goads the madman into beating Bond and forgetting about a lighter left on his desk.[43] Bond burns off his ropes, escapes certain death, and stops Drax's plan. Drax should have pocketed his lighter, but his desire to reveal himself to Bond and exert his will over the hero overrides his common sense. . . .

The second form of speechifying, the soliloquy, is performed without an audience, or in front of obedient underlings who neither interrupt nor respond to their master's musings. In the soliloquy, the supervillain gives full vent to his ego, proclaiming his greatness and promising vengeance on those who oppose him. In *The Amazing SpiderMan*, no. 5, a solitary Doctor Doom declares, "Ordinary men tremble at the mention of my name! The entire civilized world fears the menace of Doctor Doom!," and he later asserts, "When one is a master of science, as I am, there is nothing which cannot be accomplished! Sooner or later, I shall eliminate all those who dare oppose me!"[44]

The other topic of the soliloquy is the villain's relationship to the hero. In Doctor Octopus's second appearance, Ock complains that he has been committing all sorts of crimes, but he cannot get Spider-Man's attention.[45] He is essentially wondering why their relationship is not foremost in Spider-Man's life, and he resolves, like a football widow, to do more to interest his man.

The monologue and soliloquy have great value in conveying the character of a supervillain and are presented straightforwardly and without irony. . . .

Power

Supervillains are superior to and more powerful than the ordinary authorities. They have cunning, genius, resources, or extraordinary abilities that render the ordinary agents of the social order helpless to stop them, or at least that puts the authorities at a distinct disadvantage. Their superiority has several sources. Typically they have access to super-science or science-fictional technology that is far superior and greatly advanced over the technology available to the rest of society, and they typically are geniuses and create this technology themselves, or they employ geniuses—willingly or not—to invent for them. This technology can also be represented as mystical or magical power, in which case the villain is or is allied with a sorcerer. The second source of their power is great wealth, wealth that can be used to recruit and equip a private army or a squad of highly trained and effective specialists in crime; or their wealth represents the resources of a foreign power or state—the armed forces, government bureaucracy, agricultural resources, industrial power, or national resource wealth of a kingdom, nation, or empire. The third source of their power is charisma—they are able to draw mass numbers of ordinary people into their schemes or extract extraordinary loyalty from those who serve them. The last source of strength is extraordinary physical, mental, or mystical abilities, superpowers that make them more than human—super strength, invulnerability, telepathy, super speed—any of the powers that a superhero might possess.

Power is central to the definition of supervillain—if a malign individual has only the strength, wit, and other resources available to normal human beings, they are mere villains. If the resources and abilities of the police are sufficient to counter a villain's schemes, he is just a bad guy. But if a villain transcends those abilities and holds mastery of so many resources that even major world governments are working against the odds when they try to stop him, then he is a supervillain, particularly if these resources are matched to a vision that goes beyond mere avarice—if they have an ego-soaked or ego-driven mania or vision, or some great project to accomplish, especially if this project is socially transformative but will have to be forced upon an unwilling populace, and especially if it involves mass murder or a massive numbers of deaths, or if the project can be viewed, in a sick and twisted way, as art. Therefore, mission and power are the two important defining elements of supervillainy.

Identity

In a reverse with the superhero, identity is the weakest element of the definition of the supervillain and is not necessary but typical. It is a necessary aspect of inverted-superhero supervillains, since they wear costumes and have codenames.

Unlike superheroes, they often do not maintain secret identities, although they obviously have ordinary identities. They often give up their normal lives, deciding to live purely within the super world. They have abandoned the things that tie them to mundane existence and cut themselves off from normal life. Just as a secret identity helps the superhero retain ties to the larger society he protects, so does the villain's abandonment of an ordinary identity magnify his selfishness and disconnect him from the larger society he attacks.

Quite often, a villain's name raises him above the ordinary criminal. Joe Chill killed Bruce Wayne's parents, but he is just a criminal, and his name does nothing more than identify him for booking purposes. But the name Ming the Merciless, the Emperor of Mongo, tells a different story. It conveys the bearer's character—he is merciless—and gives a sense of his power (he is the emperor of Mongo). The villain's birth name often supplies some sense of grandiosity—one wonders if it is the villain's attempt to live up to his name that drives him to become a supervillain. . . .

HERO/VILLAIN RELATIONSHIPS

Supervillains relate to their corresponding heroes in a number of ways, through self-worth, as archenemies, as doppelgängers, in Oedipal pairings, as displacement of the hero's personality, and in rogues' galleries.

Self-Worth

Supervillains get their sense of self-worth from the quality of the hero they oppose. In *Detective Comics*, no. 475, the Joker surprises Rupert Thorne in the men's room:

> [T]he Penguin and myself! I suspect you're behind Prof. Strange's disappearance! But obviously, you didn't learn the Batman's identity, and that's why you yet live! I don't want that secret penetrated—ever—since it would take away my fun—the thrill of the joust with my perfect opponent. The Joker must have the Batman! Nay, the Joker deserves the Batman! What fun would there be in humbling mere policemen? I am the greatest criminal ever known! Ha Ha Ha Ha! And for anyone else to destroy the Batman would be unworthy of me![46]

The Joker rates himself by rating his opponent—he is a great criminal because he has a great hero to oppose him. Their relationship is what makes his criminal life worthwhile.

Archenemy

In the archenemy relationship, the villain is the hero's greatest opponent, typically the one he has faced most often. The archenemy relationship always comments on the nature of the hero. The defect that makes the villain villainous is exactly what the hero resists. The Red Skull stands for Nazi ideology and antidemocratic values, which the Aryan-looking *Übermensch* Steve Rogers rejects. The Joker represents a self-centered response to tragedy that Batman, who has suffered a similar tragedy and loss, must resist. On the television show *Smallville*, Lex Luthor stands for the moral shortcuts that Clark Kent must resist to avoid becoming a tyrant, as his father Jor-El seemingly wants. Perhaps the most telling archenemy relationship is that of Professor X and Magneto. Once, they were friends who shared a vision—or at least a fear—of what mutants could become in the world and of how humanity would respond. Xavier chose the path of peaceful integration, Magneto the path of violent opposition to the threat humanity posed to mutanity. In a very real sense, they have identical goals—the safety of mutantkind—but Xavier chooses the arduous, slower path of cooperation, whereas Magneto's plans would result in *Homo superior* ruling the earth and replacing *Homo sapiens*, with Magneto ruling over the mutants. Xavier is selfless and therefore a hero; Magneto is selfish, and therefore a villain.

Doppelgänger

The doppelgänger is a villain with the same powers as the hero and most often with a very similar visual look. The purest example is Professor Zoom, whose costume inverts the costume of the Flash.[47] Captain Marvel's red costume is inverted in Black Adam's black costume, as is Spider-Man's in Venom's. In some cases, the inversion is taken to a higher level, as with the armored opponents of Iron Man, a capitalist in his Tony Stark identity, and the Crimson Dynamo, a communist agent. These villains offer the toughest challenge to the hero because they have the same powers but are not bound by the heroic code.

A rare variant of this relationship exists, the opposite doppelgänger, who reverses the powers and appearance of the hero. Man-Bat, who originally appeared as a monster supervillain, inverts Batman's name and appears more as a bat than a man. The Hulk villain the Leader is small with a large cranium—he is all brain, whereas the Hulk is all body. The Silver Age Flash's first villain, Turtleman, has the opposite sobriquet to the Flash; he is the slowest man alive.

Oedipal

An Oedipal villain has a Freudian relationship with the hero; he represents the hero's relationship to his parents. The clearest example of this relationship is Superman, who primarily battles versions of his father. According to Michael Fleisher and Janet Lincoln: "The horrendous cataclysm that destroyed Krypton occurred at a time when the infant Superman was grappling with the agonizing complexity of his affectional and erotic feelings toward Lara, his mother. In Oedipal terms, the infant Superman wished his father dead so that he could possess his mother. And then, all at once, the first part of the forbidden fantasy came true: the entire planet exploded and his father died."[48] Compounding this Oedipal tension is the fact that Lara specifically rejected Kal in favor of Jor-El. In Oedipal terms, she could have rejected Jor-El by suggesting that he save himself while she and Kal remained on Krypton. This rejection is made explicit in the first initial comic book version of the origin.[49] The rocket is large enough to carry one adult along with the child. Jor-El suggests that Lara take their baby to earth, but she rejects this idea, telling Jor-El that her place is by his side. Instead of a long life on earth as Supermom to her son, Lara chooses death as an ordinary woman with her husband. Thus she rejects both Kal and the Superman he would become, banishing him to a life isolated from his past and leaving him to discover his Kryptonian heritage slowly and on his own. . . .

Superman's chief supervillain, Lex Luthor, stands out as a twisted version of Jor-El. Luthor is a leading scientist on earth, but unlike Jor-El he has turned his gifts to selfish pursuits. An even greater Oedipal aspect of their relationship is the attempt by Lex Luthor to replace Jor-El.[50] He goes back in time in order to romance Lara and become Superman's father, reasoning that a son could not oppose his father, even his father's schemes to rule the world. Therefore, Lex Luthor gains a double Oedipal resonance: he is a father figure who wishes Superman dead and who tries to take his mother away from him in order to negate his heroic persona.

Superman's other villains are generally representations of his father in the role of a leading scientist. Brainiac is an especially interesting inversion of Jor-El. Jor-El sought in a variety of ways to save his home planet. He discovered the Phantom Zone, into which Krypton could have projected its population. But the only Kryptonians who survived in the Phantom Zone were its criminals. So Jor-El's genius only managed to save the worst of Krypton. Brainiac seeks to repopulate his home planet, which has been decimated by a plague, by shrinking cities from various planets and putting them in jars with the idea of returning them to their original size in his home world.[51] Before the destruction of Krypton, Brainiac shrinks and steals its capital city, Kandor, thereby preserving the best of the planet's heritage. Where Jor-El tried to preserve the planet but only managed to save its worst element, Brainiac saved its best element through theft.

Displacement

Supervillains can represent a displaced aspect of the hero that the hero struggles with. This relationship is best represented by Batman. Like Superman's villains, Batman's opponents emerge out of Bruce Wayne's relationship with his father. Batman's relationship with his father is much less ambivalent than Superman's, but his internal struggles are much more intense. In discussing Batman, Richard Reynolds asserts: "The great Batman villains all mirror some key point in Batman's character, a point of reference which gives their villainy special purchase within the meta text of the Batman myth."[52] . . .

Batman's first supervillain, the Monk, is a twisted version of himself. The Monk's "brain is the product of years of intense study and seclusion."[53] He operates at night and can turn himself into a wolf, just as Bruce Wayne operates at night and effectively turns himself into a bat. Many of Batman's other villains suffered one bad day, as Bruce Wayne did, but their grief and anger turned inward and twisted them so that they take out their pain and hurt on society. Interestingly, like Batman, their wounds often come from criminals, but instead of turning their hatred toward crime, as Bruce Wayne did, they join criminals in despoiling society.

Alan Moore and Brian Bolland address this aspect of the Joker's criminal identity in *Batman: The Killing Joke*, . . . which argues that villainy and heroism proceed out of the same confrontation with absurdity. . . . Interestingly, when Batman goes to visit the Joker at Arkham Asylum in order to talk over their conflict in an attempt to avert it ending in the murder of one by another, he passes Two-Face, his split face divided by the barred window of his door. Gordon, Batman, Two-Face, and the Joker represent a continuum of response to law and crime. Gordon has a single face and represents law and sanity, the proper construction of authority, and an unproblematic relationship with reality. Gordon's world makes sense and is codified in the law. . . . Batman has two faces—Bruce Wayne and Batman, representing his encounter with the meaninglessness of the universe via the senseless death of a good man and woman who should not have been killed in a just universe. As Batman, his face is split between his mask (above) and face (below), thus representing his dual nature and his incomplete transition into the world of insanity. He holds half of himself back, going much further than Gordon but not fully committing to a solipsistic view of the world. He brings the Joker in; he does not kill him.

Two-Face also has two faces, but his are split vertically, the opposite of Batman's. Two-Face's faces are also permanent. He cannot slip out of his super identity as Batman can. Two-Face suffered a bad day like Batman and the Joker. He was once Harvey "Apollo" Dent, dashing and handsome crusading district attorney who worked alongside Batman before Gordon became commissioner.... The Joker has one face, a permanent joker face, and seemingly has no control or outside consideration over his actions. His is an individualistic anarchy without loyalty or consideration for others: he wants only what he wants, regardless of the consequences....

Rogues' Gallery

A rogues' gallery is a band of villains who repeatedly face off against one hero. Typically they oppose him individually, but they often team up in various combinations. The rogues' gallery reflects the hero in some way. The Flash's rogues' gallery is collection of single-powered supervillains—each villain has a central motif: cold (Captain Cold), heat (Heat Wave), mirrors (Mirror Master), the weather (Weather Wizard), and so on. The Flash also has a single superpower—speed—but he is well known for using that speed to produce a whole range of super-powered effects such as invisibility, intangibility, time travel, whirlwinds, appearing to be in more than one place, and so on. So the Flash represents many powers in one power, whereas the rogues' gallery represents a combination of single powers.

PROACTIVE AND REACTIVE

In a narrative sense, villains are proactive and heroes are reactive. The villain's machinations drive the plot. The hero reacts to the villain's threat, which justifies the hero's violence. But on a generic level, the villain is reactive; that is, supervillains are created in reaction to the hero's ability to defeat ordinary criminals in order to create narrative tension. This idea of villain inflation is raised in the film *Batman Begins* (2005) and the comic book series *Batman: The Dark Knight Returns* (1986). At the end of *Batman Begins*, Batman meets Lieutenant James Gordon atop police headquarters. Gordon expresses the concern that Batman's existence, though useful in the fight against Ra's al Ghul and the Scarecrow, pushes criminals to heighten their attacks. Batman asserts, "We can bring Gotham back." Gordon rejoins, "What about escalation? We start carrying semi-automatics, they buy automatics. We start wearing Kevlar, they buy armor-piercing rounds. And you're wearing a mask and jumping off rooftops. Now take this guy, armed robbery, double homicide. Got a taste for the theatrical like you, leaves a calling card," and he hands Batman an evidence-bagged joker playing card. Implied here is the idea that the next escalation will be from ordinary gangsters and mob leaders to masked, theatrical super criminals who will take crime to horrific new heights. Because the implied but unnamed Joker seems to be responding to the debut of Batman, it seems that Gordon may be correct. . . .

When the superhero attempts to be proactive, he essentially becomes a villain, as with Ozymandias in *Watchmen*. Ozymandias sees that the United States and the Soviet Union are headed to nuclear confrontation and so fakes an alien incursion to give the superpowers a common enemy to join forces against. His plan works, and it seems that a nuclear catastrophe is averted, but at the cost of millions of deaths as the fake alien sends out a telepathic burst that kills most New Yorkers and drives the rest mad. Ozymandias started as a superhero but ended as the greatest mass murderer in history in a proactive attempt to save the world. . . .

This brief overview of proactive superhero series seems to suggest that the superhero has to be reactive to operate effectively within the genre, at least in terms of open-ended serial narratives. Individual graphic novels or movies can discuss the proactive superhero profitably, but proactivity as a central focus seems to cause a shift in narrative strategy away from the superhero formula and toward a use of the superhero as metaphor, along the lines of literary fiction. Conversely, the supervillain must remain proactive to create the menace the superhero reacts to.

CONCLUSION

Supervillains are not unique to the superhero genre but have roots that go back through the adventure narratives of the past two centuries into epics, legends, and mythology. Although the superhero genre is a twentieth-century invention, the superhero likewise has roots in such ancient materials. What does the superhero draw from myth, legend, and epic?

Notes

1. Excerpted from Peter Coogan, *Superhero: The Secret Origin of a Genre* (Austin, TX: MonkeyBrain Books, 2006). The numeration of the endnotes reflects the placement of notes in the excerpted text and is thus different from the numeration in the original text. Alterations in format have been made in order to be consistent with other chapters in this volume, and the chapter has been lightly edited for style for the purposes of the present publication.

2. Stan Lee, introduction to *Bring On the Bad Guys: Origins of the Marvel Comics Villains* (New York: Marvel Enterprises, 1998), 8.

3. *Beowulf*, trans. Burton Raffel (New York: Signet, 1963).

4. *The Amazing Spider-Man*, no. 6 (November 10, 1963).

5. *Captain America*, no. 2 (April 1, 1941), cover art by Joe Simon. (The cover art was included in the original text. We have chosen not to reprint those images here in the name of economy, but we will herewith include the references to the image placements.)

6. Richard Slotkin, *The Fatal Environment: The Myth of the Frontier in the Age of Industrialization, 1800–1890* (Norman: University of Oklahoma Press, 1985), 53–54, 59–61.

7. James Fenimore Cooper, *The Deerslayer* (1841; repr., New York: Penguin, 1996), 465.

8. James Fenimore Cooper, *The Last of the Mohicans* (1826; repr., New York: Oxford University Press, 1998), 127.

9. Cooper, *The Last of the Mohicans*, 172.

10. *Tales of Suspense*, no. 66 (June 1965).

11. Peter H. Goodrich, "The Lineage of Mad Scientists: Anti-Types of Merlin," *Extrapolation* 27, no. 2 (July 1986), 110.

12. Goodrich, "The Lineage of Mad Scientists," 111.

13. Goodrich, "The Lineage of Mad Scientists," 112.

14. Goodrich, "The Lineage of Mad Scientists," 112–13.

15. "Mad Scientist," Wikipedia, available at https://en.wikipedia.org/wiki/Mad_scientist.

16. John G. Cawelti, *Adventure, Mystery, and Romance: Formula Stories as Art and Popular Culture* (Chicago: University of Chicago Press, 1976), 92.

17. Cawelti, *Adventure, Mystery, and Romance*, 92.

18. Cawelti, *Adventure, Mystery, and Romance*, 92–93.

19. *New Nick Carter Weekly*, no. 692 (April 2, 1910), quoting from Jess Nevins, "Fantastic Victorian Q," 2005, available at http://www.reocities.com/jessnevins/vicq.html.

20. Ben Macintyre, *The Napoleon of Crime: The Life and Times of Adam Worth, Master Thief* (New York: Broadway Books, 1997).

21. Macintyre, *The Napoleon of Crime*, 77.

22. Macintyre, *The Napoleon of Crime*, 222.

23. Arthur Conan Doyle, "The Adventure of the Final Problem," *McClure's Magazine* 2 (1894): 102.

24. *Tales of Suspense*, no. 64 (April 1965); *Avengers*, no. 16 (May 1965).

25. *Fantastic Four*, no. 18 (September 1963).

26. *Strange Adventures*, no. 126 (1964).

27. *Journey into Mystery*, no. 115 (April 1965).

28. *Batman: The Dark Knight Returns*, no. 3 (1986).

29. Ian Fleming, *Goldfinger* (1959; repr., New York: Penguin, 2002).

30. Fleming, *Goldfinger*, 185–86.

31. Ian Fleming, *Dr. No* (1958; repr., New York: Penguin, 2002), 163.

32. Fleming, *Dr. No*, 163.

33. Fleming, *Dr. No*, 163.

34. Ian Fleming, *Moonraker* (1955; repr., New York: Random House, 2003).

35. Philip Wylie, *The Murderer Invisible* (1931; repr., New York: Popular Library, 1959), 26.

36. *Superman*, no. 173 (November 1964).

37. *Superman*, no. 173.

38. Alan Moore, Brian Bolland, John Higgins, and Richard Starkings, *Batman: The Killing Joke* (New York: DC Comics, 1988).

39. Moore et al., *Batman: The Killing Joke*, 39.

40. Stan Lee, Dave Michelinie, Steve Ditko, and Erik Larsen, *The Sinister Six: Amazing Spider-Man Annual*, no. 6 (November 1969), 35.

41. Alan Moore and Dave Gibbons, *Watchmen* (New York: DC Comics, 1987), 27.

42. Fleming, *Moonraker*, 204.

43. Fleming, *Moonraker*, 213.

44. *The Amazing Spider-Man*, no. 5 (October 10, 1963).

45. *The Amazing SpiderMan*, no. 11 (April 10, 1964).

46. *Detective Comics*, no. 475 (February 1978), 12.

47. *The Flash*, no. 225 (February 1974).

48. Michael L. Fleisher and Janet E. Lincoln, *The Great Superman Book* (New York: Warner, 1978), 396.

49. *Superman*, no. 53 (August 1948).

50. *Superman*, no. 170 (July 1964).

51. *Action Comics*, no. 242 (July 1958).

52. Richard Reynolds, "Masked Heroes," in *The Superhero Reader*, ed. Charles Hatfield, Jeet Heer, and Kent Worcester (Jackson: University Press of Mississippi, 2013), 99–115.

53. *Detective Comics*, no. 33 (November 1939), 1.

CHAPTER 6

Vivisecting the Villain

A Framework for the Analysis of Enemy Image Construction in Cinema

LENNART SOBERON

> Before the weapon comes the image. We think others to death and then invent the battle-axe or the ballistic missiles with which to actually kill them.
>
> **SAM KEEN, *FACES OF THE ENEMY***

Enemies are the products of invention; they don't exist in or out of themselves but have to be created.[1] Before becoming part of a social reality, enemies' conception has to be cultivated in the minds and hearts of people. Antagonistic divisions play an important part in the structuring of discourses and thus contribute to the construction of meaning and the formation of identities.[2] We consider enemy-making as consisting of articulatory practices, constituting and organizing social relations. These processes of identity construction are part of social life, political rhetoric, and international conflict, but they are also deeply engrained in how we structure the stories we tell. As Ragnhild Fiebig-von Hase and Ursula Lehmkuhl[3] point out, antagonism is indispensable—not only ontologically but also cinematically.[4] Alfred Hitchcock famously stated, "The more successful the villain, the more successful the film."[5] Enemies often form the center around which many narratives are grafted. Following David Bordwell and Kristin Thompson,[6] we adopt a perspective of cinema as an integrated system of content and form,[7] consisting of a series of aesthetic problems and choices. The construction of villains in films is thus the result of a series of creative decisions, usually designed to elicit certain sets of emotions and affects. Cinema as a medium of mass communication has displayed potential in the identification, reinvigoration, and crystallization of enemy identities arguably unmatched in the twentieth century. Film propaganda has played a pivotal part in structuring groups into the role of villain based on their ethnicity, nationality, ideology, or any other category of identity.[8] Moreover, apart from having great significance in politics, enemies are an important locus for drama in fiction. They serve an instrumentalist function, designed to heighten tension, raise stakes, and incite conflict.

EXAMINING ENEMY IMAGES

Since the very first film villains, filmmakers around the world have utilized their best abilities in effectively crafting enemy characters. As such, by attempting to evoke a sense of threat, accentuate danger, demonize or dehumanize characters, or structure life as ungrievable, filmmakers have established and subsequently refined formal techniques, tropes, and conventions. How enemies are constructed deserves distinct scholarly attention for many reasons, not least because the repetitious presence of an enemy image reinforces ancient dichotomies of good versus evil and, over time, can solidify a negative and stereotypical evaluation of the "Other" in mass media representations.[9] Although we greatly recognize the importance of enemy image construction as a discursive practice in the ideological sense, this chapter will not go into too much detail on the symbolic power of this representational practice. The scope of this contribution rather lies in exploring enemy image construction chiefly as *cinematic practice*—namely, how enemies are represented and formally articulated in film as audiovisual narratives.

The concept of "enemy image construction" is here used to define the set of discursive and cinematic practices in operation when structuring individuals and collectives into the role of enemy—"the culturally influenced, very negative, and stereotyped evaluation of the Other."[10] This chapter makes the case that throughout the history of narrative film, filmmakers have been occupied with creative decisions regarding enemy-making. From Soviet agitprop to American action thriller films, enemy image construction has developed into something of a language—a cinematic discourse if you will. These processes will be elaborated upon utilizing the theoretical frameworks of poststructuralist discourse theory and cognitive film studies in order to position film villains as discursive constructs that interact with mental and emotional structures elicited and sustained in cinema. Here we adopt a neoformalist approach to how the formal devices within the medium are utilized by filmmakers in relation to anticipated effects. Nevertheless, constructing a framework for the analysis of enemy image construction that can account for the totality of cinema is an impossible feat. Attempting to do so regardless of the complex multitudes in modes of cinema—its genres, authors, trends, and many other types—undeniably runs the risk of overgeneralization. Generic traditions and conventions, for one, can be considered to chiefly determine how a film's hero and villain characters are portrayed.[11] While we avoid the pretense of delivering an all-encompassing model, therefore, we would like to argue that this process of enemy image construction does show some consistency over a wide variety of genres. We consider this framework specifically applicable to what Thomas Schatz defines as "genres of determined space":[12] narratives set in a symbolic arena of action (war, conflict, revenge, and other struggles for dominance) that often dictate the need for an antagonistic relation in which enemies are required to be defeated in order to achieve resolution and reach a desired state. Focusing on narratives of conflict and action, this container category can be considered to encompass a wide number of genres such as war films, fantasies, science fiction, and Westerns.

ORGANIZING STRUCTURES OF OPPOSITION

Just as our identity construction takes place through the struggle between subject positions,[13] the film viewer has the potential to oscillate through different character positions. However, through a series of textual and formal decisions, filmmakers attempt to fix these subject positions in an attempt to steer audience perception into the preferred reading of characters as enemy threat. In analyzing how these perspectives, and their matching discourses, are negotiated within cinema, we are indebted to Holger Pötzsch's theoretical approach regarding how the formal properties of war films attempt to structure emotional engagement in audience members.[14] Pötzsch conceives a useful orientation toward how films attempt to establish a certain closedness, stating: "In positioning the spectator within the discourse of a movie, these technical and narrative features reduce the paradigm for possible articulations and push reception in a particular direction."[15] Our aim lies in analyzing such formal properties and textual patterns characterizing enemy image construction as cinematic practice. By employing different narrative and stylistic components of the medium, filmmakers help steer enemy perception among audiences. We propose a framework in which narrative structures and what Thompson identifies as the five kinds of cinematic material (i.e., mise-en-scène, sound, camera framing, editing, and optical effects) are utilized in constructing characters as enemies.[16] In dissecting the process of enemy image construction, we consider this group categorization to undergo different stages in a linear process through which individual characters and groups are defined as villains. This process moves along a gradual line of narrative development; however, it should also be noted that these four stages are in equal measure part of an interconnected dynamic. To further theorize this process of enemy-making, we've partially based ourselves on Kurt R. Spillman and Kati Spillman's model for enemy image construction as a socialized process,[17] in establishing a model that reconstructs the cognitive/emotional process filmmakers attempt to establish in the construction of enemy characters in cinema.

1) Establishing difference
Layering Otherness
Deindividualization
Structuring opposition
2) Identifying enemies
Narrative designation
Enhancing opposition
3) Intensifying threat
Heightening tension
Accentuating necessity
4) Providing means for resolution
Delivering a "legitimate" solution
Executing action

In this four-tier process, the character engagement of spectators is structured both toward the narrative and to its characters. As such, the spectator is guided through gradually intensified layers of opposition. The aim of this progression is to elicit audience antipathy. Juxtaposed to this process, Murray Smith has constructed a narrative framework through which spectators are guided toward character identification, consisting of phases of recognition, alignment, and allegiance.[18] Labeling this process the "structures of sympathy," Smith conceptualizes character engagement among stages of an increasingly intensified empathic connection between viewer and character. What enemy image construction attempts to do is work against these empathic processes through a set of formal strategies cultivating opposition between spectator and character, a complex interaction of epistemological and rhetorical limitations aimed at disabling the empathic engagement of the audience through the manipulation of emotion and affect. These structures of antipathy are essential in understanding enemy image construction because "emotions are intimately tied to cognitions, and for this reason affective experience, meaning, and interpretation are firmly intertwined; and . . . emotions as experienced in films have powerful rhetorical functions and contribute to a film's ideological effects."[19] According to Carl Plantinga, emotions elicited by fiction can be direct or sympathetic/antipathetic.[20] Sympathetic and antipathetic emotions are in this philosophy dependent upon character behavior and situations. Through such constructs, filmmakers attempt to evoke different feelings and affects ranging from "pro-emotions" such as pity, compassion, and admiration to "con-emotions" such as anger, disgust, and contempt. The aim of enemy image construction essentially boils down to communicating these "con-emotions" for villain characters among spectators while minimalizing the presence of "pro-emotions."

As Plantinga notes, "there are good reasons to believe that fiction, artifact, and metaemotions in response to films have strong similarities to extrafilmic emotions, but can be altered or inflected by various filmic strategies."[21] The construction of enemies goes through four stages of structuring opposition. First, difference is established though distancing practices of Othering. This is followed/paralleled by a process of enemy designation, in which the character(s) to whom we've been introduced is/are established as villain(s). Upon this basis is built an intensifying feeling of threat, most often by setting up a series of increasingly suspenseful circumstances. In the final phase, the problem the enemy poses is addressed, and solutions to this problem are formulated, discussed, and subsequently executed. This model is most relevant for those stories that start with the inception of enemies as instigators of conflict and ending with resolution by way of their elimination—most often in the form of violent destruction. Such structures of antipathy build toward the dehumanization, and in an extreme degree even demonization, of characters and the identities they embody. This results in an emotional disenfranchisement of individuals and collectives alike through a process that limits the validity of these characters' goals and, indeed, their very existence. Accordingly, the violent actions undertaken by the hero are more easily framed as legitimate, unavoidable, or righteous.

Establishing Difference

Just as our notions of Us and Other are relational, similarly, the opposition between Hero and Enemy is part of a wider politics of exclusion.[22] The Other could be considered an essential nodal point in the discursive articulation of the enemy.[23] In order to construct enemies, structures of opposition are first established through a process of Othering—here conceptualized as a "process which serves to mark and name those thought to be different from oneself"[24]—a set of representational practices resulting in the differentiation and distancing of individuals and groups of a dissimilar identity. Othering lowers a person's position in a social/moral hierarchy by creating cognitive/emotional distance. Debra Merskin considers Othering to be a cognitive structure, offering mental schema with which to organize reality.[25] This information is often simplified and brought into relation with existing conceptions of identity.

One such mental technique playing a part in this process is stereotyping. Richard Dyer defines stereotyping as a process in which "the dominant groups apply their norms to subordinated groups, find the latter wanting, hence inadequate, inferior, sick or grotesque and hence reinforcing the dominant groups' own sense of the legitimacy of their domination."[26] Stereotypes here function as symbolic markers through which elements associated with certain identities are enlarged and applied systematically, interacting with wider layers of meaning based on our conceptions of social reality. This accentuation of Otherness is played out mostly through a game of iconography; the usage of a set of distinct visual and aural signs is a simple and efficient way to introduce the likes of character and setting. Dyer describes iconography in relation to stereotyping as "a kind of short-hand—it places a character quickly and economically."[27] The communication of these codes is usually directed to prominent dichotomies based on morality, ideology, ethnicity, gender, religion, age, and other essential markers of identity. When establishing difference, films always structure opposition on one or several of these fault lines. A fetishization of these aspects of Otherness subsequently takes place through the use of what we dub "alien iconography." These are cinematic cues delivered to an audience with little function aside from stressing the Otherness of certain characters. Equally important to point out is that these elements enter this chain of equivalence with various components, discursively connecting different identities with connotations resting on other, although similar, dichotomies. This is epitomized by the binary between civilization/savagery standing in discursive relation with the division West/Orient.[28] Imagery associated with these characteristics of Otherness feature heavily in these films. For example, in the film *Rambo: First Blood Part II* (1985), through a sly use of semantics, the Vietnamese soldiers are portrayed as being barbaric. As a type of moral exposition, all shots featuring such characters aim to stress either their hypersexuality (taking in prostitutes), primitivism (covered in sweat and mud), or savagery (torturing Rambo in a puddle of leeches).

Another way opposition is structured in this first phase is through processes of deindividualization. Sam Keen, for one, has made clear that enemy image construction works by way of abstraction.[29] By obscuring human features, personal characteristics, and individual attributes, filmmakers deny the audience any empathic identification with these characters. Whether it's *Star Wars'* iconic Storm Troopers, *Mad Max: Fury Road's* (2015) white-painted War Boys, or *Kill Bill's* (2003) Crazy 88s, the viewer encounters a horde-like group of mostly unrelatable characters defined by their homogeneity. This uniformity, in accordance with their costumed appearances, creates distance and deprives audiences of empathic access. Equally present in *Rambo II* are groups of enemy characters appearing in extreme closeups, making only fragments of their presence visible, or viewed from afar in long shot, staging them indistinctively in straight lines—strongly reminiscent of the geometric compositions of the soldiers engaging during the Odessa Steps massacre in Eisenstein's *Battleship Potemkin* (1925). Such sentiments can also be put forward aurally, by burdening characters with thick accents, inaudible dialogue, or the absence of dialogue altogether.

Identifying Enemies

As pointed out above, the question of enmity is mostly a matter of perception. According to conflict theory, essential to one's distinction between Others and enemies is the perception of danger—others become enemies if their appearance is coupled with extreme threat perception.[30] In the second stage of enemy image construction, opposition toward specific characters is enhanced through the designation of these characters' enemy identity. In this phase, enemies are formally identified. This enemy identification is established both narratively by way of their actions, and through a series of cues that audiences have learned to pick up. This stage of construction functions to further stress difference and introduces us to the morally vile nature of these enemy characters. As Daniel Forbes formulated it: "It makes sense that evil should have a particular look and style, so that we can readily identify it and understand how it fits into the narrative."[31] Understanding characters as enemies therefore relates to Bordwell's notions of "narrative comprehension": audiences continually undergo cognitive processes through which they form and revise hypotheses about the diegetic story world.[32] This perception is partially the result of the formation of background knowledge and various textual cues, each new piece of which contributes to an evaluation of previous hypotheses and judgments. As such, these films construct subject positions in which audiences orient themselves.

Narrative here forms the foundations upon which the enemy is built; its codes and structures produce a stigma that can't be shaken off. By limiting or expanding the information between audience and characters, filmmakers attempt to define the relationship between both. Pötzsch, for example, defines the Self/Other relationship in cinema through an "epistemological barrier."[33] This Husserlian take on Othering suggests that an oppositional structure is drawn around the Soldier-Self through the war film's formal properties; in the process, the diegetic subject position of the Enemy-Other is discouraged. Furthermore, these barriers keep the Enemy-Other ubiquitously absent: "hidden, inaccessible, incomprehensible yet potentially omnipresent as a deadly threat."[34] One way this happens is through focalization, wherein a subjective perception of the diegetic world is presented by one or more characters or the narrator. By being ubiquitously absent, enemy characters do not offer a focalization opportunity, and thus insight concerning the thoughts and experiences of these characters is denied. Such structures therefore relate directly to empathic involvement with characters. We understand empathy in accordance with Amy Coplan, who considers it to be a complex imaginative process relating to both cognitions and emotions that is deeply entwined with perspective taking.[35] Here, the filmmaker attempts to simulate a character's situated psychological states, including their beliefs, emotions, and desires, by allowing us to perceive the character's experiences from the character's point of view while simultaneously maintaining clear self/other differentiation. By limiting any focalization of the film's narrative from the viewpoint of the villain, a disproportional empathic alliance with the protagonist(s) is structured.

Enemy identification is further enhanced by narratively designating enemies by way of their actions. Enemy characters often get introduced to the story by exposing some of their heinous crimes to the audience (Pötzsch refers to these actions as "evil deeds"[36]). This has been a narrative trope that has been firmly established in cinema for over a century. Examples can be found in D. W. Griffith's venomous piece of Victorian melodrama *The Birth of a Nation* (1915), in which an attempted rape by the black "buck" Gus leads to the suicide of the protagonist's sister. In an entirely similar manner, many contemporary films use such gruesome crimes as an introductory moment to vilify characters and their ruthless ways. The James Bond franchise excels in applying this format. Whether it's *Goldfinger's* (1964) gold-laced Bond girl, *Licence to Kill's* (1989) Franz Sanchez feeding a secret agent to sharks, or Raoul Silva's whimsical execution of his lover in *Skyfall* (2012), all these moments function as definitive etchings of the enemy's identity as evildoer. Such patterns aim to elicit anger, disgust, and contempt toward enemy characters because of their strong assault upon our own moral codes. The more gruesome and personal these violent acts, the more any empathic alliance of the spectator is thwarted.

Intensifying Threat and Providing Means for Resolution

Once the spectator is empathically reeled in and antagonistic structures are firmly established, filmmakers employ these affective relationships to heighten tension and accentuate the necessity of defeating respective threats. Emotional knowledge is of prime importance in the formation of a feeling of belonging and exclusion, since it is deeply entwined with psychological structures.[37] Furthermore, emotion is a core component of experiencing situations of shock and suspense. As Brian Massumi states: "Emotion is qualified intensity."[38] By cultivating a degree of emotional involvement with a character's situation in combination with an appraisal of the character's goals and desires, films establish "concern-based construals."[39] The sympathy and empathy thus established for characters in previous phases provide a mode for spectators from which they can further assess and interpret narrative situations. By way of such narrative conditions and stylistic characteristics, filmmakers attempt to amplify specific affective logics among spectators.[40] We might be led to fear certain enemy characters in a similar way in which we fear the monster in a horror film,[41] but in equal measure we can be led to desire their demise out of hope that the characters we feel sympathetic toward will succeed in their goals. Toward the conclusion of *Nighthawks* (1981), for example, we are given several affective registers to fall back on when hoping for the elimination of Rutger Hauer's Red Army Faction–type terrorist Wulfgar. First we've been led to despise Wulfgar on the basis of his heinous crimes, since we've seen him commit bombings, executions, and violent kidnappings and are led to expect that his agenda remains robust. Second, through the intensive focalization from the perspective of NYPD agent Deke DaSilva, we are motivated to root for his success in apprehending the international criminal. But most of all, when the conflict escalates, we fear for the life of life of DaSilva's ex-wife Irene, whom we've gotten to know and sympathize with. So when in the closing moments of the film Wulfgar breaks into Irene's house to murder her, we interact with several affective logics, all contributing to our anticipation of Wulfgar's apprehension. Building on these affective registers, filmmakers guide us to live vicariously through emotions of fear, humiliation, and anger. Plantinga, for example, considers sociomoral disgust to be a type of "gatekeeper" emotion that can be utilized to "elicit judgments of persons rooted in stereotypes and to make salient and pleasurable conventional ways of responding to narrative scenarios."[42] Not only does the intensification of threat further enhance the hero-self and enemy-Other distinction, it also contributes to the construction of means of resolution. By way of such narrative and affective setups, legitimate scenarios are offered regarding how to solve the problem that the enemy poses. As such, through antipathic relations, the violent retribution enacted on enemies can be warranted out of necessity (survival narratives such as *Behind Enemy Lines* [2001]), morbid satisfaction (revenge narratives such as *Death Wish* [1974]) or sheer indifference (rescue narratives such as *Commando* [1985]). These violent resolutions are merely a consummation of the affective logics established earlier in the films' narratives.

CONCLUSION

This chapter has contributed to the formation of a theoretical framework for the analysis of villainous characters in cinema. With this contribution, we hope to inspire further analysis in the narrative and formal articulation of film villains.

By dividing this process into several stages of building opposition, we show that enemy image construction should be considered as a set of representational practices. Scholarly attention to this subject is needed in order to better understand how perceptions of Otherness and animosity are layered in cinema, and, as Eva Herschinger notes, this designation and reiteration of enemy identities is crucial to the construction of the sustainment of hegemonic orders.[43] Hero cults and enemy images are among the most effective instruments with which the demagogue conditions people to accept war and endure injustices.[44] Nazi Obersturmführers, Russian spies, Mexican drug lords, and Arab terrorists are just some of many enemy archetypes that have been constructed and recycled throughout the twentieth century and continue to appear persistently in popular culture. These different enemy identities should be considered as interacting at their base with the same set of discourses. Not only is this designation of certain enemy archetypes a form of social control, setting the parameters of normality and abnormality, it is also a representational strategy telling us who to hate. If we are to dismantle these processes of enemy image construction, we must first and foremost understand how such inclusions/exclusions are established in cinema.

Notes

1. Vilho Harle, *The Enemy with a Thousand Faces: The Tradition of the Other in Western Political Thought and History* (Westport, CT: Greenwood, 2000).

2. Ernesto Laclau and Chantal Mouffe, *Hegemony and Socialist Strategy: Towards a Radical Democratic Politics* (New York: Verso, 2001).

3. Ragnhild Fiebig-von Hase and Ursula Lehmkuhl, eds., *Enemy Images in American History* (New York: Berghahn Books, 1997).

4. Daniel A. Forbes, "The Aesthetic of Evil," in *Vader, Voldemort and Other Villains: Essays on Evil in Popular Media*, ed. Jamey Heit (Jefferson, NC: McFarland, 2008), 18.

5. François Truffaut and Helen G. Scott, *Hitchcock* (New York: Simon and Schuster, 1985), 191.

6. David Bordwell and Kristin Thompson, *Film Art: An Introduction* (New York: Alfred A. Knopf, 1979).

7. Kristin Thompson, *Eisenstein's "Ivan the Terrible": A Neoformalist Analysis* (Princeton, NJ: Princeton University Press, 1981), 11.

8. Richard Taylor, *Film Propaganda: Soviet Russia and Nazi Germany* (New York: I. B. Tauris, 1998).

9. Debra L. Merskin, *Media, Minorities, and Meaning: A Critical Introduction* (New York: Peter Lang, 2011).

10. Fiebig-von Hase and Lehmkuhl, *Enemy Images in American History*, 2.

11. Helena Vanhala, *The Depiction of Terrorists in Blockbuster Hollywood Films, 1980–2001: An Analytical Study* (Jefferson, NC: McFarland, 2011), 109.

12. Thomas Schatz, *Hollywood Genres: Formulas, Filmmaking, and the Studio System* (New York: McGraw-Hill, 1981), 25–27.

13. Marianne W. Jørgensen and Louise J. Phillips, *Discourse Analysis as Theory and Method* (New York: Sage, 2002), 47.

14. Holger Pötzsch, "Borders, Barriers and Grievable Lives: The Discursive Production of Self and Other in Film and Other Audio-Visual Media," *Nordicom Review* 32, no. 2 (January 2011): 75–94.

15. Pötzsch, "Borders, Barriers and Grievable Lives," 77.

16. Thompson, *Eisenstein's "Ivan the Terrible,"* 25–26

17. Kurt R. Spillman and Kati Spillman, "Some Sociobiological and Psychological Aspects of 'Images of the Enemy,'" in *Enemy Images in American History,* ed. Ragnhild Fiebig-von Hase and Ursula Lehmkuhl (New York: Berghahn Books, 1997), 55–56.

18. Murray Smith, *Engaging Characters: Fiction, Emotion, and the Cinema* (Oxford: Clarendon Press, 1995).

19. Carl Plantinga, "Emotion and Affect," in *The Routledge Companion to Philosophy and Film,* ed. Paisley Livingston and Carl Plantinga (London: Routledge, 2008), 86.

20. Carl Plantinga, "Affect and Narrative Film," in *Current Controversies in Philosophy of Film,* ed. Katherine Thomson-Jones (London: Routledge, 2016), 138.

21. Plantinga, "Emotion and Affect," 90.

22. Harle, *The Enemy with a Thousand Faces,* 21.

23. Laclau and Mouffe, *Hegemony and Socialist Strategy.*

24. Lois Weis, "Identity Formation and the Processes of Othering: Unraveling Sexual Threads," *Journal of Educational Foundations* 9, no. 1 (January 1995): 17.

25. Merskin, *Media, Minorities, and Meaning,* 32.

26. Richard Dyer, ed., *Gays and Film* (London: British Film Institute, 1977), 27–39.

27. Dyer, *Gays and Film.*

28. Edward Said, *Orientalism* (New York: Vintage, 1979).

29. Sam Keen, *Faces of the Enemy: Reflections of the Hostile Imagination* (Berkeley, CA: Catticus, 1986).

30. Fiebig-von Hase and Lehmkuhl, *Enemy Images in American History,* 2–3.

31. Forbes, "The Aesthetic of Evil," 24.

32. David Bordwell, *Narration in the Fiction Film* (London: Routledge, 2013), 39–40.

33. Pötzsch, "Borders, Barriers and Grievable Lives."

34. Pötzsch, "Borders, Barriers and Grievable Lives," 78.

35. Amy Coplan, "Empathic Engagement with Narrative Fictions," *Journal of Aesthetics and Art Criticism* 62, no. 2 (Spring 2004): 141–52.

36. Holger Pötzsch, "Ubiquitous Absence: Character Engagement in the Contemporary War Film," *Nordicom Review* 34, no. 1 (July 2013), 125–44.

37. Spillman and Spillman, "Some Sociobiological and Psychological Aspects," 57.

38. Brian Massumi, *Parables for the Virtual: Movement, Affect, Sensation* (Durham, NC: Duke University Press, 2002), 21.

39. Carl Plantinga, *Moving Viewers: American Film and the Spectator's Experience* (Berkeley: University of California Press, 2009), 80.

40. Sean Carter and Derek P. McCormack, "Film, Geopolitics and the Affective Logics of Intervention," *Political Geography* 25, no. 2 (February 2006), 228–45.

41. Noël Carroll, *The Philosophy of Horror; or, Paradoxes of the Heart* (London: Routledge, 2003).

42. Plantinga, "Emotion and Affect," 95.

43. Eva Herschinger, *Constructing Global Enemies: Hegemony and Identity in International Discourses on Terrorism and Drug Prohibition* (London: Routledge, 2010).

44. Fiebig-von Hase and Lehmkuhl, *Enemy Images in American History,* 37.

CHAPTER 7

Sorting Out Villainy

A Typology of Villains and Their Effects on Superheroes[1]

ROBIN S. ROSENBERG

SUPERVILLAINS ARE IMPORTANT INHABITANTS OF THE WORLD OF SUPERHEROES. Villains are drawn to crime—and different types of crime—for a variety of reasons. Some are simply greedy. Some are vengeful, selfish, psychopathic, or mentally disturbed in other ways. Some see themselves in the role of the hero on a mission that requires moral flexibility. Still others are sadists, causing harm for the thrill of it. Some villains are driven by a combination of these motivations.

These motivations mean that superheroes battle different types of villains, and each type of villain elicits a different challenge for superheroes and creates different types of stories. Each type of villain creates different "lessons," for both superheroes and readers or viewers, and reveals different aspects of the superheroes' mettle.

I've created a typology of villains based on their motives and actions. In what follows, I discuss how the different types of villains engage and reveal different facets of superheroes. This typology is loosely derived from the typology of evil proposed by psychologist Roy Baumeister in his book *Evil: Inside Human Violence and Cruelty.*[2]

THE STRAIGHTFORWARD CRIMINAL

The straightforward criminal seeks either material gain—in money or valuable objects—or power, and acts illegally to get it. This type of villain isn't generally "super" and so provides less of a challenge for the superhero, and consequently less interesting stories. Many of the early superhero stories typically involved this type of villain (such as Alex Greer, the crooked lobbyist from *Action Comics*, no. 1, or Alfred Stryker, the criminal at the head of the chemical syndicate from *Detective Comics*, no. 27).[3] Modern incarnations include Marvel's Kingpin, who is motivated to acquire money and power; Batman's villain, the Penguin (in comic book stories); and Catwoman, who in many stories is motivated to acquire feline-themed objects. Straightforward criminals want "more" of their hearts' desires and engage in criminal acts to get them. They generally don't harm or kill people unless they must, either to obtain their desired object or to display their power strategically. Their illegal acts are the means to their ends.

Such villains allow the superhero to fight openly for justice and the rule of law, and often these stories portray relatively clear-cut cases of right versus wrong. Stories with these villains may show superheroes as superpowered extensions of law enforcement.

THE VENGEFUL VILLAIN

A more interesting type of villain—both in terms of the story and for what he or she elicits in the superhero—is the *vengeful* villain: the thwarted criminal whose actions stem from a personal vendetta. Typically, this type of villain has it out for the superhero. The villain's conflict with the superhero is personal. This type of villain's crimes and shenanigans are motivated not simply by greed—though that may be a part of it—but by revenge. The vengeful villain wants either to eliminate the superhero or to prove him- or herself superior to the superhero. The villain typically seeks not simply to kill or beat but to outsmart, outfight, or humiliate the superhero. At his or her most extreme, the villain is only satisfied with beating the superhero where the superhero is strongest, to prove superiority in every way and seek retribution for whatever "injury" the villain perceives himself or herself to have previously sustained from the superhero. In fact, it is hurt pride that leads vengeful villains to inflict disproportionate "harm" on the superhero. It's a never-ending contest. From the superhero's perspective, the conflicts take the form of battles of wits or brawn, and the villain must be apprehended and locked up. Such battles can be a burdensome duty for the superhero, particularly when the intensity of the villain's malevolence ratchets up over time. The superhero might wish that he or she didn't have to engage in these battles but is resigned to them, as if they were some kind of repetitive chore. Examples include Reed Richards's skirmishes with Doctor Doom and Superman's with Lex Luthor. . . .

As vengeful villains seek revenge, they look for the chink in the superhero's armor. It is often these stories that allow us to see the superhero not only as a hero with powers, but as someone vulnerable and more like us. The villains typically do find some flaw. They figure out who the superhero cares about and kidnap that person. Examples abound. The Fantastic Four's Sue or Johnny

Storm gets trapped in another dimension as a way to get at Reed Richards. Mary Jane is kidnapped surprisingly frequently just to make Spider-Man squirm. Some vengeful villains learn that kidnapping is not enough. They go one step further and make superheroes choose between saving their loved one or many innocent people. This forced choice is a staple of many superhero stories, and a notable example is found in the film *Spider-Man*, in which the Green Goblin kidnaps Mary Jane to compel Spider-Man to face one of the most difficult choices a human might confront.[4]

Some straightforward criminals can become vengeful villains after the superhero thwarts their plans. Luthor traveled this exact path. In *Action Comics*, no. 23, Superman demolishes Luthor's floating fortress and wrecks the human's plans to make himself "supreme master of the world."[5] After a series of confrontations, Luthor is able (temporarily) to gain powers greater than Superman's, and instead of using that power to accomplish his goals, he spends the whole story trying to defeat and humiliate Superman. Another example of the path from straightforward criminal to vengeful villain is found in the abovementioned film *Spider-Man*: the villain, the Green Goblin, shifts to being a vengeful villain after Spider-Man turns down his offer for them to be partners in crime.[6] This rejection spurs the Green Goblin to seek revenge on Spider-Man. Just as in our world we can inadvertently create our own enemies through our actions, so too with superheroes.

THE HEROIC VILLAIN

A third type of supervillain can be thought of as a "heroic" villain in that he or she has an "altruistic" cause and an ultimate goal that is more than simply acquiring money or jewels. Heroic villains believe that they are working for some greater good; they see themselves as a hero, and the superhero as someone who thwarts their worthwhile actions and goals. They have a goal that isn't selfish, although it might be a bit twisted. Like superheroes, then, heroic villains fight for a cause. From their point of view, they are heroes, and their ends justify their destructive means.

A few examples of this type of villain stand out, with perhaps the best one being Batman's nemesis Poison Ivy, who is considered to be an ecoterrorist. She is passionate about the primacy of plant life over human life and sees herself as a defender of the weak and oppressed (namely, plants), which she sees as her children: when she harms humans, she feels that she is punishing those who deserve it, just as superheroes apprehend villains who deserve to be put away. As she says in an episode of *Gotham Girls*, "I'm an ecoterrorist of global importance. I make a contribution."[7]

Another example of a heroic villain is the X-Men's sometimes-nemesis Magneto, who uses his powers not for traditionally selfish reasons but for the betterment of mutantkind, so that mutants can get the same (and perhaps more) rights as regular humans. Should humans be hurt in the process, it's not his concern.

The third example of the heroic villain is Batman's enemy Ra's al Ghul, who seeks to make a more stable and thus "better" world. Unfortunately, his mechanism for doing so invariably involves some form of mass murder or other harming of innocents. Another heroic villain with a similar general goal and means to an end is Ozymandias from *Watchmen*, who kills millions of innocent victims in a faked alien incursion in order to unite the United States and the Soviet Union against a common enemy and thus prevent the mutually assured nuclear destruction the two countries are heading toward.[8] Note that the line between heroic villain and antihero (such as the Punisher, a vigilante who wages war against criminals) can be fuzzy and depends in part on the point of view from which the story is told.

Because heroic villains believe that they fight for right, they are different from other types of villains who recognize that their actions are illegal or immoral and thus "wrong." The heroic supervillains believe that their goals and actions are set on a higher moral plane. Because they don't see themselves as doing anything wrong, and in fact see themselves as doing "good," their actions prompt the superhero to wrestle with his or her own moral conscience about what is right and wrong. Heroic villains are fighting to right a perceived injustice or to make the world, in their view, a better place. In this way, they aren't so dissimilar from superheroes; it's just that the specifics are different regarding what constitutes an injustice, what the "better place" would look like, for whom it would be better, and at what cost.

THE SADISTIC SUPERVILLAIN

Perhaps no other type of villain is as frightening as the sadistic supervillain—the type who wreaks havoc simply because he or she can and who enjoys it. This pleasure is the main motive. Sadistic supervillains leave trails of death and destruction to get their kicks. The Joker exemplifies the sadistic supervillain, and the best example of this aspect of his character is in the film *The Dark Knight* (2008). This Joker is a self-appointed "agent of chaos" who clearly enjoys frightening and hurting others for the fun of it. His twisted sense of humor is evident in the forced-choice, life-and-death dilemma he sets up with two ships, giving passengers on each ship the power to kill everyone on board the other ship and informing them that a ticking bomb will sink both ships if neither ship acts to destroy the other. The Joker creates this horrific dilemma for the fun of watching what will happen. As he says to Batman, "I won't kill you because you're too much fun." Similarly, in other comics stories, Loki, Thor's brother, refuses to kill the thunder god so that he can go on tormenting him. . . .

Stories with sadistic villains thus induce superheroes to wrestle with their conscience about what can be sacrificed for the greater good, about whether it is possible to stay on the side of "right" when fighting someone who is so "wrong." Such stories invoke existential dilemmas for superheroes that we can relate to as we try to grapple with the "evil" in our world and understand why some people commit horrific and destructive acts.

THE SUPERVILLAIN SHAPES THE SUPERHERO

Villains aren't a monolithic group. They're motivated by different forces, they desire different goals, they use different means. Villains come in different types, each of which induces different emotions, thoughts, and struggles for the superhero. Each type of villain, then, reveals, a different aspect of the superhero. In doing so, each aspect that comes to the fore provides an added dimension to the definition of the superhero.

Notes

1. Originally published in Robin S. Rosenberg and Peter Coogan, eds., *What Is a Superhero?* (Oxford: Oxford University Press, 2013).

2. Roy F. Baumeister, *Evil: Inside Human Violence and Cruelty* (New York: Henry Holt, 1999).

3. *Action Comics*, no. 1 (June 1938); *Detective Comics*, no. 27 (May 1939).

4. Sam Raimi, dir., *Spider-Man* (Columbia Pictures, 2002).

5. *Action Comics*, no. 23 (April 1940).

6. Raimi, *Spider-Man*.

7. "Scout's Dis-Honor," *Gotham Girls*, prod. Alan Bruckner (Warner Brothers and Noodle Soup, September 2001).

8. Alan Moore and Dave Gibbons, *Watchmen* (New York: DC Comics, 1987).

CHAPTER 8

Implacable Henchmen?

From the Iliad's *Myrmidons to the Wild Hunt of* The Witcher 3

CAIT MONGRAIN AND DAVID D. PERLMUTTER

> King Radovid: You [Geralt] do not [understand] because you are not a king.
> Pawns see only their companions at their sides and their foes across the field.
> . . . [C]hess is the art of sacrificing your own pieces.
>
> **THE WITCHER 3**

INTRODUCTION: TOWARD A MORPHOLOGY OF THE MYTHOLOGY OF HENCHMEN

"Morphology" is a term used in fields as disparate as the physical sciences and literary studies to denote the study of the structure of the elements of something—whether the body of an animal or the parts of a story—and their mutual relationships. Adopting this approach can be a dangerous enterprise for the researcher or critic, however, because human beings by nature tend to see patterns in the world, a state of apophenia in which we connect even random dots of data into meaningful narratives, trend lines, or pictures. Those patterns may differ depending on our own psychology, history, culture, and society. For instance, almost every people that studied the stars concluded that "lights in the sky" could be grouped into a "zodiac." But which stars were part of what animal, spirit, or deity differed from culture to culture—as did the meanings of the movements.

When examining a particular cultural tradition, one can have some confidence that elements and patterns that consistently recur in prescribed ways across many examples are indeed occurring purposively and from the intentions of an "author." In two famous studies, Vladimir Propp's *Morphology of the Folktale*[1] and Will Wright's *Sixguns and Society*,[2] certain types of stories—the

Russian folktale and the classical Hollywood Western—are discovered to have a very limited number of recurring genre characters, events, storylines, revelations, morals, and outcomes.

The situation becomes complicated when stretching the limits of what constitutes a specific cultural tradition. One begins to ask, what is a borrowed genre element versus a natural co-occurrence because of similar circumstances? It is no surprise that a majority of critical, scholarly, and fan discourse about villains in popular culture tends to center on the "stars": the premier personages or "supervillains" themselves. After all, most texts, from books to graphic arts to movies, focus on the battle between the main characters, the hero versus the villain. But as any observer of the "super" genre knows, there are many other types of resident characters who help create the story world. Here, we focus on the evil or bad guy "henchmen" (or "minions," "lackeys," or "stooges") who are found ubiquitously, from James Bond films of the 1970s to modern Marvel superhero screen epics, and who are instantly familiar to almost anyone on the planet.

Among the most prominent qualities of henchmen are:

1. They are sketchily individualized (but easily visually identifiable). In the 1989 film *Batman*, Jack Nicholson's Joker employed leather-jacketed and hipster-capped henchmen who wore the same "uniform," and only one even had a name, perhaps revealingly a common generic one: Bob. Indeed, the fact that henchmen come in masses is one of their genre markers. They may speak—that is, in Hollywood terms have "lines"—but they tend to act as a group and notably perform (competently or incompetently) according to the orders of the lead villain. They behave like automatons even if they are mortal flesh and blood.

2. Their motivations for being henchmen are somewhat opaque. They tend to die, in droves. The act cannot quite be considered noble sacrifice; they are not kamikaze pilots. They do not seem to hold some great cause as their patriotic or ideological motivation. They often appear basically almost *dumb*, in the original sense of the word: cattle too stupid to see their own self-interest and mute in expressing it.

3. They are often preternaturally loyal to the villain, not only willing to die on a whim or toss-away order but never to question his (almost always it is a male) orders. They do not protest, hesitate, demand explanations—or a higher salary and medical benefits. They obey orders, even when fatal to themselves, and never seem to "reason why."

In short, *what gives with henchmen*? Have they simply been a shallow prop for lazy story writers through the centuries? Or have they played a more substantive role in tales told—or some variation between the extremes? Here we offer a compare-and-contrast view of arguably the first henchmen in the literary record (the Myrmidons of the *Iliad*) to one of the latest (the Wild Hunt in the video game *The Witcher*). We argue that there is depth in the details if we examine any human artistic or narrative construction, as we do here, starting with history's first and arguably greatest oral poem and ending with a popular example of the youngest new art form, the digital video game (and its ancillary graphic arts publications).

BUILDING THE ARCHETYPE FROM THE PROTOTYPE: MYRMIDONS IN THE *ILIAD*

The beginning of every story, from the invocation to the muse to "sing the tale of Achilles' anger" in the first lines of the *Iliad* to the opening shot of any television sitcom, is a variation of "once upon a time." Human beings are storytelling animals, and the morphology of such tales, from those told in hunting camps to the evening news, resonates with certain structures of content.[3] The act of telling stories itself is as rich a human praxis to study as what the stories say, for the narrative is in itself a message. More complex is the addition of what might be called proscriptions of the present coupled with such presentations of the past—but not just any past: a lost golden past in which obstacles, irritants, confusions, frustrations, and even deadly forces of the time either were not encountered or were defeated.

In a more concrete vein, Tamar Liebes and Elihu Katz, in their study of the reception of the TV show *Dallas* in Israel,[4] have suggested that while audiences may differentially interpret the meanings and significance of events or attend to different sets of information, at the same time such audiences may also find certain themes to have strong currency, because they are in a sense cross-cultural. Liebes and Katz give the example of "conflict between father and son" as one such primordial theme in television drama.

Among the archetypes of literature and media, the faithful henchman, although less storied, has a niche as far reaching and momentous as the Damsel in Distress, the Wise Old Man, or any number of stock characters in the literary panoply. Whether as the hunchbacked lackey Igor or a homogeneous army of orcs, henchmen function as the essential supplement to the villain by virtue of their very nature, embodying the traits that the latter cannot possess: (a) cringing, obsequious subservience ("Yes, all-mighty Master, I obey!") and (b) proclivity to ask the foolish question that elicits the revelation of information to the audience ("Master, where will we get the toxins to poison the city?"). The parallel to the hero's sidekick is self-evident. It is this intrinsically ancillary role that, almost paradoxically, makes the henchman essential.

In the *Iliad*, one of the oldest preservations of literature extant, the humble henchman makes an appearance in the form of the Myrmidon, a word that even now carries the meaning of "a subordinate who executes orders unquestioningly or unscrupulously" (Merriam-Webster, s.v. myrmidon). Homer's[5] Myrmidons are linked almost inextricably with Achilles, the Greek hero, described in direct connection with him in the overwhelming majority of their appearances. These men, natives of Aegina, were supernaturally created from ants, a creature who more than two thousand years ago must have had in the popular conception a denotation of mindless obedience to authority and indefatigability as much as they do today. They also, for our purposes, exhibit the characteristics we have previously described as inherent (or primordial) to henchmen:

1. The Myrmidons' individual identities are largely subsumed by their collective identity as *Myrmidons*. Although the commanders of the Myrmidons are given some small measure of distinction (e.g., "warlike" Eudorus, described as a son of Hermes and "finest of runners and fighters" [*Il.* 16.179–92]), the text emphasizes their essential unity through metaphor: wasps flying out in a swarm to defend their larvae (*Il.* 16.257–83); close-set stones in the walls of a house (*Il.* 16.210–20).
2. The motivations of the Myrmidons are nebulous and uniform: loyalty to Achilles and desire for *kleos* (glory). No single Myrmidon is given his own discrete motives for his actions, nor does the action of any single member of this group run counter to the overarching purpose of the collective.
3. The Myrmidons' loyalty to Achilles is unflappable, even in the face of the condemnation of the leader of the Greek forces, Agamemnon. When Achilles absents himself from battle, the Myrmidons follow; when he reenters the fray, so do his faithful soldiers.

In this narrative, the Myrmidons are held, alongside Achilles's presence on the battlefield, as political pawns: necessary for the victory of the Greek forces but withheld from battle to satisfy Achilles's grievance against Agamemnon. Alone, Achilles does not tip the scale in favor of the Greek contingent. In company with his Myrmidons, Achilles is critical. This is a crucial point, a subtlety often lost when we see the supervillain strut and pose: he needs his henchmen; they are necessary appendages as much as arms or legs.

The origin of the Myrmidons serves to heighten one's perception of them as a unified whole. In myth, the Myrmidons are said to have come into being through the wish of Achilles's grandfather, Aeacus. In the narrative, Aeacus, alone on an island, wishes for as many men as there are ants on the tree near him. Obligingly, Zeus accommodates this prayer by transforming the ants themselves (*murmikes* in Greek) into people (the *murmidones*).[6] Although this origin story is not referenced directly in the *Iliad*, the ant-like character-istics of the Myrmidons are emphasized by a long tradition of viewing ants as militaristic.[7] The essential unity of the Myrmidons in literature is likewise underscored by the makeup of their ranks. While primarily natives of Achil-les's homeland, the designation "Myrmidon" supersedes ethnic differences. Consider, as an example, Epigeus. Although formerly a king of Budeum, Epi-geus fled his homeland, reaching Phthia as a political refugee (*Il.* 16.569–85) and becoming a high-ranking Myrmidon commander. Here, rank outstrips national identity.

A VISUAL MOMENT: A 1200 BC COMIC RENDERING OF HENCHMEN

We must make a tangent here to remark on a singular *iconographic* puzzle regarding the Myrmidon that enthusiasts of modern comic books and graphic novels may enjoy. There is a paucity of portrayals of Myrmidons in ancient vi-sual art, at least that which survives for modern inspection, most prominently on vases and mosaics. Only one clear visual depiction exists of soldiery of the place and the period for which we normally associate the historical conflicts, participants, and locales of a "Trojan" war in western Anatolia and the Aegean region. It is found on a badly damaged and reconstructed vase from the city of Mycenae dated to around 1200 BC (fig. 4).

It is commonly referred to in the archaeological and historical literature as the "Warrior Vase." One text describes the scene as thus:

> Lines of heavily armed soldiers march across the belly of the bowl while a maiden cheers them on from under a handle. . . . The troops have a cer-tain rustic look to them, but one cannot help recalling the many poignant leave-taking scenes in Homer's poetry, and we suspect that many a tear may have been splashed in the wine taken from this rather special mixing bowl.[8]

But a modern student of comic books, graphic novels, and superhero popu-lar culture portrayals will instantly recognize in the vase's figures anthropic depictions that seem more out of 1950s *Andy Capp* and 1960s *Pogo* than that which we normally associate with the aesthetic realism of Greek and Roman art. The military historian will note immediately that this is a regular army: they are on the march, in exact calisthenic unity. Their panoply and kit are identical: helmets, cuirasses, greaves, clothing, shields, footwear, spears, even what presumably is their "purse" or lunch bag. They march in lockstep—no

Figure 4. Warrior Vase. Mycenae, Greece, ca. 1200 BC. Height: about 16 inches. From the collection of the National Archaeological Museum, Athens.

individualization is detected in any quality, from ethnicity to build. This is not a group of come-as-you-are barbarians; they are not truly even warriors. They are soldiers, uniformly acting and in uniform.

But are they Myrmidons? They certainly match the attributes of the henchmen of being dressed alike and even looking alike; they are all of the same racial caste, even to the point of similar body builds and height. But it is difficult to imagine being terrified of them as they march toward you on a battlefield. They are comic book characters. Maybe this really was a troop of Hellenic infantry that would have chopped you to pieces if you stood in their way on the plains of Ilium, but laughter might be your initial reaction—before the spears pierced your side.

Further, it is intriguing that, even as we can be quite sure about our military conclusions, the cultural and social ones fit a modern contradiction within most henchmen. On the one hand, they are meant to be fearsome, despicable, threatening, non-individualized, ready for battle; on the other hand, there is something comical about them, what literary theorists like to call ludic keying. One even has to wonder whether satire was the intention, rather than journalistic reporting or heroicizing. We argue that this inherent contradiction in the henchman—the collision and conflation of fierceness and farce, a Pantagruel without portfolio—resonates with us to the present day.

HENCHMEN, REDUX: THE WILD HUNT AND PATTERNS OF INTENTION

Although Homer's *Iliad* centers its narrative on the framing device of Achilles's rage, the narrative of the Trojan War itself arguably takes Helen, the stolen bride of Menelaus, as its nucleus. Her capture by the Trojan prince Paris (or, in some versions of the narrative, her willing abandonment of her husband) provokes the Greeks to go to war.[9] In an unusual variant, Euripides's *Helen* removes the physical Helen from the entire process, secreted away by the gods, who send a "phantom Helen" to Troy in her place.

Strikingly, however, regardless of Helen's degree of agency, the ancient narratives agree on her *culpability*. The "face that launched a thousand ships" is consistently at fault: the prize, the temptation, the sought-after treasure. Without her presence on the one side and absence on the other, the war would not have taken place, so the ancient logic follows. Further, Helen is a source of anxiety in the Greek consciousness as a powerful figure in her own right: a child of Zeus, a member of the ruling class, and the woman designated the most beautiful in the world by the goddess Aphrodite. Helen's character can be reduced to a simple, traditional trope: the powerful object, the control of which is contested. This is the essence of Tolkien's One Ring, the magic lamp of Aladdin, and, as we will discuss below, the figure of Ciri in the video game *The Witcher 3: Wild Hunt*.

The plot of *The Witcher 3*, although superficially far removed from the hexametrically rendered battlefields of Homer, bears the seed of the same narrative formula: a powerful woman is fought over by two ideologically opposed forces. The woman in question here is Cirilla Fiona Elen Riannon, daughter of the emperor and vessel of "Elder Blood," a genetic anomaly inherited from her mother's line, allowing her to travel between different worlds. Like the mythical Helen, Ciri's presence and intrinsic power incite conflict. On the one hand are the beings from the world of Ciri's formidable mother, Aen Elle elves, whose population faces destruction from the White Frost (without Ciri's unique abilities allowing them to transport their numbers to another world).

Alongside this goal, the ruler of these elves, Eredin, aims to increase his power by compelling Ciri to produce his heir. Ciri's refusal to comply and subsequent escape to the world of the game lead Eredin to pursue her with the Wild Hunt, his militaristic band of supporters. Opposed to Eredin and the Wild Hunt is a coalition headed by Geralt of Rivia, a witcher (professional killer of monsters) and the adoptive father of Ciri. Like Homer's *Iliad*, the game frames itself around not the source of the conflict (in this case, Ciri, the central character's adoptive daughter) but around the actions of Geralt, the only playable character for the majority of the game.

Although, as the game is structured, it is Geralt's (and thus, the controlling player's) decisions that determine Ciri's ultimate fate, the dialogue emphasizes the centrality of Ciri for the overall narrative and the agency she has as an independent character: at the end of the final major battle of the base game, Ciri tells Geralt that she alone can stop the White Frost and has made the choice to do so. She underscores her superior role, saying: "What can you know about saving the world, silly? You're but a witcher. This is my story. You must let me finish telling it." Furthermore, the game evokes Homer in its third-person narrative format. The loading screens of the game recapitulate the story up to that point through the voice of Dandelion, a bard.

Of interest to this study in particular is the Wild Hunt, the militant elves whose seemingly sole purpose is the completion of their leader Eredin's agenda: recapturing Ciri. These figures encapsulate the core traits of henchmen outlined above.

1. The Wild Hunt is composed of a largely nameless group of elven soldiers and their hounds, whose sudden, destructive appearances intersperse the game. Their uniform black armor—a direct reference to Myrmidons—conceals any trace of individuality, rendering them almost wholly interchangeable, while the face-covering helmets both anonymize and dehumanize them, removing both potential empathy and targeted animosity from the player's interactions with these figures. For both sides of the conflict, these figures are entirely expendable: pawns in a conflict between two worlds. Only a scant handful (in the game's "boss" battles) are even given names.

2. If the foot soldiers of the Wild Hunt have independent motivations, those thoughts are never given voice in the game. It is to be assumed that they must in some way support the goals of Eredin, but the degree to which they understand the conflict or the larger issues at play is obscure. The insignificance of individual soldiers in the game and their general ignorance is underscored in a different context. King Radovid, leader of one of the world's political factions vying for supremacy, explains the rationale behind chess as a game for kings, saying, "You [Geralt] do not [understand] because you are not a king. Pawns see only their companions at their sides and their foes across the field. . . . [C]hess is the art of sacrificing your own pieces." It would be difficult to find a better summing up of the way most villains conceive of their henchmen.

3. Unquestionably, Eredin sacrifices his "pieces" in this way. The Wild Hunt's loyalty is never in doubt, and they are killed in droves during the course of the game. Never do they attempt to escape battle or pursue their own ends. If Eredin orders them to fight, they fight; if he flees, they follow. When Eredin is ultimately defeated, the Wild Hunt is never seen again.

Figure 5. Soldiers of the Wild Hunt. Image taken from the Battle of Kaer Morhen quest. *The Witcher 3: Wild Hunt,* CD Projekt RED, 2015. Screenshot and gameplay credit to Karlissa Black, M.A.

Like the Myrmidons, the henchmen of the Wild Hunt are almost exclusively referred to as a collective unit: "the Hunt," the "Red Riders," the "specters," and so on. Again, apart from the few named commanders, no individual soldier is given a name, and their strength lies in numbers rather than individual prowess (fig. 5).

This is especially remarkable when set in contrast with the supporters Geralt rallies to his side to defend Ciri (fig. 6). Each of these figures is highly individualized, and the player must complete quests for each at a previous stage of gameplay in order to ensure the willing participation of these characters. Even if a player has provided assistance, some figures will refuse to come for their own personal reasons.[10] Their loyalty to Geralt and his cause comes from the player's actions rather than blind adherence to a powerful leader.

Looking toward the format of the oral poem, a critical aspect of this type of art form is performance. In his work *Poetry as Performance: Homer and Beyond,* Gregory Nagy explores the nature of the performed poem as "living" and emphasizes the fluidity of the oral poem, which, according to Nagy, is continuously "recomposed" rather than "reperformed."[11] For Nagy, not only is the rhapsode's performance of Homer a mimetic performance of the original composition, the rhapsode himself engages in a mimesis of Homer, becoming a composer and a performer simultaneously. Thus, necessarily, the text must be understood as multiform, and scholarly readings of the text should seek not "superiority" but "authenticity"—that is, readings consistent with oral composition.

Similarly, the video game may be likened to the oral performance, with the player serving as both rhapsode and audience in an almost unique way. By

Figure 6. The Survivors of the Battle of Kaer Morhen, left to right: Triss Merigold, Aval-lac'h, Geralt of Rivia, Yennefer of Vengerberg, Eskel. *The Witcher 3: Wild Hunt,* CD Projekt RED, 2015. Screenshot and gameplay credit to Karlissa Black, M.A.

centering the experience on the choices and actions of the player, the game builds in intrinsic multiformity—seemingly endless possible iterations branching out from the core narrative.[12] The experience of even the most rigidly structured games will vary based on the relative aptitude of the players. As a highly complex and open-ended game, *The Witcher 3* offers thousands of potential variations, with almost every quest offering real choices with significantly different outcomes, from minor interactions (Do you accept or refuse the money offered?) to decisions that radically change the outcome of the main story (Will your decisions result in the survival or destruction of your character's adoptive daughter?). The player, as both rhapsode and audience, crafts the story and the protagonist to which he or she is most receptive.

CONCLUSIONS: EXPLORING THE HENCHMAN

When we set out to examine certain aspects of the world of the henchman, we were surprised to find such a small actual focused literature on the topic. Certainly, on innumerable popular culture websites, forums, blogs, and, in antediluvian days, bulletin boards, observations and threads of discussion about recurrent themes and tropes of their appearance, behavior, and even psychology are common. But it seems in general that henchmen are ubiquitous but unobserved except in hazy conception and stereotype.

It is easy to question the motivation, and even the rational intelligence, of henchmen if we consider only the vertical, hierarchical dimension of their social relationships. Perhaps the examination of the henchman's purpose needs to be expanded horizontally, as in: "What are the known benefits (social, political, personal, and even neurochemical) of being a henchman or being a member of any extremely close-knit group, often in dangerous situations, with shared goals and values?" Maybe this is where a more plausible answer is to be found and fleshed out, because we are no longer asking why followers follow leaders—a vast literature in itself—but what are the real and tangible benefits of "hanging out" and conducting activities, even ultraviolent ones, with fellow followers. In this horizontal dimension of buddyship we find historical and biological evidence that the henchman is not implausible.

For example, if we look in the historical and anthropological literature, we find that "coalitional killing" has a long history in humans and even among other primates.[13] First, we know that any close-knit group, from a street gang to an infantry platoon, gains considerable (and pleasurable) cohesion by sticking together, especially when in conflict with another group. Cohesion is defined by who we are *not* as much as by who we are; or, more reductively, "us versus them." Henchmen, thus, may be following others rather than following orders.[14] The Greek phalanx, for example, which once set the standard for military excellence, consisted of a closely unified group of citizens, perhaps best exemplified by the Spartan military, whose population of male citizens ate, slept, and trained together in barracks from early childhood until retirement.[15] The generalization that all tight-knit military groups draw succor from what the Romans called *commilitium*, or fellow-soldiership, can be made to nearly any agglomeration of young humans (usually young males) fighting together.[16]

It is no surprise that, among the earliest images we have of actual interhuman warfare, the fighting band is distinctly shown to include members who are similarly attired and who even physically look much alike.[17] (The Warrior Vase shows this absolutely; lexical-oral descriptions of Myrmidons imply it strongly.) Even the aural dimension, perhaps related to the theme song of certain henchmen groups, is a well-known factor in group cohesion. Dancing, drilling, singing, chanting, making noise of some kind in unison builds comradeship in arms.[18] Today, new forms of media such as online, interactive venues like Facebook are similarly used by soldiers to cement cohesion.[19]

Being one of the group matters—physically and emotionally. In interviews conducted after World War II, researchers found: "More than any other single characteristic, veteran enlisted men mentioned helpfulness toward their men, and the display of personal interest in them and their problems, in describing the characteristics of the best officer they had known in combat."[20] Indeed, "takes a lot of interest in what his men are thinking" was the most frequently cited quality of the sought-after commander, and the lack of which was the most crucial detriment to morale.[21] Writing in the late first to early second centuries CE, the biographer Plutarch detailed the preference of any grunt when he described what gratified a legionnaire and what visually marked this satisfaction: "It is the most obliging sight in the world to the Roman soldier to see a commander eat the same bread as himself, or lie upon an ordinary bed, or assist in the work in drawing a trench and raising a bulwark ... [for they admire] those that partake of the same labor and danger with themselves."[22] Pliny speaks particularly of the great soldier-emperor Trajan: "They saw how you shared their hunger and thirst on field maneuvers and how their commander's sweat and dust was mingled with their own; with nothing to mark you out save your height and physique."[23] Such was the tradition, which remains with us, at least symbolically.[24]

At the same time, as we have seen, being in dangerous situations draws one closer to those who face similar obstacles and enemies; no wonder many veterans remember the friendships they formed as the best part of their military service. There are even, as evidenced by some recent discoveries made by physical anthropologists, real biochemical benefits of military comradeship. Oxytocin, a hormone that reduces stress and increases feelings of warmth and security, has been found to increase in relation to the level of imminent threat, when one group of chimpanzees confronts another; a "a bond of trust" will "physically protect them from threats."[25] As shown in other research conducted by the same team, when chimps have a comrade or partner with them as they run patrols at the border of their territory, stress hormones decreased.[26]

Bonding comes in many forms, however, and here the questions of the researcher and opportunities for the scriptwriter and game designer converge. For example, we have not explored here issues of gender or ethnic/racial identity in henchmen. Henchmen, in texts, ancient and modern, lexical-oral and visual, are almost always *male*. Historically, armies have also been so, but in fantastic genres why does not the imagination extend beyond the template? Consider, for example, Indian epics in which a goddess employs henchmen for purposes that include not only conquest of enemies but necessary sacrifice—that is, the henchmen (like male praying mantises) are served up to fulfill religious obligation. As a historian describes:

> [There are in the tales] scenarios in which death at the hands of an enemy and for the betterment of society constitutes sacrifice for and by a bloodthirsty goddess, who consumes her henchmen and renders them divine. As we shall see, both society, represented in variant modes as female, and the goddess who serves as guardian as well as emblem of society, require heroic death and slaughter; the hero-victim perfecting himself by fulfilling his duty as a male sacrifice reserves territory and, more important, those who must not be sacrificed. Achieving and conferring glory, the hero's sacrifice bears variegated

fruit.... Glory is inherited by descendants, who may claim enhanced status
and command deeper respect as generations proliferate and prosper.27

We can ask whether that "divine" status conferment is implicitly offered to the
henchmen of other traditions.

Finally, others might go further in exposing the psychosexual element in
henchmen-villain relationships. Among the works of Christopher Marlowe
we find reference to the "lovely minions" ("les mignons," or "small ones"; i.e.,
homosexual secret lovers) who supposedly led to the downfall of several English kings.28 The variations of henchmen can signify liberation, not a genre
constraint.

While we are not calling for the rise of an entire field of henchmen studies,
we do assert that anyone interested in cultural history, studies of visual and
lexical/oral content, and even politics, public affairs, criminology, sociology,
anthropology, and other disciplines should examine the evolution of the henchman. We have examined the first prototype in literature of the accompanying
band of killers of the villain, recalling that in the ancient Greek concept a "hero"
(literally a demigod) could act quite nastily and constitute what we would call
today a villain. While the modern designation of "hero" or "villain" lies rooted in
subjectivity and perspective (e.g., the Trojans would acknowledge Achilles as a
hero in the ancient sense, but certainly not in the modern one), the henchman's
role shows marked consistency across temporal and cultural barriers.

From this study we draw the following overarching observations: First, from
the earliest concept of literature, authors or producers of content have balanced
the deeds and character of an individual with masses or groups. In the *Iliad*,
battles comprise duels between heroes with thousands of soldier onlookers
who, on cue, push and stab at each other, almost always inconclusively. The
heroes make a difference. We can ask if that is a forever role for henchmen.
They can threaten and menace, and even kill lesser opponents or massacre civilians, but they rarely, if ever, take down a hero; without a villain as their soul
and brain, they collapse. Henchmen make an appearance, always, but make a
difference, never.

Second, at first glance and probably with even deeper investigation, there is
an essential problem of answering the "why" question of henchmen. Certainly,
in the *Iliad*, victory for the Greeks meant the sacking of a city, with all the benefits of plunder (of people and goods) that were accorded to victorious armies
as a norm. But the unswerving loyalty of henchmen to their villain is only very
sketchily explained in almost the entire corpus of popular culture, including
the original conception in Homer's poetry. It is almost as if there were a giant
"that's just so" inserted into the ellipsis of explaining their characterization.

Finally, the Warrior Vase contradiction is also evident some 3,300 years after it was baked and painted. If one were an average person at a cocktail party in Gotham, which was then invaded by Bane's henchmen; or a villager in western Anatolia suddenly confronted with several phalanxes of Myrmidons; or a peasant in Velen encountering the Wild Hunt, in literature and life terror would be an appropriate reaction. But there is this essential element of opéra bouffe, of the bank robber who drops his weapon and trips over his own feet, that makes us fail to take henchmen completely seriously as a threat. That key combination of fear and farce makes the henchman much more complicated than the popular stereotype and movie template.

Notes

1. Vladimir Propp, *Morphology of the Folktale* (Austin: University of Texas Press, 1968).

2. Will Wright, *Sixguns and Society: A Structural Study of the Western* (Berkeley: University of California Press, 1977).

3. Propp, *Morphology of the Folktale.*

4. Tamar Liebes and Elihu Katz, "Dallas and Genesis: Primordiality and Seriality in Popular Culture," in *Media, Myths, and Narratives: Television and the Press*, ed. James W. Carey (Beverly Hills, CA: Sage, 1988), 113–25.

5. The use of the name "Homer" as author for this text is inherently problematic for a great many reasons. For a cogent recent discussion of this scholarly problem, see Robert Fowler, "The Homeric Question," in *The Cambridge Companion to Homer*, ed. Robert Fowler (Cambridge: Cambridge University Press, 2004), 220–34.

6. In the *Iliad*, however, the term is used specifically for the soldiers following Achilles, although Achilles himself is not from Aegina but Thessaly; see Barry B. Powell, *Classical Myth*, 8th ed. (Boston: Pearson, 2015), 527; and *The Oxford Classical Dictionary*, s.v. Aeacus.

7. David D. Perlmutter, *Visions of War: Picturing Warfare from the Stone Age to the Cyberage* (New York: St. Martin's Press, 1999).

8. Curtis Runnels and Priscilla Murray, *Greece before History: An Archaeological Companion and Guide* (Stanford, CA: Stanford University Press, 2001), 99.

9. The abduction of Helen and the theme of abducted wives in myth is the subject of a recent volume edited by Lowell Edmunds: *Stealing Helen: The Myth of the Abducted Wife in Comparative Perspective* (Princeton, NJ: Princeton University Press, 2016).

10. Sigismund Dijkstra, for instance, one of the major characters from the game's city storyline, will refuse Geralt's plea for aid no matter what choices the player has made, because his political goals demand that he remain in the city.

11. Gregory Nagy, *Poetry as Performance: Homer and Beyond* (Cambridge: Cambridge University Press, 1996).

12. For an excellent discussion of the unique liminality of the game world and the ludic interaction of the player with this world, see Kristine Jørgensen's *Gameworld Interfaces* (Cambridge, MA: MIT Press, 2013).

13. Richard Wrangham, "Evolution of Coalitionary Killing," *American Journal of Physical Anthropology* 110, no. S29 (December 1999): 1–30; Richard Wrangham and Dale Peterson, *Demonic Males: Apes and the Origins of Human Violence* (New York: Houghton Mifflin Harcourt, 1996); and Lawrence H. Keeley, *War before Civilization: The Myth of the Peaceful Savage* (Oxford: Oxford University Press, 1996).

14. Jay Jackson, "Realistic Group Conflict Theory: A Review and Evaluation of the Theoretical and Empirical Literature," *Psychological Record* 43, no. 3 (1993): 395–415; Muzafer Sherif, *In Common Predicament: Social Psychology of Intergroup Conflict and Cooperation* (Boston: Houghton Mifflin, 1966), 24–61; Leonie Rösner and Nicole Krämer, "Verbal Venting in the Social Web: Effects of Anonymity and Group Norms on Aggressive Language Use in Online Comment," *Social Media + Society* 2, no. 3 (July–September 2016): 1–13; and Bertjan Doosje, Naomi Ellemers, and Russell Spears, "Perceived Intragroup Variability as a Function of Group Status and Identification," *Journal of Experimental Social Psychology* 31, no. 5 (September 1995): 410–36.

15. For a more thorough discussion of Spartan society, see Michael Whitby, ed., *Sparta* (New York: Routledge, 2002), with bibliography. For a discussion of Spartan society with a chronological organization, see Paul Cartledge, *Sparta and Lakonia: A Regional History 1300 to 362 BC*, 2nd ed. (New York: Routledge, 2002).

16. David D. Perlmutter, *Visions of War: Picturing Warfare from the Stone Age to the Cyberage* (New York: St. Martin's Press, 1999), esp. chap. 4, "Comrades," 89–116.

17. Perlmutter, *Visions of War*, 89–116.

18. William McNeill, *Keeping Together in Time: Dance and Drill in Human History* (New York: American Council of Learned Societies, 1995).

19. Lisa Ellen Silvestri, *Friended at the Front: Social Media in the American War Zone* (Lawrence: University Press of Kansas, 2015).

20. Edward Shils, "Primary Groups in the American Army," in *Continuities in Social Research: Studies in the Scope and Method of "The American Soldier,"* ed. Robert Merton and Paul Lazarsfeld (Glencoe, IL: Free Press, 1950), 32.

21. Shils, "Primary Groups in the American Army," 33.

22. Plutarch, *Life of Caius Marius*, 7.3, trans. John Dryden (1683).

23. Pliny, *Panegyricus*, 13, trans. Betty Radice (1969).

24. This discussion reprises Perlmutter, *Visions of War*, 89–116.

25. Martin Surbeck et al., "Comparison of Male Conflict Behavior in Chimpanzees (*Pan troglodytes*) and Bonobos (*Pan paniscus*), with Specific Regard to Coalition and Post-Conflict Behavior," *American Journal of Primatology* 79, no. 6 (2017): e22641.

26. Catherine Crockford, Tobias Deschner, and Roman Wittig, "What Is the Role of Oxytocin in Social Buffering: Do Primate Studies Change the Picture?" In *Behavioral Pharmacology of Neuropeptides: Oxytocin*, ed. Rene Hurlemann and Valery Grinevich (New York: Springer, 2018).

27. Lindsey Harlan, *The Goddesses' Henchmen: Gender in Indian Hero Worship* (New York: Oxford University Press, 2003), 72.

28. Jeffrey Rufo, "Marlowe's Minions: Sodomitical Politics in *Edward II* and *The Massacre at Paris*," *Marlowe Studies* 1 (2011), 5–24.

Section 2

SUPERVILLAINY IN MYTH AND LITERATURE

CHAPTER 9

Aṅgulimāla

Buddha's Original "Super Foe"

JOHN N. THOMPSON

"SUPERVILLAINS," THOSE ARCHFOES OF OUR FAVORITE HEROES, HAVE LONG been stock characters in popular culture. In his pulp novel *The Rolling Stones*, science fiction writer Robert Heinlein observes that villains give heroes purpose. Consider Superman or Harry Potter—what would either of them do without Lex Luthor or Lord Voldemort? Just as superheroes have incredible abilities, supervillains also have wondrous powers (mind control, teleportation, etc.), yet with very few exceptions they are not typically supernatural beings so much as bigger-than-life versions of real-world "villains" (dictators, gangsters, and terrorists). It thus may be somewhat surprising that some studies indicate that supervillains are *more* popular than the heroes who defeat them.[1] So *why* do we like the "bad guys" so much? Over the years, scholars have offered various explanations: supervillains help us confront our "shadow" selves (Jung), embody the fulfillments of dark wishes rooted in our id (Freud), or allow us to indulge vicariously in our inherent "will to power" (Nietzsche).[2] Regardless, just as theorists such as Joseph Campbell trace the roots of modern superheroes to traditional tales,[3] we can find precursors to contemporary supervillains in ancient myths as well.

In this paper I examine one such "proto-supervillain" from ancient India: Aṅgulimāla, a vicious murderer/brigand who, subdued by the Buddha, renounces his outlaw ways for monastic life and attains nirvana. Aṅgulimāla is well known in Buddhism, and his story has inspired various paintings, sculptures, movies, and even cartoons. What's more interesting than his popularity, however, is the fact that Aṅgulimāla, like many modern supervillains, is complex and compelling—an evil figure who is also a "victim," and who even turns out to be rather heroic. I therefore maintain that Aṅgulimāla saga reveals important truths about heroes and villains that we would do well to heed.

INITIAL POINTS ABOUT SUPERVILLAINS

The contest between good and evil is a perennial theme across all cultures—a fact that has led some scholars to speculate that this fundamental duality may have its roots in our shared cognitive and/or psychological structures.[4] In most cases, these forces are personified in the figures of the hero, the champion of order and justice, and the villain, the antagonist whom the hero must overcome. Probably the world's oldest surviving literary work concerns the Mesopotamian warrior-king Gilgamesh and his struggles against all manner of threatening monsters.[5] While such tales may include a variety of fantastic details and plot twists, in the end these stories are much the same. They are primal narratives reflecting basic struggles of daily life writ large, satisfying our longing for moral clarity and order.

One reason supervillains are so common is that without them, most of our favorite stories would not exist. Simply put, superheroes are just costumed schmucks (or thugs) without their nemeses. Indeed, the better the villain, the more heroic the hero; if you have a *super* hero, you also need a *super* villain. Stan Lee puts this quite well: "Where would Spider-Man be without the Green Goblin, Doc Ock, the Lizard, the Sandman, the Kingpin, or any of his other splendidly savage and sinister supervillains? Sure, you always need the hero, but ask yourself this: how eager would you be to read about a superhero who fought litterbugs, jay-walkers, or income-tax evaders?"[6] Our deep-seated desire for an even match between heroes and villains makes sense, as there is very little suspense in a contest where one side is hopelessly outmatched.

Clearly supervillains, like their hero counterparts, need extraordinary powers, but there is no single list of essential supervillain traits. Still, supervillains generally share certain characteristics: an abiding contempt for ordinary people's lives and values, a thirst for vengeance against perceived enemies, a threatening hideout far removed from the public, a central theme for plotting crimes, and more. Most of all, a supervillain needs a backstory (often involving tragedy) to explain what led him to embark on his life of crime.[7] While by no means exhaustive, even a cursory examination of this list suggests that supervillains are rather complex figures—often more so than superheroes.

WHO EXACTLY IS AṄGULIMĀLA?

Seeking comic book–style heroes and villains in ancient Indian culture may seem strange, but art historian Julie Romain notes that such archetypal pairings have a long history in South Asian society. As Romain observes, lavishly illustrated versions of the Rāmāyaṇa, the epic recounting the exploits of Prince

Rāma against Lord Rāvaṇa and his demonic hordes, first appeared during the sixteenth century, and these "picture books" circulated widely among the nobility. By the nineteenth century, these illustrated versions of classic tales had given way to lithographs suitable for mass reproduction and distribution, which proved incredibly popular, gradually developing into modern comic books and graphic novels. Such contemporary versions of mythic tales have legions of fans and merely continue India's illustrated narrative tradition.[8] Viewing the Buddhist story of Aṅgulimāla in "comic book terms," thus, is no great stretch.

There are several versions of Aṅgulimāla's tale in Buddhist literature. In the Pali canon, purportedly the oldest collection of Buddhist scripture, Aṅgulimāla appears in verses 866–91 of the *Theragāthā* (*Verses of the Elders*), a collection of hymns by the Buddha's disciples, yet these verses only obliquely refer to events in his life. The *Aṅgulimāla Sutta*, a sermon in the *Majjhima Nikāya* (*Middle Length Discourses*), presents a more developed yet episodic narrative. Aṅgulimāla is also mentioned in the *Mahāvagga* (*Great Chapter*), a text on monastic discipline, and several stories of the Buddha's previous lives.[9] Later commentaries such as the *Papañcasudani* and the *Paramattha-dipani* add details to the story that make for a richer, more satisfying narrative. Other texts mentioning Aṅgulimāla include the *Milinda-pañhā* (*Questions of King Milinda*) and the *Mahāvaṃsa* (*Great Chronicle*). Aṅgulimāla's story also appears several times in the *Taishō Shinshū Daizōkyō*, the standard modern edition of the Chinese canon.[10] In what follows, I piece together a version from various sources to highlight points relevant for considering Aṅgulimāla as a supervillain.

Long ago in the kingdom of Kosala, a region in the northwest of what is now India, a son was born to the wife of the court priest. This joyous occasion was marred, however, by a sinister omen: a mysterious light glittering on all the weapons in the palace. The royal astrologer declared this "the sign of the thief," a portent of the boy's destiny to become a criminal. To counter this fate, his parents named him Ahimsaka (Harmless), vowing to raise him to be pure and virtuous. The boy prospered, proving unusually strong in mind, body, and character. His parents sent him to the city of Takṣaśilā, a great commercial and cultural center, to study with the foremost teacher of the age. There, Ahimsaka's quick mind, scrupulous character, and hard work earned him the guru's favor.

Unfortunately, the other students resented Ahimsaka's prominence and vowed to bring him down. To that end they repeatedly slandered their classmate behind his back, eventually going so far as to convince their teacher that Ahimsaka had seduced his beautiful young wife. Crazed with jealously, the guru demanded that his star pupil, in accord with ancient custom, grant him his guru *dakṣiṇā* (offering): a *mālā* (garland or necklace) of one thousand human fingers.

Ahimsaka was devastated. Innocent of any wrongdoing and abhorring violence, he knew that he had a sacred duty to obey his guru or bring dishonor on his family and suffer terrible karmic consequences. Driven mad by his classmates' treachery, horror-struck by his guru's request, and enraged over his evil fate, Ahimsaka seized various weapons and fled into a forest traversed by a network of trade routes. He then began murdering people and taking their fingers, only to have his grisly trophies devoured by crows and vultures. So he took to wearing them as a macabre necklace (hence his epithet Aṅgulimāla, "necklace of fingers"). By the time he had collected 999 fingers, his victims were too numerous to count, and he had laid waste to the countryside.

At this time, the Buddha was residing at the Jeta Grove outside the town of Sāvatthī. One morning after his alms round, he learned of this highwayman terrorizing the region. Carefully setting his affairs in order, the Buddha proceeded down the road to the forest. Villagers along the way repeatedly warned him that the brigand had slain many people (including large parties of armed men), but the Blessed One, seemingly heedless of the danger, continued toward the killer's lair.

Certainly this looks like a typical superhero scenario. We have an ill-fated youth possessed of wondrous abilities who suffers a grave injustice at the hands of his fellows. In response, he experiences a psychological/spiritual breakdown and commits himself to a life of crime. Aṅgulimāla has all the marks of a supervillain: extraordinary intelligence and physical power,[11] hatred for others, and an unquenchable thirst for vengeance. From his dark hideout where he plots his crimes, he pounces upon his victims, slaying them and wearing their fingers around his neck to memorialize his bloody deeds. His campaign of terror inevitably draws the attention of our hero (the Buddha), who, true to form, moves to counter the threat.[12] Thus the stage is set for an archetypal clash.

HERO AND VILLAIN MEET

Let us return to the story. The sharp-eyed Aṅgulimāla spotted the Buddha from afar and, surprised at a lone monk wandering into his domain, gathered his weapons to dispatch this foolish holy man quickly. Things didn't go as planned, however. The Blessed One used his psychic powers (*iddhi*) to stay out of harm's reach, calmly walking while Aṅgulimāla ran furiously, yet unable to catch up. Frustrated, he halted and called out, "Stop, contemplative! Stop!" The Buddha replied, "I *have* stopped, Aṅgulimāla. *You* stop." Aṅgulimāla was amazed—the Buddha evaded his clutches merely by walking yet claimed to have stopped. Moreover, he commanded Aṅgulimāla to stop when the killer had already done so. Aṅgulimāla mused, "These Śakyan contemplatives are speakers of the truth, asserters of the truths, and yet this contemplative, even while walking, says, 'I have stopped, Aṅgulimāla. You stop.' Why don't I question him?" He then said aloud, "While walking, contemplative, you say, 'I have stopped.' But when I have stopped you say I haven't. I ask you the meaning of this: How have you stopped? How haven't I?" The Buddha explained,

> I have stopped, Aṅgulimāla,
> once and for all,
> having cast off violence
> toward all living beings.
> You, though,
> are unrestrained toward beings.
> That's how I've stopped
> and you haven't.[13]

The Buddha's words of truth had an immediate and powerful effect: Aṅgulimāla declared that he would give up his evil ways. Tossing his weapons aside, he bowed and requested to become a monk. The Buddha accepted, and together they returned to the Jeta Grove to join the rest of the *sangha*.

Aṅgulimāla dedicated himself to religious life, proving a model monk. His fellow *bhikkhus*, alarmed at first, quickly realized that their new brother deeply understood the dharma and was genuinely committed to the path. His sincerity even won the admiration of King Pasenadi, the regional ruler, who had come to capture the bandit and execute him for his crimes. In fact, the king even offered to pay for Aṅgulimāla's upkeep; the devout monk, ever correct, declined, stating his intention to pursue a life of austerity beyond what was usually required. The king departed, amazed at this ex-murderer's example.

At this point, we should note that this story departs from the stereotypical superhero narrative arc. Unlike some hero stories, this tale does not promote violence as the way to conquer evil or vice versa: the Buddha never physically engages Aṅgulimāla, nor, despite his initial resolve, does the killer lay a hand on the hero (contra the infamous Zen motto, "If you meet the Buddha on the road, kill him"). Instead, the Buddha peacefully subdues the villain, returning him to the path of the good. The result, though, surpasses all expectations. With his special powers, keen intelligence, recognition of spiritual authority, and extraordinary discipline (Aṅgulimāla is single-minded in his pursuit of the dharma), the new monk recalls none other than Siddhārtha Gautama himself, a gifted young man who underwent a radical conversion to a spiritual path that led to his becoming the Buddha. Indeed, like the Buddha, the murder-monk exudes a powerful spiritual charisma on those around him. Something strange is emerging: Aṅgulimāla seems less a villain and more a mirror image of our hero (an antihero?) whose resemblance to the Buddha is uncanny . . . and unsettling. And yet for all their similarity, the two remain very different individuals.

FURTHER PLOT TWISTS

Delving back into the tale, the killer-monk devoted himself to the routines of monastic life. He assiduously performed his daily begging rounds, accepting whatever he was given—food or rejection and harsh treatment—with equanimity. One day, he chanced upon a woman in danger of dying while in labor and felt compassion for such suffering. He reported this to the Buddha, who instructed him to return and perform a "truth act" (*satyakiriyā*) by declaring that since he had never killed any being, his life of purity and harmlessness would bring health and well-being to both mother and child. Balking at this lie (he had slain *many*), Aṅgulimāla followed the Buddha's instructions by declaring that the purity of his life *since his conversion* would bring blessings—an act that established a protection ritual (*paritta*) still used in Theravādin societies to bless pregnant women and protect new houses from evil forces.

Sometime later, Aṅgulimāla secluded himself to practice extreme asceticism, eventually attaining arhatship. Soon afterward, he was violently assaulted on his begging rounds by villagers who recognized him. Badly beaten, Aṅgulimāla crawled back to the Buddha, "his head broken open and dripping with blood, his bowl broken, and his outer robe ripped to shreds."[14] The Buddha comforted the wounded *bhikkhu*, exhorting him to bear his pain by explaining it as the fruit of the bad karma from his crimes that otherwise would have burned him "in hell for many years, many hundreds of years, many thousands of years."[15]

Finally, Aṅgulimāla experienced the "bliss of release," spontaneously breaking into song to celebrate his change to a nonviolent life by proclaiming himself Ahimsaka once again:

> "Doer of No Harm" is my name,
> but I used to be a doer of harm.
> Today I am true to my name,
> for I harm no one at all.
>
> A bandit
> I used to be,
> renowned as Aṅgulimāla.
> Swept along by a great flood,
> I went to the Buddha as refuge . . .

This has come well & not gone away,[16]
it was not badly thought through for me.
The three knowledges
have been attained;
the Buddha's bidding,
done.[17]

With this, the story ends.

The last part the story is even more curious. While our newly reformed villain has forsaken the "dark side," he still struggles, and his relationship with the Buddha betrays ongoing tensions. While on the surface this situation may resemble other hero-villain relationships (e.g., the "friendship" between Clark Kent and Lex Luthor), due to their mentor and student roles, the relationship between the Buddha and Aṅgulimāla seems rather distant. Despite living in close quarters, Aṅgulimāla and the Buddha never develop the sort of camaraderie we see between the Buddha and other monks such as Śariputra or Ananda.[18] In addition, the World Honored One scarcely acknowledges the killer-monk's gifts and spiritual accomplishments. Instead, the Buddha remains aloof, continuing to exert his authority by providing Aṅgulimāla with some cryptic (deceptive?) instructions to deal with an admittedly unprecedented situation. Furthermore, the Buddha forces the killer-monk to face harsh truths and suffer great pain. It seems that now the Buddha is the sharp-eyed figure watching at some remove. The text implies that he knows what will happen to Aṅgulimāla, yet he does not warn the new monk or make any effort to spare his protégé, and his words, while truthful, offer cold comfort. Perhaps the Buddha, like Hamlet, must be "cruel to be kind"; but more to the point, there seems to be a larger message here about the relationship between heroes and villains.

WHAT AṄGULIMĀLA TELLS US ABOUT "SUPERVILLAINS" (AND HEROES)

Aṅgulimāla's story raises many questions, regarding plot details (the sequence of incidents, particularly toward the end, seems rather confused) as well as the deeper symbolism involved. On the surface, it is a basic morality tale in which the Buddha subdues Aṅgulimāla, ending his criminal career and restoring peace while enticing the murderer into the monastic order. This life proves to be the ex-criminal's true vocation, as Aṅgulimāla becomes an arhat. Thus the tale confirms the power of *ahimsā* (nonharming) with the monk's triumph over the murderer and also shows that the path of rehabilitation is more effective than punishment. Many people cite Aṅgulimāla as proof that under the dharma no one is beyond salvation, and his tale has inspired a successful prison ministry in the United Kingdom with branches in the United States.[19]

Yet for all this, the story remains more ambiguous than most tales of super-heroes and supervillains. Certainly, the Buddha *is* a heroic figure whose life story is full of great feats. For instance, on the night of his awakening under the bodhi tree, he defeats Mara, the Indian *deva* who is something of a counterpart to the Western Satan. During his ministry, he performs various miracles (part-ing the waters of a flooding river, rising up to the heavenly abodes of the gods, healing the sick), brings peace to warring tribes, and even tames a rampaging elephant. Traditional accounts maintain that his good works and teachings benefit countless beings.[20] And Aṅgulimāla is definitely a villainous and pow-erful opponent. But as we've already seen, their resemblance is disturbing, and their roles are not so clear and distinct. What's more, both the Buddha and Aṅgulimāla seem to know this on some deeper level.

One way to understand this relationship and its implications is to read the story of Aṅgulimāla not as a run-of-the-mill superhero tale but as a story of redemption. Literally, "redemption" means buying something back or repay-ing a debt, and in an ethical or religious context the term often has Christian overtones. For our purposes, though, redemption compensates for an initial loss but does not negate it; morally, redemption does not erase evil so much as recognize it and make amends.

We find a comic book version of this theme in the example of Doctor Octo-pus (Doc Ock) from the movie *Spider-Man 2* (2004). A brilliant scientist who turns evil as a result of an experiment gone wrong, Doc Ock wreaks havoc on New York, endangering thousands of lives and nearly killing Spider-Man. Yet he cannot control the power of his own technology: his cybernetic arms turn on him, leaving him mortally injured while a nuclear device threatens the entire New York area. The battered Spider-Man cannot halt the imminent destruction of the city, and in desperation he appeals to Doc Ock's remaining humanity. It works. In the face of death, Doc Ock declares: "I will not die a monster." Taking control of his mechanical arms, he destroys the nuclear device before sinking into the Hudson River's watery depths. His final act does not negate the very real evil he committed earlier, but it shows that he recognizes what he has done and takes responsibility. Moreover, in his death he does something heroic that is beyond even Spider-Man's abilities. He has saved the day, and while this act does not fully make up for his evil deeds, still, we feel for Doc Ock and cannot condemn him absolutely.[21]

Somewhat like Doc Ock, Aṅgulimāla becomes a villain due to a tragedy and goes on to cause much harm. Eventually, he returns to the good, and ironically becomes something of a hero (a "dharma protector") by using the powers he'd honed as a villain. Yet, although Aṅgulimāla redeems himself by embracing the dharma, his good deeds, sterling example, and spiritual accomplishments do not erase his crimes or absolve him of their consequences. Karma is a bitch, beyond the control of even the Buddha himself. In fact, in some versions of the tale, Aṅgulimāla suffers recurring nightmares in which he is tormented by the ghosts of his many victims (perhaps an early narrative depiction of what we now call posttraumatic stress disorder), and he actually dies as a result of the assault by the angry villagers. So much for a Hollywood ending.

David Pizarro and Roy Baumeister observe that comic book stories of superheroes pose problems because they provide us with the cheap pleasure of exercising moral judgment in uncomplicated situations. Dubbing them a form of "moral pornography" for the way they pander to our "moralistic urges," Pizzaro and Baumeister suggest that these tales hinder our ability to recognize true evil, noting that "the real bad guys never resemble the images from the Batman movies."[22] Aṅgulimāla's story, though, resists a morally pornographic interpretation because its ambiguity resonates with our lived experience.

Drawing on Jungian psychology, one scholar writes that stories like Aṅgulimāla's make abstract moral ideas real "by turning them into the interplay between human characters. The tensions between samsara and nirvana, fixations and freedom, start to crackle with immediacy. . . . [O]ne's own life is mirrored in these dramas in a way that no amount of theorizing can achieve."[23] Such Buddhist hero tales teach us that we can never fully defeat evil but must face and work with it as best we can. The dark side remains ever present, a source of power and a temptation that requires constant vigilance from even the most upright hero. In truth, what really makes a hero heroic is recognizing how close the villain is yet being able to hold him at bay.[24]

Interestingly, this nuanced view of supervillainy dovetails with depictions of villains in contemporary comics, graphic novels, and movies. Movie producer Laura Ziskin has remarked that in Marvel there are no ultimate villains, only "people gone wrong because of some other need."[25] These humanized figures are very recognizable; our supervillains, like our superheroes, *are* us. From a Buddhist perspective, however, this is nothing new. Martial artist Nagaboshi Tomio points out that Aṅgulimāla's story was allegorized in later traditions, with the murderer representing our continual cravings for the mundane world and his bloody necklace representing our string of failures to practice dharma and attain the gifts of enlightenment.[26] Paradoxically, maybe to become Buddha we need to recognize and take hold of our inner Aṅgulimāla while keeping him at arm's length—a heroic feat indeed.

Notes

1. David A. Pizarro and Roy Baumeister, "Superhero Comics as Moral Pornography," in *Our Superheroes, Ourselves*, ed. Robin S. Rosenberg (New York: Oxford University Press, 2013), 19–36.

2. For a brief overview of some psychological theories of supervillains, see Travis Langley, "Why Do Supervillains Fascinate Us? A Psychological Perspective," *Wired*, July 27, 2012, available at https://www.wired.com/2012/07/why-do-supervillains-fascinate-us/. For an insightful discussion of how Nietzsche's theories of the Superman (*Übermensch*) and *resenttiment* help us understand the Joker, a particular supervillain who has proven to be uncannily popular, see Ryan Litsey, "The Joker, Crown Prince of Nobility: The 'Master' Criminal, Nietzsche, and the Rise of the Superman," in *The Joker: A Serious Study of the Crown Prince of Crime*, ed. Robert Moses Peaslee and Robert G. Weiner (Jackson: University Press of Mississippi, 2015), 179–93.

3. Campbell famously lays out the "hero's journey" in *The Hero with a Thousand Faces* (Princeton, NJ: Bollingen Foundation, 1949). However, it is in his series of interviews with journalist Bill Moyers that he explicitly applies motifs from the "hero's journey" to examples from popular culture such as *Star Wars*. See Joseph Campbell with Bill Moyers, *The Power of Myth* (New York: Doubleday, 1985). For a critical discussion of how Campbell's heroic monomyth both does (and does not) fit superheroes of comic books, movies, and other media, see Hougaard Winterbach, "Heroes and Superheroes: From Myth to the American Comic Book," *South African Journal of Art History (SAJAH)* 21, no. 1 (2006): 114–34, available at http://www.repository.up.ac.za/dspace/bitstream/handle/2263/10798/Winterbach_Heroes(2006).pdf?sequence=1.

4. Examples include Freud's notion of the conflict between the "life instinct" (*eros*) and "death instinct" (Thanatos), and Claude Lévi-Strauss's theory that the human mind operates via a continual dialectic between binary oppositions (hot-cold, left-right, male-female, etc.). For details, see Sigmund Freud, *Beyond the Pleasure Principle*, standard ed., trans. James Strachey (New York: Liveright, 1961); and Claude Lévi-Strauss, *The Raw and the Cooked*, trans. John and Doreen Weightman (Chicago: University of Chicago Press, 1990).

5. For a scholarly translation, see Andrew R. George, ed. and trans., *The Babylonian Gilgamesh Epic: Introduction, Critical Edition and Cuneiform Texts* (Oxford: Oxford University Press, 2003).

6. Quoted in Ben Dyer, "The Devils Get Their Due," in *Supervillains and Philosophy: Sometimes, Evil Is Its Own Reward*, ed. Ben Dyer (Chicago: Open Court, 2009), x.

7. For a tongue-in-cheek discussion of "essential" characteristics of supervillains, see Galen Foresman, "Making the A-List," in *Supervillains and Philosophy: Sometimes, Evil Is Its Own Reward*, ed. Ben Dyer (Chicago: Open Court, 2009), 23–30.

8. Julie Romain, "Heroes and Villains: The Battle for Good in India's Comics," *World of Antiques and Art* 78 (February 2010): 118–23.

9. See Mahāvagga I.41 and Jātaka 537.

10. See the *Angulimālīya Sūtra* or *Yangjuemolou jing*, T.120, translated into Chinese by the monk Gunabhadra (435–443 CE), as well as the *Yang juemo jing*, T.118, attributed to Dharmarakṣa (226–313 CE), and the *Yang jue ji jing*, T.119, translated by Fa Zhu (290–307 CE).

11. Aṅgulimāla had run down galloping horses and elephants, and killed as many as forty armed men at a time.

12. In some versions, the Buddha goes into the forest to save Aṅgulimāla's mother, who had come to bring her son food.

13. *Aṅgulimāla Sutta*, trans. Thanissaro Bhikkhu, 2, available at http://www.accesstoinsight.org/tipitaka/mn/mn.086.than.html.

14. *Aṅgulimāla Sutta*, 5.

15. *Aṅgulimāla Sutta*, 5.

16. Presumably nirvana.

17. *Aṅgulimāla Sutta*, 5–7.

18. Śariputra was the most philosophically gifted of the Buddha's disciples, often speaking with the Blessed One, while Ananda was the Buddha's personal attendant who accompanied him wherever he went.

19. See "Angulimala: The Buddhist Prison Chaplaincy," available at https://angulimala.org.uk/.

20. One of the Buddha's epithets is *jina* (hero), and Campbell even uses his life as a prime example of the "hero's journey." See Joseph Campbell, *The Hero with a Thousand Faces*, 2nd ed. (Princeton, NJ: Princeton University Press, 1968).

21. Spider-Man has a long history of trying to rehabilitate villains by appealing to their humanity. At one point, Spidey villain Sandman was even a member of the Avengers (see *Avengers*, no. 329 [February 1991]). Wonder Woman, too, has long history of trying to rehabilitate villains on Reform Island/Transformation Island, "a smaller companion to Paradise Island where criminals are rehabilitated by the Amazons. . . . Wonder Woman believed that even criminals had the potential to learn the Amazon way of life." See Tim Hanley, *Wonder Woman Unbound: The Curious History of the World's Most Famous Heroine* (Chicago: Chicago Review Press, 2014), 22. Reform Island/Transformation Island first appeared in *Wonder Woman*, vol. 1, nos. 3–4 (February–May 1943).

22. Pizarro and Baumeister, "Superhero Comics as Moral Pornography," 32.

23. Stephen Batchelor, *Living with the Devil: A Meditation on Good and Evil* (New York: Riverhead Books, 2004), 123.

24. Fans of Marvel movies may note how this idea resonates with Colossus's "hero speech" at the end of *Deadpool* (2016) when he (unsuccessfully) tries to convince the "Merc with a Mouth" *not* to kill his now defenseless enemy, Ajax: "Over a lifetime, there are only four or five moments that really matter. Moments when you're offered a choice—to make a sacrifice, conquer a flaw, save a friend, spare an enemy. In these moments, everything else falls away. The way the world sees us."

25. Quoted in Anthony R. Mills, *American Theology, Superhero Comics, and Cinema: The Marvel of Stan Lee and the Revolution of a Genre* (New York: Routledge, 2014), 151.

26. Shifu Nagaboshi Tomio, *The Bodhisattva Warriors: The Origin, Inner Philosophy, History and Symbolism of the Buddhist Martial Art within India and China*, repr. ed. (Delhi: Motilal Banarsidass, 2000), 183.

CHAPTER 10

Shakespeare's Villains[1]

MAURICE CHARNEY

I THINK THAT READERS AND AUDIENCES ALIKE ARE SURPRISED AT HOW IMPORT-ant villains were to Shakespeare. In *Othello*, for example, the nefarious Iago almost steals the show from the rightful protagonist. Iago is clever, inventive, and subtle, a quick and ingenious improviser, not qualities that Othello is not-ed for. He is also very persuasive and an excellent actor who plays many parts and can speak in many different styles to accomplish his objectives. He is also wonderfully in touch with the audience and speaks many soliloquies to make sure that the audience is fully informed about what he is doing. Iago is a plotter, like Shakespeare himself. We will never know why Shakespeare was so skillful in his creation of villains, but the question is an intriguing one.

The question has a practical side to it, because there are so many different kinds of villains (and calumniators and tyrants, too) in Shakespeare.... In this chapter, I hope to bring readers of Shakespeare and people who go to see the plays to some realization of the crucial role that villains play, even minor villains like Tybalt, Iachimo, and Angelo. They establish an elaborate network of evil—what constitutes the world of the play—in which the good characters must function. I think we are rightfully stung by how easily villains like Iago can dupe their victims.

There is a kind of gleeful gloating in Iago as he triumphs over the honest and trusting Othello. This gloating is also present in Cassius as he discovers that Brutus can be won over to the conspiracy without much effort, by fair means or foul. Evil is rampant in Shakespeare, and the villains seem to be able to overpower the virtuous characters—at least for a time—because the virtuous characters, by their very nature, are so credulous, trusting, and unsuspecting, whereas the villains are always so extremely wary. Villains are generally sub-tle and ingenious, excellent role-players and actors. It is not surprising that Shakespeare should be so suspicious of actors as creators of false appearances.

I would like to define some of the characteristics that many of the villains share. These are, of course, only tentative generalizations, since there are so many exceptions. One obvious point is that most of the villains are either murderers or capable of murder. I think what Shylock says in *The Merchant of Venice* is important here: "Hates any man the thing he would not kill?" (4.1.67). This question is unanswerable because there is no necessary link between hatred and killing, as Shylock seems to think. But among Shakespeare's villains there is an additional element of sport, as in Aaron, Richard (Duke of Gloucester and later King Richard III), Iago, and others, who think of killing as a kind of game, the primary purpose of which is to show how clever you are in outwitting your antagonist. Macbeth as a villain-hero is different, because he is so powerfully convinced of his own guilt in killing, but he kills nevertheless in his overweening ambition to be king. In this he is supported by his wife. Claudius, too, feels great guilt about his murders, but this feeling doesn't prevent him from annihilating his enemies (or his imagined enemies).

It is not surprising that many villains are creatures of will, as Iago pronounces so vigorously to Roderigo: "Virtue? A fig! 'Tis in ourselves that we are thus, or thus. Our bodies are our gardens, to the which our wills are gardeners; so that if we will plant nettles or sow lettuce, set hyssop and weed up thyme, supply it with one gender of herbs or distract [vary] it with many . . . why, the power and corrigible authority of this lies in our wills" (*Othello* 1.3.314–21). As creatures of will, villains pursue their ambitious projects with a cynical indifference to what anyone else thinks. They are fixated on themselves as the center of the universe. This is stated very simply in *Julius Caesar*. Caesar explains to Decius, a conspirator who is determined to bring him to the Capitol, why he cannot come: "The cause is in my will: I will not come" (2.2.71). It is not important that Calpurnia, Caesar's wife, has had ominous dreams, which Decius twists around with the promise of a crown for Caesar, who is finally persuaded to come—to be assassinated.

Shakespeare's villains are arbitrary and irrational in the pursuit of their wills, as if they need to consult with no one else among their many counselors. In his mad jealousy of his wife in *The Winter's Tale*, Leontes rejects all arguments to the contrary, even from those nearest and dearest to him. He is resolved to pursue his indomitable will even after the oracle at Delphi has declared against him, right up to the news that his dear son Mamillius is dead. Only this fact can persuade him to abandon his paranoid jealousy.

Linked with the villains as creatures of will is their lack of belief in anything greater than themselves. In religious terms, some of the villains are outright atheists, like Aaron in *Titus Andronicus* or even more obviously Edmund in *King Lear*. When he proclaims: "Thou, Nature, art my goddess; to thy laws / My services are bound" (1.2.1–2), it is Nature red in tooth and claw, the law of the jungle, completely set apart from Christian revelation. In the same scene, Edmund waxes satirical about his father's superstitious fears:

> This is the excellent foppery of the world, that when we are sick in fortune, often the surfeits of our own behavior, we make guilty of our disasters the sun, the moon and the stars, as if we were villains on necessity, fools by heavenly compulsion, knaves, thieves and treachers by spherical predominance; drunkards, liars and adulterers by enforced obedience of planetary influence; and all that we are evil in by a divine thrusting on. An admirable evasion of whoremaster man, to lay his goatish disposition on the charge of a star. (1.2.118–28)

To Edmund, everything depends on the force of the individual will and nothing else—certainly nothing metaphysical or religious.

Soliloquies and asides are very important to many of Shakespeare's villains, who want to be in close touch with the audience. The soliloquies are partly confessional and partly boastful, since the villains want to be considered absolutely honest among spectators—"honest" is a much-repeated word in *Othello* and *Julius Caesar*. Like Iago and Richard, Duke of Gloucester, villains wish to present themselves as plain and unadorned speakers (although they can also use slang and colloquial language when it suits their purpose). They seek not just the audience's approval but its sympathy and praise. They take pride in their cleverness and in their superiority to ordinary mortals, and they show only contempt for the credulousness of their victims.

Many of Shakespeare's villains have a low opinion of women, if not overt misogyny. In Richard III's wooing of Anne, for example, he seduces her in a kind of game or sport, but after she has exited, he has only contempt for her. He mocks her in his soliloquy:

> Was ever woman in this humor wooed?
> Was ever woman in this humor won?
> I'll have her, but I will not keep her long. (1.2.117–19)

Anne's early death is already predicted—she will be murdered by Richard.

In *Othello*, Iago eggs Roderigo on by provocative enticements about Desdemona's torrid sexual needs: "When the blood is made dull with the act of sport, there should be a game to inflame it and to give satiety a fresh appetite, loveliness in favor, sympathy in years, manners, and beauties; all of which the Moor is defective in" (2.1.225–29). In Renaissance physiology, the blood was thought to be the seat of sexual appetite. Iago says all this even though he knows that his slandering of Desdemona as a whorish creature is a product of his own imagination and that she remains, in his own words, "All guiltless"

(4.1.49). Like many of Shakespeare's villains, Iago's talk is very sexual, although he doesn't seem to have any concept of love.

Villains in Shakespearean tragedy are essential to his presentation of tragic themes, and this is also true of his histories, many of which are tragic in feeling. But the villains (and calumniators and tyrants) in his comedies pose special problems. This is nowhere more obvious than in the actions of Don John in *Much Ado about Nothing*. His calumniation of Hero, which results in her supposed death, is weakly motivated and seems anomalous in this play. Don John seems to be playing out his own vengeful and unsubstantiated impulses, as if something dire is needed to cure his melancholy. A number of villains, calumniators, and tyrants from the comedies—Shylock, Angelo, Don John, Iachimo, Lucio, Leontes, and Duke Frederick—are substantially affected by the conventions of the genre. The happy ending, for example, in comedies and tragicomedies alters the direction in which characters seem to be moving earlier in their plays. In many comedies, villainous figures serve as blocking agents to prevent the course of true love from running too smoothly. They provide necessary perturbations for the comic action. Undoubtedly, characters such as Sebastian and Antonio (and Caliban, too) from *The Tempest* and Cloten and his Queen Mother from *Cymbeline* have a function similar to Don John's in *Much Ado about Nothing*.

The word "villain" (and related forms) is extremely common in Shakespeare, for example Hamlet's exclamation about Claudius right after he has spoken with his father's ghost: "O villain, villain, smiling, damned villain" (1.5.106). But the word had less force than it does now, because "villain" in its etymological (French) sense also refers to a peasant or servant, or any base person. The *Oxford English Dictionary* defines "villain" in its double sense as "I. Originally, a low-born base-minded rustic; a man of ignoble ideas or instincts; in later use, an unprincipled or depraved scoundrel; a man naturally disposed to base or criminal actions, or deeply involved in the commission of disgraceful crimes." The first recorded use of the word is in 1303.

There is a good example of the double meaning of this word in *Titus Andronicus*, when Chiron and Demetrius discover that their mother has given birth to a black baby:

DEMETRIUS. Villain, what hast thou done?
AARON. That which thou canst not undo.
CHIRON. Thou hast undone our mother.
AARON. Villain, I have done thy mother. (4.2.73–76)

Aaron is the mentor of Chiron and Demetrius, so "villain" in this context is not a very strong word. . . .

Iago is clearly Shakespeare's most significant villain. His dramatic character is already anticipated by Aaron in *Titus Andronicus* and by Richard, Duke of Gloucester, who becomes King Richard III. Iago is extraordinary for his inventiveness and creativity. His plotting depends on improvisation, as if it is all very easy and spontaneous. For example, the handkerchief that Emilia finds suddenly falls into Iago's hands, and he then becomes amazingly successful in deceiving Othello. But we are sure that Iago really doesn't need the handkerchief. Without much effort, he could win Othello over with some other ruse. Like many of Shakespeare's villains, Iago indulges in abundant soliloquies. These put him in close contact with the audience, which is kept informed of his every move. It is important to him for the audience to like him and to sympathize with him. He doesn't consider himself a villain but rather a very clever manipulator who has many different reasons for his actions. He is a skillful actor who can play many parts, and he always expresses a kind of glee in his bravura performances. This is also characteristic of the laughing Aaron in *Titus Andronicus*.

Tarquin in *The Rape of Lucrece* and Aaron in *Titus Andronicus* are Shakespeare's first villains, from early works dating around 1594, and it is noteworthy how strongly they set the pattern for future villains. Both Tarquin and Aaron are creatures of powerful will, and both have remarkably little concern for the natural rights of other people. Tarquin is surprisingly moralistic, because he is certain that what he is doing is wrong and will have dire consequences. But he pursues the rape of Lucrece relentlessly, and Shakespeare uses abundant martial imagery in depicting him. Both Aaron and Tarquin are purposive, but they are also inventive and improvisational. Aaron is distinctively a laughing villain, like the Vice in medieval morality plays. He is redeemed from absolute villainy by his love for his black baby, but he also expresses a strong atheism. Like Edmund in King Lear, he believes only in nature. Aaron resembles Democritus, the laughing philosopher, because he is cynically amused by his evil deeds and by the stupidity and gullibility of his fellow humans. Finally, both Tarquin and Aaron are ready to rape or kill to accomplish their ends.

Richard, Duke of Gloucester (who becomes King Richard III), is endlessly creative in his villainy. He pursues the crown, and despite many obstacles he manages to kill everyone in his way. His physical deformity is closely associated with his villainy, but he woos and wins Anne as if he were a beautiful young lover. His own mother curses him. Richard is artful in killing off his enemies, and we are made to admire his histrionic skill. He is gleeful at how easy it is to manipulate appearances and how foolishly credulous everyone is. Like Iago after him, Richard is closely in touch with the audience, in whom he confides in his soliloquies. He needs the audience to admire him and to be astounded by his consummate plotting. Like a skillful actor, he can play many roles. At the end of *Richard III*, Richard is despondent, as the ghosts of the many persons he has killed come to remind him of his villainy.

Although he appears in a comedy, Shylock is clearly a villain because, once the due date for a loan he made to Antonio has passed, he refuses the money many times over, insisting on taking the pound of flesh that is stipulated in his "merry" bond. He is a purposive and determined character, and it is evident that he intends to kill Antonio right before our eyes. The flight of his daughter Jessica, who has stolen his money and jewels, to marry the Christian Lorenzo infuriates him. It is interesting that Shakespeare goes out of his way to give Shylock some justification for his hatred of Antonio, who expresses a gross anti-Semitism. Shylock has an extremely sympathetic (and much quoted) speech about the common humanity that Jews share with Christians: "Hath not a Jew eyes?" (*The Merchant of Venice* 3.1.55ff.), but we should remember that the speech ends with a call for vengeance. He is a curious, if not bizarre, figure in this play, but he relentlessly pursues the life of Antonio as if this were a tragedy of revenge and not a comedy.

In *Hamlet*, Claudius is a politic murderer who has killed his brother and usurped the throne of Denmark. He is noted in the play for his secrecy as well as his subtlety. Among his many homicidal actions, he sends Hamlet to be murdered in England; he doesn't make much effort to stop his queen, Gertrude, from drinking from the poisoned chalice; and he is responsible for the death of Laertes, and of Rosencrantz and Guildenstern. Claudius has an important soliloquy in the middle of the play in which he acknowledges his guilt, like Cain, who committed the first murder, although he is also aware that his prayer is useless, since he is not penitent. He is abetted by his chief counselor, Polonius, who is not directly a villain but proceeds by "policy," a word very much linked with villains.

Macbeth is a villain-hero, an unusual role in Shakespeare. Even while he is committing murder, he is tormented by his own guilt. This presents us with a double perspective, because Macbeth is not only a brutal murderer but also a conscience-stricken soul in spiritual torment. The first step in his ambitious pursuit of the crown is to kill King Duncan, but further murders are necessary, and Banquo and then Macduff's wife and children are hunted down. As the play proceeds, Macbeth becomes progressively less sensitive, ending in a despairing apathy. A great deal of emphasis is placed on the inability of both him and Lady Macbeth to sleep. She does not directly persuade her husband to commit murder, but she engages in an elaborate psychological process of unsexing, so that she can become a female warrior. The play ends with her madness and intense guilt. The play is very much preoccupied with gender issues, especially what it means to be a man, defined by military might.

King Lear features an abundance of evildoers. Edmund, the bastard son of Gloucester, is a free spirit who believes only in the workings of nature, like Iago and Aaron. He is a strong and determined villain, and from his atheism comes a total disregard for the lives and feelings of others; he is unconstrained by any moral imperatives. Lear's elder daughters, Goneril and Regan, are savage in their conspiracy against their aging father. When they shut their doors on Lear in the midst of a ferocious storm, they clearly don't care whether he lives or dies. Regan abets her husband, Cornwall, in the blinding of Gloucester, perhaps the cruelest scene in all of Shakespeare. Goneril and Regan both kill themselves for the love of Edmund, who doesn't plan to marry either of them. The evil deeds in this play penetrate to the very heart of a grim and uncompromising reality.

In *Measure for Measure*, the strict Angelo is promoted to become Duke of Vienna when Duke Vincentio withdraws, but Vincentio seems to be testing Angelo right from the beginning of the play. When Angelo first appears, he is represented as being extremely virtuous and cold, but he is soon tempted by Isabella, the novice of Saint Clare and sister of Claudio, who has been condemned to death for fornication. Angelo soon proposes that he will spare Claudio's life if Isabella has an assignation with him. Angelo, of course, is determined that Claudio be executed. This is at the heart of his villainy. As is fitting for a tragicomedy, the Duke in *Measure for Measure* arranges things so that Claudio is never really put to death and that Mariana, to whom Angelo was once betrothed, is substituted for Isabella in the Duke's "bed trick." The play ends not with "measure for measure," as we might expect, but with everyone pardoned, including Angelo and Lucio.

Tybalt in *Romeo and Juliet* is not a major character, but he is a caricatural villain who speaks in the language of the Italian dueling manuals that were so popular at the time. He is an affected, somewhat ridiculous figure, whom his uncle, Lord Capulet, calls a "princox." Mercutio speaks satirically of him as the Prince of Cats. Tybalt is deeply committed to the feud between the Montagues and the Capulets at the very moment when it seems to be dying down. His killing of Mercutio precipitates the tragic action. He returns intending to kill Romeo, but Romeo kills him.

Calumniators are not exactly villains but share many of their qualities. Examples include Don John in *Much Ado about Nothing*, Iachimo in *Cymbeline*, and Lucio in *Measure for Measure*, none of whom is a major character. Don John is an anomalous figure whose impulse to do evil is unexplained, so in that regard he resembles the villains in the tragedies. He slanders Hero and breaks up her marriage to Claudio. Iachimo is more fully developed as an Italianate villain, whose cleverness overcomes the innocent Posthumus in his ill-fated bet on Imogen's virtue. He resembles Iago not only in name but also in subtlety. Lucio is hardly a villain at all, but he is a satirical malcontent who vilifies the

Duke and everyone he comes in contact with. But there is an underlying idea that he sometimes speaks the bitter truth, like Thersites in *Troilus and Cressida* and Apemantus in *Timon of Athens*. The fact that the calumniators are all figures in Shakespeare's comedies somewhat mollifies their evil intents, which tend to disappear by the time of the happy ending.

Tyrants resemble villains in many ways, especially in their reliance on strong will. King Richard III and Macbeth are tyrants whom we have spoken about earlier. Another example is Julius Caesar, who speaks in the vaunting language of Shakespeare's villains; his death brings on a bloody civil war. In the first part of *The Winter's Tale*, Leontes's jealous rage brings about the deaths of his son Mamillius and his counselor Antigonus, as well as the supposed deaths of Hermione and her daughter. But the play is a tragicomedy, and his rage ends as suddenly as it began. In *As You Like It*, Duke Frederick has usurped the kingdom from his brother, Duke Senior. Oliver parallels the Duke in his oppression of his younger brother, Orlando. Both Duke Frederick and Oliver talk of killing their enemies, but in the comic world of the play, this never happens.

Note

1. From Maurice Charney, *Shakespeare's Villains* (Lanham, MD: Farleigh Dickinson University Press, 2011), xi–xix. The chapter has been lightly edited for style for the purposes of the present publication.

CHAPTER 11

Shakespeare's Supervillain: Coriolanus

JEROLD J. ABRAMS

> If [. . .] there be some one person, or more than one, although not enough to
> make up the full complement of a state, whose excellence is so pre-eminent
> that the excellence or the political capacity of all the rest admit of no compar-
> ison with his or theirs, he or they can be no longer regarded as part of a state;
> for justice will not be done to the superior, if he is reckoned only as the equal
> of those who are so far inferior to him in excellence and in political capacity.
> Such a man may truly be deemed a God among men.
>
> ARISTOTLE, *POLITICS*, III.13

CAIUS MARTIUS CORIOLANUS

Shakespeare in *The Tragedy of Coriolanus* (1607) presents one of the most
powerful supervillains in literature. The Roman soldier Caius Martius is the
son of the ambitious and war-loving Volumnia and (apparently) Mars himself,
the god of war, for whom Martius is named and from whom he derives his
superhuman powers. Martius establishes these powers in the battle of Corioles,
where he stands as one man against an entire army of Volsces and emerges victorious, earning himself the surname "Coriolanus." The Senate elects the hero
of Rome as their new consul, but Coriolanus's soaring pride and open hatred
for the citizenry also establish him as the enemy of Rome, a potential tyrant
who must be exiled. In exile, the vengeful Coriolanus joins with the enemy
Volsces in Antium and promises to burn all of Rome to the ground, causing
harm even to his own family.

Of all of Shakespeare's plays, *Coriolanus* remains perhaps the least loved—for
its graphic violence and pouring blood, its disturbing Sophoclean romance
between mother and son, and its unsympathetic and monstrous central
character. But despite the unpopularity of Shakespeare's supervillain—who

metamorphoses from man into dragon and back into man again, and dies tragically in the end—Coriolanus survives within the cultural imagination and metamorphoses yet again, to become the most popular superhero of all time: Jerry Siegel and Joe Shuster's Superman. Both Coriolanus and Superman walk among humanity as otherworldly beings, seemingly unbreakable "men of steel," each with superhuman strength, speed, olfaction, voice, vision, and even flight—each the equal of a planet, each with one mortal weakness.

MARTIUS AS ENEMY AND DEFENDER OF ROME

At the beginning of *Coriolanus*, the starving people of Rome organize to assassinate Martius:

> FIRST CITIZEN. First, you know Caius Martius is chief enemy to the people.
> ALL. We know't, we know't.
> FIRST CITIZEN. Let us kill him and we'll have corn at our own price. (1.1.7–11)[1]

But Martius stands his ground, calls the armed rebels cowards, and threatens them with their very lives. Martius despises the people because they demand food for their families and safety from their enemies but refuse to fight in the wars, and now they seek to kill their greatest defender. If only the law allowed, declares Martius, he would happily hunt down these citizens and pitch them high on his lance like game animals to be cooked and eaten:

> MARTIUS. Would the nobility lay aside their ruth
> And let me use my sword, I'd make a quarry
> With thousands of these quartered slaves as high
> As I could pitch my lance. (1.1.194–97)

The rebels would kill Martius for corn, but Martius the cannibal would kill the quarry of rebels and eat them. As Stanley Cavell writes, "The idea of cannibalization runs throughout the play."[2] Standing face to face with Martius, hearing him roar, the once brave citizens scatter like rabbits.

In these early passages and throughout *Coriolanus*, Shakespeare synthesizes Aristotle's portraits of the *megalopsychos* (the "proud man" or the "great-souled man") from the *Nicomachean Ethics* (IV.3), the *Eudemian Ethics* (III.5), and the *Posterior Analytics* (II.13); the "god among men" (a superhuman being) from the *Politics* (I.2, III.13, III.17, VII.14); and the monstrous man of the *Politics* (I.2). Like the *megalopsychos*, Martius is a proud warrior who lives apart from and looks down upon society, and who openly voices his hatred of the citizenry for their cowardice and slavishness.[3] And like the god among men, whom Aristotle in the *Politics* (III.13) claims is a "lion," compared to the citizenry, who are "hares," Martius identifies himself as a "lion," and the people as "hares" (1.1.164–81).[4] Martius also identifies the greatest warrior of Antium, Tullus Aufidius, as a worthy adversary and fellow lion: "He is a lion / That I am proud to hunt" (1.1.232–33).

After the Roman citizens disperse, Martius must also leave to defend them in battle at Corioles. Rome has the advantage with information from spies that Aufidius is marching from Antium to join the Volsces of Corioles and then attack Rome. Originally, Aufidius had planned "[t]o take in many towns ere, almost, Rome / Should know we were afoot" (1.2.22–25). Instead, the Romans attack first, but the Volsces hold their city and even force the Romans to retreat. Martius, enraged at the rout, threatens to kill his own men if they do not follow him back into Corioles. The Romans know that the mission is suicide, so they do not follow but watch in near disbelief as Martius marches alone into Corioles to stand one man against an army. Then the gates close behind him. The scene recalls Aristotle's portrait of the proud man, in the *Nicomachean Ethics* (IV.3), who will march into the greatest dangers for the greatest honors and would never fly from battle; and Aristotle's stunning image of the battle rout, in the *Posterior Analytics* (II.19), and the supreme soldier who stands alone, unflinchingly, to face an entire army.

The Roman general Titus Lartius arrives at the scene and asks the whereabouts of Martius.

> LARTIUS. What is become of Martius?
> ALL. Slain, sir, doubtless.
> FIRST SOLDIER. Following the fliers at the very heels,
> With them he enters, who upon the sudden
> Clapped-to their gates. He is himself alone
> To answer all the city. (1.5.21–24)

The Romans know that Martius must be dead. But then the gates reopen and Martius reemerges, soaked in Volscian blood. Before the battle, the Roman army knew that Martius was their greatest soldier, but now they know he is a god. As Harold Bloom writes in *Shakespeare: The Invention of the Human*, "Coriolanus … has as its protagonist a battering ram of a soldier, literally a one-man army, the greatest killing machine in all of Shakespeare."[5]

Following the initial battle, Martius is wounded and should be exhausted if not near death. But once Aufidius finally appears in view, somehow Martius seems newly energized and marches out to meet him in combat. In the battle of lions, Martius is still superior, but the Volsces tear Aufidius away while the

Romans take the city. For conquering Corioles alone, Cominius (the consul of Rome and Martius's best friend) renames Caius Martius "Coriolanus."

CORIOLANUS RETURNS TO ROME

Aristotle in the *Politics* (III.13) claims that the god among men cannot be given laws because he is a law unto himself and therefore cannot be a member of the state. He must be assassinated or exiled, or crowned absolute monarch (Aristotle's favored solution).[6] These three solutions appear by turns throughout Shakespeare's play, beginning with an early assassination attempt, followed by the possibility of rule in Rome, followed by exile from Rome for potential tyranny, followed by rule over the Volscian army as a god, and finally assassination in Antium for treason.

Upon his triumphant return from Corioles, Coriolanus marches through the streets of Rome to flowing colors and blaring trumpets. The same citizenry who once hated him and even sought to assassinate him now worship him as a god. Two tribunes, Brutus and Sicinius, who represent the people in the Senate, also behold the scene. Brutus, in particular, suspects Coriolanus to be inhabited by a god (clearly Mars).

> BRUTUS. Such a pother
> As if that whatsoever god who leads him
> Were slily crept into his human powers
> And gave him graceful posture. (2.1.214–17)

Beholding the new god of Rome, Brutus and Sicinius know that the Senate will elect Coriolanus consul and that Coriolanus will become a tyrant. But full transition of power requires both approval by the Senate and approval by the people. So Brutus and Sicinius fix their sights on the people, while Cominius makes his case in the Senate for the new consul.

In his speech to the Senate, Cominius recounts the actions of Coriolanus at Corioles, and (like Brutus) describes Coriolanus as inhabited and "doubled" (2.2.114) by a foreign spirit (again, Mars), rendering the man a god.

> COMINIUS. His sword, death's stamp,
> Where it did mark, it took. From face to foot
> He was a thing of blood, whose every motion
> Was timed with dying cries. Alone he entered
> The mortal gate of th'city, which he painted
> With shunless destiny, aidless came off,

And with a sudden reinforcement struck
Corioles like a planet. Now all's his. (2.2.105–12)

Cominius's phrase "sudden reinforcement" may suggest reinforcement of troops. But Cominius claims that Coriolanus entered "alone," and "aidless" conquered Corioles. The First Soldier earlier also claimed, "He is himself alone / To answer all the city." In fact, "sudden reinforcement" refers to a more spectacular version of what Brutus correctly suspects of Coriolanus: a god "slily crept into his human powers." Mars inhabited and animated Coriolanus, enabling him to strike the Volsces like the planet of the same name. What Brutus observed in Rome was simply the afterglow emanating from Coriolanus, following the superhuman surge of power in Corioles.

Like the *megalopsychos*, in Aristotle's analysis in the *Nicomachean Ethics* (IV.3), who will not stand to hear his praise, Coriolanus refuses to hear Cominius's speech and leaves the Senate hall while the nobility elect him consul. Coriolanus is also too proud to ask the people for their voice, which he must do if he is to become consul. In point of fact, however, Coriolanus never really wanted to be consul, and he despises the world of politics almost as much as he loves the world of battle. In battle, Mars inhabits Coriolanus and makes him a god; in politics, his mother Volumnia inhabits him and makes him her instrument. Volumnia wishes her son to be consul, and he worships his mother as a goddess, as much as he worships Mars, so Coriolanus submits to her (to the extent he can), and stands among the people and feigns humility. But Coriolanus cannot contain himself as he speaks with searing irony and all but open disgust for the people. As Aristotle writes of the proud man in *Nicomachean Ethics* (IV.3), "he is free of speech because he is contemptuous, and he is given to telling the truth, except when he speaks in irony to the vulgar."[7]

At first, the unsophisticated citizenry fail to hear the irony and grant their support to Coriolanus. But upon his departure, the tribunes inform the people about the not-so-subtle hatred and mockery in Coriolanus's false speech of request. The people then retract their support and demand the exile of Coriolanus for tyranny. Upon hearing the news of his failure, Volumnia demands that Coriolanus return to the people, kneel and beg forgiveness, and ask once again for their voice, which, of course, he cannot convincingly do. Nevertheless, he returns to the people, resolved to succeed, but Brutus and Sicinius meet Coriolanus with charges of treason, at which he explodes (as they knew he would).

CORIOLANUS. You common cry of curs, whose breath I hate
As reek o'th' rotten fens, whose loves I prize
As the dead carcasses of unburied men
That do corrupt my air: I banish you! (3.3.121–24)

The insult may appear to be hyperbole or metaphor, but after several declarations about the horrific stench of Rome, and given his superhuman nature, Coriolanus would appear to possess a superhuman power of olfaction. He simply cannot bear the smell of Rome, and if the people would banish him, then Coriolanus, as the equal of a state, will banish all of Rome and seek better air elsewhere.

So Coriolanus says goodbye to his family and leaves Rome as "a lonely dragon" (4.1.31). But instead of living like a dragon in a cave, he travels to Antium to join Aufidius with the promise that together they will burn Rome to the ground. Aufidius happily accepts his new friend and ally, while the Volscian soldiers worship Coriolanus as a god, apparently the very son of Mars: "Why, he is so made on here within / as if he were son and heir to Mars" (4.5.196–97).

METAMORPHOSIS FROM MAN INTO DRAGON

Rome knows that it is no match for the two greatest warriors in the world marching on a starving and defenseless city. So Cominius journeys to the camp of the Volsces to beg for mercy from his once closest friend. But instead of a friend, Cominius finds Coriolanus to be a cold and silent monster, strangely distant, as if his mind were elsewhere, as if he barely saw the consul of Rome kneeling before him, as if a different mind (the mind of Mars) had taken over. Cominius returns to Rome and speaks with Coriolanus's friend Menenius, who still struggles to grasp the situation:

> MENENIUS. If Martius should be joined wi'th' Volscians—
> COMINIUS. If? He is their god. He leads them like a thing
> Made by some other deity than nature,
> That shapes man better, and they follow him
> Against us brats with no less confidence
> Than boys pursing summer butterflies,
> Or butchers killing flies. (4.6.93–99)

In the *Politics* I.2 (a passage often connected with *Coriolanus*), Aristotle sets the demigod beyond the perimeter of the state: "But he who is unable to live in society, or who has no need because he is sufficient for himself, must be either a beast or a god: he is no part of a state."[8] Coriolanus, who can be no member of Rome, actually appears to be both a beast and a god. Beyond Rome, and fighting in Corioles, Coriolanus is a god of war and a cannibalistic beast. Once returned to Rome, he is still a god but appears to be more human. Here, he is the son of Volumnia, the husband of Virgilia, the father of Young Martius, a patrician of

Rome, and potentially the consul of Rome. But once cast into the wilderness, all that made Coriolanus a man steadily disappears: namely, the family, the state, and even language itself, as Aristotle establishes these species-defining traits of humanity, in *Politics* (I.2).

Now the fatherly Menenius journeys to the camp of the Volsces to beg for mercy, but he also fails and returns to recount an even more terrifying scene of Coriolanus:

> SICINIUS. Is't possible that so short a time can alter the
> condition of a man?
> MENENIUS. There is difference between a grub and a
> butterfly, yet your butterfly was a grub. This Martius is
> grown from man to dragon. He has wings, he's more
> than a creeping thing. (5.4.9–14)

The language of metamorphosis may appear to be metaphorical, but the early scene of Coriolanus inhabited by Mars and conquering Corioles alone sets the stage for an actual transformation of Coriolanus the "grub" into Coriolanus the "dragon." Shakespeare's continuous imagery of grubs, metamorphosis, butterflies, and moths can be puzzling in a tragedy about an Aristotelian great-souled man. But the concept of the *megalopsychos* actually contains this very imagery. Again, the word *megalopsychos* may be translated as "great-souled man," because *megalo* means "great" (or "large"), and *psyche* means "soul." But *psyche* may also be translated as "butterfly," and Aristotle himself uses this same term in *History of Animals* (V.19), in his study of the metamorphosis of the grub into the butterfly. Synthesizing the two figures of the great-souled man and the metamorphosing butterfly, Coriolanus appears in the imagination as a gigantic caterpillar eating Volsces in the battle of Corioles, and then by nature detaching into a chrysalis state among the Volsces of Antium, to digest himself and complete his metamorphosis into a gigantic butterfly-like dragon:

> MENENIUS. When he walks, he
> moves like an engine, and the ground shrinks before
> his treading. He is able to pierce a corslet with his eye,
> talks like a knell, and his hum is a battery. He sits in
> his state as a thing made for Alexander. What he bids
> be done is finished with his bidding. He wants nothing
> of a god but eternity and a heaven to throne in. (5.4.18–24)

The dragon terrifies the very ground with his walking. His blazing eyes shoot streams of fire that pierce enemy corslets and kill men at a glance. His low hum, for he disdains to speak, sounds like thousands of horses pounding the ground in war. Coriolanus is the equivalent of an army even when he hums in hatred for those he used to love and who love him still.

But Coriolanus has one mortal weakness against which he is defenseless. Volumnia, Virgilia, Young Martius, and their friend Valeria enter the camp. His mother bows before Coriolanus, shocking him through and through, because he worships her as a goddess: "My mother bows, / As if Olympus to a molehill should / In supplication nod" (5.3.29–31). Volumnia praises her son as a god, but begs him and commands him to grant peace to Rome and write his name into history as the hero who sealed peace with Antium rather than the traitor who murdered his family. Coriolanus is no match for his mother, and Volumnia with language alone quickly transforms the quiet dragon back into a little boy, her little boy, reducing the boy to tears in front of Aufidius and the Volsces. Conquered and sobbing, Coriolanus cries out: "O Mother, mother!" (5.3.183). The scene is heartbreaking, because Coriolanus knows that his mother has sealed his death at the hands of Aufidius for the betrayal of Antium.

After Coriolanus signs peace with Rome, he returns to Antium offering the spoils of battle and honor in peace. But Aufidius declares the Roman a traitor, a mere "boy of tears," and commands his men to kill Coriolanus, who quickly seizes back command and gives the order himself and declares victory in fame.

> CORIOLANUS. Cut me to pieces, Volsces. Men and lads,
> Stain all your edges on me. "Boy"! False hound,
> If you have writ your annals true, 'tis there
> That, like an eagle in a dovecote, I
> Fluttered your Volscians in Corioles.
> Alone I did it. "Boy"! (5.6.112–17)

Coriolanus may not have conquered Rome, but his name will be written into the annals of Antium and Rome for securing peace and conquering Corioles "like an eagle in a dovecote," while Aufidius will know fame only for ambushing a god, ignobly. So Volumnia has ensured her son's victory over Aufidius after all.

CORIOLANUS AND SUPERMAN

T. S. Eliot, in his essay on *Hamlet*, controversially dismissed Shakespeare's most popular play as "most certainly an artistic failure," because of Hamlet's wild madness and unbridled disgust for his mother, far in excess of the facts of the play. In that same essay, Eliot also praised Shakespeare's least popular play, *Coriolanus*, as his greatest achievement for its brilliant plot and powerfully tragic emotion: "*Coriolanus* may be not as 'interesting' as *Hamlet*, but it is, with *Antony and Cleopatra*, Shakespeare's most assured artistic success."[9] But while *Coriolanus* remains Shakespeare's least popular play, the character of Coriolanus transforms within what Eliot in "Tradition and Individual Talent" calls "the mind of Europe" (the literary tradition of Europe and America) to become the most popular superhero of all time: Superman.[10]

Of course, differences abound between Coriolanus and Superman. Coriolanus is a tragic hero-villain who loves war and hates peace—and hates his own people—while Superman is an epic hero who loves peace and loves America, and who fights evil for all humanity. But a fundamental identity of character underlies the differences between these two Aristotelian gods among men. Both Coriolanus and Superman possess superhuman powers of voice, olfaction, speed, strength, flight, fighting skill, and eyes that shoot beams of fire. Coriolanus draws his superhuman powers from Mars, while Superman draws his from the sun, making each an extension and conduit of greater and even cosmic powers. Coriolanus is the equal of an entire army, and even a planet (as he "struck / Corioles like a planet"), while Superman is the equal of the earth. But because he is the equal of an army, Coriolanus cannot be a full member of Rome (or Antium), any more than Superman can be a full member of America. So Coriolanus suffers exile from Rome and must disguise himself in Antium as a common man, before joining Aufidius, while Superman, who lives a dual life, disguises himself in Metropolis as Clark Kent. But even after joining the more warlike Volsces, Coriolanus remains detached and soon enters a silent and cocoon-like condition for metamorphosis, while Superman periodically retreats to his Fortress of Solitude to gather his powers.

But for all his powers, Coriolanus is helpless against his mother, just as Superman is helpless against kryptonite. When Coriolanus's origins return to him from Rome in the form of his family, he loses all his powers, and when Superman's origins return to him from his home planet of Krypton, in the form of kryptonite, he also loses all his powers. Superman is "the Man of Steel," but this steel softens in the presence of kryptonite, just as Coriolanus, the original man of steel, softens in the presence of his family. Coriolanus actually identifies himself as a man made of steel twice in the play: once before, and once after, the fight with Aufidius:

MARTIUS. O, me alone! Make you a sword of me? (1.8.77)

Coriolanus may appear to ask his men to make him into a sword, but he never "asks" his men to do anything. He commands them, always, and thinks them cowards anyway. In fact, in this line Coriolanus is praying to Mars to be made into a sword and to be wielded by Mars against Aufidius. Following the fight,

Cominius offers Coriolanus all the spoils of war, but Coriolanus refuses every-thing except his new name, and declares his hatred for all who seize on spoils, and all who praise and flatter themselves in victory (like his men). Praise and flattery and smooth words are symptoms of the sickly political culture of Rome, and the true warrior must be on his guard against them as much as against any enemy. When men of steel become men of silk, declares Coriolanus, then men are lost:

> MARTIUS. When steel grows soft as the parasite's silk,
> Let him be made an ovator for th' wars! (1.10.45–46)

But Martius himself, this man of steel, soon becomes soft like a parasite's silk, mastered by the flattering and commanding words of his mother. Solving the riddle of his mind, Volumnia unravels Coriolanus's terrible cocoon, halting the metamorphosis of the Sphinx-dragon, destroying the dragon, and leaving little but the parasite's silk, with which she (as a seamstress in the play) will stitch together the fabrics of Rome and Antium. Aristotle, in *History of Animals* (V.19), in his discussion of grubs and butterflies, identifies one "particular large grub," which is valuable for its silk: "A class of women unwind and reel off the cocoons of these creatures, and afterwards weave a fabric."[11] In *Coriolanus* 1.3, Volumnia and Virgilia sew while they discuss with Valeria war, bravery, chil-dren, butterflies, and sewing, seemingly all as one thing. Now, in *Coriolanus* 5.3, at the opposite end of the play, the Aristotelian "class of women" arrives in the camp of the Volsces to "unwind and reel off" Coriolanus's cocoon.

In the final scene, before killing Coriolanus, Aufidius declares the once man of steel nothing more than a "twist of rotten silk," with the implication that Coriolanus failed to complete his metamorphosis, because his mother har-vested his silk.

> AUFIDIUS. Breaking his oath and resolution like
> A twist of rotten silk, never admitting
> Counsel o'th' war. (5.6.97–99)

From beginning to end, Coriolanus metamorphoses from man into dragon, and then back into man again, and from man of steel into man of silk, finally to be "cut to pieces" by Aufidius and his men. But the metamorphosing char-acter of Coriolanus survives within the mind of Europe and metamorphoses once again, this time from man of silk back into man of steel, from the sev-enteenth century to the twentieth century—to become Superman, "the Man of Steel," caped and costumed not in armor and sword but (seemingly) in red and blue silk. With this final metamorphosis, the least popular Shakespearean hero-villain transforms into the most popular superhero of all time, so that Shakespeare speaks still within a new, but no less visually brilliant, and deeply philosophical form of literature, and once again flutters the dovecote of the collective imagination.

Notes

1. William Shakespeare, *Coriolanus*, ed. R. B. Parker (New York: Oxford University Press, 2008), 159. References to this edition appear within the text.

2. Stanley Cavell, "'Who Does the Wolf Love?' Reading *Coriolanus*," *Representations*, no. 3 (Summer 1983): 6.

3. Aristotle, *Nicomachean Ethics* (IV.3), in *The Complete Works of Aristotle*, ed. Jonathan Barnes, trans. Benjamin Jowett (Princeton, NJ: Princeton University Press, 1984), vol. 2, 1124b26–31, 1775. See also F. N. Lees, "*Coriolanus*, Aristotle, and Bacon," *Review of English Studies* 1, no. 2 (April 1950): 114–25; and Carson Holloway, "Shakespeare's *Coriolanus* and Aristotle's Great-Souled Man," *Review of Politics* 69, no. 3 (Summer 2007): 353–74.

4. Aristotle, *Politics* (III.13), in *The Complete Works of Aristotle*, ed. Jonathan Barnes, trans. Benjamin Jowett (Princeton, NJ: Princeton University Press, 1984), vol. 2, 1284a1–11, 2037.

5. Harold Bloom, *Shakespeare: The Invention of the Human* (New York: Riverhead Books, 1998), 577.

6. Aristotle, *Politics* (III.13), 1284a17–1284b34, 2038–39.

7. Aristotle, *Nicomachean Ethics* (IV.3), 1124b29–31, 1775.

8. Aristotle, *Politics* (I.2), 1253a29–30, 1988. See also Lees, "*Coriolanus*, Aristotle, and Bacon"; Holloway, "Shakespeare's *Coriolanus*"; R. B. Parker, introduction to *Coriolanus*, ed. R. B. Parker (New York: Oxford University Press, 2008), 8, 57; and Jonathan Crewe, introduction to *Coriolanus*, ed. Jonathan Crewe (New York: Penguin, 1999), xl–xli.

9. T. S. Eliot, "Hamlet," in *Selected Prose of T. S. Eliot*, ed. Frank Kermode (New York: Harcourt Brace Jovanovich, 1975), 47.

10. T. S. Eliot, "Tradition and Individual Talent," in *Selected Prose of T. S. Eliot*, ed. Frank Kermode (New York: Harcourt Brace Jovanovich, 1975), 39.

11. Aristotle, *History of Animals* (V.19), in *The Complete Works of Aristotle*, ed. Jonathan Barnes, trans. d'A. W. Thompson (Princeton, NJ: Princeton University Press, 1984), vol. 1, 551b10–17, 870.

CHAPTER 12

Milton's Satan[1]

JOHN CAREY

THE CONTROVERSY ABOUT MILTON'S SATAN PROVIDES AN OPPORTUNITY TO
inspect the relationship between a literary text and critical reaction to it. This
is instructive because it shows how literature works (or has worked), and how
it should not be expected to work.

A word, first, about the generation of Milton's Satan. There is very little in
the Bible about Satan. In *Christian Doctrine*, Milton collects all the available
biblical evidence in a few sentences. It amounts to little more than that Satan is
the author of all evil and has various titles.[2] As Frank Kastor has shown, it was
not until about AD 200 that official Judaism began to absorb popular concepts
of Satan.[3] From then on, appearances of Satan in literature, subliterature, and
theology multiplied. Scores of literary Satans evolved, and some of them—
notably those created by Du Bartas, Andreini, Grotius, and Vondel—possibly
influenced Milton. However, no convincing single source for Milton's Satan
has been found.

The need to create a Satan figure arises from a Manichaean view of the
moral universe. Within this mentality, as Jung has pointed out,[4] the evolution
of God as a *summum bonum* necessitates the evolution of an *infimum malum* to
account for the presence of evil in the world. It was to combat Manichaeanism
that the early church launched its doctrine that evil had no real being but was
merely *privatio boni* (privation of good).

This sophistical tenet had no appeal for Milton. He presents evil as real
and traceable to a single Evil One. The wish to isolate evil in this way argues a
particular mental configuration that seems to be associated with the belief that,
once isolated, evil may become containable or punishable. Hence has arisen the
urge to locate evil in a single kind of being, which has borne fruit throughout
history in pogrom, ghetto, and racial massacre. In Freudian terms it may be
identified as an effort of the severe and critical superego, which subjugates the
recalcitrant id. From a literary viewpoint, the isolating effort of the purifying

and punitive will is the opposite of the mentality we think of as Shakespearean, which accepts the fact that evil is inextricably enmeshed in collective human experience.

Milton's effort to encapsulate evil in Satan was not successful. That is, those readers who have left their reactions on record have seldom been able to regard Satan as a depiction of pure evil, and some of the most distinguished have claimed that he is superior in character to Milton's God. It is sometimes supposed that critical support for Satan began with the romantics, but this is not so. Roger Sharrock has shown that the notion of Satan as the true hero of Milton's epic goes back to Dryden and was a commonplace of eighteenth-century literary opinion in both France and England.[5] Arthur E. Barker finds that eighteenth-century admirers of the sublime praised Satan's "high superior nature," and so came into conflict with Addison and Johnson, who declared Satan's speeches "big with absurdity."[6] Among romantic critics, Blake, Byron, Shelley, and Hazlitt championed Satan, whereas Coleridge identified him with Napoleonic pride and sensual indulgence.[7] These critics certainly intensified and politicized the controversy, but they did not start it—nor, of course, did they finish it. In the twentieth century, anti-Satanists such as Charles Williams, C. S. Lewis, Sydney Musgrove, and Stanley Fish have been opposed by A. J. A. Waldock, Elmer Edgar Stoll, G. Rostrevor Hamilton, William Empson, and others.[8]

The correct critical reaction to this dispute is not to imagine that it can be settled—that either Satanists or anti-Satanists can be shown to be "right." For what would that mean but ignoring what half the critics of the poem have felt about it—ignoring, that is, half the evidence? A more reasonable reaction is to recognize that the poem is insolubly ambivalent insofar as the reading of Satan's "character" is concerned, and that this ambivalence is a precondition of the poem's success—a major factor in the attention it has aroused. Other texts generally recognized as "great" literature manifest similar ambivalence in their central characters. The critics who strive to prove that Shakespeare "really meant" Shylock to be essentially bad, or essentially good, would, supposing either side could prevail, destroy much of the play's power and interest. A similar ambivalence characterizes Isabella, Prospero, Othello, Lear, Falstaff, and so on. Within liberal bourgeois culture, disputability is generally advantageous to a text since it validates individual reinterpretation and so functions, from the consumer viewpoint, as an anti-obsolescence device.

To recognize that the character of Satan is essentially ambivalent is not to say that we must agree with everything the Satanists or the anti-Satanists propose. Both sets of critics misrepresent or overstate in their bid to strengthen their case. Among anti-Satanists there is a tendency to jeer at Satan and become sarcastic at his expense, as if he really existed. Williams and Lewis both manifest this. Pro-Satanists are likewise seduced into anger and indiscretion—as when Stoll, replying to Lewis, deplores the fact that criticism is nowadays "complicated by scholarship."[9] The power to entangle and excite readers is an observable feature of the Satan figure.

Satanist critics generally emphasize Satan's courage, anti-Satanists his selfishness or folly. These simplified versions of Satan ignore or evade the evidence within the poem that fails to square with them. If we wish to find a single term for the character attribute that Satan's ambivalent presentation, taken as a whole, generates, then the most suitable term seems to be "depth." Depth in a fictional character depends on a degree of ignorance being sustained in the reader. The illusion must be created that the character has levels hidden from us, the observers. By comparison with Satan, the other characters in *Paradise Lost*—Adam, Eve, even God—exist simply and transparently at the level of the words they speak. Satan does not—partly because his habitual mode is dissimulation, partly because, unlike the other characters, he exists, or has existed, within the historical span the poem covers, in a number of different modes.

These different modes are partly inherent in the biblical and postbiblical Satan material. The traditional Satan story, as it eventually took shape, involves Satan in three separate roles—an archangel, before and during the war in heaven; a Prince of Devils in the council in hell; and a serpent-tempter in the garden. Satan is thus not a single concept but a trimorph. In the earliest records of the Satan myth, the pseudepigrapha and apocrypha of the Old Testament, the three roles were, as Kastor notes, performed by three different figures.[10] The ambivalence of Milton's Satan stems partly from his trimorphic conception; pro-Satanists tend to emphasize his first two roles, anti-Satanists his third.

Further, Milton has compounded the ambivalence by making the division between the roles uncertain. Satan as archangel, before his fall, is never shown by Milton, but this stage of his existence is often alluded to, as is the fact that some of his archangelical powers remain, though we cannot be quite sure which. Hence Satan, as fictional character, gains a hidden dimension and a "past." Also, Satan as Prince of Devils is still present within Satan-as-Tempter, as is shown when Ithuriel touches the toad with his spear and Satan springs up "in his own shape" (*PL* 4.819). This means that Satan's bestial disguises need not be regarded as debasement or degradation, as some critics have viewed them, since he retains his inner consciousness despite his disguises—or seems to. This qualification has to be added, for the precise state of Satan's consciousness at various points in the action is problematic (for example, at the point where, in the debate with Abdiel, he denies that he and the other angels were created by God; see below). The reader cannot solve these problems, because no textual evidence is available that will provide access to Satan's "true" state of mind. By this device of narrative occlusion, Satan gains depth, whereas with the other characters no such interesting possibility of discrepancy opens up between inner state and outward profession or appearance.

The one part of the poem where access is provided to the "true" Satan is his soliloquy at the start of book 4 (32–113). The impression of depth is maintained throughout this soliloquy because, although Satan's mind is no longer hidden, his inner debate and self-criticism reveal him as a creature of dynamic tensions, such as the other characters of the poem notably lack. This is partly because the soliloquy is a generic transplant. Edward Phillips, Milton's nephew, tells us that it was written as part of a drama, not an epic, at a time when Milton intended to write a tragedy on the Fall. The soliloquy has the immediacy of drama, not the distance of epic. In it, Satan concedes his own criminality, and his own responsibility for his fall. He vacillates between remorse and defiance. He confesses that his rebellion was completely unjustifiable, that he had the same "free will and power to stand" as all God's creatures, and that he therefore has nothing to accuse but "heaven's free love dealt equally to all." Since heaven's love means his own damnation, he curses it ("Be then his love accursed"), but then, rationally, he turns his curse against himself ("Nay, cursed be thou"). Satan could be called evil at this point in the poem only in some attenuated sense, since he speaks the truth and curses himself as God curses him. He and God are in accord. The function of the speech within the poem's argument is to justify God; even Satan, we are meant to see, admits that God was right. But paradoxically this admission redeems Satan in the reader's eyes, so that the response elicited is, as usual with Satan, ambivalent.

As part of his "official" task of exculpating God in the soliloquy, Satan explains that even if he could repent and get back to heaven "by act of grace," it would do him no good, since, once back there, he would grow proud again ("how soon / Would highth recall high thoughts"), and this would lead to a "worse relapse" and "heavier fall." The intent of this argument, within the poem's apparent didactic strategy, is to make it seem merciful of God not to have mercy on Satan and allow him back. However, ambivalence once more surrounds the issue. For it is reasonable for the reader to ask why Satan should not learn from his fall, and be forgiven without any risk of his falling again. Why should a hypothetical but inevitable recurrence of his fall be built into his nature as part of the poem's case? The question is important, since whether Satan might ultimately be forgiven was a doctrinal issue; one church father, Origen, had opined that he would, although Milton disagreed.[11] C. A. Patrides argues that at this juncture in the poem the dramatic context demands that Satan's redemption should be entertained at least as a possibility,[12] and it is of course true (within Christian doctrine) that Satan's redemption could not be regarded as impossible for God, since this would infringe on God's omnipotence.

To retrieve the situation, Milton has to make Satan's irredeemability his own fault, and the soliloquy effects this. He emerges as a creature trapped within his own inevitably and repeatedly fallprone nature. But this means, of course, that he is trapped within Milton's fiction, of which that "nature" is a part. The fiction leads him toward a doom from which he sees a way of escaping ("But say I could repent"). Hence Satan appears to possess, from the reader's viewpoint, an autonomy that is another attribute of fictional "depth." The illusion is created that he is independent of the fiction that contains him, and unfairly manipulated by that fiction.

The most obvious sense in which Satan is trapped within an alien fiction is that the fiction requires him, though an archangelically rational creature, to take up arms against a God who is axiomatically omnipotent. Much has been made of this by anti-Satanist critics, who take Satan's hostility to Almighty power as a sign of folly. The pro-Satan critics, on the other hand, produce it as evidence of his supreme courage, since even his adversary's omnipotence does not daunt him. Neither response can, of course, be pronounced "right"; the potential of Satan to elicit both is simply a product of his habitual ambivalence. Folly and courage are, however, strictly inadequate terms for describing the behavior of Satan and the rebel angels in relation to God's omnipotence, since these terms relate to human behavior, and the fiction places Satan and his followers in a situation for which we can find no precise human counterpart.

Comparison with Napoleon and other earthly conquerors (such as Coleridge suggests) is inaccurate, since Satan's situation is more curious than any such parallel would allow. The situation the devils are in is clearly enunciated by Belial during the council in Pandaemonium in book 2. Belial acknowledges that God is not only omnipotent, and therefore proof against any attack the devils can make, but also omniscient, so that he cannot be outwitted. Neither force nor guile, Belial concludes, can be effective against such an adversary. God "views all things at one view" and "sees and derides" the devils' council even while it is in progress. The devils are performing before God as their audience and are aware of his presence even as they discuss outwitting him. This means that their behavior is not just "foolish" or "courageous"; it has an inherent fictive improbability. In order to make their behavior credible, the reader must assume that the devils make an at least temporarily successful effort at self-deception or willed oblivion: that they forget, or pretend that they are ignorant of, the predicament Belial has described. Otherwise it is not evident how they could keep up the momentum of their action.

Milton indicates that this is how he requires us to read the processes of diabolic intelligence by the way he writes about Satan at the start of book 4. As Satan flies up from hell to earth, we are told that he does not rejoice in his speed. "Horror and doubt distract" his thoughts when he remembers that "of worse deeds worse sufferings must ensue." But if Satan knows that his mission is bound to make things worse for him, why, we may ask, does he undertake it? The answer, strictly, is that he cannot escape the terms of the fiction he finds himself in. He is the victim of a breakdown of fictional logic inherent in the terms of the myth Milton is transcribing. For he is cast in a poem with an axiomatically omniscient and omnipotent God, and this means that every hostile move he makes must be self-defeating. Yet his fictional function is precisely to make hostile moves: he is the fiend, the enemy.

The unlikelihood of Satan's rebellion against God had worried biblical commentators. They were especially puzzled by Isaiah 14:14, where "Lucifer, son of the morning" is depicted as saying "I will ascend above the heights of the clouds; I will be like the most High." This text was generally taken as a reference to Satan, but it caused difficulties since it would have been irrational for Satan to aspire to be equal in power with God. As Stella Revard shows, both Anselm and Aquinas argued that Satan could not, despite the apparent meaning of the text, have wished directly for equality with God, for as a rational and perfect being he would have known this was impossible.[13] Partly because of these interpretative problems, Protestant theologians tended to deny that the Isaiah text referred to Satan at all. Calvin and Luther both read it as alluding to the King of Babylon.

Milton, however, could not evade the terms of the story by an exegetical maneuver of this sort. In the narrative he adopts, the omnipotence of God, which must have been evident to an archangelically intelligent Satan, coexists incongruously with a Satanic rebellion. Milton disguises this insuperable narrative difficulty partly by omitting any depiction of the unfallen Satan from his account. In this way, he sets aside the problem of showing perfect intelligence operating imperfectly. He also makes the story seem more likely by adapting the fallen Satan's psychology. Satan's states of awareness, we are given to understand, are murky and changeable. Thus his realization, at the start of book 4, that worse deeds will lead to worse sufferings, is presented as something he managed previously to forget: "Now conscience wakes despair / That slumbered" (4.23–24). Satan, then, manages genuinely to hope at times, although after these respites despair reasserts itself. The fallen Satan is, we gather, a creature of moods, apprehending reality through mists of self-deception and forgetfulness. This wavering, slumbering, deceptive state of consciousness is another factor that gives Satan fictional depth, concealing him from our full knowledge. It also lends credibility to his unlikely story, since the reader tends to assume that the fallen Satan's indecisiveness about God's omnipotence (perhaps, he sometimes thinks, God is only "Almighty styled" [9.137], not really Almighty) also characterized the unfallen Satan and led to his revolt. In fact, of course, the unfallen Satan could not, by definition, have been fallible in this way. But Milton's narrative strategy conceals the logical flaw.

The fallen Satan's ability to dismiss unattractive facts from his consciousness is a feature that complicates the interpretation of his argument with Abdiel about the creation of the angels in book 5 (835–64). In response to Abdiel's declaration that the angels were created by the Son, Satan insists that they were, on the contrary, "self-begot, self-raised," and that Abdiel's theory is a "strange point and new." When soliloquizing, however, in book 4 (42–44), he admits to himself that it was "heaven's matchless king" (meaning, presumably, God the Father not the Son) who created him. Some critics (Lewis, for example) have seen this later admission as proof that Satan was simply lying in the Abdiel episode. Others (such as Waldock and Empson) have interpreted it as a new perception by Satan, or a resurgence of something he has chosen to forget. We cannot adjudicate between these interpretations with any confidence, since either would be reconcilable with Satan's mental processes as the poem elsewhere shows them. It is certainly odd that the other angels present at the debate accept Satan's, not Abdiel's, version of the creation. Presumably this means either that they never had any intuitive knowledge of their creation by the Son, or that they have willfully suppressed or simply lost it. John Steadman suggests that Abdiel, like Adam, may have worked out by means of reasoning the fact that God created him.[14] But Abdiel would have intuitive, not discursive reason, so would not need to work things out. The crux remains insoluble. Satan may be lying, he may be deceiving himself, he may have genuinely lost touch with the truth. That he never knew the truth does not seem a probable interpretation, since it would contradict his archangelical knowledge (although, of course, archangels did not know everything, nor, even, did the Son, according to Milton in *Christian Doctrine*[15]—full knowledge was the Father's alone).

The depth and ambivalence Satan gains from this episode issue from an uncertainty of interpretation. The facts are not fully ascertainable. More often it is the moral evaluation of his actions that generates disagreement among readers. Three episodes have proved particularly divisive. The first occurs in book 1, when he weeps at the sight of his fallen followers and cannot speak for tears:

> Thrice he essayed, and thrice in spite of scorn,
> Tears such as angels weep, burst forth. (1.619–20)

Pro-Satanist critics interpret the tears as magnanimous compassion. But anti-Satanists point out that angels were not supposed, in orthodox theology, to weep, since tears were a sign of passion, which angels were not subject to. Alastair Fowler annotates the lines with a quotation from Andrew Marvell ("only humane Eyes can weep").[16] The tearlessness of angels certainly seems to be emphasized by Milton in book 11, where Michael shows Adam the effects that death and disease will have upon mankind in the future. Adam weeps, but

Michael remains composed and dry-eyed, and Milton remarks rather pointedly on the contrast between them. The future fate of mankind is a

> Sight so deform what heart of rock could long
> Dry-eyed behold? Adam could not, but wept,
> Though not of woman born; compassion quelled
> His best of man, and gave him up to tears. (11.494–97)

"Though not of woman born" echoes *Macbeth* (5.7), and, as Fowler notes, the echo is more than just a verbal reminiscence, for one of the chief themes of *Macbeth* is the evil that ensues from a drying up of compassion—the "milk of human kindness." This point does not, of course, redound to the credit of Michael or other tearless angels, and, though Fowler fails to note it, Milton's phrase "Tears such as angels weep" in the description of Satan weeping also has a Shakespearean original. In *Measure for Measure*, Isabella proclaims that

> man, proud man,
> Dress'd in a little brief authority,
> Most ignorant of what he's most assur'd,
> His glassy essence, like an angry ape,
> Plays such fantastic tricks before high heaven
> As makes the angels weep; who, with our spleens
> Would all themselves laugh mortal. (2.2.117–23)

This Shakespearean original might be taken (by a pro-Satan critic) as removing any culpable passion from Satan's weeping. Weeping, it seems, is what angels do in situations where men, being coarser and more splenetic, would laugh. Anti-Satan critics might point out, on the other hand, that the "proud man" in Isabella's speech is remarkably like Satan, an "angry ape" of God, so that if the echo is to be taken as more than a chance reminiscence, it would become anti-Satanic in its reverberations and would, indeed, highlight the ambivalent responses Satan's "tricks" evoke—laughter in some readers, tears in others. As usual, there is no deciding between these evaluations of Satan's action, which remains essentially disputable—although the Shakespearean echo, coming from such a context, probably enhances his depth for most readers. By weeping "tears such as angels weep," he seems more grief stricken than mere human weepers. A second instance of Satanic action—or reaction—that seems at first creditable, but that can be claimed as evidence by both Satanists and anti-Satanists, occurs when he sees Eve in Eden and is so enraptured by her beauty that he becomes momentarily good (9.460–79). He is deprived of his "fierce intent" as he watches her, "abstracted" from his own evil:

> and for the time remained
> Stupidly good, of enmity disarmed,
> Of guile, of hate, of envy, of revenge. (9.464–66)

But he snatches himself back from the brink of innocence, "recollects" his hatred, and "excites" himself to evil once more:

> Thoughts, whither have ye led me, with what sweet
> Compulsion thus transported to forget
> What hither brought us, hate, not love. (9.473–75)

The passage seems to indicate that Satan's natural tendency, when caught unawares, is to love. Beauty and delight are his natural element. Hatred is an effort of his will. This could be seen as making him either more, or less, sympathetic. Like his angelic tears, it shows his capacity for a role different from the one the fiction assigns him to. From the viewpoint of his function within the plot, the incident is extraneous. Milton did not need to include it to advance his narrative. It is a gratuitous piece of characterization, and seemingly favorable. On the other hand, since Satan chooses not to escape his diabolism, although he has the opportunity, he could be seen as the more damnable. The incident shows that he is not a destructive automaton but a creature who chooses to destroy the human race against the promptings of his better nature. Milton echoes, in the passage, both himself and Shakespeare. "Sweet compulsion" is from the vision of universal harmony described by the Genius in *Arcades* ("Such sweet compulsion doth in music lie ...," 68); and "whither have ye led me" echoes the ruined Antony after Actium ("O, whither hast thou led me, Egypt?"; *Antony and Cleopatra* 3.11.50). Both echoes can be seen as "lifting" Satan, setting him in the context of tragic love and the music of the spheres, which is what the Genius is listening to. But both echoes are also, by implication, critical of Satan, since Antony chooses to lose the world for love, whereas Satan does the opposite, and the music of the spheres signifies universal harmony, which Satan is about to destroy. As usual, he moves within a cloud of ambivalence.

A third prominent example of Satan's attaining depth through ambivalence occurs earlier in the poem's action than his "stupidly good" response to Eve, and is (if read as pro-Satanists read it) the most surprising and poignant of his utterances. When he first sets eyes on Adam and Eve in Eden, he is stricken with wonder at the human pair—not spirits, he perceives, yet "little inferior" to heavenly spirits—and feels, or says he feels, an inclination to love them. They are creatures

whom my thoughts pursue
With wonder, and could love, so lively shines
In them divine resemblance. (4.362–64)

Satan's reason for feeling that he could love Adam and Eve—that they look so like God—naturally surprises the reader, since we have been led to suppose it is God Satan hates. Though there is nothing here so clear as an echo, there seems to be a recollection of the incident in Marlowe's *Doctor Faustus* in which Mephistophilis, asked by Faustus how he comes to be out of hell, replies:

Why, this is hell, nor am I out of it.
Think'st thou that I, who saw the face of God,
And tasted the eternal joys of heaven,
Am not tormented with ten thousand hells,
In being deprived of everlasting bliss?

The similarity lies in the unexpected revelation of love or desire for God in a figure we believed to be wholly committed to the opposition. Not all critics are prepared to grant that Satan really feels any inclination to love at this point. Whereas pro-Satanists (Walter Raleigh, Stoll, Hamilton) take his response to "divine resemblance" to be sincere, anti-Satanists (Lewis, Musgrove) interpret his words as brutal irony. Since he is soliloquizing, irony is perhaps unlikely—but not impossible. As usual, we cannot take the simple step of declaring one reading correct. But we can see that Satan gains fictional depth from the dubiety surrounding the point, as well as from the possibility of his underlying love for God.

These three examples all help to make Satan seem inscrutable. So, too, does his imaginativeness. As a dissimulator, he displays imagination in ways that are unavailable to God or the other good characters. Unlike him, they do not depend on lies, so the constant imaginative effort by which Satan sustains himself is foreign to them. They remain, from the viewpoint of imagination, relatively undeveloped beings. It is no doubt true, in a doctrinal sense, that God "imagined" the universe, since he created it out of his mind. But he is not presented, in the poem, as an imaginative being. Satan is—as we note, for example, when the snake tells Eve how he found the forbidden fruit:

Till on a day roving the field, I chanced
A goodly tree far distant to behold
Loaden with fruit of fairest colors mixed,
Ruddy and gold: I nearer drew to gaze;
When from the boughs a savory odor blown,

> Grateful to appetite, more pleased my sense
> Than smell of sweetest fennel or the teats
> Of ewe or goat dropping with milk at even,
> Unsucked of lamb or kid, that tend their play.
> To satisfy the sharp desire I had
> Of tasting those fair apples, I resolved
> Not to defer; hunger and thirst at once,
> Powerful persuaders, quickened at the scent
> Of that alluring fruit, urged me so keen.
> About the mossy trunk I wound me soon,
> For high from ground the branches would require
> Thy utmost reach or Adam's: round the tree
> All other beasts that saw, with like desire
> Longing and envying stood, but could not reach.
> Amid the tree now got, where plenty hung
> Tempting so nigh, to pluck and eat my fill
> I spared not, for such pleasure till that hour
> At feed or fountain never had I found. (9.575–97)

This is all lies, of course. Satan does not like milk or apples; he never climbed a tree. But he has imagined himself into the snake's existence so vividly that we almost forget he is lying. He even takes the trouble to make the tree "mossy," imagining that would make it more comfortable for a snake to wind around. (Is this where Keats got his "mossed" apple trees in "To Autumn"?) Of course, being inside a snake may have enabled Satan to take over the snake's sensibility, which would aid his imagination. We cannot tell. Nor can we tell whether his rapt musing on unsucked teats and fair apples is prompted by the naked woman he is gazing at. (Some critics have suggested that "ewe" is a Freudian slip: "the teats / Of you.") Maybe. As usual, we cannot locate Satan's state of consciousness within a firm reading. But however we read him, his imaginativeness is impressive and allies him, of course, with the creator of the poem, Milton, who had to imagine it all.

Satan's imagination is crucial because it inaugurates the whole divergent history that is *Paradise Lost* and the story of the human race—a narrative divergent from God's original perfect creation, and a narrative that began when Sin, Satan's imagining, jumped out of his head. The episode with Sin and Death at the gate between Hell and Chaos (2.648–870) is one of the most puzzling in the poem, and the one that seems to carry us furthest into the half-light of Satan's subconscious. As he talks to Sin, she reveals a buried phase of his life, one that, even when she has recounted it, it seems he has no recollection of. He is, she tells him, her father, but also her mother. He went through birth pangs in heaven, and she sprang from an opening in the side of his head. She became his accomplice against God, but she was also his image, as the Son is the image of the Father. He had a child by her, Death, who, once born, pursued his mother and raped her. That rape begot the "yelling monsters" that now surround her.

We can recognize in all this a perverted rewriting of several of the poem's motifs. Adam is father and mother to Eve, since she was taken from his side, as Sin from Satan's head. He pursues her and unites sexually with her, as Death does Sin. In this murk of rape and incest and male birth pangs, the themes and actions of the poem swim about guiltily transformed. We have here, as it were, not just Satan's but the poem's subconscious. Its myths of origin are here released from narrative decorum and parade in spectral shapes. The theme of lethal eating (the deadly apple) finds its counterpart in this underworld sequence in cannibalism. Death wants to eat Sin, but she warns him that she would "prove a bitter morsel, and his bane" (2.808). What adds to the strangeness and profundity of the sequence is that it has not only perversion to offer but also wifely and (as nowhere else in the poem) motherly love, shown when Sin rushes between Satan and Death to prevent their fighting.

Of course, readers are at liberty to insist that the sequence is "just allegory" and that we should not bother with any of its deeper shades. However, even readers who take this line need to explain what it is an allegory of—what are the actual events that its various details correspond to? It does not take much thought to see that we are in no position to answer such a question. The status of the sequence in terms of the poem's "reality," and the level on which we are to read it, are not matters about which we can obtain any firm directives. This means that, in this strange episode as in much else, Satan slips from our knowledge. We can see that he is implicated in depths, but the nature of them eludes our understanding.

The emergence of Sin from Satan's head was Milton's way of dealing with the poem's (and Christianity's) most difficult question—how evil originated. The problem of how evil could have been created spontaneously from good exercised, as Revard points out, the minds of the church fathers,[17] and Manichaeanism grew from the belief that the evil factor, Satan, was created from a kingdom of darkness over which God had no authority. Christianity could not allow this solution, since it had an omnipotent God. But the church fathers who, like Cyril of Jerusalem, simply asserted that Satan became evil of his own free will, though created good, did not have to show it happening. Milton, too, found this impossible, and retreated into the cloudy region at hell's gate where Sin tells of events that took place somewhere other than in the poem's usual narrative mode, though we cannot tell where.

Finally, the relation of Satan to Milton's intentions (was Milton of the Devil's party? or not? or only subconsciously so?) has interested critics. Such questions are all clearly unanswerable, since we have no access to Milton's mind, let alone his subconscious, at the time of writing. That does not, of course, prevent speculation about them. We can, moreover, be sure that Satan was originally the product of Milton's psychology (he was certainly, that is, not the product of anyone else's psychology), and critics who oppose the psychological approach are usually participating in it without realizing they are doing so. Merritt Hughes, for instance, asserts that the interpretation of Satan must be cleared of all "modern psychologism" that makes him a reflection of irrational depths in Milton's nature. Milton created him, Hughes lays it down, "as an example of the self-deception and the deception of others which are incident to the surrender of reason to passion."[18] Hughes's interpretation is of course flatly intentionalist, since it assumes access to Milton's mind, and is therefore an instance of the "psychologism" he believes himself to be opposing.

Although originally the product of Milton's psychology, Satan, as he is read and interpreted, is also the product of the reader's psychology. *Paradise Lost*, like other texts, reads the reader, and Satan, as I have shown, divides readers into opposed camps. Most readers, probably, can feel sympathy with both the Satanists and the anti-Satanists. We feel that by suppressing a part of ourselves, we can disown and denounce Satan, but we also feel the power of that part of us that is having to be suppressed. This situation has encouraged critics to see the character of Satan as built over a dichotomy in Western—or human—consciousness. R. J. Zwi Werblowsky associates Satan with the drive toward science and rationalism in Western culture, and away from the female womb chaos (the Jungian *mater devorans*).[19] Maud Bodkin sees *Paradise Lost* as rendering in symbol the conflict between aspiration and a sense of one's own nothingness, basic to human experience.[20] Isabel MacCaffrey maintains that all arguments about where our sympathies lie in *Paradise Lost* are vain, since they lie both with the fallen and with the rigors of discipline necessary for our survival as reasonable beings.[21]

Freud's analysis of the modern psyche seems particularly applicable to Satan's disputable nature, as well as to the recognition that Satan is a "great" (that is, widely significant) creation. At the end of *Civilization and Its Discontents*, Freud speaks of the exorbitant development of the superego in modern culture, and particularly the ethical demands the superego makes on the individual. It requires the individual habitually to suppress his aggressiveness and his hunger for self-satisfaction:

> In the severity of its commands and prohibitions it troubles itself too little about the happiness of the ego. . . . It, too, does not trouble itself enough about the facts of the mental constitution of human beings. It issues a command and does not ask whether it is possible for people to obey it. On the

contrary, it assumes that a man's ego is psychologically capable of anything that is required of it, that his ego has unlimited mastery over his id. This is a mistake; and even in what are known as normal people the id cannot be controlled beyond certain limits. If more is demanded of a man, a revolt will be produced in him, or a neurosis.[22]

Freud goes on to argue that the unappeasable commands of the civilized cultural superego in modern man lead to whole civilizations, "possibly the whole of mankind," becoming neurotic. The controversy about Milton's Satan—what I have called Satan's essential ambivalence—is, I would suggest, evidence of that neurosis.

Notes

1. Excerpted from "Milton's Satan," in *The Cambridge Companion to Milton*, ed. Dennis Danielson (Cambridge: Cambridge University Press, 1999), 160–74. The chapter has been lightly edited for style for the purposes of the present publication.

2. John Milton, *Christian Doctrine*, ed. Maurice Kelley, trans. John Carey, vol. 6 of *Complete Prose Works of John Milton* (New Haven, CT: Yale University Press, 1973), 349–50.

3. Frank S. Kastor, *Milton and the Literary Satan* (Amsterdam: Rodopi, 1974).

4. R. J. Zwi Werblowsky, *Lucifer and Prometheus: A Study of Milton's Satan*, with an introduction by Carl G. Jung (London: Routledge and Kegan Paul, 1952), x–xii.

5. Roger Sharrock, "Godwin on Milton's Satan," *Notes and Queries*, n.s. 9 (1962): 463–65.

6. Arthur E. Barker, "'... And on His Crest Sat Horror': Eighteenth-Century Interpretations of Milton's Sublimity and His Satan," *University of Toronto Quarterly* 11, no. 4 (July 1942): 421–36.

7. Edna Newmeyer, "Wordsworth on Milton and the Devil's Party," *Milton Studies* 11 (1978), 83–98.

8. Charles Williams, introduction to *The English Poems of John Milton* (Oxford: Oxford University Press, 1940); C. S. Lewis, preface to *Paradise Lost*, by John Milton (Oxford: Oxford University Press, 1942); Sydney Musgrove, "Is the Devil an Ass?," *Review of English Studies* 21 (1945): 302–15; Stanley E. Fish, *Surprised by Sin: The Reader in "Paradise Lost"* (New York: St. Martin's Press; London: Macmillan, 1967); A. J. A. Waldock, *"Paradise Lost" and Its Critics* (Cambridge: Cambridge University Press, 1947); Elmer E. Stoll, "Give the Devil His Due: A Reply to Mr. Lewis," *Review of English Studies* 20 (1944): 108–24; G. Rostrevor Hamilton, *Hero or Fool? A Study of Milton's Satan* (London: George Allen and Unwin, 1961); and William Empson, *Milton's God* (London: Chatto and Windus, 1961).

9. Stoll, "Give the Devil His Due," 124.

10. Kastor, *Milton and the Literary Satan*, 1–17, 69–71.

11. See Harry F. Robins, *If This Be Heresy: A Study of Milton and Origen*, Illinois Studies in Language and Literature, 51 (Urbana: University of Illinois Press, 1963).

12. C. A. Patrides, "The Salvation of Satan," *Journal of the History of Ideas* 28, no. 4 (October–December 1967): 467–78.

13. Stella Purce Revard, *The War in Heaven: "Paradise Lost" and the Tradition of Satan's Rebellion* (Ithaca, NY: Cornell University Press, 1980), 45–46.

14. John M. Steadman, *Milton's Epic Characters: Image and Idol* (Chapel Hill: University of North Carolina Press, 1968), 166.

15. Milton, *Christian Doctrine*, 227.

16. John Milton, *Paradise Lost*, ed. Alastair Fowler, 2nd ed. (Milton Park, Oxfordshire, England: Routledge, 1997).

17. Revard, *The War in Heaven*, 35–36.

18. Merritt Y. Hughes, *Ten Perspectives on Milton* (New Haven, CT: Yale University Press, 1965), 177.

19. Werblowsky, *Lucifer and Prometheus*, 53.

20. Maud Bodkin, "Literature and the Individual Reader," *Literature and Psychology* 10, no. 2 (1960), 38–44.

21. Isabel Gamble MacCaffrey, *"Paradise Lost" as "Myth"* (Cambridge, MA: Harvard University Press, 1959), 182–83.

22. Sigmund Freud, *Civilization and Its Discontents*, ed. James Strachey, trans. Joan Riviere (London: Hogarth Press, 1979), 80–81.

CHAPTER 13

"More Demon Than Man"

Melville's Ahab as Gothic Villain[1]

TONY MAGISTRALE

HERMAN MELVILLE'S FICTION REVEALS HIS FASCINATION WITH ELEMENTS FROM the eighteenth-century gothic literary tradition. Merton Sealts says that Melville read Horace Walpole's *The Castle of Otranto*, William Beckford's *Vathek*, and even Mary Shelley's *Frankenstein*, as well as a number of lesser known but related gothic texts.[2] Gothicism is concerned with fallen man, often embracing and flaunting his sinful state. The genre's characteristic association with evil, the rebellion against God and optimistic virtues, and an emphasis on disorder, chaos, and ambiguity all find a developmental place in Melville's works. The gothic supplied Melville with a workable tradition: a theater that enabled and encouraged him to give dramatic life to conflicting and often darkly pessimistic philosophical positions. In his hands, the standard, eighteenth-century gothic apparatus—blood bonds with evil, haunted castles, a reliance on supernatural terror—evolved to tell a more complicated story, focusing on the profoundly tragic imperfections inherent in man and his institutions.

Melville's most ambitious use of standard gothic elements occurs in his 1851 novel, *Moby-Dick*. The environmental backdrop of the novel itself—life on board the restricted *Pequod*—possesses something of the poetic quality of the haunted house, with Ahab as the one man who is lord over it. Indeed, the ship's bond with the landlocked haunted house may be felt in nearly every description of the *Pequod*: from its weather-stained hull, its venerable bows, its spire-like masts, its worn and ancient decks, to its general atmosphere of grotesqueness and somber picturesqueness.[3] In short, the ship holds much in common with the Houses of Usher, Udolpho, or Otranto. Moreover, the eclectic collection of sailors on board the *Pequod* are as much Ahab's captives as any incarcerated maiden trying to gain exit from the gothic castle.

It is, however, within the actions and personality of the *Pequod*'s mad captain Ahab that Melville's most significant debt to the gothic genre becomes apparent. A major theme running through gothic fiction is an association of the male villain with evil forces, most specifically the Devil. Ahab emerges as an embodiment of the fallen angel demigod who in the Christian myth was variously named Lucifer, the Devil, the Adversary, or Satan. Ahab is not Satan but a human creature possessing Satan's evil pride and energy, summing up within himself, as Irenaeus said, "the apostasy of the devil." Melville's intention to beget Ahab in Satan's image can hardly be disputed. Indeed, early in the novel Elijah warns Ishmael and Queequeg to fear for their souls because a voyage with Ahab and his "shadowy figures" is certain to involve evil:

> "Yes," said I [Ishmael], "we have just signed the articles."
> "Anything down there about your souls?"
> "About what?"
> "Oh, perhaps you hav'n't got any," he said quickly.
> "No matter though, I know many chaps that hav'n't got any . . . He's got enough though, to make up for all the deficiencies of that sort in other chaps," abruptly said the stranger, placing a nervous emphasis on the word he.[4]

Connected to the gothic fascination with evil is a pervasive element of blasphemy. In Matthew Gregory Lewis's *The Monk*, Ambrosio is a Catholic monk who violates on top of an altar a woman masquerading as a nun. Vathek in Beckford's novel of the same name makes a Faustian pact with Satan in order to experience as many depraved sensations as mortal life will afford. Ahab is a continuation of this gothic tradition in that he is an "ungodly, god-like man" who is spiritually outside Christendom.[5] In Ahab, there is a well of blasphemy and defiance, of both rejection and scorn for the gods: "Who's over me?" he asks, taunting whatever inhuman forces may animate the supernatural realm.[6] We are also told that Ahab once spat in the holy goblet on the altar of the Catholic church at Santa.[7] In the course of the whale voyage—a journey that ironically commences on Christmas Day—Ahab engages in three blasphemous rituals. Each unholy rite incorporates the use of a harpoon (with Ahab serving in the role of high celebrant) clearly to present a blasphemous parody of a religious ritual. In the first of these rituals, "The Quarter-Deck," Ahab pours grog into the inverted ends of hollow harpoon heads and commands the harpooners to drink from the "murderous chalices" with this oath: "God hunt us all, if we do not hunt Moby Dick to his death."[8] And when Starbuck suggests that perhaps Ahab's quest is blasphemous, the captain snarls in a tone reminiscent of Manfred's or Melmoth's enraged pride: "Talk not to me of blasphemy, man; I'd strike the sun if it insulted me. For could the sun do that, then could I do the other; since there is ever a sort of fair play herein, jealousy presiding over all creations."[9]

The demonical nature of Ahab's quest is again suggested in "The Forge," when Ahab baptizes a scorching harpoon in the name of the Devil. And, finally, in "The Candles," Ahab uses his consecrated harpoon to aid him in a speech of defiance, asserting his unconquerable individuality in the face of nature: "Oh, thou clear spirit, of thy fire thou madest me, and like a true child of fire, I breathe it back to thee. . . . Yet blindfold, yet will I talk to thee. Light though thou be, thou leapest out of darkness; but I am darkness leaping out of light, leaping out of thee!"[10] Like Manfred on his mountain, lightning flashes and Ahab speaks directly to it, calling it his ancestor: "There burn the flames! Oh, thou magnanimous! Now I do glory in my genealogy. But thou art but my fiery father; my sweet mother, I know not."[11] In these scenes Melville relies on standard gothic visual effects and soundtracks: tremendous fire, blackness, storm, and battering seas; all are present, as are high emotion, conflicting beliefs, and a clash of personalities. Ahab once more establishes his link to the male-dominated world of the gothic genre by calling the flames his father, while denying even a knowledge of a mother's milder milk.

His nexus to evil notwithstanding, there exists another side of Melville's captain that is not entirely wicked. Like Walpole's Manfred or Lewis's Ambrosio, "Ahab has his humanities."[12] We are told that he thinks often of his bride and daughter, and his care of the pathetic Pip reveals his compassion. These instances serve to complicate our response to Ahab and further connect him to earlier gothic prototypes. Despite his imperious manner and narrowed perception of reality, Ahab possesses a streak of sensitivity and melancholia that is found in a number of earlier gothic villains. Charles Maturin's Melmoth and Lewis's Ambrosio are two illustrations of the morbidly sensitive gothic hero whose value system is considered warped because he refuses to conform to accepted social mores. The gothic novel thus prefigures the romantic movement insofar as it delineates the irreconcilable gap between individual psyche and societal constraints. The gothic hero's alienation is self imposed and socially ordained; it remains a continual source of paradox, encompassing both a sense of pride in his rising above the moral restraints of common men and a melancholic lamentation born out of prolonged isolation.

Like Manfred's, Ambrosio's, or Melmoth's, Ahab's single name suggests a lonely and sinister independence from social ties. Ahab throws overboard, loses, or smashes several social objects in the course of the voyage. Each one symbolizes the rejection of some aspect of his connection with the rest of humanity. In chapter 30, "The Pipe," Ahab realizes that he no longer can derive any pleasure from so leisurely an activity as smoking and throws his pipe into the sea. In "The Quadrant," Ahab dashes the valuable instrument to the deck and crushes it, shouting, "Cursed be all things that cast man's eyes aloft to that heaven, whose live vividness but scorches him."[13] In both scenes, Ahab, more and more obsessed with the inhuman whale, is shown displaced from human or geographical positioning in the actual world. The unsocial nature of the *Pequod's* voyage under Ahab is stressed in the ship's encounters with the other whaling vessels. Because of Ahab's obsession, the *Pequod* is not merely unsociable, but antisocial in the literal sense:

> "Come aboard, come aboard!" cried the gay Bachelor's commander, lifting a glass and a bottle in the air.
> "Hast seen the White Whale?" gritted Ahab in reply.
> "No; only heard of him; but don't believe in him at all," said the other goodhumoredly.
> "Come aboard!"
> "Thou art too damn jolly. Sail on ..."[14]

Not simply desirous of avoiding company, but actually of attacking the very foundation and values upon which a society is built, Ahab becomes a fanatical violator of both the purpose of whaling and of respect for other human beings. Ahab's attitude bears much in common with the profoundly antisocial world of the eighteenth-century gothic novel. A primary reason that the gothic novel remains significant to literary history is that it initiates the destruction of the social order and stability that was characteristic of the rest of the eighteenth century. The last decade of this century—with its emphasis on the breakdown of social ties, social hierarchy, conventions, and institutions—belongs more to the romantic generation of the century to follow rather than to the enlightened world of reason and societal organization. It is, after all, the decade that followed the dramatic French Revolution of 1789. The *Pequod*, then, is analogous once more to the haunted castle where the gothic owner spends the majority of his time, avoiding social company and tending to an assortment of perverted personal quests.

If Ahab's bonds with humanity are shown to be slowly disintegrating in the course of the voyage, his links with the satanic grow proportionately stronger. His personal crew, for example—those "shadows" that Ishmael and Queequeg see board the *Pequod*—resemble mysterious phantoms from an old gothic romance; indeed, they are refugees taken directly from *Vathek*. The crew has a symbolic significance, reflected in Ishmael's speculation: "Such a crew, so officered, seemed especially picked or packed by some infernal fatality to help Ahab to his revenge."[15] Melville's most striking use of the gothic device is his characterization of the enigmatic Fedallah, the crew's leader: "That hairturbaned Fedallah remained a muffled mystery to the last.... He was such a creature as civilized, domestic people in the temperate zone only see in their dreams."[16] Fedallah seems linked to *Macbeth*'s weird sisters, especially in his talent for surrounding himself in an air of ambiguity and in stating false prophesy. Like the forces of evil in gothic dramas, he is never clearly defined by the author but is omnipresent, lurking mainly in the background and always weaving an air of intrigue. Also, Fedallah's "presence" on board the ship grows in proportion to Ahab's nearness to the whale. We do not see him at all early in the voyage; he and his infernal crew only emerge from the *Pequod*'s shadows when it is time to go into battle against Moby Dick. Fedallah seems to represent the darkest recesses of Ahab's own psyche, emerging more as an extension of the captain's deepening madness than as an independent source of evil.

In depicting the end of Ahab's quest, Melville uses colossal effects similar to those found throughout the gothic realm. Ann Radcliffe's castles inevitably vanish into forests or tarns or the reader's imagination in the conclusions of her novels. The end of *Moby-Dick*, like so many gothic visual climaxes in Poe's tales or Walpole's *Otranto*, overwhelms the crew of the *Pequod* as well as the reader in a vortex to such intensity that it sucks everything with it, including a "living part of heaven."

> Tashtego kept his hammer frozen there; and so the bird of heaven, with archangelic shrieks, and his imperial beak thrust upwards, and his whole captive form folded in the flag of Ahab, went down with his ship, which, like Satan, would not sink to hell till she had dragged a living part of heaven along with her.[17]

The tale that Ishmael lives to tell, however, ultimately succeeds in transcending the restrictive gothic world of the late eighteenth century. The genre's scope is enlarged by Melville to include a tragic dimension: Ahab goes out not simply to avenge his accident at the jaws of Moby Dick but to revenge a world-insult, the world-wound of existence as symbolized in his leg injury: that man is a simple creature fated to dying by his very birth. Melville adds philosophical complexities to *Moby-Dick* that finally lift it out of the gothic cesspool. But through an adaptation of standard gothic apparatus, *Moby-Dick* attains the power and dimensionality of classical tragedy.

Notes

1. Reprinted from Tony Magistrale, "More Demon Than Man": Melville's Ahab as Gothic Villain," *Extrapolation* 27, no. 3 (Fall 1986), 203–7. The chapter has been lightly edited for style for the purposes of the present publication.

2. Merton M. Sealts Jr., *Melville's Reading: A Check-List of Books Owned and Borrowed* (Madison: University of Wisconsin Press, 1968), 40, 93, 103.

3. Newton Arvin, "Melville and the Gothic Novel," *New England Quarterly* 22, no. 1 (March 1949): 38.

4. Herman Melville, *Moby-Dick* (1851; repr., Indianapolis: Bobbs-Merrill, 1964), 132–33.

5. Melville, *Moby-Dick*, 119.

6. Melville, *Moby-Dick*, 221.

7. Melville, *Moby-Dick*, 134.

8. Melville, *Moby-Dick*, 225.

9. Melville, *Moby-Dick*, 221.

10. Melville, *Moby-Dick*, 642.

11. Melville, *Moby-Dick*, 642–43.

12. Melville, *Moby-Dick*, 120.

13. Melville, *Moby-Dick*, 634.

14. Melville, *Moby-Dick*, 627.

15. Melville, *Moby-Dick*, 251.

16. Melville, *Moby-Dick*, 307.

17. Melville, *Moby-Dick*, 723.

CHAPTER 14

The Bat, the Cat . . . and the Eagle?

Irene Adler as Inspiration for Catwoman

RICHARD D. HELDENFELS

A NOTORIOUS FEMALE VILLAIN WAS ONCE DESCRIBED AS "A LUNATIC . . . A criminal . . . insanely dangerous," but she had so smitten her heroic rival that his sidekick declared, "Trust you to fall for a sociopath."[1] In comic books, one might easily look at those comments and think of the complications besetting Batman and Catwoman. In fact, the description makes perfect sense when you consider how from their first encounter Batman was taken with the remorseless thief then known as the Cat. But the remarks mentioned above involve a different pairing of crime-stopper and crook: Sir Arthur Conan Doyle's Sherlock Holmes and "*the* woman," Irene Adler, in the short story "A Scandal in Bohemia."[2] The more closely you look at Holmes and Adler, the more you see the roots of Batman and Catwoman: two closely matched opponents; villains whose criminality has in both cases a sense of ambiguity; wronged women and damaged men; an attraction that is as confusing as it is powerful for the men in the equation; and an upheaval in gender roles.

Catwoman unquestionably ranks among the greatest supervillains and, next to only the Joker, as the greatest villain in the Batman canon—one who has been considered and reconsidered as often as Batman himself, from her debut in the first issue of *Batman* comics through the young Selina Kyle on the television series *Gotham*. From the beginning, Batman has at once opposed her and been attracted to her; in their first encounter, he spurns an offer from the Cat (as she was first known) to become a criminal couple, but at the same time he moons over her "lovely eyes" and wishes "maybe I'll bump into her again sometime."[3] In ensuing stories, he sees her reform and then relapse into crime, moving back and forth along the moral spectrum, leaving him uncertain—as one 1951 story has it—whether she belongs with the law or the underworld.[4]

Similarly, the opera singer Irene Adler is first cast as Holmes's foe "of dubious and questionable memory,"[5] as Watson stuffily puts it, a woman scorned and bent on revenge against a former lover in the original Doyle story. She has a photograph of herself with the king of Bohemia that could ruin his planned engagement to a Scandinavian noblewoman, and the king enlists Holmes to get the photo back before Adler releases it to the public. Although the king paints Adler as "an adventuress,"[6] the accumulated facts suggest that it is she who was "cruelly wronged"[7] by the king. The case, Watson will later admit, was "entirely free of any legal crime,"[8] and Adler has in fact been a crime victim—as the king has twice paid burglars to ransack her house. Although Holmes cannot get the photo, Adler—by then the married Irene Norton—says that she will not release it but keeps it as a safeguard against any new actions by the king. Holmes ends up admiring her, even disparaging the king by comparison. She is indeed *the* woman, much as Catwoman begins as *the* Cat.

Arguing that Adler is an antecedent of Catwoman is not mere conjecture. In addition to Holmes's many print and screen interpretations over the years, he has impacted other fictional detectives, such as TV's Dr. House (whose street address was the same as Holmes's) and, as Mary Rose Sullivan has argued, Sam Spade.[9] Batman has also left a paper trail leading back to Doyle's detective. Bill Finger, cocreator of Batman and author of the first Catwoman story, envisioned him as "a combination of Douglas Fairbanks, Sherlock Holmes, the Shadow and Doc Savage"[10] (the latter, for that matter, was based in part on Holmes as well).[11] Holmes worked as a "consulting detective" when government and police detectives were "at fault . . . and I manage[d] to put them on the right scent."[12] Batman had a habit of "making the police department look ridiculous," one 1940 comic says.[13] The costumed hero is not merely a fighter but a skilled investigator; in the earliest version of his origin, he is both physically powerful and "a master scientist."[14] Holmes, readers learn in "The Gloria Scott," fenced and boxed in college,[15] and, according to "The Yellow Face," he is "absolutely untiring and indefatigable" on a case;[16] *A Study in Scarlet* tells us that he is "an enthusiast in some branches of science" who spends hours in the laboratory.[17] Like Holmes, Batman keeps extensive files; a 1951 story including Catwoman shows him trying to decide whether she belongs in his files categorized "with the law or the underworld."[18] (Holmes's index of "all paragraphs docketing men and things" holds Adler's biography "between that of a Hebrew Rabbi and that of a staff-commander who had written a monograph upon the deep-sea fishes."[19]) And Batman has Robin in part because, Finger said, "Holmes had his Watson. The thing that bothered me was that Batman didn't have anyone to talk to, and it got a little tiresome always having him thinking."[20]

The parallels extend to villains. James Moriarty, Holmes's nemesis, is a brilliant mathematician, "a genius, a philosopher, an abstract thinker," and an "organizer" of evil.[21] The notorious early Batman villain Professor Hugo Strange is a "scientist, philosopher and a criminal genius . . . undoubtedly the greatest organizer of crime in the world."[22] In addition, just as Moriarty was "the Napoleon of crime,"[23] another early Batman villain, Dr. Carl Kruger, aims to be "another Napoleon."[24] With Catwoman, the connections are even more evident.

Adler and Catwoman are both breakthroughs. Adler is central to the first of the Holmes short stories (following the novels *A Study in Scarlet* and *The Sign of Four*); although the adventure falls later in Holmes's contradictory chronology, it nonetheless finds Holmes "upstaged and tricked, for the first and last time, by a woman," Pascale Krumm says.[25] Catwoman makes her debut in the first issue of *Batman* comics, succeeding a string of exotic, male *Detective Comics* villains for Batman including Doctor Death, the Monk, Kruger, and Hugo Strange. The only woman in that lot is Dala, a vampire working in league with the Monk; she hints that stronger women are coming—giving orders to the Monk about how to take revenge on Batman—but is still basically a supporting character.[26] Catwoman, like Adler, is a leading lady.

As I have mentioned, Catwoman and Adler are criminally ambiguous, and their actions are driven by issues other than morality; Catwoman's turn to crime was at first explained as the result of an accident causing amnesia, with Batman saying that "she really wasn't a criminal at heart."[27] Adler in her earliest rendition is not a criminal at all. Both are smart, and both employ disguises in their work. Catwoman is animal-like, and Adler, as Krumm has written, has a name that translates from the German as "eagle," associating her with a "different species" than Holmes and other people.[28]

Holmes and Adler are more than evenly matched; she is, in fact, a woman who beats him at his own game, with Sullivan concluding that he fails because "an emotional distraction has blurred his keen eyesight."[29] Batman is comparably confused by Catwoman; although he foils her jewel theft in her first adventure, he is so "emotionally distracted" that he lets her escape (even blocking Robin's attempt to stop her).[30] In each case, such behavior goes against the heroes' customary thinking. Holmes, as Watson says in "A Scandal in Bohemia," felt that "all emotions . . . were abhorrent to his cold, precise, but admirably balanced mind. . . . He never spoke of the softer passions, save with a gibe and a sneer."[31] Batman could also mock strong feelings, claiming once that "murder isn't in the Catwoman's heart. Sentiment is her weakness."[32] The distaste for feelings reminds us that Batman is emotionally damaged, traumatized by witnessing the murder of his parents. Holmes's chilliness, meanwhile, leads to "queer humours" in Watson's view, such as playing melancholy chords on his violin, engaging in pistol practice while in his armchair, and, of course, "the occasional use of cocaine . . . as a protest against the monotony of existence when cases were scanty and the papers uninteresting."[33] Such actions may be a substitute for relationships with women. "Holmes himself cannot be sensational or colorful; to be sensational would remove him from the rational world," says Jasmine Yong Hall. "But Holmes does need the sensations that his female clients provide in order to make his cases exciting."[34] Lara Pulver, who played Adler in TV's *Sherlock*, has called her character "a bit dysfunctional and a bit lost and, at times, she's vulnerable"[35]—all of which also applies to Holmes and to Batman.

Indeed, both Adler and Catwoman are remedies of sorts for the lost men they duel. After the first few Batman stories, two characters arrived who moved him away from the "winged figure of vengeance,"[36] "possessing the powers of a Satan."[37] The first, in *Detective Comics*, was Robin the Boy Wonder, who, in addition to providing a sounding board, is an orphan who becomes both Batman's ward and his crime-fighting associate. Comics historian James Steranko calls that a turning point, "forever ending the image of solitude and menace that typified the early Batman."[38] When we next see Batman, in his own title, he has new foes—not only the mad Joker but also the more complicated Cat. The latter, says Batman cocreator Bob Kane, was introduced because the stories "needed a female nemesis to give the strip sex appeal . . . a somewhat friendly foe who committed crimes but was also a romantic interest in Batman's rather sterile life."[39] (Pity Julie Madison, Bruce Wayne's fiancée in that "sterile" life.) Catwoman was also, Kane says, "a kind of female Batman, except that she was a villainess and Batman was a hero."[40] Introducing a character who had Batman cooing like a schoolboy further dampened the "solitude and menace" seen earlier in the comic series; Catwoman has continued to be used in such a fashion up through *Gotham*, a Batman prequel in which young Bruce Wayne is smitten with the street-smart, pre-Catwoman Selina Kyle, who is also one of Bruce's instructors in the ways of the world. One could easily argue in turn that Adler is a "kind of" Sherlock Holmes, using some of the same tactics and possessing a comparable strength. As the king of Bohemia says, she has "the face of the most beautiful of women, and the mind of the most resolute of men."[41] It may be no accident that she appears so early in the Holmes chronicles, softening him both emotionally and in terms of his attention to his craft. When in "The Five Orange Pips" Holmes is told that he is "never beaten," and he replies, "I have been beaten four times—three times by men and once by a woman,"[42] the consensus is that the woman is Adler.[43]

Only how much, exactly, does Holmes care for Adler, and Batman for Catwoman? In the latter, the physical attraction is there from the beginning, with Batman ordering himself to remember he has a fiancée.[44] Some writers have carried their relationship to consummation; one story has the Earth-2 Bruce Wayne marrying Selina Kyle—although the marriage ends tragically when Batman deflects a villain's bullet, accidentally striking and killing Catwoman.[45] The original Holmes-Adler relationship is more difficult to parse, since Watson says both that Holmes sees Adler as *the* woman and that "it was not that he felt any emotion akin to love" for Adler.[46] In his annotated edition of the Holmes stories, William S. Baring-Gould says that the possibility that Adler "was one he might have loved, even did love," is "hotly contested by other students of the Canon."[47] At the same time, in his speculative biography of Holmes, Baring-Gould has Holmes and Adler uniting years after "A Scandal in Bohemia" and having a child—the detective Nero Wolfe.[48] This, too, has been contested; Holmes scholar D. Martin Dakin carps that Baring-Gould's theory "not only casts aspersions on the moral character of Holmes . . . but is rendered utterly impossible by Watson's clear statement that she was deceased by then."[49]

Yes, Watson says she was "the late Irene Adler" in "A Scandal in Bohemia"; as Baring-Gould says, however, "many commentators have since expressed doubt,"[50] and some later writers have worked around it. In *Sherlock*, for example, Adler appears to have died but in fact is surreptitiously saved by Holmes himself.[51] Still, killing Adler may be less about storytelling than about dealing with a character who would be problematic for Holmes if still alive—the same reason that drove DC Comics to erase Catwoman from Batman stories for years. Carole Nelson Douglas, author of a series of novels with Irene Adler as the hero, believes that Adler was "literally too hot for Doyle as well as Holmes to handle."[52] By the early 1950s, Catwoman was too hot for DC.

When we talk about "hot," we are referring only in part to sexual attraction. To be sure, that could be considered part of the formula, and, as we have noted, Holmes's feelings for Adler have at times been interpreted as sexual. This is even more an element in Catwoman, as it has been in other female villains. Historian Mike Madrid has argued that in the Golden Age of comics, "seduction was not a weapon that an upright female hero was allowed to use, since it connoted sexual conquest," while "bad girls had an advantage. . . . Since a villainess had already cast aside society's rules by stealing, cheating or killing, sex would hardly be an inhibition for her."[53] Therefore, "with her sharp-clawed gloves and wielding a whip, Catwoman wasn't just a deadly foe but also a forbidden love interest."[54] On a larger scale, though, the heat in these villains comes from their taking of power where other women could not because the culture did not permit it. Shannon Austin has said that Catwoman and her spiritual sisters Harley Quinn and Poison Ivy "serve as examples of the correlation often drawn between female power and monstrosity. Women in power are feared by men, which precipitates men's disempowerment of them; because traditional stereotypes depict women as passive, any deviation from this norm is viewed as a threat."[55] Even more to the point here, Austin believes that the Joker tries to get rid of Harley rather than "risking her taking his power away by forcing him to care about her."[56] Indeed, in *Harley Quinn*, no. 1, the Joker tells her: "I've been reminded of what it's been like to be part of a couple . . . And I hate having those feelings. They're upsetting, confusing and worse, distracting from getting my share of Gotham."[57] For Batman and Holmes, too, it's arguable that regardless of their effect on the men's power, Catwoman and Adler are severe distractions when it's time to go to work.

Power is no less an issue, however. Adler, in seizing control of her interaction with the king, becomes a threat to his keeping and expanding his power. (One theory about Adler's death has the king as her killer, a final move to secure his future.[58]) Doyle was not immune to the standards of a male-dominated society; biographer Daniel Stashower observed that Doyle's "great delight in strong, independent women" was "in fiction, if not always in [Doyle's] life."[59] And even in Doyle's fiction, Krumm says, "[w]omen are powerless entities in all [of Doyle's Holmes] stories, except in 'A Scandal in Bohemia.'"[60] Jasmine Yong Hall has observed that "[w]omen in the Holmes stories . . . are a conduit for male power. As the object of sexual dominance, they are necessary to release that power. But they do not acquire power themselves; it is, instead, passed on to Holmes."[61] Adler passes on no such power, so her place in Holmes's world is untenable. "While for a brief time the world is turned upside down by Woman, the ultimate Male world order is finally restored," says Krumm.[62] Adds Douglas: Doyle's "mixed feelings of attraction to and fear of a liberated, artistic woman like Irene Adler led him to 'kill' her as soon as he created her."[63]

Catwoman, in turn, crashes up against the male order because, as Austin says, her sexuality gives her power and that scares the daylights out of some men. Kane sounds much like Douglas characterizing Doyle when he talks about Catwoman: "Cats are hard to understand, they are erratic, as women are,"[64] he says, although it is Batman who proves erratic when meeting the Cat. "Men feel more sure of themselves with a male friend than a woman," adds Kane. "You always need to keep women at arm's length. We don't want anyone to take over our souls, and women have a habit of doing that."[65] Madrid put it another way: sexy villainesses create a moral dilemma for men, as "bad women" who at once "captivate" and "terrify."[66] And, in the censorious 1950s, that kind of dilemma was unacceptable to many holding onto their own power.

Madrid states that "in the years after WWII there was growing pressure to make comic books more wholesome, and to clean up the salacious aspects of the stories. In this new era, Catwoman was famously declawed."[67] For example, as I have mentioned, while her criminality was blamed on an accident for a time, she went back to her evil ways, and the cat-and-bat games came with them; in one story from September 1954, Catwoman leaves Batman the utility-belt gear he needs to cheat death, and Batman once again watches her escape him.[68] But regardless of her behavior, there is still that sexual aura to Catwoman that raised censors' hackles. The Comics Magazine Association Code in October 1954 seems to allude to Catwoman again and again: "Crimes shall never be presented in such a way to create sympathy for the criminal. . . . Criminals shall not be presented so as to be rendered glamorous or to occupy a position which creates a desire for emulation. . . . All characters shall be depicted in dress reasonably acceptable to society. . . . Passion or romantic interest shall never be treated in such a way as to stimulate the lower and baser emotions."[69] No wonder that Catwoman vanished from Batman's world in 1954, returning only in 1966, following the success of the *Batman* TV series (which had its own Catwoman, first played by Julie Newmar) and the changing standards of the time.[70]

Of course, just as Catwoman found new life, so Irene Adler has never really died. She is one of the most compelling figures in the Holmes canon and, as such, has been revisited regularly, including in director Guy Ritchie's Sherlock Holmes adaptations, the TV series *Elementary*, and, as noted, the TV series *Sherlock*. Douglas calls her "fascinatingly unrealized,"[71] but it may be more accurate to say that she is misunderstood, by Doyle and by Holmes, with Krumm pointing repeatedly to Holmes's "inability to understand" not only Adler but all women.[72] That incomprehension shows on the page, where Adler is elusive, seen more through men's view of her (including the photograph of her that Holmes takes as payment for the case) than her own, with Holmes's admiration validating her. Although Catwoman eventually gained her own comic book series, her initial and ongoing attraction derives from how men see her—starting with Batman. It is then suggestive that, when presented with a powerful woman, some writers prove so at a loss to understand that they fall back on the same tropes. *Sherlock*, for one, offered an updated Adler who echoed Catwoman; the series portrayed Adler as a dominatrix,[73] a role Catwoman has also played, for example in the story "Metamorphosis."[74] Note that Batman's true love throughout his nearly sixty-year career has always been Catwoman (despite his other romances, and even having a child with another woman). At the time of this writing, Bruce Wayne has asked Selina Kyle for her hand in marriage, and she has accepted (see *Batman*, no. 32 [2017]).[75] How this plays out remains to be seen, of course, but the line from Adler to Catwoman is clearly not merely a bit of literary inspiration, but a demonstration of popular culture's ongoing struggle with gender roles.

Notes

1. Nick Hurran, dir., "The Lying Detective," *Sherlock*, prod. Sue Vertue, writ. Steven Moffat (Hartswood Films, broadcast January 8, 2017).

2. Sir Arthur Conan Doyle, "A Scandal in Bohemia," in *The Annotated Sherlock Holmes*, vol. 1, ed. William S. Baring-Gould (New York: Wings Press, 1992), 346–67.

3. Bill Finger, Bob Kane, and Jerry Robinson, "The Cat," in *Batman Chronicles*, vol. 1 (New York: DC Comics, 2005), 177; originally published in *Batman*, no. 1 (Spring 1940).

4. Bill Finger, Bob Kane, Lew Sayre Schwartz, and Charles Paris, "Catwoman: Empress of the Underworld," in *Catwoman: A Celebration of 75 Years* (New York: DC Comics, 2015), 37–38; originally published in *Batman*, no. 65 (June 1951).

5. Doyle, "A Scandal in Bohemia," 346.

6. Doyle, "A Scandal in Bohemia," 353.

7. Doyle, "A Scandal in Bohemia," 367.

8. Sir Arthur Conan Doyle, "The Adventure of the Blue Carbuncle," in *The Annotated Sherlock Holmes*, vol. 1, ed. William S. Baring-Gould (New York: Wings Press, 1992), 451.

9. Mary Rose Sullivan, "Sherlock Holmes and Sam Spade: Brothers under the Skin," in *Sherlock Holmes: Victorian Sleuth to Modern Hero*, ed. Charles R. Putney, Joseph A. Cutshall King, and Sally Sugarman (Lanham, MD: Scarecrow Press, 1996), 170–80.

10. James Steranko, *The Steranko History of Comics* (Reading, PA: Supergraphics, 1970), 44.

11. Marilyn Cannaday, *Bigger Than Life: The Creator of Doc Savage* (Bowling Green, OH: Bowling Green State University Popular Press, 1990), 15.

12. Sir Arthur Conan Doyle, *A Study in Scarlet*, in *The Annotated Sherlock Holmes*, vol. 1, ed. William S. Baring-Gould (New York: Wings Press, 1992), 160.

13. Bob Kane, Bill Finger, and Sheldon Moldoff, "The Case of the Ruby Idol," in *Batman Chronicles*, vol. 1 (New York: DC Comics, 2005), 97; originally published in *Detective Comics*, no. 35 (January 1940).

14. Bob Kane, Gardner Fox, and Sheldon Moldoff, "The Batman Wars against the Dirigible of Doom," in *Batman Chronicles*, vol. 1 (New York: DC Comics, 2005), 63; originally published in *Detective Comics*, no. 33 (November 1939).

15. Sir Arthur Conan Doyle, "The Gloria Scott," in *The Annotated Sherlock Holmes*, vol. 1, ed. William S. Baring-Gould (New York: Wings Press, 1992), 107–8.

16. Sir Arthur Conan Doyle, "The Yellow Face," in *The Annotated Sherlock Holmes*, vol. 1, ed. William S. Baring-Gould (New York: Wings Press, 1992), 575.

17. Doyle, *A Study in Scarlet*, 148.

18. Finger et al., "Catwoman: Empress of the Underworld," 37–38.

19. Doyle, "A Scandal in Bohemia," 353.

20. Steranko, *The Steranko History of Comics*, 47.

21. Sir Arthur Conan Doyle, "The Final Problem," in *The Annotated Sherlock Holmes*, vol. 2, ed. William S. Baring-Gould (New York: Wings Press, 1992), 303.

22. Bob Kane, Bill Finger, and Jerry Robinson, "Professor Hugo Strange," in *Batman Chronicles*, vol. 1 (New York: DC Comics, 2005), 100; originally published in *Detective Comics*, no. 36 (February 1940).

23. Doyle, "The Final Problem," 103.

24. Kane, Fox, and Moldoff, "The Batman Wars against the Dirigible of Doom," 66.

25. Pascale Krumm, "'A Scandal in Bohemia' and Sherlock Holmes's Ultimate Mystery Solved," *English Literature in Transition, 1880–1920* 39, no. 2 (1996): 193.

26. Gardner Fox, Bob Kane, and Sheldon Moldoff, "Batman versus the Vampire, Part Two," in *Batman Chronicles*, vol. 1 (New York: DC Comics, 2005), 50–60; originally published in *Detective Comics*, no. 32 (October 1939).

27. Finger et al., "Catwoman: Empress of the Underworld," 39.

28. Krumm, "'A Scandal in Bohemia' and Sherlock Holmes's Ultimate Mystery Solved," 194.

29. Sullivan, "Sherlock Holmes and Sam Spade," 178.

30. Finger, Kane, and Robinson, "The Cat," 177.

31. Doyle, "A Scandal in Bohemia," 346.

32. Edmond Hamilton, Dick Sprang, and Charles Mortimer, "The Jungle Cat-Queen," in *Batman: A Celebration of 75 Years* (New York: DC Comics, 2014), 54; originally published in *Detective Comics*, no. 211 (September 1954).

33. Doyle, "The Yellow Face," 575.

34. Jasmine Yong Hall, "Ordering the Sensational: Sherlock Holmes and the Female Gothic," *Studies in Short Fiction* 28, no. 3 (1991): 302.

35. Steve Tribe, *Sherlock: Chronicles* (New York: HarperCollins, 2014), 140.

36. Gardner Fox, Bob Kane, and Sheldon Moldoff, "The Return of Doctor Death," in *Batman Chronicles*, vol. 1 (New York: DC Comics, 2005), 29; originally published in *Detective Comics*, no. 30 (August 1939).

37. Gardner Fox, Bill Finger, Bob Kane, and Sheldon Moldoff, "Batman versus the Vampire, Part One," in *Batman Chronicles*, vol. 1 (New York: DC Comics, 2005), 40; originally published in *Detective Comics*, no. 31 (September 1939).

38. Steranko, *The Steranko History of Comics*, 47.

39. Bob Kane with Tom Andrae, *Batman and Me* (Forestville, CA: Eclipse, 1989), 107.

40. Kane and Andrae, *Batman and Me*.

41. Doyle, "A Scandal in Bohemia," 355.

42. Sir Arthur Conan Doyle, "The Five Orange Pips," in *The Annotated Sherlock Holmes*, vol. 1, ed. William S. Baring-Gould (New York: Wings Press, 1992), 392.

43. Baring-Gould notes that another Holmes scholar, H. W. Bell, argued against this being Adler, in part because Holmes would then have referred to "the woman" instead of "a woman." But it is commonly thought to refer to Adler.

44. Finger, Kane, and Robinson, "The Cat," 177.

45. Alan Brennert, Joe Staton, and George Freeman, "The Autobiography of Bruce Wayne," in *Catwoman: A Celebration of 75 Years* (New York: DC Comics, 2015), 199–222; originally published in *The Brave and the Bold*, no. 197 (April 1983).

46. Doyle, "A Scandal in Bohemia," 346.

47. Doyle, "A Scandal in Bohemia," 346.

48. William S. Baring-Gould, *Sherlock Holmes of Baker Street: A Life of the World's First Consulting Detective* (New York: Bramhall House, 1962), 208–12.

49. D. Martin Dakin, *A Sherlock Holmes Commentary* (Newton Abbot, Devon, England: David and Charles, 1972), 42.

50. Doyle, *The Annotated Sherlock Holmes*, vol. 1, 346.

51. Paul McGuigan, dir., "A Scandal in Belgravia," *Sherlock*, prod. Sue Vertue, writ. Steven Moffat (Hartswood Films, broadcast May 6, 2012).

52. Carole Nelson Douglas, *Good Night, Mr. Holmes* (New York: Tom Doherty, 1990).

53. Mike Madrid, *Vixens, Vamps, and Vipers: Lost Villainesses of Golden Age Comics* (Ashland, OR: Exterminating Angel Press, 2014), 14.

54. Madrid, *Vixens, Vamps, and Vipers*, 22.

55. Shannon Austin, "Batman's Female Foes: The Gender War in Gotham City," *Journal of Popular Culture* 48, no. 2 (2015), 286.

56. Austin, "Batman's Female Foes," 286.

57. Paul Dini, Yvel Guichet, and Aaron Sowd, "Harley Quinn," in *Harley Quinn* (New York: DC Comics, 2015), 28–29; originally published in *Batman: Harley Quinn*, no. 1 (October 1999).

58. Doyle, *The Annotated Sherlock Holmes*, vol. 1, 346–47.

59. Daniel Stashower, *Teller of Tales: The Life of Arthur Conan Doyle* (New York: Henry Holt, 1999), 123.

60. Krumm, "'A Scandal in Bohemia' and Sherlock Holmes's Ultimate Mystery Solved," 195.

61. Hall, "Ordering the Sensational," 301.

62. Krumm, "'A Scandal in Bohemia' and Sherlock Holmes's Ultimate Mystery Solved," 201.

63. Douglas, *Good Night, Mr. Holmes*, n.p.

64. Kane and Andrae, *Batman and Me*, 108.

65. Kane and Andrae, *Batman and Me*, 108.

66. Madrid, *Vixens, Vamps, and Vipers*, 15.

67. Madrid, *Vixens, Vamps, and Vipers*, 22.

68. Hamilton, Sprang, and Mortimer, "The Jungle Cat-Queen," 52–54.

69. "'Good Shall Triumph over Evil': The Comic Book Code of 1954," History Matters, available at http://historymatters.gmu.edu/d/6543/.

70. *Catwoman: A Celebration of 75 Years* (New York: DC Comics, 2015), 64.

71. Douglas, *Good Night, Mr. Holmes*, n.p.

72. Krumm, "'A Scandal in Bohemia' and Sherlock Holmes's Ultimate Mystery Solved," 197.

73. McGuigan, "A Scandal in Belgravia."

74. Mindy Newell, J. J. Birch, and Michael Bair, "Metamorphosis," in *Catwoman: A Celebration of 75 Years* (New York: DC Comics, 2015), 225–49; originally published in *Catwoman*, no. 1 (February 1989).

75. Tom King and Mike Janin, *Batman*, vol. 4, *The War of Jokes and Riddles (Rebirth)* (New York: DC Comics, 2017).

CHAPTER 15

Vilifications

Conjuring Witches Then and Now

HANNAH RYAN

FOR TWO HUNDRED YEARS, THE *MALLEUS MALEFICARUM*, OR *HAMMER OF Witches*, sold more copies than any other book but the Bible.[1] Written by powerful German Dominicans in 1486 as witch hunting reached its peak, the guidebook instructed Europeans how to identify and persecute witches and circulated broadly throughout Europe and the colonies. The text was uniquely influential in popularizing the construct of *witchcraft as heresy*, a crime against God, whereas previously witchcraft was understood as a lesser offense, a harmful act only among humans. Through the rise of print culture and the broad dissemination of the text, and affecting Catholics and Protestants alike, witchcraft hysteria spread globally.[2] While quantifying the impact on innocent women is a pursuit that has challenged historians for centuries, recent scholarship suggests that one hundred thousand women were persecuted as witches, many of them executed.[3] The book itself certainly proved far more dangerous than the witches it conjured.

The *Malleus Maleficarum* identifies the most dangerous type of witch as one who is also a midwife, and claims that witches posed as midwives in order to gain access to newborns. They caused miscarriages and stillbirths, feasted on infants, and infected those who survived, creating more witches.[4] The precarious position of midwives during the witchcraft frenzy is dizzying; maternal and infant morbidity rates were high, and these women bore the responsibility, with their own reputations and lives at stake. As women who transgressed the domestic sphere and worked outside the home, they were already vulnerable to suspicions of witchcraft. "Clearly," John Demos writes, "the wisest course in early modern community life—especially for a woman—was to blend in and not to seem too openly self-assertive. To be, or to behave, otherwise was to open oneself to suspicion of witchcraft."[5]

While the guidebook certainly suggests that midwives were particularly de-monized and imperiled, and leading scholars like David D. Hall have identified midwives as "especially vulnerable" to charges of witchcraft, this claim is hardly incontestable. In fact, as I shall discuss here, in the titillating world of witchcraft scholarship, there is perhaps no figure more controversial than the midwife. In recent decades, she has been adopted and rejected by competing camps of historians, with equal vitriol on both sides.

The intellectual debate regarding the persecution of midwives as witches in colonial America, particularly the strong interest among feminist scholars ad-vocating both schools of thought and how they overlap historically, signifies the value of female figures who transgressed social boundaries in their learnedness and ability to both heal and harm. Rather than offer superfluous argument to the debate over whether or not midwives were *disproportionately accused of witchcraft*, I instead survey this remarkably productive dialogue and pivot slightly to assert: these educated and trusted, yet nonconforming women were *uniquely imperiled by their learnedness and vocation*, which were critical to the survival, health, and well-being of their communities. This chapter investigates the conflict, underscores the importance and stature of midwives in foundational America, and further, explores contemporary manifestations of the healer-harmer in con-temporary popular culture. In doing so, it becomes clear that the construct of the independent, intellectual "witch" who can both heal and harm is alive and well, and remains an important, resilient talisman for feminists. Within this book's broader context of villainy, witches emerge as unique in obtaining their power through knowledge. The stakes are high: the conjuring of real women as villains puts them in serious danger. As witches are sanitized and perpetually reimagined in popular culture, this chapter acknowledges a gendered system of vilification that cost the lives and livelihoods of countless women. Within the context of our collective project, this chapter is an interrogation of the process of vilification: how have women been rendered witches in the popular imagination, historically and today? And what processes rehumanize them?

THE MIDWIFE PROBLEM

Edward Peters calls the ideological conflict at hand "the midwife problem." On the types of women most susceptible to accusation, he asserts, "unmarried or widowed older women whose neighbors suspected them of causing harm to people or property were most frequently accused, tried and convicted. Witch-craft was also thought to run in families, especially from mother to daughter, and to be prevalent in certain occupations, *not often, as once was thought, that of midwife*, but in those of lower domestic servants."[6]

Peters cites a 1990 article by David Harley, in which he positions the historians who characterize midwives as susceptible to suspicion of witchcraft as demonologists. Harley argues that midwives were largely immune to accusation because they were generally respected and valued in their communities. He writes convincingly that the myth has been blown out of proportion, supported by only a few historical examples and the sensational vilification of midwives in the *Malleus Maleficarum*, and perpetuated by shoddy second-wave feminist scholarship. Doing so, he argues, serves to "create a multitude of imaginary martyrs for the modern women's health movement."[7]

According to Harley, feminists who adopted the midwife-witch as a symbolic figure of women's historical oppression did so without data to support the claim. He downplays the influence of the *Malleus Maleficarum* on everyday life, noting that large-scale witch hunts came long after its initial publication, and argues that the suspicion of witch-midwives sacrificing infants seems rooted in myth and propaganda, not tethered to real examples of prosecuted midwives. Citing lack of proof, he contends that the suspicion was later inscribed by modern historians, yet concedes that women engaged in occupations associated with food preparation and medicine were likely most at risk of witchcraft charges.[8]

I argue that those very tasks were central to midwifery at the time; diaries reveal midwives to be gardeners, foragers, and botanists who prescribed, prepared, and treated their patients with all manner of remedies. Many were ingested, and the distinction between medicine and food did not exist then as it does now. Here, in the visual record, I invoke the iconic cauldron as the place where the midwife melts into witch. The image of an unaccompanied woman or group of women together, working over a vessel, creating medicines and tinctures from all manner of unidentifiable natural materials, ignited fears of midwives' unknown and uncontrollable power and unjustly conflated midwives with witches.

Their role, along with the responsibility they bore in matters of life and death, could have rendered them all the more susceptible as the frenzy grew. Perhaps the suspicion that may have beleaguered midwives was not well documented. But I ask: how could it have been? Laurel Thatcher Ulrich, in her Pulitzer Prize–winning book on early American midwife Martha Ballard, *A Midwife's Tale*,[9] reveals midwives to have been highly trained and skillful medical practitioners who not only delivered babies but treated every malady and injury imaginable, using medicines they created and procured. At the very core of midwifery, then as now, are pregnancy, childbirth, and lactation support; through each, midwives were charged with preserving the lives of mothers and infants, not just through services but through products, many of which were ingested. This elevated role in communities and the corresponding high levels of trust certainly buoyed midwives amid the witch hunts, but the degree to which it protected them safely above it is still unclear.

If the witch-midwife correlation is a misunderstanding, as Harley argues, how did it arise? He suggests that some women prosecuted for witchcraft were essentially misidentified as midwives, as in the case of Agnes Sampson, who, during her trial, admitted to "administering magical medicines to take away the pains of women in childbirth." Although initially identified in the records as a servant girl, due to this particular offense she was reinscribed as a midwife. She confessed to witchcraft under torture, and was garroted and burned at the stake.

The ability to ease pain during childbirth, who had the authority to do so, and with what methods are all described in the records of witchcraft trials. While Harley acknowledges that some midwives were prosecuted and executed as witches, he essentially disconnects the two categories, dismissing any connection as coincidental and demonstrating midwives' insignificant representation among the large number of executions overall. Yet, scholarship does suggest that independent, educated women were feared; administering medications and deploying methods to ease pain might also cause harm to a mother or child, and these women indeed held a unique power to nurture and heal. Carol Karlsen's authoritative text *The Devil in the Shape of a Woman* reveals that women who healed people, with surprising degrees of success, were also susceptible to suspicions of witchcraft. This phenomenon included midwives: "[A] woman who safely delivered infants that were not expected to survive might find herself accused of witchcraft. In these cases, it was not simply the effects of their actions that were at issue, but the means: the unexpected results were attributed to knowledge or skill that could only come from occult agencies."[10] An uncanny ability to heal signaled a pact with the devil. This imagined agreement between a witch and the devil further underscored the suspected women as those who transgressed boundaries socially, sexually, and religiously; making the pact involved riotous drinking, intercourse with the devil, and a renouncement of Christian baptism.[11]

Puritans believed that when the agreement was made, the witch's body would bear a "witch's teat." While the witch's teat survives in the vernacular as a reference to feeling cold, its violent origin is less known. Witch-hunting guides contended that the devil marked his witches to easily identify them, and markings near a woman's breasts and groin were considered "witch's teats" at which her animal familiars suckled. Well versed with their clients' bodies, midwives were called to testify regarding marks on the skin, whether they were normal or abnormal, old or new. Doing so did not necessarily put them at further risk but effectively required them to use their knowledge against other women. During trials, juries investigated accused witches' nude bodies, adding yet another layer of victimization, a public humiliation with terrifying consequences.[12]

Karlsen suggests that the designation of "midwife" and the way information was recorded were both ambiguous, and that the desire for quantifiable data to prove whether midwives were disproportionately accused of witchcraft is unfulfillable. "We cannot," she writes, "determine precise numbers—or how explicit a woman's identification as healer had to be to render her vulnerable to suspicion—because all colonial women provided for their neighbors as well. Medical knowledge and skills were handed down from mother to daughter, in much the same way colonists thought witchcraft arts were passed on."[13] All women were expected to learn "recipes for medicines" and how to heal basic ailments and injuries, as well as to assist in childbirth and provide their own milk and care when fellow women died in childbirth.

Yet midwives held unique positions in colonial New England as primary medical professionals in communities. As the European, patriarchal medical profession was slowly established, women healers were barred from the new training and gradually vilified as dangerous quacks. This process cannot be easily disentangled from suspicions of witchcraft.

EMPOWERMENT THROUGH RECLAMATION

The conflict itself begs the question: how have midwives and witches become so important to feminist historians? Ultimately, this process of vilification is gendered violence against women who were uniquely empowered by their learnedness, and who were rendered more vulnerable by working outside of the home and existing outside of patriarchal, societal, monetary, and religious boundaries. That they may have been buffered from suspicion because their communities valued and respected them does not preclude them from being victimized by the process of vilification. Broadly speaking, an entire profession, and the very notion that women could be medical professionals, was—and is—at stake.

During the 1970s, feminist historians cast new light on women's history; two in particular turned their attention toward women healers. Barbara Ehrenreich and Deirdre English led community-based sessions on women's health and the history of its oppression. In 1973, the Feminist Press published *Witches, Midwives, and Nurses*, a powerhouse of a pamphlet and work of scholarship inspired by these sessions. Acknowledging profound sexism in the medical profession and women's mediated understanding of their own bodies, Ehrenreich and English had become aware "of a variety of ways women were abused or treated unjustly by the medical system," as both patients, subjected to cruel treatments with little information or choice, and workers, relegated to subordinate positions and supporting male doctors. Women and girls were denied access to information about their bodies and bodily processes.[14]

In 2010, in their introduction to the volume's second edition, the authors reflect: "We were beginning to suspect that women had not always, in all circumstances, been so disempowered with respect to their own bodies and care. After all, medical technology and the medical profession that monopolized it were relatively recent historical developments, and yet somehow our female ancestors had, however imperfectly, negotiated the challenges of the female life cycle."[15] In 1972, they had convened a conference on women's health with

> the central idea . . . that the medical profession as we knew it (still over 90 percent male) had replaced and driven out a much older tradition of female lay healing, including both midwifery and a range of healing skills, while closing medical education to women. In other words, the ignorance and disempowerment of women that we confronted in the 1970s were not longstanding conditions, but were the result of a prolonged power struggle that had taken place . . . well before the rise of scientific medicine. We traced a similar power struggle in Europe back to the early modern era . . . and how female lay healers of the same era were frequently targeted as "witches."

The inexpensive booklet was wildly popular and influential, the *Village Voice* deeming it an "underground bestseller," and soon it was translated into other languages and distributed globally.[16]

Central to the pamphlet is a powerful narrative describing the ways in which midwives and other female healers were disproportionately accused of witchcraft. Among the three primary accusations were "magical powers affecting health—of harming, but also of healing. They were often charged specifically with possessing medical and obstetrical skills."[17] They cite the *Malleus Maleficarum*: "No one does more harm to the Catholic Church than midwives."[18] Positioning the midwife's process as empirical, using trial and error to treat a vast variety of illnesses, Ehrenreich and English argue that she is ideologically at odds with the church and thus a prime target of witchcraft suspicion.[19] Midwives were further oppressed by the growing establishment of the medical profession, from which they were excluded. Ultimately, Ehrenreich and English argue that the "witch hunts did not eliminate the lower-class woman healer, but they branded her forever as superstitious and possibly malevolent."[20]

In 2010, the second edition of *Witches, Midwives, and Nurses* allowed Ehrenreich and English to reconsider some of their claims, offering corrections and nuances to their initial bold assertions:

> Looking back after all these years, what strikes us about the witch hunts are not only the bizarre beliefs that inspired them and the personal tragedies that ensued, but the sheer waste of talent and knowledge that they represented.

The victims, besides the individual women who were tortured and executed, were also all the people who were consequently deprived of their healing or midwifery skills. At a time we now associate with the Renaissance in Europe and the first signs of the scientific revolution, the witch hunts were a step back toward ignorance and helplessness. . . . What could have been a proud occupation for women and a field for lively intellectual inquiry was discredited when not actually obliterated.[21]

Is it not ironic that this occurred during an era glorified for its advancements in science and medicine?

Ultimately, the 2010 edition provides a platform for Ehrenreich and English to respond to David Harley, who attempted to discredit the connection they had drawn between midwives and witches: "While agreeing that witches were often folk healers, he criticized us, based on a survey of convictions in England, Scotland, and New England (data that was *not available* when we wrote), for exaggerating the proportion of midwives among convicted witches, saying we had maligned midwives and created 'a multitude of imaginary martyrs for the modern women's health movement.'"[22]

Ehrenreich and English refute Harley's determined argument for being rooted in lack of data. "Even now, with all the archival data that has become available, it's impossible for scholars to offer statistically firm generalizations about the occupations of women accused of witchcraft: usually, the convicted person's occupation was not recorded. Yet, the association that witch hunters made between witches and midwives in Europe is inescapable." They cite instances of midwives persecuted as witches and a study of witchcraft depositions by Brian P. Levack confirming that, throughout Europe and New England, women "cooks, healers and midwives" were "vulnerable to the charge that they practice[d] harmful magic."[23] Further rebuking Harley, Ehrenreich and English invoke colonial New England witchcraft scholar John Demos, whose research shows that a quarter to a third of suspected women were known for "making and administering special 'remedies,' providing expert forms of nursing, or serving in some regular way as midwives. A few were specifically described as 'doctor women.' . . . The underlying linkage here is obvious enough; the ability to heal and the ability to harm seemed intimately related."[24]

Ehrenreich and English's original 1973 text stands as an example of productive and effective second-wave feminist activism, and its contribution to recent surges of female-centered healthcare, midwifery, and breastfeeding can only be guessed. Certainly, what began as a modest pamphlet contributed in ensuing decades to a massive reclamation of women's participation in health and medicine. Now established, senior scholars of considerable influence, Ehrenreich and English continue to make convincing claims for the persecution of midwives as witches.

Ultimately, regarding "the midwife problem" and the question of the "midwife-witch," I maintain that it is critical to acknowledge the imperiled position of midwives and their unjust vilification, and encourage a scholarly response that: (1) acknowledges the conjuring of witches as systematic form of violence against women, (2) extricates the midwife from the witch, and (3) works toward a richer understanding of the critical role midwives have played, historically and across cultures. Lest we believe that this systematic subjugation lies in the distant past, amid myriad examples at the time of this writing, consider: the common practice of banning midwives from hospital delivery rooms, the refusal by insurance companies to cover midwifery by designating it "nontraditional," and several political attempts to defund Planned Parenthood, compromising not just affordable, accessible reproductive health for more than five million clients but also the employment of thousands of female medical practitioners. Further, becoming acquainted with the process through which women were vilified can in turn nuance both the creation and the consumption of witches in popular culture today.

CONTEMPORARY MANIFESTATIONS

Consider the cackle: unrestrained, a delight in power and freedom, tinged with warning. As midwives and other learned women who transcended social boundaries were persecuted for witchcraft, the witch trope grew in the popular imagination, beloved and feared for her ability to heal and harm, stubbornly resisting oppression and violence. The following evocations of witches today—Princess Nokia, Hermione Granger, and Willow Rosenberg—demonstrate a new generation of intersectional feminism, as multidimensional women with overlapping racial, sexual, social, mental, economic, and social identities. In so doing, these characters dismantle the outdated modes through which witches have commonly been represented, reveal current forms of violence and oppression women face, display their rich interior lives, and play with agency and identity through reclamations of the witch. If witches of the past—and the women unjustly accused of witchcraft—have come to represent a violent subjugation of women, these contemporary evocations powerfully battle the systems of patriarchal oppression that initially conjured the witch. The witch is clearly an established icon of feminism; how will new evocations evolve along with the movement itself?

URBAN FEMINISM, UTOPIC VISIONS

A New Yorker of Puerto Rican descent, musician and artist Princess Nokia mines Caribbean witchcraft and evokes *brujas* (witches) to sonically and visually explore her diasporic identity and spiritual heritage of Yoruba and Santería practice, and to celebrate communities of women, particularly women of color.[25] On November 8, 2016, the day of the US presidential election, Nokia independently released the video for her track "Brujas," in which she raps, "I'm the Black a-Rican bruja straight out from the Yoruba," and rhythmically lists the rich components of her racial, ethnic, and geographic background: African diaspora, Cuban, Arawak, black, Native American, Nigerian, and Puerto Rican.

Dreamy scenes of ethereal women moving in water visually convey brujas, important spiritual figures who exist not just in the distant past but today as well. Princess Nokia herself identifies as one, and she speaks of communicating with her diseased mother, who also identified as a bruja, through her spiritual practice. These hypnotic scenes are interspersed with badass witches of pop culture, four young women visually emulating Andrew Fleming's 1996 cult classic *The Craft*[26] and replacing the four leads with Princess Nokia and three friends. Damola Durosomo hails the grouping as "pure black and brown girl magic,"[27] a concept developed by CaShawn Thompson in 2013 to celebrate women of color, their accomplishments, and their support for one another.[28] "Brujas," writes Durosomo, is a vibrant exploration of the unique cultural inheritance of Afro-Latina women, an "anthem for women in the Diaspora who feel connected to the transcendental strength manifested by powerful deities like the Yoruba Orishas."[29] In both depicting women as powerful in groups and connecting women across time and space, Princess Nokia references and venerates the coven, rapping, "Casting spells with my cousins, I'm the head of this coven."

Historical texts reveal that independent women who came together in groups were suspected of secretly participating in covens and were imperiled precisely for that activity; Princess Nokia reclaims the coven and insists that it is a place of not just power but joy, buffered from external oppression through direct warnings, and promising: "I cast a circle in white and I can vanquish your spite, and if you hex me with hate then I'ma conjure the light."

As a feminist reclamation of witchcraft, "Brujas" follows Princess Nokia's 2015 track and video "Young Girls," honoring motherhood in what Barbara Calderón-Douglass calls a "feminist paradise that is filled with strong and beautiful brown women."[30] The video, codirected by Destiny Frasqueri (Nokia's given name) and her frequent collaborator, Milah Libin (a female music video director in her early twenties), is remarkable in a number of ways, such as its body positivity, featuring a diverse group of women in what Libin calls "a visual representation of body types and colors that don't get [offered] in media and in music videos." Strength forged among groups of women is central to what Nokia has termed "urban feminism," a concept that drives her work; during live shows she insists that women, particularly women of color, come to the front of the audience and create a safe space there for one another. In "Young Girls," she connects female empowerment to witchcraft. The video begins with Nokia foraging in a forest. Over the atmospheric sounds of birds chirping and leaves rustling, she speaks meditatively: "We are old souls, protectors of the earth, guardians of children, worshippers of the moon, mermaids of the ocean, we are followers of the sun, and women of magic." In a decidedly more direct tone, she states: "We *are* witches," emphasizing the word *are* in a further act of insistent reclamation.

In the video, a shot of the sky framed by leafy trees spins gently and cuts to a utopic scene of women and girls sitting together, moving their hands in unison, led by Nokia. Dubbed over, she then speaks of devotion to protecting nature and one another, and as in the "Brujas" track, she creates a clear linkage to the women of her ancestral roots: "From deep in the Caribbean, witches, who lived by nature." As the song's languid melody begins, Nokia walks through the forest, foraging, an action that provides sustenance for humans with no harm to nature, enjoying the cool water of the creek, laughing with her friends, and playing with a little girl. The following shots are subtly moving portraits of the individual women, followed by the group moving through the forest, as Nokia sings about the joy of their collectivity and individuality. She repeatedly emphasizes the special roles and responsibilities of young girls (also the title of the track), and while the video displays portraits of the girls, framed by the forest's lush greenery, Nokia sings that these young girls will become protectors of the earth and enter this matrilineal cycle, and that they are also part of a proud spiritual lineage.

Refusing to participate in a patriarchal music industry that exploits women and flattens the diversity of their lived experiences, identities, and bodies, Princess Nokia remains unsigned and thriving on her own, and among her community of women. Having quickly gained global acclaim, she speaks to and inspires an entirely new mode of feminism and an unencumbered way of being; that she evokes authentic witchcraft of the past and present underscores the enduring, or perhaps ascending, symbolism of the witch and coven for women—particularly those who are nonconforming, independent, and have experienced oppression.

Nokia's devotion to witchcraft extends into the realms of literature and popular culture, as she has frequently expressed her love of the *Harry Potter* series through social media posts, cosplay, and interviews. In 2017, she was asked by writer Paley Martin to reflect on love, and she responded, "Love is sitting at my favorite chicken and waffles restaurant, sipping a cup of tea and reading the *Harry Potter* series. That's true love to me."[31] Within the framework of this chapter, in subverting outdated stereotypes and reclaiming the witch as independent and enlightened, lines can be drawn between Nokia the heroine of that series, Hermione Granger.

POWER THROUGH LEARNEDNESS

Among today's "villains" of pop culture, witches are unique in attaining their power through knowledge, a characteristic firmly rooted in their predecessors. J. K. Rowling's beloved character Hermione Granger is quite valued in that re-gard. From the moment readers are introduced to Hermione, she is presented as emboldened by her intelligence and desire to learn, saying, "I've learned all the course books by heart of course. . . . I'm Hermione Granger, by the way, who are you?"[32] Throughout her training, she continues to develop her power by increasing her knowledge. In Hermione, Rowling conjured the "brightest or cleverest witch of her age," one based on the author herself. She uses the skill of time travel to read even more:

> Every night, without fail, Hermione was to be seen in a corner of the common room, several tables spread with books, Arithmancy charts, rune dictionaries, diagrams of Muggles lifting heavy objects, and file upon file of extensive notes; she barely spoke to anybody and snapped when she was interrupted.[33]

Like many lonely heroines of literature, Hermione is a bibliophile who finds solace in her books, and like many witches, she grows ever more powerful in developing her life of the mind.

While she may not seem a beacon of intersectional feminism, she is othered in multiple ways in a hierarchical social structure. Rowling explains the social politics of the space she created:

> I wanted Harry to leave our world and find exactly the same problems in the wizarding world. So you have the intent to impose a hierarchy, you have bigotry, and this notion of purity, which is this great fallacy, but it crops up all over the world. People like to think themselves superior and that if they can pride themselves in nothing else they can pride themselves on perceived purity.[34]

In wizarding terms, Hermione is "muggle-born," meaning a descendant of nonmagical humans; muggle-borns are referred to derogatorily as "mudbloods" and discriminated against for their lack of purity by some "half-bloods" and "pure-bloods" who object to the presence of impure wizards and witches at Hogwarts. Rowling herself has connected such politics to the tenets of Nazism and other regimes obsessed with blood purity. As Hermione faces discrimination, her dedication to social justice increases, and after the series ends, Rowling imagines her becoming a "progressive voice who ensure[s] the eradication of oppressive, pro-pureblood laws."[35] A mudblood among purebloods, a witch among wizards, a nerd among jocks, Hermione perseveres through an inner strength cultivated in her steadfast intellectualism; the cleverest witch at Hogwarts becomes a powerful opponent of oppression.

Ultimately, Rowling's beloved witch has made a profound cultural impact; in a *Hollywood Reporter* survey of nearly two thousand film industry professionals, Hermione was voted the favorite fictional female character of all time. Emma Watson, who rose to fame playing Hermione in eight films from age eleven to twenty-one, responded to the honor: "Her empathy, her sense of integrity, her decency and resolute belief in fighting for justice and fairness— even when her earnestness made her an easy target for ridicule—they're all unwavering.... Hermione made it okay for girls to be the smartest in the room. To be a leader, the one with the plan. She's not just a role for me, she's a symbol. I am deeply proud to have played her."[36]

TOWARD DEVILIFICATION

To complicate traditionally evil characters, franchises use time-traveling techniques to provide context and character development for villains (see Tara Lomax's chapter "You Were the Chosen One!" in this volume). This approach is predicated by modern humanist assertions that few people are entirely good or evil but rather are impacted by their circumstances and experiences. Thus these projects set out to answer questions about what led individual characters to become evil, and in so doing, humanize them.

A perceived moral instability among witches engenders fearful uncertainty among mortals. The premise of some recent books and films is to uncover the root causes of why some witches have swung toward evil, such as how Elphaba became *The Wizard of Oz*'s wicked witch in *Wicked*, and how Maleficent became the evil witch of *Sleeping Beauty* in *Maleficent*. Inventing backstories for iconically evil witches underscores the unpredictable, pendular nature of witches' morality; further, doing so humanizes these characters, conveying the trauma and heartache that can cause a divergence from one's core morality. This allows audiences to understand these witches as multidimensional characters. Within the broader context of this volume, I argue for the witch backstory as a process of devilification.

Similarly humanizing and fulfilling is the practice of revisiting favorite witches of the past. The gender and labor subversion inherent in the vilification of early witches manifests clearly in Joss Whedon's beloved character Willow Rosenberg and her most recent incarnation in a single-issue comic, *Willow: Goddesses and Monsters* (2009).[37] The one-shot comic book provides *Buffy the Vampire Slayer* fans with an update on Willow: grieving her partner Tara's death, she takes time to explore the breadth of her powers and struggles with the dark magic that entices her. Like the women accused of witchcraft during the violent birth of the American project, Willow is characterized by her quest for knowledge, by her ability to both help and harm (and the instability and frequency with which she oscillates between the two), and by her nonconforming gender and sexuality.

Whedon's progressive, empathetic handling of these issues provides an opportunity to consider the initial American women who were targeted for the characteristics that now render Willow a nuanced and beloved phenomenon of pop culture. The experimental narrative provides insight into Willow's rich interior life through a journey of self-discovery, through layers of her identity, as she wishes to better understand the nature of her power. The story begins with an embedded reference to none other than fellow witch Hermione Granger, as Willow stands on a platform resembling the iconic 9¾ of *Harry Potter* fame, with the Hogwarts Express train surrounded by young wizards and witches. Behind Willow, a boy resembling Harry chats with a brown-haired girl; although she turns away from the viewer, the stack of books nearby codes her as Hermione, and in so doing asserts an interconnectedness of witches. As an entry point to this tale, Whedon contextualizes Willow first as a witch, and as a young person, a student and lover of knowledge; it is from these foundational parts of her identity that she will further explore who she is and how she feels in the wake of losing her partner.

Greeted by her guide, Muffitt, Willow embarks on a mystical journey through stratified worlds that reveal various parts of her self. In the second level, the train disappears and Willow finds herself in a field of flowers. "Wow, are you ever a dyke," says Muffitt. "That term is offensive. Or maybe it's empowering—I can't always keep up. How do you know?" asks Willow.

Muffitt explains that in this level, straight witches see a "forest of tall, thrusting trees. . . . Being a fierce 'mo has nothing to do with your power, this is you relating to the outside world." Surrounded by flowers, they turn toward a vaginal threshold, juxtaposed by the "thrusting trees" visualized by heterosexual witches in this second level. This second part of her identity is tied to her sexuality and relationships with other people, connected to her queerness. "We are going deeper than that," says Muffitt, and they do so both physically and psychologically, as they sink through the fertile ground, drop through darkness, and land hard on the ground.

Willow's witchcraft mentor Aluwyn takes over as her guide. Through a series of interactions and conflicts, Willow comes to understand that much of what she experiences in her journey and in her life is simply an illusion; she chooses to move forward as her own guide. She realizes that at her core she is nonviolent, but that she is not fully herself as she grieves. Both the conflict and memories that accompany her grief are distractions from her purposeful journey.

She is greeted by goddesses: "There are many guides on the path to wisdom, but [Willow has] one in mind." Tara is revealed, and Willow is reminded of her painful loss. But Willow refuses Tara as her guide, wanting to know what lies ahead, rather than behind, and a way to find peace in her grief. Tara represents her internal love and lightness, juxtaposed by Aluwyn's chaos and darkness; this duality epitomizes Willow's propensity as a witch to be benevolent or malevolent, to help or to harm, and her instability as she struggles through her grief. "I said I wanted to understand my power—and I do. But under that I wanted to know my fate. . . . Was I a good witch or a bad witch? Under the under, I just wanted her." Whedon crafts a complex character with a rich interior life, a witch whose power is influenced by her emotional state and who is defined by those she has loved and lost. Willow plays a prominent role in the continuing *Buffy the Vampire Slayer* seasons eight, nine, and ten.[38] In the miniseries *Willow: Wonderland*, she travels to another dimension and attempts to bring magic back to earth.[39]

CONCLUSION

Reflecting on this dialogical exercise, I am struck by how the various processes of conjuring witches have been driven not just by fear, but by desire. The initial patriarchal anxiety about the few spaces in which women worked with total independence and agency, the midwife's ability to both harm and heal, and educated and nonconforming women, together produced a burning desire to control and suppress these spaces and women. In turn, this desire fueled a process of vilification: turning women into witches. In hindsight, and with adequate archival data in hand, this particular form of vilification is gendered violence, and should ignite fury for the lives and livelihoods lost, as well as newly informed concern about how this particular villain has endured unjustly and inaccurately in the popular imagination.

Centuries later, educated and nonconforming witches like Princess Nokia, Hermione Granger, and Willow Rosenberg rise up and face that violent history, and through their creators' progressive approaches, smash the patriarchy. Reclaiming the terms used to subjugate them, they combat systems of oppression, speak truth to power, and unapologetically display their multifaceted identities. What is owed to witches of the past and present? Creators and consumers of pop culture who are concerned with equity have a responsibility to remain attentive to the ways in which individuals who exist outside of a narrow construct of womanhood are endangered by systems of gendered oppression as they mutate and surface today.

In closing, if it is true that patriarchal desire conjured witches as a means to suppress women,[40] the ways in which intersectional feminists reclaim and empower witches sends a solemn warning to be heeded: be careful what you wish for.

Notes

1. The copy I studied for this project is an original from 1494, and an important part of Cornell University's Witchcraft Collection. Comprising more than thirteen thousand books, it is today known as one of the greatest witchcraft collections in the world, thanks to Cornell's first president, Andrew Dickson White, a history professor with a scholarly interest in fanaticism who built a broad collection of various secular materials, aggressively collecting witchcraft books and objects with the assistance of archivist and personal librarian George L. Burr. We do hold an original, from 1486 as well, which is currently undergoing conservation.

2. Rosemary Ellen Guiley, *The Encyclopedia of Witches and Witchcraft*, 2nd ed. (New York: Facts on File, 1999), 222.

3. John Demos, *The Enemy Within: 2,000 Years of Witch-Hunting in the Western World* (New York: Viking, 2008), 38.

4. Henricus Institoris and Jakob Sprenger, *Malleus Maleficarum*, trans. Christopher Mackay (Cambridge: Cambridge University Press, 2009).

5. Demos, *The Enemy Within*, 43.

6. Edward Peters, "The Literature of Demonology and Witchcraft," Cornell University Library Witchcraft Collection, 1998, available at http://ebooks.library.cornell.edu/w/witch/resources.html.

7. David Harley, "Historians as Demonologists: The Myth of the Midwife-Witch," *Social History of Medicine* 3, no. 1 (April 1990): 1.

8. Harley, "Historians as Demonologists," 5.

9. Laurel Thatcher Ulrich, *A Midwife's Tale: The Life of Martha Ballard, Based on Her Diary, 1785–1812* (New York: Vintage, 1991).

10. Carol F. Karlsen, *The Devil in the Shape of a Woman: Witchcraft in Colonial New England* (New York: W. W. Norton, 1998), 9.

11. Karlsen, *The Devil in the Shape of a Woman*, 10.

12. Karlsen, *The Devil in the Shape of a Woman*, 13.

13. Karlsen, *The Devil in the Shape of a Woman*, 142.

14. Barbara Ehrenreich and Deirdre English, *Witches, Midwives, and Nurses: A History of Women Healers*, 2nd ed. (New York: Feminist Press, 2010), 7–8.

15. Ehrenreich and English, *Witches, Midwives, and Healers*, 15.

16. Ehrenreich and English, *Witches, Midwives, and Healers*, 12–13.

17. Ehrenreich and English, *Witches, Midwives, and Healers*, 39.

18. Ehrenreich and English, *Witches, Midwives, and Healers*, 45.

19. Ehrenreich and English, *Witches, Midwives, and Healers*, 49.

20. Ehrenreich and English, *Witches, Midwives, and Healers*, 57.

21. Ehrenreich and English, *Witches, Midwives, and Healers*, 21.

22. Ehrenreich and English, *Witches, Midwives, and Healers*, 17.

23. Brian P. Levack, *The Witch-Hunt in Early Modern Europe*, 3rd ed. (Harlow, Essex, England: Pearson Longman, 2006), 146.

24. Demos, *The Enemy Within*, 119.

25. I include Princess Nokia here as a character, in that she is the performing persona and stage name of Destiny Frasqueri.

26. This astute observation was made by Anna Lee, a student in my course at Cornell University, Dangerous Women.

27. Damola Durosomo, "Princess Nokia's 'Brujas' Is the Afro-Latina Anthem America Needs This Week," *OkayAfrica*, November 10, 2016, available at http://www.okayafrica.com/video/princess-nokias-brujas-afro-latina-anthem/.

28. Dexter Thomas, "Why Everyone's Saying 'Black Girls Are Magic,'" *Los Angeles Times*, September 9, 2015, available at https://www.latimes.com/nation/nationnow/la-na-nn-everyones-saying-black-girls-are-magic-20150909-htmlstory.html.

29. Durosomo, "Princess Nokia's 'Brujas.'"

30. Barbara Calderón-Douglass, "Explore Princess Nokia's Feminist Utopia in Her New Video for 'Young Girls,'" *Vice*, January 20, 2015, available at https://www.vice.com/en_us/article/bn5e88/explore-princess-nokias-feminist-dream-paradise-in-her-new-music-video-815.

31. Paley Martin, "Quickie Q&A: Prince Nokia on Fear, Love and Being a Frantic Neurotic," *Tidal*, September 21, 2017, available at http://read.tidal.com/article/a-brief-qa-princess-nokia-on-fear-love-and-being-a-frantic-neurotic.

32. J. K. Rowling and Mary GrandPré, *Harry Potter and the Sorcerer's Stone* (New York: Arthur A. Levine, 1997), 106.

33. Rowling and GrandPré, *Harry Potter and the Sorcerer's Stone*, 230.

34. J. K. Rowling, "J. K. Rowling at Carnegie Hall Reveals Dumbledore Is Gay; Neville Marries Hannah Abbott, and Much More," the Leaky Cauldron, posted by EdwardTLC, October 20, 2007, available at http://www.the-leaky-cauldron.org/2007/10/20/j-k-rowling-at-carnegie-hall-reveals-dumbledore-is-gay-neville-marries-hannah-abbott-and-scores-more.

35. "J. K. Rowling Web Chat Transcript," the Leaky Cauldron, posted by Melissa Anelli, July 30, 2007, available at http://www.the-leaky-cauldron.org/2007/07/30/j-k-rowling-web-chat-transcript/.

36. "Hollywood's 50 Favorite Female Characters," *Hollywood Reporter*, December 9, 2016, available at https://www.hollywoodreporter.com/lists/50-best-female-characters-entertainment-industry-survey-results-951483.

37. Joss Whedon and Karl Moline, *Willow: Goddesses and Monsters* (Milwaukie, OR: Dark Horse Comics, 2009).

38. Joss Whedon, Brian K. Vaughan et al., *Buffy the Vampire Slayer, Season 8 Omnibus*, vol. 1 (Milwaukie, OR: Dark Horse Comics, 2017); Joss Whedon, Andrew Chambliss, Georges Jeanty, and Karl Moline, *Buffy the Vampire Slayer, Season 9*, vol. 1, *Freefall* (Milwaukie, OR: Dark Horse Comics, 2015); and Joss Whedon, Christos Gage, and Rebekah Isaacs, *Buffy the Vampire Slayer, Season 10*, vol. 1 (Milwaukie, OR: Dark Horse Comics, 2018).

39. Jeff Parker, Christos Gage, and Brian Ching, *Willow*, vol. 1, *Wonderland* (Milwaukie, OR: Dark Horse Comics, 2013).

40. While there is certainly a history of women practicing witchcraft, this chapter focuses on vilification as a process of women being unjustly accused of witchcraft.

CHAPTER 16

Voldemort's "Unusual Evil"

ADAM DAVIDSON-HARDEN

Lord Voldemort has seemed to grow less human with the passing years, and
the transformation he has undergone seemed to me to be only explicable if
his soul was mutilated beyond the realms of what we might call "usual evil."

J. K. ROWLING, *HARRY POTTER AND THE HALF-BLOOD PRINCE*

ARTISTIC, CULTURAL TREATMENTS OF EXTREME "IMMORALITY" OR EVIL, SUCH
as those offered in literature, offer us interpretations of morality in the context
of a safely abstracted and imaginary space, and within different cosmological
and philosophical contexts. Literary treatments of morality and evil may also
be rooted in religious/supernatural or nonreligious/humanistic frameworks,
from ancient sacred texts to modern secular narratives. Such overarching systems of thought and reference within narratives are a kind of "metanarrative,"
to borrow Jean-François Lyotard's conception.[1] Characters may be portrayed as
acting within moral contexts defined by a divine standard, or as beholden only
to their own and others' moral standards, in a humanistic rather than religious
framework. By extension, the question of the origins of evil or immorality—
the reason for its existence—is also caught up in discrete cosmological and
philosophical viewpoints. The way that stories frame evil through characters
invites readers to interpret how any narrative approaches the question of why
evil exists, and how evil functions in the universe of the story.

J. K. Rowling's Voldemort character, featured in the *Harry Potter* franchise
of books and films, represents a recent example of a humanist approach to
character-based evil in literature. Voldemort's uniqueness, his brand of "unusual
evil," is rooted in its essential humanism—expressed by the character's desire to
transcend mortality as well as in the relational reverberations of his essential
psychopathic tendencies. Rowling's portrayal of Voldemort's "inhuman" influence and resonance in the lives of "good" characters situates her archvillain in
a fully profane, humanistic context. Evil is signified through a portrayal of its

rootedness in individual existential choices. Voldemort represents an essentially humanistic hermeneutics of evil, and this approach contrasts with that of an author to whom Rowling owes inspiration, namely J. R. R. Tolkien, whose "evil" characters are firmly rooted in his own fully articulated religious/divine framework. As the author's Voldemort character is developed along with the main story arc, readers are invited to gauge his "unusual evil" increasingly by its influence on the relationships between characters as exemplified by their choices, actions, and behavior.

SITUATING EVIL THROUGH NARRATIVE

In her work on narrative and evil, María Pía Lara[2] conceptualizes literature and narrative as essential means for representing morality and evil to facilitate our own hermeneutic processes of interpretation, analysis, and reflection. In this light, religious or sacred texts themselves can be seen as a form of contrived mythological narrative about human existence that wishes to place elements of our being supernaturally outside of ourselves. In the context of religious belief systems, the reader-as-believer may choose to objectify and internalize such stories as cosmologically "true," or acknowledge that they, too, are simply one among many cultural products or texts that use narrative as an artistic and cultural tool for self-reflection and interpretation.

In Western thought, the very term "evil" has an intellectual provenance in Christian theologies that struggle to reconcile a "good" God with worldly and individual evils (or "sins"), an area of debate known as "theodicy." Successive answers to the question of the "problem of evil," as it is often referred to in this context, have sought to reconcile this apparent contradiction in many ways, if the existence of a supremely good and powerful divine presence is to be accepted.[3] Augustine, an early Christian theologian, innovated the idea of the "original sin" as an early form of theodicy, pointing to the character of Adam in the Torah's book of Genesis and his initial disobedience of God as a source for all humankind being born with an inherent disposition toward sin.[4] Of course, not all literature needs to point to a divine or religious belief system to validate or support an interpretation of evil or immorality. The intellectual era known as the Enlightenment began an explosion of moral philosophy that sought to grapple with the existence of immorality and evil on a more humanistic basis.

Immanuel Kant's *Religion within the Limits of Reason Alone*[5] marked the Enlightenment's igniting of a humanist line of inquiry into morality and evil from a philosophical perspective, although his arguments may be said to accommodate religion and deism within a humanistic context (in a time when it was still slightly dangerous to speak critically of religion in Western/European cultures). For Kant, the choice of evil represented an individual deviation from the natural moral law, as against the laws of reason. Kant asserted a basic propensity to good in humanity, characterizing "radical evil" as an ethical choice in an essentially humanistic context. Nietzsche mounted his own full-scale philosophical and cosmological rebellion against Christian culture in his work; he actively sought to deconstruct prevailing conceptions of morality as residing in a specific cultural context while attacking European/Western culture and its Judeo-Christian basis.[6] Following this type of critical hermeneutic stance, one may see every story—like Rowling's *Harry Potter* saga—as offering a distinct interpretation of morality and evil that exists in its own narrative universe, which may or may not connect to broader metanarratives touching on morality, such as those rooted in theism or religious belief generally.

Mythological and religious narratives, literature considered "sacred" by the devout, offer a variety of stories that frame human morality with reference to divine command and sanction. The stories of what believers in Judaism call the Torah, for example, set up morality in the context of human submission to divine will, whether directly or indirectly mediated through prophets or other intermediaries. Rowling's universe has no direct religious frame of reference other than a passing mention of Christian cultural holidays. The moral universe of the *Potter* stories is firmly rooted in human interaction. One consequence of this orientation, when combined with the overwhelming popularity of the series, is the phenomenon of negative reactions from Christian audiences whose more fundamentalist outlook might cause them to bristle against mentions of witchcraft and magic in the context of a story that pays no outright obeisance to Christianity's narratives (despite Harry's eventual Christ-like self-sacrifice in book 7, *The Deathly Hallows*). In the 1990s, parents in the Durham District School Board in my province of Ontario attempted to have book 1 of the *Harry Potter* series banned because of its alleged representations of witchcraft. The twenty or so phone calls and complaints about *The Sorcerer's/Philosopher's Stone* were brought forward by devoutly fundamentalist Christian families who were rankled, no doubt, not least by the idea of "witches and wizards" (which we may find laughable), but also perhaps by the rooting of Rowling's story in a world that does not directly feature Christian culture as a frame of moral reference, despite the fact that holidays such as Christmas and Easter are mentioned in the books. The ban was actually in force for a time in 2000 but was rescinded that same year.[7]

In book 7, *Harry Potter and the Deathly Hallows*, we come closest to a representation of Christian culture when Harry and Hermione pass a church on Christmas Eve in the wizarding village of Godric's Hollow, where they hear Christmas carols. Despite these surface references, however, it is clear that religion plays essentially no role in the lives of the protagonists of the *Harry Potter* series, except through the oblique nod to the reality of "soul" and the "afterlife" in the universe of Rowling's narrative (a type of cosmology that embraces some metaphysics without the concept of the divine). This broadly humanistic basis of the culture of the "Potterverse" reverberates in its portrayal of evil, which itself is a type of posttheological representation. As I will suggest in the conclusion, one may wish to interpret the themes of love and self-sacrifice as tributes to Christian culture and belief. However, Voldemort's evil seems securely rooted in the context of human relationships, in a world where the idea of the divine is never even mentioned.

The *Potter* franchise's humanism contrasts interestingly with another author to whom Rowling owes inspiration, namely J. R. R. Tolkien. The sense of religious-inspired cosmology penetrating his deeply imaginative works is palpably connected with his own Catholic Christian devotion (just as is his colleague C. S. Lewis's Christian Protestantism). Whereas in Tolkien's broader world, characters are subject to the whims, favors, and powers of immortals,[8] Rowling's world features human beings having adventures with fully human consequences, in relationship to one another and a "fantastic" natural context where nature itself is imbued with magical properties. There is no divine presence pushing the characters of the Potterverse around. The protagonists are free to face trials and make mistakes, which even the most powerful of the "good" characters do, along the way. Although Rowling uses the idea of a "soul" and hints at an "afterlife," the realities and consequences of evil and morality are rooted in the human world of the story's characters.

THE HUMANISTIC EVIL OF VOLDEMORT

The Potterverse's humanism is reflected well in the portrayal of its archvillain. Voldemort might merely be a derivative contemporary successor to a long line of power-hungry, psychopathic, murderous villains if it weren't for the social context of his villainy and the existential nature of his self-directed brand of evil. First, we have his origins, that of the boy Tom Marvolo Riddle, rejected and poverty-stricken orphan to a witch mother who herself bewitched a muggle (ordinary human) father—Tom Riddle Senior—to have Tom Junior. Riddle constructs himself the identity of Voldemort as a teenager as he continues on a dark path of negative moral choices that lead to the circumstances of the whole book series, notably book 7, *Harry Potter and the Deathly Hallows*. In this book we discover that Riddle—aka Voldemort—has resorted to the darkest form of magic to create "horcruxes," thereby ripping pieces of his soul apart repeatedly in order to attempt to achieve a form of immortality (something his nemesis Albus Dumbledore remarks on in the epigraph above). This is achieved through murder, which allows the murdering wizard to enclose a ripped portion of his soul in any object, which in turn becomes a piece of the soul's "body." We learn in book 6—*Harry Potter and the Half-Blood Prince*—that in doing so Voldemort has moved beyond what Dumbledore terms "usual evil."[9] In the memory of Dumbledore's interview with the boy Riddle in the orphanage, we have a hint of Voldemort's nascent obsession with death and immortality in his comment that his mother "can't have been magic, or she wouldn't have died."[10] Voldemort's growing hatred of muggles stems from his revulsion for his muggle father, who along with his paternal grandparents is the first to fall victim to his son. The evil into which Voldemort/Riddle grows and ultimately chooses includes a Machiavellian life dedicated to accumulating power and influence through dark magic, including undertaking acts of murder, torture, and mind control to secure his goals (the three "unforgivable curses," which will be explored below).

Voldemort's choice of an evil path fits the philosophical zeitgeist of existentialism well, as reflected in the work of Kierkegaard, Heidegger, Sartre, and Beauvoir particularly, and captured well in the idea of "authenticity."[11] Existential perspectives stress the meaning of self-directed existence and the ultimate primacy of individual choices to determine one's intentions, actions, and worlds as "authentic." The idea that we take ownership over our lives and existence on a moment-to-moment basis by committing to various choices is a consistent theme that links existential thinkers. In the *Harry Potter* series, the protagonist and antagonist choose contradictory, authentic paths set in a firm social context where the consequences of their choices reverberate throughout relationships with and between other characters. Whereas evil and good, dark and light suffuse the worlds of *Star Wars* and *The Lord of the Rings* as eternal absolutes—sometimes personified by mystical or divine-type characters or forces—in the Potterverse, good and evil are situated in the humanity (or lack thereof), and deliberate acts, of Harry and Voldemort.

Rowling constructs Voldemort/Riddle as building a kind of death cult, branding his followers the "Death Eaters" and undertaking anything he can to further his vision of wizard supremacy over muggles, as well as his own control, influence, and power in the wizarding world. He creates his own nemesis in Harry Potter when he tries to murder him as a child, having heard a prophecy that a child born on Harry's birthday would be a threat to him. The arc of the series consists of Harry testing his strength as he adventures against Voldemort, battling one of his horcruxes in book 2 (*Harry Potter and the Chamber of Secrets*), facing his return in book 4 (*Harry Potter and the Goblet of Fire*), and finally personally facing him in a final confrontation in *Harry Potter and the Deathly Hallows*.

Voldemort's existential choice to follow a dark, evil path of murder and his defiance of human mortality, along with his notable psychopathic features—the inability to form true friendships and his incapacity for love—make up the core of his evil in the series. What sets Voldemort apart in his particular representation of a hermeneutics of evil is the way his horcruxes impact upon the relationships between others, in addition to his own actions. In books 2 and 7 of the series, we see the emotional effects that horcruxes can have on people who "get close" to them. Ginny Weasley, Harry's later love interest, is possessed by one of Voldemort's horcruxes in book 2, the major problem of that book that Harry must eventually solve. In book 7, after Harry, Ron, and Hermione find another horcrux, they take turns wearing it around their neck (an obvious homage to Frodo bearing Sauron's Ring of Power in Tolkien's epic *Lord of the Rings* trilogy). The consequence of this is that the three of them are affected by negative emotions, heaviness, and despair. They experience increased irritation and aggressiveness while wearing the horcrux, as though part of the essence of Voldemort's psychopathic and malignant evil can have influence on their relationships via the power of the horcrux. In this context, Voldemort's evil is modeled as a relational construct, symbolically portrayed in the horcruxes' negative influence on those close to it. In addition to this suggestive relational power of Voldemort's evil as embodied in the horcruxes, Rowling offers the additional interesting case of Harry himself *being* a horcrux, which suggests further dimensions to Voldemort's representation of evil.

In Rowling's wizarding world, three spells called the "Unforgivable Curses" are categorized as the three most immoral, evil acts a wizard can undertake. The Avada Kedavra, or killing curse, represents the most heinous of the three and is the reason why Harry is orphaned to begin the series. This is how Voldemort is able to make horcruxes, because, as we learn in book 6, the act of killing "rips the soul apart." We learn in book 7 that Voldemort never realizes that he created an unintended seventh horcrux in unsuccessfully attempting to kill Harry as a child, after his mother and father die trying to defend him. Harry himself carries a horcrux, which is the reason he can speak to snakes (a rare trait passed down through Voldemort's family line from the ancient Salazar Slytherin), feel pain in his scar related to Voldemort, and even see into Voldemort's mind when Voldemort is experiencing some powerful emotion, something he learns fully in *Order of the Phoenix*.[12] In addition to the killing curse, there is the Cruciatus, or torture curse, and the Imperius, or mind-control curse.

Harry's housing of a horcrux poses some questions about how evil can influence individual decision making and actions within the universe of the story. In book 6, Dumbledore distances himself from Harry, worrying that the growing connection between Harry and Voldemort might put Harry and himself in danger. Dumbledore has Snape attempt to teach Harry occlumency, or the shielding of one's mind from magical influence and penetration, in an effort to suppress the connection, an effort that ultimately fails; Harry finally masters his feelings in conflict with the influence of the horcrux over his conscious mind in book 7. In particular in book 6, Harry wrestles with the feelings that are arguably tied to the horcrux he carries. This feature of the story causes us to wonder whether the unintended horcrux is the reason why Harry's rage leads him to attempt the Cruciatus curse on his godfather Sirius Black's murderer, Bellatrix Lestrange, or why he also uses the Cruciatus curse on another Death Eater, Amycus Carrow, after he insults and threatens Minerva McGonagall, head of Gryffindor House at Hogwarts, in book 7.[13] In their break-in to Gringotts Bank to steal a horcrux (also in book 7), Harry also uses the Imperius curse, although this act is depicted as tactical and morally acceptable under the circumstances.[14] In the end we are left with killing (the Avada Kedavra curse) as the ultimate immoral and evil act, a line that we presume Harry never crosses, although he may have taken a life in self-defense while casting nonkilling spells while being pursued in the beginning of book 7.

After the seventh and unintended horcrux inside Harry is destroyed inadvertently by Voldemort himself near the end of book 7, Harry proceeds to protect his friends and supporters from further harm without resort to any of the "unforgivable" curses, and he eventually prevails. The presence of the horcrux inside him throughout the series is suggestive, however, when appreciated beside the aggressive actions, feelings, and thoughts he experiences while carrying it. Despite the presence of a horcrux inside him, driving him as it were toward evil, Harry chooses a path of predominantly good intentions and actions. Such a choice reminds readers of our own everyday challenges to live according to moral standards that emphasize an ethics of respect, love, and the good for oneself and others. The inhuman aspect of evil in this context is captured in its antisociality: Voldemort, as evil, represents the absence of love and the presence of a psychopathic desire for power and self-aggrandizement, in defiance of something so basically human as death.

Ultimately, the essence of Voldemort's evil is simultaneously relational and existential in its influence on the behavior of others through the horcrux. This model of humanistic evil, rooted in the morality of choices that impact human relationships, is fittingly pitted against the great "power the Dark Lord knows not" as prophesied by Sybil Trelawney to Albus Dumbledore—that is, love.[15] Love saves Harry in the form of his mother's sacrifice, and love saves his allies in the form of his self-sacrifice in book 7. Love is the reason why Voldemort cannot possess Harry without difficulty, even for a short time, at the end of book 5 (*The Order of the Phoenix*), as his own psychopathic lack of love clashes so utterly with Harry's better nature. It is possible to argue that Rowling channels Harry as a Christ figure in his act of heroic self-sacrifice, on a symbolic level. Despite this and other echoes of Christian themes and metaphysics in the Potterverse, however, ultimately Voldemort's evil is convincingly humanistic in its existential nature, rooted strongly in the series' world of human relationships.

Notes

1. Jean-François Lyotard, *The Postmodern Condition: A Report on Knowledge* (Minneapolis: University of Minnesota Press, 1984).

2. María Pía Lara, *Narrating Evil: A Post-Metaphysical Theory of Reflective Judgment* (New York: Columbia University Press, 2007).

3. Paul Ricoeur, *The Symbolism of Evil* (Boston: Beacon Press, 1969); and Paul Ricoeur, *Evil: A Challenge to Philosophy and Theology* (London: Continuum, 2007).

4. Michael Mendelson, "Saint Augustine," Stanford Encyclopedia of Philosophy Archive, Winter 2016, available at https://plato.stanford.edu/archives/win2016/entries/augustine/.

5. Immanuel Kant, *Religion within the Limits of Reason Alone*, trans. Theodore M. Greene and Hoyt H. Hudson (New York: Harper and Row, 1960).

6. Friedrich Wilhelm Nietzsche, *Beyond Good and Evil: Prelude to a Philosophy of the Future*, trans. Walter Kaufmann (New York: Vintage, 1989).

7. Devon Peavoy, "Banning Books, Burning Bridges: Recognizing Student Freedom of Expression Rights in Canadian Classrooms," *Dalhousie Journal of Legal Studies* 13 (January 2004): 125.

8. J. R. R. Tolkien, *The Silmarillion* (Boston: Allen and Unwin, 1977); and J. R. R. Tolkien and Christopher Tolkien, *The History of Middle-Earth*, vol. 3 (London: HarperCollins, 2002).

9. J. K. Rowling, *Harry Potter and the Half-Blood Prince* (New York: Arthur A. Levine, 2005), 502.

10. Rowling, *Harry Potter and the Half-Blood Prince*, 275.

11. Somogy Varga and Charles Guignon, "Authenticity," Stanford Encyclopedia of Philosophy Archive, Winter 2016, available at https://plato.stanford.edu/archives/sum2016/entries/authenticity/; and Steven Crowell, "Existentialism," Stanford Encyclopedia of Philosophy Archive, Winter 2016, available at https://plato.stanford.edu/archives/spr2016/entries/existentialism/.

12. J. K. Rowling, *Harry Potter and the Order of the Phoenix* (New York: Scholastic, 2004).

13. J. K. Rowling, *Harry Potter and the Deathly Hallows* (New York: Arthur A. Levine, 2007), 594. McGonagall uses the Imperius curse immediately afterward to restrain the unconscious Death Eaters, which invites readers to consider whether this Unforgivable Curse might be a necessary evil in the context of war.

14. Rowling, *Harry Potter and the Deathly Hallows*, 531.

15. Rowling, *Harry Potter and the Order of the Phoenix*, 831.

SUPERVILLAINY IN CINEMA AND TELEVISION

CHAPTER 17

Caligari[1]

SIEGFRIED KRACAUER

THE CZECH HANS JANOWITZ, ONE OF THE TWO AUTHORS OF THE FILM *DAS Cabinet des Dr. Caligari* (*The Cabinet of Dr. Caligari*), was brought up in Prague—that city where reality fuses with dreams, and dreams turn into visions of horror.[2] One evening in October 1913 this young poet was strolling through a fair in Hamburg, trying to find a girl whose beauty and manner had attracted him. The tents of the fair covered the Reeperbahn, known to any sailor as one of the world's chief pleasure spots. Nearby, on the Holstenwall, Hugo Lederer's gigantic Bismarck monument stood sentinel over the ships in the harbor. In search of the girl, Janowitz followed the fragile trail of a laugh that he thought hers into a dim park bordering the Holstenwall. The laugh, which apparently served to lure a young man, vanished somewhere in the shrubbery. When, a short time later, the young man departed, another shadow, hidden until then in the bushes, suddenly emerged and moved along—as if on the scent of that laugh. Passing this uncanny shadow, Janowitz caught a glimpse of him: he looked like an average bourgeois. Darkness reabsorbed the man, and made further pursuit impossible. The following day big headlines in the local press announced: "Horrible sex crime on the Holstenwall! Young Gertrude . . . murdered." An obscure feeling that Gertrude might have been the girl of the fair impelled Janowitz to attend the victim's funeral. During the ceremony he suddenly had the sensation of discovering the murderer, who had not yet been captured. The man he suspected seemed to recognize him, too. It was the bourgeois—the shadow in the bushes.

Carl Mayer, coauthor with Janowitz of *Caligari*, was born in the Austrian provincial capital of Graz, where his father, a wealthy businessman, would have prospered had he not been obsessed by the idea of becoming a "scientific" gambler. In the prime of life he sold his property, went, armed with an infallible "system," to Monte Carlo, and reappeared a few months later in Graz: broke. Under the stress of this catastrophe, the monomaniac father turned the sixteen-year-old Carl and his three younger brothers out into the street and finally committed suicide. A mere boy, Carl Mayer was responsible for the three children. While he toured through Austria, peddling barometers, singing in choirs, and playing extras in peasant theaters, he became increasingly interested in the stage. There was no branch of theatrical production that he did not explore during those years of nomadic life—years full of experiences that were to be of immense use in his future career as a film poet. At the beginning of the war, the adolescent made his living by sketching Hindenburg portraits on postcards in Munich cafés. Later in the war, Janowitz reports, he had to undergo repeated examinations of his mental condition. Mayer seems to have been very embittered against the high-ranking military psychiatrist in charge of his case.

The war was over. Janowitz, who from its outbreak had been an officer in an infantry regiment, returned as a convinced pacifist, animated by hatred of an authority that had sent millions of men to death. He felt that absolute authority was bad in itself. He settled in Berlin, met Carl Mayer there, and soon found out that this eccentric young man, who had never before written a line, shared his revolutionary moods and views. Why not express them on the screen? Intoxicated by Paul Wegener's films, Janowitz believed that this new medium might lend itself to powerful poetic revelations. As youth will, the two friends embarked on endless discussions that hovered around Janowitz's Holstenwall adventure as well as Mayer's mental duel with the psychiatrist. These stories seemed to evoke and supplement each other. After such discussions the pair would stroll through the night, irresistibly attracted by a dazzling and clamorous fair on Kantstrasse. It was a bright jungle, more hell than paradise, but a paradise to those who had exchanged the horror of war for the terror of want. One evening, Mayer dragged his companion to a sideshow by which he had been impressed. Under the title "Man or Machine," it presented a strong man who achieved miracles of strength in an apparent stupor. He acted as if he were hypnotized. The strangest thing was that he accompanied his feats with utterances that affected the spellbound spectators as pregnant forebodings.

Any creative process approaches a moment when only one additional experience is needed to integrate all elements into a whole. The mysterious figure of the strong man supplied such an experience. On the night of this show, the friends first visualized the original story of *Caligari*. They wrote the manuscript in the following six weeks. Defining the part each took in the work, Janowitz calls himself "the father who planted the seed, and Mayer the mother who conceived and ripened it." At the end, one small problem arose: the authors were at a loss as to what to christen their main character, a psychiatrist shaped after Mayer's archenemy during the war. A rare volume, *Unknown Letters of Stendhal*, offered the solution. While Janowitz was skimming through this find of his, he happened to notice that Stendhal, just come from the battlefield, met at La Scala in Milan an officer named Caligari. The name clicked with both authors.

Their story is located in a fictitious northern German town near the Dutch border, significantly called Holstenwall. One day, a fair moves into the town, with merry-go-rounds and sideshows—among the latter that of Dr. Caligari, a weird, bespectacled man advertising the somnambulist Cesare. To procure a license, Caligari goes to the town hall, where he is treated haughtily by an arrogant official. The following morning, this official is found murdered in his room, which does not prevent the townspeople from enjoying the fair's pleasures. Along with numerous onlookers, Francis and Alan—two students in love with Jane, a medical man's daughter—enter the tent of Dr. Caligari and watch Cesare slowly stepping out of an upright, coffinlike box. Caligari tells the thrilled audience that the somnambulist will answer questions about the future. Alan, in an excited state, asks how long he has to live. Cesare opens his mouth; he seems to be dominated by a terrific, hypnotic power emanating from his master. "Until dawn," he answers. At dawn Francis learns that his friend has been stabbed in exactly the same manner as the official. The student, suspicious of Caligari, persuades Jane's father to assist him in an investigation. With a search warrant the two force their way into the showman's wagon and demand that he end the trance of his medium. However, at this very moment they are called away to the police station to attend the examination of a criminal who has been caught in the act of killing a woman, and who now frantically denies that he is the pursued serial murderer.

Francis continues spying on Caligari and, after nightfall, secretly peers through a window of the wagon. But while he imagines he sees Cesare lying in his box, Cesare in reality breaks into Jane's bedroom, lifts a dagger to pierce the sleeping girl, gazes at her, puts the dagger away, and flees with the screaming Jane in his arms, over roofs and roads. Chased by her father, he drops the girl, who is then escorted home, whereas the lonely kidnapper dies of exhaustion. As Jane, in flagrant contradiction of what Francis believes to be the truth, insists on having recognized Cesare, Francis approaches Caligari a second time to solve the torturing riddle. The two policemen in his company seize the coffinlike box, and Francis draws out of it—a dummy representing the somnambulist. Profiting by the investigators' carelessness, Caligari himself manages to escape. He seeks shelter in a lunatic asylum. The student follows him, calls on the director of the asylum to inquire about the fugitive, and recoils horror-struck: the director and Caligari are one and the same person.

The following night—the director has fallen asleep—Francis and three members of the medical staff whom he has initiated into the case search the director's office and discover material fully establishing the guilt of this authority in psychiatric matters. Among a pile of books they find an old volume about a showman named Caligari who, in the eighteenth century, traveled through northern Italy, hypnotized his medium Cesare into murdering sundry people, and, during Cesare's absence, substituted a wax figure to deceive the police. The main exhibit is the director's clinical records; they evidence that he desired to verify the account of Caligari's hypnotic faculties, that his desire grew into an obsession, and that, when a somnambulist was entrusted to his care, he could not resist the temptation of repeating with him those terrible games. He had adopted the identity of Caligari. To make him admit his crimes, Francis confronts the director with the corpse of his tool, the somnambulist. No sooner does the monster realize that Cesare is dead than he begins to rave. Trained attendants put him into a straitjacket.

This horror tale in the spirit of E. T. A. Hoffmann was an outspoken revolutionary story. In it, as Janowitz indicates, he and Mayer half-intentionally stigmatized the omnipotence of a state authority manifesting itself in universal conscription and declarations of war. The German war government seemed to the authors the prototype of such voracious authority. Subjects of the Austro-Hungarian monarchy, they were in a better position than most citizens of the Reich to penetrate the fatal tendencies inherent in the German system. The character of Caligari embodies these tendencies; he stands for an unlimited authority that idolizes power as such, and, to satisfy its lust for domination, ruthlessly violates all human rights and values. . . . Functioning as a mere instrument, Cesare is not so much a guilty murderer as Caligari's innocent victim. This is how the authors themselves understood him. According to the pacifist-minded Janowitz, they had created Cesare with the dim design of portraying the common man who, under the pressure of compulsory military service, is drilled to kill and to be killed. The revolutionary meaning of the story reveals itself unmistakably at the end, with the disclosure of the psychiatrist as Caligari: reason overpowers unreasonable power, insane authority is symbolically abolished. Similar ideas were also being expressed on the contemporary stage, but the authors of *Caligari* transferred them to the screen without including any of those eulogies of the authority-freed "New Man" in which many expressionist plays indulged.

A miracle occurred: Erich Pommer, chief executive of Decla-Bioscop, accepted this unusual, if not subversive, script. Was it a miracle? Since in those early postwar days the conviction prevailed that foreign markets could only be conquered by artistic achievements, the German film industry was of course anxious to experiment in the field of aesthetically qualified entertainment.[3] Art ensured export, and export meant salvation. An ardent partisan of this doctrine, Pommer had moreover an incomparable flair for cinematic values and popular demands. Regardless of whether he grasped the significance of the strange story Mayer and Janowitz had submitted to him, he certainly sensed its timely atmosphere and interesting scenic potentialities. He was a born promoter who handled screen and business affairs with equal facility and, above all, excelled in stimulating the creative energies of directors and players. In 1923, Ufa was to make him chief of its entire production.[4] His behind-the-scenes activities were to leave their imprint on the pre-Hitler screen.

Pommer assigned Fritz Lang to direct *Caligari*, but in the middle of the preliminary discussions Lang was ordered to finish his serial *The Spiders*; the distributors of this film urged its completion.[5] Lang's successor was Dr. Robert Wiene. Since his father, a once-famous Dresden actor, had become slightly insane toward the end of his life, Wiene was not entirely unprepared to tackle the case of Dr. Caligari. He suggested, in complete harmony with what Lang had planned, an essential change of the original story—a change against which the two authors violently protested. But no one heeded them.[6]

The original story was an account of real horrors; Wiene's version transforms that account into a chimera concocted and narrated by the mentally deranged Francis. To effect this transformation, the body of the original story is put into a framing story that introduces Francis as a madman. The film *Caligari* opens with the first of the two episodes composing the frame. Francis is shown sitting on a bench in the park of the lunatic asylum, listening to the confused babble of a fellow sufferer. Moving slowly, like an apparition, a female inmate of the asylum passes by: it is Jane. Francis says to his companion: "What I have experienced with her is still stranger than what you have encountered. I will tell it to you."[7] Fade-out. Then a view of Holstenwall fades in, and the original story unfolds, ending, as has been seen, with the identification of Caligari. After a new fade-out, the second and final episode of the framing story begins. Francis, having finished the narration, follows his companion back to the asylum, where he mingles with a crowd of sad figures—among them Cesare, who absent-mindedly caresses a little flower. The director of the asylum, a mild and understanding-looking person, joins the crowd. Lost in the maze of his hallucinations, Francis takes the director for the nightmarish character he himself has created and accuses this imaginary fiend of being a dangerous madman. He screams; he fights the attendants in a frenzy. The scene is switched over to a sickroom, with the director putting on horn-rimmed spectacles, which immediately change his appearance: it seems to be Caligari who examines the exhausted Francis. After this, he removes his spectacles and, all mildness, tells his assistants that Francis believes him to be Caligari. Now that he understands the case of his patient, the director concludes, he will be able to heal him. With this cheerful message, the audience is dismissed.

Janowitz and Mayer knew why they raged against the framing story: it perverted, if not reversed, their intrinsic intentions. While the original story exposed the madness inherent in authority, Wiene's *Caligari* glorified authority and convicted its antagonist of madness. A revolutionary film was thus turned into a conformist one—following the much-used pattern of declaring some normal but troublesome individual insane and sending him to a lunatic asylum. This change undoubtedly resulted not so much from Wiene's personal predilections as from his instinctive submission to the necessities of the screen; films, at least commercial films, are forced to answer to mass desires. In its changed form, *Caligari* was no longer a product expressing, at best, sentiments characteristic of the intelligentsia, but a film supposed equally to be in harmony with what the less educated felt and liked.

If it holds true that during the postwar years most Germans eagerly tended to withdraw from a harsh outer world into the intangible realm of the soul, Wiene's version was certainly more consistent with their attitude than the original story; for, by putting the original into a box, this version faithfully mirrored the general retreat into a shell. In *Caligari* (and several other films of the time) the device of a framing story was not only an aesthetic form but also had symbolic content. Significantly, Wiene avoided mutilating the original story itself. Even though Caligari had become a conformist film, it preserved and emphasized this revolutionary story—as a madman's fantasy. Caligari's defeat now belonged among psychological experiences. In this way Wiene's film does suggest that during their retreat into themselves the Germans were stirred to reconsider their traditional belief in authority. Down to the bulk of social democratic workers they refrained from revolutionary action; yet at the same time a psychological revolution seems to have prepared itself in the depths of the collective soul. The film reflects this double aspect of German life by coupling a reality in which Caligari's authority triumphs with a hallucination in which the same authority is overthrown. There could be no better configuration of symbols for that uprising against the authoritarian dispositions, which apparently occurred under the cover of a behavior rejecting uprising. . . .

Caligari shows the "Soul at Work." On what adventures does the revolutionized soul embark? The narrative and pictorial elements of the film gravitate toward two opposite poles. One can be labeled "Authority," or, more explicitly, "Tyranny." The theme of tyranny, with which the authors were obsessed, pervades the screen from beginning to end. Swivel-chairs of enormous height symbolize the superiority of the city officials turning on them, and, similarly, the gigantic back of the chair in Alan's attic testifies to the invisible presence of powers that have their grip on him. Staircases reinforce the effect of the furniture: numerous steps ascend to police headquarters, and in the lunatic asylum itself no fewer than three parallel flights of stairs are called upon to mark Dr. Caligari's position at the top of the hierarchy. . . . Caligari is a very specific premonition in the sense that he uses hypnotic power to force his will upon his tool—a technique foreshadowing, in content and purpose, that manipulation of the soul that Hitler was the first to practice on a gigantic scale.

Notes

1. Excerpted from Siegfried Kracauer, *From Caligari to Hitler: A Psychological History of German Film* (Princeton, NJ: Princeton University Press, 1947). The chapter has been lightly edited for style for the purposes of the present publication.

2. The following episode, along with other data appearing in my pages on *Caligari*, is drawn from an interesting manuscript Hans Janowitz has written about the genesis of this film. I feel greatly indebted to him for having put his material at my disposal. I am thus in a position to base my interpretation of *Caligari* on the true inside story, up to now unknown.

3. Carl Vincent, *Histoire de l'art cinématographique* (Brussels: Trident, 1939), 140.

4. Karl Wolffsohn, ed., *Jahrbuch der Filmindustrie*, vol. 1, *Jahrgang 1922–1923* (Berlin: Verlag der Lichtbild-Bühne, 1923), 86, 46. For an appraisal of Pommer, see C. A. Lejeune, *Cinema* (London: Alexander Maclehose, 1931), 125–81.

5. Information offered by Mr. Lang.

6. Extracted from Janowitz's manuscript. See also Vincent, *Histoire de l'art cinématographique*, 140, 143–44.

7. Film license, issued by the Board of Censors, Berlin, 1921 and 1925 (Museum of Modern Art Library, clipping files); *Film Society Programme*, March 14, 1926.

CHAPTER 18

Destructive Villain or Gigantic Hero?

The Transformation of Godzilla in Contemporary Popular Culture

STEFAN DANTER

REFLECTING ON SOME OF THE MAJOR PROBLEMS THAT HUMAN BEINGS HAVE faced in recent years, one of the most striking factors is their gigantic dimension. Whether it is the amount of national debt, the extent of global economic recession, the surge of global terrorism and the ensuing refugee crisis, or the dangers of global warming that loom on the horizon: they all have in common that they appear "larger than life," affect humankind as a whole, and cannot be solved by one individual. Perhaps not surprisingly, an equivalent development can be observed in the content produced in Hollywood and exported as global popular culture. Recent box office successes show a number of movies that involve one or several larger-than-life characters filling the role of either the main hero, the main villain, or both. Films like *Transformers*, *Pacific Rim*, *The Avengers*, *Cloverfield*, and *Godzilla* all deal with destruction caused by a gigantic, villainous, and often monstrous entity. With the exception of *Cloverfield*, they also involve the subsequent defeat of said entity through other, at least equally powerful beings. An important key to the success of these movies is the increasingly sophisticated means of digital production. Without these new technologies, depicting large-scale destruction, gigantic scenarios, and larger-than-life characters would not be possible. Aside from the visual aspects on-screen, the viewing experience is further improved through techniques such as 3-D filming, state-of-the-art surround sound, and vibrating or moving seats like the D-BOX. Although it is tempting to solely attribute their popularity to such technological advances, this success also has broader cultural implications as it reflects the continued feeling of endangerment and risk that characterizes local and global contexts today.

It is precisely because contemporary problems seem to have grown in scale that enormous movie characters are so appealing. In this context, oversize heroes, villains, and monsters have become more than a source of entertainment; they are representatives of the abject posthuman and attest to the outscaling of human beings by global problems. In order to shed light on the continuing fascination with global disaster scenarios, monsters, and villains as well as the posthuman "other," this chapter will draw on several authors to provide a basic theoretical backdrop. On a more general level, this includes Slavoj Žižek's critique of twenty-first-century capitalism, Susan Sontag's theories on the depiction of disaster in science fiction, and concepts from critical posthumanism as defined, for instance, by Sherryl Vint and Neil Badmington. Focusing more on the role of the monstrous villain, I also draw on Lynette Porter's distinction between hero and villain, explorations of monstrosity taken from Jeffrey Jerome Cohen's monster theory, Michel Foucault's lectures on the abnormal, and Julia Kristeva's conceptualization of the abject. One larger-than-life creature that not only fits into these categories but also has been terrorizing audiences for more than sixty years is the gigantic reptile with a bent for destruction, Godzilla. By using two cinematic examples involving Godzilla, the 1954 Japanese original and the 2014 Hollywood remake, I want to show how monster movies can tackle problems of size and scale as well as how one such character has fared through recent global changes. As one of the most iconic figures in popular culture, Godzilla additionally offers an opportunity to analyze what the transformation of the giant lizard from a destructive and villainous monster to savior of humankind can teach us about ourselves.

One way to understand the origins of the increasing feeling of endangerment felt by contemporary subjects is to look at the workings and effects of the global financial system. For instance, Slavoj Žižek argues that global capitalism evokes a feeling of imminent collapse and that there are not one, but several versions of apocalyptic world views envisioning "humanity approaching a zero-point of radical transmutation."[1] When he identifies "ecological crisis, the consequences of the biogenetic revolution, imbalances within the system itself, . . . and the explosive growth of social division and exclusions"[2] as the four horsemen of the twenty-first-century global capitalistic apocalypse, it is particularly the realization that all of these developments are already in progress that is unsettling. Relating movies featuring gigantic heroes, villains, and monsters to other successful themes of contemporary popular culture, it appears that they form something akin to an apocalyptic trinity in conjunction with the disaster movie (e.g., *2012*, *The World's End*, *Noah*, *Interstellar*) and the increasingly popular zombie narrative, which can be seen as a fusion of the other two. Frequently tied to global biological disasters, undead, cannibalistic monsters emerge who vastly outnumber the human characters. Prominent examples are *World War Z*, *Zombieland*, and the *Walking Dead* franchise. This interconnectedness, however, cannot be the sole answer for their skyrocketing popularity and continued worldwide success. Žižek offers an explanation by pointing out that nowadays it is "easier to imagine a total catastrophe which ends all life on earth than it is to imagine a real change in capitalist relations."[3]

This ties in well with Susan Sontag's 1965 study of science fiction, "The Imagination of Disaster." While acknowledging its success, she also criticizes science fiction for making the audience comply with a logic of disaster, portraying simplistic morality, and stylizing abhorrent scenarios. For Sontag, science fiction's appeal consists in "the aesthetics of destruction, with the peculiar beauties to be found in wreaking havoc, making a mess."[4] Furthermore, she identifies science fiction material as a source for both utopian fantasies of the future and deeply rooted psychological anxieties about the destruction of humankind. Thus, the appeal of disasters and monsters is drawn from the symbolic as well as literal destruction of social, cultural, and economic structures. This is especially the case because of the high level of influence these structures have on individual lives and the fact that they are commonly regarded as fundamental to the "natural" order of society.

It is at this juncture that the movie monster (gigantic, small, or microscopic) particularly becomes a worthwhile subject of analysis. By definition, the monster is not able to become a part of society and is envisioned as "outside" or radically "other." Thus, the monster is endowed with the unique ability to question normative orders, deconstruct established categories, and subvert the structures that more often than not have created it. In his lectures on the abnormal, Michel Foucault explores the notion of the monster in terms of the legal system, stating that its "power and its capacity to create anxiety are due to the fact that it violates the law while leaving it with nothing to say."[5] The monster represents both "the impossible and the forbidden"[6] and through its mere existence breaks social, cultural, judicial, and religious laws. The judiciary is unable to tackle the issue because the act of creating monster-specific laws would legitimize the monster's place within society. It is therefore not surprising that Foucault names "natural transgression, the mixture of species, and the blurring of limits and characteristics"[7] as the aspects the monster is most commonly associated with. It possesses a great deal of subversive as well as seductive power in its capability to force human subjects to question both themselves and the structures and hierarchies they believe in.[8]

Moreover, as Jeffrey Jerome Cohen has pointed out in "Monster Culture (Seven Theses)," the monster is a rich source for the understanding of cultural phenomena because it "always signifies something other than itself: it is always a displacement."[9] Cohen's theses shed light on the information that can be gained by analyzing literary and filmic monsters and villains. Among other things, this includes their propensity to escape and return as well as their status as "Harbinger of Category Crisis."[10] The latter is largely based on their hybridity and the way their existence at the margins, while serving as the important "other" from which to construct identity, also paradoxically reveals the arbitrariness of the "cultural apparatus through which individuality is constituted and allowed."[11] The monster hence fulfills a double function by serving as a warning against the transgression of boundaries and established categories while simultaneously revealing their contingency. Rather than just inducing fear, it can also become a source of desire. According to Cohen, humans are fascinated by monstrous characters because they represent suppressed qualities and therefore appear as alter egos to the civilized self.[12] By constantly returning, haunting, and threatening said self, such representations force human beings to acknowledge their own role in the creation of monsters.

Considering the theoretical contexts explored thus far, it is impossible to ignore the psychological implications of our fascination with monsters and villains. One particularly interesting concept that can help us understand the fearful, horrified reactions monsters often evoke is Julia Kristeva's notion of the abject. She describes the abject as an element that has been excluded and, as a result, exists in a position of radical meaninglessness. Rather than to simply vanish, however, the abject continuously challenges the coalition of ego and superego that has pushed it to the margins.[13] Put differently, it inhabits a sphere between subject and object, of "being opposed to I,"[14] and is capable of questioning the locus of meaning and forcing the subject to reevaluate itself in relation to it. Abjection, on the other hand, is a process described as "one of those violent, dark revolts of being, directed against a threat that seems to emanate from an exorbitant outside or inside, ejected beyond the scope of the possible, the tolerable, the thinkable."[15] Kristeva mentions the human loathing of certain food items and the general repulsion caused by bodily fluids, sickness, and death as examples, stating that these reactions of violent rejection are the result of the subject encountering the abject. Because the abject is that which "disturbs identity, system, order. What does not respect borders, positions, rules,"[16] it has to be suppressed and excluded. With this strategy, the subject determines itself in the face of the desire that constitutes its being.[17] So while it is frequently identified with taboos and exclusion, the abject also reminds the subject that its core is constantly in danger of being altered and that it cannot fully detach itself from its many undesirable qualities. Naturally, this puts the abject in proximity of Freud's notion of the uncanny, which is frequently invoked in monster theory as well. Both concepts support the idea that human subjects are inherently fascinated by the threatening dimension of the impossible because it signifies an alternative to their current conceptualization of self. Since monsters are not expected to possess the same restraint and control, they can easily serve as foils that allow human subjects to explore the implications of unleashing desires and repressed instincts.

Before turning to analyze the character of Godzilla, which over its long career on the big screen has definitely fulfilled the requirement of being elusive,
hard to kill, and difficult to categorize, a clarification on the use of the terms
monster, hero, and villain is required. As Lynette Porter explains, the basic
distinction between a heroic and a villainous character is made by considering
their motivation and intentionality. While heroes are commonly shown to have
a strong moral compass and work for the greater good, villains are self-centered
and strive to gain increasing power, influence, or wealth.[18] Needless to say, in
Godzilla's case, it is the category of the monster that is most relevant. Porter
distinguishes between the monster and the villain, stating that even though
villains are frequently dehumanized and reduced to the status of a monster,
they nevertheless possess human traits such as the capability of rational thinking, planning, and using language. By contrast, monsters are viewed as more
animalistic, their behavior being unpredictable, reactive, or instinctive rather
than calculated. The most interesting assumption about monsters here is that
they behave monstrously because that is who they are and because they do
not have morality or a sense of right and wrong.[19] However, this perspective
is not differentiated enough to understand Godzilla's impact and role—especially when considering Foucault's arguments and referencing them with the
criticism of anthropocentrism brought forth in animal studies, ecocriticism,
and critical posthumanism in recent years. While it is certainly true that the
original incarnation of Godzilla lacked a clearly discernible intentionality, a
wholesale demotion to the status of a mindless monster on the basis of its refusal or inability to respect a human moral code would be too anthropocentric
to provide an answer. In fact, as the development of the character over the years
suggests, Godzilla does possess intentionality and consciousness. Of course,
this is not an argument to remove Godzilla from the category of the monster,
but to highlight that even a seemingly animalistic character can act villainously
despite its nonhumanity and supposed lack of rationality.

One could understand Godzilla's utter disregard for the structures and rules
created by humankind, its destructive force and gigantic size, as a very concrete
representation of what Sherryl Vint called an abject posthuman, mainly because it "emblematize[s] our current state of neoliberal crisis and biopolitical
governance."[20] The "Big G," as one frequently used nickname goes, is a deeply
ambiguous figure, a fact further emphasized by the creature's undefined gender.
It calls human agency and anthropocentrism into question through its mere
presence, transporting and performing the workings of the abject and abjection.
This is why Godzilla, and similar monsters, could also be associated with the
prominent idea of critical posthumanism, established by contributors such as
Stefan Herbrechter, Cary Wolfe, Katherine Hayles, Neil Badmington, and others.[21] Accordingly, when Godzilla raids and destroys cities, it also haunts and

invades the cultural structures that have produced the humanist subject and the idea of an autonomous, self-controlled agency. In the face of this gigantic and villainous monster, the power of the individual appears shockingly small, and none of the structures centered on the human subject, whether they are political, military, social, economic, or cultural, seem to withstand the monster's trampling feet and lashing tail.

I will now turn to an analysis of two filmic examples from the Godzilla franchise, which, as William Tsutsui has shown in his insightful study *Godzilla on My Mind*, has spawned a total of thirty-two Japanese-produced movies over a period of sixty-plus years, making it Japan's biggest cultural export as well as the longest-running franchise in world cinema history.[22] In Japan, the movies are categorized under the label of *kaijū eiga*, which directly translates as "monster movie," with Godzilla inhabiting the special subcategory of *daikaiju*, which specifically refers to its large size. As Tsutsui's analysis shows, Godzilla has undergone a variety of changes to its personality over the years. While the 1954 original was a dark, somber reimagination of the destruction of Japan during the Second World War and the threat posed by nuclear weapons and bomb tests, the following years saw Godzilla transformed into a more family-friendly giant that catered to young audiences while being stylized as a heroic protector. This choice reportedly lessened the overall quality and reduced the appeal of the movies for critics, scholars, and mature audiences. Tsutsui notes that the movies of the 1960s and 1970s featured simplistic moral messages, with the plots moving in a direction that featured countless scenes of monsters battling each other while simultaneously doing away with the depressing tone of the 1954 original. The change went as far as to omit the portrayal of human death altogether.[23] At the same time, however, the new representation initiated Godzilla's evolution into a lovable, humorous, and sometimes goofy movie hero. The result of this can still be observed today, for instance when Godzilla received its own star on Hollywood's Walk of Fame in 2004[24] or when it became honorary resident and official cultural ambassador of Tokyo in 2015.[25] Tsutsui concludes that an aesthetics of destruction is not the only source for Godzilla's appeal, instead pointing to the manifold associations viewers have developed and the ambiguity and ambivalence the lizard embodies. The following analysis will show that Godzilla is, above all, "ever available as a metaphor, ever compliant to interpretation and appropriation."[26] It will pay particular attention to the relation of Godzilla to size and scale, human agency, and the way both movies depict its assumed villainy and monstrosity.

In *Gojira*, the 1954 original directed by Ishirō Honda, Godzilla is portrayed as a giant prehistoric lizard/dinosaur hybrid who was lying dormant at the bottom of the Pacific before being woken by H-bomb tests.[27] Godzilla is thus situated thoroughly within the realm of nature, and its arrival is even tied to a thunderstorm. Its highly radioactive footprints and capability of shooting a radioactive heat ray from its mouth only add to this initial assessment, allowing us to view Godzilla in conjunction with the atomic bomb itself, as critics such as Susan Napier and Nancy Anisfield have shown.[28] Put differently, like the plutonium and uranium used for bombs, Godzilla was hidden and only became a threat once it came to the surface, causing destruction and radiation on a scale that was unimaginable before.

Godzilla's actions are all the more frightening in that they seem to be completely devoid of intentionality as defined in human terms. It appears more like a force of nature and causes destruction mainly because of its gigantic body. What is especially striking is that, in its first full-size appearance on screen, Godzilla appears to walk aimlessly through the city. Crushing buildings, ripping electrical cables, and stepping on a moving train appear arbitrary, leaving the viewer awestruck and bewildered at the sight of this gigantic, bipedal monster. The true destruction, however, only starts after the Japanese military attacks Godzilla, prompting it to rampage through Tokyo. It is at this point that its behavior shows signs of intentionality, as the destruction becomes more violent and widespread. The people of Tokyo, standing in for humanity, now face an all-powerful monster that, as in the case of the National Diet Building, literally destroys what human society stands for.[29] Godzilla's capability to cause horror is amplified by the fact that it does not communicate aside from its signature roar, which sounds thoroughly unnatural, akin to metal colliding with metal.

Compared to its human counterparts, Godzilla makes for a terrifying villain precisely because there is no common ground that would allow a comparison or some sort of empathizing. Godzilla, the gigantic, sexually ambiguous lizard without an intelligible voice, is scary both because its intentions are unclear and because it so radically transgresses or destroys all boundaries. It is both completely "other" and unknown, a villain whose motives and weaknesses aren't readily available for analysis, thus preventing an easy solution. Furthermore, the movie does a brilliant job of conveying Godzilla's gigantic scale by using low camera angles, showing screaming, running, and stumbling humans at the bottom of the screen while the creature looms large in the background. This is supported by having a human actor in a rubber suit stomping through a miniaturized version of Tokyo. None of the existing structures are fit to accommodate Godzilla, which is why it seems forever condemned to remain, in the proper sense of monstrosity, outside of society and civilization.

Despite this problematic, one of the characters, paleontologist Dr. Kyohei Yamane, objects to killing Godzilla. In a scene that reflects the trauma caused by the atomic bombings of Japan, he advocates that the creature should instead be studied in order to learn the secret of surviving a nuclear blast. As Chon Noriega explains in his analysis of Godzilla, this reflects a different approach to otherness and monstrosity within Japanese culture.[30] In contrast to their American counterparts, Japanese monsters do have individuality, a fact stressed by them having personal names. The monster's otherness is not perceived as something outside of culture but rather something that emerges from and remains part of it. Rather than stylizing the conflict as a showdown between the internalized ideals of the self and the externalized and repressed qualities of the other, the Japanese notion is to move past this separation, immersing the self within the other.[31] Thus, Yamane's statement further emphasizes Godzilla's ambiguity: while destructive, it also embodies a promise of regeneration.

In terms of audience response, critical reception, and success, *Gojira* proves to be a particularly interesting piece of postwar cinema. As Barak Kushner points out, most early reviewers in Japan disliked the film, citing a poor script and the monster's lack of personality. They did, however, praise it for having an original and interesting basic concept.[32] Despite this lack of critical acclaim, the movie was well received by audiences, becoming increasingly popular. Kushner considers *Gojira* Japan's first postwar media event, a fact underlined by the incredible following Godzilla as a character garnered in the years to follow. In Kushner's opinion, it was precisely because *Gojira* was so fundamentally and unmistakably Japanese that it could become this successful as a global franchise, earning it a place in a Japanese film industry magazine's top twenty of greatest postwar Japanese films, in spite of its mediocre critical reception.[33]

In global box office numbers, the film reportedly grossed $4.25 million.[34] Considering that the Japanese original saw limited distribution outside Japan and was only released in the United States in 1956, this does not come as a huge surprise. Renamed as *Godzilla, King of the Monsters!*, the US release was heavily edited, cutting around thirty minutes of the original, including references to Hiroshima and Nagasaki.[35] The material was replaced with scenes shot with actor Raymond Burr, who served both as a frame of reference and a narrator. The perceived need for relatable scenes featuring a North American actor and the English-language dubbing entirely eliminated important subplots and conversations essential for character development. As a result, most American reviews were rather negative, perhaps because the extensive changes skewed the original intention of the creators—to make a monster movie with a serious antiwar message—and significantly lowered the film's quality.[36]

Accordingly, most reviews mentioned the dubbing as a major point of criticism while also commenting condescendingly on the movie's overall quality. A 1956 *New York Times* review, for instance, called it "an incredibly awful film," criticizing its creators for a cheap attempt at imitating King Kong and describing its aesthetics as "a miniature of a dinosaur made of gum-shoes and about $20 worth of toy buildings and electric trains."[37] Despite the reviews and qualitative downgrades, however, the emigration to the US film market still was a success. Apparently, Godzilla's appeal was too big to be dragged down by bad edits and scathing reviews, with "children and gullible grown-ups," as the *New York Times* review called the audience, quickly becoming fascinated with its rampages. In fact, quite a few Americans only saw the original Japanese cut when it was rereleased in the United States in the context of the giant lizard's fiftieth anniversary. As one 2004 review stated, "For today's moviegoing audiences, this may not be your daddy's Godzilla movie, but chances are your granddaddy could teach you a thing or two about the context."[38] If anything, this exemplifies the importance of looking at the unedited original and taking the context of its creation into account before judging the big lizard.

Comparing the original to *Godzilla*, the 2014 Hollywood remake by Gareth Edwards, there are several striking differences.[39] To begin with, the 2014 version has raked in an impressive $529 million, a result cementing the status of the franchise's global reach.[40] Furthermore, state-of-the-art CGI and animation have greatly increased the monster's size. Godzilla, now truly a towering giant, is often shown from focalized point-of-view shots that only reveal parts of its body, conveying a sense of it being too big even for the big screen. Although this stylistic choice emphasizes the gigantic dimension of the creature, it has also garnered criticism because Godzilla is rarely shown in long shots. Furthermore, the movie designates Godzilla as a male "ancient alpha predator," who is described as both a god and a monster by different characters. In clear reference to 1960s- and 1970s-era Japanese films, this iteration of Godzilla arrives to battle MUTOs, a species of radiation-consuming parasites. Interestingly, while Godzilla is called by its usual, personalized name, the hostile monsters are only referred to in military terms: their name is an acronym of "Massive Unidentified Terrestrial Organism." This creates a strong distinction between the monstrous characters and makes a case for the audience seeing the parasites as the villains rather than Godzilla.

Keeping in line with the American theme of the movie, the only Japanese character is Dr. Ishirō Serizawa. His name references both Ishirō Honda as well as the maverick scientist Daisuke Serizawa, whose weapon, the oxygen destroyer, defeated Godzilla in the 1954 original. A voice of reason, Serizawa identifies Godzilla as a representative of a natural order whose purpose is to restore balance and, in a statement echoing contemporary posthuman ideas, tells US officials that "the arrogance of man is thinking nature is in our control, and not the other way around." To underline this, Godzilla's appearance on Hawai'i is accompanied by a full-blown tsunami, symbolically aligning it with natural disaster and forces of nature.

The movie emphasizes the gigantic size of the monsters, showing them next to skyscrapers and depicting the large-scale paths of destruction they leave behind. Despite being called a monster, Godzilla quickly assumes the role of antihero, battling the two MUTOs who devour a US nuclear missile and ener-gy supplies. Godzilla never willingly attacks any humans, and the destruction caused is more accidental than openly villainous. In one of the most telling sequences, Godzilla tries to move past a bridge when its path is blocked by the US military. It is their misfired rockets that destroy one of the bridge's cables, while Godzilla is shown gently gripping the other cable without causing any damage. The destruction of the bridge occurs when Godzilla stumbles through it in its attempt to escape the military. Despite the considerable power at its disposal, the lizard does not fight back, underlining its position as unofficial ally of humankind. The recklessness and lack of intentionality that would qualify Godzilla as a mindless monster are absent here, and whatever damage it causes is collateral. Having defeated its enemies, Godzilla temporarily becomes part of the posthuman scenario as it is shown lying in the rubble of a destroyed city. However, the monstrous antihero eventually recovers and trudges back into the ocean, leaving the humans once again in control.

This scene is exemplary for the close relation between human agency and a fascination with size, scale, and monstrosity. In Godzilla's specific case, scale also refers to the scales that shield and protect its body. Both the 1954 and 2014 movies feature stylized demonstrations of military action, which, as Tsutsui has shown, have always been an integral part of the franchise.[41] Human weaponry, however, proves utterly inefficient in the face of Godzilla's gigantic scaled body. It shrugs off rockets, bullets, and even atomic blasts, thus putting in doubt the idea of human agency and forcing human characters and audiences to stand by and watch the mayhem unfold. In the 2014 version, this effect is increased by the MUTOs' ability to emit electromagnetic pulse blasts, thus causing the US military, the most technologically advanced power in the world, to fully lose control over their fighter jets, machinery, and even nuclear arsenal. Only then do they heed Dr. Serizawa's advice and allow Godzilla to defeat the monsters. When both movies in the end feature a positive resolution to the problem of losing agency, this is only achieved through one extraordinary individual. In 1954, it was Serizawa and his oxygen destroyer, and in 2014, it was the soldier Ford Brody, who prevents a nuclear detonation and destroys the parasite's eggs. Of course, this serves as a reinstatement of the autonomous humanist subject, making the posthumanization of civilization caused by Godzilla and the audience's encounter with the abject a temporary phase rather than a dis-turbing reality.

It seems worth noting that giant monsters have played a role in comics and popular culture dating back to the pulp era of science fiction, sword and sorcery, fantasy, and horror publications (1920s–1940s) like *Weird Tales*, *Astounding Sto-ries*, *Terror Tales*, *Thrilling Wonder Stories*, and *Amazing Stories*, when Bug Eyed Monsters (BEMs) and creatures like H. P. Lovecraft's Cthulhu were a literary staple. In comics, one example is *The Thing: Weird Tales of Suspense*, published by Charlton Comics, which ran for seventeen issues from 1952 to 1954 and often featured giant monsters on their covers (and featured the early work of artist Steve Ditko). Marvel Comics in the 1950s (when the firm was known as Atlas) perfected the giant monster genre in titles like *Tales of Suspense, Uncanny Tales, Tales to Astonish, Amazing Adventures, Journey into Mystery, Astonishing, Strange Worlds*, and *Mystic*, among others. Stan Lee, Jack Kirby, Ditko, and others created monsters with names like Groot, Goom, Googam, the Heap, Orrgo, ZZUTAK, Droom, Torr, the Colossus, and Fing Fang Foom that would menace humanity.[42] *Fantastic Four*, no. 1 (1961), the title that ushered in the Marvel age of superheroes, was originally marketed as a giant monster comic (as the cover denotes). In fact, Marvel published a Godzilla series, which ran for twenty-four issues from 1977 through 1979.[43] In the 1990s, Godzilla was published by Dark Horse Comics[44] and is currently being published by IDW.[45]

In this context, the analysis of the figure of Godzilla as a multifaceted and deeply ambiguous representative of an abject posthuman has shown that despite the lowbrow entertainment that gigantic monster movies offer on the surface, there is a deeper meaning to be found when one engages with gigantic scales (literally and metaphorically). The continued fascination audiences around the world have with disasters, monsters, and zombies belies an awareness of problems that overstep accustomed boundaries and our uneasiness about our lack of power to deal with them. What is more, the importance and influence of Godzilla as a globally recognized and beloved icon shows how the distinction between monster, villain, and (anti-) hero is not always clear-cut. Godzilla is an excellent example of a nonhuman entity that requires us to acknowledge its agency and personality, especially since it is too big and ambiguous for established categories of interpretation. While enjoying the seemingly mindless entertainment offered in these movies, we nevertheless have an opportunity to engage with the potentialities that contemporary problems hold and to rethink our current structures and systems. Viewed from this perspective, having Godzilla rampaging through our lives might not be as bad we thought.

Notes

1. Slavoj Žižek, *Living in the End Times* (London: Verso, 2011), 336.

2. Žižek, *Living in the End Times*, x.

3. Žižek, *Living in the End Times*, 334.

4. Susan Sontag, "The Imagination of Disaster," in *Against Interpretation and Other Essays* (New York: Picador, 1965), 213.

5. Michel Foucault, *Abnormal: Lectures at the Collège de France, 1974–1975*, trans. Graham Burchell (New York: Picador, 1999), 56.

6. Foucault, *Abnormal*, 56.

7. Foucault, *Abnormal*, 65.

8. In *Skin Shows: Gothic Horror and the Technology of Monsters* (Durham, NC: Duke University Press, 1995), Judith Halberstam comes to a similar conclusion in her analysis of monstrosity in gothic literature and the discourse surrounding it.

9. Jeffrey Jerome Cohen, "Monster Culture (Seven Theses)," in *Monster Theory: Reading Culture*, ed. Jeffrey Jerome Cohen (Minneapolis: University of Minnesota Press, 1996), 4.

10. Cohen, "Monster Culture," 6.

11. Cohen, "Monster Culture," 12.

12. Cohen, "Monster Culture," 17.

13. Julia Kristeva, *Powers of Horror: An Essay on Abjection* (New York: Columbia University Press, 1982), 2.

14. Kristeva, *Powers of Horror*, 1.

15. Kristeva, *Powers of Horror*.

16. Kristeva, *Powers of Horror*, 4.

17. Kristeva, *Powers of Horror*, 5.

18. Lynette Porter, *Tarnished Heroes, Charming Villains and Modern Monsters: Science Fiction in Shades of Gray on 21st Century Television* (Jefferson, NC: McFarland, 2010), 36.

19. Porter, *Tarnished Heroes*, 37.

20. Sherryl Vint, "Abject Posthumanism: Neoliberalism, Biopolitics, and Zombies," in *Monster Culture in the 21st Century: A Reader*, ed. Marina Levina and Diem-My T. Bui (London: Bloomsbury, 2013), 134.

21. For an overview of critical posthumanism, see Stefan Herbrechter, *Posthumanism: A Critical Analysis* (London: Bloomsbury, 2013); N. Katherine Hayles, *How We Became Posthuman: Virtual Bodies in Cybernetics, Literature, and Informatics* (Chicago: University of Chicago Press, 1999); Cary Wolfe, *What Is Posthumanism?* (Minneapolis: University of Minnesota Press, 2010); and Neil Badmington, "Theorizing Posthumanism," *Cultural Critique*, no. 53 (Winter 2003): 10–27.

22. William Tsutsui, *Godzilla on My Mind: Fifty Years of the King of Monsters* (New York: Palgrave Macmillan, 2004), 208.

23. Tsutsui, *Godzilla on My Mind*, 62.

24. Lloyd Vries, "Godzilla Stomps onto Walk of Fame," CBS News, November 30, 2004, available at http://www.cbsnews.com/news/godzilla-stomps-onto-walk-of-fame/.

25. Benjamin Lee, "Resident Evil: Godzilla Made Official Japanese Citizen," *Guardian*, June 4, 2015, available at https://www.theguardian.com/film/2015/jun/04/godzilla-made-official-japanese-citizen.

26. Tsutsui, *Godzilla on My Mind*, 208.

27. Ishirō Honda, dir., *Gojira* (Toho, 1954).

28. Susan Napier, "When Godzilla Speaks," in *In Godzilla's Footsteps: Japanese Pop Culture Icons on the Global Stage*, ed. William Tsutsui and Michiko Ito (New York: Palgrave Macmillan, 2006), 9–20; and Nancy Anisfield, "Godzilla/Gojiro: Evolution of the Nuclear Metaphor," *Journal of Popular Culture* 29, no. 3 (Winter 1995): 53–62.

29. The National Diet Building is the official seat of the Japanese government, and its destruction is therefore possibly a political statement. While the true meaning of this episode remains open to interpretation, Tsutsui notes that its destruction was met by cheers from Japanese audiences at the time. See Tsutsui, *Godzilla on My Mind*, 94. Other commentators, such as Barak Kushner, have supported the idea of a political message being sent through the destruction by pointing out that Godzilla walks around the Imperial Palace rather than destroying it. See Barak Kushner, "*Gojira* as Japan's First Postwar Media Event," in *In Godzilla's Footsteps: Japanese Pop Culture Icons on the Global Stage*, ed. William Tsutsui and Michiko Ito (New York: Palgrave Macmillan, 2006), 49.

30. Chon Noriega, "Godzilla and the Japanese Nightmare: When 'Them!' Is U.S.," *Cinema Journal* 27, no. 1 (Autumn 1987): 63–77.

31. Noriega, "Godzilla and the Japanese Nightmare," 68.

32. Kushner, "*Gojira* as Japan's First Postwar Media Event," 42.

33. Kushner, "*Gojira* as Japan's First Postwar Media Event," 47, 49.

34. "Godzilla (1954)," Internet Movie Database (IMDb), available at http://www.imdb.com/title/tt0047034/business.

35. Sayuri Guthrie-Shimizu, "Lost in Translation and Morphed in Transit: Godzilla in Cold War America," in *In Godzilla's Footsteps: Japanese Pop Culture Icons on the Global Stage*, ed. William Tsutsui and Michiko Ito (New York: Palgrave Macmillan, 2006), 55.

36. David Kalat, *A Critical History and Filmography of Toho's Godzilla Series* (Jefferson, NC: McFarland, 2007), 25.

37. Bosley Crowther, "Screen: Horror Import; 'Godzilla,' a Japanese Film, Is at State," *New York Times*, April 28, 1956, available at www.nytimes.com/movie/review?res=9A05E6DD1F3BE23 ABC4051DFB266838D649EDE.

38. In his review, author Luke Y. Thompson highlights the dark, grim, and serious message of the movie while simultaneously pointing out that the special effects were quite convincing at the time. He does, however, also note that for contemporary and especially younger audiences, the movie might be too slowly paced to keep them glued to their seats. See Luke Y. Thompson, "Burning Japanese," *Dallas Observer*, June 17, 2004, available at http://www.dallasobserver.com/film/burning-japanese-6385294.

39. Gareth Edwards, dir., *Godzilla* (Legendary Pictures, 2014).

40. "Godzilla (2014)," Box Office Mojo, available at http://www.boxofficemojo.com/movies/?id=godzilla2012.htm.

41. Tsutsui, *Godzilla on My Mind*, 97.

42. See Gary Carter and Pat S. Calhoun, "Journey into the Unknown World of Atlas Fantasy," in *The Overstreet Comic Book Price Guide*, no. 22, ed. Robert M. Overstreet (New York: Avon, 1992), A-87–103. For reprinted comics featuring giant monsters, see Stan Lee, Jack Kirby, Steve Ditko, Don Heck et al., *Marvel Masterworks: Atlas Era Tales to Astonish*, vol. 1 (New York: Marvel Enterprises, 2006); or Stan Lee, Jack Kirby, Don Heck, Steve Ditko et al., *Marvel Masterworks: Atlas Era Tales of Suspense*, vol. 2 (New York: Marvel Enterprises, 2008).

43. See Doug Moench, Herb Trimpe et al., *Essential Godzilla: King of the Monsters* (New York: Marvel Enterprises, 2006).

44. See, as one example, Randy Stradley and Art Adams, *Godzilla: Age of Monsters* (Milwaukie, OR: Dark Horse Comics, 1998).

45. See, as one example, Chris Mowry, Matt Frank, and Jeff Zornow, *Godzilla: Complete Rulers of the Earth*, vol. 1 (San Diego: IDW Publishing, 2016).

CHAPTER 19

Harley Quinn, Villain, Vixen, Victim

Exploring Her Origins in Batman: The Animated Series

JOE CRUZ AND LARS STOLTZFUS-BROWN

AFTER THE CRITICAL AND FINANCIAL SUCCESS OF TIM BURTON'S *BATMAN* (1989) and the more moderate yet significant popularity of its sequel *Batman Returns* (1992), the reinvigoration of the Batman brand spearheaded by Warner Brothers in the 1990s introduced the character to a new generation. Amid a barrage of toys, video games, and merchandise, a vibrant reinterpretation of Batman and his mythos emerged with *Batman: The Animated Series* (*BTAS*). The show—created by Bruce Timm and Eric Radomski—became a spiritual successor to Burton's gothic style. It aired from 1992 to 1995, spawning spinoffs and cross-overs, and reshaped Batman's mythology beyond his comic book roots. The show could be considered one of the most influential animated series due to its thematic complexities and aesthetic sensibilities.[1] Due to this popularity, the Batman animated universe expanded into *The New Batman Adventures*, which premiered in 1997 and is generally bundled together with *BTAS* as one continuous story.[2] According to showrunner Timm, the series draws inspiration from different elements of Batman's intertextual universe, never shying away from its then fifty-three-year-old canon.[3] As a result, some members of Batman's rogues' gallery experienced retellings of their origin stories and expansions of established iconography.

Familiar villain the Joker in particular enjoyed renewed fan attention when paired with a doting, if psychologically unstable, partner: Harleen Frances Quinzel, better known as Harley Quinn. Her character, portrayed in a red, black, and white jester outfit, started out as a secondary member of the Joker's gang. Subsequent appearances and a seamless transition into the DC Comic Book universe cemented Harley Quinn's indispensable status as a complex and popular comic book villain/antihero.[4] She was a main character in the Warner

Brothers/Noodle Soup Flash animation series *Gotham Girls*, which focused on Batgirl and women villains during its three-season run from 2000 to 2002. Harley is featured regularly in comic book series and video games. Recently, she was in 2016's commercially successful live-action film *Suicide Squad*, and she is even a hero in the ongoing DC Comics/Mattel animated series *DC Super Hero Girls*, which launched in 2015. Although Harley Quinn has evolved from her original role as villainous sidekick into a more independent player, her stories continue to gravitate around her fixation with the Joker and his relentless abuse of her.[5] Their relationship has generated debate due to the couple's popularity with comic book enthusiasts and young audiences, as demonstrated by Robert Moses Peaslee and Robert Weiner's work on the Joker;[6] Carlen Lavigne's research on gender and Harley Quinn in the *Arkham* video game franchise;[7] and Shannon Austin's exploration of gendered violence in Batman.[8]

Although Harley Quinn has been portrayed in a plethora of media franchises, this chapter chronicles her origins in *BTAS* (including episodes on *The New Batman Adventures*) and the character's psychological complexities in her roles as a sidekick, villain, and victim of abuse. We hope to provide a critical perspective on this popular character, who originated in a children's TV show and is currently marketed to mass audiences.

Problematizing Harley Quinn and her relationship with the Joker is an important step in comic book scholarship because it addresses questions about ideology and misogyny that transcend the show itself. Women-centric comics scholarship tends to cover superheroines or antiheroines, as in the work of Richard J. Gray II or Charlotte Howell,[9] ignoring the less-empowered status of sidekicks. Research solely on villains tends to focus on straight, white men, such as Jack Fennell's work on deformed villains or Travis Langley's work on the Joker.[10] This leads to gaps in literature, despite Kate Roddy's work on Harley Quinn and female masochism and Nathan G. Tipton's discussion of the problematic Robin in *Batman: The Dark Knight*.[11] As such, Harley Quinn's complex status as a sometime villain/sometime antihero dealing with the everyday trauma of an abusive relationship—while also serving as an object of lust for male readership—is troubling, especially as "[c]omics-based franchises are marketed around this industrial construction of their audience."[12]

Due to this, we are interested in analyzing Harley Quinn as someone who experiences gendered violence—she is a victim of the Joker personally and patriarchy generally. The argument is that as long as Harley Quinn's abuse is glamorized, as long as she is stripped of agency in service of the male gaze, and as long as she is presented as an *object* to be beaten, it is important to ask: "[W]hat are the unconscious repercussions of young women [and men] embracing this narrative that men's attractiveness stems from their ability to physically overpower a lover?"[13] Harley Quinn's characterization in *BTAS* perpetuates ideologies suggesting that subservient, sexy women crave being overpowered, that women are not hurt by abuse, and that violent men are endlessly attractive. However, Harley's ardent female fan base complicates this assertion. The character enjoys overwhelming support in female cosplayer communities, especially since attendance at comic conventions nears gender parity.[14] On Instagram, the hashtags #harleyquinncosplay and #harleyquinncosplayer hold more posts than those for Batman, Superman, and Spider-Man combined. This community's loyalty to Harley suggests a renegotiation of the character's victimhood, such that she is a symbol of empowerment due to her embrace of physical violence and the threat she poses to Batman and Gotham's male-dominated law enforcement agencies.

TEXTUAL ANALYSIS

We have used a textual analysis approach in viewing *BTAS* and its associated works; such analysis finds "likely interpretations"[15] that can be made based on recurring themes within a text. As such, we will explore Harley Quinn's characterization as a sometime-villain focusing on her relationship with the Joker; the show's aestheticization of violence; and the conditional, contested nature of Harley's personal brand of villainy. These repeated themes emerged after we watched, and took notes on, each episode of *BTAS* in which Harley Quinn appears.

CHARACTER OVERVIEW AND HISTORY

Harley Quinn debuted in the first half of the first season of *BTAS* in the episode "Joker's Favor." Albeit brief, her introduction to the Batman universe established some of her defining traits. She is the Joker's approving audience; in many ways, her presence validates his.[16] At the beginning of the episode, following the Joker's monologue about his next crime, Harley ratifies his tirade by asking, "Is it to laugh, huh, *Mistah J?*," a response he ends up ignoring in order to seek further acclamation from her and his henchmen. This first interaction illustrates the obsessive nature of their relationship. Harley lives to please and cheer for Mistah J—whom she also refers to as "puddin'"—but he perceives her as ancillary to his larger-than-life Machiavellianism. Harley's subsequent appearances find her embracing simultaneous roles as the Joker's partner in crime, his on-and-off romantic companion, and as a villain in her own right (or working in tandem with other villains, generally Poison Ivy) after being repeatedly cast off by the Joker.

Even though Harley Quinn premiered in the show's first season, her origin story was not explored until "Mad Love," one of the last episodes of the final season. Appropriately titled, the episode deconstructs two contrasting kinds of "mad love": the Joker's fixation with Batman and Harley's obsessive attraction to her puddin'. In this story, she reminisces about how only Batman drains the Joker's attention away from her. Through flashbacks we learn how Harleen Frances Quinzel transformed from a professional into the Joker's pawn. She is shown as a psychiatrist interning at Arkham Asylum who catches the Joker's eye. Their first interaction occurs through the Joker's glass cell, where he rearranges Harley's name from Harleen Quinzel to Harley Quinn, "a name that puts a *smile* on my face," he adds. As Harley's infatuation with the Joker grows, she schedules therapy sessions with him. Noticing her fascination, he manipulates her with fictitious accounts about how he was psychologically and physically abused during his adolescence. After witnessing an injured Joker return to Arkham following an escape attempt thwarted by Batman, she steals a jester costume in her first act of physical aggression, assumes the identity of Harley Quinn, and breaks Mistah J out of the asylum. The story suggests that the pain of watching the Joker suffer edges her into a life of crime to be near the man she loves. Her tragically romantic origin and subsequent abusive relationship with the Joker continue to determine motivations and reasoning behind her villainous acts. She is a victimizing victim yearning for her abuser's affection.[17] During the climax of "Mad Love," Batman laughs dismissively at Harley's naïveté regarding the Joker's romantic priorities: "The Joker doesn't love anything except himself." It seems that for Harley, this is the grim reality she must face: loving a psychotic narcissist who only desires her veneration through humiliation. This is the tragedy of her character, harboring a "mad love" that fuels her sense of villainy, her prowess as a feared vixen, and her plight as an abused sidekick.

THE VICTIMIZING VICTIM, OR THE BATTERED BATTERER

Harley Quinn is a sycophant—her villainous tendencies change based on who she is around at any given moment. With or tangential to the Joker, her actions are outrageously villainous. She will steal, rob, and maim in service of the man she loves despite his lack of appreciation and care for her. With Poison Ivy, Harley Quinn's actions are more antiheroic; she adopts a more empowered outlook and demonstrates an understanding that the Joker is psychologically and physically damaging. For example, in the episode "Harley and Ivy," Harley Quinn laments being a "doormat" for the Joker, states that she should be used to pain due to being with him, and sighs wistfully when Poison Ivy tells Harley that she needs "some lessons in good old female self-esteem." When occasionally partnering with Batman, again Harley exhibits antiheroic attitudes. Harley's lack of agency seems to be a defensively learned helplessness, which, along with "anxiety, depression, psychological distress, and . . . [p]oor relationship adjustment,"[18] are effects of psychological and physical abuse. She has difficulty grasping her own sense of agency due to it being routinely revoked by the Joker.

Throughout this show, Harley Quinn's relationship with the Joker is depicted as being clearly abusive, yet she always returns to him despite positive experiences with Poison Ivy, Batman, and her own villainous independence. Regardless of how (in)competently Harley Quinn is portrayed, the Joker physically, verbally, and emotionally abuses her: force-feeding fish to her, throwing her, yelling at and berating her, and emotionally manipulating her. In the episode "Harlequinade," Harley performs a burlesque-style dance during which she details the abuse dealt her at the hands of the Joker; she dances suggestively as she sings of this violence against her while the white male audience applauds and catcalls. Harley spends much of "Harlequinade" defending the Joker to those around her, especially Batman, who offers her release from Arkham Asylum in exchange for helping to capture the Joker. She agrees with the goal of double-crossing Batman. Thus, despite her acknowledgment through song and dance that the Joker is abusive, she still defends him verbally and physically. The episode ends with forgiveness after he attempts to kill her. These instances are presented as exaggerated slapstick comedy—physical representations of the zany mentality of the Joker as opposed to a normalization of abuse.

Thus, when Harley Quinn eventually begins retaliating against the Joker's abuse by using physical violence and emotional/sexual manipulation, it is depicted as battered-woman syndrome, the "psychological theory developed to explain the behavior of women who suffer abuse from their husbands, partners, or lovers."[19] Her turn to violence is a response to how "abuse by one partner causes the other partner to modify their behavior, and the primary mechanism of control is fear."[20] The Joker's repeated, varied abuse acts as a cattle prod, forcing Harley into behaviors she may not otherwise exhibit; she is essentially coerced into villainy as a coping mechanism for the extreme damage repeatedly dealt her.

Her descent into villainy at the hands of, and conditional to, the Joker reinscribes the notion that female villains like Harley Quinn are not ugly in the traditional manner of those like the Joker, Killer Croc, or Two-Face but rather are "deformed in other ways."[21] Harley Quinn's mental state and her fetishization of the Joker are demarcated as clear signs of disturbance, but she can perform the public face of the Joker due to her "normal" appearance as an attractive blonde woman. This highlights how Harley Quinn was ultimately created as a sexy side character designed to satisfy a voyeuristic male gaze.[22]

VIXEN

Harley fits into the "canonical female body"[23] by being white, young, thin, able bodied, and endowed with Barbie-doll-esque features. Her villainy is not writ on her skin as with the Joker; she performs physical feminine perfection and subjugation while also being presented as a kind of inverse feminist role model. Harley is a reverse Wonder Woman who can handle the Joker's dark side, a villain who makes her own choices and owns her sexuality. In Harley's current title (at the time of this writing), she is independent and has gone way beyond being a pawn for the Joker, even developing a romantic relationship with Poison Ivy. She lives "life by her own rules,"[24] and that independence has helped make her one of the most popular DC characters of all time (going well beyond the animated series).[25]

Earlier, however, in addition to Harley Quinn's fulfillment as an object of titillation for a constructed male audience, her status for much of her textual existence as an abused character who seems to *enjoy* the abuse is problematic. It perpetuates the historical assumption that women are inherently "moral masochists"[26] who enjoy suffering, rape, and abuse. As Roddy argues, "this fallacy [is] a product of a patriarchy that wants both to subjugate women and to make them responsible for the pain it inflicts upon them."[27] In rare moments when Harley Quinn breaks out and acts on her own, she is always brought back into a relationship with the Joker. Finding her own agency would remove the extreme control wrought on her not only by the Joker but also by the misogynistic universe of Batman and the male gaze inherent in its creation.[28] Treating their abusive relationship as comedic glamorizes "pleasure in surrender, and the privileging of lust over respect, common interests, and the intellectual connection promotes female subordination to a controlling male partner as highly attractive and rewarding."[29]

THROUGH THE MALE GAZE

The show depicts Harley Quinn and Poison Ivy in a manner consistent with the male gaze. Their presence in the show is to act as villains, yet their actions are also uniquely gendered. For instance, both Poison Ivy and Harley Quinn enact physical violence against men who catcall them or refuse to leave them alone, as in the episodes "Harley and Ivy," "Holiday Knights," and "Girl's Night Out." Their retaliatory actions against a misogynistic culture are polysemic, leaving the audience to interpret Ivy's or Harley's assertions as villainous or heroic. While we do see the pair carrying out villainy together, it is also highly tied into traditional Western gender norms and tropes—when Harley is camped out at Ivy's house in "Harley and Ivy," the pair walk around in Oxford shirts, full makeup, and panties; in "Girl's Night Out," they go clothes-shopping together. Even their villainy cannot escape the male gaze, regardless of the characters themselves being aware of misogyny and fighting against it. They live in a highly patriarchal society and were created by a patriarchal industry, so Poison Ivy and Harley Quinn are always already constrained by the structures that brought them to life. Harley will presumably always be both a subject and an object, both a quasi-feminist asserting her agency through sexuality and chaos and an oversexualized victim of abuse whose agency is routinely stripped.[30] Ultimately, her character will continue to be problematic as long as she is an object for fans and the Joker to abuse.

The depths of the male gaze may be best demonstrated in the *BTAS* debut of Batman antihero Creeper. His origin in the episode "Beware the Creeper" shoehorns him into Harley's life as a stalker willing to fight the Joker—or Batman—to gain her attention. Like the Joker, the Creeper also fell into a vat of chemicals that turned him into a less psychotic version of the Prince of Crime. Living up to his name, the character sexually assaults Harley by forcefully licking her face and kissing her hands, all portrayed in comical manner. The episode serves to further affirm Harley's status as an object to be desired, obsessed over, and dominated. Although she consistently rejects the Creeper's advances, she does so by relinquishing her agency to the Joker, who fights the Creeper, assuring the audience that Harley is a "one-man loon."

AESTHETICIZING VILLAINY AND VICTIMIZATION

Although marketed as a children's show, *BTAS* contains significant amounts of violence, sometimes graphic. Compared with other superhero cartoons of the 1990s like *X-Men* (1992–1997) and *Spider-Man* (1994–1998), *BTAS* never hesitated to orchestrate action scenes illustrating the consequences of violent acts. According to series creator Bruce Timm, the show's tone was intended to evoke a "mixture of dark realism and action for the kids."[31] Although the violent scenes on *BTAS* generally retained a sense of realism—Batman was often shown reacting to pain from physical wounds—aggressions between the Joker and Harley evoked more caricatured reactions from the characters. Their violent interactions often employed humorous elements such as fights inspired by slapstick comedy, which trivializes abuse. Margaret Ervin Bruder catalogs these representations as industry attempts to aestheticize domestic violence by "calling attention to specific acts of violence, and the violent dimensions of the story's apparatus."[32]

In the episode "The Trial," Batman is held captive at Arkham Asylum to face trial for playing a crucial part in creating some of Gotham's most vicious criminals. With the Joker acting as judge, Harley is called to testify against the Dark Knight, and while she's on the stand, the prosecutor tricks the Joker into admitting that he once sought parole at Harley's expense. With this betrayal, Harley jumps out of her seat to strangle her puddin', calling him a "slimy rat," drawing laughter from the trial's spectators. This instance serves to remind the audience (fictional and real) that their amusement at this unstable relationship comes at Harley's expense. The Joker's dismissal of Harley is not as violent as in other scenes, but it robs her of her agency, further positioning her as a hysterical woman instead of someone grappling with an abusive lover.

Indeed, making light of violent behavior between the Joker and Harley has become a crucial attribute of their relationship. During their interactions, the comedy occurs as if to mitigate the consequences of abuse for audiences. Lilie Chouliaraki explains that the cartoonization of violence on TV materializes to "eliminate the element of human pain (in this context, the psychological and physiological consequences of domestic abuse) from the act of suffering."[33] As discussed above, Harley's burlesque number reveals graphic details of the Joker's sadistic tendencies even as it serves to distract: "Life used to be so placid, won't you please put down that acid, and say that we're sweethearts again," she muses gracefully. Just as the show implores Harley to ignore her abuse, the aesthetic structure of this musical number asks the same of the audience. Bruder suggests that spectacularized violence "engage[s] audiences' fantasies and sensibilities"[34] by masquerading the violence itself and glamorizing its artistic dimensions. Thus, audiences accept the violence due to its excessively stylistic depiction even if they are affected by its ideological implications.

The episode "Mad Love" is a notable exception to the series' tendency to humorize Harley's suffering. In it, she attempts to finally conquer the Joker's lack of desire for companionship by murdering Batman. Instead, the Joker punishes her for achieving what he never could: outsmarting, overpowering, and capturing the Dark Knight. He backhands Harley and chastises her for appropriating the pleasure of defeating Batman, a goal he alone feels worthy to attain. Moments later, he throws her out of a window, and she falls several stories down until she crashes, bleeding, in a back-alley dumpster. The construction of the scene prioritizes a sense of shock and sorrow over humor. When her body breaks the window, the only noise heard is shattering glass. The sound of a void accompanies the rest of the scene as Harley falls in slow motion, staring wide-eyed at the audience. The scene cuts to the Joker walking away from the window and dismissively declaiming: "And don't call me 'puddin.'" Perhaps one of a few moments when the show demands serious attention to the Joker's abuse, this scene aestheticizes violence while *also* creating space for the audience to contemplate the context and moral dimensions of the couple's long history of abuse. Chouliaraki argues that, in general, media content creators lack interest in contextualizing the ethics of violence in their stories, preferring to focus instead on presenting violence in a visually enticing fashion.[35] The glamorization of violence on *BTAS*, particularly involving Harley, eternalizes her role as the "masochist's playmate,"[36] depriving her of the desire to extirpate herself from the Joker and pursue her own villainous (or nonvillainous) endeavors as an agentive individual.

CONCLUSION

Much of this chapter has chronicled the multiplicities of Harley Quinn as observed through her obsessive interactions with her "creator," the Joker. Compared to other vixens defining Gotham City's hyperviolent social dynamics, Harley exists in a crime purgatory, where she engages in violent behavior to please Mistah J, but only because her agency is repeatedly taken away through the abuse she suffers—she is stuck here due to gendered violence and fights against it with the only tools she knows: her own brand of gendered violence. Harley's characterization as a battered woman, whose villainy is conditional and a site of symbolic violence against women, is worthy of study.[37] As millions of people watch popular shows and consume comics media, "media influence society (and are in turn influenced by it);"[38] portrayals of gendered violence and abusive relationships like the Joker's and Harley Quinn's, then, are not just idle comic relief.

Notes

1. Matthew Freeman, "Transmediating Tim Burton's Gotham City: Brand Convergence, Child Audiences, and *Batman: The Animated Series*," *Networking Knowledge: Journal of the MeCCSA Postgraduate Network* 7, no. 1 (2014): 10.

2. Bruce Timm and Eric Radomski, "DVD Talk," *Batman: The Animated Series*, vol. 4 (Warner Brothers, 2005).

3. Bruce Timm and Eric Radomski, audio commentary for "On Leather Wings," *Batman: The Animated Series*, vol. 1 (Warner Brothers, 2005).

4. Robert Moses Peaslee and Robert G. Weiner, eds., *The Joker: A Serious Study of the Clown Prince of Crime* (Jackson: University Press of Mississippi, 2015).

5. Travis Langley, *Batman and Psychology: A Dark and Stormy Knight* (Hoboken, NJ: John Wiley and Sons, 2012).

6. Peaslee and Weiner, *The Joker*.

7. Carlen Lavigne, "'I'm Batman' (and You Can Be Too): Gender and Constrictive Play in the Arkham Game Series," *Cinema Journal* 55, no. 1 (Fall 2015): 133–41.

8. Shannon Austin, "Batman's Female Foes: The Gender War in Gotham City," *Journal of Popular Culture* 48, no. 2 (2015): 285–95; and Shelley E. Barba and Joy M. Perrin, eds., *The Ascendance of Harley Quinn: Essays on DC's Enigmatic Villain* (Jefferson, NC: McFarland, 2017).

9. Richard J. Gray II, "Vivacious Vixens and Scintillating Super-Hotties: Deconstructing the Superheroine," in *The 21st Century Superhero: Essays on Gender, Genre and Globalization in Film*,

ed. Betty Kaklamanidou and Richard J. Gray (Jefferson, NC: McFarland, 2011); and Charlotte Howell, "'Tricky' Connotations: Wonder Woman as DC's Brand Disruptor," *Cinema Journal* 55, no. 1 (2015): 141–49.

10. Jack Fennell, "The Aesthetics of Supervillainy," *Law Text Culture* 16, no. 1 (2012): 305–28; and Langley, *Batman and Psychology*.

11. Kate Roddy, "Masochist or Machiavel? Reading Harley Quinn in Canon and Fanon," *Transformative Works and Cultures* 8, (2011): 1–26; and Nathan G. Tipton, "Gender Trouble: Frank Miller's Revision of Robin in the *Batman: Dark Knight* Series," *Journal of Popular Culture* 41, no. 2 (2008): 321–36.

12. Howell, "'Tricky' Connotations," 142.

13. Danielle Borgia, "Twilight: The Glamorization of Abuse, Codependency, and White Privilege," *Journal of Popular Culture* 47, no. 1 (2015): 162.

14. Ron Salkowitz, quoted by Rachel Grate, "Behind the Mask: What Fans Want at Fandom Conventions," Eventbrite, July 27, 2017, available at https://www.eventbrite.com/blog/ds00-fan -conventions-behind-the-mask/.

15. Alan McKee, *Textual Analysis: A Beginner's Guide* (London: Sage, 2003).

16. Roddy, "Masochist or Machiavel?," 1–26.

17. Borgia, "Twilight: The Glamorization of Abuse," 153–73.

18. Tyler B Mason, Robin J. Lewis, Robert J. Milletich, Michelle L. Kelly, Joseph B. Minifie, and Valerian J. Derlega, "Psychological Aggression in Lesbian, Gay, and Bisexual Individuals' Intimate Relationships: A Review of Prevalence, Correlates, and Measurement Issues," *Aggression and Violent Behavior* 19 (2014): 220.

19. Sarah Gibbs Leivick, "Use of Battered Woman Syndrome to Defend the Abused and Prosecute the Abuser," *Georgetown Journal of Gender and the Law* 6, no. 3 (2005): 391.

20. John Hamel, "'But She's Violent, Too!': Holding Domestic Violence Offenders Accountable within a Systemic Approach to Batterer Intervention," *Journal of Aggression, Conflict and Peace Research* 4, no. 3 (2012): 128.

21. Fennell, "The Aesthetics of Supervillainy," 306.

22. Gray, "Vivacious Vixens and Scintillating Super-Hotties," 91.

23. Diane Ponterotto, "Resisting the Male Gaze: Feminist Responses to the 'Normatization' of the Female Body in Western Culture," *Journal of International Women's Studies* 17, no. 1 (2016): 135.

24. Tim Beedle, "Laughter and Pain: Jimmy Palmiotti and Amanda Conner on Harley Quinn," DC Comics, April 28, 2016, available at https://www.dccomics.com/blog/2016/04/28/ laughter-and-pain-jimmy-palmiotti-and-amanda-conner-on-harley-quinn.

25. For more current examples of storytelling featuring Harley, see Marguerite Bennett, Laura Braga, Mirka Andolfo, and Elsa Charretier, *DC Comics Bombshells*, vol. 5, *The Death of Illusion* (New York: DC Comics, 2017); and Amanda Conner, Jimmy Palmiotti et al., *Harley Quinn Omnibus*, vol. 1 (New York: DC Comics, 2017). Various chapters in Shelley E. Barba and Joy M. Perrin's edited volume *The Ascendance of Harley Quinn: Essays on DC's Enigmatic Villain* (Jefferson, NC: McFarland, 2017) are pertinent, as follows: for a more detailed discussion of Harley's romantic intentions, see Cia Jackson, "Harlequin Romance: The Power of Parody and Subversion," 16–29; for her relationship with the Joker, see K. Scarlett Harrington and Jennifer A. Guthrie, "'That Just Proves He Wants Me Back': Pure Victimhood, Agency and Intimate Partner Violence in Comic Book Narratives," 55–69, and Amanda Hoyer, "Victim, Villain or Antihero: Relationships and Personal Identity," 107–19; and on Harley's autonomy, see Erica McCrystal, "The Motley Queen: A 'Spicy Package' of Misrule," 168–76.

26. Paula J. Caplan, *The Myth of Women's Masochism* (London: Methuen, 1985), 140.

27. Roddy, "Masochist or Machiavel?," 7.

28. Gray, "Vivacious Vixens and Scintillating Super-Hotties," 91.

29. Borgia, "Twilight: The Glamorization of Abuse," 159.

30. Austin, "Batman's Female Foes," 285–95.

31. Freeman, "Transmediating Tim Burton's Gotham City," 10.

32. Margaret Ervin Bruder, "Aestheticizing Violence; or, How to Do Things with Style," PhD diss., Indiana University, 2003.

33. Lilie Chouliaraki, "The Aestheticization of Suffering on Television," *Visual Communication* 5, no. 3 (October 2006): 261–85.

34. Bruder, "Aestheticizing Violence."

35. Chouliaraki, "The Aestheticization of Suffering on Television."

36. Anita Phillips, *A Defense of Masochism* (London: Faber and Faber, 1998), 12.

37. Laura Mulvey, "Visual Pleasure and Narrative Cinema," *Screen* 16, no. 3 (Autumn 1975): 6–18.

38. David Croteau and William Hoynes, *The Business of Media: Corporate Media and the Public Interest* (Thousand Oaks, CA: Pine Forge Press, 2001), 191.

CHAPTER 20

"You Were the Chosen One!"

Darth Vader and the Sequential Dynamics of Villainy in the Star Wars *Prequel Trilogy*

TARA LOMAX

AS THE EMBLEMATIC REPRESENTATION OF "THE DARK SIDE OF THE FORCE" IN the *Star Wars* franchise, Darth Vader is one of the most iconic supervillains in popular culture. His ultimate villainy is first established in *Episodes IV, V,* and *VI*[1] of the saga, yet the subsequent revelation of Vader's tragic origin as Anakin Skywalker in *Episodes I, II,* and *III*[2] complicates his unequivocal villainy. This is because the prequel trilogy refigures Anakin/Vader as both the predestined hero of an ancient Jedi prophecy and a victim of Sith manipulation. Vader's creator, George Lucas, contends that with the prequel trilogy, "the person you thought was the villain is really the victim and the story is really about the villain trying to redeem his humanity."[3] This chapter argues, then, that the significance of Vader as a villain is conditional on the distinct episodic continuity across which his character is developed—that is, an in medias res trilogy (the "original" trilogy) followed by an origin trilogy (the prequel trilogy). This inverted continuity is often considered merely an idiosyncrasy of the franchise that offers viewers multiple plot sequences through which to experience the saga; alternatively, this chapter contends, the *Star Wars* franchise's episodic plot structure is fundamental to understanding the dynamics of Vader as a complex villain. Following from Richard Reynolds, who considers that "[s]upervillains are the engines of diachronic continuity,"[4] this chapter examines the sequential dynamics of villainy through its association with liminality, temporality, and destiny. In occupying both the before and after, the prequel trilogy presents Vader as a liminal villain who is simultaneously Jedi and Sith, thus contributing a temporal perspective to Vader's role as villain.

The *Star Wars* franchise's thematic fixation with the nature of good and evil is critically regarded as an oversimplified dualism in which Vader is seen to archetypically represent the evil extreme. The moment Vader boards the *Tantive IV* and emerges from a haze of blaster-fire in the opening scene of *Episode IV—A New Hope*, his reputation as a supervillain is firmly impressed upon the popular consciousness. His presence is heralded by an ominous score and rumbling soundscape, and his appearance is characterized by black cyborg armor, a towering stature, and a menacing voice with machine-aided heavy breathing. Vader's ambitions involve galactic domination enhanced by the power of the Force, and his association with unrepentant evil is further affirmed by his ability to Force-choke insubordinates at a distance as well as destroy an entire planet merely as an interrogation tactic. Despite such unambiguously villainous power, it is the mysterious and obscure origins of his menacing form and behavior in *Episode IV* that upholds Vader as a straightforward and easily identifiable symbol of supervillainy. It is through this scope that Vader represents the darkest extreme of the good and evil duality that defines the thematic foundation of the *Star Wars* franchise.

As the original trilogy unfolds, however, the extremity of Vader's villainy is arguably allayed as the enigma of his character dissipates. In *Episode V—The Empire Strikes Back*, Vader is subordinate to the ultimate villain, Emperor Palpatine/Darth Sidious, and he also reveals himself to be the father of the hero, Luke Skywalker. Then, at the end of *Episode VI—Return of the Jedi*, Vader finally sacrifices himself to save his son and destroy the emperor. Nonetheless, perceived through the contained scope of the original trilogy, Vader's redemption does not work to question or complicate the nature of his villainy so much as it serves Luke's character development. This is exemplified on the planet of Dagobah in *Episode V*, when, as part of his training with Jedi Master Yoda, Luke ventures into the Cave of Evil and encounters a vision of Vader. In this scene, Luke strikes Vader down only to find Luke's own face revealed underneath the black cybernetic mask. This scene frames Vader's own struggle with good and evil as a test of Luke's own moral impulses and is therefore a pivotal moment in the hero's journey. In describing the tests and conflicts of the hero, Anna Fahraeus and Dikmen Yakalı Çamoğlu contend that what "in the end produces and constructs the hero is the battle to overcome the antagonist or opposition."[5] For this reason, the moral conflict that Vader grapples with in *Episodes V* and *VI* functions as a device that drives the hero's development. After Vader destroys the emperor, he asks Luke to remove his mask so he can tell his son, as Anakin Skywalker, "you were right about me"—responding to Luke's earlier insistence that "there is good in you." As a conclusion to Luke's journey in *Episode VI*, Vader's vindication serves to more clearly articulate the prevailing good in Luke rather than complicate Vader's villainy.

While the original trilogy is known for its focus on heroism, this is in contrast with the prequel trilogy's preoccupation with the causes and motivations of villainy. *Episodes I, II,* and *III* follow Anakin's tragic progression from a young slave to a Jedi knight who, consumed and manipulated by fear and ambition, becomes seduced by the dark side of the Force. This ultimately presents us with a villain's journey. Despite recent scholarly interest in antiheroes, the concept of a villain's journey has yet to be adequately examined. Indeed, the most significant engagement with the villain's experience comes from screenwriting mentor Christopher Vogler with his oft-cited adage, "a villain is the hero of his own myth."[6] The villain's journey perhaps differs from the hero's journey in structure, method, and goals, but it still relies on character development and identification. First introduced as a nine-year-old slave on the planet of Tatooine in *Episode I—The Phantom Menace*, the foundation of Vader's villainy is disrupted when the "ultimate villain" of *Episode IV* is depicted as a defenseless child. For this reason, Vader's origin story has incited critics like Tony Pacitti to fear that "Darth Vader could someday be shoehorned into the role of the everyman."[7] I argue that such concerns do not undermine Vader's villainy but demonstrate how the prequel trilogy destabilizes the polarities that drive the franchise's archetypal conventions.

Anakin's journey toward villainy is constituted by the culmination of several tragic circumstances and unredeemable evil actions. In *Episode I*, after revealing his upbringing as a slave, Anakin is separated from his mother as a sacrifice of pursing life as a Jedi, only to be refused by the Jedi Council because, as Master Yoda explains, there is "much fear" in him. Ten years later, in *Episode II—Attack of the Clones*, Anakin is tormented by nightmares of his mother. He returns to Tatooine to discover that she has been kidnapped by Tusken raiders, and after finding her in a tortured and ravaged state, she dies in his arms. This provokes Anakin to enact revenge by slaughtering whole families of Tusken raiders, which is a pivotal moment in his villain's journey. Finally, in *Episode III—Revenge of the Sith*, Anakin beheads an unarmed Count Dooku, saves Chancellor Palpatine, stands by as Jedi Master Mace Windu is murdered, and slaughters Padawan younglings. Each event becomes less defensible than the last and culminates in him becoming the Sith Lord, Darth Vader. However, even with the Sith name, Vader manifests conflicting forces in its association with "the negative connotations of scarcity and devastation, and the positive possibilities of 'glory,' 'daring,' and 'obligation.'"[8] The actions that lead Anakin to the dark side are arguably not premeditated but the result of inner conflict between the light and dark sides of the Force.

Anakin's inner conflicts might indeed be associated with an amplified expression of the moral thresholds that the hero encounters in their archetypal journey. At the beginning of *Episode III*, Anakin's crossroad is overtly symbolized as he wields both his blue Jedi lightsaber and Count Dooku's red Sith lightsaber in an intersecting pose, as he internally struggles with whether to follow Palpatine's order to kill Dooku. However, for the villain—and especially for Vader—the threshold is not a marker of progress or accomplishment like in the hero's journey, but represents a perpetual state of conflict. The villain's journey of the prequel trilogy might, therefore, be productively understood through Victor Turner's concept of the transition-being or liminal persona. Turner defines this role as "frequently employed to designate those who are being initiated into very different states of life."[9] To see Anakin as the liminal persona is to recognize his journey as a volatile, but eternal, rite of passage, in which his segregation from his home and mother, his marginalization within the Jedi Order (because of his deep-seated fear and his "clouded" future), and the aggregation of thresholds that lead to him turning to the dark side, all appeal to Turner's explication of the transition-being.[10] Similarly, Christopher N. Poulos considers the notion of the liminal hero, who

> embodies *some* heroic qualities (like courage under fire) while still carrying qualities that are antithetical to the presumed purity of mission embodied by the classic hero figure. . . . He is a both/and, neither/nor, betwixt/between character. He is both hero and villain. And yet, he is neither all the way good nor all the way bad. He is, as they say, an "unresolved" character.[11]

Anakin exemplifies this state of liminality in the prequel trilogy in his perpetual battle with the thresholds of good and evil. As someone potentially borne out of the Force itself, he is destined to occupy the betwixt and between of moral order and, through the temporal dynamics of the prequel, he occupies the past, present, and future of his journey simultaneously. However, to see Anakin as the liminal hero is to undermine the significance of the original trilogy in establishing Vader as iconic villain *first*, before Anakin's origin story is revealed. Vader can, therefore, more powerfully be realized as a liminal villain.

As a device for sequential storytelling, the prequel is particularly compatible with representing the liminal villain, because it can reveal the villain's background and motivations while locating it in the sequential future of the villain's journey. Nathaniel Van Yperen fittingly describes Vader as "the *future self gone bad*,"[12] which conceptualizes the temporal duality of Vader's past actions and his future identity. Prequels reveal origins through a sequential logic that complicates temporality and form, which Paul Sutton calls "the logic of 'afterwardsness,'" describing that "it possesses a peculiar dual temporality that enables it to both precede and follow."[13] The prequel device is often considered in relation to its pastness, in which it establishes a new starting point;[14] by contrast, Sutton emphasizes the after/forward progression of the prequel, which acknowledges its complex temporality as both after and before. Therefore, like Vader, prequels are profoundly liminal: "that which is neither this nor that and yet is both."[15] For this reason, the "afterwardsness" of the prequel disrupts the classic linearity of causal relations and sequential dynamics; it also informs an understanding of how Vader's villainy carries temporal dimensions.

The textual mechanism that characterizes the prequel can also be productively understood using Gérard Genette's notion of *analeptic* (or backward) continuation: "meant to work its way upstream, from cause to cause, to a more radical or at least a more satisfactory starting point."[16] This does not describe the prequel as instigating a new starting point but as being forward-moving *toward* a reaffirmed and reappraised starting point—that is, the opening of *Episode IV*. The analepsis is often applied to thinking about the "flashback" plot device; however, in seeking to emphasize its sequential dynamics, Ken Ireland proposes the notion of the "analeptic phase," which works to conceptualize the "retrospective evocation of an event" across a diachronic continuity.[17] The analeptic phase provides a much stronger basis for realizing the temporal complexity of the prequel: as being not merely a new beginning but simultaneously occupying the before and, most especially, the after. Through the logic of "afterwardsness" and the concept of the analeptic phase, Vader is provided with an origin story but not a new starting point—this adds a temporal layer to his moral liminality and, at the same time, firmly maintains his iconicity as a threatening villain in *Episode IV*.

In simultaneously occupying the before and after, the analeptic phase precipitates a moment of temporal juncture that further complicates the sequential dynamic of the prequel. Ireland calls this juncture a "hinge-point" and explains that when the "analeptic phase functions to unmask an enigma or mystery, [the hinge-point] might well occupy a pre-final position."[18] In the prequel trilogy, this hinge-point can undoubtedly be identified as the final climactic scenes of *Episode III*, in which the newly anointed Darth Vader is dramatically defeated by his former Jedi Master Obi-Wan Kenobi and left to burn in the lava-entrenched soil of Mustafar. This is a pivotal moment in the *Star Wars* franchise because it finally reveals the physical trauma of Vader's past *in its afterwardsness*, and it invokes the pressures of destiny that have loomed over Anakin's journey. As Obi-Wan looks down at Vader's almost unrecognizable body, he exclaims, "You were the chosen one! It was said that you would destroy the Sith—not join them. Bring balance to the Force—not leave it in darkness!" In this moment, destiny is complicated by analeptic temporality, because in *Episode VI*, which is previously in the saga's plot but later in the diegesis, Anakin *was* indeed the chosen one and he *did* indeed destroy the Sith. Without the original trilogy, therefore, there is no prophecy; put another way, the original trilogy *is* the prophecy. Vader's destiny is always already foretold by the original trilogy, and this further supports this chapter's earlier contention that the prequel trilogy manifests greater meaning and significance as an analeptic phase—that is, the "afterwardsness" of a past event. For this reason, this moment on Mustafar is a hinge-point that represents the trauma of Vader's role as liminal villain because, this chapter argues, Vader is as trapped by the sequential dynamics of the *Star Wars* franchise as he is constrained by his cybernetic life-support suit. The moment Vader's helmet finally clasps into place, when breathes through his life support suit for the first time, represents the ultimate temporal nexus between the original and prequel trilogies—one that Vader perpetually occupies as liminal villain.

In the animated television series *The Clone Wars* (2008–2015), which takes place between the events of *Episodes II* and *III*, Anakin's destiny as the "Chosen One" remains central to his character development. In season 3, Anakin, Obi-Wan, and Padawan Ahsoka Tano are drawn to the planet Mortis,[19] where Anakin's role as the Chosen One is tested—not for his ultimate good, but to determine whether he can balance the light and the dark sides of the Force. The episodes on Mortis explore a previously unaddressed aspect of the Chosen One prophecy: in the movies, the actual meaning of bringing "balance to the Force" is overlooked by the Jedi Order, with the assumption that balance must mean that the Jedi prevail over the Sith. However, on the planet Mortis in *The Clone Wars*, the Force is not bound up with the polarized doctrines of the Jedi and Sith but is a conduit for the Force itself, which Obi-Wan describes as yielding "an intersection unlike anything I've ever felt before." Mortis, as a liminal threshold planet, is inhabited by three Force-wielding beings: the Daughter, who channels only the lightest side of the Force; the Son, who embodies its darkest extreme; and the Father, who keeps them in balance. Compellingly, the Daughter describes her family in temporal terms, explaining: "We are the ones who guard the power. We are the middle, the beginning, and the end." With this explication, the Daughter curiously presents the temporalities of the Force out of sequential order; moreover, in beginning with the *middle* followed by the *beginning* and then the *end*, she also articulates the plot order of the *Star Wars* franchise. In this way, the powers of balance and temporality are also intertwined with the dynamics of sequential plot structure.

On Mortis, Anakin proves himself to be the Chosen One by simultaneously subduing both children. This complicates the meaning and implications of the ancient Jedi prophecy, because it questions what it means to "bring balance to the Force"; in doing so, it also hints toward the subversive notion that evil is fundamental to maintaining balance. The episodes on Mortis in *The Clones Wars*, therefore, work to activate the liminality of Anakin's journey to villainy. The Son attempts to lure Anakin to the dark side of the Force by revealing his future villainy as Vader. The Son torments Anakin with a flash-forward vision of his analeptic "hinge-point" on Mustafar from *Episode III*, and his destruction of Alderaan from *Episode IV*, as Vader's mask appears above Anakin in a gust of smoke, together with a subtle variation of the "Imperial March" theme music. Ironically, the Son tells Anakin that "the future, by its nature, can be changed," but this vision reiterates the temporal reality that, for Anakin, the future cannot be changed because the sequential dynamics of the franchise have already foretold his destiny in the original trilogy.

Despite Vader's tragic backstory, he remains an iconic supervillain. Although this chapter has explored how the prequel trilogy complicates the archetypal nature of Vader's villainy, this has far from dampened his iconic significance. Poulos's explication of the liminal hero as "an 'unresolved' character"[20] is indeed fitting for Vader, as the characterization of his villain's journey continues to interest *Star Wars* creators. Recent installments and contributions to the *Star Wars* franchise keep exploring the complexity and liminality of Vader's villainy through analeptic temporality. *Rogue One: A Star Wars Story* (2016)[21] is a standalone anthology movie that takes place directly before the beginning of *Episode IV*. In this prequel installment, Vader lives in a castle on Mustafar, tormented by his past and his origins. His appearance in *Rogue One* is also marked by a glimpse of his body without armor and vulnerably exposed inside a Bacta healing tank. In the animated series *Star Wars: Rebels* (2014–),[22] which is set prior to *Rogue One*, Vader duels with Anakin's former Padawan Ahsoka Tano and sustains damage to one side of his helmet. Revealing his tormented eye, Ahsoka recognizes Anakin's own voice calling out through the rupture in his armor. This might perhaps recall, in its afterwardsness, the moment of redemption at the end of *Episode VI*, when Vader asks to look upon his son Luke with his "own eyes." Moreover, in the comic book series *Darth Vader* (2015–2017),[23] which occurs between the events of *Episodes IV* and *V* and follows Vader as he investigates Luke's identity and parentage, Vader has his cybernetic suit malevolently shut down and harnesses the trauma of his past to bring himself back to life. This comic depicts alternating panels that recall Vader's pivotal hinge-point moment of defeat at the hands of Obi-Wan on Mustafar in *Episode III*. These examples demonstrate that the complex and vulnerable facets of Vader's villainy remain unresolved, and his character continues to be explored through experimentation with sequential dynamics and the temporal thresholds between texts.

For a contemporary audience who is familiar with the entire *Star Wars* franchise, it is difficult to divorce the original trilogy from the prequel trilogy and the knowledge of Vader's origin as Anakin and the Chosen One prophecy. After having considered the sequential dynamics of the original and prequel trilogies, then, I have reinscribed Luke's encounter with Vader in the Cave of Evil on Dagobah in *Episode V* with the temporal complexity of Vader's liminal villainy. As argued above, with only the original trilogy in mind, this scene merely serves the character development of the hero; however, by also considering the prequel trilogy, the revelation of Luke's face beneath Vader's mask takes on new meaning for the development of the villain: Luke's resemblance to Anakin at the same age draws attention to the man inside the suit—not Luke, but Anakin. As Anne Lancashire describes: "Building backwards as well as forwards, each *Star Wars* episode also revises in retrospect our readings of some aspects of the earlier films."[24] Vader's association with villainy and heroism is continually in oscillation across moral and temporal thresholds, as is the viewer's experience of him and his villain's journey. The prequel trilogy has not only provided a backstory but refigured Luke's journey as hero to also retroactively serve Anakin's journey as liminal villain. To this end, this chapter has examined how the sequential continuity through which Vader's character unfolds—from archetypal villain to liminal villain—blurs the stark division between good and evil at the thematic foundation of the saga.

By considering the concept of liminality and the prequel's temporality, it is possible to realize that Vader's villainy is not absolute, regardless of Obi-Wan's problematic declaration that "only the Sith deal in absolutes" (when even the Jedi have an absolute view of good and evil). Rather, as liminal villain, Vader disrupts the archetypal mythology that is so strongly associated with the *Star Wars* franchise. The sequential dynamics of Vader's villainy presents the polarities of good and evil as being temporally one and the same. It is this blurring that, Daniel A. Forbes explains, makes villains so intriguing:

> we recognize that often in the real world the boundaries between good and bad are not so clear—perhaps because these labels represent not so much the intrinsic characters of persons and their actions, but our own judgments about them, judgments shaped by differences in perspective and personal bias. So our interest in evil may not be so strange—it may simply be an interest in a different perspective.[25]

The notion of perspective and point of view has underscored this chapter, in which I have suggested that Vader's villainy is dependent on the sequential perspective of plot—that is, the episodic order through which Vader is viewed. Similarly, such perspective is also fundamental to Anakin's journey to the dark side, in which, what might be a moment of epiphany for Anakin as villain in *Episode III*, Chancellor Palpatine sinisterly suggests that "good is a point of view." The prequel trilogy broadens the textual point of view through which Vader's villainy can be realized. It indeed dispels some of the enigma of his evilness, but it does so by complicating sequential continuity. In this way, the temporal liminality of the prequel trilogy critically reformulates the conditions of heroism, villainy, and destiny that are all central to understanding the complexities of Vader and supervillainy more generally.

Notes

1. George Lucas, dir., *Star Wars: Episode IV—A New Hope* (Lucasfilm, 1977); Irvin Kershner, dir., *Star Wars: Episode V—The Empire Strikes Back* (Lucasfilm, 1980); and Richard Marquand, dir., *Star Wars: Episode VI—Return of the Jedi* (Lucasfilm, 1983).

2. George Lucas, dir., *Star Wars: Episode I-—The Phantom Menace* (Lucasfilm, 1999); George Lucas, dir., *Star Wars: Episode II—Attack of the Clones* (Lucasfilm, 2002); and George Lucas, dir., *Star Wars: Episode III—Revenge of the Sith* (Lucasfilm, 2005).

3. Tippy Bushkin, dir., *The Chosen One*, in George Lucas, dir., *Star Wars: Episode III—Revenge of the Sith* (2005; Sydney: Twentieth Century Fox Home Video, 2005), DVD, disc 2.

4. Richard Reynolds, *Super Heroes: A Modern Mythology* (London: B. T. Batsford, 1992), 50.

5. Anna Fahraeus and Dikmen Yakalı Çamoğlu, "Who Are the Villainous Ones? An Introduction," in *Villains and Villainy: Embodiments of Evil in Literature, Popular Culture and Media*, ed. Anna Fahraeus and Dikmen Yakalı Çamoğlu (Amsterdam: Rodopi, 2011), vii.

6. Christopher Vogler, *The Writer's Journey: Mythic Structures for Writers*, 3rd ed. (Studio City, CA: Michael Wise Productions, 2007), 68.

7. Tony Pacitti, "Pancakes with Darth: Shifting Images of Villain from Death Stars to Departments Stores," *Glimpse* 9 (Summer 2012): 70.

8. Stephen Rojcewicz, "Darth Vader: Masks, Power, and Meaning," *Journal of Poetry Therapy* 1, no. 1 (September 1987): 26.

9. Victor Turner, "Betwixt and Between: The Liminal Passage in *Rites de Passage*," in *The Forest of Symbols: Aspects of Ndembu Ritual* (Ithaca, NY: Cornell University Press, 1967), 95.

10. Turner, "Betwixt and Between," 95.

11. Christopher N. Poulos, "The Liminal Hero," *Cultural Studies/Critical Methodologies* 12, no. 6 (2012): 487.

12. Nathaniel Van Yperen, "I Am Your Father: The Villain and the Future Self," in *Vader, Voldemort, and Other Villains: Essays on Evil in Popular Media*, ed. Jamey Heit (Jefferson, NC: McFarland, 2011), 190.

13. Paul Sutton, "Prequel: The 'Afterwardsness' of the Sequel," in *Second Takes: Critical Approaches to the Film Sequel*, ed. Carolyn Jess-Cooke and Constantine Verevis (Albany: State University of New York Press, 2010), 141–42.

14. Mark J. P. Wolf, *Building Imaginary Worlds: The Theory and History of Subcreation* (Hoboken, NJ: Taylor and Francis, 2012), 207.

15. Turner, "Betwixt and Between," 99.

16. Gérard Genette, *Palimpsests: Literature in the Second Degree*, trans. Channa Newman and Claude Doubinsky (Lincoln: University of Nebraska Press, 1997), 115.

17. Ken Ireland, *The Sequential Dynamics of Narrative: Energies at the Margins of Fiction* (Cranbury, NJ: Associated University Presses, 2001), 115.

18. Ireland, *The Sequential Dynamics of Narrative*, 116.

19. George Lucas, "Overlords," "Altar of Mortis," and "Ghosts of Mortis," *Star Wars: The Clone Wars*, season 3, episodes 15–17 (Lucasfilm Animation, January–February 2011).

20. Poulos, "The Liminal Hero," 487.

21. Gareth Edwards, dir., *Rogue One: A Star Wars Story* (Lucasfilm, 2016).

22. Dave Filoni, Simon Kinsberg, and Steven Melching, "Twilight of the Apprentice," *Star Wars: Rebels*, season 2, episodes 21–22, (Lucasfilm Animation, March 2016).

23. Kieron Gillen and Salvador Larroca, *Star Wars: Darth Vader*, no. 24 (August 2016). See also Charles Soule and Jim Cheung, *Star Wars: Darth Vader, Lord of the Sith*, vol. 1 (New York: Marvel Enterprises, 2017); and Kieron Gillen, Salvador Larroca et al., *Star Wars: Darth Vader Omnibus* (New York: Marvel Enterprises, 2017).

24. Anne Lancashire, "*The Phantom Menace*: Repetition, Variation, Integration," *Film Criticism* 24, no. 3 (Spring 2000): 24.

25. Daniel A. Forbes, "The Aesthetic of Evil," in *Vader, Voldemort, and Other Villains: Essays on Evil in Popular Media*, ed. Jamey Heit (Jefferson, NC: McFarland, 2011), 13.

CHAPTER 21

TV Serial Killers

The Configuration of a New Concept of Villain

VÍCTOR HERNÁNDEZ-SANTAOLALLA AND ALBERTO HERMIDA

IN CONTRAST TO THE CLASSIC HERO AND THE VIEWER'S EXPECTATIONS OF WHAT is correct and admirable, the presence of opaque characters with double or inexistent moral standards is well established in the "quality television" fictional series. Such characters abandon their traditional supporting role or that of the enigma driving the story in order to become the true lead. The result is a dramatic change in the focalization of the discourse, redirecting interest into getting to know them better: to go deeper into their universe, discover what motivates them, and, in short, see the fictional reality through the eyes of this new concept of villain.

This ongoing change in approach, perfectly crystallized by characters like Tony Soprano (*The Sopranos*, HBO, 1999–2007), Walter White (*Breaking Bad*, AMC, 2008–2013), or Frank Underwood (*House of Cards*, Netflix, 2013–2018), reaches peak relevance with the figure of the serial killer, with whom audiences are increasingly asked to identify. Specifically, shows like *Dexter* (Showtime, 2006–2013), *Hannibal* (NBC, 2013–2015), *Bates Motel* (A&E, 2013–), *The Following* (Fox, 2013–2015), and *The Fall* (BBC Two, 2013–), among others, serve to illustrate this tendency in modern televised fiction. Thus, the main characters of these TV series generally adhere to the definition of a serial killer: a murderer who kills at least three victims in different places or at different times with a cooling-off period in between.[1] In fact, this cooling-off period is what differentiates serial murders from spree or mass murders, which happen at one time and place.

Thus serial killers escape, for example, their condition as marginal, "leftover" members of society and are admired in a variety of roles: a qualified forensic analyst for the Miami Police Department; an erudite psychiatrist of the highest prestige, respect, and recognition; a distinguished university literature professor; or a loving father. If the conventional model of the television serial killer can be represented by Errol Childress in the first season of *True Detective* (HBO, 2014)—not surprisingly, clearly a member of what is contemptuously referred to as "white trash"—then Dexter Morgan, Hannibal Lecter, Joe Carroll, and Paul Spector, among others, exemplify this reversal of the traditional face of villainy.

This chapter explores the different issues that strengthen the persuasive profile of these main characters in an interrelated way, making them the main draw of the show. First, in relation to the narrative, we explore issues such as the characters' motivations, traumas, and interpersonal relationships. We also investigate the mise-en-scène, or elements related to scenographic construction, through the configuration of the characters and the environments they inhabit. Last, in order to answer why these dark characters emerge/reemerge at this time and thus change the narrative focalization, we discuss the sociocultural context in which these series are produced.

FASCINATION WITH THE HUMANIZED MONSTER

Analyzing the monster as cultural object, Jeffrey Jerome Cohen indicates that it "quite literally incorporates fear, desire, anxiety, and fantasy (ataractic or incendiary)."[2] In the same way, and centering on serial killers in real life, David Schmid notes that, while murderers are governed by their own laws and moral codes, they stir up a mixture of fear, indignation, attraction, and admiration in the public.[3] Regarding these last two emotions, the degree of fascination inspired by these types of criminals never ceases to amaze. Take the cases of Charles Manson or Ted Bundy as examples. In the case of the latter, T-shirts were made saying "Ted Bundy is a one-night stand," songs were dedicated to him on the radio, and the "Bundyburger" was even sold in a restaurant in Aspen, Colorado.

Thus, just as some serial killers awaken a special zeal in society, the actions of television serial killers are both condemned and "applauded" by viewers. There is at the outset the paradox that the arrest or death of the criminal would cause, a priori, the end of the series; this is a main reason why the audience sides with the killer. This desire can even be understood in relation to Dexter Morgan or Light Yagami (*Death Note*, Nippon TV, 2006–2007), who are guided by a so-called need for justice. Specifically, both characters target criminals whom their respective legal systems are incapable of punishing, but circumstances force them to take different measures in order to survive.

It is perhaps more complicated, however, to understand why a viewer would identify with killers such as Hannibal Lecter, considering that his only reason for being is to eliminate anyone he himself defines as vulgar and crude. In some way, issues such as elegance, erudition, and the good taste that characterize the cannibal could be understood as a justification for the fanaticism some feel toward Lecter, as well as the exaltation of the painstaking aesthetic treatment of his violence. In fact, excuses such as this, among others, would be equally valid to "defend" the crimes of other characters such as Paul Spector or Joe Carroll: the former makes a show of his cultural heritage, citing Albert Camus, while the latter uses the figure of Edgar Allan Poe in his modus operandi. Even so, it is hard to assimilate the fact that viewers enjoy the freedom of such monsters, even if they are from works of fiction.

Moreover, the attraction felt for television serial killers has an important connection to the process of humanization they experience over the course of several episodes. The characteristics of the TV series allow the psychological development of characters to be drawn out over time, thus permitting viewers to better explore the reasons behind their monstrosity. The urgency and condensed nature of the cinematographic story disappear in favor of television seasons, which are drawn out year after year. There is neither excessive introspection nor retreat into the lives of the main characters; moreover, the viewer is frequently taken down tortured passageways that lead to existential conflicts. Far from being anecdotal, these series focus on the individuals and their internal struggles, giving the viewer reasons to empathize with them.

The trauma and extreme experiences these characters often suffer within the context of their family contribute to a certain empathy and solidarity on the part of the audience, finally leading to some degree of understanding of their actions as a last resort. For example, Dexter's "dark passenger" is defined by having witnessed his mother's murder as a child, while in *The Fall*, the origin of Spector's sociopathy is associated with his mother's suicide. In this way, even in those cases in which a psychopathology can be detected, as with Norman Bates's psychosis, it is patently obvious at all times that traumas witnessed and experienced in a family setting were fundamental in causing the illness. For Bates (in *Bates Motel*), it is not only a result of the abuse his mother receives at the hands of her alcoholic father, or the multiple rapes that she is subjected to by various characters throughout the series, but also her unhealthy overprotection of Norman, completely overshadowing him and, as a consequence, strengthening his insecurities and most extreme obsessions.

In that regard, it is significant that these serial killers—not coincidentally, all of them are white men[4]—are influenced in their actions, relationships, and crimes by their different female role models, whether a mother, a partner, or a sister. In fact, another representative example can be found in Hannibal Lecter, who, after losing both of his parents, suffered the loss of his sister, whose death is directly related to the origins of his cannibalism. Norman's fixation with the teacher he ends up killing, Carroll's with his wife, or Spector's with his ex-girl-friend should be highlighted as references to Ted Bundy's obsession with his first girlfriend, whose physical attributes determined the features of his victims. Likewise, we should underscore the special relationship that Dexter has with his stepsister and with Rita, as well as his relationship with Hannah McKay. She, we should note, is one of the few female serial killers on the small screen.

Lastly, another plot device that confers special and unconditional audience favor on these killers is the introduction of another criminal even more despi-cable than the lead: in short, the villain's villain. In this way, the pretext is reused and not only serves as a catalyst for the story but also positively influences the perception of the main character. The rival should be defeated, therefore conferring paradoxically heroic values onto the protagonist serial killer, as illustrated in the cases of Trinity in *Dexter* and Mason Verger in *Hannibal*. Such heroism adds another humanizing aspect to the protagonist killer and, as a consequence, renders him more persuasive to the viewer.

THE MISE-EN-SCÈNE OF THE SERIAL KILLER

In this configuration of the new concept of villain, supported by the aforemen-tioned internalization of personality and human experience, it is important to explore in depth one of the characteristics of audiovisual "structure" as part of that process. The peculiarities of the mise-en-scène provide a further means of character development through its impact on serial killers' appearance and their surroundings on-screen. In this way, dimensions such as art direction, costume design, characterization, actor direction, and lighting come together to embel-lish the character beyond his or her presence on the scripted page.[5] The visual representation of the serial killer is structured, in this way, as a complement to narrative development. Thus, the symbolic values that scenographic resources allow to be included in the story are assembled to "paint" a more complex and intense psychological portrait.

Specifically, the different departments required in the mise-en-scène shape the main character and his or her universe.[6] In the cases discussed here, serial killers are portrayed through a visual preoccupation with the most intimate details of their daily lives, which plunge the viewer into their unique, person-al world. This is done through the killers' physical characteristics and their particular ways of gesturing, as well as through the clothes they wear and the spaces they inhabit or frequent. These narrative strategies afford a look into the main character's life, utilizing color palettes that affect costuming, set design, and lighting guidelines and taking form in props, textures, and many other elements necessary to create the setting and atmosphere in which the serial killer lives. In short, the viewer's attraction and empathy are intimately bound to artistic strategy, an unquestionably handcrafted weapon of seduction within the story construction.

Dexter Morgan and Hannibal Lecter are paradigmatic examples of this strategy. Their visual representations are indispensable not only for building their characters but also for seducing viewers into identifying with them in certain ways. Quite independent from narrative justifications for their violent behavior, the screen image is designed to curry the audience's empathy, no matter how reprehensible or sadistic the killers' attitudes are. Each of these characters has a distinct pattern that shapes his visual look, whether it is manifest duality or the seductive force of class and good taste.

In Dexter's case, his existential polarity is essential to the production design of the series, originally conceived by Michael Corenblith and Brandy Alexander. Through the aesthetic guidelines they establish, the double life of the main character is visually represented by playing with contrasts developed on complementary levels. So, in Dexter's daily life—his simulation of an ordinary citizen—warm colors, pastel-colored clothing, sunny Miami exteriors, and high-key lighting are used, so that there are no shadows and nothing is apparently hidden. Conversely, dark colors and costumes, abandoned locations, nocturnality, and low-key lighting accompany the "dark passenger" in his bloody thirst for justice. In both cases, however, one color remains a constant nexus: blood red, which dyes the chromatic palette defining Dexter Morgan.

In turn, if such duality allows a main character to be molded on-screen, it is also important to remember that, in order to understand him in depth, we must have access to his private spaces. The more intimate the space, the deeper the insight.[7] In the case of Dexter, both the interior of his house and the plastic-covered "kill rooms" he builds for his ritual of vigilante justice reinforce his fastidious sense of order and organization, as well as his surgical, methodical precision. Such molding of a character by his domain becomes even more evident in the televised scenography of *Hannibal*.

Doctor Lecter leaves the doors to his territory wide open, leaving viewers fascinated by the remarkable things they find there. This is done based on a production design initiated by Patti Podesta and continued by Matthew Davies almost through to the end of the series' third season. Hannibal deeply seduces the viewer with the aesthetics surrounding him. The omnipresent aesthetics even infiltrate his crimes, such that even the darkest and most savage obscenity seems to be briefly touched by beauty. Hannibal, whose imposing and fastidious presence, impeccable down to the last detail, is presented in the series as the pinnacle of erudition and excellence. In his particular combination of Renaissance man and modern-day Lucifer, there exists an exquisite palate, delicately combining crime and cuisine, hypnotizing the audience with his slightest gesture. Once again, his "refuge" allows symbolic access to the interior of the beast, particularly through the architecture: the interior design and the chiaroscuro of his office, the sophistication of his kitchen, and the majesty of his dining room. In short, it is a perfect example of set design at the service of a character's psychological portrait. Hannibal's personality "impregnates" his environment, making the character more comprehensible to the viewer.

REASONS FOR THE (RE-)EMERGENCE

In "Monster Culture (Seven Theses)," Cohen proposes a strategy of "reading cultures from the monsters they engender,"[8] arguing as his first thesis that "the monster is born only ... as an embodiment of a certain cultural moment—of a time, a feeling, and a place."[9] This idea is also shared by Douglas Cowan, who, based on the idea of "sociophobics," suggests that the object, the manner in which an individual fears, and the reaction to that fear are intensely conditioned by culture.[10]

In the end, as Jeffrey Andrew Weinstock gathers based on the novella *The Monster* by Stephen Crane, "monsters are not born but made."[11] The term "monster" is derived from the Latin *monstrum* and related to the verbs *monstrare* and *monare*, which can be translated as "to show" and "to warn," respectively. In this way, Weinstock points out that "the monster is thus a kind of omen that gives shape to moral vice, reveals the will of the gods, and forecasts the future."[12] The monster is therefore a product of the sociocultural context in which it is inserted—"They ask us why we have created them," indicates Cohen[13]—but in view of the aforementioned, we should ask why they have been reborn now, moreover in the role of the main character.

From a general perspective, Robin Wood suggests that horror films—including those with a "human psychotic or schizophrenic" in the leading role—tend to be produced "in a period of extreme cultural crisis and disintegration, which alone offers the possibility of radical change and rebuilding."[14] Similarly, Adam Kotsko identifies the flowering of the television sociopath as a symptom of dissatisfaction with a broken society.[15] These societal symptoms are likewise related to the appearance of the fictional serial killer.[16] Serial killers on current television series are the product of a sociocultural context, not just genetics; their monstrosity arises from their educational and existential experience. In this sense, it is relevant to persist in the reversal of the serial killer's treatment in popular culture from supernatural to human monstrosity.

Taking a more comprehensive view and looking for the contextual origin as well as the prominence of these monstrous humans, it is important to highlight various historical events. The threat of terrorism as well as the moral crisis arising from the uncertainty caused by the terrorist attacks on September 11, 2001, are significant, as is the Great Recession that started in 2008. The relationship between the chronologies of these two events and the life cycles of the TV series described here is not coincidental. This sociopolitical and economic background coincided with the development of two pivotal shows: *Dexter* and *Breaking Bad*, which indirectly portray this critical context. In addition, both series' finales coincided with the global financial crisis in 2013, in turn followed by a number of other original series, remakes, and adaptations, specifically *Utopia* (Channel 4, 2013–2014), *The Following*, and *Do No Harm* (NBC, 2013) in January; *House of Cards* and *Cult* (The CW, 2013) in February; *Bates Motel* in March; *Hannibal* in April; *The Fall* in May; *The Bridge* (FX/Mundo Fox, 2013–2014) in July; and *The Tunnel* (Sky Atlantic/Canal+, 2013–) in October.

The economic crisis, perceived lack of safety, and other doubt-inducing circumstances experienced by society fed into televised fiction, which became progressively darker, populated by opaque characters who used duality and artifice as a mask in order to carry out their criminal activity. Zygmunt Bauman, updating the ideas of Ferdinand Tönnies and Émile Durkheim, maintains that in this way, in contrast to the comfort and safety of community, broader society is shown as a space lacking in safety and requiring constant vigilance.[17] Currently, however, the borders between community and society are weakening in such a way that average citizens no longer feel safe even in their closest circles. The state of permanent conflict, therefore, is no longer limited to the social and public environment but has entered the intimacy of the communal and familiar, where fear and distrust leak in.

Dexter, Spector, Carroll, Hannibal, Norman Bates, and even Light Yagami appear to be model citizens, respected professionals, or responsible students as well as good family members and friends. Nevertheless, their respective television series show their true identities—their real essence. Moreover, if these killers set a trend and take others down the wrong path, then the villainy spreads, subjecting larger swaths of society to a state of absolute vulnerability. Beyond the classic example of the copycat shown in *Hannibal*, Doctor Lecter's powers of persuasion seep into and transform the other characters in the series. At the same time, Joe Carroll manages to bring together an army of followers from all parts of society, waiting for his order to sow terror in his name in an almost sectarian manner. Doubt and anonymity are established, therefore, as ingredients for generalized social distrust. This is the idea that underlies some of the promotional posters for *The Following*, which features the following taglines: "Do I look like a killer?," "Even serial killers have friends," and "Friend, neighbor, killer."

THE TV SERIAL KILLER AS A NEW CONCEPT OF VILLAIN

Taking into account everything that has been mentioned here, we can conclude this chapter by taking the inverse route: starting from the context to finish up in the story. In this way, in a society in full global crisis, where moral values are questioned and a climate of widespread weariness and exhaustion leads to certain unrest, it is not difficult to understand why television viewers would let themselves be seduced to satiate their frustration with characters who champion disobedience of any restriction, rule, or ethical code. This behavior, undoubtedly, works as a means of garnering empathy and identification, serving as a justification for the audience's frenzied fascination.

Likewise, as we have detailed in this chapter, several mechanisms come together within a story to "unleash" the audience's fascination. On the one hand, the narrative conveys a deep understanding of the serial killer's daily life and establishes (usually) him as the main character in such a way that it is possible to get under his skin, understand his motivations, and investigate his humanization. On the other hand, as far as scenography is concerned, the mise-en-scène is used to full advantage on-screen, as it shows such characters to be attractive individuals, seductive while at the same time enigmatic, and able to awaken feelings from the most superficial admiration to the most visceral passion.

In conclusion, these aspects come together to form a new profile of villainy in which the reprehensible acts of the main characters, whether potential or seasoned serial killers, do not put the audience off. Therefore, as viewers are submitting to their charms, they cannot help but perpetuate a discourse that feeds the very contextual issues that originated them.

Notes

1. Ronald M. Holmes and Stephen T. Holmes, "What Is Serial Murder? The Character and the Extent," in *Contemporary Perspectives on Serial Murder*, ed. Ronald M. Holmes and Stephen T. Holmes (Thousand Oaks, CA: Sage, 1998), 1–4.

2. Jeffrey Jerome Cohen, "Monster Culture (Seven Theses)," in *Monster Theory: Reading Culture*, ed. Jeffrey Jerome Cohen (Minneapolis: University Minnesota Press, 1996), 4.

3. David Schmid, "Idols of Destruction: Celebrity and the Serial Killer," in *Framing Celebrity: New Directions in Celebrity Culture*, ed. Su Holmes and Sean Redmond (Milton Park, Oxfordshire, England: Routledge, 2006), 308.

4. Philip Jenkins, "Catch Me Before I Kill More: Seriality as Modern Monstrosity," *Cultural Analysis* 3 (2002): 2–3.

5. Vincent LoBrutto, *The Filmmaker's Guide to Production Design* (New York: Allworth Press, 2002).

6. Félix Murcia, *La escenografía en el cine: El arte de la apariencia* (Madrid: Fundación Autor, 2002), 87.

7. Josep Rosell, "El decorado, radiografía del personaje: Reflexión-contradiccón," in *Constructores de ilusiones: La dirección artística cinematográfica en España*, ed. John D. Sanderson and Jorge Gorostiza (Valencia, Spain: Ediciones de la Filmoteca, 2010), 27.

8. Cohen, "Monster Culture," 3.

9. Cohen, "Monster Culture," 4.

10. Douglas E. Cowan, *Sacred Terror: Religion and Horror on the Silver Screen* (Waco, TX: Baylor University Press, 2008), 171.

11. Jeffrey Andrew Weinstock, "American Monsters," in *A Companion to American Gothic*, ed. Charles L. Crow (Chichester, West Sussex, England: Wiley Blackwell, 2014), 41.

12. Weinstock, "American Monsters," 41.

13. Cohen, "Monster Culture," 20.

14. Robin Wood, "An Introduction to the American Horror Film," in *The American Nightmare: Essays on the Horror Film*, ed. Robin Wood and Richard Lippe (Toronto: Festival of Festivals, 1979); cited in Barry Keith Grant and Christopher Sharrett, eds., *Planks of Reason: Essays on the Horror Film* (Lanham, MD: Scarecrow Press, 2004), 123.

15. Adam Kotsko, *Why We Love Sociopaths: A Guide to Late Capitalist Television* (Alresford, Hampshire, England: Zero Books, 2012), 94.

16. In fact, as Philip Jenkins points out, serial killers are described as "monsters" or "beasts" by authors like Robert K. Ressler and Tom Shachtman in *Whoever Fights Monsters* and *I Have Lived in the Monster*; Donald James in *Monstrum*; Steve Jackson in *Monster*; and Carlton Smith in *Shadows of Evil*, among others (Jenkins, "Catch Me Before I Kill More," 10–13).

17. Zygmunt Bauman, *Community: Seeking Safety in an Insecure World* (Cambridge: Polity Press, 2001), 1–2.

CHAPTER 22

The Kingpin

A *"Princely" Villain for Social and Political Change*

RYAN LITSEY

THE VIEWER IS THREE EPISODES INTO THE FIRST SEASON OF THE HIT NETFLIX series *Daredevil* before they are finally introduced to the villain at his moment of creation. The scene begins with a solitary figure, staring, contemplating a blank canvas that hangs in an art gallery. Described as the "rabbit in a snow storm," the canvas seems simple yet symbolizes the moment of creation. In the same way a painter must start with a blank canvas, so must the character we see looking at the "rabbit in a snow storm." Until this point, however, the name of this character has not been spoken, and when asked how the canvas makes him feel, he replies, "alone." He is alone because only a person of a certain *virtù* can undertake the type of creation he is about to begin. Wilson Fisk, more commonly understood as the Kingpin, is looking at the canvas and imagining a new Hell's Kitchen, one he will help create from the decay of the Chitauri attack. It is in the moment of creation that the Kingpin represents a new type of villain.

Peter Coogan, earlier in this volume, argues that the supervillain can be any of five basic components or typologies: the monster, the enemy commander, the mad scientist, the criminal mastermind, and the inverted superhero.[1] However, there are a few rare villains that fit a new typology, a typology that has some links to the hero more than a villain. That is not to say that these villains are heroes, but rather to contend that there may be a heroic element in their ultimate goal, whether the villain is cognizant of it or not. This new typology of villain is that which serves as a force for political and social change.

There are very few of these in the comic arts universe. Magneto could be considered a villain of this type as well. These are villains who through their individual virtue/actions bring about a change in society. The Kingpin serves as an agent for social and political change and possesses the type of virtue necessary to create order from chaos, a villainous heroic virtue. The reason the

Kingpin does not fit into the Coogan typology is twofold: first, he has a split personality more akin to a hero, and second, he possesses a unique type of virtue. In order to understand how the villainous virtue of the Kingpin can be a galvanizing force for social and political change, it is important to understand how his virtue comes about. The emergence of villainous virtue comes from an understanding of Fortuna, fate, and the role Fortuna plays in society. The villain for social and political change is best understood in this context and through the writings of an often maligned sixteenth-century Italian philosopher, Niccolò Machiavelli, and his villainous character, the Prince.

Machiavelli published his most famous book in 1531. At the time, it served as a handbook for a newly anointed prince to better understand how to consolidate and hold power even during turbulent times. However, over the years further examination has revealed that the virtue of the Prince, or *virtù* as Machiavelli calls it, is not in gaining or holding power. True virtù is to usher in a free and civil society. This is the role of the Kingpin as an agent for social and political change. His virtù as a villain serves to bring forth a new civil society. In order to see how the Kingpin can actually benefit society through extreme villainy, we must first understand what typology of prince the Kingpin would be for Machiavelli. The answer to this comes in chapter 9, "Civil Principality." The civil principality is for citizens who rise to power through the favor of their fellow citizens. The Kingpin is the Prince who rises as a result of favor from the citizens. In the scene where Anatoly meets the Kingpin for the first time, the audience is shown the violence the Kingpin is capable of, but the Kingpin is also a fictional cover used by Wilson Fisk. The individual Wilson Fisk is the chief organizer and rebuilder of Hell's Kitchen after it was heavily damaged during the Chitauri attack. Wilson Fisk is a man so loved by the people that he is almost elected mayor or prince of this society. Machiavelli writes, "[A] wise prince should think of a method by which his citizens, at all times and in every circumstance, will need the assistance of the state and of himself; and then they will always be loyal to him."[2] Nowhere is this more evident than in the fact that Fisk's construction company is the primary rebuilder of Hell's Kitchen, to say nothing of the fact that the Kingpin is the sole force keeping the different criminal factions in line. What arises from this situation is a troubling duality within the Kingpin. Machiavelli foresaw this eventuality:

> For there is a such a gap between how one lives with how one ought to live that anyone who abandons what is done for what ought to be done learns his ruin rather than his preservation: for man who wishes to make a vocation of being good at all times will come to ruin among so many who are not good. Hence it is necessary for a prince who wishes to maintain his position to learn how not to be good and to use this knowledge or not use it according to necessity.[3]

The quotation sets the stage for understanding how the Kingpin's duality develops: one persona to do the work of being good and another to do what is necessary to preserve Hell's Kitchen and his place in the hierarchy as the Prince. The Kingpin, then, in order to keep power, must be feared rather than loved. Since he cannot be "all good," then the only reliable force in Machiavellian terms is fear. Hence the need for the dual identities: he needs the Kingpin as villain to generate the fear. This is most evident in the first three episodes of Netflix's *Daredevil*, during which the mere mention of his character strikes fear into even the most hardened criminal. The duality creates an area for the development of villainous virtue. Machiavelli writes:

> A new prince cannot observe all those things by which men are considered good, for in order to maintain the state he is often obliged to act against his promise, against charity, against humanity, and against religion. And therefore, it is necessary that he have a mind ready to turn itself according to the way the winds of Fortune and the changeability of affairs require him.[4]

In writing this, Machiavelli changed the understanding of virtue. No longer is virtue connected to the higher good. It is not justified as a thing in and of itself. Virtue has become virtù, the skill that a prince has to hold and maintain his power. Machiavelli later admits: "Let a prince act to seize and to maintain the state; his methods will ways be judged honorable and will be praised by all."[5] For the Kingpin and Machiavelli, any acts that seek to seize or maintain the state are effectively honorable and good, like when the Kingpin kills drug dealers who threaten his criminal empire—the criminal empire that enforces control over the gangs in Hell's Kitchen. Murdering them with fierce brutality conveys fear, which is useful, and the murder is necessary to maintain the empire. Also, as Fisk lies about his role as the Kingpin, or hides the records of what his construction company is doing, he finds it perfectly reasonable if it helps maintain the status quo in Hell's Kitchen. Fisk demonstrates a deeply paternal desire to improve Hell's Kitchen throughout the series. He views himself as a savior. He wants to clean it up. The end result of this type of princely virtù is to separate the Prince from those whom he rules. He is above them, and since his principality was gained through civility, he stands above them with none being his equal. This singular position is important for confronting Fortuna, and it is this confrontation that both brings the Prince into being and is eventually his downfall.

Machiavelli describes Fortuna as a woman, a destructive force within the state of nature. She's a combination of natural forces and a certain playfulness. Fortuna destabilizes society because society is unable to confront the uncertainty she brings. Machiavelli writes:

> And I compare her to one of those ruinous rivers that, when they become
> enraged, flood the plains, tear down the trees and buildings.... [E]veryone
> flees from them, everyone yields.... The same things happen where Fortune
> is concerned; she shows her force where there is no organized strength to
> resist her.[6]

Machiavelli further describes the female attributes of Fortuna. She is a force that
needs to be "taken" by an impetuous man. She needs to be seduced by a special
princely character. The gender specificity of Fortuna aside, her sheer force is an
apt description of the Chitauri. Aliens from outer space invaded from a hole in
the sky and, until the Avengers responded, there was no organized force to resist
such an attack. Hell's Kitchen got the worst of it. In such a case, only a singular
force like the Prince possesses the capability to bring civil society back from
the brink of destruction. The only counter against a force the world has never
seen before is a person of equal power who is removed from the conventional
moral hindrances of society. In order to confront the state of nature, the Prince
must possess characteristics that distinguish him from citizens of a republic.
The Prince must be able to do what is necessary in order to rein in Fortuna and
provide sufficient stability to enable the rise of civil society. The true virtù of
the Prince is his capacity to do what is necessary to serve as an agent of social
and political change. How is the change brought about? Examine for a moment
the characteristics of the Prince and his relationship to Fortuna.

A prince such as the Kingpin, who is as ruthless as Machiavelli describes,
will admittedly be more feared than loved. For Machiavelli, fear is a more stable
emotion than the fickle love. Through his actions and sheer disregard for the
conventional morality of civil society, the Kingpin has distinguished himself as
separate from "regular" society. As a singular actor, he has positioned himself
to adequately deal with the winds of change, understood as Fortuna. However,
he has also distinguished himself in the eyes of the society he wishes to rule.
He has demonstrated a callous disregard for the rules and order of society. In
his attempt to separate himself from the rest of society, he has also become a
pariah. In a society where traditional authority is absent (since aliens invaded
and threw New York into chaos), what remains to bring stability is princely
virtù. The virtù of the Kingpin lies in Machiavelli's understanding of political
power. For Machiavelli, there are two types of political power: liberation and
stabilization. For the citizens of Hell's Kitchen, the traditional political forces of stabilization are incapable of dealing with Fortuna in the form of the
Chitauri, which means there is a need for a new liberating political force. The
force that rises is contained within the virtù of the Prince. John Pocock writes
concerning virtù:

Since by his own act the Innovator [the Prince] inhabits a delegitimized context, where Fortuna rules and human behavior is not to be relied on, he is obliged to take the short view and continue to act ... then action is virtù; when the world is unstabilized and the unexpected a constant threat, to act—to do things not contained within the structures of legitimacy—was to impose form upon Fortuna. Aggression was the better part of value.[7]

Combating the unpredictability of Fortuna is the reason why at the beginning of *Daredevil* we see the importance of Wilson Fisk in helping Hell's Kitchen heal after the attack. The Kingpin is the force that rises when traditional political structures cannot combat what happened. Anecdotally, the introduction of the character Vanessa also occurs at the moment of creation. The development of their relationship follows a similar path to that taken by the Prince in his wooing of Fortuna. Vanessa serves as the embodiment of Fortuna, and as Fisk wins her heart, so does society begin to recognize the evils of the Princely Fisk. The rise of the virtù of the Kingpin and the development of his character is what moves society in a different direction. The downside to being a force for political and social change is that the process can often be very ugly. For Machiavelli and the Kingpin, though, it is a necessary process. The process comes about as a result of how the unique villainous virtù of the Kingpin positions him in a place separate from society.

The virtù of being able to do what is necessary also has a side effect of distinguishing the Kingpin from everyone else and not necessarily in a "good" way. The evil that he undertakes is so bad that the citizens of society begin to question if he is the best ruler society can offer. It is at this moment that the true nature of the Kingpin as a villain for social and political change becomes apparent. Nowhere is this encapsulated more effectively than in one of the most critical scenes in the first season. The scene occurs in episode 13. The Kingpin is being transported to prison in the back of a truck. He begins a monologue with an admission that he is not a religious man; he reads more out of curiosity than anything else (Machiavelli argued that the Prince should use religion as a tool in this way, something to pacify or add legitimacy to an argument rather than an ideal). The Kingpin tells the story of a man who was walking on the road to Jericho, when another man of ill intent attacked him. There are a few key points to take from the initial setup of the story. The traveler is a citizen on his way to a city, outside of the "boundaries" of civil society since he is on the road. By being outside of the city when the highwayman attacks him, he is actually being attacked in the state of nature itself, or as Machiavelli would argue, he was subjected to the whims of Fortuna. The traveler is brutally beaten and left for dead on the side of the road. He is passed by holy men, who do nothing. He is also passed by government officials, who offer no help because the traveler is in the state of nature where civil society cannot help him. Eventually, a Samaritan comes and helps the man. The Samaritan admittedly is called a "good man." He offers aid and money to help ensure the traveler's survival. He returns the traveler to the safety of the city. As the Kingpin continues the story, he tells the guards that he had believed himself to be the Samaritan, but over time, he came to realize that he is in fact the man of ill intent who brutally beat the traveler. The use of this story is deliberate, as it also serves to inform the audience about the origin of the common phrase "a good Samaritan," which has powerful connotations in society. This phrase would not exist if this traveler had not been beset on the road by "ill intent." It is at this moment that we can see how the virtù of the villain can serve as a catalyst for social and political change.

The Kingpin/Wilson Fisk was so disturbingly evil that society itself turned against him. Machiavelli's Prince is not a model for maintaining power but rather a vehicle that ushers in republican government. This is why the Prince must be so removed from the citizens of the principality. The Prince has no morals; the Prince acts out of necessity. The Prince is the ill intent, a highway criminal who attacks good citizens when they find themselves outside of the city. The reason the Prince does this is because, in order to battle Fortuna, he must be removed from life as a citizen, and sometimes that means bad things happen to good citizens. When a hole in space opened up above the city, New York was cast into the state of nature to be preyed upon by ill intent. However, as the Prince lays waste to the city, he also has the effect of keeping the forces of Fortuna at bay. It is in this moment when Fortuna is assuaged and the Prince is doing what must be done out of necessity, through acts of unspeakable evil, that the citizens of the republic come to realize that the Prince does not represent a favorable method of governance. The amorality, the lying, the violence, and the fear are not stabilizing political forces. This leads to the "good Samaritan" and the citizens themselves casting the Prince out. The virtù of the Kingpin, the true agent of change, is that he gives life to justice. Justice is often described as being both blind and carrying a sword. The Daredevil is the pinnacle example of blind justice: a violent hero who cannot see, but who in the end allows the stability and legitimacy of the law to take the Kingpin into custody. It is only through the Princely virtù of the Kingpin acting as a villain for social and political change that the citizens of Hell's Kitchen are able to give rise to peaceful governance protected by justice itself.

Notes

1. Peter Coogan, *Superhero: The Secret Origin of a Genre* (Austin, TX: MonkeyBrain Books, 2006). See also Coogan's chapter in this volume, excerpted from *Superhero*.

2. Niccolò Machiavelli, *The Portable Machiavelli*, ed. and trans. Peter Bondanella and Mark Musa (Harmondsworth, Middlesex, England: Penguin, 1979), 110.

3. Machiavelli, *The Portable Machiavelli*, 127.

4. Machiavelli, *The Portable Machiavelli*, 135.

5. Machiavelli, *The Portable Machiavelli*, 138.

6. Machiavelli, *The Portable Machiavelli*, 159.

7. John Greville Agard Pocock, *The Machiavellian Moment: Florentine Political Thought and the Atlantic Republican Tradition* (Princeton, NJ: Princeton University Press, 1975), 177–78.

Section 4

SUPERVILLAINY IN COMICS AND SEQUENTIAL ART

CHAPTER 23

Comics Codes and Parameters for Villain Construction in Sequential Art

ROBERT G. WEINER AND THE COMICS MAGAZINE ASSOCIATION OF AMERICA

IF EVER THERE WAS A REAL-LIFE VILLAIN IN THE HISTORY OF COMICS, IT WAS psychiatrist Fredric Wertham (1895–1981). His 1954 volume *Seduction of the Innocent* argued that juvenile delinquency was linked to reading comics (in particular, those dealing with crime and horror, but also superhero comics).[1] Rather than first publishing his arguments in a peer-reviewed journal, Wertham published an excerpt in *Ladies' Home Journal* (November 1953).[2] While American comics since their inception have attracted social critique,[3] it was Wertham's tirade against them that garnered the most notoriety. It is odd that Wertham would single out comics as being a cause of deviant behavior, because he understood *true* deviancy, having been a consultant on the trial of the notorious cannibal, child serial killer Albert Fish (although, one could argue that, perhaps because of this case, Wertham saw crime and horror comics as encouraging the kind of behavior Fish engaged in). Carol Tilley has argued that Wertham falsified his research to fit his own attitude toward comics.[4]

As a result of this growing consensus against comics and parent outrage, neighborhood burnings occurred, and the federal government held congressional hearings in 1954 (which were televised, featuring Wertham and several industry professionals) to investigate how comics contributed to juvenile delinquency and moral corruptibility.[5] While ultimately the government did not step in to regulate the comics industry, the damage had been done. The industry itself took the initiative and created its own self-censoring mechanism, the Code of the Comics Magazine Association of America. Despite stepping up to create the code, the industry was crippled, with companies scaling their operations down or going out of business completely. Many writers and artists were purged in the aftermath: David Hajdu, in *The Ten-Cent Plague*, catalogs several hundred people in a fourteen-page list who "never again worked in comics after the purge of the 1950s."[6] Comics were then quickly replaced by rock 'n' roll music and films like *The Wild One* (1953), *Rebel without a Cause* (1955), and *Blackboard Jungle* (1955) as being the causes of juvenile delinquency.

As one can see below, the Code sanitized comics and forced those companies lucky enough to stay in business to come up with creative ways to keep readers (and compete with television). For some, this period marked a "mediocre, confusing period between the comics of the 1940s (Golden Age) and the second rise of the super heroes in the 1960s." For other fans, the 1950s were "the most exciting era in the medium's history."[7] It largely depends on how one wants to interpret the events pre- and post–Comics Code.[8]

The Code was revised in 1971 due to the fact that "Marvel Comics . . . broke new ground by producing a mainstream comic book dealing with drugs" and releasing it to the newsstands without code approval (*The Amazing Spider-Man*, nos. 96–98 [1971]). By publishing these issues, "Marvel Comics forced the Comics Magazine Association to reevaluate the comics code that had been in effect with no changes since 1954. . . . Stan Lee, Marvel's editor in chief, received a letter from the Department of Health, Education, and Welfare asking the company to do a *Spider-Man* story about the dangers of drugs. . . . Because the comics code forbade any mention of narcotics or their use, the story did not get code approval, but Marvel decided to publish the story anyway" without the Code's seal.[9] Publishing this story helped loosen some of the rules to keep up with the changing times.[10]

In 1989, the Comics Code was again revised to reflect the fact that many more adult-oriented and serious comics were being released (e.g., *Watchmen*, *Dark Knight Returns*, *Killing Joke*, *Maus*),[11] and also, in large part, to accommodate the proliferation of independent comic book stores, which stocked materials through the direct market and thus allowed for more comics with mature themes and content. In 2001, Marvel quit the association, stopped using its seal, and started its own rating system. DC and Archie Comics followed suit, and although DC quit the Code in 2011 (thus nullifying the Code completely), the Code was more or less a thing of the past by 2009.[12]

CODE OF THE COMICS MAGAZINE ASSOCIATION OF AMERICA, INC.[13]

Adopted October 26, 1954

Preamble

The comic book medium, having come of age on the American cultural scene, must measure up to its responsibilities.

Constantly improving techniques and higher standards go hand in hand with these responsibilities.

To make a positive contribution to contemporary life, the industry must seek new areas for developing sound, wholesome entertainment. The people responsible for writing, drawing, printing, publishing, and selling comic books have done a commendable job in the past, and have been striving toward this goal.

Their record of progress and continuing improvement compares favorably with other media in the communications industry. An outstanding example is the development of comic books as a unique and effective tool for instruction and education. Comic books have also made their contribution in the field of letters and criticism of contemporary life.

In keeping with the American tradition, the members of this industry will and must continue to work together in the future.

In the same tradition, members of the industry must see to it that gains made in this medium are not lost and that violations of standards of good taste, which might tend toward corruption of the comic book as an instructive and wholesome form of entertainment, will be eliminated.

Therefore, the Comics Magazine Association of America, Inc., has adopted this code, and placed strong powers of enforcement in the hands of an independent code authority.

Further, members of the association have endorsed the purpose and spirit of this code as a vital instrument to the growth of the industry.

To this end, they have pledged themselves to conscientiously adhere to its principles and to abide by all decisions based on the code made by the administrator.

They are confident that this positive and forthright statement will provide an effective bulwark for the protection and enhancement of the American reading public, and that it will become a landmark in the history of self-regulation for the entire communications industry.

Code for Editorial Matter

General Standards: Part A

(1) Crimes shall never be presented in such a way as to create sympathy for the criminal, to promote distrust of the forces of law and justice, or to inspire others with a desire to imitate criminals.

(2) No comics shall explicitly present the unique details and methods of a crime.

(3) Policemen, judges, government officials, and respected institutions shall never be presented in such a way as to create disrespect for established authority.

(4) If crime is depicted, it shall be as a sordid and unpleasant activity.

(5) Criminals shall not be presented so as to be rendered glamorous or to occupy a position which creates a desire for emulation.

(6) In every instance good shall triumph over evil and the criminal punished for his misdeeds.

(7) Scenes of excessive violence shall be prohibited. Scenes of brutal torture, excessive and unnecessary knife and gunplay, physical agony, and gory and gruesome crime shall be eliminated.

(8) No unique or unusual methods of concealing weapons shall be shown.

(9) Instances of law-enforcement officers dying as a result of a criminal's activities should be discouraged.

(10) The crime of kidnapping shall never be portrayed in any detail, nor shall any profit accrue to the abductor or kidnapper. The criminal or the kidnapper must be punished in every case.

(11) The letters of the word "crime" on a comics-magazine cover shall never be appreciably greater in dimension than the other words contained in the title. The word "crime" shall never appear alone on a cover.

(12) Restraint in the use of the word "crime" in titles or subtitles shall be exercised.

General Standards: Part B

(1) No comic magazine shall use the word "horror" or "terror" in its title.

(2) All scenes of horror, excessive bloodshed, gory or gruesome crimes, depravity, lust, sadism, and masochism shall not be permitted.

(3) All lurid, unsavory, and gruesome illustrations shall be eliminated.

(4) Inclusion of stories dealing with evil shall be used or shall be published only where the intent is to illustrate a moral issue and in no case shall evil be presented alluringly, nor so as to injure the sensibilities of the reader.

(5) Scenes dealing with, or instruments associated with walking dead, torture, vampires and vampirism, ghouls, cannibalism, and werewolfism are prohibited.

General Standards: Part C

All elements or techniques not specifically mentioned herein, but which are contrary to the spirit and intent of the code, and are considered violations of good taste or decency, shall be prohibited.

Dialogue

(1) Profanity, obscenity, smut, vulgarity, or words or symbols which have acquired undesirable meanings are forbidden.

(2) Special precautions to avoid references to physical afflictions or deformities shall be taken.

(3) Although slang and colloquialisms are acceptable, excessive use should be discouraged and, wherever possible, good grammar shall be employed.

Religion

(1) Ridicule or attack on any religious or racial group is never permissible.

Costume

(1) Nudity in any form is prohibited, as is indecent or undue exposure.

(2) Suggestive and salacious illustration or suggestive posture is unacceptable.

(3) All characters shall be depicted in dress reasonably acceptable to society.

(4) Females shall be drawn realistically without exaggeration of any physical qualities.

NOTE. It should be recognized that all prohibitions dealing with costume, dialog, or artwork applies as specifically to the cover of a comic magazine as they do to the contents.

Marriage and Sex

(1) Divorce shall not be treated humorously nor represented as desirable.

(2) Illicit sex relations are neither to be hinted at nor portrayed. Violent love scenes as well as sexual abnormalities are unacceptable.

(3) Respect for parents, the moral code, and for honorable behavior shall be fostered. A sympathetic understanding of the problems of love is not a license for morbid distortion.

(4) The treatment of live-romance stories shall emphasize the value of the home and the sanctity of marriage.

(5) Passion or romantic interest shall never be treated in such a way as to stimulate the lower and baser emotions.

(6) Seduction and rape shall never be shown or suggested.

(7) Sex perversion or any inference to same is strictly forbidden.

Code for Advertising Matter

These regulations are applicable to all magazines published by members of the Comics Magazine Association of America, Inc. Good taste shall be the guiding principle in the acceptance of advertising.

(1) Liquor and tobacco advertising is not acceptable.

(2) Advertisement of sex or sex instruction books is unacceptable.

(3) The sale of picture postcards, "pinups," "art studies," or any other reproduction of nude or seminude figures is prohibited.

(4) Advertising for the sale of knives or realistic gun facsimiles is prohibited.

(5) Advertising for the sale of fireworks is prohibited.

(6) Advertising dealing with the sale of gambling equipment or printed matter dealing with gambling shall not be accepted.

(7) Nudity with meretricious purpose and salacious postures shall not be permitted in the advertising of any product; clothed figures shall never be presented in such a way as to be offensive or contrary to good taste or morals.

(8) To the best of his ability, each publisher shall ascertain that all statements made in advertisements conform to fact and avoid misrepresentation.

(9) Advertisement of medical, health, or toiletry products of questionable nature are to be rejected. Advertisements for medical, health, or toiletry products endorsed by the American Medical Association, or the American Dental Association, shall be deemed acceptable if they conform with all other conditions of the Advertising Code.

Notes

1. Fredric Wertham, *Seduction of the Innocent: The Influence of Comic Books on Today's Youth* (New York: Rinehart, 1954).

2. Fredric Wertham, "What Parents Don't Know about Comic Books," *Ladies' Home Journal*, November 1953, 214–20. See also Fredric Wertham, "What Parents Don't Know about Comic Books," A Crisis of Innocence: Comic Books and Children's Culture, 1940–1954, available at http://crisisofinnocence.library.ryerson.ca/index.php/items/show/479.

3. For a detailed history and discussion of the initial negativity surrounding the formidable early years of American comics, see David Hajdu, *The Ten-Cent Plague: The Great Comic Book Scare and How It Changed America* (New York: Farrar, Straus and Giroux, 2008).

4. Carol Tilley, "Seducing the Innocent: Fredric Wertham and the Falsifications That Helped Condemn Comics," *Information and Culture: A Journal of History* 47, no. 4 (2012): 383–413.

5. For a detailed look and transcription of the congressional hearings on comics, see Greg Theakston, ed., *Comics on Trial*, vol. 1, *Juvenile Delinquency Hearings, April 21, 22, and June 4, 1954* (New York: Pure Imagination, 2011).

6. Hajdu, *The Ten-Cent Plague*, 337–51.

7. Bill Schelly, *American Comic Book Chronicles: The 1950s* (Raleigh, NC: TwoMorrows Publishing, 2013), 6.

8. For detailed look at the history of the Comics Code, see Amy Kiste Nyberg, *Seal of Approval: The History of the Comics Code* (Jackson: University Press of Mississippi, 1998). See also Schelly's discussion of the congressional hearings and how the Code affected comics in *American Comic Book Chronicles*, 106–30.

9. Nyberg, *Seal of Approval*, 139. See also Joe Sergi, "Tales from the Code: Spidey Fights Drugs and the Comics Code Authority," Comic Book Legal Defense Fund, July 18, 2012, available at http://cbldf.org/2012/07/tales-from-the-code-spidey-fights-drugs-and-the-comics-code-authority/.

10. "Comics Code Revision of 1971," Comic Book Legal Defense Fund, available at http://cbldf.org/comics-code-revision-of-1971/. See also Nyberg, *Seal of Approval*, 170–74.

11. "Comics Code Revision of 1989," Comic Book Legal Defense Fund, available at http://cbldf.org/comics-code-revision-of-1989/. See also Nyberg, *Seal of Approval*, 175–79.

12. Vaneta Rogers, "The Comics Code Authority: Defunct Since 2009?," *Newsarama*, January 24, 2011, available at https://www.newsarama.com/6897-the-comics-code-authority-defunct-since-2009.html.

13. Senate Committee on the Judiciary, Comic Books and Juvenile Delinquency, Interim Report, 1955 (Washington, DC: Government Printing Office, 1955), available at https://en.wikisource.org/wiki/Comic_book_code_of_1954.

CHAPTER 24

Excerpt from "The Sun God and the Dark Knight"[1]

GRANT MORRISON

AS EVERYBODY KNOWS, THE JOKER WAS BATMAN'S MOST ENDURING, ACCOM-
modating, and iconic nemesis. Foreshadowing David Bowie, Madonna, and
Lady Gaga, he shared Batman's chameleonic ability to adapt his routine to
suite the tastes of the day. In his first appearance (*Batman*, no. 1, 1940), the
"Grim Jester" was a sour-faced homicidal maniac who left chilling clues for the
police. Ten years later, he'd become a chortling crime clown robbing banks in
his Jokermobile. In the eighties, he was a gender-bending serial killer, and in
actor Heath Ledger's 2008 film portrayal, he appeared as a punk-influenced
agent of performance-art-inspired chaos. The Joker's ruined mug was the face
at the end of it all, the makeup melting on the funeral mask of Von Aschenbach
in Visconti's *Death in Venice*, the grinning skull caked under troweled layers
of cosmetics. Corrupt and unhealthy, protopunk, proto-Goth, he was skinny,
pale, hunched, and psychopathic. He was Johnny Rotten, Steerpike, Bowie
strung out in Berlin, or Joel Grey in *Cabaret*. The Joker was the perfect dissolute
European response to Batman's essentially can-do New World determination,
toned physique, and outrageous wealth. While Batman cut a swath through
blackened streets and leapt between skyscrapers, the Joker had to hunch beneath bare bulbs like a heroin addict facing a nightmare comedown with an
acid tongue and a graveyard wit. He dressed like a riverboat gambler, his face
composed to suggest some unhallowed marriage of showbiz, drag culture, and
the art of the mortician. If Batman was cool, the Joker was cooler. The pair
shared the perfect symmetry of Jesus and the Devil, Holmes and Moriarty,
Tom and Jerry.

Bill Finger wrote the Joker with relish, finding, as he did with Batman, fresh
and unremittingly inventive ways to reintroduce the villain. His narrative cap-
tions took on a deliciously creepy-crawly tenor any time the Clown Prince of
Crime made an entrance:

THE JOKER—GRIM JESTER, ARCH-CRIMINAL, MASTERFIEND . . .
AN EMBER OF LIFE GLOWS WITHIN THAT GHASTLY SHELL OF HU-
MAN CLAY . . . AND THE ICY CLAWS OF FEAR AND APPREHENSION
CLUTCH TIGHTER ABOUT THE HEARTS OF THE DENIZENS OF THE
WORLD!! ONLY THREE DARE TO PLAY THE GAME OF CARDS WITH
THIS MAD, EVIL GENIUS—THE FEARLESS BATMAN, THE HEROIC
ROBIN, AND THE BEAUTIFUL, LITHE CATWOMAN . . . TO THE WIN-
NER BELOW THE PHAROAH'S GEMS . . . THE LOSER—GETS DEATH!!

The rest of Batman's rogues' gallery personified various psychiatric disorders
to great effect: Two-Face was schizophrenia. Catwoman was kleptomania. The
Scarecrow was phobias of all kinds. By psychoanalyzing his enemies with his
fists, Batman may have hoped to escape the probing gaze of the analyst himself,
but it was not to be. There was, after all, something deeply mad about Batman.
Superman made a kind of sense in a hopeful, science fiction way: a do-gooding
orphan from another world who decided to use his special alien powers to help
the people of his adopted world achieve their greatness. The decision of the
rich but otherwise powerless Bruce Wayne to fight crime dressed as a bat took
a bit more swallowing. After witnessing the senseless murder of his parents (a
story revealed in *Batman*, no. 1), the young Bruce would have been forgiven
for spending his inheritance on drink, drugs, hookers, and therapy, but instead
he chose to fight crime on his own somewhat unconventional terms. Madness
haunted Batman from the start.

Notes
1. Excerpted from Grant Morrison, *Supergods: Our World in the Age of the Superhero* (London:
Jonathan Cape, 2011). Reproduced by permission of The Random House Group Ltd. © 2011.

CHAPTER 25

Disability and the Silver Age Supervillain[1]

JOSÉ ALANIZ

Deformed persons are commonly even with nature; for as nature hath done ill by them, so do they by nature; being for the most part, as the Scripture saith, void of natural affection; and so they have their revenge of nature. . . . [T]herefore it is good to consider of deformity, not as a sign which is more deceivable, but as a cause which seldom faileth of the effect. Whosoever hath anything fixed in his person that doth induce contempt, hath also a perpetual spur in himself, to rescue and deliver himself from scorn; therefore all deformed persons are extreme bold.

FRANCIS BACON, "ON DEFORMITY"

VIRTUALLY ALL SUPERVILLAINS OF THE SILVER AGE AND AFTER, EVEN MORE than their heroic counterparts, come off as blatant caricatures: cackling, hand-rubbing megalomaniacs uniformly bent on world domination, often misshapen in some way, motivated exclusively by power-lust and/or greed. As foils, they play a vital oppositional role in the genre, often acting as "engines of diachronic continuity"[2] to the heroes' "status quo" inclinations.[3] Peter Coogan, too, sees them as inversions of the superhero, with their own "selfish, anti-social" mission tied to a "personal defect" that spawns a "superiority complex."[4]

Moreover, supervillains—following the gothic tradition of revealing the inner deformity of the soul through the disfigurement or spectacular otherness of the body—simplistically reify the ableist reader's unconscious anxieties and prejudices regarding difference (racial, gender-related, nationalist, class-based, or physical).[5] As Paul Longmore characterizes it:

Physical handicaps are made the emblems of evil. . . . Giving disabilities to villainous characters reflects and reinforces, albeit in exaggerated fashion, three common prejudices against handicapped people: disability is a punishment for evil; disabled people are embittered by their "fate"; disabled people

Figure 7. The origin of the Mole Man (*Fantastic Four*, vol. 1, no. 1, November 1961).

resent the nondisabled and would, if they could, destroy them. In historic and contemporary social fact, it is, of course, nondisabled people who have at times endeavored to destroy people with disabilities. As with popular portrayals of other minorities, the unacknowledged hostile fantasies of the stigmatizers are transferred to the stigmatized.[6]

Several scholars have characterized the villain as a bearer of aspects (moral, ideological, corporeal) that the hero disavows.[7] Such a status grants the villain tremendous freedom but also condemns him to isolation and inhumanity. This transgressive outsider status corresponds to a significant degree with that of disabled people, long considered "historical scapegoats."[8] Such thinking has naturalized the notion of deformed and disabled figures as villains, what Ato Quayson terms "disability as bearer of moral deficit/evil."[9] In sum: "villainous" disabled characters often cited by disability scholars, such as Ahab, Captain Hook, Dr. No, and Dr. Strangelove, seem possessed of traits straight out of the ableist's worst nightmare: malformed, malevolent, mighty.

Golden Age supervillains such as Batman's enemies the Joker, Two-Face, and the Penguin typically manifest the "deformed malefactor" type, while the Marvel Silver Age's first supervillain, the Mole Man, makes society's contempt for the misshapen the originary motivation for his evil plans to rule the earth. In "The Fantastic Four!" (*Fantastic Four*, vol. 1, no. 1, November 1961, Lee/Kirby), the Mole Man—only subsequently was his true name, Harvey Rupert Elder, revealed—recounts his story: shunned by his peers, who mock his stunted, large-nosed appearance, he flees society in search of the earth's center, where a fall causes him to lose most of his vision but where he eventually gains control of an army of monsters with which to terrorize the surface world.[10]

Artist Jack Kirby's layout on the page illustrating the villain's biography underscores, through contrasting portraits and panel size, the isolation and loathing he suffers (fig. 7). At the top left, the Mole Man's tiny head begins his sorry tale of an outcast, while immediately below three small horizontal panels show different "normal" people's cruel reactions to him, as they stare directly at the reader: "What? *Me* go out with *you?*" a woman says. "Don't make me laugh!" "I *know* you're qualified, but you can't work here!" scoffs a besuited gentleman. "You'd scare our other employees away!" "Hey, is that your face, or are you wearin' a mask? Haw haw!" jokes a caddish-looking fellow. The direct address puts the reader in the villain's place, to witness firsthand the public's "bad staring" at the physically different, which, as Rosemarie Garland-Thomson (referencing Susan Sontag) notes, "fails to make the leap from a place of discomfort, shock or fear toward empathetic identification."[11]

The next four panels depict the Mole Man (in medium and long shot) traversing desolate regions of the earth on his quest, while in the last panel—when he has found the earth's center after his fall and blinding—his face appears in closeup, with impressionistic shadows, against a red background of "power lines." "I was *stranded* here . . .," he concludes, "like a human mole!!" The large, closeup portrait (the most intimate picture yet of the Mole Man's face) stands in opposition to, and in a sense supersedes, the many smaller, diverse images of him and the normals elsewhere on the page; it seems to announce that he has found his true, unified identity and purpose at last—a purpose beyond the petty, hurtful prejudice of those who scorn him.

The effect is one of transformation, from the tiny upper-left head shot of the Mole Man in the same visual space as the normals (although due to his visor and cowl still standing apart from them) to the dominant, large closeup portrait of his new, blind, triumphant self at the bottom right. The page functions as a visual chronicle of abreaction to trauma; moreover, the water, cave, and tunnel imagery identify this as a scene of rebirth—the impressionistic shadows on the Mole Man's final rendering make him, among other things, resemble a neonate. The deformed supervillain: conceived, born of, shaped by "normate" derision, with no place among humanity.[12] Kirby's layouts convey, not without sympathy, the villain's compelled outsider position. As Reed Richards says in the story's closing panel, after the Mole Man has presumably perished, "There was no place for him in our world."[13]

Other Silver Age villains undergo similar transformations from disabled alter ego to grotesque fiend, such as Curt Connors turning into the Lizard (first appearance *Spider-Man*, vol. 1, no. 6, November 1963, Lee/Ditko) and Kirk Langstrom becoming Man-Bat (*Detective Comics*, vol. 1, no. 400, June 1970, Robbins/Adams)—in both cases, it is the experiments these scientists perform to cure their impairments (Connors wants to restore an arm lost in war, Langstrom to keep from going deaf) that lead to the creation of their evil identities.[14] The Brain (*Doom Patrol*, vol. 1, no. 86, May 1964) represents an extreme case of this type: a lab accident reduces the unnamed scientist to a brain floating in a nutrient bath, wreaking vengeance on the world entirely through technology and second parties—a malevolent near-total amputee/quadriplegic.

In short, disabled supervillains in the Silver Age evince some of the innovations in psychological complexity observed in the heroes, and in some cases share in the dramatic pathos of figures like Ben Grimm or the Hulk. But they of course go much further in their bitter reactions to the injustices they suffer, while the needs of the genre for antagonists and moral nemeses impose strict limits on sympathy for their plight.[15]

THE FACE OF DOOM

Garland-Thomson identifies the disabled villain as a distortion of American values, a sort of hyper-individualist gone amok, both morally and physically. Melville's Captain Ahab, whom she calls "perhaps the quintessential disabled figure in American literature," conjures in the reader both a sublime admiration and terror through his superhuman obsession and Nietzschean will to power. At the same time, his amputated limb flouts notions of autonomy and physical perfection central to US identity, as previously discussed. The captain thus constitutes a monstrous contradiction:

> Ahab is, perhaps above all else, different from other men. At once compelling and repelling, he represents both the prospective freedom of nonconformity and the terrible threat of antinomianism. The outer mark of his difference is his ivory leg, and the inner manifestation is his monomaniacal fury.... [But h]is disabled body testifies to the self's physical vulnerability, the ominous knowledge that the ideology of individualism suppresses.[16]

Such attributes appertain to the foreign-born Silver Age tyrant Doctor Doom, archnemesis of the Fantastic Four, whose bodily deformity seems of a piece with his anti-American threat—and, I will argue, incarnates a "gender threat" as well. In his "origin story" (*Fantastic Four Annual*, vol. 1, no. 2, September 1964, Lee/Kirby), Doom first appears as an angelic Gypsy boy in the central European country of Latveria. When his father, a renowned healer, is killed by the reigning monarch, young Victor von Doom swears that "all mankind shall pay" for the murder of his father (and the earlier murder of his mother). The boy soon learns that his mother had been a great witch, and he embarks on learning the family trade, despite the misgivings of his kinsman Boris.

Victor grows into a handsome swindler with the "features of a demi-god and the cunning of a demon!,"[17] wreaking vengeance on all Latveria by selling people bogus "trick" merchandise. He also displays a tremendous talent for creating duplicate selves, in the form of ultrarealistic androids. He eventually winds up at State University in America, where the arrogant Doom coldly rebuffs a bright freshman, Reed Richards, and his offer to room together. To his misfortune, Doom also rejects Reed's advice that he recheck some miscalculations on a secret science project involving "matter transmutation and dimension warps"—the machine blows up, disfiguring the once-handsome foreigner and getting him expelled.[18]

Devastated by his deformity, Doom vows to hide his visage from all the world and joins a mysterious order of monks in the Tibetan mountains. He ultimately takes over the sect and has them fashion an imposing suit of armor for him, with a dread iron mask to forever conceal his ravaged face. So anxious is Doom to don the facial covering that he orders it seared, still hot from the forge, onto his bare flesh. From that moment, Doom declares himself reborn as the scourge of a world that hated and vilified him, pledging to take over first his home country of Latveria and then dominate all humankind.[19]

Doctor Doom falls in with the standard literary representation of the "monstrous" disabled, whose physical differences, Longmore notes, "typically involve disfigurement of the face and head and gross deformity of the body ... [expressing] disfigurement of personality and deformity of soul. Once again, disability may be represented as the cause of evildoing, punishment for it, or both."[20] All this in spite of the possibility that Doom's original "disfigurement" in the experiment gone wrong may not have been so severe after all. "[S]ome have speculated," writes Tom Brevoort in the introduction to *The Villainy of Doctor Doom*,

> that, if you were to peel away that cold metal and take a gander at the features underneath, you'd see only the slightest scar marring an otherwise handsome visage—but that tiny imperfection is all it took to drive Doom to a life of villainy and hatred.[21]

Yet even if this were the case, the hypernarcissistic Doom still subsequently chooses to destroy his slightly damaged face with the burning mask rather than tolerate a "tiny imperfection," thereby reinscribing ableist prejudices of the body's perfectibility.[22] That Doom never gives up those prejudices is reflected in his maniacal obsession with restoring his "perfect" face—but always in some exterior imago. In the 1978 "Overthrow of Doom" storyline by Marv Wolfman, Keith Pollard, and others, he fashions a statue of himself that will "set the new standards for masculine beauty throughout the globe";[23] clones himself a "son," emphasizing his beauty;[24] and uses another (unscarred) statue of himself to control the world through mesmerism.[25]

Despite such schemes, Doom clings just as obsessively to the safety of his mask, even *sleeping* in it.[26] He often cites his disfigurement as the source of all his failures and misfortunes in life (e.g., *Fantastic Four*, no. 200, 22, 43; *Fantastic Four*, no. 199, 23), even comparing it to the Thing's ugliness.[27]

How to resolve these fraught views of Doom's face/mask—by Doom himself? How can Doom despise the very features that have driven him not only to madness but, on several occasions, to the brink of world domination? Has he indeed followed in the footsteps of tragic literary deformities like Frankenstein's monster, Quasimodo, Polyphemus? We can assay an answer through a reading of a climactic chapter in Doom's history and an examination of the techniques used to portray Doom's face since Kirby's time; for what lies behind Doom's mask has resonances for several Silver Age supervillains.

Figure 8. Jack Kirby depicts Doom without showing his disfigured face (*Fantastic Four*, vol. 1, no. 85, April 1969).

Figure 9. Doom first dons his mask—searing his face (*Fantastic Four Annual*, vol. 1, no. 2, September 1964).

First of all, we can say that so much ambiguity remains over the exact nature of Doom's initial injury in his college lab explosion because—in one of the great in-jokes of superhero comics—his face has almost never been depicted postblast.[28] For example, in "Within This Tortured Land," when Doom poses for a portrait, Kirby draws him holding a mirror over his face.[29] But much earlier, in the origin story, we can already observe Kirby progressively obscuring Doom's face with various props as the fateful moment of the accident approaches. By the page before the explosion, Doom's face, as visual element, has clearly transcended the mere storyline and entered another signifying realm.[30] The first time Doom "turns" to the reader after the accident, in fact, he is wearing his new mask, declaring: "From this moment on, there *is* no Victor von Doom! He has vanished . . . But in his place there shall be another . . . Dr. Doom!"[31]

What is it that remains forever off-frame or concealed by Doom's imposing mask? What is the face of Doom?

As art and drama historians point out, the word "person" derives from the ancient Greek *persona*, which describes the masks actors donned during classical dramatic performances. "*Persona*, 'the mask,' is related to personality, the self or ego we reveal to the world," writes George Ulrich. "Masks have the ability to conceal, change, or transform the 'person' behind the image into something or someone else other than who we are."[32]

In the case of Doom, the iron mask concealing his "ravaged" features—which no Silver Age reader had ever seen—works to hide another iconic emblem of classical myth: the gaze of the Medusa. Disability scholar Lennard Davis has likened the act of seeing the disabled to the dread and fascination of the horrid Gorgon, whose countenance petrified its victims:

Figure 10. Susan Richards/Invisible Woman glimpses Doom's ravaged visage (*Fantastic Four*, vol. 1, no. 236, November 1981).

The "normal" person sees the disabled person and is turned to stone, in some sense, by the visual interaction. In this moment, the normal person suddenly feels self-conscious, rigid, unable to look. The visual field becomes problematic, dangerous, treacherous. The disability becomes a power derived from its otherness, its monstrosity, in the eyes of the "normal" person.[33]

Something similar to this seems to happen on the few occasions when Doom slips his guard and allows others to see him without his mask, as when Sue Richards, the Invisible Woman, catches a glimpse of his face—and is stupefied.[34]

Yet, like the basilisk, Doom seems the most susceptible of all to the horrid spectacle of his own destroyed visage. Davis further relates the act of gazing upon the radical otherness of the disabled body to a regressive episode, a return to the Lacanian mirror stage, in which the child initially experiences the body as fragmentary, with discreet and uncoordinated organs and limbs. Only by taking on an "armor" (read: "identity") and entering the Symbolic Order does he manage to contain that threat of fragmentation.

But the different, disabled corpus inverts that process, forming a direct imago of the repressed fragmented body. The disabled body causes a kind of hallucination of the mirror phase gone wrong. The subject looks at the disabled body and has a moment of cognitive dissonance, or ... cognitive resonance with the earlier state of fragmentation.... [R]ather than seeing the object of desire, as controlled by the Other, the subject sees the true self of the fragmented body.[35]

Figure 11. The unmasked Doom is driven insane by innumerable reflections of his face (*Fantastic Four*, vol. 1, no. 200, November 1978).

This description lends itself to a productive interpretation of a climactic scene in "When Titans Clash!," the culmination of the epic "Overthrow of Doom" arc by Wolfman and Pollard, presented in *Fantastic Four*, no. 200 (November 1978). In the story, an infuriated Doom sees his various schemes to make a perfect, unscarred clone of himself who will "inherit" the throne of Latveria; to telepathically dominate the United Nations (and hence the world) through a specially equipped statue of himself (again, without the scarred face); and, last but not least, to destroy the hated Fantastic Four, all fail. In a final, bare-knuckle, no-holds-barred showdown with Reed Richards (aka Mr. Fantastic), Doom is stripped of his mask and stands helpless before a million reflections of his obliterated face staring back at him from his massive crystal Solartron, the iridescent power source for his many weapons.[36] His self-image at such odds with the "fragmented" bodily reality, there is no room for misrecognition; the sight drives him insane—his Medusa's gaze thrown back at him.

Furthermore, Doom's mask itself, concealing and impersonating the disabled supervillain's "monstrous" identity, forms a multipronged threat to the male subject. Rhonda Berenstein, writing on classic horror cinema, emphasizes the transgender aspects of the "monster" and its appeal to "cross-over" spectators, a viewing practice she calls "spectatorship-as-drag." Working from Judith Butler's concept of the performativity of gender, Berenstein argues that the monster in classic horror film comes to represent a "sexually ambiguous" other, a moment of bisexual rupture in the "safe space" of the cinema. As she writes:

> Spectatorship-in-drag . . . transposes horror's sex and gender ambiguities to the spectating domain. Part of horror's and drag's draw for spectators is opening a space for an attraction to figures that revel in sex and gender fragmentation, and posit something more than the conventional sex-role and gender options available to men and women in American patriarchy.[37]

The monstrous Doctor Doom carries precisely that trace of sexual vagueness (cowl, monk's dress, reproduction by cloning, dandy-like preoccupation with his body, a good "maternal" leader to the nation of Latveria), while his iron mask contains nothing less than the face of the Medusa, the classical symbol of the castrating female gaze (taken up as an empowering trope by feminist critics such as Hélène Cixous).

In conclusion, if the Silver Age superhero represents a (superficially) hypermasculine, ableist compensation for male physical disability and lack at a time of masculine anxiety (the Cold War), then the supervillain—its foil and structuring Other—on some level must represent the return of that repressed, body-disrupting, feminizing force. Moreover, this dread figure embodies not just castration anxiety (through an all but undepicted, polyvalent signifier of

Figure 12. Byrne's portrait of Doom, with scarred flesh visible (*Fantastic Four*, vol. 1, no. 247, October 1982).

sexual difference) but the threat of the Mirror Stage's fragmented, unresolved self—in other words, the unmasking of lack in all senses.

The masked, deformed Silver Age supervillain, Doctor Doom perhaps most suggestively of all embodies exactly these dangers to the male subject. Doom's mask as drawn by John Byrne shows the malevolent, contingent nature of that mask: the penetrating eyes, with traces of scarred flesh just visible, barely held back by the iron faceplate, which presses up against the so-called unhealing wound.[38] Too powerful and overdetermined a signifier, the double threat of castration and physical disability can never be shown, only hinted at, disavowed, deflected, literally marginalized by placing it ever and only just "off-frame."

Many Silver Age supervillains in the Marvel universe in essence repeat the pattern of Doctor Doom vis-à-vis their masks—which become their personae. For one thing, so many of them sport masks, and almost never remove them: Psycho-Man, Diablo, Annihilus, Ultron (an android whose face looks like a mask), the Celestials, Galactus. The more powerful the figure, in fact, the less likely he will be to show his face beneath the mask. In some cases, like that of the Destroyer, removing the mask is impossible without risking *annihilation*. The Red Skull, in a literalization of the metaphor, actually adopts his mask *as* his face, when he falls victim to his own "Dust of Death."[39]

In short, the villains—like the heroes—of Marvel's Silver Age insistently have something to hide: physical disability, feminizing threat of castration, the subversion of the gender order itself. And through every means at his disposal—overcompensating superpowers, fantastic resolutions, searing iron masks to hold back the Medusa's gaze—to hide in plain sight is precisely what the villainous supercrip does.

Notes

1. Excerpted from José Alaniz, *Death, Disability, and the Superhero: The Silver Age and Beyond* (Jackson: University Press of Mississippi, 2014). The chapter has been lightly edited for style for the purposes of the present publication.

2. Richard Reynolds, *Super Heroes: A Modern Mythology* (Jackson: University Press of Mississippi, 1992), 50.

3. Reynolds, in *Super Heroes*, notes:

Heroes are generally obliged to defeat at least one supervillain per issue, but the events which lead up to the confrontation are normally initiated by the supervillain. The hero is in this sense passive: he is not called upon to act unless the status quo is threatened by the villain's plans. . . . The common outcome, as far as the structure of the plot is concerned, is that the villains are concerned with change and the heroes with the maintenance of the status quo. (50–51)

On the villain as proactive and heroes as reactive, see also Peter Coogan, *Superhero: The Secret Origin of a Genre* (Austin, TX: MonkeyBrain Books, 2006), 110–15.

4. Coogan, *Superhero*, 77, 79, 83.

5. As Leslie Fiedler writes: "[I]n the throes of paranoia and projection, we convince ourselves that the crippledness of the cripple is an outward and visible sign of an inward invisible state"; Leslie Fiedler, *Tyranny of the Normal: Essays on Bioethics, Theology and Myth* (Boston: David R. Godine, 1996), 41. Among the key literary figures he lists under such a heading: Shakespeare's Richard III, Captain Ahab, Long John Silver, Quasimodo, Captain Hook, and several James Bond villains. Incidentally, Quasimodo (Quasi-Motivational Destruct Organism) is also the name of a Marvel supervillain introduced in 1966.

6. Paul K. Longmore, *Why I Burned My Book and Other Essays on Disability* (Philadelphia: Temple University Press, 2003), 133–34.

7. For example, in his Lacanian reading, Christopher Murray sees the routine "castration imagery" humiliation of the villain by the hero as a form of therapy, "with the banishment and containment of the inner demons (fear, hatred, and impotence) represented in the villain"; Christopher Murray, "Superman vs. Imago: Superheroes, Lacan and Mediated Identity," *International Journal of Comic Art* 4, no. 2 (Fall 2002): 202. Coogan's structuralist approach, too, sees the villain expressing "displaced aspects" of the hero; Coogan, *Superhero*, 103–9.

8. David T. Mitchell and Sharon L. Snyder, *Narrative Prosthesis: Disability and the Dependencies of Discourse* (Ann Arbor: University of Michigan Press, 2000), 20.

9. Ato Quayson, *Aesthetic Nervousness: Disability and the Crisis of Representation* (New York: Columbia University Press, 2007), 42.

10. Stan Lee, Jack Kirby et al., *The Essential Fantastic Four*, vol. 1 (New York: Marvel Comics, 2001).

11. Rosemarie Garland-Thomson, *Staring: How We Look* (Oxford: Oxford University Press, 2009), 187.

12. The Mole Man visually stands apart from the Fantastic Four and "normal" bodies throughout the story, both physically and spatially: he appears in one panel in the opposite corner from a "beautiful" classical statue of a man (Lee and Kirby, *The Essential Fantastic Four*, vol. 1, 21); he is introduced in a separate, rather incongruous panel in medium close-up when Johnny and Reed discover the Valley of the Diamonds (19); his green costume contrasts sharply with the Four's magenta garb; and his five-panel action-to-action staff contest with Johnny (or Reed; the man is not identified) is staged such that the two remain in place even as they move dynamically, enhancing the impact of their stark physical differences.

13. Lee and Kirby's Mole Man owes a debt to Franz Kafka's short story "The Burrow" ("Der Bau," published posthumously in *Beim Bau der Chinesischen Mauer* [Berlin: Gustav Kiepenheuer Verlag, 1931]), about an unnamed creature's alienation and dread of the world beyond the confines of its subterranean home. Most readers have read the creature as an anthropomorphized mole.

14. It bears mention that, oddly, the Lizard's appearances correlate with instances of Spider-Man's body "destabilizing," as if the villain's own corporeal mutability had a contagion-like effect on the hero's. In one case, Spider-Man sprains his arm so that he must—absurdly—wear a sling as he fights (*Spider-Man*, nos. 44–45, 1967); and in another, he famously grows four extra arms (*Spider-Man*, nos. 100–102, 1971).

15. The Kristevan abject has useful applications to the supervillain as described here; see Julia Kristeva, *Powers of Horror: An Essay on Abjection*, trans. Leon S. Roudiez (New York: Columbia University Press, 1982).

16. Rosemarie Garland Thomson, *Extraordinary Bodies: Figuring Physical Disability in American Culture and Literature* (New York: Columbia University Press, 1997), 44.

17. Polly Watson, ed., *The Villainy of Doctor Doom* (New York: Marvel Comics, 1999), 5.

18. This episode's fraught Oedipal drama bears some mention, since later continuity would reveal that Doom had been trying to contact his mother, who lay trapped in the transdimensional realm of Mephisto, with the failed device. Reed Richards—whom Doom always blames for the experiment's catastrophic outcome—thus represents the interfering, domineering father who ever foils the son's desired return to the maternal.

19. This history leads Coogan to taxonomize Doom as a "mad scientist" and "renegade commander" brand of supervillain, and to deemphasize the role played by his disfigurement (Coogan, *Superhero*, 61, 85). As I argue in this chapter, he should also fall in the "monster" category.

20. Longmore, *Why I Burned My Book*, 135.

21. Watson, *The Villainy of Doctor Doom*, iii.

22. For the fascistic overtones of this episode, and Kirby's seeming awareness of them, see the "Doom's Scratch" section in Craig Fischer, "Fantastic Fascism? Jack Kirby, Nazi Aesthetics, and Klaus Theweleit's *Male Fantasies*," *International Journal of Comic Art* 5, no. 1 (Spring 2003), 334–54. On supervillain narcissism, see Coogan, *Superhero*, 85–90.

23. Stan Lee and Jack Kirby, "Within This Tortured Land," *Fantastic Four*, vol. 1, no. 85 (April 1969), 16.

24. Marv Wolfman and Keith Pollard, "The Son of Doctor Doom!," *Fantastic Four*, vol. 1, no. 199 (October 1978), 30.

25. Marv Wolfman and Keith Pollard, "When Titans Clash!," *Fantastic Four*, vol. 1, no. 200 (November 1978), 37.

26. Larry Lieber and Wally Wood, "The Invaders!," *Astonishing Tales*, vol. 1, no. 4 (February 1971), 5, 7.

27. Marv Wolfman and Keith Pollard, "Invasion!," *Fantastic Four*, vol. 1, no. 198 (September 1978), 15.

28. The exception: John Byrne's "revisionist" account of Doom's origin story in "True Lies"; *Fantastic Four*, vol. 1, no. 278 (May 1985). He depicts Doom's face after the experiment explosion, revealing that he had suffered only a scar along his cheek, thus reconciling Lee and Kirby's conflicting approaches to the character. (For succinct accounts of this convoluted history, see Craig Fischer and Jay Fludd's article on Doom at http://www.ffplaza.com/library/?issue=ff@2.) But Byrne does not represent Doom's face once he has donned the hot iron mask and seared his features, presumably beyond recognition.

29. Stan Lee and Jack Kirby, *Fantastic Four*, no. 85 (1969), 17.

30. Lee and Kirby, *Fantastic Four*, no. 85, 9–11.

31. Lee and Kirby, *Fantastic Four*, no. 85, 11.

32. George Ulrich, "Masks," *LORE* 39, no. 3 (Fall 1989), 2–9.

33. Lennard Davis, "Nude Venuses, Medusa's Body, and Phantom Limbs: Disability and Visuality," in *The Body and Physical Difference: Discourses of Disability*, ed. David T. Mitchell and Sharon L. Snyder (Ann Arbor: University of Michigan Press, 1997), 55.

34. John Byrne, "Terror in a Tiny Town," *Fantastic Four*, vol. 1, no. 236 (November 1981), 35.

35. Davis, "Nude Venuses, Medusa's Body, and Phantom Limbs," 60.

36. Wolfman and Pollard, "When Titans Clash!," 44.

37. Rhonda Berenstein, "Spectatorship as Drag: The Act of Viewing and Classic Horror Cinema," in *Viewing Positions: Ways of Seeing Film*, ed. Linda Williams (New Brunswick, NJ: Rutgers University Press, 1995), 261. For a different, non–queer theory approach to the horror cinema monster's ambiguity, see Noël Carroll, *The Philosophy of Horror; or, Paradoxes of the Heart* (New York: Routledge, 1990). His arguments pertain to Doctor Doom no less than do Berenstein's.

38. See, for example, John Byrne, "This Land Is Mine!," *Fantastic Four*, vol. 1, no. 247 (October 1982), 22.

39. Compare these Silver Age villains to their pre–Cold War Golden Age counterparts: so many of them—Lex Luthor, Sinestro, Yellow Claw, Two-Face, the Penguin, Bizarro, Master Man, Lady Lotus, Mister Mxyzptlk—go unmasked.

CHAPTER 26

Art Imitates Life

Nixon as Villain in the Pages of Captain America

RICHARD HALL

HEROES ARE REAL. THE ONLY REASON WE KNOW THIS TO BE TRUE IS THAT VIL-
lainy is real. All of human history—up to and including the evening news—is
replete with examples of humanity's darker potential. Villains in popular fictions
represent these frightening and even dangerous aspects of human nature. These
fictional villains—like their heroic counterparts—are hyperidealized portrayals
of what we consider "evil" or "criminal." Voldemort is an extreme example of
Adolf Hitler. Doctor Doom is an extreme version of Joseph Stalin. Audiences
enjoy their fictions because they, to a degree, provide a cathartic release of our
deeper fears. When Batman returns the Joker to Arkham Asylum, the audience feels a sense of relief that the world, for the time being at least, is safer.
Occasionally, however, a real-life event so deeply touches society's fears and
anxieties that the creators of popular fiction feel compelled to address it in their
respective fictions. This chapter seeks to examine how the real-life criminal
activity of President Richard Nixon surrounding the Watergate scandal was
addressed in the pages of *Captain America* comic books.

In his study of heroes and villains, Mike Alsford pointed out: "To collapse
into villainy is not to be taken over by the 'beast within' but to have our connection with others compromised."[1] Perhaps the best example of this perspective
on villainy in the real world lies within the realm of politics. In democratic
societies such as the United States, elected officials depend greatly on their connection with their constituents. To lose the faith of those who elected you is the
most dangerous pitfall of elected office. History contains numerous examples
of political officials who have lost the faith of the people through unethical,
criminal, or outright "evil" activities. In American history, such occurrences
have often bled into the realm of popular culture, whether through political

cartoons in early colonial times, to television screens in the twenty-first century, and in between, the pages of comic books.

The 1960s were the most turbulent decade in American history since the Civil War, the social and political movements of the period both dramatically changing American society and laying the groundwork for everything that followed.[2] Social movements on behalf of racial and ethnic minorities and, by decade's end, women, were viewed by some as the greatest threat to the status quo since the end of slavery. Political assassinations and the escalation of the war in Vietnam caused millions of Americans to question government authority like never before. By the end of the decade, the status quo was striking back. In 1968, Richard Nixon narrowly defeated liberal Democrat Hubert Humphrey and radical conservative Independent candidate George Wallace to win the presidency, with promises to end the Vietnam conflict and restore law and order. While eventually succeeding at the former, he would become synonymous with the latter's antithesis.

Watergate was one of the most serious political scandals in American history. On June 17, 1972, five men working for the Committee to Reelect the President (the CRP, or, unofficially, CREEP), on behalf of Nixon's reelection campaign, broke into the offices of the opposition Democratic National Committee, located in the prestigious Watergate Hotel and Office Complex in Washington, DC. The arrest of the five burglars soon led to the arrest of their two supervisors, G. Gordon Liddy and E. Howard Hunt. Initially, the story was not widely covered, and President Nixon won his reelection bid in what was, at the time, the largest electoral victory in American presidential history. Eventually, however, the dogged investigative journalism of Bob Woodward and Carl Bernstein at the *Washington Post* led to clear connections between the burglars and the president's campaign. For eighteen months, the nation was consumed by the investigations into the president, his advisers, and their alleged crimes. Finally, on August 8, 1974, President Nixon announced on national television that he would, the following day, become the first president of the United States to resign from his office. Nixon would spend the last twenty years of his life as a symbol of government corruption, his name synonymous with all that was wrong with government and politics. At the height of the congressional investigation, American society increasingly turned against the president, demanding that he be punished to the fullest extent of the law—something that, thanks to a pardon from his successor, Gerald Ford, would never happen.[3]

The Watergate scandal itself would prove to be only the tip of the criminal iceberg that was the Nixon administration. Through the investigations into campaign activity, many more irregularities were brought to light. Nixon had utilized his power to attempt to discredit critics such as Daniel Ellsberg, who had, in 1971, released the controversial *Pentagon Papers*. Nixon had attempted to connect the would-be assassin of political rival George Wallace to the Democratic Party. Nixon had even gone so far as to compile an "enemies list," comprising individuals ranging from reporters to celebrities, and used his power to attack some of these perceived enemies. At one point, in the released Oval Office tapes, Nixon is heard ordering the burglarizing of the Brookings Institution to steal a report that could be used against former president Lyndon Johnson.[4] Although not directly involved in the planning or execution of the Watergate break-in, Nixon immediately afterward used his position as the most powerful political figure in the world to subvert and even block the investigation in an attempt to protect himself and his administration. By the time he resigned, Nixon had been exposed as a verdant example of absolute power corrupting absolutely.

By 1971, the war in Vietnam had expanded into Cambodia. The once largely peaceful hippie movement had given rise to more radical—and occasionally violent—groups such as the Weather Underground, the White Panthers, and the Black Panthers, while civil rights movements moved beyond African Americans in the South to the American Indian movement, the Chicano Power movement, and on to the women's and gay rights movements. In comics, a new generation of young writers and artists had taken over the industry, desiring to use their talents to promote an agenda of equality and social justice. At DC Comics, the creative team of Denny O'Neil and Neal Adams first portrayed President Nixon and Vice President Spiro Agnew in a negative light in the pages of *Green Lantern/Green Arrow*, no. 83. In the story titled "And a Child Shall Destroy Them," a villainous man, introduced only as "Grandy," drawn by artist Neal Adams to look exactly like Agnew, runs a grade school where the children are controlled by the powerful mind of a young girl known only as "Sybil." Sybil bears a more than striking resemblance to Nixon (the distinct nose and high forehead specifically) and blindly follows the orders of her guardian. Grandy claims to be "a person who wants order . . . and nothing is so disordered as the average school! . . . [I] punish those who can't respect order!" By the story's end, Sybil—tired of being used to hurt people—brings an entire wing of the school crashing down on herself and Grandy. The schoolmaster, Mr. Belmore, exclaims: "The whole West Wing is in ruins!"[5] The allusions to the Nixon White House are palpable. O'Neil's and Adams's disdain for the Nixon administration as early as 1971 is quite clear.

At the height of the Watergate scandal, in late 1973, writer Steve Englehart embarked in the pages of the Marvel comic *Captain America and the Falcon* on a multi-issue storyline revolving around a sinister "Secret Empire" that seeks to take over the American government from within. As the story unfolds, Captain America is repeatedly portrayed in the mass media as being "un-American." This plan is put into motion by the Committee to Regain America's Principles

(CRAP), operated by Quentin Harderman, a not-too-subtle reference to CREEP and Nixon chief of staff, H. R. Haldeman.[6]

In one television ad, the fictional committee claims: "For years, Captain America has been a one-man vigilante committee, attacking anyone he deemed a criminal. Some were clearly such—but others were private citizens—men the legal agencies had never molested."[7] This is a clear allusion to the crimes that had been exposed concerning the White House targeting political enemies. As the public face of the Secret Empire, CRAP seeks to turn the public against their most trusted hero, Captain America, utilizing the ancient strategy of divide and conquer. At first confused by these attacks, Captain America eventually learns from Professor Charles Xavier, leader of the mutant supergroup the X-Men, that the ultimate goal of the Secret Empire is to control the country by confusing the people through the use of popular media and propaganda.[8] A frequent strategy of the real-world Nixon administration throughout the Watergate scandal was to attempt to discredit the media—particularly the left-leaning *Washington Post*—as being partisan and having an agenda to destroy the president. By the time of the "Secret Empire" storyline, however, Nixon's strategy had failed, and Americans were more convinced every day that their president was, indeed, a criminal.

In *Captain America and the Falcon*, no. 175 (1974), the organization's leader, "Number One," is exposed as actually being someone of importance whom Cap immediately recognizes. When Cap chases the outlaw into the Oval Office, the villain reaches into a desk drawer, pulls out a pistol, and commits suicide, but not before confessing: "High political office didn't satisfy me! My power was still too constrained by legalities! I gambled on a coup to gain me the power I craved—and it appears that my gamble has finally failed! I'll cash my chips, then!"[9] While the comic book never actually shows Nixon's face (or even states his name), Cap's reaction upon discovering Number One's secret identity makes it clear to the reader who he really is. Rather than being publicly exposed and arrested, Number One chooses to commit suicide. The storyline results in Captain America questioning what America has become, and whether he can continue to act as a symbol of the country.[10] Coming months before Nixon would resign, the reader can see how far the president had fallen in the eyes of many Americans.

Captain America stories in the early 1970s, following the trend of most comic books at the time, had already been taking a more "realist" approach to storytelling before the Watergate scandal broke, which makes commentary on Nixon and Americans' feelings toward him somewhat inevitable. Nixon had already been established as the president in *Captain America* comics beginning as early as issue no. 144 (December 1971). In that issue, appearing with Agnew, Nixon is established as the person overseeing SHIELD (the Strategic

Hazard Intervention and Espionage Logistics Directorate), and he explains to SHIELD director Nick Fury the lengthy legislative process involved in approving increased funding for the spy agency. At that time—and for a few more appearances over the course of the following year—Nixon was simply the president, with no sign or suggestion that he was in any way a "villain"; there was, of course, no such serious suggestion in real life. Once Watergate became a household word, however, Englehart would—along with a large segment of Americans—turn against the commander in chief, and remove him from office months before his actual resignation.

What is evident, then, in the pages of the Secret Empire storyline is what now seems an extremely plausible conspiracy—a secret society of powerful individuals utilizing the American media in an attempt to gain total control of the country—spearheaded by a real person who was, at the time, the most powerful political figure in the world. Throughout the Watergate investigations, it became increasingly clear that the real-world Nixon was in every way capable of the type of fictional villainy that was attempted by his comic book counterpart. The usual catharsis was nonexistent, unless the real-world villain was in some way brought to justice—which, of course, would not happen.

In the early 1970s, the primary audience of comic books was still children. Older readers—teenagers and college students in particular—had started reading comic books in greater numbers over the previous decade, and they would certainly be able to connect the Secret Empire storyline to what was unfolding in newspapers and on the evening news every day. It is reasonable to assume, however, that even some younger readers could probably make connections with what they heard adults talking about or saw referenced on television. Americans' faith in their leaders was permanently damaged and would only worsen over the next several decades. When asked why he chose to address Nixon in the pages of *Captain America*, Englehart said: "The problem [in the 1970s] was that Cap was supposed to stand for America when people were ashamed of America. . . . [U]ltimately, Cap stands for American ideals, [which in the 1970s meant] 'America can do better!'"[11] Nixon had forever tarnished the image of the federal government, and of those in political power.

Published reader response at the time was not exclusively critical of the Nixon administration. Ralph Macchio of New Jersey—who would grow up to become editor of Marvel Comics by the 1990s—thanked Marvel for placing some of the blame for America's problems on the shoulders of Americans themselves.[12] Warren Blum, also of New Jersey, wrote: "The real problem [in America] is not corrupt government but the apathy that led to the situation."[13] An evident point in the Secret Empire storyline was that if Americans were led like sheep to slaughter, it was because they allowed themselves to be. In response to Macchio's letter, the editorial staff wrote: "Cap has always been a mouthpiece for his writers' political views."[14] The Marvel writing bullpen had become almost legendary for its "hipness" and liberal leanings, long hair and blue jeans having long replaced crew cuts and suits as standard office wear.[15] Mike Luckenbill, a college junior from Pennsylvania, called for *Captain America and the Falcon*, no. 175, to be required reading in college classes, presumably for exposing the real-life political corruption within the US government.[16] It seems to have been important to many at the time that young readers be made keenly aware that evil was possible in their own reality and that it was not simply an entertainment device.

After Captain America's experience in this storyline, he retired the superhero identity that he had proudly borne since World War II, donning, instead, the mantle of Nomad, the "Man without a Country." By 1975, Americans had grown weary of reality. The civil unrest and political assassinations of the 1960s, Vietnam, the OPEC oil embargo, and now Watergate had left much of the American population emotionally and mentally exhausted, likely driving American morale to an all-time low. Comics readers overwhelmingly demanded a return to standard escapist "rockem-sockem" superhero stories.[17] Comics publishers came to believe that their overreliance on realism was the primary reason for declining sales. Americans needed to escape.[18] By the bicentennial celebrations of 1976, Americans had been inundated with sociopolitical realism in their popular media, including television programs like *All in the Family* and feature films such as *All the President's Men* (1976), based on the best-selling book that shed light on the heroes of the Watergate scandal, the reporters Woodward and Bernstein. The remainder of the decade would see the market success of outright and unapologetic escapism, from television's *Buck Rogers in the 25th Century* and *The Six Million Dollar Man* to the movie phenomenon of *Star Wars*.

What therefore seems clear in the wake of the Nixon storyline in the pages of *Captain America* is that the preponderance of American readers preferred to keep their villains in the realm of fiction. When faced with our own demons in reality, the normally cathartic release of seeing fictional villains brought to justice instead breeds fear and anxiety that we are not safe; in reality, there are no heroes to swoop in and save the day. If we allow our real-life villains to bleed into the realm of fiction, what would stop our fictional villains from bleeding into the real world? It might then become possible for an egomaniacal billionaire villain like Lex Luthor to become president of the United States, as he would in 2001.[19]

Once trust is broken, it is extremely difficult to regain, and Nixon completely pulverized the trust of many Americans in their government institutions. Although in hindsight Watergate actually did much to underscore the strength of the Constitution, this would not have been the primary feeling at the time. Not only was the president individually criminal but he was supported by a staff of people who were equally willing to abuse their positions in direct violation of the law. Even once he was caught, Nixon was able to avoid justice through the pardon granted by his successor, which, to an already dubious American public, undoubtedly appeared to be corrupt in and of itself. Nixon succeeded in not only separating himself from society but also in tainting the presidency specifically—and government as a whole more generally—in the eyes of the public. The distrust and even hatred that so many Americans feel toward the federal government in the twenty-first century could easily be argued to be a result of the real-life crimes of Richard Nixon; and the fictionalization of those crimes in the pages of *Captain America* at the time only goes to symbolize how deep into society the ramifications of Nixon's actions had bled.

Villainy will always exist in the real world. Usually, consumers utilize their respective favorite fictions as an escape from the stresses of daily life. Popular culture, however, is most significant when it most closely reflects the society that produced it. From time to time, a real-world event so shocks society that the creators of popular fictions feel an overwhelming compulsion to express their concerns and anxieties in the pages or frames of their respective media. At those times, our fictional heroes are given the opportunity to bring justice to our actual demons. This type of crossover provides society with a deep sense of catharsis at a time when it is most desperately needed. As Englehart himself noted, "So I had asked myself, 'Who is Captain America?,' and had found an answer for the man. Thing was, America was moving from the overarching Vietnam War toward the specific crimes of Watergate. I was writing a man who believed in America's highest ideals at a time when America's President was a crook. I could not ignore that."[20] He saw a problem, and he addressed it.

Notes

1. Mike Alsford, *Heroes and Villains* (Waco, TX: Baylor University Press, 2006), 121.

2. Terry H. Anderson, *The Movement and the Sixties: Protest in America from Greensboro to Wounded Knee* (New York: Oxford University Press, 1995), xiii; Allen J. Matusow, *The Unraveling of America: A History of Liberalism in the 1960s* (New York: Harper and Row, 1984), x; and Van Gosse and Richard Moser, eds., *The World the 60s Made: Politics and Culture in Recent America* (Philadelphia: Temple University Press, 2003), 8–9.

3. Peter N. Carroll, *It Seemed Like Nothing Happened: America in the 1970s*, 3rd ed. (New Brunswick, NJ: Rutgers University Press, 2000), 140–60.

4. Bruce J. Schulman, *The Seventies: The Great Shift in American Culture, Society, and Politics* (Cambridge, MA: Da Capo Press, 2001), 43–44.

5. Denny O'Neil, Neal Adams, and Dick Giordano, *Green Lantern/Green Arrow*, no. 83 (May 1971).

6. Bradford W. Wright, *Comic Book Nation: The Transformation of Youth Culture in America* (Baltimore: Johns Hopkins University Press, 2003), 245.

7. Steve Englehart and Sal Buscema, *Captain America and the Falcon*, no. 169 (January 1974).

8. Steve Englehart and Sal Buscema, *Captain America and the Falcon*, no. 173 (May 1974).

9. Steve Englehart and Sal Buscema, *Captain America and the Falcon*, no. 175 (July 1974).

10. Englehart and Buscema, *Captain America and the Falcon*, no. 175.

11. Richard Hall, interview with Steve Englehart, January 27, 2008.

12. Ralph Macchio, "Let's Rap with Cap," *Captain America and the Falcon*, no. 179 (November 1974).

13. Warren Blum, "Let's Rap with Cap," *Captain America and the Falcon*, no. 180 (December 1974).

14. Editor, "Let's Rap with Cap," *Captain America and the Falcon*, no. 179 (November 1974).

15. Robin Green, "Face Front: Clap Your Hands! You're on the Winning Team!," *Rolling Stone*, no. 91, September 16, 1971, 28–34; and Richard Hall, interview with Gary Friedrich, September 5, 2009.

16. Mike Luckenbill, "Let's Rap with Cap," *Captain America and the Falcon*, no. 181 (January 1975).

17. Richard Hall, "The Captain America Conundrum: Issues of Patriotism, Race, and Gender in "Captain America" Comics, 1941–2001," PhD diss., Auburn University, 2011, 155–60.

18. Wright, *Comic Book Nation*, 245.

19. Jeph Loeb and Tony Harris, *Superman: Lex 2000*, no. 1 (January 2001).

20. Steve Englehart, "Captain America II: 153–186," available at http://www.steveenglehart .com/Comics/Captain%20America%20169-176.html.

CHAPTER 27

The Absence of Black Supervillains in Mainstream Comics[1]

PHILLIP LAMARR CUNNINGHAM

ALTHOUGH I WAS ONLY THREE YEARS OLD WHEN IT DEBUTED IN 1977, *STAR WARS: Episode IV—A New Hope* made a lasting impression on me. Like many impressionable children, I immediately became enthralled with the grand spectacle, and that Christmas, my toy chest was filled to the brim with *Star Wars* action figures and starships. Of all the characters in the film, my immediate favorite was Darth Vader, the brooding, asthmatic Sith Lord. From the moment the black-armored Vader entered the opening scene, he became—and remains—my all-time favorite *Star Wars* character.

Vader's status as my favorite *Star Wars* character was at its peak when, a few years later, *Star Wars: Episode VI—Return of the Jedi* (1983) arrived in theaters. Over the course of the intervening years, as my awareness of race began to develop, my mother revealed to me that Darth Vader was "black." Like many unaware and naïve *Star Wars* fans, my mother had assumed that legendary actor James Earl Jones—who provided Vader's deep, menacing voice—was the man behind the mask.[2] The fact that the most powerful man in the galaxy was supposedly black obviously was great news to me, a burgeoning young black film buff and comic book reader who rarely got to see or read about immensely powered black folks in popular media.

With this in mind, one can imagine the great disappointment I felt, near the conclusion of *Return of the Jedi*, when Luke Skywalker removed his father's mask to reveal the glaringly bright countenance of a white Anakin Skywalker! Of course, I had already been given a hint that this might occur in *Star Wars: Episode V—The Empire Strikes Back* (1980) when Vader revealed to Luke Skywalker that he indeed was his father; however, I simply had dismissed this as a lie. Nonetheless, as the credits rolled, I had no other choice but to accept that the greatest, most powerful villain of my generation was, like virtually all of his progenitors, a white man.

This realization—that all of the greatest supervillains are white—would be heightened when I became an avid comic book reader. My uncle Mike, a pretty good artist in his own right, returned from his stint in the army with a trunk full of comic books, all of which I read enthusiastically. He had all the greats—*Batman*, *Spider-Man*, *Superman*—along with a few others like low-key classics *OMAC: One Man Army Corps* and *Sgt. Rock*. However, amid his collection was *Black Lightning*, the first comic I had read that featured a black superhero. While I thoroughly enjoyed *Black Lightning*, eventually I found it troubling because the title character—who fought crime in the slums of Superman's Metropolis—was not as powerful as his counterparts, and his villains were lame and white. Even his archnemesis, the black crime lord Tobias Whale, was an albino![3]

Flash forward some twenty-plus years, and mainstream comics still remain without many black supervillains. While black superheroes have managed some progress (perhaps punctuated by the brief yet impactful run of DC Comics' black imprint Milestone during the early to mid-1990s), black supervillains have yet to experience such a boon.[4] Thus, this chapter aims to discern the reasons for such a long, pronounced absence of black supervillains in mainstream comics.[5] As I shall postulate here, this absence largely emerges from a host of narratological constraints that have influenced other genres of popular media, particularly film. I shall conclude by considering the problematic nature of racialized villains while also championing a call for the inclusion of more.

DEFINING BLACK, DEFINING SUPERVILLAIN

The decision to pursue this topic largely came out of a question I asked several of my friends who read comics: "Can you name a major black supervillain?" I posed the question without any qualifications of what I meant by *black* or *supervillain*. Nonetheless, I typically received one of two answers from my friends: (a) "I can't think of any *major* ones . . ."; or (b) "Well, there's Apocalypse." These limited responses are not surprising given the nature of the question and the reality that black supervillains are few and far between. Of course, this contention of black supervillain scarcity rests largely on qualifying the terms *black* and *supervillain*. A consideration of the aforementioned Apocalypse provides me with an opportunity to delimit both terms.

Admittedly, defining *black* is rather difficult and often leads to essentialism. However, for the purposes of this essay, *black* shall refer to those people whose origins are in sub-Saharan Africa, especially the descendants of African slaves in the United States. Making this distinction is important because, while there are a number of supervillains who emerge from Africa or are of African descent, the vast majority are not phenotypically black. As Jared Diamond notes in his influential yet highly controversial *Guns, Germs, and Steel*, many conflate being African with being black: "Most Americans and many Europeans equate native Africans with blacks, white Africans with recent intruders, and African racial history with the story of European colonialism and slave trading.... [B] lacks are the sole native Africans familiar to most Americans, because they were brought in large numbers as slaves to the United States."[6] However, these assumptions about the blackness of Africa largely misconceive the continent's racial diversity. Diamond notes: "Even before the arrival of white colonialists, Africa already harbored not just blacks but ... five of the world's six major divisions of humanity."[7]

Most supervillains with African origins—like Apocalypse—typically emerge from or have ties to ancient Egypt.[8] As one can imagine, given their well-known wealth and power, the pharaohs have served as a source of inspiration for a number of villains. Apocalypse, perhaps the X-Men's most powerful foe, emerges from the Age of the Pharaohs. The immensely powered mutant was born En Sabah Nur in the "harsh, unforgiving desert of ancient Egypt." Other supervillains—DC Comics stalwart Captain Marvel's nemesis Black Adam, for example—have similar origins. However, viewing supervillains such as Apocalypse and his ilk as black is indeed problematic.

The blackness of ancient Egypt has long been subject to heated debates in academic circles. For example, as recently as 2007, the skin color of the most well-known of the pharaohs, King Tut, was a source of controversy. During the King Tut exhibition at Philadelphia's Franklin Institute Science Museum, Temple University's Molefi Asante, the self-described "founder of the theory of Afrocentricity," among other scholars, contested the reliability of a forensic reconstruction of King Tut's head and shoulders.[9] The reconstruction—which includes a disclaimer about the accuracy of skin color—depicts a browned yet not discernibly black King Tut.[10] For scholars such as Asante, concerns about the divorcing of Egypt from Africa and the denial of any black African influence on ancient Egyptian culture are strong and certainly justified given the frequent depictions of Egyptians as European (perhaps best exemplified by Elizabeth Taylor's portrayal of Cleopatra in the 1963 film).[11] Given the continued, heated discourse on the racial makeup of the ancient Egyptians, it seems unwise to wholly classify them as black (or any other race, for that matter). As such, considering the ultrapowerful Armageddon, who actually was born with gray skin, as black is equally problematic.

Given that most superheroes operate in urban locales within the United States, the few black villains in mainstream comics are African American and tend to originate from these spaces as well. Most black villains were created as foes to the few black superheroes, and, as I shall elucidate in the next section, because black superheroes are predominantly street-level vigilantes, their villains are limited in terms of power and purpose. Admittedly, there is no general consensus on the term; compendiums such as Mike Conroy's *500 Comic Book Villains* and Gina Misiroglu and Michael Eury's *The Supervillain Book: The Evil Side of Comic Books* do not distinguish villains such as Paste-Pot Pete (later the Trapster), who trapped heroes such as the Fantastic Four and Spider-Man in his superadhesive glue, from Doomsday, the massive monster who "killed" Superman.

However, equating the likes of Armageddon and Doomsday with characters such as Paste-Pot Pete does not seem logical. Granted, most of the villains in mainstream comics are merely aliased or masked common-criminal types (bank robbers, gangsters, etc.), or henchmen for military or terrorist outfits. This is not surprising considering that, as scholars Nickie D. Phillips and Staci Strobl conclude in their analysis, organized crime and violent street crime are the two primary crime themes in comic books.[12] Given how common these types of characters are, it seems that we should distinguish them from other foes who are far more powerful: criminal masterminds (Kingpin, Lex Luthor), leaders of global terrorist organizations (Baron Zucker of HYDRA), military leaders (the Red Skull), immensely powered mutants (Armageddon, Magneto), intergalactic tyrants (Darkseid), and world eaters (Galactus), among others. Of these latter types, which for the purposes of this chapter I shall refer to as "supervillains," very few black villains can be classified as such. While characters such as Armageddon—with his immense power, influence, and determination to conquer the world—epitomize the term "supervillain," black villains rarely measure up to such standards.

NARRATIVE CONSTRAINTS ON BLACK SUPERVILLAINY

The scarcity of black supervillains is inextricably linked to the equal scarcity of black superheroes in mainstream comics, particularly those who have had an ongoing series. As one might imagine, black villains were created primarily as antagonists to those few black superheroes who have had their own ongoing series (although popular titles such as *Daredevil* and *Spider-Man* also have produced several black villains). For example, most of Marvel's black villains originate from either the *Black Panther* series or the *Luke Cage* series, both of which feature black protagonists.[13] Since DC Comics has historically failed to sustain a series with a black protagonist (outside of its Milestone imprint, in which the characters originally were not part of the DC universe), it is not surprising that its comics have far fewer black villains than does Marvel.[14]

As scholarship on black superheroes has noted, the modern black superhero emerged out of the turbulent late 1960s–early 1970s. This period also saw the rise of blaxploitation films, low-budget affairs geared toward the previously ignored black audience. This period gave rise to comics such as Marvel's *Black Goliath*, *Black Panther*, and *Luke Cage, Hero for Hire* and DC's *Black Lightning*, all of which, to a degree, maintained some of the tropes of the blaxploitation films, most notably a hypermasculine protagonist who operates in a gritty inner-city setting.[15] Like the antiheroes of the blaxploitation genre, these super-heroes' ties to traditional heroics were always in question: Captain America's partner the Falcon began life as a pimp/gangster named "Snap" Wilson; Luke Cage gains his powers after being experimented on while in prison (albeit for a crime he did not commit); and Black Lightning is as wanted by the police as the villains he fights.

While the villains of the blaxploitation era were often various forms of the Man, the living embodiment of the white power structure, the protagonists of these films frequently would clash with black villains as well. For example, in Ossie Davis's *Cotton Comes to Harlem* (1970), one of the genre's earliest films, rugged detectives Gravedigger Jones (Godfrey Cambridge) and Coffin Ed Johnson (Raymond St. Jacques) take down the crooked Reverend Deke O'Mal-ley (Calvin Lockhart), a charismatic black reverend selling fraudulent trips back to Africa to the poor residents of Harlem. Similarly, black superheroes would often combat black villains, many of whom were aliased or costumed petty criminals. For example, Shades and Comanche—who were among Luke Cage's first villains—were mere hoods; the former had acquired a visor that shot concussive beams (similar to that of X-Men leader Cyclops), and the lat-ter was adept with a bow and arrow. Like several of Luke Cage's black villains (Diamondback, Mangler, and Spear, for example), they had ties to Cage while he was imprisoned. Most were low-level mobsters (many were operatives of the criminal organization the Maggia), racketeers, and thieves, motivated by financial gain or revenge against Cage.

Because of their origins as common thugs, most black villains—like their superhero counterparts—are often inadequate for adventures beyond the street corners and rooftops of the inner city. This is largely due to the industry's tendency to use black superheroes (and characters, in general) as a means to address social issues that its primarily white, nigh invulnerable superheroes could not. As Rob Lendrum notes in his essay on 1970s black superheroes, "Su-perman is ineffective at dealing with [street-level crime and social issues]."[16] As evidence, he echoes Umberto Eco's earlier criticisms of Superman as a defender of the status quo: "Superman never engages in political or social struggles, he only defeats evil that attempts to seize private property. In fact even his civic consciousness has ignored an entire area of Metropolis populated by African Americans, making him complacent in an oppressive system."[17] Thus, he dis-tinguishes black superheroes—in this case, Black Lightning, who primarily fights crime in Suicide Slum, the ghettoes of Superman's Metropolis—from their white counterparts by asserting that tackling street and organized crime is an essential part of their character. Lendrum writes: "The masculinity of the black heroes then, encompasses a code of morality that includes an obligation to protect the black community in a better way than has been offered by white agencies prior. . . . The black heroes battle an assortment of criminals and super-villains in their politically charged battle to protect the ghetto streets."[18] Lendrum's contention falls in line with what writer Tony Isabella—creator of Black Lightning and Marvel's Black Goliath—states about his creation: "[Jefferson Pierce] became Black Lightning because his sense of morality, his sense of social responsibility, wouldn't allow him to withhold his gifts, all his gifts, from his community. He comes from a background that tells him that, if you can help, you must help. He's a devout Christian who puts his belief into deeds."[19] As a result, most of the villains faced by heroes such as Luke Cage and Black Lightning are more akin to Reverend Deke O'Malley—albeit with the occasional superpower or weapon—than to Armageddon.

Beyond limiting their goals to organized or street crime, the situating of black villains in the ghetto has had two other effects that prevent them from being major supervillains. First, it has vastly limited the powers and abilities of these villains. For the most part, black villains typically rely on their fighting prowess or access to weaponry. Marvel, in particular, has a litany of black villains who carry heavy weaponry: the aforementioned Comanche, who is proficient with a bow and arrow; the unfortunately named Butcher T. Washington, a weapons expert with a heavily armed tank at his disposal (granted to him by Dionysius in order to combat Hercules); the aptly named Ammo and Shotgun; and several others. This tendency undoubtedly emerges from the experiences of black soldiers who served in Vietnam, and the complete dominance of heavyweight boxing by black fighters (Muhammad Ali, George Foreman, "Smokin'" Joe Frazier, Ken Norton, etc.) in the 1970s.[20] Ammo and Shotgun, for example, are noted Vietnam veterans (with the latter having served alongside Marvel's resident gun-wielding vigilante the Punisher), as is Superman foe Bloodsport.

However, outside of being able to fight and to use conventional and advanced weaponry, black villains—like many black superheroes—are most noted for their raw strength. Of course, superhero comics are rife with larger-than-life, inhumanly strong characters; however, this is particularly true of black villains. The portrayal of hypermasculine black men not only is a requisite of the genre but also is an integral part of racist ideology. As Jeff Brown notes:

> But not all Others have been constructed as equal by the dominant masculine ideology. While the gay man, the Jewish man, the Asian man (and many other "Others") have been burdened by the castrated softness, the black man

has been subjected to the burden of racial stereotypes that place him in the symbolic space of being *too* hard, *too* physical, *too* bodily.[21]

While Brown is speaking specifically of black superheroes like Luke Cage (whose skin is literally as hard as steel), his findings also apply to black villains. Take for instance characters such as "Big" Ben Donovan, one of Luke Cage's earliest nemeses. Although he possesses no superpowers nor has been augmented in any fashion, Donovan nonetheless stands nearly eight feet tall; his hands are large and strong enough to palm Daredevil's face and lift him off the ground (as he does in *Marvel Knights*, no. 12)! When black villains are empowered with superhuman abilities, tremendous strength is usually one of them, as is the case with Tombstone, a giant black albino with filed teeth and rock-hard skin, and Man-Ape, who gained super-strength by "[b]athing in the [white] gorilla's blood and eating the gorilla's flesh."[22]

A heavy reliance on brawn does not fully distinguish black villains from nonblack villains, does not imply that black villains do not have other abilities or powers, nor does it necessarily imply that there are no black villains who utilize their intelligence. There are plenty of nonblack villains—prominent examples are Spider-Man villains Ox and the Rhino—who are literally mindless brutes. There are black villains who possess unique abilities outside of the scope of super-strength, such as Moses Magnum, whose "body generates seismic force which amplifies his natural strength and attunes him to seismic vibrations." Furthermore, there are those black villains who are highly intelligent, like Black Manta and Thunderball, who, prior to his criminal career, was gamma ray physicist Dr. Eliot Franklin.

However, what does distinguish black villains from their nonblack counterparts is that their great power and intellect rarely (if ever) coincide. Whereas supervillains such as Armageddon, Doctor Doom, Lex Luthor, and Magneto wield both great power and great intellect, black villains often are forced to choose between the two. One need only look to the aforementioned Thunderball, who, despite his genius-level intellect, relies primarily on his strength, has resorted to utilizing a ball and chain as a weapon, and commits crimes with his band of ruffians, the Wrecking Crew.[23] Moses Magnum, perhaps the closest Marvel has gotten to a true black supervillain, is also incapable of wielding great intellect with great power. Before inheriting the ability to generate seismic waves, Magnum was "the world's foremost independent weapons manufacturer."[24] However, due to his many failures (and despite having actually conquered a small African nation for a short period), Armageddon rendered Magnum incapable of controlling his powers. As a result, characters such as Moses and Thunderball lend further credence to what Jeff Brown writes of the linkage between black men and hypermasculinity:

Moreover, the more one's identity is linked to a hypermasculine persona based on the body, the more uncultured and uncivilized, the more bestial one is considered to be. . . . [B]lacks have historically and symbolically been represented as pure body and little mind. . . . Because of this racist ideological paradox, blacks in Western culture have been forced to shoulder the burdens of the body itself. In contemporary culture black men are often seen more as beasts, as rapists, as gangsters, as crack-heads, and as muggers—literally as bodies out of control—than they are as fathers, as scholars, as statesmen, and as leaders. It is perhaps this split between the mind and the body that marks one of the greatest threats of (self-) destruction facing blacks today.[25]

This is particularly true in the case of black comic book villains such as Magnum Moses and Thunderball, neither of whom can seem to rectify their powerful minds with their powerful bodies. Both are quite literally black bodies out of control: Magnum can no longer be on solid ground without causing a tremendous earthquake; Thunderball's power is linked to his proximity to his partner Wrecker's magic crowbar.

Beyond greatly limiting the powers of black villains, situating them in urban locales has also, in many regards, made many of them redeemable figures. Many black villains do not stay villains, and even those who remain so are seemingly justified in their villainy. Undoubtedly the product of white liberal guilt and the comic industry's sudden interest in addressing social issues in the 1970s, the rise of black superheroes coincided with the rise of somewhat sympathetic black villains. As the origins of many of the black villains who emerged out of this period (and even later) suggest, many were victims of circumstance or sought redress through crime for crimes committed against them. For example, before embarking on a life of crime, Chemistro, one of Luke Cage's early foes, was Mainstream Motors chemist Curtis Carr. Carr had developed the Alchemy Gun, a device capable of transforming one substance into another (e.g., wood to rubber). When company president Horace Claymore became aware of the project, he unjustly fired Carr in an attempt to keep the gun for himself. As a result, Carr (as Chemistro) decided to seek revenge against the company— though he was ultimately foiled by Luke Cage and crippled after accidentally transmuting his own legs into dust. However, later, he reforms and assists Cage in foiling the second Chemistro.[26] Thunderball has a similar story: according to his official biography, "Dr. Eliot Franklin was a genius-level physicist, nearly on par with Bruce Banner. He even designed a miniature gamma-ray bomb, a feat that eluded Banner. However, his invention was stolen by an unscrupulous executive at Richmond Enterprises, and Franklin was imprisoned after an attempt to steal it back."

In fact, the black inventor who is incapable of capitalizing off of his creations was indeed a frequent trope of black villains. This feature is writ large in the former Spider-Man villain Rocket Racer. Rocket Racer is the epitome of the redeemable black villain: an inventive mind whose social circumstances forced him into a life of crime only later to embrace a role as a superhero. In his bio, his origin reads: "After his mother suffered a heart attack and was hospitalized, Robert Farrell began to feel the financial strain on his family. His talent for science and technology seemed to indicate a promising future; however, he designed a weapon-equipped costume and a super-charged skateboard only to turn to a life of crime as a means of making some fast cash." However, after facing and losing to Spider-Man on several occasions, he finally reformed and eventually became a superhero.

Of course, the vengeful (even if justifiably so) black man is such a popular trope in mainstream comics largely because writers seemingly have very little else upon which to draw. The most prominent black men in American culture were, for quite some time, the beleaguered, defeated black worker and the hoodlum. Whereas writers have a veritable treasure trove of conquerors, historical figures, movements, and mythologies upon which to rely in the creation of nonwhite villains, such has not been the case for villains coded particularly as black. Of course, many comic supervillains are derived from historical conflicts such as World War II and the Cold War largely because of the resonance those events have had in American culture. Nazism, for example, has produced some of the greatest comic book supervillains, particularly Captain America's archnemesis the Red Skull (who frequently is among the top-rated villains in polls). Communism has also produced its fair share of supervillains, such as Fantastic Four villains the Red Ghost and the Soviet Super Soldiers. Furthermore, Greek and Egyptian mythologies have been grist for the mills as well, as the gods of both traditions have been frequent villains (and heroes) in both the Marvel and DC universes. Nonetheless, despite having parallels upon which writers could indeed draw, creators have yet to do so for black villains.[27]

NO BLACK SUPERVILLAINS IS A GOOD THING, RIGHT?

If the black villains upon whom I have focused here seem somewhat antiquated and stagnant, it is for good reason: there has been very little creation of new black supervillains or development of existing ones since the litany of those who appeared in the 1970s. Those who have emerged since then, in many regards, differ little from their predecessors. While there indeed has been much progress in terms of the number of and portrayal of black superheroes (though there are still very few black superhero comics), black supervillains have not fared well in recent years.

Perhaps the most noteworthy black villain to emerge since the 1970s is Geoffrey Wilder of Marvel's hit series *Runaways*. The series focuses on the adventures of a group of superpowered teenagers who have discovered that their parents are members of a secret cabal of villains—the Pride—allied by a pact to bring about the end of the world. Wilder is the leader of the Pride, which has cornered the market on organized crime in Los Angeles since the 1980s (in *Runaways* continuity, at least). As leader of the Pride, Wilder seemingly wields great power and influence and is indeed the most dire threat to the teenage adventurers.[28]

Nonetheless, Wilder's power is not without serious limitations. For starters, the Pride are actually the servants of the Gibborim, a clan of god-like giants who act as the Pride's benefactors. The Gibborim, who seek the end of humankind but are too weak to appear on the physical plain long enough to do so, have agreed to spare six members of the Pride and allow them to rule in a posthuman world as long as they do their bidding in the present. Thus, Wilder's power is not inherent but granted.

Being granted power, of course, is not necessarily detrimental to being a powerful supervillain. However, of the members of the Pride, Wilder and his wife Catherine are the ones with the most humble beginnings and glaring lack of actual powers or special abilities. The other families of the Pride had some form of or access to a significant superpower even before their meeting with the Gibborim: Frank and Leslie Dean were actually humanoid aliens who can fly and use solar power to do other feats; Gene and Alice Hayes were both telepathic mutants; Robert and Tina Minoru were black magic sorcerers; Victor and Janet Stein were mad scientists; and Dale and Stacey Yorkes were time travelers. However, the Wilders were just common thieves. As such, Wilder's reliance on the Gibborim, his lack of actual power, his stereotypical origins as a common hood, and, perhaps most importantly, Pride members' untimely deaths at the hands of their children undermine any notion that he is a major supervillain. That Wilder and the other black villains before him fail to become major supervillains is of no surprise, especially given the mainstream comic industry's historic struggles portraying minorities.

As a result, one might wonder why I even would question the absence of black supervillains. After all, one need look at the history of perhaps the greatest archetype for the modern supervillain, Fu Manchu, as evidence of the dangers of racializing villains. As Karen Kingsbury notes in "Yellow Peril, Dark Hero," Fu Manchu "was indeed built on an all-too-familiar framework of racist, imperialist assumptions regarding Asians."[29] As Kingsbury suggests, Fu Manchu's creator, Arthur Sarsfield Ward, formulated him as a reaction to rampant street crime in London's Limehouse district and fears of the Chinese arising from the Boxer Rebellion.[30] Undoubtedly, Fu Manchu was the product of intense racial animosities, and he has proven to be the poster child of the dangerous Other and the Yellow Peril.[31]

Furthermore, as Marc Singer notes, superhero comics have always had a problematic track record with depictions of race. He writes:

> Comic books, and particularly the dominant genre of superhero comic books, have proven fertile ground for stereotyped depictions of race. Comics rely upon visually codified representations in which characters are continually reduced to their appearances, and this reductionism is especially prevalent in superhero comics, whose characters are wholly externalized into their heroic costumes and aliases. This system of visual typology combines with the superhero genre's long history of excluding, trivializing, or "tokenizing" minorities to create minority superheroes who are marked purely for their race.[32]

As Singer's remarks suggest, superhero comics are inherently dangerous ground upon which to represent race. As such, what Anna Beatrice Scott writes of comics in particular and Stuart Hall writes of popular culture in general rings true: neither seems like solid ground upon which to look for true representations of race.[33]

That stated, while I do not wish to romanticize superhero comics or overemphasize their influence, I do believe that they can provide a means with which to challenge preconceived notions about blacks. Like many other forms of popular media, comic books have been singularly focused: as a result of movements by the likes of activists such as Jesse Jackson and the NAACP, since the 1970s popular media has overcompensated for its lengthy history of negative depictions of black folks by either greatly limiting or outright eliminating roles in which black men and women portray villains. However, doing so is no more progressive than the tokenism to which Singer refers; in fact, what appears to some as altruism is more akin to an inability (or refusal) to develop complex black characters. However, as Brown indicates in his work on Milestone Comics, "black scholars and cultural critics see the need to develop new models of black masculinity, models that counter the dominant stereotypes not by reforming the hypermasculine image of the black male into an image of refinement, restraint, and desexualization, but by incorporating the associated properties of the mind (e.g., intelligence, control, wisdom) into the popular presentation of black male identity."[34] One way in which to do so has been achieved—to a degree, as Brown suggests—in the portrayals of more contemplative superheroes in the Milestone universe. Conversely, the same could be achieved in developing complex, contemplative, and powerful black supervillains.

Notes

1. Reprinted from Phillip Lamarr Cunningham, "The Absence of Black Supervillains in Mainstream Comics," *Journal of Graphic Novels and Comics* 1, no. 1 (2010): 51–62. The chapter has been lightly edited for style for the purposes of the present publication.

2. Although James Earl Jones provided Vader's voice in the original *Star Wars* trilogy and in virtually every other appearance of Darth Vader in popular culture, British actor David Prowse primarily portrays Vader in the original trilogy. However, in *Star Wars: Episode VI—Return of the Jedi*, Sebastian Shaw plays the unmasked Vader. Besides various stunt doubles, the only other actor to portray Vader in the films was Hayden Christensen, who filled the role of Vader's alter ego, Anakin Skywalker, in *Star Wars: Episode II—Attack of the Clones* (2002) and *Star Wars: Episode III—Revenge of the Sith* (2005).

3. Furthermore, Tobias Whale is an obvious nod to Marvel Comics' Kingpin, the rather large (and white) crime lord who would prove to be an archnemesis to Daredevil and Spider-Man. Kingpin first appeared in *The Amazing Spider-Man*, no. 50 (1967). Tobias Whale first appeared in *Black Lightning*, no. 1 (1977).

4. That said, mainstream comics seem to be experiencing some regression in terms of black superheroes. Marvel only has three black superhero titles, *Black Panther, Doctor Voodoo*, and *War Machine*, that are ongoing; DC currently has none (although its Vertigo imprint features a black revision of *The Unknown Soldier*, which cannot be considered a superhero title in that its protagonist is an insane Ugandan doctor). Among the major independents, Image Comics' long-running superhero title *Spawn* featured a black man as the lead character until recently, and Image also ran several volumes of the black superhero comic *Shadowhawk*. Otherwise, there are virtually no other black superhero titles in circulation. Fortunately, the lack of serials has been tempered somewhat by the rise in status of several superheroes in group titles. For example, Luke Cage is currently the leader of the New Avengers; and Black Lightning, after a stint as the secretary of education (under Lex Luthor), is an important member of the Justice League of America.

5. In this chapter, I privilege DC and Marvel Comics, as they are the two most popular comic book presses. Admittedly, there is a heavy emphasis on Marvel, for I am most familiar with Marvel Comics. However, this emphasis is also reflective of the relative dearth of black supervillains in DC Comics. Furthermore, the independent press has not provided many notable examples of black supervillains. Along those lines, there will be a heavy emphasis on black male villains and black masculinity given that, as one might imagine, there are even fewer black female villains than black male villains.

6. Jared Diamond, *Guns, Germs, and Steel: The Fates of Human Societies* (New York: W. W. Norton, 1998), 377.

7. According to Diamond: "The five major human groups to which Africa was already home by AD 1000 are those loosely referred to by laypeople as blacks, whites, African Pygmies, Khoisan, and Asians" (*Guns, Germs, and Steel*, 378). The only division not to emerge from Africa is the Australian Aborigines and their descendants.

8. Many of Marvel's villains from Africa also come from Wakanda, the fictional African kingdom ruled by Black Panther, Marvel's first black superhero to be featured in his own serial. Another African villain, and arguably Marvel's most powerful black supervillain, Moses Magnum, is from Ethiopia. The blackness of Ethiopians also has been questioned, though certainly not to the same degree as that of the ancient Egyptians.

9. Dr. Molefi Kete Asante, "Biography," available at http://www.asante.net/biography.

10. The disclaimer reads: "The features of [Tutankhamen's] face are based on scientific data. But the exact color of his skin and the size and shape of many facial details cannot be determined with full certainty." Photographs of the reconstruction can be seen at *National Geographic Magazine's* website: http://ngm.nationalgeographic.com/ngm/0506/feature1/index.html. See also Joel Rose, "King Tut Exhibit Prompts Debate on His Skin Color," NPR, August 28, 2007, available at https://www.npr.org/templates/story/story.php?storyId=13992421.

11. Afrocentrism and the blackness of Egypt have been the subject of much heated debate within scholarly circles. I cannot do justice to the myriad of issues involved in the debate in such a limited space. In "Defending the Paradigm," Adisa Alkebulan provides an in-depth analysis and literature review of key texts in the debate. Although Alkebulan is defending Afrocentrism as an approach, he also carefully articulates arguments against it. Adisa A. Alkebulan, "Defending the Paradigm," *Journal of Black Studies* 37, no. 3 (2007): 410–27. (Editor's note: Controversies around Cleopatra's racial identity and skin color remain open, as exemplified by contemporary discussions around who should play her in an upcoming new film. See Jonathan Borge, "Here's Why the Internet Doesn't Want Lady Gaga or Angelina Jolie to Portray Cleopatra," *Oprah Magazine*, January 15, 2019, available at https://www.oprahmag.com/entertainment/tv-movies/a25907570/cleopatra-movie-lady-gaga-angelina-jolie-beyonce/.)

12. Nickie D. Phillips and Staci Strobl, "Cultural Criminology and Kryptonite: Apocalyptic and Retributive Constructions of Crime and Justice in Comic Books," *Crime, Media, Culture* 2, no. 3 (2006): 314.

13. The series initially began as *Luke Cage, Hero for Hire* (nos. 1–16) in 1972. The series retained its numbering but changed its title to *Luke Cage, Power Man* (nos. 17–49) in 1974. Iron Fist, whose own self-titled series was cancelled, began pairing with Luke Cage in issue no. 48 of *Luke Cage, Power Man*, and his name was added to the title beginning with issue no. 50 (1978) and would remain until the series was canceled after issue no. 125 (1986).

14. Interestingly enough, the Milestone Comics serials, despite being created and written by predominantly black writers, also did not feature many black villains, let alone supervillains. However, the Milestone series were DC's most successful to feature black characters, as the DC universe comics such as *Black Lightning* failed to last beyond thirteen issues. Recently, the Milestone characters have been incorporated into the mainstream DC universe; however, this has yet to result in any new ongoing series for any of these characters.

15. Arguably, Milestone Comics emerged out of the second wave of blaxploitation, the popular "hood films" of the early 1990s. The influence of films such as John Singleton's *Boyz n the Hood* (1991) and *Menace II Society* (1993) can clearly be seen in Milestone's *Blood Syndicate*, for example, which centers on a superpowered street gang.

16. Rob Lendrum. "The Super Black Macho, One Baaad Mutha: Black Superhero Masculinity in 1970s Mainstream Comic Books," *Extrapolation* 46, no. 3 (2005), 396.

17. Lendrum. "The Super Black Macho," 369.

18. Lendrum. "The Super Black Macho," 369–70.

19. Markison Naso, "Tony Isabella: Black Thought." *Comics Bulletin*, available at http://www.comicsbulletin.com/features/107042750449064.html.

20. Herman Graham III notes: "In the early years of American involvement in Vietnam, African Americans enlisted and reenlisted at higher rates than did whites and even displayed a more favorable opinion of the draft"; *The Brothers' Vietnam War: Black Power, Manhood, and the Military Experience* (Gainesville: University Press of Florida, 2003), 15. Furthermore, as James E. Westheider notes, black soldiers in Vietnam received a great deal of praise for their fighting abilities: "As they had in previous wars, African Americans in Vietnam once again demonstrated their abilities as warriors. They compiled an impressive record in the early years of the war, and

the military noticed it. In 1967, [General William C.] Westmoreland went out of his way to praise the valor and skill of African Americans under his command. His appraisal of black fighting prowess may have surprised and even irritated some of his audience, but it was the opinion of most officers in Vietnam, black or white"; James E. Westheider, *The African American Experience in Vietnam: Brothers in Arms* (Lanham, MD: Rowman and Littlefield, 2007), 51.

21. Jeffrey A. Brown, "Comic Book Masculinity and the New Black Superhero," *African American Review* 33, no. 1 (1999): 28.

22. Despite being six foot seven inches tall, 215 pounds, Tombstone, unlike many of his predecessors of that size, did not initially have superhuman strength or rock-hard skin. He acquired these powers after exposure to chemicals. However, before he acquired these abilities, he still was quite strong and had filed teeth.

23. The Wrecking Crew—Bulldozer, Piledriver, Thunderball, and Wrecker—share superhuman strength, which was accidentally bestowed upon them by Karnilla, the Norn Queen, and one of Thor's archenemies. In order to utilize their power, the Crew must be in close proximity to Wrecker's crowbar, which is where all of Karnilla's magic is concentrated. On several occasions, Thunderball has sought (and briefly held) sole control of the crowbar. To Marvel's credit (although this vacillated between writers), Thunderball is usually distinguished as the smartest, most ambitious member of the Wrecking Crew, even though he is not the de facto leader.

24. Magnum was granted his powers from Armageddon in return for lifelong servitude. After being thwarted by Luke Cage in his attempt to mine energy from the earth's core, Magnum falls into a crevice, where he is rescued by Armageddon.

25. Brown, "Comic Book Masculinity," 30.

26. The second Chemistro is actually Carr's former cellmate, Arch Morton. The third Chemistro is Carr's younger brother, Calvin Carr.

27. Arguably, outside of the common street tough, the voodoo priest has proven to be another common trope for black villains. Villains such as Black Talon, Empress, and Hougan, among a host of others, all utilize a stereotyped form of voodoo.

28. In *Runaways*, vol. 2, no. 18, Wilder apparently kills Gertrude Yorkes, one of the teenage adventurers and daughter of two of his fellow Pride members.

29. Karen Kingsbury, "Yellow Peril, Dark Hero: Fu Manchu and the 'Gothic Bedevilment' of Racist Intent," in *The Gothic Other: Racial and Social Constructions in the Literary Imagination*, ed. Ruth Beinstock Anolik and Douglas L. Howard (Jefferson, NC: McFarland, 2004), 105.

30. Kingsbury, "Yellow Peril, Dark Hero," 105–6.

31. Fu Manchu has also served as inspiration for a number of comic book supervillains, namely the Mandarin and Yellow Claw.

32. Marc Singer, "'Black Skins' and White Masks: Comic Books and the Secret of Race," *African American Review* 36, no. 1 (Spring 2002): 107.

33. Anna Beatrice Scott, "Superpower vs. Supernatural: Black Superheroes and the Quest for a Mutant Reality," *Journal of Visual Culture* 5, no. 3 (2006): 295–314; and Stuart Hall, "What Is This 'Black' in Black Popular Culture?," *Social Justice* 20, nos. 1–2 (51–52) (Spring–Summer 1993): 104–14.

34. Brown, "Comic Book Masculinity," 30.

Making America Great Again, You Foolsssss

Neoliberal Snake Charmers in Marvel's G.I. Joe: A Real American Hero

J. RICHARD STEVENS

> G.I. Joe is the code name for America's daring, highly trained special mission
> force. Its purpose: to defend human freedom against Cobra, a ruthless terror-
> ist organization determined to rule the world.
>
> "THE COBRA STRIKES," *G.I. JOE: A REAL AMERICAN HERO*

THE PRECEDING MANTRA, PRESENT WITHIN THE THEME SONG OF EVERY EPISODE
of the Sunbow and Marvel Productions cartoon *G.I. Joe: A Real American
Hero* (which appeared from 1985 to 1987, and 1989 to 1991), frames the G.I. Joe
mission as the defense of human freedom against a defined terrorist group.
But who is this organization that warranted the formation of one of the early
symbols of the rising trend toward militainment?[1] As all good villains do, Cobra
represents the antithesis of the G.I. Joe team. The clash between "the Ultimate
Weapon of Democracy"—the description from the cover of the first issue of
Marvel Comics' *G.I. Joe: A Real American Hero* (*G.I. Joe: ARAH*)[2]—and the
forces of Cobra frames the identity of the Joe team, the narrative structure of
the comic series, the Hasbro toy line, the advertisements for the toy line, and
the cartoon series.

But the framing of this "ruthless terrorist organization determined to rule
the world" seems quite at odds with conceptions of terrorism contemporary
to the 1980s franchise, and upon closer inspection, the key players within the
organization, its structure, and even its stated goals bear more resemblance
to the neoliberal ethos of the Ronald Reagan administration itself than to its
clandestine nonstate opponents. Although the basic narrative of the *G.I. Joe*
text might appear simplistic, a deeper analysis reinforces the observation that

"popular fiction is rather more complex than it looks at first sight."[3] Recognizing in the observations of Antonio Gramsci and Stuart Hall that media texts contain rich sites of cultural critique,[4] this chapter explores Marvel Comics' framing of the Joe and Cobra teams, which appears to present a striking critique of neoliberalism as an ideology—one that enshrines itself in Americana while actually undermining the values and tenets of twentieth-century American values.

This critique at times seems almost ironic, given that Hasbro utilized the renewed sense of patriotism championed by Reagan's election to promote war-themed action figures and toys. While promoting those products, Marvel writer Larry Hama's comic series simultaneously explores many mature themes about military command structure, stressing personal journeys and reconciling sins from the past, combining the paradox of the hypermasculine metatext with the hypomasculinity critique present in many post–Vietnam War narratives of the 1970s. In the comic series, almost all the original Joes (certainly each of the officers) are Vietnam vets, and flashbacks to their military service in Southeast Asia appear prominently in the comic narrative. And, like most comic book heroes, many of the characters in *G.I. Joe: ARAH* are orphans or have suffered significant family loss.[5] Hama is himself a veteran, and themes of honor and ability are threaded throughout the series, consistent with classic military masculinity.[6] Within the comic book narrative, the G.I. Joe unit serves as a surrogate family for many Joes, and the mission serves as a sacred trust with the nation, as articulated in a letter written by one of the main characters, Snake-Eyes, in *G.I. Joe ARAH*, vol. 1, no. 155:

> I had the privilege and honor of serving with men and women I could depend on literally. I have had comrades lay down their lives for me, and I would have gladly laid down mine for them. How many other occupations engender such camaraderie? But then—this "Bearing of arms in defense of the constitution of the United States of America" is not really a profession per se . . . it is a trust.[7]

In 1982, Hasbro reintroduced its G.I. Joe toy line (resurrecting the world's first action figure, which premiered in 1964 and was continually offered in different forms until the mid-1970s) with an unusual marketing campaign. Hasbro had determined that using animation in its promotional materials to appeal to boys was key to their toy line's success, but animation in children's products was restricted because children were seen as a special audience that needed protection.[8] To skirt FCC regulations, Hasbro approached Marvel Comics to create a comic book series, which it then advertised with animated promotions in television ads. As Hama explained, Hasbro wanted an angle on being able to advertise [G.I. Joe], which is how the Marvel connection came in. . . . There were only a few seconds of animation you could have in a toy commercial, and you had to show the toy, so people wouldn't get totally deluded. . . . [Hasbro] realized that a comic book was protected under the first amendment and there couldn't be restrictions based on how you advertised for a publication.[9]

Hama developed each of the major characters and storylines around Hasbro's action figures, and a tight coordination between Hasbro, Marvel, and advertising firm Griffin-Bacal was formed to embed toys in comic books, comics that were then promoted on television using fully animated commercials, animation that was also used in the advertisements for the toys[10] and, eventually, the 1983 cartoon series. Although the comic series was originally proposed as part of a strategy to evade television regulations, the series became immensely popular in its own right, running 155 issues.[11]

The 1980s-era G.I. Joe franchise utilized a self-reinforcing strategy among its versions to promote and sell Hasbro products, resulting in the brand reinforcement becoming stronger across multiple texts rather than specific narratives or continuity in storytelling. Notably, the narrative structure and characters in the comic book series differ in stark ways from the cartoon series. Prior to writing *G.I. Joe: ARAH*, Hama had been developing for Marvel a series called *Fury Force*, based around an elite squad of soldiers (led by Marvel spy character Nick Fury's son) hunting down the evil forces of the terrorist organization Hydra.[12] Many of the elements and characters from *Fury Force* appear to have been pressed into the initial *ARAH* lineup. This evolution might account for the similarities between Cobra and Hydra, Marvel's terrorist organization composed of former Nazi agents. Like Hydra, Cobra officers wear standardized uniforms (and Cobra's more closely resemble Nazi uniforms) and carry standard-issue weapons. Like Hydra, Cobra relies on a series of secret bases and clandestine sleeper-cell structures for its operations.

Within the comic, the rise of Cobra begins with one man, who, bitter about a lifetime of financial struggle and resentful of those who wield power, launches a crusade against "the wheels of big government," which opposed his pyramid scheme. He forms Cobra as "an underground organization that will bypass government restrictions, and garner power through terrorism and extortion."[13]

As he travels from town to town in the role of a small-time salesman, he holds meetings in which he recruits disillusioned people. At one of the earliest rallies, Cobra Commander declares, "War is an extension of politics and politics is an extension of economics! If the government says that an honest man can't work as much as he wants to and earn as much as he wants to—it's wrong! And we have a right to fight back if we want to!"[14] These goals are pursued in part through terrorist acts, but the other tools in the organization's strategy include propaganda, economic interference, and culture-war argumentation:

> Do not let the false rumors of our military mishaps alarm you! Cobra is WINNING! When the citizenry loll back on their fat haunches and hire the poor minorities to do their dirty work, we WIN! When love of money eclipses moral conviction, we WIN! When good men see the ascension of evil and do nothing, we WIN!
> Our household cleaning product pyramid scheme grows exponentially! It is a money-making juggernaut! It is based on man's willingness to exploit his neighbors! Our nationwide "greed is good for you" seminars are filled to capacity and our media department has succeeded in selling ten more mindless sitcoms to the networks to further lower the intelligence of America! Armies of Cobra accountants advise millions of Americans to cheat on their taxes, denying funds to the government, and prompting cuts in defense spending![15]

In this passage, Cobra Commander appears to be reinforcing a criticism of the neoliberal trends in contemporary America by using negative critiques of the results of those trends as goals purported to undermine American values. By the time of the conflict portrayed in the first issues of the comic narrative, Cobra does not merely seek armed conflict with the status quo but rather presents a multipronged strategy of American subversion. Military encounters with G.I. Joe do occur, and the organization does mobilize troops for military engagements, but the tactics, goals, and culture of the Cobra organization seem at odds with those of a "terrorist organization."

EXPLORING THE TERRORISM OF COBRA

In examining the roots of terrorism, political scientists question how to define "terrorism," its causes, and the underlying goals of various groups who use its tactics.[16] Although early studies were preoccupied with the moral dimensions of terrorist tactics, more recent work approaches terrorism as a rational, utility-oriented strategy aimed at achieving specific political ends. For example, Audrey Cronin argues that "terrorism always has a political nature. It involves the commission of outrageous acts designed to precipitate political change."[17]

Only in the broadest sense are Cobra's goals political. When Cobra Commander gives speeches (which happens often), criticisms of the status quo are offered, but political solutions beyond amassing power are rarely articulated. In *G.I. Joe: ARAH*, vol. 1, no. 33, Cobra Commander addresses his troops, explaining the strategy of sending covert operatives to pose as average citizens:

[A]nd now even as I speak, hordes of Cobra crimson guardsman are infil-
trating themselves into the very fabric of American life! They are lawyers,
bankers, insurance salesmen and community leaders! And soon they will
accomplish what armed might can never do . . . they will take over this
country legally!

Oh, it will take time . . . but we have the patience! And we have the hearts
and minds of our youths . . . who will march into the future we forge for them
with the assurance that they will be the masters of the earth![18]

The elaborate plan, drawn out over decades, does not appear to have an agenda
for substantive political change but merely seeks to provide power for unstated
ends. Whether terrorist strategies are used to stimulate an overreaction from
particular targets,[19] to coerce such targets into policy change,[20] or to mobilize
support within sympathetic populations,[21] terrorism is defined as a calculated
instrument undertaken by an individual or group for strategic objectives.[22]

Within the narrative of the comic book series, Cobra exists primarily as a
paramilitary force, albeit one that is as well equipped, if not better equipped
than the Joe team (given Hasbro's goal to sell toys presented in the narrative,
a constant influx of new hardware on both sides of the conflict served that
intent). While Cobra does carry out acts consistent with terrorism (kidnapping, using explosives, manipulating public opinion with the media), its stated
intent does not appear consistent with political goals normally associated with
terrorist groups. Cobra Commander begins his career as a disgruntled used
car salesman—his frustration at his lack of financial success is a driver for the
creation of Cobra, and financial gain (and control of systems to allow more
acquisition) seems to be the most consistent Cobra goal.

Terrorism is typically conceptualized as nonstate actors engaged in asym-
metrical tactics, although disagreements exist about the exclusion of state actors
from the definition.[23] Some scholars consider both state and nonstate actors,
distinguishing between "grievance terror," which challenges institutions of power, and "institutional terror," which maintains the status quo.[24] Cobra operates
mostly as a stateless actor that somehow works from a position of strength
instead of weakness (in most combat scenarios, Cobra forces outnumbers G.I.
Joe forces). However, in *G.I. Joe: ARAH*, vol. 1, no. 41, Cobra actually becomes
a state actor when the group tricks G.I. Joe into detonating explosives on an
ocean fault line, creating an island outside international boundaries.[25] Cobra
claims the island and demands United Nations recognition in order to operate
legitimately and freely upon it. However, even from this state-actor position,
Cobra's tactics are not utilized to maintain a status quo, continuing to launch
schemes and missions to acquire resources, amass political capital, and influence the world's economy in its favor.

Another significant departure from the frames of terrorism concerns the degree to which Cobra resists such stereotyping vis-à-vis contemporary real-life events. In 1982, the United States had recently witnessed the Iranian hostage crisis—Hama even includes imagery from these events, positing that Snake-Eyes originally was scarred during a failed attempt to liberate the hostages.[26] In early-1980s action films and novels, terrorists were disproportionately portrayed as Arab or Muslim.[27] Even research into terrorism of that era tended to explore the phenomenon through a "good versus evil" moral paradigm that largely ignored power[28] and lent itself to ethnic stereotyping in order to construct a sense of cultural superiority.[29]

By contrast, Cobra is overwhelmingly composed of Caucasian operatives. Cobra Commander is presented as an average middle-class American. Destro (James McCullen) is a Scottish nobleman. The Baroness (Anastasia Cisarovna) is a white woman from "somewhere in Europe." Dr. Venom appears to be a white American scientist. Dr. Mindbender is white. Firefly is white and French. Major Bludd is white and Australian. Raptor is a white American. Scalpel (Andrew R. Walker) is a white American. Copperhead is white and from Florida. Crystal Ball is from the fictitious nation of Romalia, and Scarface (like all Cobra troopers) appears to be a white American. Even characters like Wade Collins, who served on the Vietnam long-range recon patrol that also included Stalker, Snake-Eyes, and Storm Shadow, is white. In fact, a good portion of the long-term Cobra plot to infiltrate various American institutions and industries revolves around the recruitment and deployment of white nuclear families selected to appear as average middle-class Americans.

In *G.I. Joe: ARAH*, vol. 1, no. 4, the Joe team combats a Montana paramilitary militia,[30] a group funded by but otherwise unaffiliated with Cobra. Not only is the militia white, but it is organized around a white couple, who are determined to start World War III with nuclear weapons so that they can emerge afterward to remake "a new world in [their] image."[31] Even when Joe and Cobra forces clash in Middle Eastern countries, such as their battle in Libya,[32] both forces are pressed to transport military equipment and personnel from the United States to join the battle. In fact, the Joe team rarely battles in the Middle East, and even during the period contemporary to the real-life Operation Desert Storm, the Joes battled Cobra in a fictitious Middle East country (Benzheen) on behalf of the Arab population.[33]

COBRA'S NEOLIBERAL FAILINGS

Although Cobra occasionally performs certain tropes of the "foreign terrorist," such as when the Baroness refers to Cobra's opponents as "capitalist lackeys,"[34] its organization is most active in the United States and is usually far more consistently neoliberal in its ideology than G.I. Joe, in the sense that neoliberalism embodies the advocacy of economic privatization, deregulation, free trade, and reductions in government spending in order to increase the role of the private sector in the economy and society. Cobra Commander began Cobra when a promotional scheme of his was deemed a pyramid scheme, and he lamented the regulatory structure preventing him from selling products as he wished. He utilizes his skill at recruiting and salesmanship to build Cobra as a network but consistently demonstrates a lack of tactical proficiency when it comes to leading troops in battle.[35]

In the first fifty issues, a significant site of exploration is the small town of Springfield (purposely presented as a small town that could be in any state), the secret location of Cobra's primary headquarters. On the surface, Springfield appears to be an idealistic representation of midwestern Americana. But just under the surface, Cobra personnel are ever present. In issue no. 10, Billy (a young boy who would turn out to be Cobra Commander's son) explains to the Joe team that Springfield had once been a quintessential American town until the "soap people" came:[36] they initially recruited the town's citizens into the Amway pyramid scheme and then indoctrinated them into Cobra's organization. "They were very convincing," he says. "They made it seem very 'un-American' not to want to get involved."[37] While the community remains outwardly an idealized American town, it is now masking hidden rooms with weaponry, a population that surveils itself, a "Cobra Scout" organization for youths who keep tabs on the adults, and secret entrances to an underground Cobra base.

This dichotomy not only presents an uncomfortable insidious relationship between a false outward perfection and an internal brutality, but it also frames the tenuous relationship between the appearance of order and the fractured competition brewing within. True to the neoliberal ideology, each leader within the Cobra organization is in constant struggle against the other leaders. Particularly after the introduction of Destro in issue no. 13,[38] the main leadership remains perpetually mired in a web of competing plots to seize control of the organization. In issue no. 16, a series of panels explores the thoughts of each leader, as they sit around a table together just after Major Bludd has been introduced to the group:

COBRA COMMANDER. He's a despicable bootlicker, everything that Destro isn't, and that's why he must destroy Destro for me.
BLUDD. Ah well. A job is just a job but it seems a dead waste to terminate a fellow like Destro whilst letting live spineless leeches like Scar-Face . . .
SCAR-FACE. Was I wrong in siding with Destro? Is Major Bludd the commander's new favorite?

DESTRO. Even through this mask of stainless steel, I fear my face betrays me. Does the Commander suspect my feelings for the Baroness? Will he act against me first ... or her?

DR. Venom. Both Destro and Cobra Commander are preoccupied in forcing me to choose between them. It's distracting them from the real menace: Dr. Venom!

BARONESS. So many contradictory plots and ambitions! How can I use them to my advantage?[39]

These plots undermine Cobra's efforts on the battlefield. Continually locked in contests for ultimate control of Cobra, the leaders regularly squander superior technological weaponry, tactical advantages, and larger troop numbers. Such conflicts do not extend below the leadership level, where the troops are held in line with a pseudo-religious fervor. At regular intervals in the series, Cobra Commander stages large ceremonial gatherings of troops with sermon-like speeches.[40] This organizational structure, with elites of varying degrees of expertise and qualifications privately engaged in a realpolitik struggle among themselves for control over an unquestioning and unthinking network of values-enforced loyalty, seems to serve as a parody of the neoliberal currents associated with the deregulation and supply-side economic arguments common in the early 1980s.

In sharp contrast to these internal problems of culture is the value system presented by the G.I. Joe team. Built around an extended family model of shared sacrifice, duty, and the honor of public service, the bonds between the members of the Joe team appear to be deeply personal and professional at the same time. Whereas Cobra suffers heavy losses or leaves comrades behind with little commentary, losses among the Joe team are portrayed as deeply significant and traumatic, such as the death of General Flagg during a Cobra invasion of the Pitt,[41] which results in a somber full-dress-uniform burial ceremony.[42]

Although the internal values of the Joe team are not extended to the public at large, the team members see their service as a part of American democracy. For example, in issue no. 38, members of the Joe team are assigned to rescue Dr. Adele Burkhart, a scientist who repeatedly criticizes the military establishment throughout the series. As the Joes prepare for the mission, Ripcord and Stalker consider her criticism:

RIPCORD. I hear this Dr. Burkhart hates the military and that she's got some far-out political views. In fact, I hear she's against everything we're fighting for!

STALKER. Wrong. What you're fighting for is Burkhart's right and every other American's right to believe in whatever they want to—providing it don't hurt anybody else! Personally, I think Dr. Burkhart is an uppity, self-centered, pretentious old windbag and if I even suspected for one second that our saving her would alter her convictions one iota . . . I'd lose every shred of respect I have for her![43]

The importance of serving the public good and the institutions of the United States remain a consistently expressed value of the Joe organization, even when those institutions or members of the public themselves oppose the Joes' mission. Through its struggle with Cobra, particularly as a military unit supported by government funding, G.I. Joe becomes a symbolic guardian of the military-industrial establishment as well as a protector of national security and the social status quo (loosely connected to "democracy" and "human freedom" in the rhetoric of the characters). This guardianship seems in strong contrast with the claims of Cobra's antiregulatory and chimerical moralistic crusade, particularly when it comes to questions of military trust and service.

Perhaps no moment in the series examines this conflict so starkly as the Cobra invasion of the small town of Millville in *G.I. Joe: ARAH*, vol. 1, no. 100.[44] As Cobra embarks on its scheme to have the citizens turn over their life savings to Cobra in exchange for "a new prosperity! New jobs, new industry, new commerce! All coupled with an end to crime and immorality!,"[45] a US military veteran speaks out, yelling:

> Cobra is a terrorist organization! I'm a veteran and I'm telling you that Cobra stands for everything that American soldiers have shed their blood to stop for two hundred years! You can't sell out your heritage of freedom for job security and free day care![46]

To this challenge, Cobra Commander responds by attacking the veteran's status:

> This low-life is telling you I'm un-American? What nerve! He's probably a chronic unemployable with psychotic tendencies! I'm American as apple pie and motherhood! I believe in free enterprise, that's the American Way.[47]

The dialogue, arguing that pro-business attitudes—and not the public service of military veterans—are the heart of American values, would be a key argument at the core of Hama's writing throughout the series. The veteran is taken away by Cobra troops, but after he is rescued by members of the Joe team, he addresses his fellow citizens again:

> All you kids in my youth program at the community center, you know that if you go out on the street and deal drugs, you can have tons of money, gold chains, fancy cars . . . the only thing you won't have is pride or respect. You rejected that side of street life because you had some sense!

You are now about to learn that same lesson about your basic freedoms! The rights that were your gifts from your forebears ... most people take their liberties for granted. They would gladly trade in the freedoms that were won with blood from Bunker Hill to Gettysburg for cheap promises of security and law and order![48]

Through conflicts between G.I. Joe and Cobra, the struggle between emerging neoliberal values and the postwar center-left consensus generates a clash of values occurring at the heart of the American system. Hama, a veteran, uses his characters to articulate the competing value systems within each ideology base, and in particular their effects on the military establishment and the service-men and servicewomen within. Although Cobra represents the embodiment of the neoliberal approach, with the leveraging of private industry and market competition, this approach consistently leads to a decentering of individual worth, the rejection of honor and tradition in the face of political expediency, and the exchange of duty to the social contract for the passive consumeristic desire for provided security. Although Cobra is labeled a terrorist organization in an attempt to position its threat as external, the clash between it and G.I. Joe reveals the incompatibilities between terrorism and Cobra's ideology, tactics, and goals. Instead, Cobra represents a threat that originates internally, undermining the American social contract by betraying the trust of those who fight to defend the freedoms necessary for a democratic society.

Notes

1. Robin Andersen, *A Century of Media, a Century of War* (New York: Peter Lang, 2007), 243–57.

2. Larry Hama and Herb Trimpe, "Operation: Lady Doomsday," *G.I. Joe: A Real American Hero*, vol. 1, no. 1 (June 1982).

3. Philip Schlesinger, Graham Murdock, and Philip Elliott, *Televising Terrorism: Political Violence in Popular Culture* (London: Comedia, 1983), 158.

4. Antonio Gramsci, *Selections from the Prison Notebooks* (London: Lawrence and Wishart, 1971); and Stuart Hall, Dorothy Hobson, Andrew Lowe, and Paul Willis, eds., *Culture, Media, Language* (London: Hutchinson), 1980.

5. Alexander Clarkson, "Virtual Heroes: Boys, Masculinity and Historical Memory in War Comics," *Thymos: Journal of Boyhood Studies* 2, no. 2 (September 2008): 181.

6. Karen J. Hall, "A Soldier's Body: GI Joe, Hasbro's Great American Hero, and the Symptoms of Empire," *Journal of Popular Culture* 38, no. 1 (2004): 34–54.

7. Larry Hama and Phil Gosier, "A Letter from Snake-Eyes," *G.I. Joe: A Real American Hero*, vol. 1, no. 155 (December 1994): 19–20.

8. Donald F. Roberts, "Children and Commercials: Issues, Evidence, Intervention," in *Learning from Television: Psychological and Educational Research*, ed. Michael J. A. Howe (London: Academic Press, 1983), 112–44.

9. Christopher Irving, "The Swivel-Arm Battle-Grip Revolution: How G.I. Joe Recruited a New Generation of Comic-Book Readers," *Back Issue* 1, no. 16 (June 2006): 15–16.

10. Eric Clark, *The Real Toy Story: Inside the Ruthless Battle for Britain's Youngest Consumers* (London: Random House, 2007), 215–16.

11. In fact, after the series was discontinued in 1994, Dark Horse Comics acquired the license and published two four-issue miniseries in 1995 and 1996. Devil's Due then acquired the license in 2001 and released a four-issue limited series though Image Comics, which grew into an ongoing series of forty-three issues and several limited series before the license expired in 2008. IDW acquired the license in 2008 and began its own series (and continuity) before in 2010 relaunching a second ongoing series as a continuation the Larry Hama storyline with the Marvel series' numbering. Both the IDW continuity and the Hama continuity continue in IDW publication today.

12. John Michlig, *GI Joe: The Complete Story of America's Favorite Man of Action* (San Francisco: Chronicle Books, 1998), 190.

13. Larry Hama and Rod Whigham, "Judgments," *G.I. Joe: A Real American Hero*, vol. 1, no. 38 (August 1985): 6.

14. Hama and Whigham, "Judgments," 7.

15. Larry Hama and Frank Springer, "Beached Whale," *G.I. Joe: A Real American Hero*, vol. 1, no. 29 (November 1984): 5–6.

16. Bruce Hoffman, *Inside Terrorism* (New York: Columbia University Press, 2006); Paul Wilkinson, *Terrorism versus Democracy: The Liberal State Response* (London: Frank Cass, 2001); and Harmonie Toros, "Terrorists, Scholars and Ordinary People: Confronting Terrorism Studies with Field Experiences," *Critical Studies on Terrorism* 1, no. 2 (2008): 279–92.

17. Audrey Kurth Cronin, "Behind the Curve: Globalization and International Terrorism," *International Security* 27, no. 3 (Winter 2002–2003): 33.

18. Larry Hama and Frank Springer, "Celebration!," *G.I. Joe: A Real American Hero*, vol. 1, no. 33 (March 1985): 14.

19. Paul Rogers, *A War on Terror: Afghanistan and After* (London: Pluto, 2004), 156–58.

20. Robert A. Pape, "The Strategic Logic of Suicide Terrorism," *American Political Science Review* 97, no. 3 (August 2003): 344.

21. Brian M. Jenkins, "The Organization Men: Anatomy of a Terrorist Attack," in *How Did This Happen? Terrorism and the New War*, ed. James F. Hoge Jr. and Gideon Rose (New York: Public Affairs, 2001), 13.

22. Arie W. Kruglanski and Shira Fishman, "Terrorism between 'Syndrome' and 'Tool,'" *Current Directions in Psychological Science* 15, no. 1 (February 2006): 45–48; and Lawrence Freedman, "Terrorism as a Strategy," *Government and Opposition* 42, no. 3 (Summer 2007): 314–39.

23. For example, see John Horgan and Michael J. Boyle. "A Case against 'Critical Terrorism Studies,'" *Critical Studies on Terrorism* 1, no. 1 (2008): 56–57; and Michael Stohl, "Old Myths, New Fantasies and the Enduring Realities of Terrorism," *Critical Studies on Terrorism* 1, no. 1 (2008): 5–6.

24. James H. Wittebols, "Media and the Institutional Perspective: U.S. and Canadian Coverage of Terrorism," *Political Communication* 9, no. 4 (1992): 267.

25. Larry Hama and Rod Whigham, "Pit-Fall," *G.I. Joe: A Real American Hero*, vol. 1, no. 53 (November 1986).

26. Larry Hama and Mike Vosburg, "A Nice Little Town Like Ours ...," *G.I. Joe: A Real American Hero*, vol. 1, no. 10 (April 1983): 11.

27. Edward W. Said, *Covering Islam: How the Media and the Experts Determine How We See the Rest of the World* (New York: Pantheon, 1981); Susan M. Akram, "The Aftermath of September 11, 2001: The Targeting of Arabs and Muslims in America," *Arab Studies Quarterly* 24, nos. 2–3 (Spring–Summer 2002): 61–119; and Jack G. Shaheen, *Reel Bad Arabs: How Hollywood Vilifies a People* (New York: Olive Branch), 2001.

28. Gabriel Weimann, "The Theater of Terror: Effects of Press Coverage," *Journal of Communication* 33, no. 1 (March 1983): 38–45.

29. Edward W. Said, *Orientalism* (New York: Vintage, 1978).

30. Larry Hama and Herb Trimpe, "Operation: Wingfield," *G.I. Joe: A Real American Hero*, vol. 1, no. 4 (October 1982).

31. Hama and Trimpe, "Operation: Wingfield," 9.

32. Larry Hama and Mike Vosburg, "Destro Returns!," *G.I. Joe: A Real American Hero*, vol. 1, no. 18 (December 1983).

33. Larry Hama and Ron Garney, "Escalator to Armageddon," *G.I. Joe: A Real American Hero*, vol. 1, no. 110 (March 1991).

34. Herb Trimpe, "Operation: Sea-Strike!," *G.I. Joe: A Real American Hero*, vol. 1, no. 8 (February 1983).

35. For example, see Larry Hama and Marie Severin, "Swampfire!," *G.I. Joe: A Real American Hero*, vol. 1, no. 28 (October 1984).

36. Hama and Vosburg, "A Nice Little Town," 13.

37. Hama and Vosburg, "A Nice Little Town," 16.

38. Larry Hama and Mike Vosburg, "Last Plane from Rio Lindo," *G.I. Joe: A Real American Hero*, vol. 1, no. 13 (July 1983).

39. Larry Hama and Mike Vosburg, "Night Attack!," *G.I. Joe: A Real American Hero*, vol. 1, no. 16 (October 1983), 5.

40. Some prominent examples include Larry Hama and Herb Trimpe, "Walls of Death!," *G.I. Joe: A Real American Hero*, vol. 1, no. 7 (January 1983): 9–10; Larry Hama and Rod Whigham, "The Battle of Springfield," *G.I. Joe: A Real American Hero*, vol. 1, no. 50 (August 1986): 7; and Larry Hama and Andrew Wildman. "The Traitor Strikes!," *G.I. Joe: A Real American Hero*, vol. 1, no. 137 (June 1993).

41. Larry Hama and Mike Vosburg, "Joe Triumphs!," *G.I. Joe: A Real American Hero*, vol. 1, no. 19 (January 1984).

42. Larry Hama and Mike Vosburg, "Like Chimney Sweepers Come to Dust . . .," *G.I. Joe: A Real American Hero*, vol. 1, no. 22 (April 1984): 13–15.

43. Hama and Whigham, "Judgments," 5.

44. Larry Hama and Mark Bright, "Seeds of Empire!," *G.I. Joe: A Real American Hero*, vol. 1, no. 100 (May 1990).

45. Hama and Bright, "Seeds of Empire!," 2.

46. Hama and Bright, "Seeds of Empire!," 11.

47. Hama and Bright, "Seeds of Empire!," 11–12.

48. Larry Hama and Mark Bright, "The New Guard," *G.I. Joe: A Real American Hero*, vol. 1, no. 101 (June 1990): 16.

CHAPTER 29

The Outing of Superman; or, How I Learned to Love Bizarro as a Trans Monster

DAN VENA

BRIAN AZZARELLO AND LEE BERMEJO'S *LEX LUTHOR: MAN OF STEEL* IS AN UN-conventional Superman story. Told exclusively from Lex Luthor's perspective, it presents fans with a sympathetic portrayal of the Metropolis villain, revealing his struggles to understand himself as human in the shadow of a demigod. When explaining his contempt for Superman, Luthor states, "Not a man. Not even close. Yet most accept him like a member of the family. . . . He's made himself appear so much *like* us he has *almost* everyone forgetting he's *not* one of us. Almost."[1] To him, Superman is an alien outsider impeding the progress of humanity with his acts of bravado and control. So reliant has humanity become on the hero to usher them out of crisis, they have forgotten what it means to be human: to struggle for survival. For Luthor, Superman threatens to eradicate the very core of human identity. Bermejo's artwork further serves to demonize the hero; he is drawn with an inhumanly metallic, steel-hard body and glowing red eyes. Here, Superman is illustrated as Luthor knows him to be, as the superhero "ought" to be seen. The striking visuality of Superman's body is presented in the series as the primary signifier of the hero's Otherness. For Luthor, Superman's body is a grotesque parody of the human form; its foreign physiological makeup aligns the hero with the monstrous.

Inspired by the Man of Steel's long-standing foe, this chapter seeks to reaffirm Luthor's emphatic positing of the hero as a monster. Adopting a supervillainous methodology that relishes in the desire to expose, this chapter scrutinizes the imperative to consistently cast the hero as "one of us" while failing to acknowledge the corporeal differences that do in fact make him alien. However, unlike previous interpretations of Superman's Otherness, this chapter adopts a "trans" reading position that attends to the ways in which the figure may come to represent a trans monster.[2] In locating the body as the primary site of difference, a trans reading highlights how these alternative bodily materialities produce markedly different understandings of identity. The imperative then to expose Superman as a trans monster is meant as a validating assertion of cultural space by a trans fan.

In order to out Superman as a trans monster, this project will reconcile with the continued imperative to repress the horrors of the superhero's body, which code him as materially and corporeally Other. Within the comic text, these fears are consistently displaced onto the more visibly abject figure of Bizarro. Often positioned as the superhero's most harmless and inept foe, Bizarro nonetheless retains the power to frighten because of his monstrous appearance. Rather than positioning Bizarro as a figure altogether removed from Superman or as an easy foil for the hero to play against (as is common in comic narratives), I suggest that we understand the villain as the hero's Freudian double, with the former embodying the latter's own unintelligibility. Here, Bizarro signals and enacts what Superman cannot, namely the hero's own profound sense of corporeal otherness, one that is uncannily akin to the ways in which trans bodies defy supposedly "natural" logics of corporeality.

It is important to recognize that the use of the word "trans" within this chapter is meant to signal a preoccupation with material organization that locates the body as the focal point of anxiety. Trans individuals who move across constructed gender lines and/or who use medical intervention to physically alter the body destabilize the firm social investment in a properly sexed subject. In moving across culturally intelligible ideas of female and male, or to another gender location entirely, trans individuals unravel the fabrics of corporeal logic that organize the body around a visibly legible (and always stable) sexual morphology. As prominent trans scholar Susan Stryker points out, the emancipatory monstrosity of the trans body resides in its ability to reorganize material and semiotic relations. Borrowing from Donna Haraway, Stryker describes the promise of the monster as the ability to exceed frames of legibility and representation, in which the monstrous body refuses corporeal stability in favor of multiplicity.[3]

In challenging questions of ontological stability and natural ordering, the trans body has been linked to Mary Shelley's Frankenstein's monster, who similarly represents a categorical crisis (i.e., dead flesh made living). The trend to compare trans persons to Frankenstein's monster was initiated in the late 1970s and early 1980s by radical lesbian feminist scholars Mary Daly and Janice Raymond as a means of delegitimizing trans persons (trans women and trans feminine people in particular) and their gender identities.[4] Under their paradigm, trans persons are positioned as horrific constructions of a hubristic medical system that aims to exploit the very materiality of gender for political profit. For these authors, trans persons are simply objectified human matter who coercively submit to the reshaping of their bodies so that they may fulfill their own fetishistic parodies of the "opposite" gender. In the early 1990s, Stryker penned an emblazoned response to these scholars, reclaiming the subject position of the monster. As she asserts, both her body and that of Frankenstein's monster can be seen as an unnatural construct of science, as "flesh torn apart and sewn together again in a shape other than that in which it was born."[5] She notes how, like the monster, trans persons are also understood as "less than fully human due to the means of [their] embodiment."[6] Yet, instead of resenting this comparison, she relishes it, politically aligning her rage with that of the monster's and suggesting that, like the creature, she too will continue to fight against the very conditions that render her body abject. Thus for Stryker, to be a trans monster is to challenge the very systems of power that define the limits of the (sexed and gendered) body.

LOVE IN THE TIME OF DUPLICATOR RAYS

The allusion to the Frankenstein myth, which frames Stryker's poetic retort, is similarly found in Bizarro's origin story, which can be read as a Space Age interpretation of the gothic novel. Having become a well-known character in the serialized *Superman* newspaper strips, a young version of the blundering supervillain was initially featured in *Superboy*, no. 68 (1958), before adult Bizarro appeared in *Action Comics*, no. 254 (1959). In the latter Golden Age telling, mad scientist Lex Luthor attempts to create a clone of Superman by exposing the hero to a duplicator ray. Conceptualized to be an exact material copy of the hero, the clone is supposed to help Luthor destroy Metropolis and Superman's reputation in the process. However, what is birthed from the ray is an imperfect, "bizarre" imitation of the hero.[7] Equally gifted with Superman's extraordinary abilities and moral determination to aid those in danger, the clone lacks the hero's intelligence, capabilities, and conventional looks. So even though Bizarro eventually chooses to reject Luthor's authority, his frequent attempts at heroism often fail, as the very sight of the creature repulses those he intends to save. Within the world of the comic text, Bizarro's inability to replicate Superman both physically and behaviorally code him as an ersatz duplicate of the original hero.

The desire to understand Bizarro as a failed copy of Superman corresponds to Daly and Raymond's reactionary rhetoric, which argued that trans individuals are simply clones of so-called real women and men. For these two authors, trans persons lack the assumed signs of authenticity (again, either physically or behaviorally) that affirm their claims to a specific gender. Echoes of this attitude carry forward to today—as S. Bear Bergman notes, "the great and terrible truth of transgender life, [is] that they will never let you be real, ever again"—since trans persons are continually positioned as "knock-offs" of the "real thing."[8] Indeed, even Bizarro comes to recognize himself as something altogether Other in opposition to the defined real referent of Superman. In the Golden Age comic, after gazing into a mirror and being repulsed by his own appearance, Bizarro violently smashes the panel and pronounces his own intelligibility: "Me not human . . . Me not creature . . . Me not even animal!"[9] Unable to understand *what* exactly he is, Bizarro similarly perceives himself as failing to approximate the more authentic Superman.

However, when we refract the Bizarro story through a markedly trans lens, we resist the underlying impulse to hierarchize identities based on authenticity. As my villainous plot begins to take shape, I argue that we should not see Bizarro as simply a failed replica of Superman but rather as the hero's Freudian double, an extension of the same identity. Here, I avoid the imperative to vertically rank Bizarro and Superman, with one more genuinely real than the other, and instead locate the two figures along the same horizontal spectrum. As a result, we can begin to trouble the established distinction between Superman as hero and Bizarro as villain and conceptualize both characters as equally monstrous. Figures of categorical crisis, Bizarro and Superman together represent the same unruly and excessive corporeality that the (trans) monster embodies. Seen as a harbinger of definitional confusion, the (trans) monster's form cannot be easily categorized or contained.[10] Similarly, both hero and villain share in this ambiguity, each playing Jekyll to the other's Hyde.

Within Freudian psychoanalysis, the double figures as a twinned representation of the self and a symbolic splitting of the ego; that which is repressed is made physically manifest in the other. Emerging from the depths of the subconscious, the double can be considered an uncanny phenomenon, whereby its emergence signals something that "ought to have remained secret and hidden but has come to light."[11] An allusion to this concept is echoed in James Whale's 1931 cinematic adaptation of Shelley's novel, wherein Dr. Frankenstein states, "So far he's been kept in complete darkness. Wait till I bring him into the light."[12] While almost figuring as an "uncanny" duplicate of Freud's sentiment, the film's dialogue refers explicitly to the monster as expressed by his maker. As established by the Frankensteinian paradigm, the monster can typically be read as a physical manifestation of a disturbing element within its creator, one that repression fails to contain and that must ultimately resurface (be brought into the light).[13]

Using this model, I suggest we disregard the narrative logistics of Bizarro's creation, as he is in fact Lex Luthor's progeny, and instead author him as Superman's double. Sharing in the same genetic makeup, Bizarro and Superman figure more literally as the self divided into two—again, rather than pairing him with Lex Luthor, who rarely maintains any relationship to the creature in the comics. What happens then when we view Bizarro as a physicalization of Superman's own (failed) repression? And what exactly does Bizarro represent within the Man of Steel? What secret is buried inside that Kryptonian unconscious?

I suggest that Bizarro signals and enacts Superman's own sense of corporeal and psychological difference. Where many readers may want to forget or minimize that Superman is an alien among humans, Bizarro makes the otherness of Superman's identity visible. Dead flesh made living, the character is often illustrated as having chalk-white skin that appears to be stone-like in nature and crudely chiseled into shape. Whereas Superman is a sleek, sophisticated Man of Steel, Bizarro is a fumbling creature of poorly etched proportions. We can read the inverted nature of Bizarro's appearance as a solidifying characteristic of the creature as double, since the monster's outward appearance commonly physicalizes the creator's own repressed inner character.[14] Here, the horror of the psyche is projected outward and becomes the horror of the flesh; Bizarro's body is Superman's as it "should" be.

Although character, creator, and reader alike rarely wish to acknowledge it, Superman is in fact an unnatural body brought to life—if, that is, we define "natural" in relation to supposedly normative human morphology and ability. Instead of acknowledging this difference, it is easier to project the fears one may associate with a body that defies logic or containment (Is it a bird? A plane?) onto a creature that stands at a notable physical and behavioral difference from our beloved hero. Yet, the oddity or strangeness of Superman's body can be overlooked (again, the presentation and behavior of the body being key here) because he chooses to use his powers for good rather than for evil. Superman perhaps goes so far as to present a model human, capable of demonstrating the power of humanity through grandiose acts of valor and compassion. However, we can also read these deeds as a continued performance of overcompensation, actions meant to absolve the hero of his own sense of otherness, to make his difference less visible, and to appease particular moral and social norms. It is easier, then, to cast the anxieties one may have about Superman's body onto the hypervisible Bizarro, whose monstrous appearance enables him to become a supposedly "proper" receptacle for exorcising cultural anxieties over excessive bodies. Put simply—Superman can *pass*, while Bizarro cannot.

As understood within the trans community, passing refers to an individual's ability to be consistently read as non-transgender (or cisgender).[15] Under this model, the onus is problematically placed upon the transitioning individual to conform to an established social script of acceptable gender presentations and behaviors (rather than to dismantle the oppressive conditions of gender and sex in the first place). By comparison, Bizarro can be read as failing to perform hero correctly and is thus consequently outed as a villain and as a monster. Try as he might, because of his appearance and his actions (Bizarro often fails at saving the day), he stands out as the opposite of the more conventional Superman. Similarly, trans individuals who cannot or do not want to conform to normative expressions of gender are also maligned as visibly Other and as failing to embody normative gender categories. One's trans status thus becomes deeply enmeshed with the visuality of the body, the assumption being that one can always tell who is and who is not transgender. The same can be said of Bizarro, whose appearance and haphazard attempts at heroism immediately code him as foe, regardless of his own understanding of his identity.

For instance, in John Byrne's 1986 *Superman* reboot, *The Man of Steel*, Bizarro understands himself not as a duplicate of Superman but that he in fact *is* Superman, and, accordingly, attempts to rescue ill-fated citizens of Metropolis.[16] The title of the comic's fifth issue, "The Beast Within," further highlights a preoccupation with doubling and identity, as we can read Bizarro as the "beast" within Superman. Indeed, even the central plot device revolves around visuality and perception; Bizarro eventually rescues a blind Lucy Lane (Lois's sister), who is moments away from stepping off a roof ledge in an attempt to take her own life. Assuming that Superman has saved her, Lucy swoons over the hero until it is later revealed that in fact a bizarre, lookalike creature rescued her. Although distressed over potentially lusting after a monster, Lucy admits that coming into contact with Bizarro's dust-like skin has returned some of her vision.[17] Bizarro, upon overhearing Lucy's admission, engages Superman in a battle to the death in order to save his newly beloved. Laid overtop the final panel, in which Superman and Bizarro collide, is the text "Shoom," which can be read as a conscious effort not to depict the violence of Bizarro's final moments. However, the buildup to the panel, in which both figures are dramatically positioned at a distance from each other on the same linear plane, also allows one to read the scene's last panel as the final melding of Superman and Bizarro. It thus may appear that hero triumphs over monster by successfully and forcibly repressing the psychic horrors of the former's own otherness, but the panel's ambiguity also serves to hide the horrors of psychic repression: through his physical destruction of Bizarro, Superman himself becomes the violent monster.

Shattered into tiny particles of dust by the hero's might, Bizarro knowingly sacrifices himself so that Lucy's vision may be restored. The motif of visibility, or rather recognition as visibility, which is played out in Byrne's series is also a staple motif of the *Superman* narrative in general: Clark Kent must wear glasses to disguise himself, Superman has X-ray vision, and Lois's journalistic pursuits involve unmasking the truth. However, in Byrne's text, the importance of vision is specifically linked to the idea of identity and monstrosity. Here, Lucy's blindness allows for a temporary acceptance of the monster and his body.[18] She "sees" his authentic inner self, only to be deceived later by the exterior body

Bizarro himself feels trapped within. The trans rhetoric of being "born into the wrong body" is palpable here, but so is the countertrope of deception in which the trans individual is blamed for the supposedly "false" presentation of the body, which may be performed as one gender but maintain the morphological characteristics of the other sex (if we adhere to a strict binary).

Within the world of the comic, then, we may read Bizarro as a physical manifestation of Superman's own closeted identity. While the hero's body may seem more human (certainly more human than Bizarro's), it is in fact alien and unknowable. Yet, when you strip away the cape, perhaps in a heated moment of intimacy, the difference of his body becomes hard to conceal. In a hyperbolic satire of such a moment, James Niven's "Man of Steel, Woman of Kleenex" exposes the horrific consequences of having a super body in bed. The author notes: "Consider the driving urge between a man and a woman, the monomaniacal urge to achieve greater and greater penetration. Remember also that we are dealing with Kryptonian muscles. Superman would literally crush Lois Lane's body in his arms, while simultaneously ripping her open from crotch to sternum, gutting her like a trout."[19] This visceral detailing of Superman's sexual intimacy positions the hero in a grotesque light. His figurative ravaging of Lois can be read as proof that difference (as signaled by his alien origins) destroys normality. The body then becomes part of Superman's larger deception: posing as Clark, we understand him to be human and to experience the body as a human, but Superman and the ability of his body cannot and do not abide by human understandings of physiology. The unintelligible nature of the monstrous or excessive body is thus exacerbated by its engagement with another; not only is fear a reaction to seeing the monster, it is also a response to witnessing what Bizarro/Superman does or rather who they do "it" with. Within Bizarro's narrative, the creature is often, perhaps ironically, treated as a benign, asexual being who seeks companionship more than carnal intimacy (staying consistent with the virginal overtones of the Superman franchise). However, Niven certainly conceptualizes Superman's sexuality as altogether abject and terrorizing; in this rendition, Superman *is* the monster.

Whether it is Superman's encounter with Lois or Bizarro's exchange with Lucy, engaging in the act of intimacy "outs" the body as something other than that which it originally appears to be. For trans individuals, to engage with a lover similarly requires one to reveal the supposed truth of their identity via the body. To physically expose the body is to expose the self, or rather one's past self. For trans folks, the placement of scars on the body or the presence or lack of certain sexual organs often act as subtle or obvious "giveaways" of one's birth-assigned sex. So to put one's body on display in front of a lover is therefore to be placed in a compromising and deeply vulnerable position, wherein one opens oneself up to ridicule, hostility, or violence. Into the hands of the other is given the ability to either authenticate the trans individual's identity or to reject the presentation of the body outright, thereby rendering the trans person as a so-called "fake" or "liar." Much like in Byrne's retelling of Bizarro's origins, the other often wields the power to either make or (literally) break the individual (as the case may be). In the comic, Lucy, although first disgusted by the creature, comes to recognize him as a hero.[20] She confirms who Bizarro knows himself to be: Superman.

Here, monster and hero finally merge into one another; unable to be divorced from each other, Bizarro and Superman figure as extensions of the same identity. By positing Bizarro as Superman's Freudian double (and vice versa), I resist the persistent urge to stabilize the hero's indeterminate physiology and identity via the creature's more visibly excessive corporeality.[21] I argue that a trans reading of these figures actively works against clean categorization and hierarchical opposition in favor of destabilization (a favorite tool of the supervillain trade). To read Bizarro and Superman through a trans lens is to therefore open oneself up to the chaos of monstrosity and multiplicity.[22]

Notes

1. Brian Azzarello and Lee Bermejo, *Lex Luthor: Man of Steel* (New York: DC Comics, 2005), n.p.

2. To clarify, the term "outing" is used here in a reclamatory fashion by a trans-identified author who recognizes in Superman a shared experience of corporeal otherness. The Luthor-inspired project of "outing" Superman as a monster stems from a larger body of work that aims to "trans" (rather than queer) the Superman narrative. See Dan Vena, "How to Build a Transsexual Superman: A 'Reading-Together' of Superman's Emergence alongside Histories of Eugenic Science and Gender Confirmation Surgeries," *Studies in the Fantastic*, no. 4 (Winter–Spring 2016–2017). Also see Dan Vena, "Rereading Superman as a Trans F/Man," *Transformative Works and Cultures*, no. 25 (2017), available at https://journal.transformativeworks.org/index.php/twc/article/view/1063/859.

3. See Donna Haraway, "The Promise of Monsters: A Regenerative Politics for Inappropriate/d Others," in *Cultural Studies*, ed. Lawrence Grossberg, Cary Nelson, and Paula A. Treichler (New York: Routledge, 1992), 295–337.

4. See Mary Daly, *Gyn/ecology: The Metaethics of Radical Feminism* (Boston: Beacon Press, 1978); and Janice Raymond, *The Transsexual Empire: The Making of the She-Male* (London: Women's Press, 1980).

5. Susan Stryker, "My Words to Victor Frankenstein above the Village of Chamounix: Performing Transgender Rage," in *The Transgender Studies Reader*, ed. Susan Stryker and Stephen Whittle (New York: Routledge, 2006), 245.

6. Stryker, "My Words to Victor Frankenstein."

7. Otto Binder and Al Plastino, "The Battle with Bizarro," in *Superman in the Fifties* (New York: DC Comics, 2002), 130; originally published in *Action Comics*, no. 254 (July 1959).

8. S. Bear Bergman, *The Nearest Exit Is Behind You* (Vancouver: Arsenal Pulp Press, 2009), 72–73.

9. Binder and Plastino, "The Battle with Bizarro," 130.

10. In fact, Bizarro himself oscillates pronoun usage, whereby he is referred to as both "him" and "it" in the comics.

11. Sigmund Freud, "The Uncanny," in *The Standard Edition of the Complete Psychological Works of Sigmund Freud*, vol. 17 (1917–1919), *"An Infantile Neurosis" and Other Works*, trans. James Strachey (New York: Vintage Classics, 2001), 240.

12. James Whale, dir., *Frankenstein* (1931; Universal City, CA: Universal Pictures, 2014), Blu-Ray.

13. Franco Moretti, *Signs Taken for Wonders: Essays in the Sociology of Literary Forms*, trans. Susan Fischer, David Forgacs, and David Miller (London: Verso, 1983), 102–3.

14. Abigail Lee Six and Hannah Thompson, "From Hideous to Hedonist: The Changing Face of the Nineteenth-Century Monster," in *The Ashgate Research Companion to Monsters and the Monstrous*, ed. Asa Simon Mittman with Peter J. Dendle (Burlington, VT: Ashgate, 2012), 240.

15. The concept of passing has a lengthier history than can be discussed here, especially in relation to race, ethnicity, and nationalism. Due to these histories, the supposed "success" of a trans individual to pass as non-transgender or to be read as cisgender is always tied to larger intersecting axes of identity including but not limited to race, class, and ability.

16. In Byrne's miniseries, Bizarro is given a new origin story. Here, the creature is an imperfect clone fashioned from Superman's DNA, not a duplicating ray. See John Byrne and Dick Giordano, *The Man of Steel*, no. 5 (December 1986).

17. This plot point is taken from *Superboy*, no. 68 (November 1958).

18. This trope can again be traced to Shelley's novel, specifically the moment when the creature is temporarily taken in and schooled by a blind patriarch. It is only after the elderly man's children catch the two interacting (and explain to their father what the creature looks like) that the man shuns the monster.

19. Larry Niven, "Man of Steel, Woman of Kleenex," in *All the Myriad Ways* (New York: Ballantine, 1971), III, available at http://www.rawbw.com/~svw/superman.html.

20. The particular moment of having the self recognized and validated through the Other's eyes is not unfamiliar to the Superman mythos. In an earlier Golden Age comic (*Superman*, no. 96), Superman meets a young girl who, because of her lack of sight, refuses to believe in his existence. The hero then takes it upon himself to restore the girl's vision so that he may prove his own existence.

21. See Clare Pitkethly, "The Pursuit of Identity in the Face of Paradox: Indeterminacy, Structure and Repetition in Superman, Batman and Wonder Woman," *Journal of Graphic Novels and Comics* 3, no. 2 (2012): 216.

22. A draft of this work was originally completed under the supervision of Dr. Jane Tolmie. Thanks goes to Dr. Tolmie and also to Dr. Eleanor MacDonald, who both provided sage guidance and support throughout the writing process. As well as to Robin Alex McDonald for the extra pair of eyes. The duration during which the original draft of this work was completed was funded through Canada's Social Science and Humanities Research Council.

CHAPTER 30

A Darker Truth Underneath

Bucky Barnes and Captain America

NAJA LATER

CAPTAIN AMERICA HAS BECOME A METONYM FOR THE HEROIC IDEAL. HIS TITULAR connection to the American nation risks the conflation of superheroism with American self-righteousness, exceptionalism, and nationalism.[1] Tension between the genre's conventions and its intrinsic political context forces *Captain America* narratives to present both self-reflexively. In embodying the superheroic ideal of America, Captain America—aka Steve Rogers—must always be better than America itself. This distinction is necessary for the narrative of American progress and functions to some degree to distance Rogers as a war hero from the villainy committed by the United States in foreign affairs. However, the process of establishing this distinction necessitates Rogers's reflection upon wrongs committed by his country and, accordingly, by himself. Rogers's capacity for doubt and self-reflection are strong markers of his heroism and offer more productive ways of discussing heroism and Americanism critically than reading Rogers in total opposition to his foreign nemeses.

This self-reflexivity occurs often in *Captain America*'s history: one of the longest-running arcs to bring it to the surface is that of Bucky, Rogers's Golden Age sidekick.[2] Stories of Bucky from the Silver Age to his revival as the Winter Soldier in the 2000s create a far darker context for Rogers's history as a war hero.[3] Bucky's identity shifts from boy sidekick to child assassin; from mind-controlled villain to antihero; from tragic backstory to reluctant inheritor of the Captain America title. This is possible through a liminal fluidity intrinsic to the sidekick figure, whose unfixity destabilizes the hero in more complex ways than an oppositional hero-villain dichotomy. The influence of Bucky's instability on Rogers consequently muddies the political narratives that similarly uphold America's fabled virtuousness, especially in times of war.

Bucky's narrative deconstructs the archetypes of the genre to challenge the conflation of (Captain) America and heroism, highlighting the significance of the sidekick and the antihero to expose the potential for villainy in America's mythic identity.

The ambivalence and complexity of Captain America operates in relation to his reputation as an exemplary "good" superhero. Christopher Robichaud argues that Captain America is known to be a paragon, a boy scout, and a moral exemplar.[4] He does not appear to operate in shades of gray—only red, white, and blue. On the pages of Marvel comics, Rogers is a pillar of the superhero community, memorialized by teammates not only as "one of the greats," but "the greatest."[5] The film *Captain America: The First Avenger* (2011) is hinged on the premise that Steve Rogers is the perfect supersoldier because he is "a good man": his goodness is simply an innate, unshakeable trait that uniquely qualifies him for superheroism.[6] However, this leads to an ethically troubling and narratively boring tautology: Steve Rogers is Captain America because he is good, and he is good because he is Captain America.[7] It echoes a nationalist logic that America is good because it fights bad people, and people who fight America are bad. Robichaud's study of moral relativism accounts for a slightly more complex view of Rogers's moral program: in these difficult times, Rogers's steadfast commitment to his classic virtuousness is even more admirable. Robichaud claims that Rogers's "struggles to wrest moral knowledge from the world prove no less heroic and difficult than [his] physical struggles in battling the bad guys."[8] While Robichaud oversimplifies the rich and complicated history of both American politics and comics in the 1960s, the argument that Rogers's heroism is not innate but a challenging and continuing process is sound. A closer look at *Captain America* comics evidences decades of struggle with the righteousness of both Rogers's and America's causes. These struggles are often played out in ways that deconstruct the conventions of the superhero narrative: in so doing, these comics are using Captain America to challenge dominant American narratives.

A popular method of quantifying Rogers's heroism in scholarship is by analyzing the relative moral positions of his allies and enemies. While this can lead down the tautological route—Hitler bad; guy who punches Hitler, good— examples abound in which the supporting characters of *Captain America* are used to challenge and complicate the conventions of heroism and villainy.[9] Christian Steinmetz and Neal Curtis have both applied this methodology effectively, though neither give close attention to Bucky.[10] I argue that Bucky is highly valuable to consider due to his historical role as an archetypal sidekick. Every iteration of Bucky since the Golden Age converses with the dominant narratives of both comics and politics, inviting but also sabotaging the cultural memory that upholds the fixity of good and evil. This creates a highly self-reflexive engagement with the generic lore of the superhero, prompting a corresponding engagement with the lore of American nationhood.

The radical dysfunction that Bucky causes begins in 1964, in Stan Lee and Jack Kirby's *Avengers*, no. 4.[11] Lee's proclaimed hatred of sidekicks resulted in a famous—and endlessly reiterated—scene in which Bucky is not only killed off, but shown to *have been* killed off in 1945.[12] This move initially appears to be an ironic departure from the straight-faced camp of the Golden Age's mythic formula. The Silver Age, as with every age of comics, worked consciously to right the wrongs of its predecessors: sometimes by cleaning up the challenging content that led to the Golden Age's downfall, but often by scratching its squeaky-clean surface with rich irony. Rogers's 1964 revival as a more cynical Cap seems at first glance to be conditional upon the absence of Bucky's *gee-whiz* hijinks. This interpretation assumes that the sidekick's narrative function was to galvanize the wholesomeness of the hero. Bucky's hero worship models the presumed young-male reader's interpretation of Cap, while his youthful innocence rubs off on the hero. Neil Shyminsky critically assesses this as the sidekick's "discursive work," in which the sidekick may reaffirm the superhero's archetypal qualities.[13] Shyminsky's study focuses on reading queerness and masculinity in the hero and sidekick, describing how, through the sidekick, the hero is "made to seem more potent, masculine, and unassailable."[14] The Campbellian types of "hero" and "helper" ostensibly serve mutually affirming roles; however, according to Shyminsky, the sidekick's duty as a narrative fulcrum Others himself and the hero in significant ways.[15] Steinmetz notes that Bucky's hero-affirming work was received uncritically during the Golden Age.[16] This would seem to have informed Lee's distaste for Bucky when he complicated Marvel heroes in the Silver Age, but equally likely in motivating Bucky's demise was the industry-crushing moral panic centered on comics and the vulnerability of young boys in the 1950s.[17] Steinmetz describes how Bucky's active, gun-toting role in the battlefield became morally questionable; Shyminsky cites the homoerotic reading of the sidekick as a factor in the scorched-earth censorship of the 1950s.[18] These dual readings demonstrate how, even in the bold primary colors of the Golden Age, memory of the sidekick slips between innocence and corruption, destabilizing in the process the moral health of the hero.[19]

In spite of Bucky's death being such a fixture in superhero lore, Lee in no way annihilated Bucky. Bucky had not appeared in comics for a decade when Lee reintroduced him with a cataclysmic flashback, and Lee's subsequent work on both *Avengers* and *Captain America* feature Bucky incessantly through flashbacks and memories.[20] Bucky becomes Rogers's motivation, his weakness, and the vessel for Rogers's empathic availability to readers—the latter one of the biggest ongoing risks in writing Cap. Robert G. Weiner details the colossal impact Bucky has on Rogers's psyche, assessing Rogers's symptoms of posttraumatic stress disorder as a definitive element of the character since the Silver Age.[21] When Lee removes Bucky as a sidekick, he shifts Bucky into the new archetypal role of "refrigerated" girlfriend.[22] In *Tales of Suspense*, though, Lee was writing new stories of Cap's wartime adventures with Bucky in classic sidekick form.[23] Bucky's absence was emphasized through his lingering, liminal presence that haunted Rogers throughout the Silver Age. This allows Rogers to self-reflexively agonize over the ethical quandary of sidekicks, expressing guilt over his own role in allowing a child to accompany him in a war zone: what Weiner emphasizes as "the responsibility he felt for Bucky's death."[24] Meanwhile, in the pages of *Tales of Suspense*, Bucky has transformed from tween to teen, armed to the teeth and never without his tommy gun. In flashbacks since the Silver Age, Bucky—if he appears at all—follows this trajectory of growing grittier and more cynical.[25] Some examples use this to contemptuously overwrite the light-hearted camp of the Golden Age, while others confront the strict conventions of superhero verisimilitude surrounding the superhero's accountability. Rogers frequently voices his guilt in *Avengers* comics beginning from 1964, with a more thorough reflection in *Captain America*, no. 105, in 1968:

> He *begged* me to let him be my partner . . . and I *agreed!* I should have known *better!* My life was *dangerous!* I lived . . . and *still* live . . . with *death* dogging my heels at every *second!* I had *no right* to ask him to share the hazards![26]

By 1990, Rogers was lamenting: "[V]iewed with the clarity of hindsight, it seems pretty irresponsible of us to have had kid partners at all."[27] Bucky remains at the margins of *Captain America* for forty years, a terrible reminder that the greatest of heroes can be wrong. As Marvel's most iconic sidekick slips into the liminal, his continuing power as Rogers's fulcrum leverages Marvel's most virtuous hero into equally liminal zones.

While Robichaud would claim that these expressions of doubt demonstrate Rogers's moral goodness through the virtuous practice of self-criticism, I argue that this happens due to an always already problematic dynamic in the superhero metamyth. When the superhero is placed at the extreme of a spectrum, the opposite end of which has the supervillain, there appears the problem of where to place the sidekick, a curiosity here manifested in the liminal persistence of Bucky after his death. It would be easy to claim that Bucky is more interesting as a ghost, and later an antihero, but his character is so effective precisely *because* of the sidekick's much-derided role and the troubling ambiguity it holds. Shyminsky identifies this as a fundamental generic problem, in which the sidekick exposes fault lines in "the *entire* tradition of masked superheroes."[28] The attempt to banish Bucky in the Silver Age only increases his power of liminality, where he takes on a surprisingly gothic capacity to trouble normative boundaries. Rogers's persistent longing and guilt over Bucky draws him into the moral grays that jeopardize a straightforward correspondence to the virtuous characterization of Americana that he ostensibly represents.

Bucky finally returns from the dead in Ed Brubaker's 2005–2012 run of *Captain America*.[29] Brubaker's writing reintegrates the many facets of Bucky: the rosy-cheeked boy of the Golden Age, the teenage scrapper from *Tales of Suspense*, and the Bucky that wasn't dead in 1945.[30] Brubaker's run begins by revising the Golden Age Bucky as a facade for the sake of propaganda.[31] In a chilling flashback, Rogers narrates Bucky's "real" origin story:

> The official story said he was a symbol to counter the rise of Hitler Youth . . . and there was *some* truth to that, but like all things in war, there was a *darker* truth underneath. Bucky did the things I *couldn't*. I was the icon. I wore the *flag* . . . but while I gave speeches to the troops in the trenches . . . he was doing what he'd been trained to do . . . and he was *highly* trained.[32]

Steve Epting's art shows a teenage Bucky slashing the throat of one Nazi; throwing a knife into the back of another; and garroting a third. This is an extreme example of the argument Shyminsky presents:

> The transgressions of the sidekick are possible and even acceptable because the sidekick, as a hero-in-training or non-hero, is never totally familiar with the conventions of heroism and often deviates from the conventionally correct course of action in a way that the hero never would or could.[33]

This thesis could remain intact, were it not for the catastrophic shattering of both Bucky's and Rogers's identities that followed. Brubaker's revision of the sidekick as child assassin leads to the greater revelation that Bucky's body was found and resuscitated by the Russians in 1945.[34] Having lost his memories, Bucky was retrained as the Winter Soldier and worked as their assassin. Cryogenically frozen when he wasn't needed, Bucky operated covertly throughout the Cold War until, in 2005, he encountered Rogers for the first time in fifty years.[35] Rogers—himself suffering memory problems surrounding Bucky's death—restored Bucky's memories, but a guilt-ridden Bucky remained hidden in the shadows as an antihero.[36] Rogers was assassinated in 2007, before they could reconcile, and Bucky uncertainly took up the mantle of Captain America. When Rogers was revived, Bucky reluctantly continued with his blessing, until being placed on trial for war crimes and faking his own death, returning to the margins as a spy. This arc catapults Bucky from sidekick to villain, to antihero to hero, and back to antihero, stopping by child soldier and Russian assassin along the way. When Bucky takes the shield, the hero and sidekick-villain-antihero occupy a single body, epitomizing the sidekick's potential to unfix the categories surrounding him. Although Rogers claims that young Bucky "did the things I *couldn't*," Rogers's success as Captain America is contingent upon not only a sidekick cleaning up his image but a sidekick cleaning up after him. Even as modern-day Bucky continues his hero-worship of Rogers, the "darker truth" exposes how Bucky's violence has always drawn Rogers into troubling acts of duplicity and complicity.

Brubaker's arc foregrounds the wartime context that may always be read in *Captain America*, connecting Cap's World War II origins with the Cold War and overshadowing both with the contemporary War on Terror. The moral grays that Rogers has wrestled with surrounding Bucky thus far correspond to the morally questionable military and intelligence strategies of the United States during the Cold War and the War on Terror. As Brubaker explores the continuity of *Captain America*, it highlights an uncomfortable consequentiality between these three wars: this tension over continuity and inconsequentiality is described by J. Richard Stevens as reflective of a fundamental struggle of superhero seriality.[37] America's self-characterization as the righteous side relies on a narrative *dis*continuity in American history—that each war bears no consequence—but Brubaker weaves consequence through both comics storytelling and political history. Bucky's Russian handlers, Vasily Karpov and Aleksander Lukin, were survivors of a World War II attack on their village by the Nazis.[38] Rogers and Bucky failed to stop the attack, triggering the chain of events that lead to Karpov and Lukin weaponizing Bucky against Rogers. In 2005, Lukin grudgingly teams up with Cap's World War II Nazi nemesis the Red Skull, taking advantage of random terrorist cells to bomb East Coast cities and destabilize the American public's faith in Rogers.[39] This political continuity draws uncomfortable connections between the aftermath of World War II and the rise of communism, and between US interventions in the Middle East and the rise of dictators and terrorist factions. The revelation that Bucky was alive as an assassin in the 1960s demands a reexamination of the Silver Age's political backdrop: the Cold War as indirect, invisible, violent, and unconscionable. This narrative stains the collective memory of World War II as a "good" war, an ideology Matthew Vernon interrogates in his study of the *Captain America* films.[40] Vernon criticizes the myth that American involvement in World War II was virtuous, patriotic, defensive, and bloodless.[41] This nostalgic ideal, Vernon argues, is used to justify involvement in present wars as a potential to course correct and return to "the heroic narrative of twentieth-century American international interventions."[42] Vernon highlights how this narrative was formed by a strategic "memory and storytelling," discussing how the *Captain America* movies and the character of Rogers both engage—at first uncritically, and later subversively—with how strategic nostalgia is a duplicitous act of the state.[43]

Rogers is repeatedly forced to examine his complicity, accountability, and responsibility, catalyzed by the problematic sidekick returning to the fore.[44] Wrenched from the mythic innocence and virtue Jason Dittmer describes, Rogers is forced to confront hard truths about his and his nation's role in the Cold War and World War II.[45] The highly affective and frustrated relationship between Rogers and Bucky from 2005 to 2007 articulates the myopic characterization of America as an innocent victim of terror.[46] Dittmer studies how, from 2001 to 2004, *Captain America* comics attempt to participate in this jingoistic narrative, but Brubaker's reintroduction of Bucky demonstrates the growing cynicism and instability of this myth, instead looking inward at the deep-seated problems of America, war, and heroism.[47] The Winter Soldier's bombing of Philadelphia is due in part to Rogers's failure to assume responsibility and recognize the political consequences of his interference as a foreign agent, a problem seldom acknowledged by superhero verisimilitude or US political figures.[48] Rogers's use of Bucky's secret role as his left hand makes a neat allegory for the frequent US involvement in proxy wars. That Bucky's training would later be used against the United States is a recurring consequence of US intervention, particularly that which led up to the rise of the Taliban. Even this narrative being contingent on Bucky's loss of memory is a scathing criticism of cultural memory's malleability surrounding the US narrativization of its war history.

Rogers's and Bucky's corrupted memories problematize the "Golden Age" of both comics and the real World War II, confronting a challenging truth: that America's cultural memory of that war has been molded into a narrative of good versus evil. Vernon describes "memory politics" as the key challenge the Winter Soldier presents, when the return of these memories "threatens to supplant the cogency of the prevailing narrative."[49] Rogers's narration recontextualizes the diegesis of the Golden Age as propaganda, directly acknowledging what Vernon calls "the informational potential of the state which rapidly accelerated through [World War II] and became a major part of the US government's strategy in the Cold War."[50] America—and the Captain America that is *better than* America—trained and employed a child soldier to do the state's dirty work while promoting a heroic cover story that mythologized the nation.[51] Rogers becomes, retrospectively, an antihero at best, demonstrating the capacity Shyminsky describes for the sidekick's fluidity to reorient the superhero.[52] As Rogers is drawn closer to Bucky, the dynamic between them casts him as villain, and even when he may be redeemed or forgiven, the nation he represents may not. The more Rogers's and Bucky's memories are restored, the further their narratives grow from the mythology of patriotism.

Bucky is the catalyst that forces us to reread the considerable distance between the surface narrative of heroism and the darker truth underneath. The inevitable political context of *Captain America* makes the comic a productive site for reading the subversive potential of the sidekick to unsettle other generic archetypes and their ideological functions. The dysfunctions and fissures that Bucky's difficult history exposes in conventional superhero storytelling are applied to the contentious status of collective memory and the political narrative of America. Complex continuity between the Golden Age, the Silver Age, and current comics collides with inconvenient truths between the contemporary wars they reflect. Through Bucky, we see a far more challenging narrative of good and evil than can be drawn between superhero and villain; or between America and its enemies. Bucky heralds the confronting truth that villainy cannot be isolated to foreign bodies: instead, it is a consequence and contingency of the narrative of American heroism.

Notes

1. The relationship between Captain America and national identity is researched by Jason Dittmer, with particular attention to the post-9/11 context. This chapter uses Dittmer's framework of reading Steve Rogers's allegorical potential as difficult and fluctuating, but pays particular attention to how the sidekick figure of Bucky causes many of these difficulties. Jason Dittmer, "Captain America's Empire: Reflections on Identity, Popular Culture, and Post-9/11 Geopolitics," *Annals of the Association of American Geographers* 95, no. 3 (2005): 626–43.

2. James Buchanan "Bucky" Barnes's shifting identity means that he uses a number of names fluidly. "Bucky" is both his civilian name and his sidekick identity; for purposes of clarity, I will refer to the character as "Bucky" throughout.

3. This chapter focuses on Marvel comics' main Earth-616 universe and the scripting of those comics. While many talented artists, Jack Kirby foremost among them, contribute to the self-reflexive generic and political criticisms being researched, they occur in a significantly different context, which would benefit from being the primary case study of a later work.

4. Christopher Robichaud, "Bright Colors, Dark Times," in *Supervillains and Philosophy: Sometimes, Evil Is Its Own Reward*, ed. Ben Dyer (Chicago: Open Court, 2009), 61, 70.

5. Jeph Loeb, Ed McGuinness, Dexter Vines, and Jason Keith, *Fallen Son: The Death of Captain America*, no. 2 (June 2007).

6. While Rogers's sketchy ethical framework sees relatively little challenge in the first film, Matthew Vernon provides an excellent analysis of how *Captain America: The Winter Soldier* (2014) prompts critical reflection upon the development of the character. Joe Johnston, dir., *Captain America: The First Avenger* (Marvel Studios, 2011); Anthony Russo and Joe Russo, *Captain America: The Winter Soldier* (Marvel Studios, 2014); and Matthew Vernon, "Subversive Nostalgia, or Captain America at the Museum," *Journal of Popular Culture* 49, no. 1 (2016): 116–35.

7. And, as we know, only a Sith deals in absolutes.

8. Robichaud, "Bright Colors, Dark Times," 70.

9. This being said, *Captain America* comics and US politics in 2016 indicate that the rudimentary analysis "Hitler bad" could afford to be restated in stronger terms.

10. Neal Curtis, *Sovereignty and Superheroes* (Manchester: Manchester University Press, 2016), 35; and Christian Steinmetz, "A Genealogy of Evil: Captain America vs. the Shadows of the National Imagined Community," in *Captain America and the Struggle of the Superhero: Critical Essays*, ed. Robert G. Weiner (Jefferson, NC: McFarland, 2009).

11. Stan Lee, Jack Kirby, George Roussos, and Stan Goldberg, *Avengers*, no. 4 (March 1964).

12. Stan Lee, *Origins of Marvel Comics* (New York: Simon and Schuster, 1974), 17.

13. Neil Shyminsky, "'Gay' Sidekicks: Queer Anxiety and the Narrative Straightening of the Superhero," *Men and Masculinities* 14, no. 3 (2011): 289.

14. Shyminsky, "'Gay' Sidekicks," 298.

15. Shyminsky, "'Gay' Sidekicks," 290, 298.

16. Christian Steinmetz, "A Genealogy of Absence and Evil: Tracing the Nation's Borders with Captain America," master's thesis, Georgia State University, 2008, 47.

17. David Hajdu, *The Ten-Cent Plague: The Great Comic-Book Scare and How It Changed America* (New York: Farrar, Straus and Giroux, 2008).

18. Steinmetz, "A Genealogy of Absence and Evil," 47; Shyminsky, "'Gay' Sidekicks," 293–94.

19. Robert G. Weiner demonstrates that Rogers's mental health is impacted as heavily as his moral health by the trauma of losing Bucky. Weiner's study of the later Winter Soldier arc details Rogers's corrupted memories of Bucky: this usefully reflects such disparate readings in the collective memory of the Golden Age. Robert G. Weiner, "Sixty-Five Years of Guilt over the Death of Bucky," in *Captain America and the Struggle of the Superhero: Critical Essays*, ed. Robert G. Weiner (Jefferson, NC: McFarland, 2009).

20. These are but a few examples of Lee's 1960s comics that feature Bucky: Stan Lee, Don Heck, Dick Ayers, Chick Stone, and Stan Goldberg, *Avengers*, nos. 7, 9 (August–October 1964); and Stan Lee, Jack Kirby, Dan Adkins, and Syd Shores, *Captain America*, nos. 105, 107 (September–November 1968).

21. Weiner, "Sixty-Five Years of Guilt," n.p.

22. Gail Simone coined the term "women in refrigerators" to describe the trope of killing a superhero's first romantic interest as a way of developing his character. Bucky mirrors this trope in all but an overtly romantic backstory, and his shift from sidekick to possible former lover is one of many examples of his slippery roles that compromise Rogers. Indeed, Rogers's feelings over Bucky are often directly positioned as the reason for his romantic failures with women, as Weiner notes. Gail Simone, "Women in Refrigerators," March 1999, available at http://www.lby3.com/wir/index.html; Weiner, "Sixty-Five Years of Guilt," n.p.

23. Stan Lee, Jack Kirby, et al., *Tales of Suspense*, nos. 63–65, 67, 69–71, 75, 82 (November 1964–October 1966).

24. Mark Waid, Doug Braithwaite, Anthony Williams, Dan Green, Scott Koblish, and Matt Hicks, *Captain America: Sentinel of Liberty*, no. 12 (August 1999).

25. Weiner, "Sixty-Five Years of Guilt," n.p.

26. Lee et al., *Captain America*, no. 105.

27. J. Richard Stevens claims that this is "the first time Cap critically considers his own earlier texts"—but it was only the first time he did it so candidly. J. Richard Stevens, *Captain America, Masculinity, and Violence: The Evolution of a National Icon* (Syracuse, NY: Syracuse University Press, 2015), 200; and John Byrne, Paul Ryan, and Bob Sharen, *Avengers West Coast*, no. 56 (March 1990).

28. Shyminsky, "'Gay' Sidekicks," 304.

29. Ed Brubaker, Steve Epting, Michael Lark, Mike Perkins, Butch Guice, Luke Ross, Frank D'Armata, Mitch Breitweiser, Mike Deodato, and Chris Samnee, *Captain America*, nos. 1–50, 600–619 (January 2005–August 2011).

30. Brubaker also revives, at least implicitly, Lee's subtext of Bucky being Rogers's long-lost lover. This further problematizes a reading of Rogers as a straightforward—and straight—ideal of the American superhero. Michael Buso presents a study of how supervillains are often queer-coded to oppose a morally upright, heterosexual hero, and how this dichotomy is queered and subverted. The correspondence in the conservative American narrative between heterosexuality and virtue makes the queer subtext of *Captain America* a fascinating example of how Rogers and Bucky complicate the mythology of American history, while their implicit intimacy emphasizes the

influence Bucky has over Rogers. Michael Buso, "A Dark, Uncertain Fate: Homophobia, Graphic Novels, and Queer Identity," master's thesis, Florida Atlantic University, 2010, 3.

31. Brubaker, Epting, and D'Armata, *Captain America*, no. 19 (August 2006).

32. Brubaker and Lark, *Captain America*, no. 5 (May 2005).

33. Shyminsky, "'Gay' Sidekicks," 298.

34. Brubaker, Epting, Perkins, and D'Armata, *Captain America*, no. 11 (November 2005).

35. Brubaker, Epting, Perkins, and D'Armata, *Captain America*, no. 8 (September 2005).

36. Brubaker, Epting, Perkins, and D'Armata, *Captain America*, no. 19 (August 2006).

37. Stevens, *Captain America, Masculinity, and Violence*, 7

38. Brubaker and Lark, *Captain America*, no. 5 (May 2005).

39. Again, bodily slippage abounds in this arc: the Skull initially occupies a cloned body of Rogers, later transferring his consciousness to share with Lukin. As events progress, the Skull takes over Rogers's original body, and Rogers's body becomes the villain: only Bucky can restore Rogers to himself. Brubaker, Epting, and D'Armata, *Captain America*, no. 2 (February 2005).

40. Vernon, "Subversive Nostalgia," 116.

41. Vernon, "Subversive Nostalgia," 117.

42. Vernon, "Subversive Nostalgia," 117.

43. Vernon, "Subversive Nostalgia," 116.

44. This arc influences the concurrent *Civil War* comics in 2007, in which Rogers sides against federalizing superheroes: the state cannot hold superheroes accountable because it does not hold itself accountable. Rogers ultimately surrenders upon realizing the consequences of the conflict on innocent lives, and his subsequent assassination demonstrates the disillusionment with the dominant narrative of American righteousness in the War on Terror. Mark Millar, Steve McNiven, Dexter Vines, and Morry Hollowell, *Civil War*, nos. 1–7 (July 2006–January 2007).

45. Dittmer, "Captain America's Empire," 637.

46. For example, see John Ney Rieber and John Cassaday, *Captain America*, nos. 1–6 (June–December 2002).

47. Dittmer, "Captain America's Empire," 634–41.

48. Brubaker, Epting, and D'Armata, *Captain America*, no. 6 (June 2005).

49. Vernon, "Subversive Nostalgia," 130.

50. Vernon, "Subversive Nostalgia," 125.

51. As Shyminsky notes, a disturbing overtone of pederasty between the hero and child sidekick can potentially throw the hero into an even darker realm of villainy than child soldiers. Brubaker avoids this by firmly stating that Bucky is sixteen to twenty-one years old during World War II, which potentially redirects the queer subtext toward a criticism of the legally mandated narrative of heterosexuality in American soldiers.

52. Shyminsky, "'Gay' Sidekicks," 303, 304.

CHAPTER 31

Excerpts from *Japanese Demon Lore*

Oni from Ancient Times to the Present[1]

NORIKO T. REIDER

AN OVERVIEW: WHAT ARE *ONI*?

In an English-language treatment of *oni*, it is tempting to seek comparisons in Western demonology. Indeed, the concept of *oni* and the history and development of their representation have some striking affinity to the demonic entities that populate Judeo-Christian myths and the various figures from older Greco-Roman, Celtic, Anglo-Saxon, Germanic, and Norse traditions that became "demonized" as Christianity spread through the European continent, the British Isles, and finally Iceland. Such a comparison, a worthy task in itself, is, however, beyond the scope of this chapter. It suffices to say that the Western adjective "demonic," while the closest Western term to describe *oni*, falls short of capturing the full idea of these creatures.

The popularity and longevity of the *oni* myth is no doubt partially based on the beings' conventional demonic accoutrements, which have remained relatively constant through the ages: they are dreadful supernatural beings emerging from the abyss of Buddhist hell to terrify wicked mortals; their grotesque and savage demeanor and form instill instant fear; and their omnipresence in the sociohistorical and cultural archive of Japan is directly attributable to the moral, social, and religious edification that stories about *oni* engender. But there is a lesser-known side to the *oni* that will also be examined here—the *oni* as harbingers of wealth and fortune. This widely disparate dichotomy begs a fundamental question: "What are *oni*?" . . .

ONI IN MANGA, ANIME, AND FILM

In contemporary Japan, a virtual world of anime (Japanese animation), film, and games offers *oni* and other *yokai* unlimited potential. Manga (graphic novels)—a close relative of anime and an essential component in contemporary Japanese pop culture—is also fertile soil for *oni*. Japanese manga were popular in the prewar period, but it was only after the war that the industry fully recognized its potential, most notably with the publication of Osamu Tezuka's (1928–1989) *Tetsuwan atomu* (*Astro Boy*).[2] In 1995, comic books were a billion-dollar industry in Japan, accounting for 40 percent of all books and magazines sold. Overseas as well, a San Francisco–based Japanese manga and anime company that translates Japanese work into the English language was a four- or five-person operation in 1986; by 2007, it had grown to a staff of 130.[3] Many anime are based on stories that appeared first in manga. Indeed, Japan's first animated television series was the aforementioned *Astro Boy* in 1963.

Susan Napier writes: "[A]nime, with its enormous breadth of subject material, is ... a useful mirror on contemporary Japanese society, offering an array of insights into the significant issues, dreams, and nightmares of the day."[4] In this varied array of subject materials, *oni* and *yokai* are important ingredients to help understand the Japanese, as well as the broader human psyche.

As human knowledge of earth expands, and as the world becomes smaller, *oni*'s trope moves beyond this planet. Perhaps because it is less believable today that *oni* would inhabit far-distant mountains and rivers in Japan, a contemporary *oni* is often portrayed in media as a creature from a different time and/ or space. An *oni* is an alien, a hybrid of earthlings and some different species, or simply a different species on earth from the very long past, the future, or, if from the present, then from a different temporal dimension. An *oni*'s existence has also become entwined with cutting-edge technologies such as electronics, mechanics, and robotics. In cyberspace, *oni* often cohabit with humans as urban dwellers. Geopolitics may change, but the *oni* is still an alienated "other." Some *oni* are looking for a companion ... and others exist as allegories or social commentaries. Just as the subject matters treated by contemporary representative pop cultural media vary greatly, the *oni*'s representation varies widely.

APOCALYPTIC AND ELEGIAC *ONI*

According to Susan Napier, the most significant modes of anime are those of apocalypse, festival, and elegy, and distinctively Japanese in the Japanese vision of apocalypse is the sense of the elegiac.[5] She writes specifically the "Japanese vision of apocalypse" because the end of the world in the Judeo-Christian tradition—the final battle between the binary concept of righteous forces against evil, with a select few going to heaven and the rest falling into hell—does not exist in the Japanese tradition.[6] Still, "while Buddhist and Shinto scriptures do not contain visions of good frightening evil at the end of the world, the Buddhist doctrine of *mappo* or 'the latter days of the Law' does revolve around the notion of a fallen world saved by a religious figure, the Maitreya Buddha."[7]

Apocalyptic fiction became quite popular in the late 1960s and 1970s as rapid economic growth came to Japan, and with it came pollution and societal anxiety. Various apocalyptic fictions were created with a background of societal intransparency and other disasters facing humankind.

One of the pioneering artists portraying apocalyptic and elegiac modes of manga through the utilization of *oni* and demonic creatures is Nagai Go (born 1945). Nagai often depicts *oni* as members of a different tribe from the mainstream Japanese race or as creatures born out of grudge, enmity, and suffering. For example, the *oni* in the manga *Oni 2889 nen no hanran* (*Oni the Rebellion in 2889*), which appeared in December 1969, is a synthetic human—a creation of human technology. Similar to "replicants" in the film *Blade Runner* (1982), the *oni* are absolutely supposed to obey the humans. But the *oni* rebel against the humans and their cruel treatment.[8] While the setting is literally futuristic, the core concept of an *oni* as a marginalized being borne out of grudge, enmity, and suffering remains unchanged. In the following, I have chosen two of Nagai's representative works whose protagonists are *oni*: *Debiruman* (*Devilman*, 1972–1973) and *Shuten Doji* (1976–1978).

Debiruman

Debiruman is one of Nagai's most influential and popular works. This *oni*, as the name "Devilman" itself indicates, is more akin to the Judeo-Christian "devil" than to Japanese *oni*. The author uses the translation *akuma ningen* for Devilman rather than something like *oni bito*, and the architectural framework of *Devilman* is predominantly Christendom. Indeed, when Nagai's representative works are compiled, *Devilman* is often categorized by itself, separate from his "*oni* series" that include *Oni the Rebellion in 2889* and *Shuten Doji*.[9] Yet, various *oni* aspects that appear in *Devilman* make this story part of *oni*, as we shall see later. *Devilman* ran as serials of manga and TV anime almost simultaneously, but the manga serial is much more violent and cruel, with many atrocious scenes typified in the dismembering of Miki's body (Miki, a main character, is the protagonist's love).[10]

The basic plot of the manga version of *Devilman* is as follows: a long time ago, demons, an indigenous race, ruled the earth, but a cataclysm imprisoned demons in ice. The demons are skilled transformers, or more precisely amalgamators (*gattai*) who combine with other beings, and their pleasure is to kill sentient beings. The time moves to the present day, and the place is Japan. The protagonist is Fudo Akira, a gentle, righteous, but timid teenager. Ryo, Akira's best friend, one day tells Akira that the demons that had been imprisoned in the glacier are resurrected and will destroy humans to get the earth back. In order to save humankind, Akira transforms into Devilman by allowing himself to be possessed by one of the most powerful demon warriors, called Anion. As Devilman, Akira has a human heart and the demonic power of Amon; he is not shy anymore. Devilman battles against various demons to protect humans, but then demons begin indiscriminate amalgamation, murdering countless humans. Examining this mysterious phenomenon, a Nobel Prize winner for biology, Professor Rainuma, concludes that the demons are actually humans. In a plot twist resembling a medieval witch hunt, humans, who have heard the professor's statement, start to torture and kill suspicious people and those who may turn into demons. To complicate the story, Ryo turns out to be Satan, whom the demons worship as their god. Akira/Devilman decides to form the Devilman's army to counter the demons' indiscriminate attacks on humans. Eventually the humans all kill each other out of distrust. With no humans left on earth, the final campaign of Armageddon begins, with the Demons' army led by Ryo/Satan against the Devilman's army. After twenty years, when the final battle is over, Ryo/Satan speaks to Akira/Devilman. He explains that long ago, God tried to destroy the demons that were ruling the earth. Satan went against God's will and stood on the side of the demons. Victorious demons went into a long sleep in the ice—they were not encaved in the ice against their will—but when they woke up, humans were devastating the earth, so the demons decided to destroy humans. Satan realized that what the demons did was exactly the same as what God had tried to do to the demons earlier. After Ryo/Satan's confession, he apologizes for his action to Akira/Devilman, but Akira/Devilman dies of his battle wounds.

Devilman's appearance resembles Mephistopheles, a devil that appears in a lithograph of Faust by French artist Eugène Delacroix (1798–1863), or Lucifer, King of Hell, an illustration for Dante's *Divine Comedy* by Gustave Doré (1832–1883). As the term "Armageddon" suggests, the framework of the story is based upon biblical literature, especially the Revelation of Saint John the Divine. Indeed, when Akira declares that he is going to form the Devilman's army to do battle against the demons, Ryo compares Akira's idea to the Armageddon, explaining,

> It's in the Revelation of Saint John the Divine. God tells His prophesy to John who was on Patmos and told him to write the prophecy down. Satan, who was encased in the ice by God's desire, will be resurrected after the time of

eternity and will bring calamities with his army. God's army will meet Satan's army. All the beings on earth will be divided into two groups: good and evil. This battle is called "Armageddon."[11]

It should be noted that a part of Ryo's statement above, "Satan, who was encased in the ice by God's desire," comes from *The Divine Comedy* by Dante Alighieri (1264–1321). In *The Divine Comedy*, Satan is bound in the ice to his midpoint in the place just past the last circle of Cocytus, the ninth and final circle of Hell called Judecca. The Revelation of Saint John the Divine simply states that Satan is chained and thrown into an abyss to be sealed for a thousand years. Nagai freely adapts famous descriptions from the works of Christian literature and mixes them to meet his needs, making the work more appealing to a wide audience.

Interestingly, in response to Ryo's statement, Akira believes that his Devilman's army corresponds to God's army in the book of Revelation. But his army loses the campaign at the end the story. The meaning of the term "Armageddon" is widely known among contemporary Japanese, mainly as a result of an incident in 1995 in which a religious/cult group called Aum Shinrikyo attempted to force Armageddon by planting sarin gas in Tokyo subways, killing twelve commuters and injuring many others. But when *Devilman* was serialized in the mid-1970s, the notion of Armageddon was unfamiliar to most Japanese. It was in that sense a fresh concept in the manga world.

So why is the *Devilman* story considered an *oni* story in spite of its overwhelmingly Judeo-Christian theme? To begin with, there is no "good" or "evil" in support of just one religious belief in this story. As mentioned earlier, *oni* and the Judeo-Christian devil are distinctly different. The devil or Satan as evil exists in opposition to God, without whom the devil does not exist. But even interpreting "good" in terms of righteousness against "evil," there is no absolute "good" against absolute "evil" in *Debiruman*. Neither Satan's army nor Devilman's army is the completely righteous one.

While Akira is Devilman, he has the virtuous Akira's heart and soul. He is more akin to an *oni* with its own righteousness in his heart.[12] As we have seen, *oni* have both positive and negative aspects, and the demons in *Devilman* also possess both positive and negative sides. Despite Ryo's explanation that "the demon's purpose in life is to kill. The demon does not possess 'love.' They are indeed devils,"[13] some major demon characters such as Serene and Kaimu *do* understand love. In fact, the death scene of Serene and Kaimu, who offered his life to Serene, is quite elegiac. In the anime version of *Devilman*, Akira dies at the very beginning, and it is the brave demon warrior Devilman who protects Mild and her family against other demons. Indeed, Ryo tells Akira, "[d]evils existed. The legends of *yokai* that exist all over the world such as devils, *oni*, werewolves, vampires, *tengu*, *kappa* [water imps]—aren't they demons?" To this,

Akira responds, "come to think of it, Japanese *oni* look like an amalgamation of humans and oxen."[14] I should mention that in Japan in the 1970s, the word *gattai* (amalgamation) was a very popular, catchy word, especially among children. While shouting "Gattai!," children would pretend to transform into something different; one transforms into something else, into something more powerful, by amalgamating with another being. It is human to desire to transform oneself into a more desirable or powerful being. . . .

As the story develops, such familiar motifs as "demonic people" become foregrounded. For example, in one episode, American cavalry possessed by demons massacre a Native American tribe. When Devilman arrives on the scene of murder, the cavalrymen look at him and cry, "It's a devil!" But Devilman shouts at them: "No, the devils are within you!"[15] So readers may anticipate Professor Rainuma's statement: "The true identity of demons is humans." The professor's explanation for the cause of human demonization, however, reveals a contemporary societal tendency. He explains: "The humans' strong desire has changed the biological cells of human bodies and has transformed themselves into demons. . . . The accumulation of contemporary men's pent-up frustrations turned them into demons."[16] In other words, it is the angry, frustrated human psyche that takes the shape of demons. This is an interesting theory when one considers the country's situation then: Japan was just starting to enter an affluent phase, and yet various societal anxieties such as the political unrest of the 1960s and the environmental pollution that came with the rapid adoption of modern conveniences accompanied the development. Aggravation and uneasiness toward the present and the future, along with an identity crisis, took the physical form of the demon. The professor's statement triggers the "human hunt," similar to the "witch hunt" of the medieval period of Western civilization. "Suspicion will raise bogies" is a reaction that is repeated throughout human history.

Devilman's influence has been enormous on later manga and anime works, including *Shin seiki Evangerion* (*Neon Genesis Evangerion*, 1995–96), a spectacularly successful manga and anime serial.[17] *Devilman*, which essentially portrays a series of great battles for hegemony over the earth, may be taken as an allegorical war story. Nagai writes: "I started to look at *Devilman* as a symbolic story of wars. For example, Miki is Akira's fiancée who waits for Akira's return at home, the members of the Devilman's army are combatants, and humans are civilians." But then, he quickly adds,

> sometimes there are some people who swallow my story [at face value]. So I will clearly declare here. This symbolism is just one result of a "simulation game." . . . *Devilman* is not a prophecy—it is a simple manga that I created.

Don't ever think that Japan is planning wars, and don't be deceived by weird cult groups![18]

Nagai is saying that *Devilman* is a creation for entertainment, and understand-ably he does not want *Devilman* to be an inspiration for an ideologue or a cult group that may become dangerous to the public. This statement, in turn, speaks to how manga and/or his creation may influence modern readers' ways of thinking and acting so much so that the author has to draw the readers back to its pure entertainment value.

Shuten Doji

While *Devilman*'s oni is written in the framework of Christendom, *Shuten Doji* is clearly cut from Japanese *oni* cloth, right down to the *oni*'s traditional mas-culine appearance with horns. Serialized in *Shonen Magajin* (*Boys' Magazine*) from 1976 to 1978, *Shuten Doji* is a story whose time and space span the tenth through the twenty-first centuries, from the earth out into the universe, to the realm of *oni*. Although the title, *Shuten Doji*, is pronounced the same as the medieval Shuten Doji (drunken demon), Nagai uses different characters for his *Shuten Doji*, which literally means "a child handed from heaven." Indeed, the protagonist, Shutendo Jiro, is so named because "the child was handed [to his parents] from heaven," and his name also reflects the most famous *oni*, Shuten Doji.[19] Nagai's *Shuten Doji* is roughly divided into three parts: the first is a school-horror taking place in present-day Japan; the middle part is a psychic action story that depicts Shutendo Jiro and his friends fighting against a dark religious group that worships Daiankoku shiyajarai (the Great Evil Deity of Darkness and Death); and the third part is written entirely in science fiction mode—with spaceships, cyborgs, time machines, and so on—in which Shuten-do Jiro travels through time and space.

The story starts with the sudden appearance of a gigantic *oni* handing over a baby to a couple, Mr. and Mrs. Shiba, who are visiting Mr. Shiba's ancestral grave to report their marriage. The *oni* leaves the baby with the couple, saying that he will come back to retrieve him after fifteen years. The baby is named Shutendo Jiro after the famous *oni*, Shuten Doji. Fifteen years later, Jiro notices his supernatural powers, and two horns grow on his head. Then, strange crea-tures start to attack him, and Jiro realizes that he must be an *oni*, but he does not know where he came from or why he exists.

In order to find out who he is and also to follow his destiny, he sets off to the *ongokukai*, the *oni*'s realm. Jiro is accompanied by Goki (literally "protector of the *oni*"),[20] an *oni* who exists solely to protect him.

Like Devilman, the *oni* in *Shuten Doji* are endowed with the ability to copy the shapes, characters, and memories of any sentient beings.[21] Nagai's *oni*— both the demons in *Devilman* and the *oni* in *Shuten Doji* portrayed in the mode of science fiction—are more sophisticated and multitalented than the traditional *oni* representations. As in *Devilman*, an apocalyptic thought rises up ominously in *Shuten Doji* as a delinquent says: "The future of humankind is limited. Only gods or demons survive in the end. Weak humans are destined to perish.... We saw an *akuma* [devil], a being of the evil realm. Its appearance terribly resembled a legendary *oni*!"[22] This is a tangent point of *Devilman* and *Shuten Doji*. Further, an army of *oni* that attacks Jiro when he is about to enter the realm of *oni* is in fact composed of demons similar to those that appear in *Devilman*. As Devilman cries out to the humans, "The devils are within you," their mental state then creates the *oni* within their minds. Indeed, the basic premise of *Shuten Doji* is that negative human emotions such as anger and spite, which essentially do not hold mass, create an *oni* that has physical mass in this world.

It turns out that the *ongokukai* was inside Mrs. Shiba's mind. Mrs. Shiba subconsciously created the *ongokukai* out of her anger and her grudge against the *oni* who took Shutendo Jiro away from her. Mr. Shiba explains: "The *owgokukai*, the realm of *oni*, is the realm of grudge" (*owgokukai* is pronounced the same as *ongokukai*, but the first character is now replaced by a character meaning "grudge"). The mind-bearing "grudge" phenomenalized the shape of *oni*. The *ongokukai* is the world of grudge that Mrs. Shiba created when the *oni* took Jiro away from her.[23] Mrs. Shiba also created Goki and Senki, another superstrong *oni* who protects Shutendo Jiro from vicious *oni*. It is usually an *oni* that slays other *oni*.

Mrs. Shiba had always known that Jiro would be taken away from her, but when Jiro was physically removed after fifteen years, she was so shocked that she was diagnosed with *yukaku kannen*, or "overvalued ideation." According to Mrs. Shiba's psychiatrist, overvalued ideation afflicts ordinary people when they receive an enormous mental shock. The shock is so traumatizing that a patient no longer responds to any outside stimuli. Thus, Mrs. Shiba's mind stopped at the time of Jiro's disappearance, and she can only think of her grudge against the *oni* who has taken her boy away.[24] This traumatic experience created Daiankoku shiyajarai (the Great Evil Deity of Darkness and Death), who exists to draw the universe into the world of darkness and who is worshipped by an evil religious cult.[25] Mrs. Shiba is the Daiankoku shiyajarai. As time moves back and forth rather casually in *Shuten Doji*, what happens in the present affects the past; the causal relationship is reversed. Goki explains that the *oni*'s world was created suddenly in metadimensional space from nothingness.[26] This is because the *oni* world was created in Mrs. Shiba's mind when Jiro was taken, and her state of mind has affected what had happened before: that is, the creation of the Daiankoku shiyajarai, fighting against strange creatures, and other events. Nagai writes:

> I started to write the story as an adventure fantasy with a motif of *oni*, ... but a structure changed in the middle. ... I think the *oni*'s accumulated grudges over the millennia made the story change. Originally an *oni* was something that the authorities considered nonhuman and punished arbitrarily. ... *Shuten Doji* eventually made me think what an *oni* is, how an *oni* affects the human mind, and the violence of love and hate.[27]

According to Nagai, a person with a grudge becomes an *oni*. He believes that the *oni* really existed—not as a different species of beings but as humans, as a human being is the *oni*'s true identity.[28]

The ending of *Shuten Doji* is literally full of lights, with a happy reunion scene between Jiro and Mr. and Mrs. Shiba. It is seemingly a happy ending. But is it? What about those who died for Shutendo Jiro, or, to be more precise, those who were physically killed in the world that Mrs. Shiba created? Mrs. Shiba's angst and spite triggered the killing spree. ... Yet, Mrs. Shiba's case seems more frightening because the grudge stems from "motherhood"—a supposedly nurturing nature. The Great Mother has two aspects, and Mrs. Shiba's Daiankoku shiyajarai personifies the destructive aspect. The relationship between mother and son is said to be strong in Japan. While Nagai does not mention anything about the destructive power of motherhood, the *Shuten Doji* story can be interpreted as a sharp criticism of the mother-son relationship. If motherly love turns vicious, for any reason, it creates an *oni*. While the mother's instinct to protect her child is strong, if it becomes excessive, "motherhood" can destroy its surroundings, taking the many characters involved with it. Whether intended or not, this is a message that may touch one's heartstrings. ...

MODERN FEMALE *ONI*: POWERFUL, YET COMPROMISED

Urusei Yatsura: The Cute Sexy Oni

We saw above one devastatingly evil female *oni* called Daiankoku shiyajarai living in the mind of Mrs. Shiba, a mother. The evilness of Daiankoku shiyajarai may be compared to a black hole of the universe in its darkness. On the other hand, a completely lovable *oni*, a sexy ogress named Lum, appears in the manga series entitled *Urusei Yatsura* (*Those Obnoxious Aliens*). When Takahashi Rumiko, the author, created *Urusei Yatsura*, she combined the aliens of science fiction with the traditional Japanese *oni*. Her protagonist is Lum, a modern, nonterrestrial version of Japanese *oni*. The series first appeared in 1978 in a boy's weekly manga magazine called *Shonen Sunday* (*Boys' Sunday*). *Urusei Yatsura* was such a phenomenal success that it ran over nine years and was also turned into a TV series from 1981 to 1987. After the TV series ended, six feature-length movies and eleven original video animations (OVAs) were made. Just like any other successful manga, *Urusei Yatsura* was also released in book form, counting thirty-four volumes altogether, and later the series was also published in the *bunkobon* (pocket edition) format. Abroad, *Urusei Yatsura* was published in North America from 1989 to 1998 and has been translated into Italian, Spanish, and Cantonese.[29]

Both manga and anime series of *Urusei Yatsura* open with a fleet of technologically superadvanced *oni* invaders arriving on earth. The invaders challenge earthlings to fight a one-on-one battle of *om-gokko* (a game of tag) for the destiny of humankind. For humans to be saved, the randomly selected challenger, Moroboshi Ataru, a lecherous teenage Japanese boy, enters the battle. If Ataru can hold the ogress Lum's horns in his hands, he wins the game. Lum turns out to be cute and overflowing with sex appeal, but after a series of mishaps, Ataru wins the game, and Lum declares that she is his loving and devoted wife.

The ogress Lum is replete with the traditional *oni*'s attributes discussed above. She wears a traditional *oni* outfit of tiger skin. She has two horns on her head. Instead of a big mouth to eat humans in one gulp, she has cute canine teeth, indicating a sexual appetite. Her mouth becomes conspicuously large when she finds out about Ataru's lecherous behavior. She acts as if she were going to devour Ataru—demonstrating a trace of cannibalistic background. Lum can fly, just like the *oni* at Modoribashi Bridge is reported to do. Although Lum herself does not transform into any nonrecognizable creature, her former fiancé, Rei, who is still so enamored of her that he comes after her from his home planet, transforms himself into a huge tiger- or ox-like monster when excited. Ordinarily, Rei is an *oni* with an incredibly good-looking human appearance (with two horns and a tiger-skin outfit). Hailing from a different planet and intent on invading the earth, Lum's *oni* cohorts are obviously beyond the reach of the emperor's control. The alien *oni* also have many customs that differ from those of human earth dwellers. Lum's body emits electricity like lightning—a traditional *oni* power—and that is her weapon. When she becomes jealous or angry, she uses her electric power most effectively to injure her target. As *oni* can also bring wealth, Lum has brought wealth to her real-life creators (the author and the companies who published her manga and produced the TV shows and films in which her popular character was featured).

Born in 1957 and one of Japan's most popular manga artists, the author, Takahashi Rumiko, has rendered an *oni* that is entirely modern. Lum is an alien-*oni* who is capable of piloting an advanced spaceship. She is also a sexy *oni*, cute and coquettish with a curvaceous figure and huge eyes. Lum often wears a tiger-skin bikini, showing her attractive figure most effectively. Lum's image is not unlike a teenage version of an ukiyo-e *yamauba*, although she does not exactly look like a Japanese or, for that matter, any specific race.[30]

Lum is portrayed as a lovable and devoted (self-claimed) wife. Timothy J. Craig writes that one of the features of "Japan's popular culture is its closeness to the ordinary, everyday lives of its audience."[31] Lum-*oni*'s likeability increases all the more because she behaves just like ordinary human women, in spite of her supernatural electric powers and flying ability; she becomes jealous, cries, laughs, and gets mad, so a mainstream audience can automatically relate to her. Interestingly, her likeability partially comes from conforming to societal norms while she simultaneously creates social tension. Susan Napier writes that *Urusei Yatsura* reflects an aspect of contemporary Japanese society in that increasingly empowered Japanese women in the 1970s and 1980s are contained through comfort contrivances. Napier notes:

> The chaotic world that Lum often unwittingly creates is an amusing one when confined to the theatre of fantasy, but the subtext has a threatening quality to it, suggesting that in the real world women are increasingly uncontrollable as well. The inherent threat of Lum s powers . . . is ultimately mitigated by the essentially traditional relationship she has with Ataru. Lum's (women's) destabilizing power is contained through her total commitment to her man, suggesting that, no matter how independent and aggressive she may become, she is still profoundly tied to a traditional male-female dynamic. . . . [H]er emotional subordination to him ultimately guarantees that she will occupy the traditional (i.e., comforting) female subject position.[32]

With a popular following in various media, Lum is a tribute to the modern-cosmopolitan age. With the show's catchy theme song and copious spin-off marketing efforts, the *oni* Lum has proven to be a true economic commodity for Japan. She is a veritable entertainment franchise that ultimately celebrates the capitalistic and commercial accomplishments of the modern era. . . .

Yasha and Dog in InuYasha

While traditional *oni* with horns on their scalps are visible, *yamauba* and such *oni* variants as *yasha* (yaksha) and *tsuchigumo* (earth spiders) appear to be taking active roles in cyberspace. A *yasha* is an Indian-originated Buddhist *oni*. A good example of *yasha* in pop culture is *InuYasha* (dog demon), an extremely popular Japanese manga among teens of various countries including the United

States. Appearing first in Japan in 1997, the manga was so successful that it was made into a television anime series and inspired three feature-length films. The author is none other than Takahashi Rumiko, the creator of *Urusei Yatsura*. InuYasha, which literally means "dog-*yasha*," is the male protagonist of the series, and a half-*yokai*. InuYasha was born of a human mother and sired by a full-fledged *yokai*; he yearns to be the same. At the beginning of the *InuYasha* series, the heroine, Kagome, a fifteen-year-old girl living in present-day Tokyo, is sent to the past by a *yokai* through an ancient well in her family's compound. Arriving in the sixteenth-century Warring States period of Japan, Kagome discovers that she is the reincarnation of Kikyo, a deceased priestess who guarded the miraculous Shikon jewel—which has the power to fulfill any ambition of man or *yokai*. Fifty years before, InuYasha tried to steal the jewel to become a thoroughbred *yokai*, but Kikyo prevented it and put InuYasha into a deep sleep by shooting him with a sacred arrow. Now the Shikon jewel is reborn into Kagome's body, and InuYasha has awakened. *Yokai* of various kinds also start to fight for the jewel, and during the clash the jewel is shattered and its shards scattered across Japan. Kagome and InuYasha team up to retrieve the shards before they fall into the hands of their archenemy Naraku, who manipulates various *yokai* to try to obtain the shards.

Abe Masamichi comments in his study of *yokai* that "all *yokai* are the ruins of humans. *Yokai* continue to exist both inside and outside humans. They wish to return to a human form, but are unable to do so. They live in fields, mountains, seas, grasses and trees, full of sadness at not being able to return to a human form"[33] Ironically, both InuYasha and Naraku (half-*yokai*) desire to be full-fledged *yokai*, knowing that this will increase their powers and strength. Likewise, all the *yokai* characters in *InuYasha* look down on humans as weaklings. This may simply be a contemporary story element, or it could be a social satire or commentary on humankind's preoccupation with the acquisition of strength and power. These are contemporary *yokai*.

InuYasha's name reveals the characteristics of his *yokai* side. He has a keen sense of smell, dog-like ears, claws, and a white mane. Kuroda Hideo notes that during the medieval period, Japanese typically kept a dog as a pet or a hunting animal. At the same time, dogs were also looked upon as a way to maintain public hygiene, because they ate food scraps and corpses or carrion. Consequently, the dog became a symbol of the graveyard and the city. Kuroda further points out that dogs play a role as guides to the other world. In *Kobo daishigyojo ekotoba* (*Pictorial History of Priest Kobo: The Fourteenth Century*), for example, a white dog and a black one are depicted beside a deity who guides Priest Kobo Daishi to sacred Mount Koya.[34] Also, the story from *Uji shui mo-nogatari* (*A Collection of Tales from Uji*) entitled "About an Uncanny Incident Involving Seimei and a Dog Belonging to the Chancellor of the Buddha Hall" reveals how a white dog saved his master's life with its supernatural power.[35] Thus Kuroda concludes that a dog was considered to have supernatural power and was like a transboundary animal, between this world and the other world.[36] InuYasha's father was a powerful *yokai* of a huge white dog. After his demise, his carcass—a gigantic white skull and bones—served as a demarcation realm between this world and the nether land, which is his graveyard. InuYasha also goes to his father's burial ground on two occasions: once, on a mission to find a special sword made from his father's fangs; and next, in search of a Shikon shard. On the first occasion, the key leading to the boundary realm where his father's corpse resides was hidden in InuYasha's body. In this sense, one may say that InuYasha, a white dog, led a team to the different realm, just like the white dog did for Priest Kobo.

The term *yasha* conjures up something violent and ferocious, and this is what InuYasha becomes when his *yokai* side dominates; he acts like a wild animal without knowing what is good or bad. In Buddhist mythology, *yasha* was subdued by Bishamonten (Vaisravans), one of the Buddhist guardians of the four cardinal directions, and became Bishamonten's kin to protect the true law of Buddha.[37] Interestingly, in *InuYasha*, this side, as a protector of the good, is becoming increasingly visible, particularly when he protects Kagome, who purifies the Shikon shards on behalf of good. He feels for Kagome, but he cannot forget Kikyo, who urged him to become a human being with the power of the Shikon jewel and who died fifty years before, protecting it. InuYasha's character develops from a loner to a team player, and he has a hidden desire for companions. The narrative that he is no longer a lonely individual appears in one of his theme songs as well. . . . Modern fiction reflects the present-day societal phenomenon of individuals' desire for connections or relationships. Manga and anime also capitalize on this longing to identify the audience with the characters. While yearning for power, people long for some lasting relationship, and this holds true in the world of *yokai* or *yasha*, perhaps all the more so because an *oni* and its variants are marginalized to begin with.

Tsuchigumo (Earth Spider) in InuYasha

InuYasha's archenemy is called Naraku, and he, too, is after the Shikon shards to garner greater demonic power. The name Naraku is a Japanese term for hell. As his name suggests, Naraku is an entirely hellish character and the central force of malevolence in the story. Like InuYasha, he is a half-*yokai* who wants to become the most powerful thoroughbred *yokai*, a fate achievable only through the power of the shards. Naraku was formerly a human being named Onigumo (*oni* spider). In the manga version, Onigumo appears in the story as a horribly disfigured man with terrible burns. It is explained in the anime version that

Onigumo was a wicked bandit with a large spider mark on his back. He had attempted to obtain the Shikon jewel under Kikyo's protection by manipulating his boss, the bandit leader. But his plan failed, and the infuriated boss threw a bomb at him, disfiguring his whole body. Onigumo was left to die of his burns, but ironically Kikyo found him and saved his life. While Kikyo was tending to Onigumo's wounds, his base desire for Kikyo consumed him and he gave up his body to realize his lustful wish. *Yokai* devoured Onigumo's body and soul, but Onigumo's wish was never realized. He was later reborn as Naraku with a latent lust for Kikyo. Onigumo in Naraku is represented by the spider's mark on Naraku's back. Naraku despises Onigumo's weakness, specifically his feelings for Kikyo, and attempts to get rid of him in various ways. Yet, the mark always reappears or resurfaces on Naraku's back. The *oni* in Onigumo certainly represents his demonic character, and the symbolic spider reveals cultural memories.

Those cultural memories are *tsuchigumo*, earth spiders. It is commonly accepted among scholars that the term "earth spider" refers to uncultivated indigenous people who lived before the heavenly descendants claimed their authority. *Tsuchigumo* is an appellation used derogatorily in ancient Japanese literature for those who defied imperial (central) authority.[38] For example, Emperor Jimmu, on his eastward expedition to claim his heavenly authority in Kojiki, with his men smites a great number of resisting indigenous pit-dwelling tribesmen described as earth spiders.[39] An overwhelming majority of earth spiders fought and were eliminated in bloody battles; only a few survived by apologizing profusely and escaping capital punishment.[40] An earth spider defies central authority and has different customs and manners, and different physiological features, from the mainstream body culture. In that sense, the earth spider is considered to be one of the most ancient types of *oni*.[41] As for the origin of the term, Itsubun Settsu Fudoki (a missing writing from the Topography of Settsu Province, known from other literary sources) notes: "In the reign of Emperor Jimmu, there was a villain called *tsuchigumo*—he was given the disdainful name of earth spider because this person always dwelled in a pit."[42] Pit dwelling is strongly associated with *tsuchigumo*.

This also applies to the aforementioned InuYasha Onigumo, who lived in a dark cave below the cliff—a form of pit dwelling. As an abandoned outlaw, terribly disfigured from burns, Onigumo was already socially, culturally, and even physically marginalized when he was in the cave. As the manga series continues, the image of an earth spider as a marginalized being persists in the minds of young readers, and without reading Japanese classical literature or related research materials, cultural memory surrounding earth spiders is thus carried on to new generations.

Notes

1. Reprinted with permission of the author from Noriko T. Reider, *Japanese Demon Lore: Oni from Ancient Times to the Present* (Logan: Utah State University Press, 2010), available at https://ia800303.us.archive.org/3/items/JapaneseDemonLore/JapaneseDemonLore_djvu.txt. The chapter has been lightly edited for style for the purposes of the present publication.

2. Tezuka is widely regarded as the godfather of manga.

3. "Are Made-in-Japan Manga and Animation About to Be Blindsided?," *Japan Close-Up*, June 2007, 15.

4. Susan Napier, *Anime from Akira to Princess Mononoke: Experiencing Contemporary Japanese Animation* (New York: Palgrave, 2000), 8.

5. Napier, *Anime from Akira to Princess Mononoke*, 199.

6. Napier writes: "What sets Europe and America apart from Japan, however, is that they share the common tradition of the biblical book of Revelation, the themes and imagery of which have become the fundamental version of the apocalyptic narrative: a final battle between the forces of the righteous and the forces of Satan, the wholesale destruction of the world with the evil side being cast into hell, and the ultimate happy ending with the evildoers condemned and the righteous believers ascending to the kingdom of heaven. Traditional Japanese culture has never shared in this vision" (Napier, *Anime from Akira to Princess Mononoke*, 194).

7. Napier, *Anime from Akira to Princess Mononoke*, 196.

8. Nagai Go, *Nagai Go kaiki tanpenshu*, vol. 1, *Oni* (Tokyo: Chuo Korensha, 1995), 12.

9. See, for example, Nagai's *Debiruman wa dare nano ka* (Tokyo: Kodansha, 2004). When Nagai's work is classified according to genre, both *Devilman* and *Shuten Doji* are categorized under *denki* (strange stories; romance) with an English subtitle, "legend."

10. Nagai has a broad spectrum of subjects. While he is celebrated for violent manga, he is also famous for comical, sexy, and/or erotic manga such as *Harenchi gakuen* (*Shameless School*, 1968–1972) and *Kyuti hani* (*Cutie Honey*, 1973–1974). The *Devilman* serial comes almost in between *Shameless School* and *Cutie Honey*. For an insightful observation on *Cutie Honey*, see Napier, *Anime from Akira to Princess Mononoke*, 73–76.

11. Nagai Go, *Debiruman*, 5 vols. (Tokyo: Kodansha, 1997), 4:186–87.

12. This is reminiscent of a group of folktales called *Oni no ko Kozuna* (*Kozuna, Oni's Child*), in which the protagonist, Kozuna, is kind to humans. Kozuna is a half-*oni* and half-human child, and it is implied that the kind side is his human side. His cannibal *oni* side is latent, but Kozuna asks to be killed whenever he feels an urge to eat humans. Kozuna is an *oni* with a human heart.

13. Nagai, *Debiruman*, 1:114.

14. Nagai, *Debiruman*, 1:100–101.

15. Nagai, *Debiruman*, 3:186–87.

16. Nagai, *Debiruman*, 4:254–55.

17. Oizumi Mitsunari, *Anno Hideaki sukizo Evangerion* (Tokyo: Ota Shuppan, 1997).

18. Nagai, *Debiruman wa dare nano ka*, 48–51.

19. Nagai Go, *Shuten Doji* [*A Child Handed from Heaven*], vols. 1–3 (Tokyo: Kodansha, 2001); vols. 4–5 (Tokyo: Fusosha, 1998); vol. 6 (Tokyo: Fusosha, 1997). See 1:41.

20. Like many other manga artists, Nagai creates interesting names for his characters. This Goki, for example, is pronounced the same as En no Gyoja's Goki, literally "posterior demon," but, written in a different character, the name means a "protector of the *oni*."

21. Nagai, *Shuten Doji*, 1:382.

22. Nagai, *Shuten Doji*, 1:370–72.

23. Nagai, *Shuten Doji*, 6:238–39.

24. Nagai, *Shuten Doji*, 4:293–94.

25. Nagai, *Shuten Doji*, 2:167–68.

26. Nagai, *Shuten Doji*, 4:67–68.

27. Nagai Go, *Nagai Go SAGA: Sakuhin hyoronshu* (Tokyo: Fuyosha, 2003), 206.

28. Nagai, *Debiruman wa dare nano ka*, 103.

29. Dani Cavallaro, *The Cinema of Mamoru Oshii: Fantasy, Technology, and Politics* (Jefferson, NC: McFarland, 2006), 48–49, 51, 55.

30. Napier, *Anime from Akira to Princess Mononoke*, 24–25. Napier is insightful about the anime figure. She notes that

> a number of Japanese commentators have chosen to describe anime with the word *mukokuseki*, meaning "stateless" or essentially without a national identity. Anime is indeed "exotic" to the West in that it is made in Japan, but the world of anime itself occupies its own space that is not necessarily coincident with that of Japan. . . . [A]nother aspect of anime's *mukokuseki* quality in many eyes is the extremely "non-Japanese" depiction of human characters in virtually all anime texts. This is an issue among American audiences new to anime as well, who want to know why the characters look "Western." In fact, while many anime texts do include figures with blond hair, it is perhaps more correct to say that rather than a "Western" style of figuration, the characters are drawn in what might be called "anime" style. . . . This style ranges from the broadly grotesque drawings of characters with shrunken torsos and oversize heads of some anime comedy to the elongated figures with huge eyes and endless flowing hair that populate many romance and adventure stories. While many of them are blond or light brunette, many have more bizarre hair colorings such as pink, green, or blue.

31. Timothy J. Craig, ed., *Japan Pop! Inside the World of Japanese Popular Culture* (New York: M. E. Sharpe, 2000), 13.

32. Napier, *Anime from Akira to Princess Mononoke*, 147.

33. Abe Masamichi, *Nihon no yokaitachi* (Tokyo: Tokyo Shoseki, 1981), 7.

34. Kuroda Hideo, *Zoho sugata to shigusa no ehiisei-shi* (Tokyo: Heibonsha, 2002), 35.

35. "[Fujiwara Michinaga] had a particular pet, a white dog, which would go along with him and never leave his side. One day it was with him as usual, and just as he was about to go through the gate it ran round and round in front of his carriage, blocking his path and refusing to allow him in. Michinaga asked Abe Seimei what the dog's behavior meant. Seimei replied, 'If you pass over it, you will suffer harm. The dog possesses supernatural powers and was warning you.'" Douglas Mills, trans., *A Collection of Tales from Uji: A Study and Translation of Uji Shui Monogatari* (Cambridge: University of Cambridge Press, 1970). For the original Japanese text, see Kobayashi Yasuharu and Masuko Kazuko, eds., *Uji shui monogatari*, vol. 50 of SNKBZ (Tokyo: Shogakukan, 1996), 450–51.

36. Hideo, *Zoho sugata to shigusa no ehiisei-shi*, 236.

37. Aramata Hiroshi and Komatsu Kazuhiko, *Yokai soshi* (Tokyo: Kosakusha, 1987), 40.

38. See, for example, Tsuda Sokichi, *Nihon koten no kenkyii*, vol. 1 of *Tsuda Sokichi zenshu* (Tokyo: Iwanami Shoten, 1963), 188–95.

39. See Kurano Kenji and Takeda Yukichi, eds., *Kojiki, Norito*, vol. 1 of *NKBT* (Tokyo: Iwanami Shoten, 1958), 157. For an English translation, see Donald D. Philippi, trans., *Kojiki* (Princeton, NJ: Princeton University Press, 1969), 174–75. Also see Sakamoto Taro, Ienaga Saburo, Inoue Mitsusada, and Ono Susumu, eds., *Nihonshoki I, II*, vols. 67, 68 of *NKBT* (Tokyo: Iwanami Shoten, 1965–1967), 1:210. Its English translation is found in W. G. Aston, trans., *Nihongi: Chronicles of Japan from the Earliest Times to A.D. 697* (1896; repr., London: George Allen and Unwin, 1956), 129–30.

40. For example, one *tsuchigumo* named Omimi in the district of Matsuura of Hizen Province promised to give food to the emperor as tribute; Uegaki Setsuya, ed., *Fudoki*, vol. 5 of *SNKBZ*

(Tokyo: Shogakukan, 1997), 335–36. Another *tsuchigumo* called Utsuhiomaro in the Sonoki district of the same province even saved an imperial ship; Uegaki, *Fudoki*, 345.

41. Baba Akiko, *Oni no kenkyu* (1971; repr., Tokyo: Chikuma Shobo, 1988), 170. In the picture scroll entitled *Tsuchigumo soshi* (*Story of the Earth Spiders*, early fourteenth century), a gigantic *oni*, sixty feet tall with many legs, which lives in a cave, turns out to be the enormous spider. I should add that the accompanying painting to the *Story of the Earth Spiders*, however, portrays two gigantic *oni* with only two legs. For the narrative of *Story of the Earth Spiders*, see Komatsu Shigemi, Ueno Kenji, Sakakibara Satoru, and Shimatani Hiroyuki, eds., *Tsuchigumo soshi, Tengu soshi, Oeyama ekotoba*, vol. 19 of *Zoku nihon emaki taisei* (Tokyo: Chuo Koronsha, 1984), 162; for the painting, 7. Further, in Tsukioka Yoshitoshi's picture entitled *Minamoto no Yorimitsu tsuchigumo wo kiru-zu* (*Minamoto Yorimitsu Striking the Earth Spider*, 1892), the earth spider has three claws, which is reminiscent of *oni*.

42. Uegaki, *Fudoki*, 437.

Figure 13. Superman wears the Soviet hammer and sickle ("Red Son Rising," *Superman: Red Son*, no. 1, June 2003, 46).

CHAPTER 32

Where Did Superman's White Hat Go?

Villainy and Heroism in Superman: Red Son

W. D. PHILLIPS

> [T]he Cold War was a tragedy that turned men of similar, immense potential
> into mutually destructive villains at the cost of their integrity.
>
> SARA MARTIN, "THE SILENT VILLAIN"

SHORTLY AFTER 1910, WHILE IN HIS MID-THIRTIES, IOSIF VISSARIONOVICH Dzhugashvili began using the name Joseph Stalin, taking on the Russian word for steel as a symbol of strength as well as industrial might. He was Russia's "Man of Steel." Around the turn of the millennium, Scottish comic book writer Mark Millar reimagined the history of America's "Man of Steel"—Superman—as the surrogate son and ideological heir of Stalin. Moving Kal-El's crash landing back twelve hours in earth time, Millar relocates Superman's adoptive community from Smallville, a farming town in America's heartland, to the collective farms of Ukraine—Russia's own breadbasket.

Superman: Red Son is a three-book miniseries published in 2003 as part of DC Comics' Elseworlds imprint.[1] In principle, these stories work similarly to Marvel's "What if" stories, allowing writers and readers to imagine existing characters in situations that fall outside the canon established by previous writers and maintained by the editors. *Red Son*, on the surface, asks readers to reconsider what the world might have looked like if America's heroic Man of Steel had, from a young age, been influenced by Russia's despotic Man of Steel; if the Soviet hammer and sickle replaced Superman's *S*-like symbol of hope (fig. 13), and if "Truth, Justice, and the American Way" was supplanted by "Stalin, Socialism, and the International Expansion of the Warsaw Pact."[2]

The miniseries not only reimagines Superman's history and character based on this apparently simple shift, but also that of other key DC characters connected to the Superman universe, including Lois Lane, Lex Luthor, Batman,

Wonder Woman, and Green Lantern; several historical figures such as Stalin, John F. Kennedy, and Marilyn Monroe; and the history of Russia, the United States, and the world. In doing so, Millar and his collaborators grapple with questions of villainy and heroism in this redefined political landscape. In separating Superman's idealized morality from his ideological association with America, this comic book raises questions of morality's source (innate or learned) and, more significantly, the influence that political ideologies have on our conceptions of "good" and "evil" and ends versus means. These were particularly effectual themes for the post-9/11 environment in which the series was released.[3]

Published in three monthly installments, *Red Son* sets the action in three different reimagined historical moments: "Red Son Rising" (set in 1953), "Red Son Ascendant" (1978), and "Red Son Setting" (2001). Millar presents the reader with the "ends versus means" subtext quite early, through the character of Lex Luthor, Superman's frequent nemesis, who is introduced simultaneously playing twelve chess games, learning Urdu, and reading Machiavelli's *Il Principe/The Prince* ("Rising," 5). Machiavelli, known as "a teacher of tyrants," lived and published in Italy in the early sixteenth century. *The Prince*, as Ryan Litsey's chapter on Daredevil's Kingpin in this collection addresses at greater length, is generally understood to be "a treatise designed to teach a ruler the art of government."[4] What sets it apart, both in its time and still today, is that he preaches the necessity of evil for effective, enduring leaders. "It is necessary to a prince," Machiavelli writes, "to learn to be able not to be good, and to use this and not use it according to necessity."[5] Machiavelli divorces questions of morality from his study of effective political leadership and, as a result, comes to the conclusion that the ends *always* justify the means and that there are no means too severe, so long as the desired result is achieved.[6] Millar was not, of course, the first storyteller to use Machiavelli's treatise to characterize his villains; perhaps not surprisingly, Stalin himself is described as a disciple in Arthur Koestler's work of historical fiction, *Darkness at Noon*.[7]

The kinds of questions of good and evil that Machiavelli and, by proxy, Millar raise were off limits to comic books for much of their history. The formation, in 1954, of the content-regulating "Comics Code" stipulated clearly that "[i]n every instance good shall triumph over evil."[8] What is implicit in such an edict, however, is that "good" and "evil" are self-evident conditions with a clearly delineated boundary. It was only the shift in readership and distribution in the mid-1980s in conjunction with larger shifts in popular culture that ultimately relaxed the creative parameters and allowed comic book writers around that time to begin—in such works as *The Dark Knight Returns* (1986) and *Watchmen* (1986–1987)—to question directly the cultural assumptions of both the superhero's innate "goodness" and the supervillain's base "evil."[9] *Superman: Red*

Son falls within this larger body of American comics interrogating a previous generation's representations of identity, ideology, and nation through their imagined heroes and villains.[10] Published in series in 2003 and in collected form in 2004, *Red Son* also asks readers to reflect on contemporary post-9/11 issues related directly to questions of means versus ends—here particularly that of national security versus mass surveillance. Superman, utilizing the full expanse of his powers but following here the autocratic model of Cold War Russia, is reimagined as the ultimate Orwellian Big Brother (fig. 14).[11]

Red Son follows the conventions of superhero comics, despite its subversive reimagining of Kal-El as a Soviet "super-weapon" ("Rising," 1), keeping Superman at the center of the narrative to the point that he remains the narrator of his own tale.[12] Although this Superman is neither a traditional comic book hero nor a typical antihero, the narrative structure of the series nonetheless remains consistent with melodramatic hero/villain adventure stories that have been in regular circulation since at least the nineteenth century. Over the course of the three issues, Superman faces off against a series of foes, all but one of which are already familiar to DC readers. In traditional comics, and Western melodrama more generally, these oppositions are a result of the basic "good" and "evil" nature of the protagonist/hero and antagonist/villain(s).[13] In *Red Son*, however, we can read these more as a series of partial, incomplete doppelgängers that collectively indicate the various aspects of Superman's character, his heroism and villainy, and the morally ambiguous space connecting the two. Moreover, Millar and his collaborators use this sequence of interpersonal conflicts as an opportunity to raise broader questions of leadership, hero worship, surveillance, terrorism, and the degree to which the ends justify the means.

The term "supervillain" is employed only once in *Red Son*, at the trilogy's climax and the point where Superman's defeat of America's forces looks assured (fig. 15). It is used to describe a rogues' gallery of grotesque villains—the Parasite, Doomsday, Livewire, the Atomic Skull, and so on—that have been incorporated here as a series of Luthor's creations "designed to assassinate Superman and restore the fading fortunes of the United States of America" ("Ascendant," 5). Unlike Superman, whose human form indicates his innate humanity, these foes were originally designed, like many other fictional monsters, to manifest their ethical distance from the hero through their physical differences (think Frankenstein's monster, Mr. Hyde, and the like—particularly their representation in visual media). As in conventional Superman stories, these supervillains are all ultimately defeated, the human surrogate vanquishing the monstrous threat.

To better understand Millar's characterization of this Superman and to investigate some of the other topics that interested him in the writing of *Red Son*, I want to briefly look at the remaining series of characters whom he positions

Figure 14. Superman as Orwellian Big Brother ("Red Son Setting," *Superman: Red Son*, no. 3, August 2003, 1).

Figure 15. The "supervillains" ("Red Son Setting," *Superman: Red Son*, no. 3, August 2003, 27). Note the US Capitol in the background, which they are defending.

in opposition to his Soviet Superman. The first, and the lone antagonistic character unique to this storyworld, is Pyotr Iosif Roslov, a prototypical communist villain, head of Soviet Security Services, and illegitimate son of Stalin.[14] As the heir apparent to Stalin, Pyotr's jealousy of Superman's ascendance to Stalin's right hand and then to supreme leader largely defines his character. Superman ultimately corrals Pyotr and subjects him, like all other internal dissidents, to "pioneering neurosurgery" that renders them "Superman robots"—simpletons, if also "productive workers" ("Ascendant," 38; "Setting," 3). Pyotr's forced transformation into lobotomized slave labor points to one of the key issues facing Superman as a superior being and autocratic leader, a question taken up much earlier by Machiavelli: where should such a divinely anointed leader draw the "moral line" if they wish to maintain total control over a population that is not fully amicable to their methods or goals? For Pyotr, and Stalin, the answer was simply to meet resistance with greater violence, including murder. For Superman in *Red Son*, the line is drawn at forced pacification. Here, then, Superman draws our attention to one of the implicit rules for superheroes, one that has traditionally served to differentiate them from the supervillain: their unwillingness to take human life.[15] Even as Superman follows the letter of the law in *Red Son*, he clearly deviates from the spirit of the law. In doing so, he points to those questions of means and ends—does making the world peaceful and safe justify this kind of mind control? If he makes life easier for billions by rendering a few thousand intellectually harmless, is that not sufficient reason? Does mindless physical existence still constitute life? Does Superman's intellectual distance from common humanity render these reduced cognitive capacities irrelevant from his perspective (i.e., would a "normal" person feel remorse in lobotomizing rather than euthanizing a vicious dog so that it plays well with others)? Since Superman ultimately admits to Brainiac: "I could have had my utopia overnight if I'd hammered the world into submission with my fists" ("Setting," 17), he can be understood to have demonstrated restraint, but he does so only with the expectation that the whole world will ultimately see the benefit of *willfully* coming under his control. Still, these are not questions we ask of a conventionally heroic Superman.

The first superhuman foil that Superman faces, near the end of "Rising," is Bizarro, here depicted as Luthor's first attempt at creating an American superhuman. Crafted from Superman's own DNA, it is an imperfect duplicate nonetheless. Like the other monsters created by Luthor later, Bizarro's physical grotesqueness identifies him as inferior. Seeking equivalence in the new "superhuman arms race" ("Rising," 41), Luthor crests him with the US insignia as counterpoint to Soviet Superman's hammer and sickle. Satirically, his freakish appearance is revealed only after Luthor presents him with the following fanfare: "Norman Rockwell, apple pie, stars and stripes and the fourth of July ... The President asked me to design a figure who might encapsulate all these things" ("Rising," 31). Like Frankenstein's monster, it is a horribly flawed aggregate; like Dorian Gray's reflection, it reveals a decaying image—of America (fig. 16).

When Superman defeats his facsimile, Luthor goes into a violent spasm. The reason, however, is not that he had created only a lesser copy of the Soviet alien but rather that this inferior version still "had the tenacity to beat me at chess" ("Rising," 43). This sets the neoliberal competitive stage between Luthor and Superman, which extends to both the textual and extratextual considerations of America and Russia, socialism and democracy, surveillance and personal liberty, and so on, throughout the remainder of *Red Son*.

While Superman's fight with Bizarro serves as the action climax of the first issue, the principle conflict in the second is presented by Batman. The son of murdered political dissidents (they were passing out anti–Superman Day leaflets), he grows up in a Superman-controlled Russia. While issues of poverty and hunger that were endemic at the end of "Rising" have been solved by Comrade Superman by the start of "Ascendant," Batman represents that aspect of the population unhappy with the methods of governance and especially their restrictions on personal freedoms. Mocking the official propaganda published against him, Batman self-identifies as a "terrorist organization" ("Ascendant," 9); Superman refers to him in the narration as "a force of chaos in my world of perfect order. The dark side of the Soviet dream" ("Ascendant," 11). Moreover, just as Luthor will state later, he presents the reader with the idea that the

Figure 16. Bizarro ("Red Son Rising," *Superman: Red Son*, no. 1, June 2003, 37). Note the silhouetted depiction of Superman behind him, which foreshadows the Big Brother shift in the later issues.

human mind is the most powerful weapon of all, able ultimately to stand up to superhuman force(s). For a brief moment, in fact, Batman bests both Wonder Woman and Superman. He is only defeated by Wonder Woman's willingness to defer to the Man of Steel and to sacrifice herself for his benefit.[16] Batman's story further points to the estrangement that Superman and Wonder Woman both feel as superior beings, with Superman having already referred to himself as "a god" ("Ascendant," 2) who is "growing bored with human conversation" ("Ascendant," 15), and Wonder Woman screaming, "Get the hell out of my way little man!" at Batman as she strives to save Superman ("Ascendant," 37).

Rounding out his reimagined Justice League opponents, Superman is also opposed in the miniseries' climactic battle by both Hal Jordan's Green Lantern Corps and the Amazonians (led by Wonder Woman, now disillusioned with Superman). Superman easily dispatches both. Their fight against the Soviet Superman is clearly a result of their ignoble manipulation by Lex Luthor, now president of the United States. We can thus read the Green Lantern Corps as representing a domestic military force and the Amazonians a foreign army aiding America's fight. In the post-9/11 War on Terror, with a multinational military response under the direction of American leadership, this is particularly cogent.[17]

Brainiac, long a nemesis of Superman, plays a small but significant role in *Red Son*. Having shrunk Stalingrad and encased it in a test tube (an allusion to Kandor's fate in the comics canon), Brainiac is decapitated and later reprogrammed by Superman to both help him rule and keep him company as he slides into solitude in his Winter Palace.[18] In the end, though, Brainiac reveals to Superman that he has only been posing as the subordinate in order to maintain a position of influence and sway the world leader toward his own form of total global domination. As another alien form, Brainiac acts as the moral relativist against Superman's moral absolutism in the use/abuse of superior alien powers on humankind. Brainiac sees no problem in shrinking an entire city and its population down and then encasing it in a bottle for preservation. Superman challenges his colleague, arguing, "you took away what made them human" ("Setting," 16). But the reader here should recognize that the size and forced captivity of Stalingrad's population is not necessarily the essence of their humanity, at least not more so than the free will that Superman himself has incrementally denied his own subjects. When Superman stops short of total victory in his assault on the American forces, Brainiac challenges him with a moral quandary only available to such an all-powerful dictator: "But you can't stop now when you're on the brink of utopia, Superman. Denying them perfection is more morally corrupt than enforcing it" ("Setting," 32). Superman balks at Brainiac's claim and is subdued by the alien before being saved by Luthor. Brainiac, however, has one last move: his ship switches to autodestruct, and the resulting explosion would destroy the earth.[19] Superman responds with a final, heroic gesture, steering the ship into deep space, to his own apparent demise.

Finally, then, the American Lex Luthor emerges victorious over the Soviet Superman. By this point, however, their national allegiances are merely ornamentation for the questions of heroism and villainy in political leadership and militaristic intervention that the story is posing. The relationship between these two characters in *Red Son* complicates any simple good/evil or hero/villain dyad. Superman, though ideologically positioned as a trainee of Stalin (Stalin notes early in the book: "He [Superman] was raised to believe in everything that I stand for" ["Rising," 18]), is also clearly defined at the beginning as morally grounded in serving all humanity to the best of his abilities, saving Metropolis—an American city—from imminent destruction. Luthor, in contrast, is described from the very start as "the smartest man alive" ("Rising," 5), but also as lacking the super*hero*'s basic sense of responsibility to not kill lesser humans; it is he who puts the lives of the citizens of Metropolis, including his own wife, at risk just to test Superman's moral compass (and to extract DNA from which to create a clone).[20]

According to Christopher Robichaud, the concept of the hero is a normative one, representing what *ought* to be.[21] By extension then, a villain—as the converse of the hero—represents what ought *not* to be. Moreover, Robichaud argues that, for superheroes, negative duties (e.g., not hurting people) are more influential in the determination of behavior than positive duties (e.g., helping people). What this means is that traditional superheroes find it morally onerous to act toward the greater good when those actions are directly responsible for others being harmed. Thus, "the great responsibility that comes with their great power isn't a duty to use that power as a superhero, it's at most an obligation not to harm others by misusing it."[22] Said another way, the true moral responsibility that Superman, Luthor, and all of our superhuman characters face is not to become a superhero but simply to not become a supervillain! Yet at the same time, their advanced capabilities drive them to act and not just sit idly by.[23] This seemingly forces them to decide, implicitly or explicitly, between behaving like a superhero or a supervillain. It does not, however, require that they choose the same outcome each time.

Employing this in our analysis of Superman as the Soviet leader, we note again that he violates the principle of negative duties and, even if he is unwilling to kill, he is still fully willing to harm (lobotomize) numerous individuals in the service of a greater good. Luthor, of course, is equally willing to violate his negative duties in favor of his individual ambitions. It is not until the very end, when Superman recognizes his flawed methodology, that *any* of the chief characters in *Red Son* appear willing to abide by such negative duties and avoid harming some for the good of the many. Further, Superman's return to *superhero* in his final, heroic act only occurs after it is revealed to him that his actions as a ruler have been that of a *supervillain*. (Luthor of course does this for his own ends, and the sacrifice Superman makes immediately allows Luthor to finally achieve his goal of becoming the smartest being on the planet.)

"The hero—who usually wins—cannot exist," Anna Fahraeus and Dikmen Yakalı Çamoğlu remind us, "without an opponent in one form or other. The villain embodies this opposition.... The conflict that in the end produces and constructs the hero is the battle to overcome the antagonist or opposition, and resolve the transgressions that disrupt harmony, order, etc."[24] By this definition, it is Lex Luthor who emerges as the hero, as he is the one who wins in the end, defeating both Brainiac and Superman, and who also "resolve[s] the transgressions that disrupt harmony" in his establishment of the perfect, unified world that Superman never could complete.[25] This is the final question of means versus ends.[26] Luthor rose to the position of president only to have a better platform from which to attack Superman. To secure his position, he first makes America "great again," even as he despises his own populace and indeed all of humanity. With his fifty-year goal of becoming earth's smartest being finally achieved, Luthor assumes the role of global leader and returns to the Winter Palace, where he mines Superman's and Brainiac's documents. Turning to solving the kinds of problems that have eternally baffled humankind, he combines his own insights with theirs, establishing a global utopia while also carrying a 100 percent approval rating, both of which even Superman had been unable to accomplish. In doing so, he elevates humanity and confirms his own belief that only a human can lead humankind to greatness. According to the definition presented here, Luthor is ultimately the hero, the superhero, of *Red Son*.

This brings us to the final question—what, then, characterizes Superman as the superhero's opponent and thus our supervillain? For Luthor and Batman, and ultimately for Superman, the law of self-governance is critical to understanding heroes and villains in *Red Son*.[27] For each of these characters, and arguably the book itself, any act of alien interventionism necessarily enfeebles the ruled and vilifies the ruler. Millar, writing during the buildup to the American coalition's invasion of Iraq, has Superman tell Braniac, at the miniseries' climax: "We weren't born here and we've no right to interfere" ("Setting," 32). Depicted as a Cold War Soviet ruler, Superman is necessarily conceived as an empire builder, and his behavior reinforces this (only America and Chile remain outside his control at the beginning of "Ascendant"). However, America, in both the Cold War and the War on Terror, is equally culpable of empire building and thus, by extension, also to be understood as a supervillain rather than superhero. It is therefore the ideology of interventionism, which Kal-El assumes through both domestic surveillance and international militarism, rather than any national allegiance or political affiliation that ultimately nominates him, from his ascension to the mantle of Soviet leadership at the end of "Rising" to his assumption of the role of sacrificial savior at the climax of "Setting," as the reigning supervillain of *Superman: Red Son*.

Notes

1. Mark Millar, *Superman: Red Son* (Burbank, CA: DC Comics, 2014). In addition to Millar's role as writer, Dave Johnson and Kilian Plunkett receive chief credit as the artists.

2. "Truth . . ." was part of the introduction for *The Adventures of Superman* radio series (1940–1951); "Stalin . . ." is Millar's replacement (Millar, *Superman: Red Son*, "Red Sun Rising," 4). All further citations from *Superman: Red Son* will be from the 2014 compilation edition and will be included parenthetically in the body of the chapter, referring to issue title and corresponding page number, which I counted manually since the 2014 compilation of the trilogy from which I worked had no page numbers.

3. Several of these themes can be recognized in Millar's other work at the same time in *The Authority* and *The Ultimates*; Douglas Wolk, *Reading Comics: How Graphic Novels Work and What They Mean* (Cambridge, MA: Da Capo Press, 2007), 100.

4. William R. Thayer, "Machiavelli's Prince," *International Journal of Ethics* 2, no. 4 (July 1892): 477.

5. Niccolò Machiavelli, *The Prince*, ed. and trans. Harvey C. Mansfield, 2nd ed. (Chicago: University of Chicago Press, 1998), 61; cited in Harvey C. Mansfield, "Strauss on *The Prince*," *Review of Politics* 75, no. 4 (Fall 2013): 643n4.

6. Catherine H. Zuckert, "Machiavelli's *Prince*: Five Hundred Years Later," *Review of Politics* 75, no. 4 (Fall 2013): 493–96; and Mansfield, "Strauss on *The Prince*," 643.

7. Arthur Koestler, *Darkness at Noon*, trans. Daphne Hardy (1940; repr., Harmondsworth, Middlesex, England: Penguin, 1985), 81. Quoted in Philip Boobbyer, *The Stalin Era* (London:

Routledge, 2000), 207. Koestler's novel is historical fiction set in Soviet Russia in 1938, during the Stalin-led Great Purge.

8. "Code of the Comics Magazine Association of America, Inc.," adopted October 26, 1954, available at https://en.wikisource.org/wiki/Comic_book_code_of_1954. This and other aspects of the code were largely responsible for the ascendance of the superhero genre to its juggernaut status within the medium.

9. Wolk (*Reading Comics*, 100), also credits Dan Jurgens's *Booster Gold* (1986). The introduction of increasingly complex heroes and villains, such as we find with Stan Lee in the 1960s and particularly in Chris Claremont's work on the *X-Men* series in mid-1970s, precedes this but lacks the direct challenge to the conventional presentation of character motivations and means versus ends philosophical wrestling that is visible starting in the mid-1980s. Terrence R. Wandtke, "Introduction: Once Upon a Time Once Again," in *The Amazing Transforming Superhero! Essays on the Revision of Characters in Comic Books, Film and Television*, ed. Terrence R. Wandtke (Jefferson, NC: McFarland, 2007), 18.

10. Comics were certainly not alone here. In fact, the similarities to American cinema are notable in the establishment of the Hays Code in the early 1930s, which restricted film's ability to engage such questions until it was abandoned in favor of the ratings system in the late 1960s. American filmmakers, particularly those associated with the Hollywood Renaissance, spent much of the following decade questioning the conventions of classical Hollywood's genres, including, of course, definitions of hero and villain.

11. This is also foregrounded in Tom Desanto's introduction to the collected volume. See also Mervi Miettinen's excellent chapter on *Superman: Red Son* in her dissertation "Truth, Justice, and the American Way? The Popular Geopolitics of American Identity in Contemporary Superhero Comics," PhD diss., University of Tampere (Finland), School of Language, Translation and Literary Studies, 2012, 191–207.

12. Reading *Red Son* as a part of the unreliable narrator genre would be an interesting and possibly productive exercise.

13. For a robust consideration of melodrama in nineteenth-century Western literature and theater, see Peter Brooks, *The Melodramatic Imagination: Balzac, Henry James, Melodrama, and the Mode of Excess* (New Haven, CT: Yale University Press, 1976). The title of this chapter recalls the incorporation of melodrama's Manichaean schema into the costume design of twentieth-century Western films, with the heroes in white hats and the villains in black hats.

14. "With Russian Communists being the most frequent enemy in American comic books during the early years of the Cold War, the 'Ruskies' inherited characteristics used to define the previous European enemy of America, the Nazis. . . . The main avenue of characterization, ideologically speaking, lay in resurrecting the Nazis' depravity and transferring it to the Communists"; Nathan Vernon Madison, *Anti-Foreign Imagery in American Pulps and Comic Books, 1920–1960* (Jefferson, NC: McFarland, 2013), 166.

15. Mark D. White, "Why Doesn't Batman Kill the Joker?," in *Batman and Philosophy: The Dark Knight of the Soul*, ed. Mark D. White and Robert Arp (Hoboken, NJ: John Wiley and Sons, 2008), 5–16; Aeon J. Skoble, "Superhero Revisionism in *Watchmen* and *The Dark Knight Returns*," in *Superheroes and Philosophy: Truth, Justice, and the Socratic Way*, ed. Tom Morris and Matt Morris (Chicago: Open Court, 2005), 29–41; and Christopher Robichaud, "With Great Power Comes Great Responsibility: On the Moral Duties of the Super-Powerful and Super-Heroic," in *Superheroes and Philosophy: Truth, Justice, and the Socratic Way*, ed. Tom Morris and Matt Morris (Chicago: Open Court, 2005), 177–93.

16. This scene alone could be used to support the patriarchal hierarchy of both comics and the Western culture it reflects and engages. I fully suspect this was intentional on Millar's part and can be read as a critique on this Superman's character as well as a criticism of hero worship in

both socialist and democratic modes of ruling, especially when we take Luthor's and Kennedy's representations as US presidents here into account as well.

17. The action climax of the miniseries in which Superman and Brainiac attack Washington, DC, occurs in late summer/early fall of 2001; although the exact date is not specified, the choice in this context seems to hint at September 11. In addition, as history would have it, the first issue of *Red Son* was released on April 30, 2003, one day before American forces claimed the invasion of Iraq phase of Operation Iraqi Freedom completed.

18. Alan Moore did a similar thing with Doctor Manhattan in *Watchmen*, in which he becomes increasingly disassociated from humanity, ultimately taking up residence in his Martian palace. Jean Gray, when presented with this kind of power as Phoenix, goes crazy. The superhero's need for community is discussed by Mark Waid in his essay "The Real Truth about Superman: And the Rest of Us, Too," in *Superheroes and Philosophy: Truth, Justice, and the Socratic Way*, ed. Tom Morris and Matt Morris (Chicago: Open Court, 2005), 3–10.

19. My personal interpretation is that Luthor reprogrammed Brainiac's ship to switch to autodestruct during the time he was trapped inside it, before cutting the power to save Superman.

20. Luthor, here as in canon, sees other humans as pawns in his games. Following Freud, he views others only as resources to be exploited. See Sara Martin, "The Silent Villain: The Minimalist Construction of Patriarchal Villainy in John Le Carré's Karla Trilogy," in *Villains and Villainy: Embodiments of Evil in Literature, Popular Culture and Media*, ed. Anna Fahraeus and Dikmen Yakalı Çamoğlu (Amsterdam: Rodopi, 2011), 33; see also Mike Alsford, *Heroes and Villains* (London: Darton, Longman and Todd, 2006), 120.

21. Robichaud, "With Great Power Comes Great Responsibility," 178; and Jeph Loeb and Tom Morris, "Heroes and Superheroes," in *Superheroes and Philosophy: Truth, Justice, and the Socratic Way*, ed. Tom Morris and Matt Morris (Chicago: Open Court, 2005), 16.

22. Robichaud, "With Great Power Comes Great Responsibility," 186.

23. Jeff Brenzel, "Why Are Superheroes Good? Comics and the Ring of Gyges," in *Superheroes and Philosophy: Truth, Justice, and the Socratic Way*, ed. Tom Morris and Matt Morris (Chicago: Open Court, 2005), 159.

24. Anna Fahraeus and Dikmen Yakalı Çamoğlu, "Who Are the Villainous Ones? An Introduction," in *Villains and Villainy: Embodiments of Evil in Literature, Popular Culture and Media*, ed. Anna Fahraeus and Dikmen Yakalı Çamoğlu (Amsterdam: Rodopi, 2011), vii.

25. This is true to the point that Millar, borrowing an end suggested by Grant Morrison, makes Luthor into the ancestral heir of Jor-El and hence Kal-El, reimagining the escape craft as a time machine. It is only in Luthor's recategorization as a superhero that such a lineage makes sense in the Superman universe.

26. This is similar to the evaluation of Ozymandias's methods and results and his nomination as the ultimate hero in *Watchmen*.

27. I wonder if Millar, as a Scotsman, should be placed in this group as well.

CHAPTER 33

From Perfect Hero to Murderous Villain

A Comparative Analysis between the Fallen God Heroes of
Irredeemable *and* Injustice: Gods Among Us

MATTHEW McENIRY

THE TERM "GOD HERO" IS USED TO DESCRIBE THE MOST POWERFUL BEING(S) in a comic universe. These unique beings embody abilities envied by lesser heroes that villains cannot compete against, and that demand incredible self-control to wield responsibly. One such hero is DC Comics' own Superman, a boy scout in comparison to the brooding character of Batman, the warrior Amazon Wonder Woman, the brash Flash, or the logical Cyborg. His powers include the ability to fly at tremendous speeds, nigh invulnerability, superhuman hearing, stamina, speed, strength, smell, vision, super-breath, heat vision, and the ability to recharge through solar radiation absorption.[1] To the people of Metropolis and elsewhere in his world, Superman is the picture of absolute good. But what if being good no longer worked for a hero like this? What if a catastrophic event turned his world upside down, and he realized that being a boy scout and allowing others to go about their business unfettered was the reason for his profound loss? That is the story of Tom Taylor's series *Injustice: Gods Among Us*, wherein one of the most profound questions of comics history is addressed: what if Superman went bad? Mirroring this situation, Mark Waid's series *Irredeemable* tells the story of the Plutonian, a Superman-like hero who, without warning, becomes a villain. The series illustrates the pressures of ultimate power, the need for secrecy, and the results of what happens when trust is broken. This comparative analysis will peek into the minds of two gods as they wield their powers, and will reveal the detrimental results on the heroes, parents, innocents, governments, and worlds caught in the middle

Neither Taylor's Superman nor the Plutonian immediately snap; they both initially lead lives that those around them could admire. In *Injustice*, no. 1, Superman is elated to learn that Lois is pregnant, and to hear two heartbeats instead of one. His emotions are apparent even to Batman, because he's "grinning like an idiot."[2] It's not until the end of this issue that something is amiss: Lois is missing, and Batman is called to assist with the search, an event that eventually cascades into tragedy. The Plutonian, likewise, is an upstanding citizen of Sky City, the place where he revealed himself as a hero. His protective demeanor is so ingrained in the community that its welcome sign reads: "Welcome to Sky City: Protected by the Plutonian."[3] In flashback scenes throughout the series, we see that the Plutonian is extremely welcoming of new superhumans, so much so that he forms them into the group Paradigm. They are eventually welcomed by the world in a press conference on the White House lawn, along with a flashy presentation and show of cooperation.[4] His favorite, who becomes a pseudo-kid sidekick, is Samsara. During a friendly visit with Samsara, the Plutonian finds him distraught. Samsara has just received a communication from scientists at Sky City Research stating that a children's plague, which had killed hundreds before it was stopped by Paradigm, originated from technology given to them by the Plutonian.[5] Unable to lie convincingly to Samsara about the situation, he realizes that his status as a hero in the eyes of his best friend has been erased. The Plutonian flies out to the research station in an effort to quell his anger over Samsara's lost trust in him, but grief overwhelms him and he loses control willingly and purposefully, massacring millions in the process.[6]

The events of *Injustice: Gods Among Us* start with deception and, as with the Plutonian, end with overwhelming grief turned to anger. The Joker is the catalyst; he begins the crisis by poisoning Superman with kryptonite-laced scarecrow gas, causing him to hallucinate a threatening doomsday, which he carries into outer space. Suddenly, he hears "two heartbeats coming from one person—stop beating."[7] Superman realizes too late that he has inadvertently killed his wife, Lois Lane, and their unborn child. He watches in horror as a nuclear device, hidden in Metropolis and tied to Lois's heartbeat, detonates.[8] Ground zero of the detonation is where Superman cradles the body of his wife, consumed by his grief and overwhelmed by sorrow. Wonder Woman finds him and encourages him by stating, "You are not responsible ... that madman orchestrated the whole thing."[9] Superman realizes that justice must be done because the personal loss and the devastation is too great to allow it to go unpunished. Meanwhile, in the custody of Batman, the Joker marvels at what he has wrought in Metropolis and for its hero. Most notable is his comment on what Superman might become: "He's a god who has deluded himself into believing he's a man, what will he turn into?"[10] Batman's retort, that "there are some things even you can't corrupt, Joker," is quickly proven wrong as Superman bursts into the room, emanating a mix of rage, emotional devastation, and guilt.[11] Superman, tired of the excuses, punches through Joker's chest cavity as the psychopath gives one last laugh and Batman looks on in shocked horror.[12]

Irredeemable and the events that lead the Plutonian to unleash his powers are more internal, a conflicting battle within himself that finally reaches a point of no return—the loss of Samsara's trust. His rage and anguish are evident during his violent confrontation with the offending researchers as he yells:

> No one trusted me like he did! And you took that away from me! I didn't mean for Jackson to happen! Is that how this works? I made one stupid mistake, and now I have nothing? Now no one will ever look up to me again? After all the good I have done? Stop it! Stop looking at me like I'm some bomb that could go off at any time! Is that what you think I am? Is that what you want me to be? Is it? Fine.[13]

The final frame illustrates the Plutonian in the foreground and the devastation of his Sky City in the background. The scene of devastation clearly portrays the betrayal he feels from those he trusted and the abandonment by the one person he had nurtured. This is the birth of the omnicidal, godlike villain.

The two heroes are now out of control, but they were not alone in their formerly altruistic efforts. Superman had the Justice League and the Plutonian had Paradigm. How were these groups affected by the sudden change that came upon the leader they had looked up to? A clear division manifests in the Justice League. Batman can't believe that the man he thought an incorruptible force has allowed his anger to get the best of him. Many heroes of the Justice League fall in with Superman and his idea for a new world order, which promises to prevent war and violence. Raven, Hawkgirl, Wonder Woman, Cyborg, Flash, Green Lantern, Shazam, and eventually Damien Wayne unite under this new rule. On the opposing side, Batman, Batwoman, Green Arrow, Black Canary, Nightwing, Captain Atom, Martian Manhunter, Black Lightning, Aquaman, and Huntress intend to resist this establishment.[14] Superman's desire is to instigate a new regime to rise up that encourages peace between all nations. He goes as far as suggesting that the heroes of the day have failed the world. His address to the globe is one of personal conviction inspired by intense loss:

> To those who would do the same, those who would hurt others, know that I will come for you. I don't care about your lands or your beliefs. I don't care about your petty squabbles. I don't care if you're a madman or a terrorist, a king or a president. You do not have the right to take innocent lives. I am calling for an immediate world-wide ceasefire. All hostilities will stop immediately—or I will stop them. It's over.[15]

With this declaration, Superman decides to remove the free will of those who may do harm to others. He and his team demonstrate their willingness to accomplish this by taking various significant actions. They neutralize the threat of Aquaman and his underwater nation; they take Black Adam's power away, effectively killing the ancient being; and they banish the god of war, Ares. Superman helps to instill within governments a fear of doing wrong. When Batman confronts him, Superman declares his action an achievement: "They should be too scared to hurt each other."[16] Counter to the argument, Batman worries that, by killing the Joker, Superman has blurred the line between right and wrong. Eventually, Superman becomes personally responsible for more than just the Joker's death. Nightwing, Martian Manhunter, and Green Arrow are all victims to Superman's rage and brutality. In an attempt to quell the hero rebellion at its source, Superman breaks Batman over his knee, fracturing several vertebrae and leaving him helpless.[17] It is only through the intervention of an unexpectedly supercharged Alfred that Batman is rescued and carried off to recover and continue the resistance.[18]

The Plutonian's team, Paradigm, is in a much more dangerous position. The first few panels of issue no. 1 begin with the Plutonian vaporizing the Hornet along with his wife, baby, and daughter. The Plutonian mocks the Hornet's pleas for mercy because she's just a girl, bellowing that he knows exactly what she is, "a carbon bag of atoms and bioelectricity."[19] Unhinged from the reality of responsibility, the Plutonian carves a swath through his former teammates. Inferno, Metalman, Gazer, Samsara, and Hornet are taken out in the first few days. Those remaining—Qubit, Kaiden, Bette Noir, Gilgamos, Charybdis and Scylla, and Volt—are left trying to survive. With only the slightest chance of success, they split up to try to discover as much information about the Plutonian (known to them as Tony) as possible.[20] To their credit, they succeed in finding out pieces of Tony's life formerly hidden from them. Tony had a secret identity as a radio producer, and a girlfriend, who had revealed his true identity to her colleagues, hiding in the ruins of Sky City.[21] The team uncovers facts about his childhood, his multiple foster parents, the origin of his powers, and his progression into becoming the Plutonian. Qubit, the team's technology savant, is able to locate Tony's volcanic hideout. This discovery leads to Bette Noir guiltily divulging that she and Tony had slept together after using a mystical candle that made him mortal. Using that information, she crafts a bullet from the same mystical candle.[22] Despite this cunning plan and an otherworldly demonic hunter as a formidable adversary, Qubit saves Tony, despite opposition from Paradigm.[23]

It is during this fracturing of unity that their long-dead teammate, Hornet, is successful in pulling off his contingency plan. Interstellar aliens, collectively named the Vespa, return to earth to imprison the Plutonian as part of a bargain made with Hornet for teleportation technology and planetary coordinates to helpless planets.[24] Unfortunately, even they are unable to contain the Plutonian for long and are forced to abandon him in an insane asylum in the heart of a star.[25] With the Plutonian being gone for months, the world tries to rebuild with the help of what's left of Paradigm.[26] After a series of events that include the Plutonian returning and wreaking devastation across earth, Qubit figures out how to appeal to his spirit of survival. Teleporting the mystical bullet into his heart, Qubit promises Tony that he'll set him up "with a new life, a clean slate, a second chance. I erase your mistakes."[27] But first, Tony must cleanse the world of life-threatening radiation that has been unleashed, a by-product of a failed desperation move by the world's remaining governments to remove the Plutonian.[28] After the Plutonian saves the earth one final time, we see that the radiation has ravaged his body beyond repair. Qubit, knowing that this would happen, harvests the pure idea of what the Plutonian was supposed to be and sends it out to hundreds of realities and worlds in the hope that "someone, somewhere . . . can stumble upon the notion that is you . . . make it theirs . . . and get it right this time."[29]

The similarities between the Plutonian and the Superman of *Injustice* are uncanny. Both governments try to limit the heroes through extreme measures, both involving the parents of the respective heroes. There is a sense of contagious helplessness and primordial fear around the respective worlds that Superman and the Plutonian inhabit. One is a tyrant, the other a psychopath, but neither has lost his way. To them, their individual tragedies have made the path forward clearer. Superman wants a world of peace, one in which superheroes are able to permanently dispose of all threats to humanity, whether from a supervillain or a rogue militaristic country. Superman attempts to work within a system of nonviolence, which includes his own interventions. Attempting to eliminate global conflicts by interfacing directly with leaders seems an efficient approach. However, those nations simultaneously must forfeit their free will. Superman's loss is so focused on the madman who disrupted his life and ended Lois's that he no longer cares what anyone else might think. The result is not a democracy; it is his word.[30]

Superman also finds Batman's ways to be cowardly. A hands-off approach is no longer acceptable; the criminals must be permanently neutralized so they can never hurt anyone again. Gotham can no longer harbor them or attempt to treat them. The assault on Arkham Asylum, orchestrated by Superman, is meant to punish unworthy criminals. The Arkham inmates are transferred to secret locations, and the team standing with Superman begins "blundering into every major conflict on the planet."[31] Superman himself sits the leaders of Israel and Palestine down to agree to terms; Wonder Woman appears in Burma to stop the conflict there; a show of force from Green Lantern and Shazam enforces peace in Syria; and Raven shows up "amongst the warring nomadic tribes of Sudan . . . where she literally terrified them into submission."[32] In a secret discussion with the US president, Batman sees that the end of bloodshed isn't the takeaway from these events. It's impossible to stop it all completely: "[T]he reason for the fighting is still there, the religion, the land disputes, the ancient feuds."[33]

With conflicts suddenly stopping, but without anyone to enforce the peace agreements that are drafted, the world lives in fear not only of recurring conflict but of the judgment of gods. Toward the end of the series, however, Superman is no longer a creator of peace but rather an enforcer of his own will. Superman has manipulated his allies into enslaving the world, because he knows what's better for humanity. Whether that's allowing Wonder Woman to shirk off her inhibitions, harnessing Cyborg's and Hawkgirl's sense of justice, or appealing to Shazam's internal child, Superman is a master at ensuring obedience from his team. Focused on preventing death from anywhere, he identifies Batman as the source of his misery and seeks to end him by any means necessary. The opposing heroes' strategy against Superman is met with increasing resistance when both Martian Manhunter and Green Arrow are killed. How could Jor El have unleashed this force upon the earth? How could Clark Kent have turned away from the ideologies that were instilled in him earlier in his life?[34] We see Superman's selfishness arise from the need to justify what was taken from him in the beginning. He's no longer able to turn away from the tragedy inflicted upon him; vengeance must be exacted and the all else made right, forcefully if needed. It is within this new regime that people's free will is diminished; the price of peace will be costly.

The Plutonian, on the other hand, has no such illusions of helping people. His narcissistic attitude during the series is a symptom of holding in so much contempt and hatred for his fellow men and women. While a supremely powerful being, the Plutonian is flawed, as he is unable to control his powers in a finite way. His super-hearing allows him to hear when people need him, but it also exposes him to criticism. His body is impenetrable, but his strength is so vast that he's unable to meaningfully have a relationship. Fans and lovers must admire him from afar, always reminding the Plutonian that, although he's part of a super team, he'll always be alone when it comes to personal desires. Without a manifestation of trust and admiration, the Plutonian becomes sullen, and to escape from his responsibility for so many lives he builds a hideout in the core of an active volcano and takes trips to the moon for silence.[35] While the Samsara event triggers his downward spiral, this is just the culmination of a series of sorrowful life experiences that have led to the assassination of his character.

The Plutonian started as a probe with the powers of alien gods, "designed to wander amidst the populace, sampling its attributes and mirroring its emotional spectrum."[36] The probe manifested into a child when it came upon a flawed mother with a desperate desire to right her wrongs, at least at the moment. Her shame was that she had killed her child early on, and the invulnerability of the Plutonian baby compelled her to relive her shame repeatedly. She then ended her life, throwing the Plutonian into foster homes where he never fit in.[37] His abilities showed themselves at the most inopportune times, such as squeezing a foster brother too hard, thereby crippling him, and killing a bully with a simple push; meanwhile, he witnessed the development of his foster mother's brain cancer. He had a stint as a feral child, nicknamed Wolfboy, and the aggressiveness he experienced out in the wild was something he tried hard to forget, because it reminded him of how cruel he could be.[38]

The Plutonian doesn't allow many of his friends to get too close, lest they see his dark side. Only during an intense lovemaking session as a mortal is the Plutonian made vulnerable, allowing Bette Noir a glimpse of what is hidden deep within him, something she also saw during their first hostile confrontation, "god laughing at us."[39] The Plutonian becomes a master manipulator when his inhibitions no longer hold him back. He goads his former teammates into revealing themselves for a final but lethal confrontation. He both uses and disposes of partners he meets at the insane asylum, drawing on their talents to further his goals and desires until they lose their value as assets. He attempts to learn more about the universe, its secrets, and the origins of his creator parents by stalling for time and inquiring into the methods of their scientific experiments. He operates without a conscience and has no qualms about betraying friendships or acquaintances. Although the Plutonian's actions seem dictatorial, he doesn't want to rule over anyone; he only wants the world to fear him, because that's better than him fearing the world. He no longer wants to be bound by the rules and constraints of the society that he's adapted to, so he starts to tear it down to fit the image that he's accepted. The Plutonian acts like a god, creating a new world and instilling it with his feelings of fear, helplessness, and impending doom. There is no better villain to live in such a world than a former hero who once lived with those concerns during his upstanding life.

Both Superman and the Plutonian, in their respective series, illustrate that even those with tremendous godlike power cannot alter free will without consequence. For Superman, the loss of his wife and unborn child create a burning desire to shield others from such tragedy, but in the process, he creates a regime that directly opposes free will. Superman becomes a tyrant god, and despite his best intentions, creates a world government out of fear, overwhelming power, and the enforcement of peace through violence. The Plutonian becomes a wrathful god, no longer hindered by the constructs of the world that he once protected. He is let down by the people he attempts to serve, he craves unconditional love but can't receive it, he wants to help everyone he can but is unable, and he needs to be trusted and seen as a role model. Although Samsara's abandonment is the catalyst for his downfall, the Plutonian has no hope from his inception as a human being. The flaws he carries with him throughout his life negatively impact his psyche to the point of breaking. His final act of saving the earth is based upon the hope that he'll be given a second chance to prove to everyone that he is worthy of love.

Notes

1. "Kal-El (New Earth)," Fandom, DC Database, available at http://dc.wikia.com/wiki/Kal-El (New_Earth).

2. Tom Taylor and Jheremy Raapack, *Injustice: Gods Among Us*, vol. 1, January 15, 2013, 16.

3. Mark Waid and Peter Krause, *Irredeemable*, no. 8, November 2009, 5.

4. Mark Waid and Peter Krause, *Irredeemable*, no. 9, December 2009, 5–7.

5. Waid and Krause, *Irredeemable*, no. 8, 15.

6. Waid and Krause, *Irredeemable*, no. 8, 15–17.

7. Tom Taylor and Mike S. Miller, *Injustice: Gods Among Us*, vol. 3, January 27, 2013, 18–19.

8. Taylor and Miller, *Injustice*, vol. 3, 20–22.

9. Tom Taylor and Mike S. Miller, *Injustice: Gods Among Us*, vol. 4, February 5, 2013, 10.

10. Taylor and Miller, *Injustice*, vol. 4, 19.

11. Taylor and Miller, *Injustice*, vol. 4, 20.

12. Taylor and Miller, *Injustice*, vol. 4, 22.

13. Waid and Krause, *Irredeemable*, no. 8, 18–19.

14. Tom Taylor and Jheremy Raapack, *Injustice: Gods Among Us*, vol. 18, May 14, 2013, 21–22.

15. Tom Taylor and Mike S. Miller, *Injustice: Gods Among Us*, vol. 6, February 19, 2013, 22.

16. Tom Taylor and Mike S. Miller, *Injustice: Gods Among Us* vol. 10, March 19, 2013, 8–9.

17. Tom Taylor and Mike S. Miller, *Injustice: Gods Among Us*, vol. 36, September 17, 2013, 3–4.

18. Taylor and Miller, *Injustice*, vol. 36, 19–22.

19. Mark Waid and Peter Krause, *Irredeemable*, no. 1, April 2009, 6–11.

20. Waid and Krause, *Irredeemable*, no. 1, 27.

21. Mark Waid and Peter Krause, *Irredeemable*, no. 2, May 2009, 8–9.

22. Mark Waid and Diego Barreto, *Irredeemable*, no. 14, June 2010, 19.

23. Mark Waid and Diego Barreto, *Irredeemable*, no. 15, July 2010, 20–22.

24. Mark Waid and Peter Krause, *Irredeemable*, no. 18, October 2010, 20, 26.

25. Mark Waid and Peter Krause, *Irredeemable*, no. 22, February 2011, 19–20.

26. Mark Waid and Peter Krause, *Irredeemable*, no. 20, December 2010, 20.

27. Mark Waid and Diego Barreto, *Irredeemable*, no. 37, May 2012, 8.

28. Mark Waid and Diego Barreto, *Irredeemable*, no. 30, October 2011, 20–24.

29. Waid and Barreto, *Irredeemable*, no. 37, 20–21.

30. Brian Buccellato and Tom Derenick, *Injustice: Gods Among Us, Year Five*, vol. 3, January 5, 2016, 20.

31. Taylor and Raapack, *Injustice*, vol. 18, May 14, 2013, 8.

32. Taylor and Raapack, *Injustice*, vol. 18, May 14, 2013, 9–10.

33. Taylor and Raapack, *Injustice*, vol. 18, May 14, 2013, 11.

34. Tom Taylor and Mike S. Miller, *Injustice: Gods Among Us*, vol. 34, September 3, 2013, 22.

35. Mark Waid and Peter Krause, *Irredeemable*, no. 7, October 2009, 21–22.

36. Mark Waid and Diego Barreto, *Irredeemable: Redemption*, part 1, no. 32, December 2011, 14–15.

37. Waid and Barreto, *Irredeemable: Redemption*, part 1, no. 32, 20–21.

38. Waid and Barreto, *Irredeemable: Redemption*, part 1, no. 32, 23.

39. Mark Waid and Diego Barreto, *Irredeemable*, no. 13, May 2010, 19.

CHAPTER 34

Distortions of Supervillainy, Radical Interiority, and Victimhood in Sam Kieth's *The Maxx*

TIFFANY HONG

THE MAXX, LIKE SO MANY OTHER PRODUCTIONS OF THE 1990S, IS CURRENTLY enjoying a resurgence and return to cultural relevance in a remastered IDW edition (with new colors by Ronda Pattison) in celebration of the twentieth anniversary of its first printing with Image Comics. At first glance, it is replete with conventions of the 1990s superhero comic, from the steroid musculature of the character design, to the inky layouts and equally dark thematic concerns. *The Maxx* remains equal parts provocative, disturbing, and inscrutable because of Sam Kieth's confrontation between the psychological landscape and the conditions of the superhero genre itself: the inherent schizophrenia of the masked split identity, the interdependent triangulation of hero/villain/victim, and the necessity of victimhood as a precondition of heroism and rescue. *The Maxx*'s main conceit—that the titular superhero is in reality a mere inhabitant of a rape survivor's unconscious writ large—destabilizes the genre's assumptions of narrative hierarchy and linearity: that is, the prioritization of voice and narrative authority from hero, to villain, to the oft-silenced or absent victim, and heroic action as a response to or a preempting of villainous action. These conventions are deliberately obfuscated in their representation to the reader: our superhero arguably has no independent existence, let alone an anchor to reality; our villain is seemingly omniscient and stands almost outside the diegetic universe; and the interiority of our "victim" expands to occupy and define the entire narrated world.

Notably, the reading experience is focalized, directed, and even edited by the villain of the series: the serial rapist-murderer and mystical shaman Mr. Gone. In tandem with this, Kieth's aesthetics—particularly his use of panels, insets, colors, and gutters—almost weaponizes the technical aspects of sequential art in order to impose the scattered, unreliable, and atemporal experience of trauma itself on the reader. The reader of *The Maxx* is subsumed into the multiple echelons of mimetic reality that are simultaneously produced and rejected in their very manifestation, compelling us—through our narratological and epistemological reliance on the villain—to deconstruct the insularity and legitimacy of these assigned roles: hero/villain/victim, and passive/objective reader.

The very first pages of *The Maxx*, vol. 1, establish the permeability of boundaries between narration and the narrated (fig. 17). The image is bordered with uneven, almost organic keyhole "intrusions" into the page's solitary panel: this unusual framing alerts the reader that this is mediated reality, although at this point we are not privileged with knowledge of the mediating authority (Kieth? The narrator? The Maxx?). We are compelled to gaze into an impenetrable cardboard box, the shape and positioning of which approximates a muted television screen. At the same time, caption boxes in what we will come to identify as Maxx's signature font and color invite us into the diegetic world by means of "voiceover," as he (disadvantageously) compares the cast of *Cheers* to "the shows in [his] mind."[1]

This semiotic understanding, nevertheless, is soon dispelled by the entrance of secondary authority figures, policemen who alert Maxx (and us) that what we have been signaled to recognize as internal monologue has in fact been "audible" all along: "Sometimes, it's *luck* that saves them. Sometimes it's *fate*. Yeah. *Usually*, it's fate. But, sometimes, it's me."[2] The policemen truncate Maxx's real-time noir narration of his own performance, transitioning to a white, standardized speech bubble with a "And sometimes it's *us!*" that disabuses us of our genre-dictated suspension of disbelief.[3] What is odd is the unproblematized reversion back to a lettering mode now exposed as transparent or externalized, as Maxx enunciates through the same signature caption box: "Damn, I was talking out loud again."[4]

"Reality" is further fragmented by the comic's manipulation of generic expectations through the initial setup of hero, villain, and victim. In much the same way that we as comic readers acknowledge the semiotic logic that signals us to read dialogue versus internal monologue through iconography repeated into objective meaning (speech bubbles being indicative of audible text), the experienced reader is familiar with tropes and their inevitable trajectories: in this case, the woman in a dark alley (fig. 18). First of all, the artwork reflects our perverse complicity—visually, narratively, tangibly, with the turn of the page—following the cliché: an impossibly sexualized woman occupies the top left corner, positioned to the full advantage of our scrutiny, our pitying but lurid, knowing gaze. Neil Cohn writes: "In a sense, a sequence of narrative images acts as a simulation of how an individual might view a fictitious visual scene"; we are implicated in and by perspective.[5]

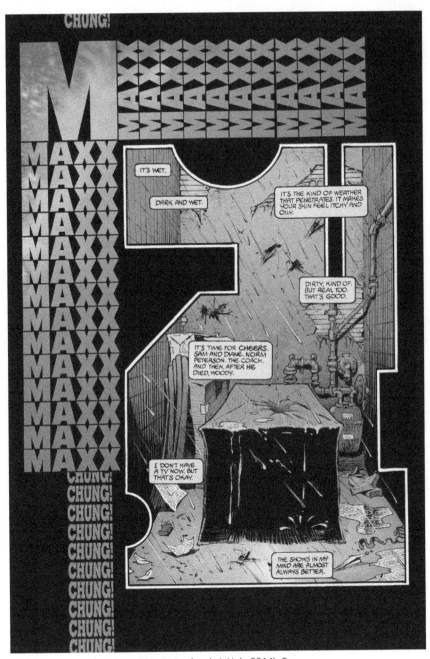

Figure 17. From *The Maxx: Maxximized*, vol. 1 (July 2014), 5.

Figure 18. From *The Maxx: Maxximized*, vol. 1 (July 2014), 6.

Second, her anticipated victimization is deferred—twice. Maxx heroically, dramatically (narrating aloud his own heroism, as no one else will) rescues her from her would-be attackers. Our base, anticipatory complicity is transformed into vicarious revelry in just off-panel violence (communicated through lettering that graphically splatters and drips out of its speech bubble, destabilizing once again the established boundaries of what is represented and what is shown). We have no choice but to accept the artist's depiction as our referent for reality, just as the policemen impose order on the clearly delusional Maxx, but our assumption of the conflated rational and the real is perturbed by the rescuers' inability to see the woman—a critique of the effacement of victims from superhero narratives—who is left to be violated off-panel (her words similarly trailing off the page) by Mr. Gone. Elizabeth MacFarlane elucidates sequential art's particular suitability to navigating the porousness of competing realities: "The transition from the real world to the imagined world in comics can be achieved far less awkwardly because of the third diegetic level of the image. The transition is seamless, from the 'lens' trained upon our authentic author/character, to tracking the movements of that character's imagined nightmare."[6] Mr. Gone supernaturally masks the anonymous theater-going woman (herself a would-be consumer of mimetic reality) from all but Maxx and ourselves; the lettering and art deprive us of recourse to an objective sensory litmus. The villain's and his minions' (the blind Iszes) very nature is a play on perception: Mr. Gone's cape is seemingly inseparable from himself and the shadows, and the Iszes appear to human eyes to embody the costumes they wear; in parallel fashion, our titular superhero (despite his clichéd, autonarrated rhetoric) has failed to "save the girl," and seems to play the hero nowhere but in his own demented reality (fig. 19).

With Maxx, we then segue into the Outback through a series of "CHUNG!"s and "MAXX"s that intrude from a black background into the drawn panels; the visualized onomatopoeia—an approximation of an approximation—appears to originate outside mediated (framed) "Reality" and in fact functions to transition the setting to a white-paneled landscape that seems to exceed its very boundaries (fig. 20). Even when sequences in the Outback are "framed," the borders are recognizably and iconographically a part of the jungle-themed Outback, with its palm fronds and string-bound sticks. Moreover, the white background (the default color) signals space and expanse, whereas the black background of Reality confines and boxes us in. In fact, the jungle panels and insets feature borders that are themselves artistic and that refuse tidy categorization into assigned space. In Reality, conversely, the frame often seeps into the panel itself, minimizing and intruding into the panel's privileged spacing over the border or gutter. Thierry Groensteen iterates the equivalence of framing and internal narrative logic: "To close the panel is to enclose a fragment of

Figure 19. From *The Maxx: Maxximized*, vol. 1 (July 2014), 11.

Figure 20. From *The Maxx: Maxximized*, vol. 1 (July 2014), 12.

space-time belonging to the diegesis, to signify the coherence. To change the frame is often the equivalent, for the reader, of causing a displacement in space, then in time—or in these two dimensions at the same time."[7] Kieth's integrated borders and overflowing gutters repudiate this neat division of realities and spatiotemporal dimensions.

The visuals of *The Maxx* embody the mutual permeability of Reality and the Outback—Julie Winters's reified psychological terrain—and parallel our focalizers' and thus our ability to properly differentiate or prioritize the two as visual information. Without recourse to linguistic signifiers of speaker, tense, or relationship to reader, as in a purely textual, diegetic work such as a novel, focalization in the comic is diverted into the narrative and the (visually) per-spectival modes. That is to say, (a) who is telling us the story (whose voice, point of view, caption boxes), and (b) from whose perspective is this story shown to us (what camera angles, what shots, what proximity, to borrow from a cinematic vocabulary)? With the comic panel, we are always already in present tense, our gaze already co-opted, focused, typically controlled by a diegetically external hand ("the Artist"). *The Maxx* vacillates between multiple narratives, voices, and time lines that vie for our immediate sympathies and prioritization in our retroactively imposed chronology. The artwork, lettering, and narrative trajec-tory deliberately obfuscate the fallacy of a singular, objective author(ity), as we alternately occupy the consciousness of Julie, the Maxx, Mr. Gone, and Sara, all of whom unknowingly (with the exception of Gone) participate in and affect the coherence of one another's externalized psyches (fig. 21).

The comic's usage of the inset is remarkable: where the inset typically pres-ents a zoom in to the action on a splash page, Kieth deploys them in *The Maxx* to approximate depth within a two-dimensional medium. His insets often penetrate the main artwork in an X-ray fashion that exposes the overlapping but spatially equivalent worlds of Reality and the Outback. The insets serve not to focus on details within the background page but to utilize the artistic approximation of depth as a means of underscoring the shared spatial dimen-sion of the two intersecting worlds that refuse a flat-plane graphic hierarchy of foreground and background. "Indeed, the image, to the degree that it relies on the perspectival code and practices the staging of the planes, creates the illusion of three-dimensionality. The text, on the other hand, frees itself from this mimetic transcendence, respecting and confirming the bi-dimensional materiality of the writing surface."[8] Kieth complicates Groensteen's qualifica-tion through a palimpsest of "realities" penetrating the Cartesian perspective of the whole image: a Goodyear blimp is simultaneously a flying air whale, visually dissected by the use of insets and overlayered panels. The comic in these instances often does away with borders altogether, further removing the technical cues that alert us to the containment of visualized spaces: in other

Figure 21. From *The Maxx: Maxximized*, vol. 1 (July 2014), 56.

words, we are no longer certain of which world seeps into which, and which is our anchor reality.

With Maxx immediately established as an unreliable narrator and super-hero, Julie Winters is next discounted as the reader's guide into the narrative. In an image that echoes the foreboding full-body shot of our first victim (the theater-going woman in the first issue), we are introduced to Julie, who is

Figure 22. From *The Maxx: Maxximized*, vol. 1 (July 2014), 43.

instantly subjected to criticism within the comic itself as an anticipation of the "unreality" of her comic book apparel. Her dress and her self-empowerment are for her (and now us) inextricable: her client compares her to a "hooker," to which she imperiously responds: "I *have* a job. While you have a blanket with *vomit* on it."⁹ Sara later elucidates, to Julie's displeasure, that she works as a "freelance social worker" simply to maintain control over a less fortunate clientele (fig. 22).¹⁰ Julie is eventually kidnapped by Mr. Gone and subjected to his laughably clichéd embodiment of male sexual revenge. Even as she deconstructs her own visual in characteristically metatextual fashion (deflating Gone's anticipation of enacting vengeance on the unattainable idealized female figures of his youth), her image is simultaneously, inevitably sexualized so that Gone's projections are reified, with our cooperation as proxies. We cannot help but gaze at her—and our first female victim—in the manner Gone intended; it is the text that overwrites this intended signification as ridiculous and thus untenable in its lack of originality.

Julie is a notably postmodern character who constantly scrutinizes the hackneyed nature of her own plotline and her own depiction—while regurgitating victim-blaming slogans and decontextualized feminist theory. It is significant that she refuses to acknowledge, articulate, or narrate her own experience of rape, reverting to direct avoidance, cynical Psych 101 deconstructions of her

Figure 23. From *The Maxx: Maxximized*, vol. 1 (July 2014), 21.

own narrative arc, or echoes of mottos like, "If you don't act dumb, you don't get hurt."[11] In *The Maxx*, no. 6, she and Sara's mother debate Paglia versus Steinem, and in the same issue, Julie offers a metacommentary on the dialogue about the prevalence of sex and violence in the media, musing, "Someone could read *pin-ups* just in the way I'm standing here" while positioned in a Frazetta-homage pose.[12]

Early on, the comic compels us to occupy various subject positions as readers—of the stories that victims/heroes/villains tell themselves and others—and simultaneously dismantles the mechanisms (visual and narrative) by which we are taught to trust our narrator, to expect genre conventions, to compartmentalize and prioritize information, and to construct archetypal rescue trajectories. Again in issue no. 1, we are *coerced* into an automatic perspective that we later recognize as simultaneous with that of the villain—not the hero or victim—of the series (fig. 23). Before Glorie is raped by Gone in the laundromat, we are introduced to her character as she is being harassed by her boyfriend Tommy, who insists on "touching privileges" and who rehearses a speech on the exclusivity of their relationship and his consequent right to her body while Gone rapes and tortures her off-panel, signified by the same graphic lettering attributed to his first victim.[13] To augment the irony, Glorie—in consciously sexualized apparel and poses—toys with a dagger that her father has bequeathed her "f'r *protection*"; the failure of patriarchal possession/protection is played out by Maxx and Gone for control of Julie Winters.[14]

Maxx's and Julie's narratives exceed them in different ways: Maxx is subsumed into Julie's storyline (indeed, he is terrified that he does not exist outside of it), and Julie performs her own "strength" with steely self-delusion: she speaks in borrowed words, and invites only to deflate the projection of the male gaze by emphasizing her belly and biting her toenails, defiantly engaging the repulsive excessive and the abject. Her particular brand of empowerment at the expense of others as a demonstration of agency is a string of barren speech acts that the teenage Sara quickly dismantles. Julie surrounds herself with those even less fortunate in a parasitical assertion of her relative power and continued invulnerability. Her repression is so successful that her interiority, her (literal) dimensionality, her motivation, are all relegated to a narrative that snowballs out of her conscious control. Julie's psyche continues this necessary arc of trauma and recovery as an entirely separate storyline, with attendant characters with whom she is forced to interact only through the repeated intervention of Mr. Gone.

Mr. Gone is our villain, but he is also our most reliable "in" to the story. Indeed, he is everyone's "in," as he is a sort of mystic psychical sorcerer who can access everyone else's Outback/interiorities and control the passage and the *timing* of information. Mr. Gone is constantly telling stories: to Julie, to Maxx, to his daughter Sara, to his victims, to the reader. He is the only one who understands the increasingly fragmented narrative of the comic book itself. At the same time, he is a serial rapist and murderer who is literally disembodied early on and must concentrate his power in his voice alone (that is, his manipulation and his shamanistic magic). The comic positions Gone as a character at the same time that it privileges him as a narrator. Gone addresses "us" directly as he narrates a fight scene between Maxx and Mako, whom the former dourly acknowledges as one of the Savage Dragon's D-rate villains. Once again, the visuals are satirized in the text, as the Gone voice (he's been beheaded at this point) sexualizes and moralizes on the violence depicted: "Ain't it great when they talk dirty?"[15] As ad hoc narrator, he delights in the stock trajectory of the protagonist being beaten before ultimately triumphing that it "justifies anything th'hero does t'him later ... no matter how gross!"[16] In *The Maxx*, no. 9, he exists as a recording (he manifests on "this plane" as a talking bag of clay, as a rotting head, as tapes, as a computer file—narrative voice distilled), addressing his victim as "you."[17] In *The Maxx*, no. 10, he tells a story from inside Julie's head (which he can literally occupy and access in a way and at a time that Julie herself cannot). Sarah Richardson condemns "[t]he implicitly aggressive act of representing others and speaking on their behalf [as] a form of imperialism, an appropriation of another's voice"; Gone literalizes this violation by traversing the materialized, geographically concentrated nexus of Julie's Outback.[18]

The series' most powerful pages occur in Mr. Gone's own autobiography, which is itself mediated through his daughter Sara and later through Julie, both of whom access the text expressly because Gone defers their curiosity with "I only ask that you not read it until I'm finished."[19] In Richardson's analysis of

Maus and *Fun Home*, she argues that "[t]he multiplicity of voice in this hybrid medium refuses the clear ordering of a straightforward confession-absolution dynamic"; while not an autobiographical comic in the same vein, *The Maxx* disturbs us with its infinitely discursive villain and focalizer, whose omniscience—his occupation of others' literalized subconscious terrain—is reversed, with limited potential for reparation, in his testimony.[20] Gone works through his hatred of women in "real time," arriving at the revelation of his deeply repressed memories at the same time that this information is conveyed to the diegetic readers (fig. 24). In a beautiful sunset-colored sequence in *The Maxx*, no. 26 (that reflects Mr. Gone's Outback "uniform" of a cheetah-print hat and coat), Kieth uses a sixteen-panel framework to obliquely yet graphically depict the incestuous rape of a young boy. Bruno Leucine writes:

> The page seeks to circumscribe the limits of pleasure through formalization. It must enclose (signify) the inexpressible, and thereby confer it to the reality. … Voyeur, the reader is equally constrained to interiorize with this constant laceration of space the processes of sadism itself.[21]

The unrepresentable (and, for Gone, inarticulable) fluctuates between an objective camera view, matter-of-factly documenting the leading action; the patterns of the wallpaper on which the infant Gone fixates during the act; and the overlapping red panels that approximate the child's silent scream, the psyche fragmented through the panels and the reversion to a frantic, childlike scrawl as a graphic inhabiting of the boy's inability to represent or understand his violation. The panels fluctuate between "reality," the wallpaper, and the child's fragmentation in silent but increasingly frenetic intervals, this emotional destruction "contained" and "ordered" by the cold pattern of the paneling itself. We switch perspectives, but most damningly occupy Aunt Ruth's—the victimizer's—gaze.

The Maxx is such a difficult experience because it implicates us into the narrativization of trauma itself through the comic's experimental manipulation of perspective, voice, and generic tropes. Hero, villain, and victim are all dismantled as constructs, as stable or independent identities, as actors in established trajectories, and we are ricocheted within these contradictory and unreliable subject positions in an interrogation of our own complicity and authorial reliance.

It is Mr. Gone (a reformed Mr. Gone, nonetheless) who concludes the various narrative threads of the story itself in the final issues. He leaves behind a record for posterity, when everyone else will magically disappear and occupy parallel but interlinked narratives with no memory of this plane of diegetic existence. The trailer home in which the main characters all die or disappear—from existence, from the comic—is contained within a snow globe that appears on a

Figure 24. From *The Maxx: Maxximized*, no. 26 (December 2015), 20.

Gone-like character's desk. He performs the ultimate narratological triumph, distilling and containing the story as we know it within the actual narrative (the continuing and mediated world of the comic book, which ends in this alternate/parallel but now anchor reality, our beloved characters bereft of their memories, existing only as echoes of a narrated world that the text has now displaced). We are left with a palimpsest of competing mediated realities, crystallized into a snow globe, a symbol of a contained, inscrutable, and microcosmic universe made material.

Notes

1. Sam Kieth, *The Maxx: Maxximized*, vol. 1 (San Diego: IDW Publishing, July 2014), 5.

2. Kieth, *The Maxx: Maxximized*, vol. 1, 7–8.

3. Kieth, *The Maxx: Maxximized*, vol. 1, 7–8.

4. Kieth, *The Maxx: Maxximized*, vol. 1, 7–8.

5. Neil Cohn, *The Visual Language of Comics: Introduction to the Structure and Cognition of Sequential Images* (London: Bloomsbury Academic, 2014).

6. Elizabeth MacFarlane, "Narrative Possibilities in Australian Autobiographical Comics," in *Negotiating Culture through Comics*, ed. Maciej Sulmicki (Oxford: Inter-Disciplinary Press, 2014), 71–87.

7. Thierry Groensteen, *The System of Comics* (Jackson: University Press of Mississippi, 2009).

8. Groensteen, *The System of Comics*.

9. Kieth, *The Maxx: Maxximized*, vol. 1, 16.

10. Kieth, *The Maxx: Maxximized*, vol. 1, 78.

11. Kieth, *The Maxx: Maxximized*, vol. 1, 23.

12. Sam Kieth, *The Maxx: Maxximized*, vol. 2 (San Diego: IDW Publishing, October 2014), 27.

13. Kieth, *The Maxx: Maxximized*, vol. 2, 21.

14. Kieth, *The Maxx: Maxximized*, vol. 2.

15. Kieth, *The Maxx: Maxximized*, vol. 2, 32.

16. Kieth, *The Maxx: Maxximized*, vol. 2, 39.

17. Sam Kieth, *The Maxx: Maxximized*, vol. 3 (San Diego: IDW Publishing, February 2015), 5.

18. Sarah Richardson, "'Perseveration on Detail': Shame and Confession in Memoir Comics," in *Negotiating Culture through* Comics, ed. Maciej Sulmicki (Oxford: Inter-Disciplinary Press, 2014), 105–21.

19. Sam Kieth, *The Maxx: Maxximized*, no. 24, October 2015, 19.

20. Richardson, "Perseveration on Detail," 105–21.

21. Groensteen. The System of Comics.

Afterword

Gloriously Flawed Saviors

RANDY DUNCAN

WE ALL HAVE A BIT OF THE VILLAIN IN US. THE SHADOW, THE ID, WHATEVER YOU want to call it—there is a part of each of us that wants to break the rules imposed by civilization. But most of us do not. Perhaps this is due to that other part of us that is moral, is good. Or, perhaps it is because we fear being ostracized or incarcerated.

And that's why we're attracted to villains. They break the rules. They do what we dare not do.

Isn't that also true of superheroes? They do things we cannot do and might not dare, even if we could.

Supposedly what separates heroes from villains is the ethical, responsible use of power. Yet, superheroes have always abused power to some extent. They are vigilantes acting outside the justice system when they feel it is justified. They do not respect boundaries. They do not need a search warrant to burst into a villain's hideout. They cross national borders in their quinjets or beam down anywhere in the world from their satellite headquarters. They do not worry about legalities like Miranda rights. Assault and battery is their stock in trade.

Certainly, comic book villain Lex Luthor has the genius and the resources to create a powerful artificial intelligence that orbits the earth monitoring superheroes and calculating their vulnerabilities. But wait, that wasn't Luthor; that was *Batman*. Supervillain Doctor Doom might create an amoral clone of a mighty hero to enforce his idea of justice—and send anyone who dares to oppose him to an inhumane prison in another dimension—but these were the actions of *Iron Man*. Batman and Iron Man eventually realize that they have crossed a line that should not have been crossed and regret their actions. In similar situations, Doom and Luthor only regret that their plans failed, they do not question their intentions. While brilliant, billionaire superheroes might exhibit a bit of egomania, the most notable supervillains usually display massive megalomania.

A Rudyard Kipling poem popularized the phrase "the White Man's Burden," but European nations had long been justifying their empire building with the claim that the lighter-skinned peoples of the world had developed a superior civilization and that they had a moral obligation to impose that civilization on "less fortunate" regions. They were, in fact, arguing that "with great power there must also come great responsibility"; not in a humble "just a kid from Brooklyn" (or Queens) sort of way, but with a sense of privilege and superiority. The manner in which Lex Luthor and Victor von Doom frequently declare themselves to be the smartest person on the planet is a symptom of their megalomania, but the claim itself might be accurate. They *are* truly exceptional. They have the ability to do so much good for the world. In fact, Doom and Luthor believe that because they are the smartest, most capable beings on the planet, they have a responsibility to make the world a better place. It is their intention to remake the world "as it should be."

So it is that the best supervillains do not consider themselves to be evil. Just the opposite. Whether he starts off as a well-meaning young man who wants to use his scientific genius to help Superboy, or a sociopath who murders his parents for the insurance money, Luthor usually becomes a man who genuinely wants to make Metropolis, and sometimes the entire world, a better place. Doom, as king of Latveria, wants to protect his subjects, and when he briefly becomes emperor of the earth, he eliminates nearly all strife and deprivation. The best supervillains are tragic characters. They are saviors, but for the fatal flaws that make them villains. The flaws that prevent such would-be saviors from realizing their potential are usually the classic flaws of tragedy—hubris and envy.

Lex Luthor (in most comic book versions) is a self-made man; he worked to become rich and powerful. It is not surprising that he is envious of Superman, who was given all his abilities just by showing up on earth. Luthor is known worldwide and is certainly the most admired man in Metropolis. Until Superman arrives.

The envy turns to hate.

In a 1983 story, Luthor is on the far side of the galaxy, living on a planet where he is revered because the inhabitants believe that his scientific genius has averted planetary disasters. The grateful people have not only built statues in his honor, they have renamed their planet Lexor. Luthor has a loving wife and a beautiful baby boy. Yet, happiness eludes him. As he carves a giant face of Superman into the side of a mountain, just so he can blow it up, Luthor thinks, "the insatiable hatred I feel for him has never ceased to consume my every waking moment." At the climax of 2011's "The Black Ring" storyline, Luthor possesses god-like power, the ability to bring absolute bliss to the entire universe, including himself. Superman pleads with him to "be the hero you were always capable of being." Luthor knows that any negative thought or action will cause him to lose his infinite power. Yet, Luthor cannot help himself—he uses his power to try to kill Superman, and loses everything.

Victor von Doom believes himself to be a hero and the Fantastic Four's leader, Reed Richards, to be a villain who keeps him from achieving the power and recognition he deserves. Doom also considers himself to be a man of honor, but he is driven to extremes to prove he is better than Reed. Doom grudgingly admits that Reed might be close to his equal as a scientific genius, but Doom is also a master of the mystic arts. In the 2003 "Unthinkable" storyline, Doom captures the Fantastic Four and subjects them to horrendous tortures while Reed is trapped in a library filled with tomes of magic lore. Reed, a scientist who denies the existence of magic, can only save his family if he masters magic. Doom wants Reed to be humbled, and Reed does eventually swallow his pride and admit he is an imbecile when it comes to magic. Luckily for Reed, Doctor Strange has provided him with a mystic artifact that is powered by humility, and Doom is defeated once again.

Luthor and Doom seem destined to endlessly repeat the cycle of envy, hatred, and defeat. However, in 2016 both Lex Luthor and Victor von Doom appear to overcome their tragic flaws and become . . . superheroes? Luthor was offered the throne of Apokolips and could have had all of its formidable resources at his command. Yet, he chose to return to Metropolis. In the wake of the apparent death of Superman, Luthor says that he is trying to be a better man. Wearing a powerful suit of armor emblazoned with the S symbol and draped in Superman's cape, Luthor intends to be "a symbol of inspiration" for humanity as the new Superman. Luthor has the advantage of being a hero in a world in which the Kryptonian he despises does not exist. Until, that is, another (perhaps the real) Superman arrives in Metropolis. Can Luthor remain a hero when he is once again overshadowed by a true Superman? A five-page story in *Action Comics*, no. 1000, hints that he cannot.

When a cataclysmic comic event fractures and destroys not only the universe in which (most) of the Marvel heroes live but all the alternative realities, Victor von Doom forges the remaining shards of the multiverse into a new reality and a new world—a world that he rules as its god-emperor. Ultimately, Doom finds that attaining the ultimate power he had always craved is not fulfilling, and he seeks a new path. The opportunity comes when, after a brutal battle with Captain Marvel, a severely injured Tony Stark uses his biotechnology to put himself in a coma. Victor von Doom modifies his own armor and attempts to fill the role of Iron Man. Although making the right choice is often difficult for Doom, his effort to be good seems genuine. He has the advantage of operating in a world in which the usual target of his envy and hatred, Reed Richards, is absent and presumed dead. Doom still has some of his old arrogance, and watching his struggle to overcome his natural instincts is interesting, but it is not fascinating. He seems but a shadow of his former self.

However, the old Doctor Doom is likely to return soon. In order to "starve out" the Fox *Fantastic Four* film franchise, Marvel cancelled the *Fantastic Four* comic book in 2015: Ben and Johnny join other superhero teams, while Reed, Sue, and their kids have been totally absent from Marvel comics and are presumed dead. However, Disney is in the process of acquiring the film holdings of Twenty-First Century Fox, and by the time this book is published, the *Fantastic Four* comic book will have been revived. Once Reed Richards returns, Victor von Doom will no doubt be driven to prove his superiority over his hated rival. The would-be hero will once again become a ruthless adversary.

And that's good for superhero fans. Superheroism is rather lackluster without a resentful, megalomaniacal, self-aggrandizing antagonist. In other words, a gloriously flawed supervillain.

CONTRIBUTORS

JEROLD J. ABRAMS is associate professor of philosophy at Creighton University in Omaha, Nebraska. He writes in aesthetics, philosophy of film, and philosophy of popular culture. Recent publications include "Hitchcock and the Philosophical End of Film," in *Hitchcock's Moral Gaze*, ed. Steven Sanders, Barton Palmer, and Homer Pettey (State University of New York Press, 2016); "Aristotle and James T. Kirk: The Problem of Greatness," in *The Ultimate Star Trek and Philosophy*, ed. Jason Eberl and Kevin Decker (Blackwell, 2016); "Submitting to Superior Aliens," in *The X-Files and Philosophy*, ed. Robert Arp (Open Court, 2017); and "Aesthetics in Mary Shelley's *Frankenstein*," in *Journal of Science Fiction and Philosophy* (2018).

JOSÉ ALANIZ, professor in the Department of Slavic Languages and Literatures and the Department of Comparative Literature (adjunct) at the University of Washington, Seattle, writes and teaches on disability studies, ecocriticism, and comics studies. He has authored two books, *Komiks: Comic Art in Russia* in 2010 and *Death, Disability, and the Superhero: The Silver Age and Beyond* in 2014 (both published by the University Press of Mississippi). He chaired the Executive Committee of the International Comic Arts Forum, the leading comics studies conference in the United States, from 2011 to 2017.

JOHN CAREY is a British literary critic, and postretirement (2002) emeritus Merton Professor of English Literature at the University of Oxford. He has twice chaired the Booker Prize committee, in 1982 and 2004, and chaired the judging panel for the first Man Booker International Prize in 2005. He is chief book reviewer for the *London Sunday Times* and appears in radio and TV programs, including *Saturday Review* and *Newsnight Review*.

MAURICE CHARNEY is Distinguished Professor of English at Rutgers University. He is the author or editor of twenty books, including *How to Read Shakespeare*, *Classic Comedies: Texts and Commentaries*, *Shakespeare's Roman Plays*, and *Sexual Fiction*.

PETER COOGAN is the director of the Institute for Comics Studies and co-founder and cochair of the Comics Arts Conference, which runs during the San Diego Comic-Con International and WonderCon. Coogan, who earned his PhD in American studies from Michigan State University, is a lecturer in American culture studies at Washington University in St. Louis.

JOE CRUZ is a PhD candidate in mass communications at the Donald P. Bellisario College of Communications at Pennsylvania State University. Cruz is the current research assistant of the Don Davis Program in Ethical Leadership and a former corporate communications fellow at Johnson and Johnson. Cruz's scholarship investigates how political engagement and nationalistic discourses manifest in online spaces. He has also published and presented about ideology in comic books and comic strips, and emerging political discourses in popular culture.

PHILLIP LAMARR CUNNINGHAM is assistant professor of media studies and codirector of the sports studies interdisciplinary minor at Quinnipiac University, Connecticut, and a scholar of black popular culture. He earned his PhD in American culture studies at Bowling Green State University in Ohio and his master's in English from Temple University, Pennsylvania.

STEFAN DANTER is a PhD candidate and assistant professor at the University of Mannheim. His PhD thesis analyzes how critical posthumanist theory can be applied in a rereading of literature ranging from realism to contemporary science fiction. It analyzes how concepts of autonomy have changed over time and how human agency can be reframed into a more relational concept taking nonhuman entities (e.g., animals, objects) into account. He is also part of the research project Probing the Limits of the Quantified Self, which is funded by the German Research Foundation. His main research interests are posthumanism, monster studies, technology studies, theories of quantification, game studies, and science fiction.

In addition to being a card-carrying Potterhead, **ADAM DAVIDSON-HARDEN** currently teaches English, special education, and social sciences at the secondary (high school) level near his home of Kingston, Ontario, Canada, where he lives with his wife and two boys aged thirteen and ten (both of whom are of course well acquainted with the Potterverse). As a university professor, Davidson-Harden has taught in the areas of peace, conflict, and development as well as cultural studies, education policy, and social/ecological justice. In addition to his academic work, Davidson-Harden is a published essayist, songwriter, and poet. His current work in progress includes an analysis of Foucault's Collège de

France lectures relevant to Christianity as a force of "subjectivation," readings in Marx, board game design, songwriting, left/green political activism, and occasional rereadings of *Harry Potter and the Deathly Hallows*.

RANDY DUNCAN, PhD, is professor of communication and director of the Comics Studies Program at Henderson State University, Arkansas. He is coeditor, with Matthew J. Smith, of *Critical Approaches to Comics: Theories and Methods* (Routledge, 2011) and *The Secret Origins of Comics Studies* (Routledge, 2017); coauthor, with Smith and Paul Levitz, of the widely used textbook *The Power of Comics: History, Form and Culture* (Bloomsbury, 2015); and coauthor, with Michael Ray Taylor and David Stoddard, of *Creating Comics as Journalism, Memoir and Nonfiction* (Routledge, 2015). Duncan is cofounder, with Peter Coogan, of the Comics Arts Conference, held each summer in San Diego. In 2009, Duncan received the Inge Award for Outstanding Comics Scholarship, and in 2012 he received the Inkpot Award for Achievement in Comics Arts. Duncan and Matthew J. Smith are editors of the Routledge Advances in Comics Studies series.

RICHARD HALL is an adjunct professor of history at Texas A&M International University in Laredo, Texas. A veteran of the United States Army, where he served with the Multinational Force and Observers in Sinai, Egypt, he received his bachelor's and master's degrees in history from Texas A&M International University in 2001 and 2004, respectively, and his PhD in history from Auburn University in Auburn, Alabama, in 2011. His dissertation research examined issues of race, gender, and patriotism in *Captain America* comic books from 1941 to 2001. He has taught classes examining American intellectual history through the prism of comic book superhero narratives. He is a contributor to the pop-culture database, *Pop Culture Universe: Icons, Idols, Ideas*, published by ABC-CLIO; and the author of *The American Superhero: Encyclopedia of Caped Crusaders in History* from the Greenwood imprint of ABC-CLIO (2019).

RICHARD D. HELDENFELS first wrote at length about detective fiction in his undergraduate thesis at Princeton University; the thesis earned a B+ and Heldenfels earned his BA. More recently, he received a master's in English from the University of Akron, where he is an associate lecturer. That is in addition to more than forty years of writing about popular culture, including as an award-winning critic and columnist for the *Akron (OH) Beacon Journal* from 1994 to 2016. A former president of the Television Critics Association, he is also the author of *Television's Greatest Year: 1954* (1994) and coauthor with Tom Feran of *Ghoulardi: Inside Cleveland TV's Wildest Ride* (1997) and *Cleveland TV Memories* (1999). He contributed "More Than the Hood Was Red: The Joker as

Marxist" to *The Joker: A Serious Study of the Clown Prince of Crime* (2015) and writes an entertainment column for the Tribune News Service.

ALBERTO HERMIDA holds a PhD in communication studies from the University of Seville. After years of academic study at universities in London, Brighton, and Los Angeles, he is currently assistant professor at the Faculty of Communication at the University of Seville. His main research interests focus on analysis of audiovisual discourse, TV series, visual digital culture, and new communication technologies. He has published academic papers in journals like *Information, Communication and Society* and lectured at international conferences. Recently, he has published the paper "Beyond the Technological Dystopia: Surveillance and Activism in *Black Mirror* and *Mr. Robot*" (*Index Comunicación*, 2016); and edited a book about the representation of serial killers in TV series (*Asesinos en serie(s)*, Síntesis, 2015), and another book related to the aesthetics and narratives of Spanish new-wave cinema (*Imágenes resistentes*, Maclein y Parker, 2016).

VÍCTOR HERNÁNDEZ-SANTAOLALLA holds a PhD with distinction in communication studies from the University of Seville. He is currently assistant professor at the Faculty of Communication at the University of Seville and a member of the Research Group on Political Communication, Ideology, and Propaganda. His research interests focus on the effects of mass media, ideology and popular culture, political communication, propaganda, surveillance, and social media; and the analysis of advertising discourse. He has lectured in international conferences and published papers in international journals like *European Journal of Communication* and *Information, Communication and Society*. Recently, he has published a book about mass media effects (Editorial de la Universitat Oberta de Catalunya, 2018). He has also edited two books about the TV shows *Breaking Bad* (Errata Naturae, 2013) and *Sons of Anarchy* (Laertes, 2017), and another about the representation of serial killers in television series (*Asesinos en serie(s)*, Síntesis, 2015).

A. G. HOLDIER is a graduate student in philosophy at the University of Arkansas and an ethics instructor for Colorado Technical University. His research interests lie at the intersection of philosophy, theology, and aesthetics with a particular focus on philosophical eschatology, as well as the ontology of creativity and the function of stories as cultural artifacts. He has published on the practical implications of the aesthetic elements within models of the afterlife, theodicy, animal ethics, and practices of forgiveness.

TIFFANY HONG is a research associate at the Center for East Asian Studies at the University of Kansas. She received her PhD in East Asian languages and literatures (Japanese) from the University of California, Irvine. Currently, she is working on a monograph that examines the narratology of Murakami Haruki through the visual rhetoric of sequential art studies. Her work has appeared in *Room One Thousand* (University of California, Berkeley, College of Environmental Design), *Image [&] Narrative*, and the *Journal of Graphic Novels and Comics*.

STEPHEN GRAHAM JONES is the Ivena Baldwin Professor of English at the University of Colorado Boulder. Jones is the author of several novels and story collections, including *Mapping the Interior* (Tor.com, 2017), *My Hero* (Hex Publishers, 2017), *Mongrels* (HarperCollins, 2016), *The Night Cyclist* (Tor.com, 2016), *The Fictions of Stephen Graham Jones: A Critical Companion*, edited by Billy J. Stratton (University of New Mexico Press, 2016), *The Faster Redder Road: The Best UnAmerican Stories of Stephen Graham Jones* (University of New Mexico Press, 2015), *After the People Lights Have Gone Off* (Dark House Press, 2014), *Not for Nothing* (Dzanc Books, 2014), *States of Grace* (SpringGun Press, 2014), *The Least of My Scars* (Broken River Books, 2013), *Sterling City* (Nightscape Press, 2014), *Flushboy* (Dzanc Books, 2013), *The Elvis Room* (This Is Horror, 2014), *The Gospel of Z* (Samhain Publishing, 2014), *Three Miles Past* (Nightscape Press, 2013), *The Last Final Girl* (Lazy Fascist Press, 2012), *Growing Up Dead in Texas: A Novel* (MP Publishing, 2012), *Zombie Bake-Off* (Lazy Fascist Press, 2012), *The Ones That Got Away* (Prime Books, 2011), *It Came from Del Rio* (Bunnyhead Chronicles) (Trapdoor Books, 2010), *Demon Theory* (MacAdam/Cage, 2006), *Ledfeather* (Fiction Collective 2, 2008), *The Long Trial of Nolan Dugatti* (Chiasmus Press, 2008), *Bleed into Me: A Book of Stories* (Native Storiers: A Series of American Narratives) (University of Nebraska Press, 2005), *All the Beautiful Sinners* (Rugged Land, 2010), *The Bird Is Gone: A Manifesto* (Fiction Collective 2, 2003), and *The Fast Red Road: A Plainsong* (Fiction Collective 2, 2000), among others. He also has nearly three hundred short stories published, in various media from literary journals to truck-enthusiast magazines, from textbooks to anthologies to best-of-the-year annuals. Jones has been an NEA Fellow and a Texas Writers League Fellow; has won the Texas Institute of Letters Award for Fiction, the Independent Publishers Multicultural Award, the Bram Stoker Award, and four This is Horror Awards; has been a Shirley Jackson Award finalist and a Colorado Book Award finalist; and has had his work named one of *Bloody Disgusting*'s Top Ten Horror Novels of the Year. His areas of interest, aside from fiction writing, are horror, science fiction, fantasy, film, comic books, pop culture, technology, and American Indian studies. Jones received his BA in English and philosophy from Texas Tech University (1994), his MA in English from the University of North Texas (1996), and his PhD from Florida State University (1998). Jones's current projects are a paleoanthropological thriller set in Boulder, a slasher, and another slasher.

SIEGFRIED KRACAUER (1889–1966) was a German writer, journalist, sociologist, cultural critic, and film theorist. He has sometimes been associated with the Frankfurt School of critical theory.

NAJA LATER is a sessional academic at the University of Melbourne and Swinburne University of Technology, Australia. She researches intersections between pop culture and politics, with a focus on superheroes and horror. She is a co-founder of the All Star Women's Comic Book Club.

RYAN LITSEY is the head of Document Delivery and Interlibrary Loans with the Texas Tech University Libraries. He earned a bachelor of arts and a master of arts in political science from California State University, Northridge. He also holds a master of science in library and information sciences from Florida State University. His interest in comics came after reading the iconic *Watchmen* in graduate school while studying postmodern political thought. One of his most popular works appears in *The Joker: A Serious Study of the Clown Prince of Crime*. In this chapter, Ryan argues that the Joker is a symbol of Nietzsche's Übermensch and is in fact the true hero in the Batman comic series.

TARA LOMAX is a sessional lecturer in the School of Film and Television at the Victorian College of the Arts in Melbourne, Australia. Her research focuses on entertainment franchising and transmedia storytelling in contemporary Hollywood, with publications in the edited collections *Star Wars and the History of Transmedia Storytelling* and *The Superhero Symbol*, and the journal *Quarterly Review of Film and Video*. She is completing a PhD in screen studies at the University of Melbourne and also teaches cinema studies at the Royal Melbourne Institute of Technology.

ANTHONY SAMUEL (TONY) MAGISTRALE has been a professor of English at the University of Vermont since 1983. He received a BA in 1974 from Allegheny College, and from the University of Pittsburgh an MA in 1976 and a PhD in 1981. He has written several books about Stephen King and Edgar Allan Poe. He is also a poet. In 2011, he received Literary Laundry's Award of Distinction for his poem "Dora Maar."

MATTHEW MCENIRY is the data management and metadata assistant librarian at Texas Tech University. He has published on video game preservation and is the coeditor of *Marvel Comics into Film: Essays on Adaptations Since the 1940s*.

He is currently editing three other books on comic characters/universes and hopes to one day be as prolific a scholar as his mentor in academia and comics, Rob Weiner. Matthew lives in Lubbock, Texas, with his awesome wife Rachel and their dog Ace.

CAIT MONGRAIN received her master's degree from Texas Tech University in 2015, with a thesis entitled "The Spectacle of the 'New': Novelty in the Roman Arena as a Literary Trope." Since graduating, she has worked at Texas Tech as an instructor of classics, primarily teaching Latin, and as the editorial assistant for the *American Journal of Philology*. Her research has focused on Roman imperial historiography and biography, Roman satire, literary depictions of spectacle, and narrative theory. In the fall of 2018, she began pursuing a PhD in classics at Princeton University.

GRANT MORRISON is a Scottish comic book writer and playwright. He is known for his nonlinear narratives and countercultural leanings in his runs on titles including DC Comics' *Animal Man, Batman, JLA, Action Comics*, and *All-Star Superman*; Vertigo's *The Invisibles*; and Fleetway's *2000 AD*. He is the current editor in chief of *Heavy Metal*. He is also the cocreator of the Syfy TV series *Happy!* starring Christopher Meloni and Patton Oswalt.

ROBERT MOSES PEASLEE is chair and associate professor in the Department of Journalism and Creative Media Industries at Texas Tech University. He and Robert G. Weiner coedited *The Joker: A Serious Study of the Clown Prince of Crime*, published by the University Press of Mississippi, and *Web-Spinning Heroics: Critical Essays on the History and Meaning of Spider-Man*, as well as *Marvel Comics into Film: Essays on Adaptations since the 1940s* with Matthew McEniry.

DAVID D. PERLMUTTER is professor and dean of the College of Media and Communication at Texas Tech University. Perlmutter is the author or editor of ten books on political communication, new media technologies, and higher education published by, among others, Palgrave, Oxford, and Harvard University Press. He has written several dozen research articles for academic journals as well as more than four hundred essays for US and international newspapers and magazines such as *Campaigns and Elections*, the *Christian Science Monitor, Editor and Publisher*, the *Los Angeles Times*, the *Philadelphia Inquirer*, and *USA Today*. He has edited a book series and served on the editorial boards of several major journals and publishing concerns. Perlmutter has been interviewed by most major news networks and newspapers, from the *New York Times* to CNN, ABC, and *The Daily Show*. He has talked about popular culture on podcasts like the Tolkien Professor and Monster Talk.

WYATT D. PHILLIPS is assistant professor of film and media studies in the Department of English at Texas Tech University. His research primarily addresses the political-economic and business histories of American media, with a particular focus on cinema. He has published in *Film History*, *Genre: Forms of Discourse and Culture*, the *Journal of Popular Television*, and collections on film genre, film adaptation, early cinema, and popular culture. His current book project considers the industrial history of American film genre production and circulation and the ascendance of genre in the economic vernacular of twentieth-century mass media.

JARED POON is assistant director at the Ministry of Culture, Community, and Youth in Singapore. He earned his master's in philosophy from the University of Florida in 2009 and his PhD from the University of California, Davis, in 2014.

DUNCAN PRETTYMAN is currently a doctoral student at Texas Tech University's College of Media and Communication. Prettyman's research looks at how different structural features of video games affect the way they are processed by their players. In particular, his research looks at how different avatar characteristics, such as avatar race and sex, can affect the way games are processed.

VLADIMIR PROPP (1895–1970) was a Soviet scholar of folktales. His work, including *Morphology of the Folktale* (1928, translated into English in 1958 and 1968), was formative to the functional analysis of narrative structure. From 1932 until his death, Propp was a member of the faculty at Leningrad State University.

NORIKO T. REIDER is professor of Japanese at Miami University, Ohio, where she teaches and writes about Japanese tales of the supernatural and folklore; classical, medieval, and early modern Japanese prose and drama; Japanese film; and Japanese history and culture. She earned her MA and PhD in Japanese language and literature from Ohio State University.

ROBIN S. ROSENBERG is a clinical psychologist with psychotherapy and coaching practices in San Francisco and Menlo Park, California, and New York City. She received her BA in psychology from New York University, and her MA and PhD in clinical psychology from the University of Maryland, College Park. She writes about psychology for a general audience, typically using fictional characters to illustrate psychological concepts and phenomena.

HANNAH RYAN holds a PhD in the history of art and visual studies from Cornell University and serves as assistant professor at St. Olaf College in Northfield, Minnesota. She researches representations of women and children within the visual and literary culture of the transatlantic. Through a decolonial and intersectional feminist approach, her dissertation is a sociopolitical history of infant feeding in the Americas told through visual culture, situating breast milk as a substance of particular value. Additionally, she has curated exhibitions of contemporary female artists, including *Ana Mendieta in Exile: Selected Films*, for which she wrote the accompanying catalogue, and Coco Fusco, *Empty Plaza*. She contributed sections to Ananda Cohen-Aponte's book *Paintings of Colonial Cusco*, and a chapter to the edited volume *Making Milk: The Past, Present, and Future of Our Primary Food* published by Bloomsbury Academic. She was awarded the 2017–2018 American Association of University Women Dissertation Fellowship and named an AAUW Fellow.

LENNART SOBERON works as a researcher and teaching assistant for the Faculty of Communication Sciences at Ghent University, where he is a member of the Centre for Cinema and Media Studies. His research concerns the representation of contemporary conflicts in cinema and focuses on the construction of enemy images in American war and action films. He has published on themes of enemy "Othering," genres, and political economy. He also gives film introductions and lectures in the local cultural scene, and is the cofounder of Kinoautomat, a Ghent-based cinephile platform.

J. RICHARD STEVENS is an associate professor in media studies at the University of Colorado Boulder. He is the author of *Captain America, Masculinity, and Violence: The Evolution of a National Icon* (2015) and is currently working on his second book, *Transforming Culture: Hasbro, Marvel, and the Rise of Hyper-commercial Media Franchising*. Stevens's research delves into the intersection of ideological formation and media message dissemination, comprising studies such as how cultural messages are formed and passed through popular culture, how technology infrastructure affects the delivery of media messages, communication technology policy, and related studies in how media and technology platforms are changing American public discourse.

LARS STOLTZFUS-BROWN is currently a PhD candidate in mass communications at Pennsylvania State University. They are interested in the political economy of popular culture, particularly the intersections of labor, representation, and corporate strategies. Stoltzfus-Brown also researches how media separatist communities like the Old Order Amish selectively utilize media for identity formation and socialization.

JOHN N. THOMPSON is professor of philosophy and religion at Christopher Newport University, Newport News, Virginia, having earned his PhD in the cultural and historical study of religion at the Graduate Theological Union in Berkeley, California. A self-styled "man of letters" (although not the type from TV's *Supernatural*), Thompson regularly teaches in the Honors and Asian Studies Program, and has broad interests in Asian cultures and religions as well as myth, symbol, and ritual. He has written two books on Buddhism, edited a volume of essays on politics and religion in Asia, and published various articles and reviews in a wide array of journals and books, including several pieces on philosophy and popular culture. Currently he lives in Williamsburg, Virginia, with his beautiful wife and daughters, an evil cat, and a goofy dog. In his spare time, Thompson practices martial arts, plays guitar, and hacks away at the vegetation taking over his yard.

DAN VENA is a Vanier Canada Graduate Scholar completing his PhD in cultural studies at Queen's University, Kingston, Ontario. He locates his academic interests within the spheres of visual and popular cultures, merging together trans, queer, and feminist approaches to an array of topics including horror cinema, representations of monstrosity, and histories of medical pathology. He has published on the topic of gender, sexuality, and the superhero in the journals *Transformative Works and Cultures* and *Studies in the Fantastic*, as well as in the anthology *Plant Horror: Approaches to the Monstrous Vegetal in Fiction and Film.*

ROBERT G. WEINER is popular culture librarian at Texas Tech University and teaches for the Honors College. He and Robert Moses Peaslee coedited *The Joker: A Serious Study of the Clown Prince of Crime*. He has published numerous articles on various popular culture topics and is author/editor/coeditor of *Python beyond Python: Critical Engagements with Culture*; *Marvel Graphic Novels: An Annotated Guide*; *Graphic Novels and Comics in the Classroom: Essays on the Educational Power of Sequential Art*; *Web Spinning Heroics: Critical Essays on the History and Meaning of Spider-Man* with Robert Moses Peaslee; and *Marvel Comics into Film: Essays on Adaptations since the 1940s* with Peaslee and Matthew McEniry.

INDEX

Page numbers in **bold** indicate an illustration.

9 781496 826473